ESSENTIAL FIEL

to humanitarian and conflict zones

Afghanistan

SERIES EDITOR: EDWARD GIRARDET

CO-EDITOR: JONATHAN WALTER

Published for ICHR by

CROSSLINES Communications, Ltd.

GENEVA and DUBLIN

First published in Switzerland by *CROSSLINES* Communications, Ltd.

Cover photo: J. Hartley/UNICEF

Design and layout: Nikki Meith, *Maximedia* Ltd.

Please address all enquiries to:

CROSSLINES Essential Field Guides,
International Centre for Humanitarian Reporting,
Villa de Grand-Montfleury, 1290 Versoix,
Geneva, Switzerland.
TEL: +41 (22) 950 0750 FAX: +41 (22) 950 0752
E-mail: info.ichr@itu.ch Website: http://www.ichr.org

ISBN 2-9700176-0-1

Printed in France at Imprimerie Sadag, Bellegarde

Contents

CONTENTS

Maps

Preface

This pilot edition on AFGHANISTAN represents the first in a series of Essential Field Guides to Humanitarian and Conflict Zones. Edited and produced by *CROSSLINES* Communications Ltd. for the International Centre for Humanitarian Reporting (ICHR), a not-for-profit media Foundation headquartered in Geneva, Switzerland, it has been compiled with the assistance of numerous groups and individuals worldwide. Principal funding was contributed by the Conflict Management and Prevention Division of the Netherlands Ministry of Foreign Affairs, with an additional gift from UNESCO. This pilot edition will serve as a template for future handbooks on humanitarian and conflict/post-conflict zones elsewhere. All proceeds from the sales of the Essential Field Guide to AFGHANISTAN will be used towards publishing updates on the Internet and in future print editions.

The principal goal of the Essential Field Guide series is to promote more well-informed interventions in conflict and post-conflict zones and to encourage greater and more balanced media coverage in these regions. The series is therefore targeted at a broad range of players both in the field and outside the region, from reporters, aid workers, local NGOs, human rights advocates and environmentalists to donors, diplomats, academics and business representatives. We seek to provide the sort of reliable on-the-ground information, background resources and practical advice that will help those reporting the story but also those involved in humanitarian intervention and political assessment to gain a better grasp of the situation. Furthermore, the guide offers accessible information on key sectors of interest, leading players, practical advice on living and working in the region, contact lists and pointers to where you can find out more, whether books, websites or research institutes.

The creation of the Essential Field Guide series emerged out of personal experience. As many colleagues from the *BBC*, the *New York Times, Le Monde, El Pais* or *Der Spiegel* covering wars and other humanitarian situations will agree, this is the sort of information that journalists and producers in particular could have used on many occasions, especially when covering areas where information is scattered and one has no special contacts. The same goes for numerous relief coordinators, volunteer doctors or human rights lawyers who suddenly find themselves thrust into conflict zones with scarcely 24 hours' notice.

The Essential Field Guide series is also designed for those who know the region well, but who may wish to expand the breadth of their overall knowledge. We hope to encourage journalists and aid coordinators to explore new areas which directly, or indirectly affect their own fields of expertise. Increasingly, for example in Afghanistan, the issues of peace-building and the repatriation of refugees are being tackled in a broader and more holistic way, taking into account the complex interrelations between political, social, economic and environmental realities.

To respond to the increasingly fragmented nature of humanitarian and conflict situations in the post-Cold War period, it is clear that more pragmatic approaches are required if the international aid community is to have any form of lasting impact. Invariably, this will mean the need for more effective partnerships among key players, be they international aid agencies or local NGOs. Relief workers can no longer operate without taking into account the needs of longer development and human rights. Nor can they afford to neglect the impact of refugee influxes on the environment or the effect of deforestation on local agricultural and health conditions.

At the same time, donors must be prepared to provide so-called 'development' assistance to countries caught up in conflict and without stable or recognised governments by involving local communities. Aid agencies, too, must be more willing to cooperate with journalists. Even if the media's coverage is critical, it functions as a necessary and vital link to the general public. All of which implies an urgent need for better and more reliable information. To that end, we hope this series of guides will contribute.

We are not trying to create the complete guide to Afghanistan but rather a key information resource. If the guide succeeds in serving as an essential information tool which can help make a difference, then we have succeeded in what we set out to do. Obviously, such information is only useful so long as it remains accurate. For this reason, the editors appeal to those involved in Afghanistan, particularly aid organizations, to keep us updated on their activities and contact changes.

You can further help us by joining or otherwise supporting the International Centre for Humanitarian Reporting. We welcome readers' comments to help us correct mistakes or provide more useful input – this project can only continue with your help. We shall provide a free copy of the guide for any significant contributions used by the editors. Updates will be published on a regular basis on the Essential Field Guides page of the ICHR website (http:// www.ichr.org) and will be included in any new editions.

We look forward to hearing from you.

The Editors, May 1998

Acknowledgements

The Editors and the International Centre for Humanitarian Reporting (ICHR) would like to thank the project sponsors for generous support:

Principal Sponsors:

Conflict Management and Prevention Division,
Netherlands Ministry of Foreign Affairs.

UNESCO (United Nations Educational, Scientific and Cultural Organization), Paris

Co-sponsors:

Agency Coordinating Body for Afghan Relief (ACBAR), Peshawar.
International Committee of the Red Cross (ICRC), Kabul.
Swedish Committee for Afghanistan (SCA), Peshawar.
United Nations Office for the Coordination of Humanitarian Assistance to Afghanistan (UNOCHA), Islamabad.

We would also like to thank the following agencies and individuals:

All the agencies which took the time to reply to our questionnaires, Charles MacFadden and Liz Spencer of ACBAR for all their advice and support, Sharifi of ACBAR Kabul for tireless contact-making on our behalf, Yvan Boyjoo of Aid for Aid for his great maps, the Danish Committee for Aid to Afghan Refugees for their hospitality in Herat, Dr Anthony van der Bunt of Help the Afghans Foundation for his advice on personal health, Handicap International for some very luxurious accommodation in Kandahar, the Mine Dog Detection Centre for the worst two days' drive in Central Asia, Médecins Sans Frontières for welcoming a total stranger at the dead of night in southern Afghanistan, Walter Klemm of the Food and Agriculture Organization for advice on the agriculture infobrief, Mark Rowland of HeathNET International for his contributions on malaria, Michel Ducraux of the ICRC for free flights and advice, Anders Fange of the Swedish Committee (SCA) for his hospitality and editing, Gul Nur at the Swedish Committee Guesthouse in Peshawar for his company and great cooking, Mohammed Taher and Salaam Khan of SCA Ghazni for food, company and impressive displays of kick-boxing, Sandy Gall's Afghanistan Appeal for a bed and a lift to Jalalabad, Nancy Dupree and Brigitte Neubacher of The Society for the Protection of

Afghanistan's Cultural Heritage for their cultural guidance, Samantha Reynolds and her team at UNCHS (Habitat) for providing a very warm welcome in Bamiyan, Rupert Colville of UNHCR for his contribution to the refugees overview, Jeremy Hartley of UNICEF for the use of his wonderful photographs, Alfredo Witschi-Cestari and Sarah Russell of UNOCHA for the loan of office space, free flights and logistical support, Brad Hanson at the US Consulate in Peshawar for his support, Gordon Adam and Jeff Carmel for their help editing, Stephen Barber for compiling the website listings, Chris Bowers and Sue Pfiffner for help with proofreading, Brenda Kellem for typing up the Dari phrasebook, Michael and Kim Keating for their generous and mad hospitality in Islamabad, Moira Rushby for her cheerful patience in processing and editing copious contact lists, Shaffi for talking our way through some tricky roadblocks, Fernando Soares for his work on graphics and promotion, and finally Peter Hulm and Nikki Meith for their editing, layout and outstanding hospitality back in Switzerland and without whom this book would never have appeared.

Edward Girardet would specifically like to thank his wife, Loretta Hieber-Girardet, for her extraordinary patience, encouragement and love while undertaking this project, particularly when it never seemed to end.

Jonathan Walter would like to dedicate his share of the book to his long-suffering girlfriend Charlotte Johnstone, with a big hug.

The Editors

Edward Girardet is a journalist, writer and producer who has reported widely from humanitarian and war zones in Africa, Asia and elsewhere. As a foreign correspondent for the *Christian Science Monitor* and *US News and World Report* based in Paris, he first began covering Afghanistan several months prior to the Soviet invasion in 1979. Since then he has travelled throughout much of the country, often by foot. Girardet has written and edited several books, including *Afghanistan – The Soviet War*. An avid outdoorsman, he has produced numerous television current affairs segments and documentaries on subjects ranging from the war in Angola to lost tribes in Western New Guinea and conservation in Africa for major North American and European broadcast networks, such as the *BBC* and *PBS's MacNeil-Lehrer NewsHour*. Girardet is currently Editor of *CROSSLINES Global Report* and President of the International Centre for Humanitarian Reporting, a Geneva-based media Foundation.

Jonathan Walter graduated in Comparative Religions from Cambridge University, followed by a Masters in Philosophy. As an officer in the British Army's Brigade of Gurkhas he worked in military intelligence in Brunei and South East Asia for three years, and coordinated routine surveillance of the Sino-Hong Kong border. As community aid director for a major British charity based in western Nepal, he developed participatory rural programmes in school building and water systems construction. Walter has travelled widely throughout Asia and Africa, working as a volunteer in the Zambian bush and among the Samburu tribe of northern Kenya. A keen climber, sailer and explorer, he has led a number of expeditions to the Himalayas, Indonesia and Borneo. Having spent a year researching and co-editing this guide, he is currently working for a conflict-resolution project operating in the Horn of Africa and Central America.

OVERVIEWS

J. Hartley/UNICEF

Introduction: an unending conflict

By Edward Girardet

Ever since the first revolts erupted against the communist regime of the People's Democratic Party (PDPA) in the summer of 1978, well over one million Afghans have been killed, not including the countless men, women and children who have succumbed to disease, malnutrition, exposure and other indirect effects exacerbated by war conditions. Some six million Afghans were forced to flee the country as refugees, most of them during the decade-long Soviet occupation (1979-1989). Another two million or more have found themselves displaced at various points during the war as refugees within their own homeland. Since the departure of the Soviets, many have managed to return to their homes, but renewed bouts of fighting and shelling continue to produce fresh waves of misery as civilians seek to flee the sheer horror inflicted on them by rival Afghan factions. (SEE REFUGEES, HEALTH, AGRICULTURE)

As a journalist who has covered Afghanistan intermittently since September 1979, less than three months prior to the Soviet invasion, it is sad indeed to find myself still reporting and writing about this debilitating conflict. Nearly two decades of war have left the country in utter ruin. Military assaults, indiscriminate shelling and looting but also neglect, erosion and other forms of destitution caused by the abandonment of whole villages or the uncontrolled cutting of forests have all played their part in destroying or severely damaging many of its once thriving urban and rural areas, cultural sites and natural resources. (SEE CULTURE, FORESTRY, RELIEF & DEVELOPMENT) The bulk of Afghanistan's basic infrastructure such as roads and hospitals lies in a sorry state of repair with little or nothing working. (SEE ECONOMICS)

For the newcomer to Afghanistan, but also for the veteran aid *afficionados* or reporter *wallahs* who have wandered in and out of this Central Asian country since the early years of this crisis, it is crucial to maintain a historical and cultural perspective on the war. (SEE HISTORY) Admittedly, Afghanistan is a difficult place to understand. As many of us have found, Afghanistan grows on you with a passion. It is a defiant and often contradictory nation whose people exhibit an array of characteristics ranging from touching hospitality, warmth and even tolerance, to shameless opportunism and selfishness. To say the least, it is a frustrating country. And as the British, Russians, Pakistanis, Americans and other outsiders have discovered, Afghans are also an impossible people to control.

Nevertheless, journalists and aid workers need to make a greater effort to fathom the Afghan way of thinking and the circumstances that have caused this extraordinary nation to be ravaged with such vehemence. While many of us, including this writer, tend to use simplistic terminology such as "the Taliban are a hardline, Islamic movement with little room for flexibility" or "Afghans believe that...," it does little justice to the extreme complexity of this society to talk in generalizations, or even worse, to ignore the issues at hand. One French nurse in Kabul adamantly insisted that she did not consider it vital to know anything about Afghan politics nor its tribal and ethnic background as it would only interfere with her humanitarian work. Such attitudes, however, can lead to disastrous consequences not only for the way aid is implemented but potentially for the security of relief workers themselves.

The essays and information briefs in this Essential Field Guide seek to help readers broaden their grasp of what is happening in this Central Asian nation. Ahmed Rashid's essay on regional players, for example, may help readers better understand the continuing internationalization of the Afghan conflict. Just as Michael Keating's overview on aid politics may help clarify the nature of international humanitarian assistance to Afghanistan. Or John Butt's analysis of the Taliban and its origins.

The conflict in Afghanistan has gone through several stages. During the first part of the war from mid-1978 to the end of 1979, when Afghanistan found itself embroiled in growing civil strife, much of the destruction – such as the bombing of Herat in retaliation for the March 1979 uprising or the massacre at Kerala (Kunar province) on 20 April 1979, when over 1,000 men and boys were brutally gunned down – was conducted by communist-led Afghan government forces supported by Soviet advisors.

Within weeks of taking power in April 1978, the new regime of President Nur Mohammed Taraki of the PDPA's Khalq ('Masses') faction had begun imposing social reforms with a ruthlessness that angered many, including potential reform-minded supporters. Purges, arrests, and the assassination of dissidents from all segments of Afghanistan's political and religious spectrum soon followed. Such actions quickly provided the beginnings of a nationwide uprising. For their part, the rebels (or *mujahideen* as they became known) began – at first sporadically – to launch attacks against PDPA symbols such as police stations, army posts and government officials, including teachers. These soon spread to include schools, administrative offices, highways and even

Jeff Danziger

development projects – in fact, anything perceived to be a product of the PDPA regime. By Christmas 1978, at least a dozen provinces were in revolt.

When Soviet troops invaded Afghanistan on 27 December 1979, the war turned into a national resistance struggle. During their ten-year occupation (1979-1989), Red Army forces, in conjunction with Afghan regime troops, were responsible for massive destruction of the countryside. They also severely damaged numerous disputed urban areas ranging from parts of Kandahar in the south to the northern town of Anawa in the Panjshair Valley. The Soviets regularly conducted large-scale offensives involving as many as 12,000 troops supported by helicopter gunships, MiG jetfighters and tanks against towns and villages believed to be affiliated with the guerrillas. These operations involved the deliberate destruction of houses, irrigation systems and fruit orchards as well as the planting of landmines and booby traps.

Such actions constituted a policy designed to force civilians either to accept government control, or to leave. Referred to as "migratory genocide" during the 1980s by many observers, at least one third of the Afghan population fled the Soviet war. This policy caused whole regions to be abandoned by most of their inhabitants, leaving ghost settlements in their wake. The effects are still painfully evident today with numerous villages and hamlets abandoned or marked by shattered buildings, dead trees, and crumbling irrigation ducts.

Following the departure of the Soviets in February 1989, the Soviet-Afghan war reverted once again to that of a civil conflict. However, it was a war that continued to involve outside players, including the Americans, Pakistanis, Iranians and Saudis. Arab-backed Islamic fundamentalist groups from Saudi Arabia,

Algeria and Egypt, for example, had become increasingly involved during the latter days of the Soviet occupation and still sought to retain their influence among several of the fundamentalist Afghan factions. As Ahmed Rashid illustrates, to describe Afghanistan today as a country caught up only in an "internal conflict" – as legalists citing international law would define it – shows little understanding of the situation.

After the Soviet withdrawal, Pakistan's military Inter Services Intelligence organization (ISI) was particularly keen to ensure a quick Pashtun-led mujahed takeover of Kabul. ISI pressured the guerrilla factions to take Jalalabad by military means before moving on to the Afghan capital. This heralded a new turn in the war. There was a rise in attacks against the major towns which, until then, had remained relatively unscathed by the direct effects of war. There was also a dramatic increase in fighting among the mujahideen. Inter-factional strife had always existed, but as some observers correctly pointed out during the late 1980s, there was an acute danger of Afghanistan turning into a Beirut-style conflict.

As a result, Kabul began to suffer growing damage from mujahed attacks with rising casualties among civilians. Remarkably little damage had actually occurred during the Soviet occupation. Following the capture of Kabul in 1992, the struggle for control among the different groups disintegrated into a nonsensical mad dogs' war with little regard for its inhabitants. The large-scale destruction one can see today in Kabul is overwhelmingly the result of bitter internecine strife at different times since the early 1990s, particularly among the forces of Hekmatyar Gulbuddin's Hezb-e-Islami, the Hazara Hezb-e-Wahdat, the Taliban and the Northern Alliance of Burhannudin Rabbani and Ahmed Shah Massoud as well as the mainly Uzbek troops of Abdul Rashid Dostum. Incessant, indiscriminate shelling, rocket assaults and aerial bombing by Afghans against Afghans have destroyed whole areas of the city. Thousands of civilians have been killed and wounded, while tens of thousands more had to flee, losing everything they possessed in the process, particularly during the brutal assaults in late 1993 and early 1994. Following even more bitter fighting, the Taliban finally moved into Kabul in September 1996. By early 1998, the struggle for Kabul was far from over with the Taliban pitted against the "Northern Alliance" and the Hezb-e-Wahdat.

Now in its 20th year of conflict, Afghanistan is directly affected by war only in certain parts of the country; surprisingly to many outsiders, much of Afghanistan is actually at peace. Overall, however, the war has set back Afghanistan decades. Notwithstanding considerable advances in education, health and other forms of development during the 1960s and 1970s, any sense of nationwide improvement has been on hold since the early days of the Soviet occupation. The worsening security situation in the early 1980s obliged the Afghan government to halt most of its development efforts, many of them financed by the Soviet Union and East bloc countries, plus some questionable forms of assistance provided by UNESCO and several other UN agencies. International aid to Afghans in resistance-held areas was largely based on emergency relief. While humanitarian support since the early 1990s has done much to help ameliorate conditions in many areas, it is clear that only limited forms of reconstruction ranging from the rebuilding of homes to the rehabilitation of irrigation networks can be undertaken under present conditions. (SEE AID POLITICS, AID IN THE 1980s)

As a nation, Afghanistan now appears to exist only as a pawn on the chessboard of strategic ambition. For those of us who remembered the extraordinary sense of warmth, congeniality and culture of this people prior to the outbreak of war, but also during much of the national resistance against the Red Army occupation, many Afghans now come across as tired and depressed. Ordinary people, it appears, have little to say in the determination of their own future. They are being held hostage by an array of interest groups ranging from armed Afghan political factions, drug traffickers and weapons dealers to outside powers such as Pakistan and Iran. Despite the utter war-weariness of the grassroots population, these groups persist in inflicting further conflict as part of their own greed and self-interest – be they political, regional, economic or religious. (SEE DRUGS)

As long as war persists, Afghanistan will never really be able to move forward. Unless the feuding factions overcome their current differences, and foreign interests such as Pakistan and Iran halt their interference, the country is likely to remain a backwater of development for years to come. Even if aid groups are able to conduct significant projects in the many zones of peace that exist, or oil companies take steps to build trans-Afghan oil and gas pipelines, an end to the fighting is prerequisite. Resilient as they are, Afghans will probably not manage to survive other than on an *ad hoc* basis. Their chances of undertaking any substantive long-term planning that will enable them to pull their country out of its current quagmire are slim.

***Edward Girardet** is currently Editor of* CROSSLINES Global Report *and has reported on Afghanistan since 1979. He is also author of the book* Afghanistan: The Soviet War.

War without borders

By Ahmed Rashid

After nearly two decades of continuous warfare and unparalleled bloodshed, no country in the modern era has been the victim of such outright foreign interference by superpowers and its regional neighbours as Afghanistan. From the Soviet invasion of Afghanistan in December 1979 to today's continuous flow of arms from neighbouring countries to all the warlord parties, ordinary Afghans feel justified when they claim that the civil war is being fuelled as much by their uncompromising power-hungry warlords as by foreign powers.

As a consequence, Afghanistan's present civil war is not merely a complex history of social, political and ethnic conflict but also a litany of the shifts and strategies of neighbours as they arm, fund and influence their various proxies inside the country. The former Soviet Union dragged Afghanistan into the front line of the Cold War after its invasion, leading the United States to forge a broad coalition of Islamic and Western states to back the Afghan mujahideen.

The United States alone provided an estimated six billion dollars worth of military and humanitarian aid to the Afghan resistance during the war. Nearly two dozen countries backed the mujahideen with some form of military aid, channelled to them through Pakistan, which emerged as a temporary home for the mujahed leadership and some three million Afghan refugees. The Soviet Union meanwhile grouped together the countries of Eastern Europe and the Soviet Socialist Republics of Central Asia to back the Afghan communist regime in Kabul.

The withdrawal of Soviet troops in February 1989 did not lead to an immediate cessation of superpower involvement. Both the Soviet and the Western blocs pumped in even more military hardware to both sides of the Afghan political divide, in an attempt to preserve the *status quo*. After Kabul fell to the mujahideen in April 1992, just a few months after the break-up of the Soviet Union, the

US and Russia finally cut off their military aid. For a brief moment, Afghanistan's western and northern neighbours – Iran, Russia and the five Central Asian Republics (CARs) – let the Afghan warlords fight out their power struggles on their own.

However, Pakistan continued military support to the main Pashtun factions, especially the Hezb-e-Islami faction led by Gulbuddin Hekmatyar which attempted to capture Kabul from the largely Tajik forces under President Burhannudin Rabbani. As the civil war intensified, other countries resumed playing a greater role inside Afghanistan. Russia and the CARs, especially Uzbekistan, supported the Afghan Uzbek forces of General Rashid Dostum in his attempt to maintain a buffer state in the north between the fundamentalist Pashtuns in the south and Central Asia.

The emergence of the Taliban at the end of 1994 created the most widespread consternation amongst Afghanistan's northern neighbours since the withdrawal of Red Army troops in 1989. The Taliban bought a new factor into the equation – a messianic and uncompromising message of Pashtun-based Islamic fundamentalism and expansionism, the like of which the region had never witnessed before. It gave rise to accusations from Central Asian leaders and Iran that the Taliban would try and extend their influence to Central Asia. Moreover, the fact that the Taliban movement was Pashtun-driven and backed by Pakistan and Saudi Arabia rekindled the same suspicions amongst the CARs and Iran as had existed in the 1980s.

For the past two decades, Pakistan's Afghan policy has been to back the major Afghan Pashtun parties. The Pashtun tribes straddle the porous Afghan-Pakistani border and Islamabad's fears that Pashtun nationalism or fundamentalism might advocate a future Pashtun state carved out of the two countries has dominated its concerns. At the same time, Pashtuns play an influential role in Pakistan's military, bureaucracy and the intelligence services. The fact that Kabul was under Tajik domination for the first time since the short-lived reign of Bacha Saqao in 1929, and that the divided Afghan Pashtuns had lost their historically dominant role in Afghanistan, created considerable unease amongst Pakistani Pashtuns in high office. A Pashtun regime in power in Kabul was not just a source of pride for Pakistani Pashtuns, but also an assurance that the Afghan Pashtuns would not consider other territorial options. These factors prompted Pakistan to switch support from Hekmatyar to the newly emerging Taliban in 1995.

Pakistan persuaded Saudi Arabia to do the same. Riyadh's major policy concern was the containment of Iranian and *Shi'a* influence in Afghanistan. The Saudis, wary of Iran's growing support to the non-Pashtun ethnic groups and supportive of the Taliban's anti-*Shi'a* stance, backed the Taliban with finances and other material aid.

Iran was convinced that the US and Saudi Arabia were backing the Taliban as part of a strategic plan to encircle Iran. Until the Taliban capture of the western city of Herat, just 70 miles from the Iranian border, Iran along with Pakistan had supported the anti-Rabbani alliance in which Tehran's proxy, the *Shi'a*-based Hezb-e-Wahdat drawn from the minority Hazara group, played a major role. However, the defeat of Wahdat outside Kabul at the hands of Massoud's forces, Iran's historic mistrust of the Pashtuns along with the perceived US and Saudi backing for the Taliban, forced Iran to open a serious dialogue with Rabbani and offer him military support.

The Taliban's capture of Herat and Persian-speaking western Afghanistan in September 1995 dramatically altered the strategic balance in the region. As perceived by Iran, it gave the Pashtuns outright control of western Afghanistan for the first time. Herat was once part of the Persian Empire and remained closely linked culturally, linguistically and economically to the Persian court for centuries. Iran considered that its strategic backyard had been taken over by an ethnically alien and virulently anti-*Shi'a* force.

Russia, which faced the burden of a continuing civil war in Tajikistan, believed that it must contain both Pashtun domination of Afghanistan and the spread of Islamic fundamentalism to Central Asia. Russia could not easily forget that the exporters of fundamentalism into Central Asia during the 1980s were Pashtun mujahideen rather than their Tajik or Uzbek counterparts.

In 1996, even before the Taliban captured Kabul, Iran, Russia and Uzbekistan began to send considerable military and financial aid to Rabbani. Russian planes arrived in Kabul regularly from Tajikistan, Russia and Ukraine with Russian arms, ammunition and fuel but also brand-new banknotes. Iran, meanwhile, had developed an air bridge from Meshad in eastern Iran to Kabul, flying in armaments and fuel to the Rabbani government. Iran also set up five training camps south of Meshad and along the Afghan border for some 7,000 fighters belonging to Ismail Khan, the former ruler of Herat who had been ousted by the Taliban. These fighters, re-equipped by Iran, would be used in late 1996 to open a new front against the Taliban in Badghis province, north of Herat. India also allied itself with Rabbani, largely as an attempt to undermine its old enemy Pakistan. Overall, however, Indian support for Rabbani has remained minimal.

Uzbekistan, the strongest military power in Central Asia, stepped up support for General Dostum's buffer mini-state. Dostum was a fellow Uzbek, who had developed close personal links with Uzbek President Islam Karimov. Uzbekistan's perception was that as long as the Taliban posed no threat to northern Afghanistan, they posed no threat to Central Asia either. Uzbekistan's attitude changed dramatically following the Taliban conquest of Kabul in 1996 and its move northwards.

Turkmenistan, a self-declared neutral state that shares some 300 kilometres of border with western Afghanistan, had developed excellent working relations with Ismail Khan. His defeat and the arrival of the Taliban on their borders initially created great unease, but the Turkmen quickly established a working relationship with the

Taliban in Herat where they maintained a Consulate. Turkmenistan was the only Central Asian state which refused to attend the extraordinary summit of the Commonwealth of Independent States (CIS) after the Taliban capture of Kabul. Despite considerable Russian pressure, they refused to condemn the Taliban.

As fighting intensified across the country, however, the Turkmen were faced with serious threats. For the first time ever in July 1997, some 9,000 Afghan Turkmen crossed the border into Turkmenistan seeking shelter from the fighting. Although the refugees soon returned home, the continuing war was now affecting Turkmenistan's frontier border regions.

The situation in Tajikistan has been far more complicated. Since 1991, both Hekmatyar and Massoud had backed various factions of the Tajik Islamic opposition trying to overthrow the Dushanbe government. But in 1995, Rabbani established working relations with Dushanbe in order to line up more support for his government. Rabbani visited both Moscow and Dushanbe and urged all sides in the Tajik civil war to step-up peace negotiations. Tajikistan was thus deeply disturbed by Rabbani's ousting from Kabul. The arrival of the Taliban in the north had a major salutary effect on the Tajik civil war. It forced all sides in the conflict and Russia to quicken the pace of negotiations out of fear of the Taliban. A settlement between the Tajik government and the opposition was finally reached in Moscow on 27 June 1997. This allowed Rabbani's forces to use Tajikistan as a receiving point for the military aid Russia and Iran were providing. Massoud was granted Kulyab airbase in southern Tajikistan to be able to supply his forces at the front.

The extent of this outside interference worried the Americans who, after a lapse of four years, once again began to take an interest in trying to resolve the Afghan conflict. The US Assistant Secretary of State for South Asia, Robin Raphael, launched an initiative in the spring of 1996. Raphael visited the three power centres of Kabul, Kandahar, Mazar-e-Sharif and three Central Asian capitals. During a United Nations Security Council debate on Afghanistan on 10 April – the first to be held after seven years – the US led an initiative along with other states in supporting the idea of an international arms embargo on Afghanistan. The Americans wanted to use an arms embargo as a lever to persuade all the involved regional countries to agree to a common platform for non-interference in Afghanistan. At the same time, they wanted to lend greater weight to UN efforts to convene a conference attended by all the Afghan factions.

But in an election year, Washington's aims in the quagmire of Afghanistan remained limited. Its principle policy concern – the containment of Iran's growing involvement in Afghanistan and Central Asia – was too obviously transparent to disguise. Despite US attempts to keep Iran out, Tehran was accepted as a major player by all neighbouring states including Pakistan. The US was also concerned about the support given by various Afghan factions to Islamic terrorist groups who were active in the US and Saudi Arabia and the growing drugs trade emanating from Afghanistan. These issues, however, were still not important enough on the US foreign policy agenda to create a major US peace initiative for Afghanistan.

The climax of the regional opposition to the Taliban came immediately after their forces swept into Kabul in September 1996. Iranian President Al Akbar Rafsanjani explicitly warned the Taliban to restrain themselves. "This is a disaster and we strongly regret it. We have repeatedly advised the Afghans that war is not the right way to solve their problems but unfortunately they don't let go. Afghanistan has turned into a complicated and un-solvable issue in the region," Rafsanjani said. Iranian newspapers were even more vehement. "The Taliban capture of Kabul was designed by Washington, financed by Riyadh and logistically supported by Islamabad," said the Jomhuri Islami daily newspaper.

Russia immediately galvanised support from all the Central Asian states. "Russia notes with alarm the danger that this conflict poses to the international community and its destabilizing effect in the region. The Taliban victory only aggravates the crisis for Afghanistan," said a Russian Foreign Ministry statement. In Tajikistan, the 25,000 Russian troops on the Tajik-Afghan border were placed on high alert. President Karimov of Uzbekistan warned the Taliban not to attempt to cross the Amu Darya (Oxus river) which divides Afghanistan from Central Asia. Publicly, he announced that Uzbekistan would offer material support to the ousted Rabbani government and General Dostum. At an emergency summit meeting in Almaty on 4 October, 1996, Russia and the Presidents of Kazakhstan, Kirghizstan, Tajikistan and Uzbekistan warned the Taliban to stay away from northern Afghanistan or face a severe response. The Taliban defiantly dismissed the threat.

The second climax in less than a year for the neighbouring states was the Taliban's brief capture of Mazar-e-Sharif on 24 May 1997. Virtual paranoia swept through Central Asia. The bloodshed on their doorstep – Mazar is just 70 kilometres from the border – created the spectre of war and thousands of Afghan refugees crossing into their territory. Military security was heightened throughout the region. Iran appealed to the UN to intervene and openly urged Russia, the Central Asian States and India to help the anti-Taliban alliance.

The Taliban's lack of diplomatic understanding of how the real world works increased regional fears. Rather than appeasing their concerned neighbours, the Taliban remain deliberately provocative. They made no effort to moderate their social policies to win greater support in the West. Instead, they deliberately made them harsher and rather than succumb to some of the demands of their allies such as Pakistan, who urged them to talk to the opposition, they rejected any suggestion of compromise. The Taliban's foreign policy was thus marked by the extremism that symbolised their social policies and radical views on Islam. Concessions and compromise were impossible.

Pakistan continued to support the Taliban ensuring that Islamabad became increasingly isolated in the region as Afghanistan's other neighbours stepped up support for the anti-Taliban alliance. At the same time, however, Pakistan undertook extensive diplomatic forays to try and convince the Taliban to negotiate. The lack of any real response from the Taliban signalled to the international community and the regional states that Pakistan appeared to be losing any influence it had once enjoyed, or thought it had, over the Taliban.

The Taliban's attitude towards foreign policy – or its lack of one – became a major cause for worry amongst Afghanistan's neighbours. Regional leaders such as Uzbekistan's President Islam Karimov publicly stated that the Taliban sought to conquer Central Asia. The question of whether the Taliban are an expansionist force and intend to carry their revolution beyond Afghanistan's borders still remains the principle issue of concern for Central Asia and Russia.

Some Taliban leaders in Kandahar, fighters at the frontline and administrators in Kabul do espouse, but in varying degrees, an expansionist foreign policy. The Taliban's highly idealistic view of the new Islamic regime that they would bring about was reinforced by the simple if naïve belief that people across the region were just waiting to receive them with open arms. But this idealism – of wanting to recreate a strong Muslim *umma* or community guided by a Taliban ideology – was not tempered with any knowledge about the history, geography and complex social structures in the region. And judging by the Taliban handling of the Uzbeks, Hazaras and Tajiks in Mazar, they appear hardly prepared to deal with the complexities posed by ethnicity in Afghanistan and Central Asia.

The Taliban generation of mujahideen, or fighters for Islam, were brought up on the 1980s' diet of Islam's fight against communism and the Soviet Union, which the Afghans spearheaded. It comes replete with the conviction that the collapse of the Soviet Union was solely caused by the Afghan *jihad*. Since then, the West and the rest of the Muslim world have betrayed Afghanistan and not given Afghans their due.

For the Taliban, educated only in *madrassas,* or Islamic schools, the end of the Cold War created more enemies and more conspiracies. These include the conviction that US and Russian imperialism and secularism are destroying Palestine, Chechnya and Bosnia; Hindu India is suppressing the Kashmiris; the dictators in Central Asia are refusing to let their people follow the Islamic path; and the UN is refusing to recognise the Taliban and thereby conspiring against Islam. This somewhat paranoid world picture for the Taliban is compounded by the latent anti-*Shia'ism* inculcated from their Deobandi *madrassas* in Pakistan, which pits the Taliban directly against Iran.

Afghanistan's neighbours had developed other new interests which pitted them against each other. The idea of a gas pipeline between Turkmenistan and Pakistan that would cross Taliban-controlled southern Afghanistan at first created intense competition between two oil company consortia – one led by the American giant Unocal and the other led by the Argentinian company, Bridas. Both companies have spent considerable time, effort and money in wooing the Afghan factions but particularly the Taliban. The pipeline issue has also pitted Iran and Russia against Pakistan. Iran feared that such a pipeline would be an American attempt to dominate its border region and avoid the more logical exit route for the energy-rich Central Asian states which was through Iran rather than Afghanistan. Russia wished to maintain its dominance over Central Asia's energy resources

All the countries in the region feared the destabilizing effects caused by the increased production of heroin in Afghanistan, which has helped finance the warlord armies but also has created drug Mafiosi in all these states as the heroin was smuggled through Iran, Pakistan and Central Asia to Europe. (SEE DRUGS) The enormous trade in weapons across Afghanistan and into neighbouring states, and the sanctuary given by the Afghan warlords for terrorists and militant Islamic opposition groups from the regional countries were equally destabilizing.

Equally contentious was the vast smuggling trade that has developed across Afghanistan and fed into the entire region. Land-locked Afghanistan was allowed to import duty-free goods via the Pakistani port of Karachi, but this permission was hugely abused as smuggled goods traversed back into Pakistan before being smuggled into Central Asia and Iran. The shattered Afghan economy has been, and still is, predominantly dependent on smuggled foodstuffs, fuel and other consumer goods from the regional states. In all these states, the Afghan smuggling trade has led to large-scale loss of customs revenues and created periodic shortages of essential goods, especially foodstuffs. (SEE AGRICULTURE)

The continuing civil war in Afghanistan is clearly a major factor in destabilizing the economies and social structures of the already fragile neighbouring states. Yet none of them is prepared to sacrifice the short-term political advantage gained from backing one Afghan proxy or the other. They are failing to explore the more long-term approaches that will be necessary to bring an end to the fighting and lead to a sustainable peace. Bringing peace to Afghanistan, however, involves more than just getting the warlords to talk to each other. It involves a pressing need to persuade all regional countries to cease their interference in that country.

In the midst of this mayhem and the continued involvement of outside powers, the Afghan population continues to suffer as the warlords refuse to compromise and are continually armed and backed by one power or the other.

Ahmed Rashid *is South and Central Asia correspondent for the* Far Eastern Economic Review *and* The Daily Telegraph, *based in Lahore. He is also a contributing editor to* CROSSLINES Global Report.

The Taliban phenomenon

By John Butt

When the Taliban – the Islamic Students Movement – appeared on the Afghan scene in late 1994, they took the world by storm. There was little understanding of where the Taliban came from, what they represented, who they were and where their appeal lay. Three years on, they are not much better understood than they were when they first became evident.

One thing is clear: November 1994 does not represent the birth of the Taliban. They were on the scene well before then. "Do you remember when you came to Kandahar in April 1992?" the Governor of Kandahar province, Mawlawi Mohammed Hassan – widely considered number two in the Taliban movement – asked me in the course of a conversation we had early in 1997. He mentioned my visit then to the village of Mullah Pasanay, elevated to Chief Justice of Kandahar province by the Taliban and a leading light behind the Taliban movement. "Well, we were organized then. We thought we would give the 'gun-slingers' (the term used in Kandahar to describe the mujahideen) a chance to get their act together. We did not make our move until we had lost all hope."

What Mullah Hassan said is consistent with evidence of Taliban organizations existing throughout Afghanistan, at least since the late 1980s and even before then. These were usually organized on a provincial level. Though the majority of Taliban are from the Pashto-speaking areas of Afghanistan, there were also organizations of Talibs from predominantly non-Pashtun provinces such as Takhar, Badakhshan and Baghlan.

Nevertheless, the bulk of the Taliban came from the Pashtun provinces, and particularly the Pashtun strongholds of Greater Paktya (Khost, Paktya and Paktika), Wardak, Ghazni and Kandahar. The predominantly, but not exclusively, Pashtun nature of the Taliban is evident in their name. 'Taliban' is the Pashto plural for 'Talib.' In Arabic and Persian, the plural of the same word is 'Tulaba.' 'Talib' is originally an Arabic word meaning 'seeker.' The Prophet of Islam urged believers to 'seek' knowledge, even if it meant going to China. The word has thus become commonly used for a seeker of religious knowledge – a religious student.

The tradition of travelling in order to gain knowledge can also be traced to the above statement of the Prophet. It is because of this tradition that Afghan students have become used to travelling, first to India and then to Pakistan, for acquiring knowledge of religion. Prior to the partition of India in 1947, students of religion used to travel to the centres of learning in Deoband (Darul Uloom, Deoband) and to a lesser extent Delhi (Darul Uloom Aminiyya).

Deoband and Afghanistan

The affinity of the Deobandi school of learning, in particular, to Afghanistan goes back to the early 20th Century. The Taliban are heirs to this traditional affinity. Not only has there been a steady stream of scholars from Afghanistan receiving education at Deoband; "freedom fighters" – among them independence-minded scholars of the Deobandi school – have also been regular visitors to Afghanistan.

Foremost of these was Mawlana Ubaidullah Sindhi, a leading Indian religious scholar who remained in Afghanistan from 1916 to 1923. Despite his own progressive nature, the Deoband school from which Mawlana Sindhi hailed has always been associated with traditional thinking in Afghanistan. Deoband represented the wing of Indian Muslim thinking which was suspicious of Western education, and sought to strengthen traditional Islamic education in the face of what was seen as an onslaught from the secular West. It was this same mentality which came up with the slogan, at the time of the introduction of secular education in Afghanistan under Amir Amanullah Khan in the 1920s:

> *"Those who go to school,*
> *Do so just for money.*
> *They will have no place in heaven,*
> *But will flay around in hell."*

Until the independence of India and Pakistan, the "Afghan connection" of the Deobandi school was synonymous with anti-British sedition. In its efforts to keep British imperialism at arms-length, Afghan rulers always treated Deobandi figureheads with at best grudging respect, sometimes bordering on disdain.

Even before Mawlana Sindhi moved to Afghanistan, the head of the royal *madrassa* (religious school) in Kabul – a Deoband graduate by the name of Abdul Razzaq – tried to mount anti-British operations on the Frontier. He was prevented from doing this by Amir Habibullah (1908-1919), who did not wish to unduly aggravate the British rulers in India.

This same policy was followed by Amir Amanullah Khan (1919-29), who actually banned any religious scholars with a foreign education – including Deoband – from teaching in Afghanistan. This decision followed considerable pressure on the Amir from British rulers in India, to expel Mawlana Sindhi and his group of Indian rebels from Afghanistan. This he did in 1923, but not before Mawlana Sindhi and his companions had played a crucial role – on the Afghan side – in the fighting leading up to the independence of Afghanistan in 1919.

It was at this time that a chain of religious schools – the *madrassas* – started operating in the northwest frontier regions of British India. These same schools, some eighty years on, have spawned the Taliban. Still, until 1947, the ultimate aim of Afghan religious students was to receive their education at the main centres of learning in Deoband and Delhi. Following the independence of India and Pakistan, leading scholars of the Deobandi school opted to open *madrassas* in Lahore, Karachi and Akora Khattak in Pakistan's North West Frontier Province. With the establishment of these *madrassas*, there was a gradual increase in the number of students from Afghanistan crossing the Durand Line to receive Islamic education.

After 1947, as the centre of learning for Afghan religious students moved from India to Pakistan, there was a sea-change in the political focus of the Deobandi movement in the frontier regions of Pakistan and inside Afghanistan itself. While the British had remained in India, there were two main aims of the movement: the more scholastic and spiritual minded aimed to consolidate Islamic learning in the face of British-sponsored Western education, while on a political level, some Deobandi scholars sought to assist the anti-British forces struggling for independence. When the British left the subcontinent, the Deobandis focused their attention on the secular forces in Pakistan and later in Afghanistan itself.

During the 1970s, there was a continuing flow of religious students travelling from Afghanistan to Pakistan to receive religious knowledge. Many of these studied in the main centres of learning, in Karachi (New Town Darul Uloom and Darul Uloom Karachi), Lahore (Jamiya Ashrafiyya), Peshawar (Jamiya Ashrafiyya and Darul Uloom Sarhad), as well as various smaller institutions spread around the frontier provinces of Pakistan and Baluchistan. The number of these *madrassas* increased dramatically with the beginning of the Afghan war in 1978, and the Islamization policies followed by the President of Pakistan, Mohammed Zia-ul Haq.

Traditionalists and Islamists

The Taliban movement represents the return of the traditional, *madrassa*-based Islamic scholar to the Afghan political scene. Until the Taliban came to prominence, it was the Islamists who combated the rising forces of secularism and, later, communism in Afghanistan. It is important to understand the distinction between *traditionalists* – epitomised by the Taliban – and *Islamists* – represented by such parties as the Jamiat-e-Islami of Professor Burhannudin Rabbani (the former alliance president of Afghanistan ousted from Kabul by the Taliban in September 1996) and Hezb-e-Islami of Gulbuddin Hekmatyar. The Taliban were educated in religious schools – *madrassas* – while the Islamists are generally products of the state education system.

The Taliban are traditionalists – seeking to return to the purity of the teachings of the Koran and the *Sunnah*, the practice of the Prophet. The Islamists, meanwhile, are modernists in that they are seeking a contemporary, albeit political, interpretation of Islam. The Taliban, being products of religious *madrassas* in Pakistan, are more inclined towards that country, while the Islamists have mostly received higher religious education in Al-Azhar University in Egypt, where they have been influenced by the political thinking of the Muslim Brotherhood. The Islamists – particularly the Hezb-e-Islami of Gulbuddin Hekmatyar – have been able to form highly organized political parties whereas the Taliban are still not organized along party lines.

However, there is evidence of the Taliban being organized on a provincial basis from the time of the *jihad* (holy war) against the Soviet army and Communist government in Afghanistan. Organizations of Taliban took the form more of regional associations than political parties. For example, the Jamiat-e-Tulaba-e-Paktya-wa-Khost was a rough association comprising those religious students pursuing studies in Pakistan, originally hailing from the provinces of Paktya and Khost in southeastern Afghanistan. Every now and then, these students would come from their various *madrassas* in Pakistan and gather in their native provinces of Afghanistan. One such gathering was held in Khost shortly after the capture of that province by the mujahideen in 1991. The gathering attracted many thousands of religious students from *madrassas* in Pakistan, who came to their native province for a "turban-tying" *(dastar bandi)* ceremony – their official initiation into the ranks of the *ulama*, the scholars of Islam.

This gathering of Taliban was symptomatic of similar organizations existing elsewhere in the country which represented a huge, and, at that time, latent force. In Khost, the Taliban were represented in the administration which ruled the province during the mujahed interregnum, between the fall of Najibullah's government in the province and the Taliban takeover in late 1994. A leading light in the Taliban movement, Abdul Hakim Sharai, was Chief of Security in the province during this time. Later, he was to become Governor of Zabul province under the Taliban.

Taliban were also influential in the administration of Mawlawi Mansur in Paktya. Mawlawi Mansur, belonging to the Harakat-e-Inqilab-e-Islami (Revolutionary Islamic Movement) of Mohammed Nabi Mohammedi, was murdered in Hezb-e-Islami controlled territory in 1993. Later, the party of Mohammedi, a leading scholar of the Deobandi school of thought, was to defect almost entirely to the Taliban. However, for the most part, Taliban throughout Afghanistan remained isolated from power until the Kandahar Taliban made their move in late 1994.

Tribals and non-tribals

Following the takeover of Kabul in September 1996, the Taliban advanced towards the Shomali plain, stretching towards the Hindu Kush north of Kabul. It was here that their advance was halted. The resistance they met in the Shomali plain came from ordinary villagers, as well as from supporters loyal to Ahmed Shah Massoud. In a way, this resistance was surprising. The Shomali plain had produced Bacha Saqao, a Tajik who in 1929 led a regime remarkably similar in its religious hue to the Taliban themselves. One might have thought that the people of Shomali would have rallied to the support of the Taliban. That they did the opposite was because the Shomalis did not see the Taliban as a religious movement. Instead, they saw in the Taliban shades of the tribal confederation which, under the future king Nadir Shah, had unseated Bacha Saqao.

For non-tribal fundamentalism, represented by Bacha Saqao, the transition to the Islamism of Burhannudin Rabbani was more logical than a reversion to the traditional, more tribal Islam of the Taliban. To a certain degree, by the time of the fall of Kabul, the Taliban movement had been hijacked by tribal, ethnic and even nationalist elements. Yet it still had considerable support from the Islamic scholars who had earlier in the century provided the groundswell of support for Bacha Saqao. Such is the complex alignment of conflicting forces which makes for the extraordinarily entangled state of Afghan politics today. If the Taliban had been able to project a more purist Islamic image, they might have been acceptable to the people of the northern plains. By projecting a tribal image, or being projected as such, they became totally unacceptable.

When the Taliban launched their aborted takeover of the north of Afghanistan in May 1997, among the first to recognise them was the government of Saudi Arabia. For two reasons this might have seemed a strange decision. The Saudis had spent much of the 1980s trying to spread their own particular puritanical brand of Islam – *Wahabiism* – in Afghanistan. Why then should they promote a different brand – that of the Taliban?

Secondly, the Taliban were continuing to give shelter to the most famous of Saudi dissidents – Osama bin Laden. Why should they recognise a regime which was giving refuge to its sworn enemy? There is a degree of conjecture in one's answer to both these questions. It may be that Saudi support for the Taliban should be seen more in geopolitical than in religious terms, and is part of the continuing rivalry with Iran for influence in Afghanistan. (The Iranian government is one of the main supporters of the anti-Taliban coalition). One may speculate that, as far as the Saudi regime is concerned, Osama bin Laden is relatively harmless in the care of the Taliban. The Saudis may well have received assurances from the Taliban that he would not pose a threat to Saudi interests while living under their protection.

Regarding the Taliban's approach and beliefs, it is true that in the past the Saudi government provided support to *Wahabiite* tendencies in Afghanistan. This may well have proven a chastening experience for the Saudis. It was clear that the people of Afghanistan were opposed to *Wahabiism* as such. The vast majority of Afghans had no time for a brand of Islam which renounced the *Hanafi* school of thought, to which all *Sunni* Afghans adhere. Many Afghans, however, became affiliated to *Wahabi* groups but usually for opportunist reasons, such as money.

From this point of view, the puritanical Deobandi interpretation of Islamic teachings may have appeared as an acceptable compromise to the Saudis. On most questions of dogma, the position of the Deobandis is quite similar to that of the *Wahabis*, though with considerable concessions to Afghan tradition and custom. Most importantly, the Deobandis strictly adhere to the *Hanafi* school of thought to which Afghans swear allegiance.

On the question of the Islamic status of shrines, for example, the Taliban adopt a more cautious approach than the *Wahabis*. While the *Wahabis* insist that the building of shrines, and visits to them, are un-Islamic and polytheistic practices, the Taliban have shown more deference to age-old Afghan traditions on this question. Not wishing to disturb a hornet's nest, they have not stopped people from visiting shrines. However, as they consolidate their hold on areas, there are signs that they are imposing what they see as a more Islamic code of conduct at shrines, particularly as far as praying to God, and not to the shrine itself, is concerned. The reverence of relics, particularly the cloak of the Prophet, which they used to sanction the position of their leader Mullah Omar as Commander of the Faithful, is even more liberal in comparison to strict interpretation of the *Wahabis*.

As for the seemingly extreme measures of the Taliban, which have attracted considerable publicity in the West, they are understandable in the context of the *Hanafi* school of thought. Without going into each particular measure, it might be enlightening to see where the thinking behind such measures as the confinement of women, and their cloaking in the all-enveloping "shuttlecock" *burqa*, comes from. In the principles of *Hanafi* jurisprudence there are two fundamental tenets, both of which are extremely important in understanding Taliban thinking. The first is that an action may not be *haram* – 'forbidden' – in itself, but it becomes so if it is likely to lead to an *haram* action. The concealment of women can be seen in the light of this principle. Women are expected to cover themselves, not because this is desirable in itself, but in order to prevent immorality.

Another principle which lies behind many of the edicts of the Taliban is that of an action being 'permissible' (*ruskhah*) and 'honourable' (*azeemah*). It is 'permissible', for example, to take a life for a life, but the 'honourable' thing to do is to forgive. In Afghan tribal tradition, this principle has often been turned upside down. For example, taking a life for a life has come to be considered honourable. Often, the Taliban impose an action which they see as honourable – as opposed to permissible – though it might be arguable whether this is seen from a strictly Islamic, or from a tribal, point of view.

One may argue with many measures of the Taliban, even from an Islamic point of view, but it is quite clear that the phenomenon of the Taliban was not artificially created. The Taliban have deep roots in Afghan society. Because these roots were indigenous to Afghan society, others may have decided that they were a force worth supporting.

John Butt*, founder editor of the BBC's radio soap opera for Afghanistan,* "New Home, New Life", *is an expert in Islamic theology with long experience of Afghanistan.*

Aid politics: dilemmas of humanitarian assistance

By Michael Keating

There can be little doubt about the profundity of Afghanistan's humanitarian crisis. The country holds Asia's, even the world's, worst records in a number of fields, including infant and maternal mortality, life expectancy, adult and female literacy, access to safe water, the estimated number of landmines, the proportion of mentally or physically disabled people, the numbers dependent upon food support, and the number of refugees and internally displaced people. It is estimated that well over a million people have been killed, and 700,000 women made widows in the fighting over the last 20 years.

Facts are scarce, but the evidence speaks for itself. The difficulties in gathering data are such that Afghanistan was actually dropped from rankings in the 1997 edition of the *United Nations Human Development Report*. This relegation is perhaps symbolic of the lack of international interest in Afghanistan's social problems, and of the ignorance about how Afghan society is coping, or failing to cope, with its continuing nightmare.

The days when Afghanistan was glamorous for the aid community have long gone. In the years immediately after the Soviet invasion, there was a cause – to show solidarity with the under-equipped rural mujahideen's resistance to the blunt might of the Soviet Army – that attracted not only every self-respecting war reporter but thousands of humanitarian aid workers, many of whom had visited and fallen in love with the country and its people as tourists. They were prepared to endure terrible hardship and danger to bring basic services, usually medical, to embattled communities. There was an innocence about assistance that gradually evaporated as the 1980s wore on and as aid became less a gesture of solidarity and more enveloped in politics, particularly once the United States stepped up its involvement in the war from the middle of the decade. (SEE AID IN THE 1980s)

Today, there is little innocence left. There is no obvious cause, other than the purely humanitarian. The aid community has become less idealistic, more self-conscious, more wary of its own role and the impact that its activities are having on Afghanistan. In part, this is owing to recognition that, in a country whose industrial productivity has collapsed and employment market evaporated, the aid industry is no longer peripheral; after agriculture, it is the second biggest sector of what is left of the licit economy. (Illicit drug production and trafficking represent Afghanistan's largest overall sector. SEE DRUGS) Dilemmas for humanitarians abound. Some of these predate the arrival of the Taliban on the scene, but nearly all have been intensified by their arrival.

Key dilemmas

The most fundamental dilemma is whether the humanitarian effort is contributing to – or at least facilitating – the conflict. There is something both alarming and perverse about the possibility that the net effect of the assistance effort may be to make it easier for the authorities to sidestep or abdicate their responsibility for the welfare of ordinary people.

It is an open question to what degree authorities in Afghanistan have ever seen provision for the social welfare of the population to be a basis of their legitimacy, notwithstanding Islamic injunctions and tradition in this regard. Certainly, during the days of the Soviet occupation, the mujahideen were not noted for giving social issues a priority. In the late 1980s, when aid funds seemed abundant, dozens of Afghan NGOs came into being under the aegis of the resistance parties. Although some were staffed by Afghan technocrats with the noblest motives, many seemed to exist to soak up funds rather than to deliver any verifiable service. The availability of funding for NGOs in any case owed much to the West's overall political objective of supporting the resistance to eject the Soviets from Afghanistan.

But even today, when there is no such political motor to drive western donor generosity, aid workers cannot help but wonder what the political impact of their hard work is. One western ambassador came back from a trip to Kabul in September 1997 with a story to illustrate the point. He was kept awake much of the night by successive planes landing and taking off from the airport – presumably not delivering cuddly toys. Bleary eyed, in the morning he met medical NGO workers struggling to resist pressure from the Taliban authorities who were demanding that they pay the salaries of government health workers. For the Taliban, but also other political factions, there is an attitude that the aid agencies are the ones who should pay for social services thus enabling government funds to be directed towards the security forces.

Some would argue that the Taliban have repeatedly demonstrated powerful commitment to the welfare of the population – that indeed, this has motivated their cause from the beginning. The Taliban

The Frontier Post 4 March 1990

themselves repeatedly point out that security has improved, particularly for women, in areas under their control. (SEE WOMEN) But the Taliban's and international community's notions of what comprises social wellbeing are hardly comparable. Attendance at mosques and provision of facilities for female medical patients cannot be measured on the same scale. (SEE TALIBAN)

But one might argue that the Taliban – and other Afghan leaders – are not alone. Their abdication of what is normally thought of as social responsibility is matched by a failure of the international community to accept responsibility for the overall humanitarian crisis. As is argued elsewhere in this book (SEE WAR WITHOUT BORDERS), the Afghan conflict has been characterized by an extraordinarily high degree of external interference. There would appear to be little domestic or international pressure upon those governments interfering in Afghanistan's internal affairs to desist, even though such governments are often paying a high price as a result of the continuation of the Afghan war, as smuggling, corruption, drug addiction and terrorism seep back into their own lands.

Exasperated aid workers often ask why greater pressure is not brought to bear on Afghanistan's neighbours to create the external conditions for peace. It is difficult not to assume that Afghanistan simply no longer matters – that it is merely a dim flicker on the global geopolitical radar screen. And that to the degree that it does matter, the suffering borne by hundreds of thousands of Afghans is of little consequence in the larger scheme of things.

This naturally raises another dilemma. Should the international community's political activities be more integrated with its social, economic and development work, or might that risk compromising and politicizing humanitarian activities?

In the late 1980s, UN humanitarian and development workers were under instruction to make a clear distinction with Afghan interlocutors between their work and that of the high-level political negotiators such as Diego Cordovez. But by late 1997, with the work of the UN Special Mission on Afghanistan apparently going nowhere, and the Taliban showing steely determination to achieve a military solution, the separation is often described as a 'disconnect.' Whether because of the mandate handed to the UN Special Mission on Afghanistan, or the manner in which its Special Representative has chosen to animate it, the perception is that, at least until the involvement of Ambassador Brahimi, UN peacemaking efforts had been confined for too long to a narrow and fruitless world characterized by ceasefires, exchanges of prisoners and talks about talks.

Reservations about the UN's agenda

Reservations about the UN's political role have raised doubts on a number of scores. First were doubts that issues relating to the deteriorating conditions under which humanitarian workers are obliged to operate were not being pursued by the Special Representative – the assumption being that only he was in a position to do so with sufficient authority. Second were concerns that the issues of human rights and gender equality raised by the Taliban – and for many, long overdue in Afghanistan – were not being factored into political discussions with Afghan leaders. But third, and most substantially, were worries that the UN was failing to address the bigger picture – the geopolitical and economic context within which both the conflict and the assistance effort take place.

The perceived 'disconnect' is therefore between the international community's professed concern for the victims of the conflict and its failure, through its chosen vehicle, the UN Special Mission on Afghanistan, to square up to and open dialogue with the parties, whether in neighbouring states or with their powerful allies, whose actions, or failure to act, are arguably prolonging the war. But how, in operational terms, can the 'reconnect' be made?

Any suggestion that aid be a bargaining counter in the pocket of the UN political negotiator raises the contentious issue of the validity of making aid subject to conditionality. Few would dispute that it is quite reasonable for the international community to hold out the prospect of major reconstruction funding as a carrot to bring parties to the table. But the apparent disregard of the authorities for aid, and the absence of development funding, means in reality that the only bargaining counter is humanitarian assistance.

The International Committee of the Red Cross (ICRC) has traditionally had a clear and fixed position – that political considerations should in no way compromise the provision of humanitarian assistance or prevent the agency from reaching people in need. (SEE ICRC) This position is being tested to breaking point by the Taliban – for example, in their insistence that female health facilities be segregated, regardless of the resource and practical implications that this has for those trying to meet women's needs. If the ICRC is compelled to suspend some of its activities, it is more likely to be on grounds of breach of contract than human rights, such is the agency's commitment to fulfilling the humanitarian imperative. But the UN has a far less fixed position, and has found itself dancing around this dilemma for years.

The issue of conditionality is the slipway to a further set of dilemmas. The subject of conditionality more usually arises in the context of human rights and the treatment of women. Is it reasonable or realistic to expect the public and politicians in western countries to provide aid to a country whose authorities have regressive human rights and gender policies? The closer to the field one gets, the less obvious the answer to this question becomes.

The challenge of the Taliban

The Taliban are not the first Afghan authorities to abuse human rights. It is often remarked that little concern was expressed by western politicians in the past, either in the 1980s or more recently since the rise of the Taliban – until they shocked the world by capturing Kabul. Not much notice was paid in early 1996 when in Herat the Taliban refused to meet female staff from aid agencies, banned all women from working except in the health sector and refused to countenance any discussion about reopening girls' schools. Nor, one might argue, do politicians seem to be so vociferous about official gender discrimination in other countries, least of all important oil-rich Muslim ones. (SEE HUMAN RIGHTS)

Others point out that while the Taliban have totally unacceptable attitudes towards the place and role of women in society, even by Islamic standards, the impact of these is confined to Kabul and a few areas of the major towns. They argue that the Taliban, like waves of Afghan ideologues before them, including the communists, are few in number and neither have the power, nor can afford, to alienate the vast majority of the population, with whom they have reached a *modus vivendi*. This has meant, for example, that where female education is locally valued, it is permitted. Indeed, a study by the Swedish Committee for Afghanistan in the summer of 1997 showed that the proportion and total number of females in SCA-supported schools in six southern provinces had actually increased over the previous 10 years. (SEE EDUCATION)

But whatever the mitigating circumstances, the brazenness of Taliban gender policies can only be received by the international community (but also by many Afghans themselves) as an insult to the women – and, one would hope, men – of the world who have struggled for equal opportunity and the full realization of human rights. On the spot, there is broad consensus on the need to adopt a principled but non-confrontational attitude towards Afghan authorities over the issue of women. But explaining the nuances of this to a distant public which consumes news reports that verge from the horrific to the ridiculous about restrictions upon women will be an almost impossible task. This dilemma is here to stay.

However, aid agencies could make their lives easier. Many demonstrate remarkably little understanding of who the Taliban are, and the Pashtun culture from which they spring. This is a poor basis for any form of dialogue, whatever the intended outcome. The range of responses to Taliban edicts by aid agencies has created confusion and given the impression, which in some cases may be fair, that agencies are not themselves committed to respecting and implementing international human rights norms and standards. The Taliban themselves have grounds for accusing the agencies, some of whom do not exemplify commitment to gender equity in their own staffing and operations, of inconsistency and even hypocrisy.

The issue of conditionality is made no easier by the difficulty of drawing the line between humanitarian and non-humanitarian assistance. Where does rehabilitation fit in? No-one would dispute that providing emergency food to the hungry is an activity protected from any form of conditionality by International Humanitarian Law. But what about giving the hungry the means – an income, perhaps some tools, or help with irrigation, or seed and fertilizer – to reduce their dependency upon handouts? Is it even ethical, whatever the political hue of the authorities, to limit aid to humanitarian assistance when it is clear that rehabilitation work is both possible and arguably essential to prevent hundreds of thousands of Afghans from becoming beggars in their own land?

But perhaps the biggest dilemma of all facing the assistance collectivity is how to deal with a group which claims to be a government and which controls most of the country, but which, in reality, is more usefully described as a movement and which has demonstrated no significant administrative capacity.

The internal dynamic of the Taliban movement remains obscure to outsiders and makes the Chinese politburo look transparent. Aid agencies, not least the UN, naturally seek government counterparts but are repeatedly frustrated by what they see as the indifference or ignorance of Taliban authorities towards them and the sectors in which they work – whether in health, education, agriculture or otherwise. Communication between ministries would seem to be rare, and agreements struck with officials in Kabul often seem to hold no sway either in other parts of the country or, in some cases, in the street outside. The Taliban do little to support what remains of the country's demoralized civil service which, amazingly, manages to carry on in some cases.

How should the aid community react to this absence of governmental interlocutor? It has done so in a variety of ways – for example, at one extreme, by bypassing central authorities altogether; or by treating them as a source of, effectively, non-objection certificates but certainly not as an administrative partner; or, at the other extreme, by seeking Taliban endorsement and involvement in programming decisions.

There are other problems which at first glance may seem lesser in scale but which pose enormous practical and political dilemmas. Much of the assistance community, the ICRC being a notable exception, is based in a neighbouring country, Pakistan. There are good practical and political reasons for this. But it makes simply travelling to Afghanistan an almost political act. Moreover, there is nothing like being on the spot, in the Afghan environment, for decision-making, and inevitably there is something artificial about assistance by remote control. The logistical and communication problems are formidable and compounded by the absence of Afghan infrastructure.

Another formidable problem is finding and supporting female UN or NGO staff, Afghan or international. Working inside Afghanistan is not easy for anyone, and infinitely more difficult for women in the current environment. Security is one issue. In addition, special arrangements are needed tor local transportation, in offices, and at meetings. Agencies have long discussions about how far they should go to respond to local authorities' diktats or sensitivities. At what point do practical arrangements become unprincipled accommodation, or amount to an abandonment of educated Afghan women's own liberal traditions, which have just as much validity as other Afghan traditions?

The eyes of the world

Many of these dilemmas are common to other prolonged crises but in Afghanistan they seem to be in sharper focus than elsewhere. This may in part be due to sustained international media interest in Afghanistan, largely limited to the military situation and to reporting of restrictions upon women by the Taliban. Their introverted ways and zealotry never cease to intrigue and outrage world public opinion. Indeed, the Taliban's beliefs and behaviour, powerfully advertised in a series of incidents such as the stringing-up in September 1996 of former President Najibullah from a traffic light in downtown Kabul or, a year later, the detaining of European Commissioner Emma Bonino and CNN correspondent Christiane Amanpour, seem to have an almost mesmeric fascination in a world preoccupied by altogether more mundane concerns.

There may be greater focus on Afghanistan, too, certainly for those in the world of international relations and aid, as the result of a decision by an obscure but powerful UN committee to single out Afghanistan as a test case for improving the world's ability to address and resolve the problems of countries in crisis.

In April 1997, the Administrative Committee on Coordination (ACC) – which includes the UN Secretary-General and the Executive Heads of UN Programmes, Specialized Agencies, the World Bank and the IMF – met in Geneva for one of its regular meetings. Its members agreed to strengthen efforts in crisis countries where the UN operates political programmes mandated by the Security Council or the General Assembly. It chose two countries as test cases – Afghanistan and Mozambique (although the latter was subsequently changed). Sadako Ogata, UN High Commissioner for Refugees, was said to have been the most vocal in support of the choice of Afghanistan, not that surprising as Afghans represent one of the largest and oldest refugee caseloads in the world.

The decision by ACC members to choose Afghanistan was a happy one in that, probably unbeknown to them, much had been going on in the region already to bring all the players in the international aid community together to address some of these very dilemmas. In January 1997 an international forum had taken place in Ashgabad, Turkmenistan, to try to get some consensus on the objectives, principles and elements of external assistance to Afghanistan.

But whether the ACC had quite realized what it was taking on by choosing Afghanistan is another question. The Taliban phenomenon has added a further dimension to all the dilemmas that the international community is facing in "failed states." Some of these dilemmas will never be resolved but a concerted attempt is now being made in Afghanistan at least to manage them better. The Strategic Framework for Afghanistan, prepared in late 1997, which resulted from the ACC's decision, is a major step forward in this regard. (SEE UN STRATEGY) It attempts to make explicit the responsibilities for the prolongation of the social, economic and humanitarian crisis in Afghanistan, and to place the assistance community's work in a realistic geopolitical and economic context. It proposes a holistic approach in which political and non-political efforts to achieve peace inform each other and in which the aid community's work is based upon recognition of comparative advantage, common identification of needs, agreement on priorities and consistent implementation of human rights principles and norms.

More specifically, it makes a number of proposals, including a common vision for the whole assistance community: the creation of productive livelihoods; a single assistance programme for all actors, operating under a single board of stakeholders; a unitary funding mechanism; an independent monitoring and evaluation mechanism; and an enhanced coordination role for the UN, both at the national and at the regional level inside Afghanistan. This, of course, is heady and radical stuff with implications not just for the way the international community works inside Afghanistan but for its business in all complex emergency countries.

Inevitably there will be resistance to this agenda. Some donors, no matter how much they may bay for reform of the UN, will resist or baulk at the implications of a unitary funding mechanism for assistance to Afghanistan, if only because the money comes from so many different bureaucratic sources, each with their own regulations and procedures. An additional complication may also be posed by the enhanced role being offered to donors as stakeholders; being absent from Afghanistan, many simply do not have the local capacity to respond. Many donors also are likely to be more sensitive to the concerns of their national NGOs, some of whom, in the absence of a diplomatic community inside Afghanistan, have exceptional influence in shaping donor foreign policies.

The NGOs are often the most critical of the UN's performance in the field. They consider the UN to be expensive, cumbersome and having staff ill-suited to the difficult jobs they have been given. Some NGOs have a better institutional memory than UN agencies and are highly critical of the UN's overall performance in the last decade. This began with the UN's heralding of a massive, and, as it turned out, totally premature reconstruction programme after the Geneva Accords were signed in 1988; and it continued through to the Action Plan for Immediate Rehabilitation which was overshadowed by a particularly vicious, and perhaps the most destructive, phase of the civil war. More recently, NGOs felt they had little input into the United Nations Development Programme's P.E.A.C.E. Initiative ("Poverty Eradication And Community Empowerment"), launched in early 1997. Their wariness about the Strategic Framework process is therefore hardly surprising.

NGOs, particularly international, have also been critical of the apparent inability of UN agencies to coordinate among themselves, particularly the way in which the UN has handled the Taliban phenomenon, not least of all in the fields of education and healthcare. They have seen the way different UN agencies have interpreted the various thunderous proclamations from distant headquarters on how to handle the human rights and gender issues and are exasperated by what they consider to be the accommodation that the World Health Organization (WHO) in particular has reached with the Taliban authorities.

It is therefore no surprise that NGOs are unlikely to be thrilled at the prospect of the UN taking on an even greater coordination function – let alone the idea that assistance funding to them should be through a unitary funding mechanism. Nor will they be easily persuaded by the UN's offer to include them in overall management and policy-making – firstly, because they doubt some UN agencies' integrity in this regard, and secondly because they are the first to admit the problems that NGOs themselves face in reaching common positions, or in representing themselves through a single body.

Existing NGO coordination structures, notably the Peshawar-based Agency Coordinating Body for Afghan Relief (ACBAR), despite funding problems, have proved to be invaluable networking, information exchange and policy fora, but none can claim to be representative of the geographically and culturally diverse range of NGO bodies. Indeed, most would argue that it is the variety of NGOs – Western, Islamic, Afghan, rights-centred, delivery-focused, emergency-oriented, developmental and so on – that constitutes the sector's strength, and that to attempt to homogenize this group for whatever purpose is both impractical and counterproductive.

But ironically, the greatest resistance to the proposals being made in the Strategic Framework will probably be from within the UN. Despite the operational flexibility that many UN agencies have shown inside Afghanistan, most are notoriously protective of their mandates, resistant to fundamental change, and suspicious of predatory behaviour by their sister agencies. Within Afghanistan, effective coordination will be possible if the individuals involved have a positive attitude towards coordination, and if a relatively new discipline – professional coordination – is given a chance to work.

The higher up the UN system one goes, the more resistance there will be, as institutional agenda and executive egos clash. Ultimately, the authority of the Secretary-General, backed up by Member States, will be needed to push through the agenda being proposed in the Strategic Framework. But even then, cynics – or sages – will warn against any underestimation of the independence of individual agencies, many having their own Executive Boards consisting of governmental representatives who may or may not have any truck with their compatriots or peers on other Executive Boards.

Afghanistan is thus currently the crucible for many dilemmas facing the global assistance community, including how to operationalize UN human rights and gender equity principles, how to reconcile these principles with the dictates of International Humanitarian Law, how to reorder the way in which the assistance actors work with each other in complex emergency situations, and how to re-energise and reform the UN, not least with a view to more muscular approaches to saving future generations from the scourge of war. The way these dilemmas are handled, if not resolved, in Afghanistan could have ramifications well beyond the local scene.

***Michael Keating,** formerly Director of Media Natura Trust (London), is currently a communications specialist with UNOCHA in Islamabad. This essay has been reproduced from* Fundamentalism Reborn? Afghanistan and the Taliban, *William Maley (Editor), Hurst & Co. (London, 1998) by kind permission of the publishers.*

Exile for a cause: the plight of refugees

By Peter Marsden, with files from Rupert Colville and Edward Girardet

Afghanistan has produced one of the largest refugee movements since the end of World War II, sending over five million refugees to the neighbouring countries of Pakistan and Iran as well as to Europe, North America and India. The first Afghans began fleeing communist repression within weeks of the 1978 *coup d'etat* by the Khalq ('Masses') faction of the People's Democratic Party of Afghanistan (PDPA), the overwhelming majority heading for Pakistan's North West Frontier Province. By the time of the December 1979 Soviet invasion, some 400,000 had crossed the border into Pakistan and another 200,000 into Iran. The exodus quickly became a flood; an estimated 1.9 million had fled by the end of the first year of the occupation, constituting the largest single group of refugees in the world.

By the early 1980s, Soviet counter-insurgency methods were leading to what many observers at the time saw as a deliberate form of "migratory genocide." From 1985 to 1990, according to estimates of the United Nations High Commissioner for Refugees (UNHCR), a staggering 6.2 million Afghans – including children born in exile – were living in Pakistan and Iran alone: just under half the world's refugee population. By the end of 1997, 2.7 million refugees remained in Pakistan, Iran and other regional countries. Although heavily diminished by refugee returns, the exile population still represented the single largest refugee caseload in the world. Since October 1979, UNHCR has spent well over one billion dollars on Afghan refugees in Pakistan and another $150 million in Iran. The World Food Programme (WFP) has donated nearly $1.4 billion in Pakistan alone while billions more have been donated by various donor governments and aid agencies on bilateral humanitarian programmes. (SEE AID POLITICS)

On the surface, Afghanistan's massive refugee flight may seem to have been largely a response to what was – and often still is – clearly a heavy military onslaught on the population. It is easy to view the return as determined by a combination of improved security and suitable economic conditions. Important as these considerations have been, interviews with refugees in Iran and Pakistan and with returnees in Afghanistan indicate that religious and historical factors weighed much more heavily in the balance.

The origins of the refugee situation in Afghanistan can be traced as far back as the early part of this century when King Amanullah, who ruled from 1919-1929, attempted to introduce a process of reform aimed at improving the position of women and girls. He failed, however, to consult with and involve the traditional tribal and religious leadership of the country. He also failed to ensure the necessary military support to secure a degree of compliance. His reforms were barely introduced before he met with armed opposition and had to abdicate. Amanullah's successors immediately cancelled his reforms and adopted a more conservative approach, taking their lead from the religious establishment of *ulama* and *mullahs.* (SEE HISTORY)

It was not until the 1950s that the reform movement resurrected itself under Prime Minister Mohammed Daoud. Backed by the Soviets, Daoud strengthened his government's armed forces, while at the same time engaged in debate with the religious leaders. As a result, he was able to secure certain concessions through a combination of force and persuasion before falling from office in 1963. Nevertheless, his efforts culminated in the 1964 Constitution which was agreed by a large assembly, representing all parts of Afghanistan, and, among other provisions, accorded legal equality to both women and men.

The reform process proceeded steadily during the 1960s and 1970s within a climate of growing political ferment and radicalism, inspired by student movements elsewhere in the world. Two

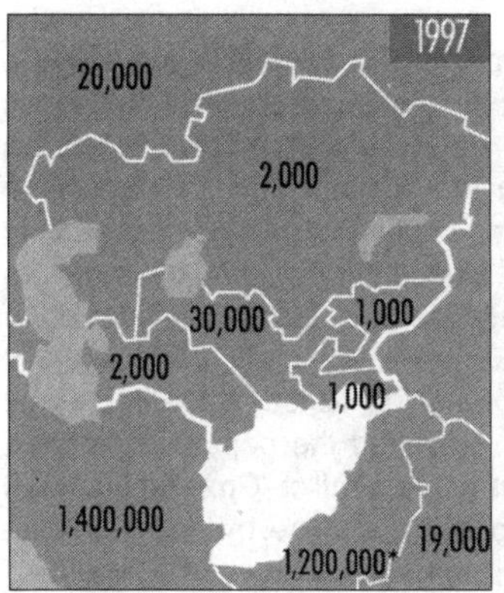

Afghan refugee numbers at July 1997. From 1996 onwards, estimates of the Afghan refugee population in Pakistan include all those residing in refugee villages, whether registered or unregistered. All figures for Iran are based on government estimates. A very small proportion of Afghan refugees in Iran lives in camps.

UNHCR, July 1997

particular movements emerged: one, socialist, looked to Moscow for guidance; the other, radical Islamist, drew on the thinking of the Muslim Brotherhood and of Islamic thinkers from the Indian subcontinent.

When Daoud ousted King Zahir Shah in 1973, and proclaimed himself President, he initially sought the backing of the socialist movement, which had formed the PDPA. He also leaned heavily on Moscow and encouraged an accelerated process of Soviet political, economic and military engagement in Afghanistan. Tensions, however, soon arose between Daoud and the PDPA over the pace of reform and his attempts to suppress the movement finally resulted in the April 1978 Saur Revolution.

The communist PDPA was quick to impose land reforms and to introduce a female literacy programme but used excessive force in the process. They demonstrated an arrogant and gross insensitivity to societal religious and cultural norms. There was an immediate backlash from all sections of rural society, with very clear echoes of the response to Amanullah's reforms.

But this time, the level of armed conflict was considerably more acute. The communists brutally put down the wave of armed insurrections which manifested themselves throughout the country, provoking a call for holy war or *jihad*. The existence of the *jihad* justified not only the taking up of arms against the PDPA but also a process of migration, on the religious grounds that the believers had been wronged. This followed the example of a migration which Mohammed and his followers had undertaken.

The military actions of the PDPA provoked an early exodus of refugees in 1978 and 1979 to the neighbouring Islamic countries of Iran and Pakistan, which regarded it as their Islamic duty to provide hospitality to those seeking exile. They also provided active support to the *jihad* by supplying arms to men of fighting age and by facilitating their regular transit across borders to engage in attacks on communist forces. The radical Islamist parties, which had emerged in Kabul in the 1960s, were quick to capitalize on the Islamic dimension to the conflict and assumed an increasingly leading role from bases in Pakistan and Iran.

This situation fed into the paranoia of the Soviet Union over the possibility of encirclement along its southern borders. The Islamic Revolution in Iran of 1978 had deprived the United States of a strategically important base in the region. Moscow may have speculated that the armed uprising could be exploited by the US to establish a military presence in Afghanistan. This and other factors led to a chain of events which culminated in the Soviet invasion of Afghanistan.

Both the invasion and the repression inflicted by the Red Army and Afghan government forces provoked the population further, resulting in a rapid intensification of the conflict. Growing numbers sought exile in Pakistan and Iran to the point where, by the mid-1980s, Pakistan accommodated 3.27 million refugees and Iran 2.9 million.

Some Afghans attempted to remain in their villages but found it increasingly difficult to withstand the bombardment and armed entry into their homes by the Soviet forces. It was common for families to flee to the mountains, where they would reduce their food intake to the absolute minimum in order to survive, while the men returned to fight as mujahideen and to keep the land under cultivation as best they could. Some villages fared worse than others. Within the same district, certain areas of strategic importance would be reduced to rubble while others were barely touched and life could continue with a degree of normality.

Only a small handful of primarily French and British humanitarian organizations provided a trickle of clandestine crossborder assistance during the early 1980s to civilians seeking to survive inside Afghanistan. The overwhelming majority of aid organizations and donors preferred to offer so-called 'official' assistance to refugees only, mainly in Pakistan. United Nations agencies, for example, refused to become involved in any form of crossborder relief. According to some observers, this lack of international assistance to help civilians withstand the impact of war inside Afghanistan actually contributed to the refugee exodus as many people had little option but to leave. (SEE AID IN THE 1980s)

When the Soviet Union announced its decision to withdraw its forces by February 1989, much of the international community expected the Soviet-backed regime of President Najibullah to fall almost immediately. They also anticipated, not unreasonably, that this would result in the immediate return of the six million refugees in Pakistan and Iran, with the ending of the *jihad*. The UN geared itself up for a massive relief operation in support of the returnees.

However, the government did not fall until the Soviet Union itself collapsed and the flow of arms and other resources supplied by Moscow came to an end. In the meantime, the UN, working closely with NGOs, sought to prepare the ground for the eventual return of refugees through programmes aimed to rehabilitate the agricultural base of Afghanistan. This resulted in a trickle of refugees, mostly men, returning to their villages from Pakistan for the summer to rebuild their homes and get the land working again before wintering in the refugee camps.

On the other hand, the families who had spent the war in the mountains of Afghanistan returned home as soon as the Soviet troops left. They started the process of reconstruction long before the aid agencies arrived to offer assistance. At this stage, however, there was no return from Iran.

When the Soviet-backed government was replaced by the mujahed-led Islamic State of Afghanistan in April 1992, the *jihad* was finally over. The summer of 1992 saw a return of refugees from the North West Frontier Province of Pakistan on a massive scale, tempered only by the gradual realization that disunity within the mujahideen was going to result in further conflict.

The ending of the *jihad* was a trigger for refugees in Iran to commence their return, particularly those who had fled from the villages of Farah province to the desert encampments on the other side of the frontier. In December 1992, the Iranian government agreed on a repatriation programme aimed at returning all its 2.9 million refugees by the end of 1995. This was initially encouraged by the stability offered in Herat by the mujahed leader, Ismail Khan. By the end of 1993, much of Herat's exiled population had returned. The remaining population of Farah was sent back as their homes and camps were bulldozed.

Continued conflict, however, inhibited further return from Iran in 1994 and 1995. The capture by the Taliban of the whole of western Afghanistan in September 1995 brought the return process to a halt. Efforts by UNHCR to assist refugees from northern Afghanistan to return via Turkmenistan met with a total lack of interest. Refugees from the north indicated that the chronic level of insecurity across the northern and central provinces represented a major deterrent to their return. Instead, people started to go back to Iran in their thousands to escape the restrictions imposed by the Taliban and the deteriorating economic situation following the takeover.

There was also a substantial flow of migrant workers from 1993 onwards, as younger members of returnee families left Afghanistan to look for work in Iran, while their elders continued the long process of reconstruction. A significant population growth among Afghans brought on by improved healthcare in Iran made it difficult to achieve self-sufficiency in spite of substantial progress in restoring the agricultural base in western Afghanistan, as in many other parts of the country.

The advent of the Taliban had a positive effect on the return of refugees to Kandahar and southern Afghanistan. Prior to the capture of Kandahar in October 1994, the city and surrounding region had been subject to chronic instability. The Taliban brought absolute security to a wide area. People started returning in large numbers to revitalise the urban economy and work on the land. However, the initial failure of the Taliban to take Kabul in 1995-1996 led to fears that the Islamic movement might not be able to maintain their hold. As a result, the return process became more cautious.

A factor in this trend of accelerated return was the final ending, in September 1995, of aid agency rations and services for the refugees living in Pakistani camps. When the refugees had first arrived towards the end of the 1970s, they had been accommodated in camps along the length of the border and provided with tents, various food items, kerosene and kitchen equipment. They had quickly built their own mud homes and compounds, with or without assistance, and had gradually found work to supplement their rations. Schools, clinics and water supply systems were established in the camps. Over time, the rations were reduced to the point where only wheat and kerosene were provided. The allocation per head of these items also declined. This was reduced even further over the 1992-1995 period. The ending of the rations coincided with a decision to require refugees to contribute towards the costs of water, education and health services.

The decision to wind down and then end the rations and free services was based on the premise that the refugees were in a position to be self-sufficient, at least at the level of the poorest amongst the population of Pakistan. The UN sought to minimize hardship for disadvantaged groups by providing an allocation of cooking oil for women attending clinics, children attending school etc. But a study undertaken by the British Agencies Afghanistan Group (BAAG) in refugee camps near Peshawar in December 1996 indicated that a significant proportion of the population were living at a very marginal level. Many were having to look for work on a daily basis and some would go for long periods without finding work. It did not appear that the safety net system provided through the allocation of cooking oil was preventing large numbers of refugees from being dependent on the charity of their neighbours in the refugee camps.

The picture in Iran is very similar. When refugees had originally fled there, most had been sent to live in the major cities, particularly Meshad, where they were expected to find their own housing and to look for work within certain designated menial occupations. They were given access to free medical and education services and entitlements to generous subsidies on basic food and other items available to the Iranian population.

Once the repatriation programme started in 1992, the Iranian government began to place restrictions on the Afghan population, particularly in relation to their right to operate businesses and to work in certain occupations. A worsening economic situation in Iran made it necessary for subsidies to be reduced and for the population to be forced to contribute increasingly to the costs of education and health services. The economically marginal position of many Afghans also led to acute suffering. Those who fled in recent years, in response to the Taliban occupation, flooding in central and south-western Afghanistan and the fighting in Kabul, have had to survive without access to subsidies or services and without the limited protection which refugee documentation accords. A study undertaken in July 1996 of refugees in Meshad and Tehran gave a picture of a highly marginal level of existence, much as in Pakistan, in which intermittent daily labouring is the principle source of income.

In both countries, some women have been forced by adverse circumstances to look for work even though this may not have been a part of their lives prior to exile. Many of them have to engage in tailoring, embroidery and other forms of piecework at a fraction of the very low rates of pay which men receive. In the refugee camps of Pakistan, women have found themselves subject to greater restrictions on their mobility than had been the norm in their villages. In the cities of Iran, women have often had to fend for themselves

The Frontier Post 12 August 1991

without family support in a difficult and sometimes hostile urban environment.

Both Iran and Pakistan have demonstrated ambivalence towards the refugees. The welcome of the early years was clearly linked to the acceptance of an Islamic duty and to the provision of military support to the mujahideen. The decision to accommodate refugees in camps was part of this. The Iranian decision to establish camps for the refugees from Farah was also part of this, even though refugees from other parts of Afghanistan had to ensure their own survival in Iran's urban centres.

The response to the mujahed takeover of Kabul in 1992 and the subsequent struggles of power has been coloured by the respective strategic interests of the two countries, so that Iran has discouraged return to Taliban-controlled areas and Pakistan has kept to a minimum the number of refugees which it has accepted as a consequence of fighting in Kabul. As a result, there has been a significant increase in the number of internal refugees, or so-called "internally-displaced persons" (IDPs), in Afghanistan since 1992. Afghans who have sought refuge in Kabul and other areas inside the country – and thus do not qualify technically as refugees – have either become the responsibility of the ICRC, UNHCR and other agencies, or must fend for themselves.

The first major movement of IDPs was to Mazar-e-Sharif, following the rocketing of Kabul in August 1992. The rockets which literally rained on Kabul in January 1994 led to the creation of two enormous refugee camps near Jalalabad and to a further exodus of Afghans fleeing to live in Nasir Bagh camp near Peshawar. The Taliban capture of Jalalabad and Kabul in September 1996 resulted in 50,000 refugees fleeing to Pakistan and the subsequent capture of the Shomali plains north of Kabul by the Taliban from January 1997 onwards expanded the population of Kabul by 200,000. Fighting in Badghis, in northwestern Afghanistan, has created movements with an ethnic basis, as Pashtuns have travelled to Herat to escape from the advancing Uzbek forces and as Turkmen have attempted to cross the border to escape from the Taliban.

***Peter Marsden** is Information Coordinator for the British Agencies Afghanistan Group, based at the Refugee Council in London. Rupert Colville is Regional Press Officer for UNHCR, based in Islamabad.*

Media coverage: frontline or fringe?

By Edward Girardet

In an editorial on 1 June 1982, the *New York Times* wrote that the world's attention span for conflicts and humanitarian crises was estimated at 90 days. Commenting on the continued Soviet occupation of Afghanistan nearly two-and-a-half years after the December 1979 invasion, the newspaper noted that Afghanistan had all but slipped from sight. "But still the war goes on," it observed. "The Russians, incredibly, are no nearer victory than at the start, when experts blandly forecast that their modern army would subdue primitive tribesmen in months. It is bigger news than a bored world realizes."

Looking back, this assessment appears sad but also ironic. By early 1998 as we go to press, the Afghan war is well into its 20th year, albeit once again in the form of a civil conflict. The Soviets finally pulled out in February 1989, soon involving themselves – as Russians – in another war, Chechnya. There they began using the same brutal methods against the civilian population as they had in Afghanistan, but also suffered the same horrendous setbacks at the hands of Chechen partisans as they had at those of the mujahideen. As for the *NYT's* observation on the world's attention span, even 90 days now seems a generous timeframe given the media's current obsession with nine-second sound bites and highly competitive 'live' saturation coverage of events.

When fighting first broke out in summer 1978 with local Afghan groups opposed to the communist regime in Kabul staging increasing numbers of attacks against the government, it marked the outbreak of an intermittent but devastating civil war. It also signalled the first civilian departures of a mass exodus that would quickly snowball into one of the world's largest refugee crises since World War II. The early stages of this war received relatively little international press coverage. Only the occasional wire reports or feature stories referred to police stations being hit, party officials assassinated, or hippie buses taking the odd sniper bullet from mujahideen hiding out in the mountains, resulting in several tourist deaths and injuries. It was only when the American ambassador in Kabul was killed in February 1979, followed by the lynching of a large group of Soviet advisors in Herat, that the Afghan war began to have international repercussions. One then began to see a growing trickle of stories about an emerging Central Asian war.

Yet it was only with the Red Army invasion in December 1979 that the world media began to focus its attention *en masse* on Afghanistan – and then, over the years, only in intermittent bursts. As a major war, Afghanistan never quite made it. Nevertheless, not unlike Vietnam in the 1960s and early 1970s, Afghanistan was, and still is, in some respects, a poignant landmark conflict for journalists. It is a war that has managed to move, despite all odds, with the times, in terms of both how it is fought and how it is reported. As with current or recent conflict areas such as Somalia, Rwanda, Kurdistan, Liberia, Sri Lanka and Sudan, Afghanistan continues to inspire irregular surges of coverage although hardly for as long as the *NYT's* statutory three months.

Both in 1996 and 1997, Afghanistan witnessed periods of relatively good reporting with major European and American news organizations ranging from French television and *CNN* to the *Süddeutsche Zeitung*, *The Times* and the *NYT* lending prominent coverage to the humanitarian plight, the continuing war, and the Taliban phenomenon. Of course, some media, notably the *BBC*, *Voice of America, Reuters, Agence France Presse,* and the *Associated Press,* have provided relatively consistent coverage since the start of the Afghan war nearly 20 years ago. All have reporters or stringers still working out of Kabul and Islamabad. According to the International Committee of the Red Cross (ICRC) and other humanitarian agencies, the coverage had become almost 'embarrassingly' good. In 1997 alone, well over 800 foreign journalists made the trip to Pakistan or Afghanistan to cover the story.

Journalists point out that slump periods in the news agenda, Taliban repression against women, alleged links to Afghanistan among Islamic extremists in North America, Europe, Saudi Arabia and elsewhere in the world, the country's global position as the number one producer of heroin and other opium products, and its recently heralded strategic importance as a pipeline host for oil and natural gas from Central Asia to the Indian Ocean have all contributed to this spread of coverage. Improved road and air facilities, including flights and vehicles provided by the ICRC, the United Nations and other relief agencies from Peshawar to the interior, have prompted editors to commission more reporting from the region.

When the Soviets first invaded in 1979, there was an obvious explosion of media coverage. Journalists, producers, photographers and cameramen, both male and female, flocked by the hundreds to

Kabul and other parts of the country to report the Red Army incursion. Others travelled to Peshawar and the refugee camps along the Pakistan-Afghan frontier. For several months, it was possible to cover both sides of the story. However, this became increasingly difficult as the Soviet-backed Afghan regime cut back on visas, particularly to those who had reported with the mujahideen. Such one-sidedness always has been a major drawback in the coverage of the Afghan war. While some newspapers sought to include reports from Moscow or from the Afghan capital by other correspondents, it was virtually impossible for one journalist to cover both the Soviets and the guerrillas. A similar situation exists today given the growing difficulties of reaching non-Taliban areas.

As a result, journalists seeking to cover the conflict itself travelled clandestinely with the mujahideen. Without doubt, there was a strong element of romanticism in the covering of a war which involved 19th Century conditions, horse caravans through the mountains and drinking tea with desert nomads on the one hand, and dealing with helicopter gunship and MiG attacks on the other. Afghanistan also had its fair share of "war cowboys", and not just amongst the journalist community. Many aid workers and various Afghan *wallahs*, too, were enthralled by the excitement of trekking 'inside.' Today, such frontline intrepidness still intrigues. One American gem dealer, who regularly travels into Afghanistan, unabashedly advertises himself as the "Indiana Jones of the '90s."

Some journalists, particularly those representing partisan conservative interests in the United States or Europe, assumed blatantly anti-Soviet stances paying little attention to the faults or excesses of the so-called "Freedom Fighters", and providing what was essentially extremely poor reporting. A not-so-different militancy, justified or not, is found among some writers who openly condone or condemn the Taliban without bothering to seek a more balanced understanding of the phenomenon. Considerable recent reporting fails to take into account that the Taliban is nothing particularly new nor is it fervently embraced by many Afghans who purport to support the movement. Not unlike the influences commanded by previous groups, including the Khalq or Parcham factions of the Kabul communists or the Hezb-e-Islami of Gulbuddin Hekmatyar, the Taliban appears to owe much of its sway to a combination of typical Afghan opportunism, payoffs and fear, but also deep-rooted frustration with the war.

The Soviet war also attracted journalists who appeared more interested in the "Great Game" itself. Some often dabbled with various Western intelligence services or even took part in the fighting. Others had themselves photographed brandishing kalashnikovs or aiming anti-aircraft guns, a real no-no if you don't want to be accused of being a mercenary or a spy. In general, however, many among the foreign press corps, including the freelancers, proved both conscientious and professional in their reporting.

They sought to furnish a coverage that was as accurate and as balanced as could be expected under exceptionally difficult circumstances.

Unlike in Vietnam, journalists could not simply fly in and out of conflict areas by helicopter. And unlike the Gulf War – many of whose correspondents not only relied on highly sanitized military propaganda for their information but also found themselves severely restricted in their movements even when with Allied forces – the Afghan media *wallahs* had to depend largely on their own ingenuity and stamina. For a small but significant portion of the press corps, it was often a matter of trekking for days, weeks, even months across mountains and deserts to report the story. Many, however, particularly those representing television networks, simply did not have the time to undertake serious crossborder reporting trips. As a result, the majority of visiting journalists based most of their coverage on trips to Peshawar with short excursions, usually of a few days, to mujahed bases inside Afghanistan in order to obtain 'frontline' bylines. Mobile satellite television and telephone units, just beginning to make an appearance during the late 1980s, did not really figure in reporting from the field. Television networks such as *CBS, BBC, NBC, ITV, ZDF* and *Antenne 2 (now France2)* had to rely mainly on freelance cameramen and women for the bulk of their footage.

As a correspondent for *The Christian Science Monitor* and American public television's *MacNeil-Lehrer NewsHour,* for example, this writer often travelled with a freelance crew for as many as six weeks. Unable to file from the mountains, one had to wait until one returned to Peshawar or Paris to produce a series of lengthy articles plus two or three television reports. *Le Monde, The Washington Post, TIME, The Guardian, The New York Times, Der Spiegel, Corriere della Sera, El Pais* and other newspapers and magazines did the same. In fact, such trips probably provided far better informed and 'quality' reporting than much of the 'live' coverage during the Gulf War, Somalia or Rwanda. One had time to talk to people and assess the situation from the field while combining it with information obtained from various embassies, relief agencies and other sources based in Pakistan, India, Paris or London.

During much of the Soviet occupation, media coverage from inside Afghanistan was provided by a small clutch of European, American, Australian, New Zealand, Japanese and other correspondents, probably no more than 100 throughout the year. When the Americans began providing more overt crossborder military aid to the mujahideen during the mid-1980s, there was a noticeable increase in international media coverage. The fact that more US and European humanitarian funding was also available prompted a significant rise in the number of aid agencies setting up shop in Peshawar, Quetta and among the refugee camps. They, too, engendered greater coverage for the humanitarian story by encouraging journalists from their own countries ranging from Sweden to Mexico to visit local operations.

The fact that some of these agencies, intent on cashing in on the new wave of funding, developed numerous 'refugee' projects for projects' sake while ignoring the humanitarian needs inside the country, was not necessarily picked up many journalists who simply "passed through." As a result, considerable sums of money were wasted on worthless projects or siphoned off by corrupt elements within Pakistani government and Afghan resistance organizations.

The increased US involvement in the war was one of the principal reasons why the American media suddenly showed renewed interest from 1986 onwards. Much of the reporting, however, particularly with regard to US policy, could have been, and should have been, far more critical. Too many American journalists visiting the region, or writing from Washington and New York, relied too heavily on what they were being told by the State Department, the Central Intelligence Agency, the Pentagon, the White House, the US Agency for International Development (USAID) and other sources, including various "Beltway Rat" think-tanks in Washington. The reporting was often grossly inaccurate or poorly informed, usually the result of disinformation. Some of the relief agencies in Peshawar, especially those which had no operations inside Afghanistan, cultivated curious links with the US government and were equally uninformed about the situation or knowingly contributed to the disinformation process. USAID was particularly anxious that a united front be maintained by the press *vis à vis* the Soviets. The agency bitterly resented any critical reporting of its operations, many of which were little more than fronts to support the mainly fundamentalist mujahed groups in the name of anti-Soviet political expediency.

During the Soviet war, most of the more reliable information about what was happening inside Afghanistan was provided by Western journalists and humanitarian relief workers operating crossborder. Many, including Americans, strongly criticised the way US aid, both military and humanitarian, was being delivered. Others preferred to ignore it as it skewed their image of freedom-loving Afghans determined to throw off the Red Army yoke.

At Pakistan's behest, huge amounts of weaponry and ammunition were directed to the likes of Gulbuddin Hekmatyar's Hezb-e-Islami faction and other, mainly Pashtun but also Arab-backed extremists. Much of this was simply stockpiled to be later deployed in Afghanistan's new civil war, much of it directed against hapless civilians in Kabul. Some well-informed US State Department and USAID officials concerned by the detrimental effects of this American aid had sought to encourage more outspoken reporting of deficiencies in US policy but were either ousted, transferred elsewhere or threatened. The information was there. Too many, however, failed to heed the realities.

When the Soviets left, so did most of the journalists. When the mujahideen finally took Kabul after several false alarms and misadventures, they came back in droves. Yet somehow, the war did not end cleanly with the raising of the green Islamic flag in the Afghan capital. Instead, as forecast by some observers, particularly the more experienced humanitarian representatives and conflict analysts, a Beirut-style civil war began to materialise. There was too much stored weaponry and too many unresolved factional interests ranging from a blatant thirst for power to lucrative drug and arms trafficking activities to allow Afghans to return to their homes in peace. (SEE DRUGS) And so Afghanistan became "yet another war" with sporadic media coverage. This was interspersed by bouts of saturation coverage such as "Afghanistan revisited" documentary films or newspaper reports on drug wars or Islamic extremism.

As a war embarking on its third decade, Afghanistan may find itself back in the media spotlight not so much because the world is feeling sorry for Afghans, but because of its traditional strategic importance as a crossroads for the West, the former Soviet Union and the region. (SEE WAR WITHOUT BORDERS) The United States, Russia, the Central Asian Republics, Iran, Pakistan, India, Saudi Arabia and other players all suddenly seem more openly interested in the fact that Afghanistan has a key role to play as a conduit for oil and natural gas pipelines but also regional communications and trade links.

With the Taliban making it increasingly difficult for camera teams and photographers to work, Afghanistan is in danger of becoming a 'closed' or inaccessible conflict, at least in certain parts of the country. (SEE JOURNALISM) But at least the Taliban's repressive actions against journalists – and women – are attracting attention. Afghanistan also appears to be attracting more than just weary international eyebrow raising. The issues now at the forefront, be they the way the Taliban is reacting, the way the drug trade is expanding or the political interests that are emerging, could conceivably all help end the conflict but also prolong it. Either way, the country's humanitarian plight no longer needs to jostle alone for world attention. Once again, Afghanistan is beginning to figure on the global Richter scale of strategic and economic importance, but not necessarily for the right reasons. Perhaps more than ever, humanitarian concerns representing both the Afghan people and the international community might best be served by a more critical press able to keep such issues open to public scrutiny.

Edward Girardet *is currently Editor of* CROSSLINES Global Report *and has reported on Afghanistan since 1979.*

Defiance and oppression: the situation of women

By Christine Aziz

From her throne in Herat, Queen Gawhar Shad ruled an empire that stretched from the Tigris river to the borders of China. Historians acknowledge that her husband, Shah Rukh, was a weak man, and that she was the ruling force. Queen Gawhar led a cultural renaissance with her lavish patronage of the arts, attracting artists, architects, poets and philosophers to her court. Shah Rukh died in 1447, but his wife continued to rule for a further decade until she was murdered in her eightieth year.

For the women of Herat, Queen Gawhar Shad is a powerful reminder of a time when women in the region were able to command power and influence the destiny of men. Through the centuries they have made regular pilgrimages to her tomb, leaving gifts for their Queen who has become part of Afghanistan's folklore which celebrates women and their strength and courage.

No one visits the tomb these days. The women of Herat have been effectively held under house arrest by the Taliban, a radical and primarily Pashtun Islamic movement, which took control of Herat on 5 September 1995. (SEE TALIBAN) The city fell without a fight and overnight Herat's women, used to a history of emancipation, were ordered to stay at home. Schools and universities were closed to them and they were forced to leave their jobs. If they went outside they had to wear the *burqa*, which covered their bodies from head to toe.

Throughout this century, Afghan women have been used to demonstrate the ideological and religious whims of successive governments and ruling warlords. This has been made visibly apparent to the world's onlookers through the symbolism of the veil. Afghan women have slipped in and out of it from one decade to another according`to the male dictates of the day.

The beginning of the 20th Century saw the role of women in Afghanistan expanding beyond the home. Between 1919 and 1929,

Amanullah Khan ruled as King of Afghanistan. (SEE HISTORY) His desire to modernize the country included the gradual emancipation of women. "Religion does not require women to veil their hands, feet and faces, or enjoin any special type of veil. Tribal custom must not impose itself on the free will of the individual," he said.

Female emancipation was accelerated by General Mohammed Daoud who became Prime Minister of Afghanistan in 1953. Women were encouraged to play an active part in government and join the workforce. In 1959, women were able to enrol as students at Kabul University. This increased visibility of women did not weaken the long-held Afghan tradition that women are at the heart of the family, the most important institution in Afghan society. The honour and status of the family lie with the women, who are controlled and protected by men. The extent to which they are allowed to participate in society beyond the family is determined largely by which ethnic group they belong to, and where they live. For example, Hazara and Tajik women have more freedom than Pashtun (or 'Pathan') women.

In 1973 Daoud ousted his cousin King Zahir Shah and became President of Afghanistan. The issue of a woman's place in society went to the very heart of the Afghan civil war in 1978. One of the main reasons for the outbreak of the fighting was the new communist government's insistence on forced literacy and mixed education for women. The invasion of Afghanistan by Soviet troops the following year led to the acceleration of the emancipation of many Afghan women. The ten-year Soviet occupation offered them greater opportunities in education, professional training and work – especially to middle-class and urban women. While thousands of women took advantage of these opportunities, there were many others who helped in the formation of the mujahideen in June 1979 – just months before the arrival of the Red Army. These women and later recruits would play an important role in the successful attempt to free their country from Soviet occupation.

Nooria Jehan was one of them. A veteran mujahed, she sweeps into the room of a small villa in Kabul, her feet and hands the only visible part of her body, except for a glimpse of her eyes behind the embroidered grill of her *chador*. In a dramatic gesture she flings the curtain of material up and backwards so that the hem falls behind her shoulders revealing her face with its aquiline nose, piercing eyes and mocking smile. Women rise from the *gelim* cushions scattered around the walls to embrace her in greeting. In her forties and mother of seven children, Nooria belies the West's cliché of the passive Muslim woman.

Forceful and expressive she begins to tell her story in Farsi. No doubt her companions have heard it many times before, but they sit spellbound. Nooria is one of the many women who fought against the Soviet occupation and helped oust the pro-Soviet Kabul regime of President Najibullah in 1992 in favour of President Burhannudin Rabbani and his military commander, Ahmed Shah Massoud. Two of her seven children were killed resisting the Soviets. "The Russians came to occupy our land, and there was a mission for all of us as parents to train and bring up our children to resist the occupation," she said. "They came to play with the dignity of women so we had to protect ourselves and children and other women. If they are occupying our land it means we have no right to do what we want with our land, our property, our country, with our children, with education, with economy, military resources. When I say 'dignity' for women, it goes with all things rooted in our country."

Until the arrival of the Soviets, Nooria had been a young mother concentrating on bringing up her children. She first became involved in the *jihad* (holy war) by distributing "night letters" – resistance pamphlets to civil servants. "These people had no access to the activities of the mujahideen," Nooria recalls. "After one year, the mujahideen asked me to take part in terrorist activities and gave me a gun, but I found it difficult to go out and just shoot people. So I learned explosive techniques and began supervising and teaching the younger men. I was leading them into Ministries, like the Ministry of Defence, aiming directly at Russian offices. We would stick explosives under the Russians' tables and chairs."

Early one morning, the Soviets came to her house and arrested her. "They said I was a leader and sentenced me to 18 years' prison," she said; but after two years, she was released in exchange for an Afghan communist and a Soviet who had been held by Massoud.

While women like Nooria were fighting alongside the mujahideen, there were others, particularly urban educated and working women, who although not supportive of the communist regime, were fearful of losing their new-found freedoms in the event of a mujahed victory. In 1989 hundreds of women were enlisting in the militia and regular army units. Horror stories of what happened to women like them in the hands of Islamic fundamentalists were circulating through the towns. A fundamentalist leader had sprayed acid in the faces of women university students in Kabul and a woman driving a minibus to a village had been dragged from the vehicle and knifed to death by Islamic traditionalists.

Sofia is younger than Nooria, and admits to feeling very sad when she looks through photographs taken when she was a school girl during Communist rule. "We used to wear socks with skirts. Look!" she said incredulously, "We were free to go out in the streets. There was more freedom for girls then. You could wear trousers and socks as well, at the university. We never wore anything too short though. We were modest and loved to adapt Western fashions to our tastes from magazines. It was fun."

The resignation of communist President Najibullah and the takeover by Rabbani in 1992 changed all that. The mujahideen declared an Islamic Republic of Afghanistan in Kabul and once more the female population became the initial target of change to illustrate the Republic's Islamic reforms. Women's rights were no longer part of the constitution. "In the beginning it was very strict," recalled

J. Hartley/UNICEF

Shazia, an aid agency secretary, until the Taliban forced her out of her job. "They put out a message on the television that we should cover our hair, not use lipstick or stand in groups laughing in public. They said it was not good for us to work. They stuck flowers over the faces of women on the television, so we couldn't see them. We were frightened and stayed in doors. I didn't go to work. But it was very difficult because my family rely on my salary. Then we started coming out, and we were defiant. We wore lipstick and would let our scarves slip and flirted with men on purpose. Some women were attacked, but slowly things began to get better and we went back to our work and to our education." (SEE HUMAN RIGHTS)

The Rabbani government has always acknowledged the support of women in its opposition to the Russians, and was quick to realise that unless women were allowed to work thousands of families would starve. Afghan women have born the brunt of 20 years of war and internecine strife. In Kabul alone, 30,000 women are widowed and the sole providers of food for their families. Most of them are dependent on relief handouts provided by NGOs, the Red Cross and Crescent Movement and the UN. Sediqa, 50, is one of thousands of women who have lost husbands. She lives with her nine children, 13 grandchildren and three sons-in-law in a three-room apartment. The family home was destroyed in a rocket attack in 1996 and her husband was killed. The apartment, on a large estate built by the Russians, was badly hit during fierce fighting between the various mujahed factions in 1994. "I have lost everything", she says, "My daughters' husbands are government employees, but their salaries are not enough. We are barely alive."

According to Amnesty International, thousands of unarmed civilian women have been killed by unexpected and deliberate artillery attacks on their homes. The vast majority have been killed in Kabul. Most Afghan women have taken no active part in the fighting yet their homes and neighbourhoods have been constantly bombarded. During the fighting between rival mujahed factions in 1992 and 1994 women became innocent targets. Women related to men sought by various mujahed groups, or who resisted abduction or rape, were deliberately and arbitrarily killed. Scores of young women have been taken as wives for commanders or sold into prostitution. Others have 'disappeared' or been stoned to death. One family in the old Microrayon area of Kabul told how members of General Dostum's faction entered their home in March 1994 "There were 12 of them all carrying kalashnikov rifles with their faces covered. They asked us to give them our daughter. We refused. One of them lifted his gun and shot our daughter in front of our eyes. She was only 20 and had just finished her high school," the mother said.

During this period, women working in professional jobs in government offices were targeted by various mujahed groups who considered that education under the Russians had poisoned women's minds and turned them against Islamic principles. These women's offices and homes were raided and women were abused and raped. Hundreds of professional women joined the mass exodus from Afghanistan in 1994. Most of those left behind have fled their country since the arrival of the Taliban.

Coping silently with post-traumatic stress and dealing with the everyday struggle to feed their families and keep them warm in freezing winters, Afghan women also face danger every time they step out into the street. They are regular victims of landmines. If they are lucky they will find themselves being treated at a Red Cross hospital; if not they will endure amputation without pain killers and little possibility of false limbs. Many Afghan men do not see the need for the wives to have a prosthesis fitted because they say it does not matter if they have to stay at home. (SEE LANDMINES)

Prior to the arrival of the Taliban, an estimated 8,000 women students had enrolled at Kabul University. (SEE EDUCATION) Seventy percent of the teachers in Kabul were estimated to be women but have been ordered to stay at home. Forty percent of the 150,000 children attending school in Kabul were girls. (SEE REACH) To the women of Afghanistan, the Taliban are yet another regime which has used them as ideological tools, destroying whatever rights they had managed to hang on to. As citizens of the Islamic Republic of Afghanistan which ruled from Kabul, women had been able to work and study alongside their brothers. They were not allowed to travel abroad, had to cover their heads in the streets and could not drive cars. "These were small prices to pay for the right to work and be educated," said Dr Ester, a former surgeon at Kabul's largest hospital.

In every region overrun by the Taliban, their first act is to issue a decree banning all women from public places, their jobs and institutions. "Women, you should not step outside your residence," warns a notice issued to the women of Kabul by Mawlawi Rafiullah Moazin, general president of the Religious Police. "If you go outside the house you should not be like women who used to go with fashionable clothes wearing much cosmetics and appearing in front of every man before the coming of Islam...If women are going outside with fashionable ornamental and charming clothes to show themselves, they will be cursed by the Islamic *shari'a* and should never expect to go to heaven."

What, one wonders, would the head of the Taliban's Religious Police think of the Afghan heroine, Malalai, who (unveiled) in July 1880 carried the Afghan flag into battle, after her fellow soldiers were killed by the British? Her spirit is echoed in the defiant voices of many Afghan woman. In Bamiyan, for example, Hazara women are organizing themselves into militia groups to fight Muslim extremists. They have seen what has happened to their sisters in Taliban-run areas and do not want the same fate. The region in which they live is poor and cut off in the winter by heavy snows, but the women are defiant. They are also setting up a university, despite a severe lack of resources.

In the same spirit, a passionate and courageous appeal was made by a female academic to the Taliban to let women go to work and school. Sidiqa Sidiq, a professor of archaeology in her fifties, quoted extensively from the Koran to tell the newly-arrived Taliban leaders that they were wrong to order women to stay at home. "Based on the orders of the Holy Koran, I am requesting all the concerned brothers and individuals to release us from this detention and these chains and let us continue our education and our jobs. Under the Islamic law that is the prime need for the development of our ruined homeland," she said, adding an appeal to Afghan women to fight for their rights: "Oh sisters, we have to be determined and must not be like our grandfathers expecting assistance from our compatriots abroad and from foreign organizations and countries, because they are shouting only for political propaganda."

Sidiqa's cynicism regarding the foreign response to the plight of women of Afghanistan may well be justified. The human rights abuses committed by the Taliban against women were ignored by the world's media until the militia's arrival in Kabul, and Western journalists witnessed the public whipping of women with bicycle chains because they had not worn their *burqas* correctly. The female populations of Kandahar and Herat had been living under the same conditions for at least two years beforehand.

The Taliban clearly flout the United Nations declaration which calls for the universal application to women "of rights and principles with regard to equality, security, integrity and dignity of all human persons." But UN officials in Afghanistan have consistently failed to take up the issue of female rights with Taliban leaders. The pressure group, Equality Now, has reported that several UN agencies operating in Jalalabad suspended all female Afghan employees in early 1997 under pressure from government and rebel forces, thus contravening the UN Covenant on Civil and Political Rights to which Afghanistan is a signatory. In August 1997 the Taliban instructed medical NGOs in Kabul to stop treating female patients in existing hospitals and transfer them to the partially destroyed Rabia Balkhi health centre where they would be treated separately. (SEE HEALTH) "The centre was not fit for patients, and for two months while we argued with the Taliban, there was nowhere for the women to be treated," said one aid worker whose agency refused to cooperate with the Taliban request, along with other health agencies. Only the World Health Organization (WHO) agreed to comply with the Taliban request and offered funds to refurbish the centre. "We finally convinced the authorities to allow women into Kabul's hospitals. But it was a very serious situation as some women could not be treated for two months," the aid worker said.

In the main, it has been left to individual agencies to voice support for the women. Approximately 75% of women's programmes have been affected because skilled Afghan women are needed to access, run and monitor assistance. Save the Children Fund (UK), for example, withdrew from Herat, and British agency, Oxfam, suspended its water and sanitation programme in Kabul. The agencies cited operational difficulties concerning access for both expatriate and local women as the problem. It has been a slow process amongst international agencies to unite under standard international rights for women. (SEE AID POLITICS) At this time of writing, the Taliban have just forbidden any foreign Muslim women from entering Afghanistan without accompaniment by a male family member.

Several weeks prior to the Taliban's arrival in Kabul, Nooria made it clear that as a devout Muslim, she saw them as as much of a threat to the dignity of Afghan women as the Soviets had been. "We will fight them as we fought the Russians and their Western ways. The Taliban think they will be able to force us into our homes at gunpoint like they did the women of Herat. They are mistaken."

Brave words indeed, but these are different times. Rabbani and his mujahideen have fled the city and the women are alone. The women of Kabul are exhausted after years of scavenging food for their families, moving from place to place as each home gets blown up, while at the same time coping with post-traumatic stress. They have everything to fight for, but they have nothing left to fight with. "We are the forgotten women of a forgotten war," Nooria said.

Yet the resilience and courage of Afghan women manifests itself every day, and is perhaps one of the few hopes left for Afghanistan: the welcoming smile from a woman who wants to invite you into her home to share what little she has; the determination of so many young women to continue their studies in makeshift buildings and often secretly, so they can acquire skills to rebuild their country; the quiet defiance of women in the face of tyranny.

***Christine Aziz** is a freelance journalist working out of Amsterdam and London.*

Human rights: two decades of abuse

By Charles Norchi

Over half a century ago United Nations member governments adopted the Universal Declaration of Human Rights, launching the modern human rights movement. The movement was born of tensions between the individual and the state. Previously there had been no international recourse to remedy deprivations of fundamental rights. So a set of arrangements and procedures external to the state, and to which a person could appeal, were devised. In the wake of the Nuremberg Trials following World War II, norms were codified, governmental and non-governmental international organizations and institutions were established, and human rights was on the international agenda. The principle underlying all human rights is simple: how a government treats its own citizens within its own borders is no longer only that government's business. In Afghanistan, with the exception of intrepid journalists and a few NGOs, this principle has been ignored. In fifty years of the modern human rights system and since the adoption of the Universal Declaration, few populations have experienced the degree and breadth of human rights deprivations as have the people of Afghanistan.

The international human rights system has failed many people in many places, but it has perhaps failed the Afghans more than any other population. In the last twenty years, Afghans have experienced assaults upon the body and spirit, on their culture and society. These human rights abuses have left open and irreparable wounds. In the last two decades, every human rights standard codified by the international community has been violated in Afghanistan.

For two reasons, Afghanistan has never fitted the Western human rights model. First, although the point of human rights is to protect the individual, the system revolves around states. The thinking has been that states are the primary violators and a properly organized state – with a constitution, courts, independent judiciary and so on – was the best way to protect people against human rights abuses. But the 'state' has never been relevant to Afghanistan. The Afghan state has always been weak and either tolerated, opposed or ignored by the greater population. The only states relevant to the human and civil rights of Afghans have been invaders. Second, many international human rights standards are very Western (the Universal Declaration of Human Rights was mostly drafted in Eleanor Roosevelt's New York City apartment). For ordinary Afghans these are more aspirational than real. However, human rights ideas do resonate because a value which underpins all of human rights is highly important to Afghans – respect. Many customary legal codes of *Pashtunwali* (the Pashtun tribal code) revolve around respect, as do the modern human rights treaties and conventions. But these have been largely destroyed by war and continuous assaults upon human dignity. This has been a fundamental setback to righting human rights wrongs in Afghanistan.

The dismal Afghan human rights picture is framed by the loss of self-determination. This is a fundamental human right. Afghanistan has always been a land on everyone's way to somewhere else, from Tamerlane's army to Czarist and British forces. But of all the invaders it was the Red Army of the Soviet Union which first and fully deprived Afghans of the fundamental human right to self-determination. That deprivation continues, but it began when Afghans fell victim to the Brezhnev Doctrine, which goes something like this: when external and internal forces hostile to Socialism try to turn the development of a given Socialist country in the direction of restoration of the capitalist system, when a threat arises to the cause of Socialism in any country – a threat to the security of the socialist commonwealth as a whole – this is no longer merely a problem for that country's people, but a common problem, the concern of all Socialist Parties.

On this basis, Soviet troops entered the country and Afghanistan fully lost her right to self-determination as guaranteed under international law.

The Soviet Army set the stage for a long downward human rights spiral. Red Army tactics were brutal and flouted every human right precept. Initially, aerial bombardment with combined Soviet-Afghan ground operations were used against the growing Afghan resistance. Helicopter gunships became the Soviet military's workhorse. They ferreted out mountain-based guerrillas, but were increasingly used against villages and refugee caravans. As the war progressed civilians became targets of attacks. Crops were burned, fields were carpeted with anti-personnel mines, entire villages razed, and non-combatants killed. Troops in a position to distinguish between mujahideen and civilians were not only failing to identify civilians, they were directly attacking women and children.

The Soviet period was notable for discernible patterns of human rights abuses. Human rights organizations concluded there were

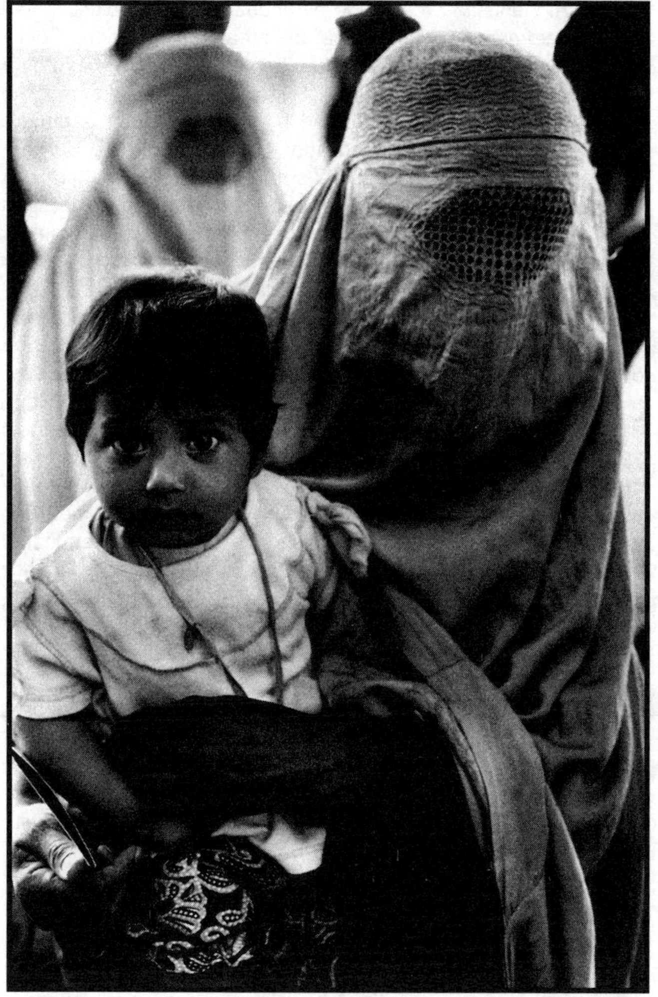

J. Hartley/UNICEF

three patterns violating the laws of human rights in armed conflict. In each pattern, civilians were objects of attack in violation of the Geneva Conventions. The first pattern was intentional depopulation of areas of strategic value. The second was the killing of individual civilians as part of a general attack on the civilian population of a village. The third pattern was one of intentional attacks on individual civilians, such as village elders or religious leaders, usually as a form of punishment or warning.

Heavy bombardment of the Pakistani, Iranian and Soviet border regions was intended to protect frontiers from mujahed-supported infiltration. It also prevented injured civilians from seeking refuge outside Afghanistan. One village in Kunduz province was decimated by bombardment in order to clear the area and establish a Soviet post. The village was bombed and then surrounded at night by a mixed force consisting principally of Soviet troops who attacked the next day. Many persons were killed in the bombardment and more were killed in the land-based attack. The crops were burned, livestock killed and most of the houses destroyed. This pattern was repeated. A two kilometre-wide band was cleared along the northern Salang Highway to protect the movement of troops and equipment from the Soviet Union to Kabul. The attacks were designed to clear the areas of all persons, including civilians.

Frequently, individual civilians were chosen for execution by Soviet troops. Persons were killed in retaliation for a mujahed operation especially if there were Soviet casualties. Civilians were also executed upon suspicion of being related to a mujahed. Village elders or religious leaders were rounded up and killed. While most village leaders were shot, some were burned alive. Prison treatment was horrendous. Most prisoners who were not summarily executed were tortured. Rape was widespread, of both men and women. Countless children disappeared, many to be re-educated in Soviet schools. And millions of landmines were scattered across the country. Many mines were purposely placed in civilian areas, around wells, in agricultural fields and as booby-traps in homes. (SEE LANDMINES) No human rights or humanitarian law standard remained unviolated.

The Soviet Army ravaged Afghanistan for a decade. In that brief period, the catalogue of abuse was formidable – massacres, indiscriminate shelling, targeted bombing of civilians including fleeing refugees, summary executions, reprisal killings, torture, rape, abuse of children, destruction of food supplies, loss of freedom of religion, expression and association. If the Soviets did not actually commit genocide in Afghanistan, they came very close. The country would not recover from the collective shock. When the Soviets turned north and marched home, the abuses continued. From then on Afghans fell into two human rights camps: victims or perpetrators.

After so many years of resisting and fighting the Soviets, Afghans yearned for peace and respect for their human dignity. They got neither. The mujahed march into Kabul only marked another period of human rights abuses. Greed for power led to factional fighting. Afghans once again fled their homes, and feared arrest, imprisonment and torture. Summary executions of Afghans suspected as disloyal to one faction or another became commonplace. Civilians again fell victim to indiscriminate bombardment.

Following the departure of Soviet troops, conflict had been localized. However the unprecedented intensity of a new armed conflict touched nearly the entire country and was resulting in the loss of life of untold numbers of innocent civilians. Political leaders formed new alliances in attempts to retain or acquire political power. For the civilian population these alliances were deadly. In his last report, the United Nations Human Rights Commission Special Rapporteur referred to the situation in Afghanistan as a "country in which the power struggle creates more of an equilibrium of anarchy than an equilibrium of people's government."

And anarchy reigned. Many mujahed units were accountable only to local commanders. They set up checkpoints to stop travellers and rob them. Looting of shops and people's homes became rampant. There were widespread accounts of rape and torture. The mujahideen were unprepared to govern and either could not, or would not, control their fighters' intimidations and attacks upon the civilian population. A high-level resistance activist dejectedly shook his head over the many years he had devoted to the *jihad*. "What was the point?" he wondered. "We fought so hard for our freedom against the Soviets and now our so-called leaders are squabbling over money and power. I am being asked to support killers who are killing their own people." From the Soviets to the mujahideen, as far as human rights were concerned, it was *déjà vu* once more.

Many individuals working for human rights became targets. One such person was Mirwaiz Jalil, an Afghan BBC correspondent. He provided critical reporting and a steady stream of human rights information. One day Jalil was dragged from his car on the outskirts of Kabul and shot 22 times. When his body was recovered it carried more holes than flesh. The Secretary-General's Representative in Islamabad, Mr Mousouris, stated: "When Afghanistan is trying to recapture international support needed for the reconstruction of the country, the murder of a journalist who offered impartial information about the current tragedy of his country can only be considered as perpetrated by enemies of Afghanistan." Not only had Afghans lost their most basic human rights, they were losing anyone who could perform the essential service of conveying the human rights picture to the world. (SEE MEDIA, JOURNALISM)

The rise of the Taliban from the *madrassas* (Islamic schools) and refugee camps in Pakistan was, in some respects, caused by the widespread human rights abuses perpetrated by the mujahideen. In their view, the new Afghan government did not respect and protect the people. This was un-Islamic. Because ordinary Afghans were fed up with the human rights situation, the Taliban met with little resistance in most places. (SEE TALIBAN)

But as the Taliban seized control of more and more areas, they imposed a rigid 16th Century brand of Islam, previously foreign to most of the population. Girls were sent home from schools, the university was shut down, female doctors were ordered out of the hospital. (SEE WOMEN) There were cases of women needing medical treatment being turned away from hospital; men were ordered to grow beards. Anything deemed un-Islamic was prohibited and punished. The Taliban cracked the whip in the name of Allah. (SEE TALI-*BANS*) But there was little relation between the exercise of power and the forging of a religious Islamic state. The Taliban are largely uneducated in matters of Islam or government.

The human rights problem in Taliban-controlled areas of Afghanistan is that religion has become a convenient mask for the application of power.

Now, as during the time of the Soviets, the human dignity of Afghans is under assault. Millions of landmines continue to cause numerous and grave injuries to the civilian population. Indiscriminate bombardments kill large numbers of civilians. There are extreme restrictions on the freedom of association and expression, on the rights of women, and an environment of extreme religious intolerance. The country lacks a constitution containing human rights provisions. Professional and organized courts and a trained judiciary are nonexistent. Trials are conducted on an *ad hoc* basis. Accusations are likely to culminate in executions.

Changes in regime do not affect Afghanistan's obligations under international law generally, nor under human rights law and humanitarian law. Afghanistan is still party to important international human rights instruments, including the International Covenant on Civil and Political Rights, the International Covenant on Economic, Social and Cultural Rights and the Convention Against Torture and Other Cruel, Inhuman or Degrading Treatment or Punishment, as well as the Geneva Conventions of 12 August 1949. The government is bound by the Universal Declaration of Human Rights. However, no governmental or administrative authority exists to ensure the protection of human rights enshrined in any international instrument.

One massive human rights abuse has been the decimation of Afghan culture. Afghan culture is a human rights victim of chaos and war. Gone is the glue which held the fractious pieces of Afghanistan together. The revered codes of honour and respect have been obliterated. This is bad for human dignity because by its emphasis on respect, the traditional culture was a basis for the promotion of human rights and a foundation for rebuilding civil society. (SEE CULTURE)

As the world observed the 50th anniversary of the Universal Declaration of Human Rights and the human rights system embarks on the 21st Century, it is leaving Afghanistan behind. The people of Afghanistan were the last victims of the Brezhnev Doctrine. But the human rights assaults on people who helped win the Cold War are horrific.

Perhaps the greatest human rights abuses will be the ones that lie ahead. Few human rights NGOs are active in Afghanistan, governments are reluctant to invest in building a human rights culture, and there is little human rights reporting. Afghanistan's human rights future depends on all of this and on training Afghans. They must be taught how to promote human rights standards along with the technical skills of fact-finding, interviewing, handling evidence, reporting, compilation and dissemination. Afghanistan's human rights future lies with its people rather than with the United Nations human rights machinery or what is called the "human rights community." Rather than a policy of purposeful engagement with the Taliban, external groups and organizations are finding it convenient to shelve Afghanistan's human rights problems because of differences over Western standards. The tragedy is that after fifty years of modern human rights, Afghan lives will continue to be nasty, brutish and brief.

***Charles Norchi** is an international lawyer based in New York, focusing on human rights. He is a director of the International Centre for Humanitarian Reporting.*

Landmines/Part I: an enduring legacy

By Timothy Weaver

Pattern I. Someone steps on a buried anti-personnel mine. The blast blows off the foot, shredding the bone and tissues of the leg up to and often above the knee. The other leg, genitals, buttocks and arms are lacerated. Fragments from the mine itself, and dirt, gravel, clothing, skin and bone are blasted up into the body. The unlucky ones are killed outright.

Pattern II. A ground-level fragmentation mine is set off by a person tripping a wire. Metal fragments are blown out in an arc that can tear a body to shreds. The victim suffers multiple puncture wounds, superficial or deep, depending on how far they are from the mine. The unlucky ones are killed outright.

Pattern III. Farmers planting rice, children playing, and deminers clearing fields have their hands blown off and are blinded when they inadvertently touch or pick up anti-personnel (AP) mines. The unlucky ones are killed outright.

Mine injuries are not always fatal. It depends on the nature and purpose of the mine. Many AP mines are designed to maim rather than kill; others such as the bouncing mines that spring up to waist height before detonating, have a 100% "kill ratio" when set off.

Since 1979 in Afghanistan people have had to live with the fear that the next step they take could be their last. As the war has gone through successive phases, the danger posed by mines has been ever-present. Demining programmes, started after the withdrawal of the Soviet Army in 1989, have cleared some areas. The civil war that followed, and that continues to this day, has limited the demining process. Landmine use has become ever more indiscriminate, with little central control over deployment, and scant effort made to map or mark minefields, or to clear areas no longer of tactical value.

The task of mapping and clearing was first taken up by international agencies. Teams of army engineers arrived in Pakistan in 1989 to teach refugee Afghans the principles of mine awareness, mine detection and mine-clearing. Nearly ten years later, the United Nations is still labouring at the same Herculean task, through the work of the United Nations Office for the Coordination of Humanitarian Assistance to Afghanistan (UNOCHA) Mine Action Programme. Even in peaceful circumstances the problems confronting the deminers would be formidable.

The UNOCHA programme focuses on mine clearance training, mine awareness, minefield surveying and mine clearance. Eight NGOs (six Afghan, one Iranian and the internationally renowned HALO Trust) implement the programme.

The immediate problem is the clearing of minefields, but the landmine problem will not end when they have lifted the last mine. A survey by CIETInternational, a New York-based NGO, found that in some provinces 12% of the population had been involved in a mine-blast incident. Afghanistan will pay the personal, economic and social costs of these incidents for decades to come.

Afghanistan was the first conflict in which mines were looked at as a weapon of terror. The horribly mutilated men, women and children who arrived at the border hospitals of Pakistan, sometimes after days of travelling, made the point eloquently that civilians were now more at risk from mines than combatants. They were also easier targets.

In their attempts to subdue the local population and to cut off the mujahed supply routes, the invading Soviets had used mines extensively. They mined outposts defensively, while ground and air forces mined villages, border regions and supply routes.

They mapped defensive minefields, but the AP "butterfly" mines dropped from the air were by their very nature impossible to control.

The withdrawal of the Soviet forces led to a worsening of the situation. What little control there had been over the use of mines now disappeared completely. The Soviets left behind large stockpiles of arms and ammunition, including landmines. All the combatants have used and reused them – often wildly, crudely and cruelly – over the years since 1989.

Moreover, since the fall of President Najibullah, weapons and ammunition, including mines, have continued to find their way into Afghanistan through Iran, Pakistan and the former Soviet republics to the north, supplied by various countries seeking to influence the balance of power in the future Afghanistan.

As frontlines have shifted rapidly, control of minefields has changed hands several times. This has led to confusion about the exact size, content and position of many minefields. People can point out the general areas of mine infestation, but mapping and clearance teams must do the exact locating.

At the end of the 1980s Afghanistan was already tagged as the most heavily mined country in the world. That was before the fighting spread to the towns, which have become the battlegrounds for the warring factions. (In 1996 UNOCHA identified 252 new mined areas in Kabul). Now aid agencies have to consider major urban

J. Hartley/UNICEF

reconstruction and development. Clearing built-up areas, where mines and UXO (unexploded ordnance) may be buried beneath piles of rubble, is more difficult than working in rural areas.

New minefields are constantly being uncovered. In 1996 UNOCHA's demining programme surveyed more than 100 square kilometres (sq.km) of previously unknown minefields. Their surveys (dated November 1997) point to a total mined area of 725 sq.km, of which 324 sq.km are "high priority" areas for demining (these are areas where civilians face the greatest risk: residential and commercial areas, farmland, irrigation canals and roads). Some 123.7

sq.km of minefields have been cleared, and a further 116 sq.km of battlefields have been cleared of UXO (as at September 1997). The UNOCHA programme has overseen the destruction of 150,900 AP and AT (anti-tank) mines and 515,153 pieces of UXO. (Estimates that there are ten million mines planted in Afghan soil are no longer considered credible).

While the fighting continues, the warring factions are laying new minefields. They use mines for defence, but do not lay them in patterns – there is no indication of real planning, recording, marking or mapping. Opposition groups have been reluctant to give up the weapons, while one prominent cleric of the Taliban, which controls much of the country, has stated that the use of mines is un-Islamic and should be banned. However, this difference in outlook probably reflects their respective offensive and defensive military postures rather than their ideals.

Meanwhile, Afghanistan's hospitals and aid posts are full of mine victims. UNOCHA estimates that unexploded bombs or mines kill or injure ten people every day.

Medical resources have always been meagre and the war has cut into them heavily, leaving them woefully inadequate. The treatment of the injured drains the medical system, while the fighting disrupts and destroys medical facilities and supply lines.

Treatment for mine victims does not stop when the doctor sews up the wound. There is a long process of rehabilitation. Artificial limbs have to be made and fitted. Physiotherapy sessions must be organized. Trauma counselling may be necessary. All this places further burdens upon the health services.

People have to learn to live with permanent disablement. (SEE DISABILITY) They face the prospect of being a burden to their family. They face poverty – many families are forced into debt to meet the costs of medical treatment for mine victims. This would be hard enough to cope with, even in peacetime. The internecine warfare that wracks the country exacerbates these difficulties.

The war has broken down communities and family groups. In many areas the rural pattern of life has changed irrevocably. Families with mine victims suffer economic hardship; breadwinners and labourers are lost to mines, so that the fields are then lost to the families. They are unable to tend them. The cities provide the only alternative, and families move from rural to urban areas where they may enjoy marginally better access to health services and employment opportunities.

The war against the Soviets has bled into a nationwide civil war; the cities themselves have become battlegrounds. Inevitably the city streets and buildings have been mined during the seesaw battles since the pro-Soviet regime of Najib fell in 1992. Urban mines have an immediate impact. People are blown up, particularly children while searching for firewood or playing. Families are made homeless. Despite the deaths, the city-dwellers are not yet being mined into exile. The heaviest contamination, and consequent depopulation, occurs in rural areas.

The immediate effects of landmines may be seen on the streets of Afghanistan and in the refugee camps of Pakistan – men, women and children hobbling around on crutches.

The long-term effects have been to turn a country that was once self-sufficient in food production into one that is dependent on foreign food aid. It has prevented farmers from returning to work on the land. It has blown apart the migratory patterns of the Kuchi nomad traders. It has helped keep refugees in foreign camps, idling their lives away far from home and depending on aid donors' compassion.

It is all too likely that the combatants will continue to use mines for the future, and use them irresponsibly. However, the long experience of the Afghan NGOs and UNOCHA means that they can rapidly survey and mark areas once the fighting has moved on. The clearing is a longer process altogether.

As ever, international funding is crucial to the success of the programme. The annual budget for 1998 is $23.5 million. However, the protracted war is testing the patience of donors. Without an end to the conflict in sight, it seems international donors are unwilling to fund aid and development. In 1997, the UNOCHA deminers were prepared to accept a 30% salary cut to offset a $3 million shortfall in funding. The cut was averted by making other savings in the programme, including reducing the level of daily allowances.

Yet every mine cleared and destroyed is a step forward, despite the continued fighting. Donors and fund-raisers must realize that the people responsible for the conflict least appreciate their efforts, and that decisions should not be based upon the reactions, or lack of response from those wielding power now. The various faction leaders in Afghanistan have shown that they care little what effect their struggle for power has on the country. Threats to restrict or withdraw international aid will not deter them.

What donors and fund-raisers must consider is whether they are prepared to abandon the Afghans, most of whom want peace. Demining will have to be undertaken whatever the circumstances; the UNOCHA programme has shown that Afghans are willing to do this for themselves. They are not yet in a position where they can do it without the support of international funding.

Timothy Weaver *is a London-based journalist and cameraman with Frontline Television.*

Landmines/Part II: progress in clearance

By Rae McGrath

On 2nd January 1990, the first United Nations-sponsored mine clearance team, belonging to the newly-formed NGO, Afghan Technical Consultants (ATC), began work in Kunar province. Seven and a half years later there are 1,665 staff from five Afghan-managed organizations directly involved in mine clearance and technical survey throughout the country. (The total workforce, including support staff, numbers over 3,500).

The success of the programme can be attributed to several factors of which, undoubtedly, the most critical is the survey process. The Mines Clearance Planning Agency (MCPA) was established in 1989 in order to ensure that minefields were surveyed in advance of clearance and priorities allocated, and that cleared areas were properly recorded. This process is now far in advance of any system in use elsewhere in the world. Largely because it has developed within the context of the national programme, it has managed to adapt its operations in response to the needs and progress of the implementing agencies.

In the first six months of 1997 MCPA teams surveyed and permanently marked more than 13.3 square kilometres (sq.km) of mined land. This area was approximately 350,000 square metres less than the total area cleared by the four Afghan clearance NGOs in the same six-month period (13,693 square metres). Thus, subject to continued and sufficient funding, it appears that MCPA is perfectly capable of maintaining a flow of surveyed land for clearance.

There are some restrictions on surveys, however, which may cause a problem in the longer term. MCPA requires that a request from the owner of the land be received before a survey commences and, in cases where the owner is absent or makes no request, mined land may remain unsurveyed. It is this factor which prevents Herat City, for example, from becoming totally mine-free.

The programme is probably the only truly indigenous landmine response in the world. The United Nations Office for the Coordination of Humanitarian Assistance to Afghanistan (UNOCHA) provides an international link and overall programme direction. With the exception of an ordnance disposal specialist based in Kabul, the small expatriate team within UNOCHA are largely involved in an oversight role vital to continued international funding.

The achievements in Afghanistan are all the more impressive when viewed in the context of a country still at war. Not only has much of its infrastructure been destroyed, but well over 2.5 million people have been displaced as internal refugees. The practical engineering problems facing the demining teams are no less daunting. In many urban and village areas where earth walls have collapsed through bombing, the clearance process can best be equated to the work of archaeologists, with mines often located two or more metres deep. Operations in rural areas can be equally problematic. Overgrown fields and irrigation systems are often covered with rusting barbed-wire entanglements which may disguise tripwires. In some minefields, the undergrowth is too dense to allow the use of tripwire feelers. The accident rate remains high in comparison to work in other countries but has fallen considerably in the past three years.

Dogs play an increasing role in clearance operations. Although the Aardvark Flails are rarely deployed, adapted commercial machines, such as backhoes, are used in suitable areas. This practice is likely to expand as more machinery becomes available. The UK demining NGO, HALO Trust, is piloting a mechanized clearance process to sift rubble for mines and unexploded ordnance in Kabul City, funded by the European Community Humanitarian Office (ECHO). HALO Trust, however, is not fully integrated into the UNOCHA Mine Action Programme for Afghanistan.

Probably the most difficult consideration for the programme planners is prioritization of clearance – the practice being far more complex than the theory. Land is categorized under five general headings:

- Agricultural
- Grazing
- Residential
- Irrigation
- Roads

Over 50% of the total area cleared in the first six months of 1997 was classified as grazing land. A further 30% was arable land. A United Nations Food and Agriculture Organization (FAO) and World Food Programme (WFP) Special Report on Crops and Food Supply published in August 1997 suggests that making the clearance of agro-land a priority is justified. "The existence of mines remained a constraint on planting in some areas although demining has already released some of the better land," the report noted.

Remaining high priority mined area to be cleared as at September 1997.

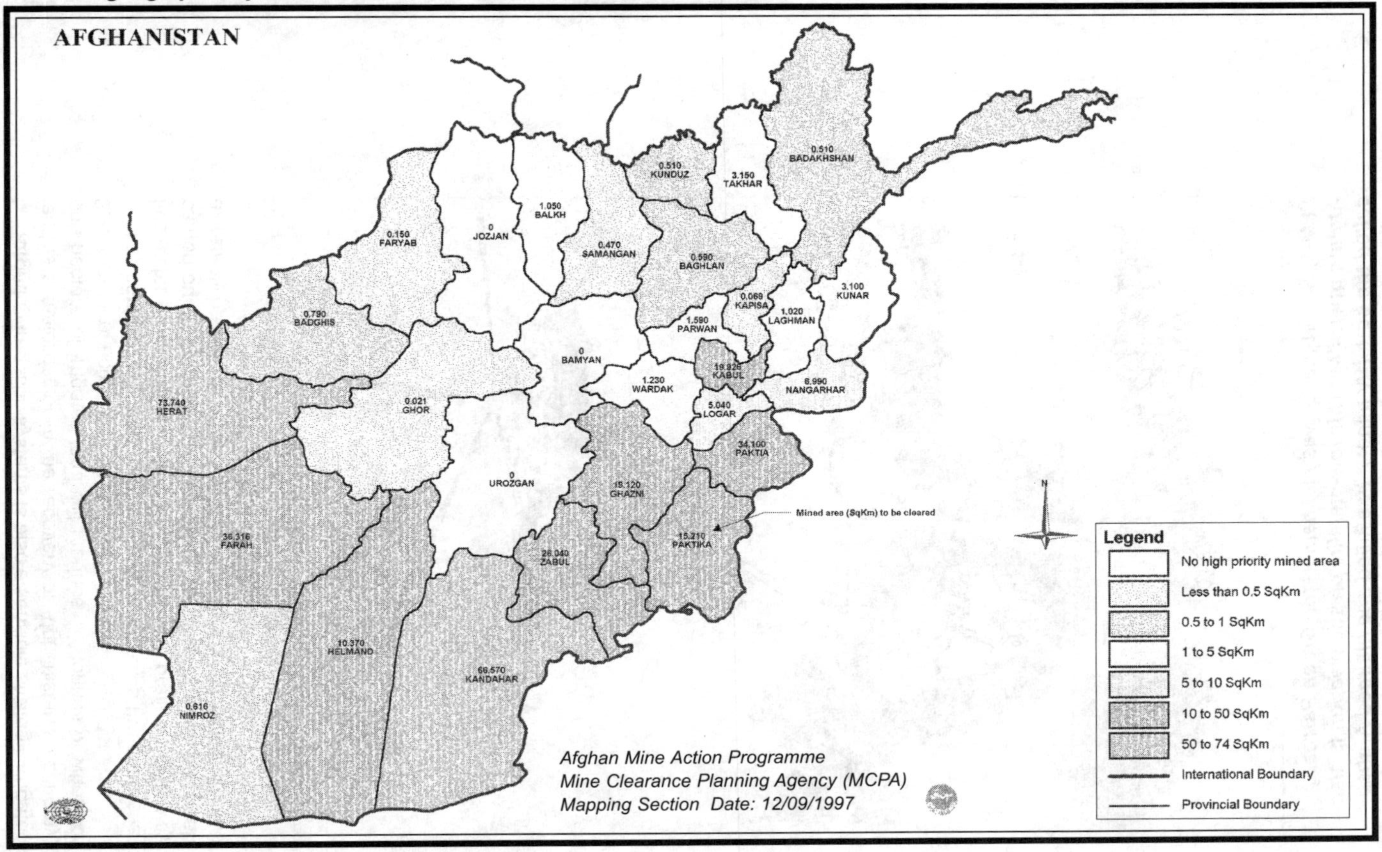

Afghan Mine Action Programme
Mine Clearance Planning Agency (MCPA)
Mapping Section Date: 12/09/1997

Targeting irrigation systems is also a sensible strategy. Irrigated land is a major factor in the recovery of Afghanistan's economy; one hectare of irrigated land will produce 1.7 tonnes of wheat or 2.22 tonnes of rice.

The continued fighting, and use of landmines, is the one negative factor facing the eradication programme. A preliminary survey carried out in August 1997 found that Badghis province has been extremely heavily mined during the recent fighting. More than 20,000

PFM-1, Soviet-made, was nicknamed the Green Parrot by Afghan guerrillas. This low-metallic plastic weapon is also called the butterfly mine. It has killed and maimed Afghan children who mistake it for a toy. *Illustration by Pamela Blotner*

people have fled to Herat from Badghis and their return will certainly be delayed and made dangerous as a result of this recent landmine dissemination. A serious concern relates to the important irrigation area along the Murghab River covering an area of up to 20,000 hectares, which was the scene of heavy fighting. The socio-economic impact of mine-laying in that area may present the clearance organizations with a major and urgent challenge when the security situation allows work to begin.

Subject to the limitations imposed in some areas by continuing war and landmine use, the Afghan programme is benefiting from its intensive on-the-job training. Many of the deminers have been clearing mines six hours a day, six days a week for more than five years. Some have been working as long as seven years. Such experience is unique and bodes well for the future.

Rae McGrath *founded MCPA and the UK-based Mines Action Group.*

The ethnic and tribal composition of Afghan society

By Ali Wardak

The ethnic and tribal composition of Afghan society strongly reflects the geographical location, population, subdivisions, and social and economic organization of the various tribal and ethno-linguistic groups within the country. Nearly 20 years of war, however, have had a profound impact on the ethnic/tribal composition of Afghan society. The terms tribe and ethnic groups are used in a very general sense: they refer to the specific Afghan ethno-linguistic groups that are commonly known in the country as *qawm* (tribe, people), *wolas* (tribe, people) and *taifa* (ethno-linguistic group, tribe).

As there has never been a systematic census in Afghanistan, little or no reliable data exists regarding the total population of the country and its various tribes/ethno-linguistic groups. This is one reason why the subject remains a controversial one. The question of population distribution and numbers has become highly politicised in recent years, particularly among the various Afghan groups. In the absence of factual data, estimates do exist. But as recent accounts by writers associated with rival Afghan factions often remain dubious, the estimates used here are those documented by well-established and experienced Western academic researchers on Afghanistan. The larger Afghan ethno-linguistic groups (Pashtun, Tajik, Hazara and Uzbek) are described in more detail than the smaller ones; similarly, the order in which they appear is also based on this criterion.

To understand Afghanistan's ethnic-tribal make-up, it is crucial to look at the geographic distribution of its various groups. The map on ethnic and tribal groups in this field guide indicates geographical locations of the various Afghan ethno-linguistic groups within the country. It does not, however, show the more complex picture of inter-tribal mixing. Nor does it illustrate the coexistence of different groups in many urban centres. Trade and commerce, universities, government institutions and employment opportunities have pulled hundreds of Afghans from different ethnic/tribal backgrounds to live and work side by side for generations in the larger towns and cities. Inter-marriages and participation in shared cultural, religious and social activities further tended to strengthen citizenship at the expense of ethnic/tribal affiliations. Interestingly the recent displacement of refugees (e.g. Tajiks and Uzbeks fleeing the north during the Soviet war to Pashtun areas in the east) to the traditional locations of other groups has further increased tribal interaction and interdependence.

Pashtun

The majority of Afghan Pashtuns have traditionally lived in the south and east of Afghanistan. While relatively small communities of Pashtuns are settled in the north and west of the country, several thousand live a fully nomadic life. Tribal Pashtuns constitute the largest ethnic group in Afghanistan. British writer Anthony Hyman (1992) estimates that the total number of settled Pashtuns in Afghanistan is seven million, whereas American anthropologist Louis Dupree (1980) estimated the population at 6.5 million. Around 12 million Pashtuns also live across the border in Pakistan, mainly in the North West Frontier Province (see Binder 1996). Also known as "Pathans," they were artificially cut off from their Afghan cousins by the "Durand Line" drawn up by the British in 1893. Writers generally divide Afghanistan's Pashtuns into *Durrani* and *Ghilzai* branches; these are further divided into many sub-branches or sub-tribes most of which are suffixed with *zai* or *khil*. Pashtuns are, by and large, *Sunni* Muslims and speak *Pashto* – one of the two official languages of Afghanistan.

The overwhelming majority of settled Pashtuns are farmers. And it is mainly the farm, the orchard, the water-spring and canal, the water-mill, animal husbandry and the manufacturing of basic agricultural tools around which the Pashtun economy and society are organized. At the heart of this social organization is the Pashtun *kalay*, or village. The average *kalay* is a small socio-economic unit that normally consists of a few extended families that are directly related to a common ancestor (the average size of a *kalay* ranges from about 50 to 200 individuals). It is usually a self-sufficient socio-economic unit within which people are not only related to one another through blood ties, but also through established reciprocal relationships. They share agricultural tools, goods, gifts, favours and services.

The norms of reciprocity are generally governed on a more immediate and local level by *trabgani*. This refers to the code of behaviour within which members of each *kalay* cooperate and compete with one another; it is a source of both cohesion and division among the kin in different circumstances (*trabgani* is mistakenly interpreted as rivalry by some commentators). But on a more general level, reciprocity in the Pashtun *kalay* is governed by the centuries-old Pashtun code of behaviour, *Pashtunwali*; this refers to the general norms of behaviour for a Pashtun as an individual in society. One pair of experienced Western 'Afghanologists' describe *Pashtunwali* in this way:

> *"In addition to the basic requirements of Islam, Pashtuns observe the code of* Pashtunwali. *It is simple but demanding. Group survival is its primary imperative. It demands vengeance against injury or insult to one's kin, chivalry and hospitality toward the helpless and unarmed strangers, bravery in battle, and openness and integrity in individual behaviour. Much honour is given to Pashtuns who can successfully arbitrate the feuds that are endemic among them. Fines and blood money are devices frequently used to limit violence among rival families.* Pashtunwali *is a code that limits anarchy among a fractious but vital people. It has influenced other groups within the country who must deal with similar environmental and social realities"*
>
> *Source: Newell and Newell 1981*

Whether *Pashtunwali* has influenced other Afghan tribal/ethno-linguistic groups in the country or not, many of its demands such as hospitality, bravery and individual integrity are central elements of the general Afghan culture; they are shared by all Afghans whatever their ethnic background may be. Such values constitute the basis of the moral order and of (informal) social control in Afghan villages, clans and tribes, which have historically resisted the penetration of successive governments' mechanisms of (formal) social control. Pashtuns have contributed significantly to Afghan culture and society; they have historically resisted the attempts of foreign military powers to subjugate them. For two centuries from Ahmed Shah Durrani in 1747 to President Daoud who was overthrown in 1978, Pashtuns ruled Afghanistan as *Amirs* and Kings. Alongside other Afghan tribes, many Pashtuns fought with considerable success against the Red Army invasion forces during the Soviet occupation of Afghanistan.

According to some observers, however, clan or tribal loyalties prevented resistance fighters from adopting more effective regional tactics against the Soviets, with Pashtun groups often preferring to operate in a more localized (and limited) manner. Nevertheless, some leading Pashtun commanders such as Abdul Haq of the Hezb-e-Islami's Younis Khalis faction managed to overcome such parochialism by organizing highly mobile guerrilla groups operating inside Kabul itself as well as throughout the eastern region. The mujahed party of Gulbuddin Hekmatyar's Hezb-e-Islami, and the Taliban Movement, are both predominately Pashtun – as was the former *Khalq* faction of the communist People's Democratic Party of Afghanistan. (SEE KEY PLAYERS)

Tajik

Afghan Tajiks are predominantly settled in the north and northeast of Afghanistan. Considered to represent more a cultural than an ethnic group, the total estimated number of largely Mediterranean-looking Tajiks in Afghanistan is estimated at around 3.5 million (Dupree 1980; Canfield 1986; Hyman 1992). The estimated 600,000 *Farsiwans* of the western Afghan city of Herat are sometimes referred to as Tajiks. Moreover, a much larger number of Tajiks (around six million) live in neighbouring Tajikistan. The Afghan Tajiks are predominantly *Sunni* Muslims and speak *Dari* (Afghan Persian) – one of the two official languages of Afghanistan.

Working mainly as farmers in fertile mountainous valleys and foothills, the social organization of the Tajik economy and society resembles that of the settled Pashtuns of Afghanistan: the largely kinship-based Tajik *deh* (village), the basic unit of collective action, is socially organized around the agricultural farm, vineyard, orchard, water-mill, canal/spring, and the processing of agricultural products. Within the *deh*, Tajik villagers are not only tied to one other through kinship relationships, but also through the institutionalized reciprocity which their agricultural economy requires. They exchange favours, services, gifts, agricultural products and tools which create strong mutual obligations among the donors and recipients.

The rules of reciprocity are generally spelled out by *abdurzadagi*. This refers to the established code of behaviour which guides members of the village-based kin-group on whom to cooperate with, whom to compete with, whom to marry, and – in short – how to live as an individual in the community. The moral and social values associated with *abdurzadagi* often coexist in a symbiotic relationship with the localized religious values expressed in the village mosque, which is an important part of the moral and social order of the *deh*.

On a broader level, the Tajik inhabitants of valleys and small regions which consist of several villages often trace their roots to one or more common ancestor(s). However, they refer to themselves by the regional (i.e. *Panjshairi*, *Ghorbandi*) rather than ancestral name, as is the case among the Pashtuns. Therefore, the social boundaries of this regional affiliation are not very rigidly drawn – whoever lives in the region may assume its regional identity. For this reason, some scholars categorize this form of social formation as 'peasantised' rather than 'tribalised' (See Canfield 1986).

Despite the fact that the Tajiks are mainly farmers, many of them migrated to and settled in urban areas, particularly in Kabul. Urban Tajiks were able to benefit from modern educational and technical facilities in the capital city and to achieve very high standards of educational and professional qualification. Many educated Tajiks occupied high-ranking positions in successive Afghan governments and played vital roles in the functioning of those administrations. As one writer put it:

> *"Because they [Afghan Tajiks] make up the bulk of the educated elite and possess considerable wealth in Kabul and Herat, they have significant political influence. Their influence lies predominantly in the government ministries, public services, and trade bodies." (Javad 1992)*

Indeed, the development of modern Afghanistan's economic, cultural, and educational institutions owes much to the dedication of many talented Tajiks; their contribution to Afghan culture and society has been tremendous. Moreover, the Tajiks contributed very significantly to the Afghan resistance movement against the Soviet invading forces. Journalists travelling with mujahideen often commented on the ability of the Tajiks of the north to operate in a more mobile fashion across the region than their fellow Pashtun fighters to the south. Some of Afghanistan's best-known and most effective guerrilla commanders, such as Ahmed Shah Massoud and Ismail Khan, are Tajiks. (SEE KEY PLAYERS)

Hazara

The Afghan Hazaras live predominantly in the central mountainous region of Afghanistan known as Hazarajat. While the Hazaras have until recently constituted a significant part of the population of Kabul, a large number of them have settled permanently in the Pakistan city of Quetta. According to Hyman (1992) Afghanistan's Hazara population is estimated at around 1.5 million (Canfield's [1986] estimation is 1,000,000), whereas Dupree's [1980] is 800,000). The Hazaras speak *Hazaragi* which is a dialect of *Dari*. As *Shi'a* Muslims, they are mostly followers of the *Ja'faria* ('Twelver') school.

The Hazaras are divided into several sub-tribes or social units. The most prominent are: *Daizangi, Daikondi, Daimirkosha, Daifolad, Daikalan, Daidehqan, Daimirdad, Daiquzi, Daimirak, Daichopan, Daikhotai, Daimordagan,* and *Daizeniat.* The prefix *Dai* is similar to *Khi* and *Zai* in the Pashtun tribal system which are used to draw social boundaries between various sub-tribal and large kinship-based social units. Thus, social relationships among the Hazaras are generally organized within these social units.

As predominantly herders and farmers, the social and economic organization of the Hazara *deh* (village) is similar to that of the Tajik *deh*. It is usually a geographically bounded area that comprises a number of extended families with members of various villages tracing their common ancestral roots to a sub-tribe or clan. As among Pashtuns and Tajiks, the *maliks, khans* and particularly *sayeds* exercise a considerable amount of authority in Hazara society. The *sayed,* who is considered to be a descendant of the Prophet (and usually a religious scholar), is the centre of authority. In practice, the *sayed* is a preacher, teacher, spiritual leader and interpreter of religious laws and doctrines. He also plays an important role in the resolution of conflicts and disputed settlements.

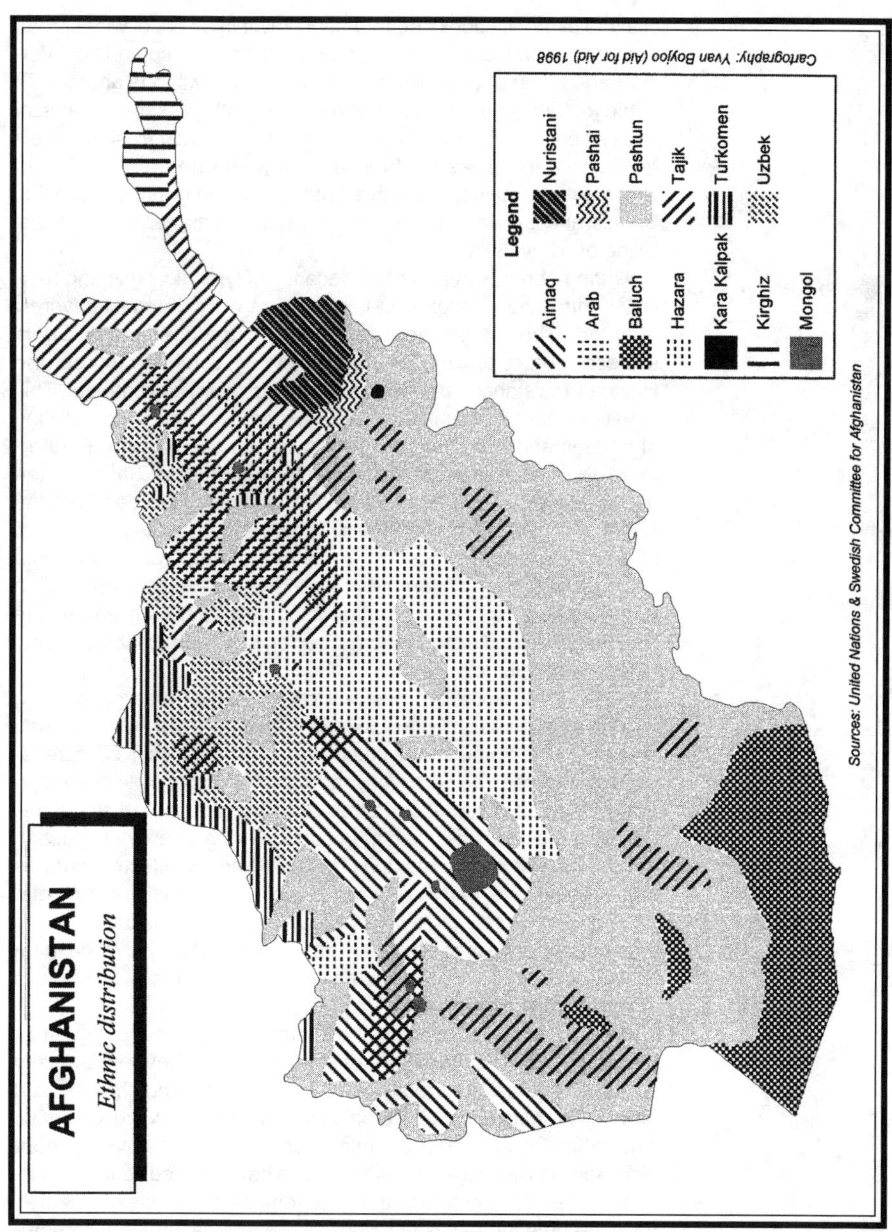

However, the social organization of the Hazara economy and society is also closely related to the consolidation of Afghanistan as a centralized state, which led to the forced subjugation of all the state's internal opponents. Amir Abdur Rahman, who in 1880 became King of what is now known as Afghanistan, was obsessed with the centralization of government power in an era of widespread anarchy, when local *khans, mirs, pirs* and *mullahs* controlled different parts of the country and continually fought with one another. To achieve this goal, Abdur Rahman used all possible means of repression. This included deportation of his *Ghilzai* Pashtun rivals to the remote areas of *Turkistan* (now the northern region of Afghanistan), inciting negative religious sentiments between the *Sunnis* and *Shi'as*, and the use of direct military force and brutal killing of all rivals.

During Abdur Rahman's two decades of tyrannical rule and ruthless centralization, Afghanistan's Hazaras were the most severely affected. The government employed its predominantly *Sunni* subjects, particularly the Pashtun tribesmen, to forcibly repress the Hazaras' resistance to the King's emerging central government. This resulted in the confiscation of Hazara lands, the large-scale looting of houses and the killing of numerous men and women. Furthermore the Hazaras were discriminated against as *Shi'as* (often performing the most menial of jobs) and largely excluded from the social, cultural and political life of wider Afghan society. This state of affairs gradually assumed an institutionalized form while successive Afghan governments (with the exception of Amanullah Khan) looked on. They did little or nothing to put an end to the discrimination and exclusion practised against this sizeable minority of their own subjects.

All this discrimination has led to the gradual emergence of a Hazara communal self-consciousness as a distinguishable cultural and religious community – a community which has received increasing strength from the hard work and social solidarity of its members. Many Hazaras in Kabul and other cities became successful entrepreneurs, businessmen and merchants. They also proved, much to the surprise of many Pashtuns, to be extremely effective fighters both against the PDPA regime as well as against the Soviets. According to outside observers who have travelled with the Hazaras, their performance in recent years has almost certainly allowed them to rise up from their previous positions as underdogs to adopt a strong identity of their own.

Those Hazaras living in the central mountainous region of Hazarajat, with its harsh weather and terrain, have steadfastly struggled against the cruelty of man and nature. They have mixed farming, herding and skilful crafting in wool, fur and wood to survive self-sufficient in extreme climatic conditions. However, recent blockades of Hazarajat by Taliban forces have created serious shortfalls in basic food commodities, and tens of thousands of Hazaras have become increasingly reliant on the international aid community to avoid starvation during winter months. In Kabul, ethnic tensions between Hazaras and Taliban – exacerbated after the May 1997 debacle in Mazar-e-Sharif – have forced many Hazaras to flee the capital. The main Hazara political party is Hezb-e-Wahdat, currently based in Bamiyan and led by Karim Khalili. (SEE KEY PLAYERS)

The Frontier Post 6 June 1997

Uzbek

Afghanistan's Uzbeks live in the northern plains of the country, separated from Uzbekistan by the Amu Darya (Oxus River), and cut off from the rest of Afghanistan by the high snow-topped Hindu Kush mountains. Only in the 1960s was this part of Afghanistan linked to the rest of the country through the building of the Salang tunnel. These fertile northern areas are also known as *Turkistan* and form a naturally-bounded homeland for the Afghan Uzbeks. The total number of Uzbeks, according to Hyman (1992), is estimated at 1,300,000, although Dupree (1980) put the figure at one million. A far larger number of Uzbeks (approximately 23 million) live in Uzbekistan. The Uzbeks of Afghanistan are *Sunni* Muslims, and speak *Uzbeki*.

Similar to the Pashtuns, Afghanistan's Uzbeks mix farming with herding. The vast northern plains represent some of the most fertile farming land in the country, and, with irrigation from the Amu Darya, are particularly suitable for growing rice and cotton. (SEE AGRICULTURE) Cotton production, processing and trade used to be one of the main sources of national income, and played an important role in the economic development of the northern cities of Mazar-e-Sharif and Kunduz. In addition, the Uzbeks produced high quality *karakul* lamb fleeces and hand-woven rugs. The *karakul* wool was exported to Europe and soon became another important source of income for the Uzbek producers/traders as well as for the national Afghan economy, despite growing competition from countries such as Namibia.

Similarly the rugs and carpets which were produced mainly by the Uzbek (and Turkmen) women found a lucrative outlet in

European markets, particularly in Germany, Britain and the former USSR. Moreover, the production of gas, oil, and fertilizer in northern Afghanistan created hundreds of jobs. The wealth and economic resources of the predominantly Uzbek north made its population relatively self-sufficient and attracted labourers, traders and skilled professionals from all over the country.

The self-sufficiency of the Uzbeks, alongside the geographical remoteness from Kabul of their northern region, has traditionally played an important role in their limited interaction with central governments and official institutions. Although successive governments have been represented throughout the northern provinces by governors, judges, magistrates and the military, the centre of Uzbek authority, economy and social organization has always been the *qishlaq*, or Uzbek village. Similar to the Pashtun *kalay*, and the Tajik and Hazara *deh,* the *qishlaq* is usually situated in a demarcated geographical area that comprises more than one extended family, the members of which have a common ancestor.

The economic and social organization of the *qishlaq* is unique. Social relationships revolve around the ways that peasants in the *qishlaq* relate to the *arbab* (landlord). Members of the Uzbek *qishlaq* are generally peasants who work on the *arbab's* land. The former are not only economically dependent on the *arbab*, but also socially and politically dependent, since the *arbab* is usually an influential figure who has links with government institutions. The peasants thus need the *arbab's* help both in community matters and in dealing with officials. The *qishlaq* provides the fundamental social context for political and social action: it is the traditional structure of authority with its main figure being the *arbab*. The social organization of the *qishlaq* and the *arbab* are in turn closely linked to the local mosque – an important agency of social control within the village.

The Uzbeks have contributed outstandingly to the Afghan economy, culture and society: their rugs, *karakul* goods, cotton and other and agricultural products constituted the backbone of the economy. They have also produced strong military personalities, such as General Dostum, one of the most powerful players on the Afghan scene but also one of the least trusted. (SEE KEY PLAYERS) The majority of ordinary Uzbeks were also particularly active in fighting against the invading Soviet forces.

Turkmen and Aimaq

Afghan Turkmen share a close Turkic cultural and linguistic affinity with Afghan Uzbeks. The Turkmen in Afghanistan live in those northern and northwestern provinces of the country which border Turkmenistan. According to Hyman (1992), the total number of Afghan Turkmen is estimated at 600,000, although Dupree (1980) puts the figure at 125,000. Some 3.52 million Turkmen live in Turkmenistan. Both the Turkmen and Uzbeks of Afghanistan are *Sunni* Muslims; Turkmen speak *Turkmeni* – a Turkic language which is closely related to *Uzbeki.*

The Turkmen of Afghanistan are a semi-sedentary people who mix herding with farming. The raising of lambs for *karakul* fleece used to be a major source of income. *Karakul* pelts and the very fine rugs and *gelims*, which Turkmen women produced, represented some of the most important Afghan exports to Europe and the USA.

Major Turkmen sub-tribes are: *Tekke, Yomud, Lakai, Saroq Chakra, Salor, Mawri, Tariq* and *Ersari*. Although the Turkmen are predominantly semi-nomadic (many fully-nomadic), and therefore more geographically mobile than Uzbeks, the social organization of these two ethnic groups is very similar.

Afghan Aimaq are scattered throughout the northwest and central regions of the country. *Aimaq* means 'nomad' in Turkic, but the mobility and power of their chiefs was curtailed by Amir Abdur Rahman, who put them under the control of the Governor of Herat in the 1880s. Their total number is estimated to be around 800,000. (Dupree 1980; Hyman 1992). Traditionally the Aimaq are herders and carpet weavers. Several thousand also live in Iran, where they are referred to as *Berberi*. Major Aimaq sub-tribes are *Jamshidi, Firozkohi, Zohri, Taimuri* and *Taimani*. Since the Aimaq in Afghanistan live in close proximity with other Afghan groups, notably the *Farsiwan* of Herat, and the Turkmen, Uzbeks and Hazaras, they have generally adopted the culture of the group that is immediately their neighbour. Afghan Aimaq are predominantly *Sunni* Muslims, and most speak *Dari*.

Baluch and Brahui

Divided, like the Kurds, between three countries – Pakistan, Iran and Afghanistan – the Baluch have a tradition of rebellion against central governments and harbour ambitions to create a separate state of Baluchistan. Since the mid-1970s some 2,500 Baluch guerrillas, fighting for autonomy in Pakistan, took refuge in southern Afghanistan. But their struggle for independence has seldom received international support and has faded after political repression by all three countries.

Afghan Baluch and Brahui live predominantly in the southwestern provinces of Nimruz, Helmand and Kandahar. Their total number in Afghanistan is estimated at around 300,000 (Dupree 1980, Hyman 1992). A larger number of Baluch are also settled in Baluchistan, a province of Pakistan, and several thousand more live in Seistan province of Iran. Most Afghan Baluch belong to the *Rakhshani* tribe, which includes a number of sub-tribes such as the *Sanjarani, Harut, Sarabandi, Nahrui, Miangul, Gumshzai, Sumarzai, Yamarzai* and *Salarzai*.

Although the majority of Baluch are semi-sedentary, some live as caravaneers and nomads. Their social and economic organization is not significantly different from those of other Afghan ethnic/tribal groups who survive on small-scale farming and herding. However, since the Baluch live on Afghanistan's porous borders with Pakistan and Iran, and can travel between the three countries without bothering about frontier regulations, some are involved in small-scale crossborder trade and smuggling. Although Afghan Baluch speak their native *Baluchi* tongue, many also know *Dari* and/or *Pashto.* They are *Sunni* Muslims.

The Brahui, who live in the southwestern region of Afghanistan, resemble the Baluch both culturally and in their general lifestyle. In fact, many Brahui consider themselves a subgroup of the Baluch (Wirsing 1987). Some work as tenant foragers and herders for Pashtun or Baluch landlords. The main Brahui sub-tribes are: *Mamasani, Zirkandi, Aidozi, Lowerzi and Yagozi*. Although Brahui is the native language of this Afghan group, most of its members also speak either *Pashto* or *Baluchi*. They are *Sunni* Muslims.

Nuristani, Pashai, Pamiri and Kirghiz

The Nuristani, whose total number is estimated at 100,000 (Dupree 1980, Hyman 1992), live in the mountains of eastern Afghanistan. They maintained their ancient paganism until 1896, when they were forcibly converted by the sword to Islam by Amir Abdur Rahman. With the change of religion, the name of their traditional homeland (Kafiristan – Land of the Infidels or nonbelievers) was changed to Nuristan (Land of Light – Islam). It is with this new cultural identity – Nuristani – that they now strongly identify, even creating their own government during the Soviet-Afghan war, including a foreign ministry to issue visas to visiting journalists and aid workers, and a finance ministry to tax passing caravans. On a local level, however, the Nuristani refer to themselves by the name of the valley or area in which they live, for example *Waigali, Krueni, Wamai* etc.

Nuristan is located in the middle of the Hindu Kush mountain range, in the provinces of Kunar and Laghman. It occupies four valleys, each with its own distinct dialect – Kati, Waigali, Ashkun and Parsun. Due to the rugged topography of the region (Nuristan contains some of Afghanistan's few remaining forests) it has limited arable land on which the population work as small farmers. Terraced farming is also mixed with goat-herding and forestry, but the economy is very much one of subsistence.

As settled farmers/herders, the social organization of Nuristani society does not appear to be significantly different from most of the other Afghan ethnic/tribal groups, with one notable exception: women are considered of equal importance to men in the daily life and work of the community.

As with other groups, the extended family and clan networks constitute the basis of social order. Despite Islam, Nuristanis have retained various elements and institutions, including clandestine wine-making, from their ancient culture which make them stand out as an unique Afghan social group. Traditionally they leave their dead exposed to the elements for a whole year before burying them and planting over the grave a carved wooden effigy which the spirit of the deceased occupies. (SEE CULTURE) They normally wear their traditional clothes even outside Nuristan and speak a distinct language – *Nuristani*, containing elements of Indian and Iranian tongues. Nuristanis are *Sunni* Muslims, and were the first group to declare rebellion against the Kabul-based Marxist PDPA government in October 1978. Subsequently the area became an important transit base for mujahed operations and has remained largely autonomous ever since.

Towards the eastern mountains of the Nuristan region live another Afghan ethnic/tribal group, the Pashai. The general outlook of the members of this Afghan group is very similar to that of the Nuristanis. However the Pashai speak their own a separate language – *Pashai.* Due to the geographical proximity of the Pashai to the Pashtuns in Kunar province, some Pashai also speak *Pashto*. The social and economic organization of the Pashai is very similar to that of the Nuristanis. They are *Sunni* Muslims too.

Further to the north of the Nuristan region live two other relatively small Afghan ethnic/tribal groups – the Pamiri and the Kirghiz. While the Pamiri are generally settled farmers and herders in and around Badakhshan province, the Kirghiz are a largely nomadic people who live in huts very close to the Chinese border. The total number of each group is estimated to be several thousand. However, hundreds of Kirghiz families migrated to Turkey after the occupation of the Wakhan Corridor (the panhandle of northeastern Afghanistan) by the Soviet forces in 1980. While all Kirghiz are *Sunni* Muslims, some Pamiris are followers of *Shi'a* (Ismaili) Islam. The Pamiri speak the *Pamiri* dialect of *Dari,* while the Kirghiz speak a *kipchak Turkic* dialect.

Other settled ethnic and tribal groups

Other than the ethnic/tribal groups that have been so far discussed, several other smaller groups further add to the cultural richness of Afghan society. These include Qizilbash, Mongols (also referred to as Moghuls), Arabs, Gujars, Kohistanis, Wakhis and Jats.

The total number of all these Afghan ethnic/tribal groups according to Dupree (1980) does not exceed several thousand. Although some of these Afghan groups such as Jats have retained their distinct lifestyle and language, the rest have by and large adopted the cultures of the neighbouring dominant ethnic group. Among these groups, the urbanite Qizilbash (*Shi'a* Muslims) have held very important professional and bureaucratic positions in Afghan official institutions. Ismailis are another group living in northern parts of the country, but are not considered to be Muslim by many conservative Afghan or fundamentalist groups.

Afghanistan has also been home to several thousand Hindus, Sikhs and Jews. These groups lived and worked mainly in Afghan urban centres such as Kabul, Kandahar and Herat. They greatly contributed to Afghan trade and business, but after the Soviet invasion of Afghanistan in 1979, many left the country.

Nomads

Afghan nomads – *Kuchi* – are an important feature of Afghan society and culture but do not represent a specific ethnic/tribal group. Instead, it is their unique fully-nomadic lifestyle that separates the

Kuchi from the rest of the settled population of the country. Afghan nomads are mainly comprised of Pashtuns (80% according to some estimates) along with some Baluch and Kirghiz. Estimates of the numbers of Kuchis range from 500,000 to three million.

Most Afghan nomads have traditionally been herders and traders, with sheep and camels constituting their main property. Baluch and Pashtun nomads generally spend winter in Pakistan and move to Afghanistan in spring when the weather is warmer. Their tradition of widespread grazing lands has occasionally led to conflicts between nomads and villagers. Some villagers complained that the surrounding grassland was overgrazed and exploited by the nomads who were aliens. Some non-Pashtuns also saw the seasonal presence of the predominantly Pashtun nomads as a form of Pashtun expansionism.

However, some settled local populations established enduring economic relationships with the nomads. In exchange for locally-produced grain, fruit and vegetables – as well as grazing rights – the nomads traded tea, sugar, mutton and goat meat, wool and dairy products. This exchange was particularly extensive between the nomads and the populations of remote and isolated villages, where Kuchis were often used as a means of communication and transportation to the outside world. According to Dupree (1980) the nomads' huge animal stock also fertilized the deserts and hillsides which would have otherwise remained barren. Dupree (1980) emphasises that, far from being a burden to the land, nomads "... live in a symbiotic, not parasitic, relationship with man and nature in Afghanistan."

Whatever the effect of Afghan nomads on the rest of the society, the past two decades of war in the country has had serious implications for the nomadic population of Afghanistan. Most Kuchis were unable to continue their traditional existence after the Soviet invasion of Afghanistan. Many of them remained as herders or traders (mainly in the transport sector) in the North West Frontier region of Pakistan, or fought alongside the mujahideen inside Afghanistan.

Although travellers and locals have witnessed the presence of large numbers of nomads during 1997 in the southern and eastern regions of Afghanistan, the presence of millions of landmines has severely limited the scope of their traditional migration patterns. Kuchis are believed to have lost about 35,000 animals to mines, which works out at 25 beasts (worth around US$3,000) per household. (SEE NOMADS IN NO-MANS-LAND)

War and the population of Afghanistan

The past 20 years of continuous war in Afghanistan have had serious consequences not only for its population but also for the social, political and economic organization of Afghan society. Recent figures from the United Nations High Commissioner for Refugees (UNHCR) suggest that while about two thirds of Afghans have returned to their homeland, the continuation of hostilities among the various

Afghan factions has displaced thousands of others within the country. Estimates made by the International Committee of the Red Cross (ICRC) show that apart from the displacement of about 120,000 residents from Kabul to Jalalabad, from October 1996 to August 1997 a further 311,000 persons were displaced within other parts of the country.

These internally-displaced persons (IDPs) have mainly been forced to move from Badghis to Herat, from Shomali to Kabul and from Kabul to the Panjshair Valley. The "internal refugees" in Herat are predominantly Pashtuns and Baluch, whereas those in Jalalabad are largely Tajiks and other non-Pashtuns. But what is important, according to aid workers and visitors, is that the non-Pashtuns in the predominantly Pashtun Jalalabad, and the Pashtuns and Baluch in the predominantly *Farsiwan* Herat *are* received as fellow Afghans and *do* enjoy considerable assistance from the local population. In some cases, locals of the 'host' cities provide shelter to and even share their own houses with the displaced Afghans.

These observations are very important. They would seem to indicate that despite the apparent division of the country along ethno-linguistic and politico-sectarian lines, the ordinary people in Afghanistan still feel that they are bonded to one another in several ways. Indeed, shared religion, customs and moral values, clothing and general lifestyle, and more importantly a shared interest in the establishment of peace and social order, are all common grounds that unite the ordinary Afghan population.

Despite the exploitation of religion and ethnicity as vehicles for seeking positions of power by the various factional leaders/warlords, the forces of unity among the ordinary Afghan population remain strong. The *long-term interests* of the ordinary Afghan population in peace and unity are more likely to override the *short-term interests* of the few in fuelling inter-ethnic strife and civil war. Thus the forces of unity and peace are more likely to decide the future of Afghanistan. However, the long-term prospects of unity and stability lie in a multi-cultural Afghanistan in which its ethnic and tribal diversity is a source of strength, progress and cultural richness – an Afghanistan that can rebuild itself, take its place in the international community, and be prepared to face the challenges of the next millennium.

***Ali Wardak** – an Afghan specialist – is a lecturer in criminology at Glamorgan University, Wales.*

A brief history of Afghanistan

By Chris Bowers

> *"If you do not wield a sword, what else will you do?*
> *You, who have suckled at the breast of an Afghan*
> *mother!"*
>
> *Afghan couplet*

Afghanistan lies at the crossroads of South and Central Asia; its northern plains an extension of the steppes of Turkistan, the Hindu Kush mountains an adjunct to the Himalayas, its southern deserts a prelude to the Persian Gulf. Linguistically, culturally and ethnically Afghanistan's northern Uzbeks, Turkmen and Tajiks look northwards to Central Asia, the centrally-located Hazaras look westwards to Iran, and the southern and eastern Pashtuns and Baluch find more resonance to the east in Pakistan. Although distinct from them, each group and region has more in common with its neighbours over the border than with each other.

A few rulers, most notably Abdur Rahman Khan at the cusp of the century, have managed to bind the Afghans into rule from Kabul, but arguably none left behind a reliable, coherent governing state system. With the mixture of lofty disdain and sharp perception often evident in British Imperial commentary, Sir Henry Rawlinson wrote, "the nation consists of a mere collection of tribes, of unequal power and divergent habits, which are held together more or less closely, according to the personal character of the chief who rules them. The feeling of patriotism, as known in Europe, cannot exist among Afghans, for there is no common country." One might almost add that there has not been much of a state either.

One of the foremost authorities on Afghanistan, the late Louis Dupree, suggests that Palaeolithic Man probably lived in the caves of what is now northern Afghanistan as long as 50,000 years ago. Afghanistan provided the backdrop to the emergence of two of the world's religions. Legend has it that Zoroaster, the founder of the modern Parsee religion, was born in the north of the country. Historians seem surer, however, with the story that Zoroaster (or Zarathustra as he was also called) was killed either in or near Balkh in around 522 BC. Zoroaster is thought to have converted to his religion the parents of Darius the Great, the ruler of the Achaemenid Empire at its height. From the south of Afghanistan, Greek and Indian influences merged to create the rich Gandhara Buddhist culture. Surfacing first in the Afghan region, it spread (as Mahayana Buddhism) through much of the Far East.

Scholars have identified 25 ruling dynasties which have swept through Afghanistan. Alexander the Great and his armies passed through on the way to India from Persia. Cyrus the Great, Genghis Khan, Tamerlane and Babur all rampaged through Afghanistan on the way to somewhere else. A few patterns emerge. Few, if any, of the invaders stayed for any length of time, nor did they attempt to establish colonies. Less surprisingly, several left behind traces of their passage. Some fair-skinned, blue-eyed Nuristanis claim their features as evidence of descent from Alexander's soldiers. The Mongoloid features of the Hazara people suggest descent from Genghis Khan's soldiers. ('Hazaar' translates as one thousand in Persian: it is widely believed in Afghanistan that Genghis Khan left behind detachments of troops one thousand strong to defend various outposts and that these soldiers were the ancestors of the Hazara people.)

The Uzbeks and Turkmen in the north see their history in terms of a much broader Turkic identity. The ancient khanates of Maimana, Shibarghan and Andkhoi, south of the Oxus River (Amu Darya) were the poorer, smaller relations to the grander Uzbek power centres of Khiva, Bokhara and Samarkand north of the river. Buddhism took root about 1,800 years ago in modern-day Nangarhar, Kabul and Bamiyan provinces. The ancient Buddhist site at Hadda, just outside Jalalabad, is a testament to the indiscriminate nature of the Afghan-Soviet war, the wanton vandalism and looting that sometimes accompanied it and the splendours of the original site. (The author last saw the Hadda site in the autumn of 1991. Many of the statuettes of the Buddha had been chipped off the side of the temple or defaced. The main statues had long succumbed to the effects of history or the odd shell. When the author related this to an Afghan acquaintance in the Kabul bazaar, his dismay was compounded when the Afghan reached under the counter and offered for sale one such statuette with assurances that it was genuine).

In the 16th Century three empires emerged, sporadically fighting each other: the Safavids from Iran, who ruled parts of western Afghanistan; the Moghuls from India, who made Kabul their capital; and the Shaibanid Uzbeks, whose kingdom stretched from the plains north of the Hindu Kush far into Transoxiana. In 1747, Nadir Shah of Persia was assassinated and the three empires lapsed into decline. One of Nadir Shah's lieutenants, Ahmed Shah Durrani, seized his chance and became the first ruler whom the Afghans can claim as their own: he controlled – or perhaps *influenced* is a better word – territory which loosely corresponds to modern-day Afghanistan. He was able to seize some bounty and used it to enrich and augment the forces at his disposal. Opportunism, paying off tribesmen and mercenaries with loot and holding out the prospect of more have pretty much guaranteed success to a whole succession of Afghan warlords over the centuries. Short-term success, that is. Ahmed Shah Durrani was a Pashtun from the Abdali tribal grouping, the bitter rivals of the Ghilzai Pashtuns. For all but a few years, the Durrani provided the rulers of Kabul until 1978, to the exclusion of not only the Ghilzai, but also all other ethnic groups. Some authors date 1747 as the beginning of an Afghan political entity, but it is an argument hard to sustain. Ahmed Shah Durrani, whose base was in Kandahar, was essentially a *primus inter pares*, who by a combination of charisma and circumstance held swathes of territory under his sway. But in no real sense did he have any governing structures. His personal bodyguards were Turkic-speaking Qizilbash (literally 'redheads') rather than Pashtuns.

After his death, Ahmed Shah's empire disintegrated as warring branches competed for the succession: a swirling and ever-changing confusion of broken and remade alliances set the political scene, and to some extent, still form an important undercurrent to Afghan governance. At the beginning of the 19th Century, Afghanistan had no legal existence and no formal borders. These were finally drawn up in the last decade of the century and were contested throughout the preceding decades, principally in reaction to the advances of foreign powers. As Ludwig Adamec puts it, "Modern Afghanistan was born as a result of foreign occupation." Its terrain and the existence of two imperialistic neighbours defined its borders.

Throughout much of the 19th Century, various dusty, isolated Afghan fortresses – Herat, Kandahar or Ghazni – were dubbed the "Key to India" by British military strategists. Britain feared that the steady march southeastwards of the Russian armies through Central Asia was designed not only to subjugate the people there but also to open up invasion routes towards India. Even resurgent Afghans posed problems to India's defences. Ahmed Shah Durrani, among others, made frequent incursions into the fertile north Indian plains. The British efforts to forestall the Russian advance by intrigue, sorties by intelligence officers, diplomacy, straight bribery and direct military intervention were dubbed the "Great Game" by the British writer Rudyard Kipling, and taken up with almost missionary zeal by some of the most flamboyant adventurers of British and Russian history.

The lack of a state structure or system of formal governance cost Afghanistan dear during this period. Abdur Rahman Khan at the end of 19th Century described Afghanistan as a goat between the two lions of Russia and Britain. But as Lord Lytton, a Viceroy of India, put it, "Afghanistan is a state far too weak and barbarous to remain isolated and wholly uninfluenced, between two great military empires such as England and Russia." Russian soldiers never crossed the Oxus in earnest, but it is not surprising that British military planners should have succumbed to something resembling paranoia. While the borders of British India remained reasonably stable, the Russians moved south capturing Novo Alexandrovsk on the north-eastern shores of the Caspian Sea in 1834, Tashkent in 1865, Samarkand three years later, Krasnavodsk in 1869 and Tekke Turkoman in 1881. By 1885 they had arrived along most of the northern banks of the Oxus River through a combination of conquest and treaty. As the British became increasingly nervous, the two countries almost went to war over the demarcation of a small village of just a few hundred souls called Panjdeh, north of Herat.

In an effort to bring the unruly Afghans under control and to shore up the western approaches to India, British armies twice invaded Kabul within the space of forty years. Both times to no avail: the first ended in spectacular military defeat, the second in fruitless intervention. After capturing Kabul in 1839 and returning the hated Shah Shuja to the throne, the British retreated to Jalalabad in January 1842. Of more than 16,000 troops and camp followers who left Kabul only one doctor (and, later, some escaped prisoners) made it the one hundred miles back to Jalalabad, after some of the most disastrous leadership ever seen from a British general and constant harrying ambushes through the snowy mountain passes led by Wazir Akbar Khan. (For a colourful, humorous but semi-fictional account of this episode see the 'Flashman' novel, by the British writer George MacDonald Fraser).

Another British army invaded later that year and by way of revenge blew up Kabul bazaar. In 1878, the British returned when, as British author Jan Morris writes, "another presumptuous Amir embarked on a flirtation with the Russians, another British Resident was murdered, another British army was defeated and another punitive force stormed back to Kabul in revenge." By now, the Afghans, although poorly equipped with ancient rifles, had developed a fearsome fighting reputation, a ferocious antipathy to foreigners who tried to rule them and a disdain for any Afghan rulers who came to power on their backs. The Afghans valued their independence above all else. The war and skirmishes against the British and Russians served to knit together the nation. From the aggressor's point of view, the interventions proved less than worthless; in the words of a British report: "as a result of two successful campaigns, of the employment of an enormous force, and of the expenditure of large sums of money, all that has yet been accomplished is the disintegration of the State which it was desired to see strong, friendly and independent."

Whether by design or accident, Afghanistan became a buffer between the Russian and British empires, albeit with Britain guiding its foreign policy. Towards the end of the 19th Century both sides accepted it as such, and saw their interests in it remaining so. Between Abdur Rahman Khan's coming to power in 1880 and his death in 1901, Afghanistan took recognisable shape. Its crucial northern and eastern borders were drawn up and a process of nation-building was started, although in a ruthless fashion. Abdur Rahman Khan established a formative cabinet and developed the framework of a civil administration. He pacified the interior, although how much actual control he exerted is not clear. In an inspired move, he expelled some rival Pashtun tribes *en masse* to the north of the country. Once there, well away from their centres of power and outnumbered by Uzbeks and Persian-speaking 'Tajiks', they had little option but to serve the interests of Kabul by policing the north. Abdur Rahman Khan was clearly more ready to depend on his erstwhile, but Pashtun, enemies rather than on Uzbeks and Persian-speakers native to the north who fell more under the aegis of their local khans – even though the latter had officially been defeated by Abdur Rahman. (Interestingly, when Afghan Uzbek forces revolted against President Najibullah in 1992, one of the reasons given was resentment that a Pashtun, whose family had been resettled in the north by Abdur Rahman Khan, was in command of the government garrison of Mazar-e-Sharif.) In 1893 the eastern border was clarified between British India and Afghanistan. Known as the Durand Line, after the principal cartographer, it was to become much more controversial than its northern counterpart, drawn up three years later. Suffice to repeat the words of Sir George Macartney, surveying the scene from Kashgar: "So fiercely independent and jealous were the Afghans and so turbulent in their domestic politics, that their borders," which he describes elsewhere as being so ambiguous and contradictory as to be almost incomprehensible, "offered unlimited scope to intrigue and aggression by a foreign power." The division, particularly of Pashtun tribes – and even families – in the east, was to prove of great significance for Afghanistan in the 1960s and still has a ripple effect on Afghan-Pakistani relations today.

With its borders finally set and a rudimentary governing system in place, Afghanistan joined the community of nations at the turn of the century very much as an isolated backwater on the world stage. Its collision with the modern world did not go very smoothly. It was one of the few countries in the world, and probably the only in Asia, which during World War Two was neither occupied nor belligerent. It was not considered important enough. There was no all-weather road connecting the north with the south, until Nadir Shah built one in the 1930s. There was no University until the 1960s. The first formal school in Kabul was constructed by Habibullah Khan at the turn of the century. There was no railway. Up to today, the only railway ever built in the country was a few miles of track near Zahir Shah's palace in Kabul. It was never connected to any other railway.

In his book *Age of Extremes*, the British historian Eric Hobsbawn wrote that, "the destruction of the past, or rather of the social mechanisms that link one's contemporary experience to that of earlier generations, is one of the most characteristic and eerie phenomena of the late 20th Century." If for one country in the world this was less true then surely it was Afghanistan. History and tradition still ruled the roost. Amanullah Khan, who ruled Afghanistan from 1919 (Independence from Britain) until 1929, tried to drag the country kicking and screaming into the modern world, only to be ejected from power by a scandalised *ulama*. Amanullah had travelled to western capitals where the gulf between an ever-developing Europe and his backward and remote kingdom was brought home to him in the starkest of manners. Afghanistan was virtually untouched by industrial development. Upon his return he incited widespread outrage when he unveiled his wife, Surraiya, in public, after forcing the tribal elders to abandon their *shalwar kameez* and turbans for morning suits and black ties. Amanullah was influenced by his contemporaries Kemal Ataturk of Turkey and Reza Khan of Iran. While all three were trying to bring in broadly similar reforms, the Turkish and Iranian leaders only ventured to do so once they had consolidated the state's (and their personal) power by building up strong armies. Amanullah, a man ahead of his time and naïve in equal measure, did not and was chased from power by a ragtag group of bandits led by Bacha Saqao, a Tajik, after a tribal uprising. Later Afghan rulers, Babrak Karmal and Najibullah in particular, have tried to portray themselves as the modernizing but more pragmatic heirs of Amanullah Khan.

Bacha Saqao was the first non-Pashtun to rule Kabul since 1747. He lasted less than one year. In 1933, Zahir Shah inherited the throne after his father, Nadir Shah, was killed in a blood feud. He ruled for 40 years and is, at the time of writing, still alive in Roman exile. He attained the throne at 18. Power rested with his uncles for 20 years. But, again, Afghanistan was to be buffeted by foreign factors largely beyond its control.

The British withdrawal from India in 1947 and the consolidation of communism in the Soviet Union changed for ever the delicate balance on which Afghanistan's status as a buffer state depended. With the creation of Pakistan, the scales tipped inexorably north. The demarcation of the eastern border back in 1893, resented at the time by a powerless Kabul, now came back to sour relations between Afghanistan and Pakistan. Kabul considered that the demise of British India in effect abrogated the Durand Line. Afghanistan's was the only dissenting voice in the vote which admitted Pakistan to the United Nations.

But what did Afghanistan actually want? Many Pashtuns harked back to the days of Ahmed Shah Durrani when Afghans controlled Peshawar. For them, the border should have been pushed back to include all of the Pashtuns in Pakistan's North West Frontier Province and entailing the creation of 'Pashtunistan' – in fact, little short of the dismemberment of Pakistan. Kabul understood 'Pashtunistan' to mean annexation; others saw it as a new independent country; others still, some sort of autonomy. Daoud Khan, King Zahir's cousin, became Prime Minister in 1953 and took a hardline stance pro-Pashtunistan. Daoud's policy caused untold damage to Afghanistan in the short- and longer-term. In the early 1960s, relations became so bad that the border with Pakistan was

Tony Auth © 1992, The Phildelphia Inquirer

closed for a time. The immediate effects of the border closure in 1961 were easy enough to predict: a sharp rise in border tension and a cut in trade. Eastern Afghanistan depended then as it does now on exchange with Pakistan. However, within ten days of the border closing, the Soviet Union offered to buy the harvest that would have gone to Pakistan. Daoud took them up on that.

Since the departure of the British and the end of its empire heyday, the United States had stepped in to try to redress the balance with the Soviet giant to the north. But, from Afghanistan's point of view there was little equality between the two. The closure of the border led to a reduction in American aid to Kabul due to Washington's increasing closeness to Pakistan.

Already America was being outspent in aid terms three-to-one by Moscow. The Soviet Union was also the only customer for one of Afghanistan's few mineral assets: its natural gas fields in the far northwest. Afghanistan totted up a large debt to the Soviet Union which, in turn, was in a position to dictate the price it would pay for the gas coming out of the pipeline that Moscow had paid for and built. Throughout the 1950s, 1960s and 1970s, Afghanistan was drawn ever closer economically to the Soviet Union. Politically, there was no great affection for communism in Afghanistan; the 1917 Revolution of the proletariat held no resonance whatsoever for Afghans. A significant number of people in the north had fled there from Soviet attacks against the Basmachi rebels in the 1920s and were familiar with the ruthlessness of the Red Army. Nevertheless, from the mid-1960s onwards, the Soviet Union tried to draw Afghanistan into its political orbit. It had no real competition.

Despite the personal dynamism of Daoud, Afghanistan was as weak a state as can be imagined and ripe for the picking. Zahir Shah was weak and was expected to be weak. The traditional troika of authority in rural Afghanistan – the *khan*, the *malik* and the *mullah* – only had use or need for a King who would adjudicate when a dispute arose. They did not wish the King to intervene in their business, nor did the King go out of his way to challenge this view. The royal family, meanwhile, kept a stranglehold on positions. Those cousins and distant relatives who were not governors would become generals. The Durrani Pashtuns kept things to themselves. Daoud tried to liberate the political class, but his Pashtun chauvinism gave it nowhere to go but north. He created some of the conditions for "equal opportunities," but failed to create an actual meritocracy. Kabul's attempts to deal with a famine in 1971 in the far west of the country were tragically ineffective. To many Kabuli intellectuals, frustrated by their antiquated regime, it underlined the need for urgent reform and a decisive step forward. A slow-burning fuse was lit in the early 1960s and smouldered beneath the hopelessly outdated royal system of governance. It would lead to some dramatic and ultimately explosions. The pace of change accelerated unrecognisably: in the space of thirty years from 1964, when Zahir Shah brought in some limited democratic reforms (which in effect made him a constitutional monarch), Afghanistan became a Republic (1973), a Democratic Republic (1978), a Soviet client (1979) and an Islamic state (1992). Yet, despite the speed of change – or perhaps because of it – the political class was tiny and based almost exclusively in the capital. Kabul was an island politically divorced from the countryside.

At its peak prior to the Soviet invasion and while it was in power, the pro-Moscow People's Democratic Party of Afghanistan (PDPA) is thought to have had fewer than 7,000 members. Kabul University, the country's first, was established in 1964. Most of the key figures of the 1980s and 1990s were former classmates. Moscow sought to build up its influence in Kabul through two main channels: the army and the PDPA. Between 1956 and 1977, up to one third of the entire officer corps of the army was trained and educated in the USSR. Many were recruited into the KGB or the GRU, the military intelligence wing. The Americans tried halfheartedly to keep pace with the growing Soviet influence. Daoud used to joke that he would light his American cigarette with a Russian match, but any idea of a happy balance was an illusion. Washington seemed to acknowledge that Afghanistan had a much closer natural relationship with its northern neighbour.

Unfortunately for the PDPA, the two branches of Soviet espionage seemed to be in competition and had sharply different, even conflicting, approaches. Virtually at its birth, the PDPA split into two factions: the Khalq ('Masses') and the Parcham ('Banner'). The two were at times separate parties rather than factions and, given the chance, persecuted and at times tortured each other mercilessly. American analyst Anthony Arnold argues persuasively in his book *Two Party Communism* that the Khalqis owed their allegiance to the GRU and the Parchamis to the KGB. The Khalqis, led by Nur Mohammed Taraki and Hafizullah Amin, concentrated their recruitment among the armed forces. The Parchamis focused on teachers and social intellectuals. Both saw the need for a dramatic step forward to bring Afghanistan out of a 'museum.' With Soviet help, the Khalqis had already taken part in the palace coup of 1973 in which Daoud overthrew his cousin Zahir Shah and established a Republic. By April 1978, they had the field to themselves.

Although it seems clear that the Soviets had taken part in the planning of the 1978 coup, its precise timing seems to have taken them by surprise. Moscow felt that Daoud had double-crossed them by ditching members of the PDPA from his inner cabinet. The April 1978 coup (also known as the "Saur Revolution") was an accidental and somewhat botched affair. The shooting to death of a prominent Parchami by unknown gunmen led to demonstrations in Kabul orchestrated by the PDPA.

Somewhat alarmed, Daoud arrested Taraki and Amin a few days later. Remarkably, Amin was not kept under close control and was allowed to receive several visitors. To these people, he reportedly issued the pre-arranged instructions to start the coup on the morning of 27 April. The palace was shelled and confused fighting broke out between various factions and divisions, but by the next morning the Khalqis had won. Daoud and his family were shot to death in the palace, so bringing to an end more than 230 years of almost unbroken Durrani Pashtun rule.

Taraki, a Ghilzai Pashtun, was declared the head of the Revolutionary Council of the Democratic Republic of Afghanistan, after several days of internal dispute and wrangling. Places were given to Parchamis but the facade of unity was not to last. Within a few months, the leading Parchamis were sent abroad as ambassadors – a communist form of exile. In much the same way as Amanullah had done decades before, the Khalqis attacked the centuries-old traditions of rural Afghanistan head on and with as little sensitivity. One government minister caused outrage by offering public prayers to the souls of Marx and Lenin. With just a few decrees, the new authorities took land away from landowners and redistributed it to peasant farmers totally disrupting the rural and social relationships that had been unchanged for generations.

The countryside was in uproar. Women were forced to take part in literacy campaigns that consisted of reciting party propaganda slogans. A personality cult was built around Taraki. The first major rebellion occurred in the western city of Herat in the spring of 1979. Government buildings were attacked and Soviet advisers lynched. The Soviets were unhappy with the way things were being run by their wayward and inexperienced charges in Kabul. Defections from the Afghan army were becoming increasingly frequent. Relations between Amin and Taraki were becoming increasingly strained, as the regime became more and more vicious in the treatment meted out to foes, real or potential. In February 1979, in an incident which has yet to be fully explained, the US Ambassador, Adolph Dubs, was taken hostage in Kabul and then shot to death by Afghan police forces while apparently trying to free him.

The opposition to the Khalqis was uncoordinated and diverse but became increasingly disruptive. The revolt against the Khalqis in the countryside is seen by many as being as much a reaction to an administration in Kabul trying to impose its will in areas where it was not welcome and where it was not usually present, as against a specific ideology in itself. In other words, the rebellion was against governance *per se*, unwarranted interference as far as many rural Afghans were concerned, as much as it was against communism. Most Afghans in the provinces simply wanted to be left alone. Only in Kabul had the 20th Century had a belated impact.

The Taraki-Amin split became worse. The Soviets seemed to have sided more with Taraki and persuaded him to rid himself of Amin. The plan was betrayed to Amin who got his blow in first, and the life of the first Communist leader of Afghanistan was snuffed out ingloriously by a pillow pressed to the face. Amin assumed power and the Soviets found themselves with a serious problem. A few months later, on 27 December 1979, the Soviets invaded, killing Amin in the process and installing Babrak Karmal, the leader of the Parcham faction.

***Chris Bowers** is a former BBC correspondent in Kabul.*

INFOBRIEFS

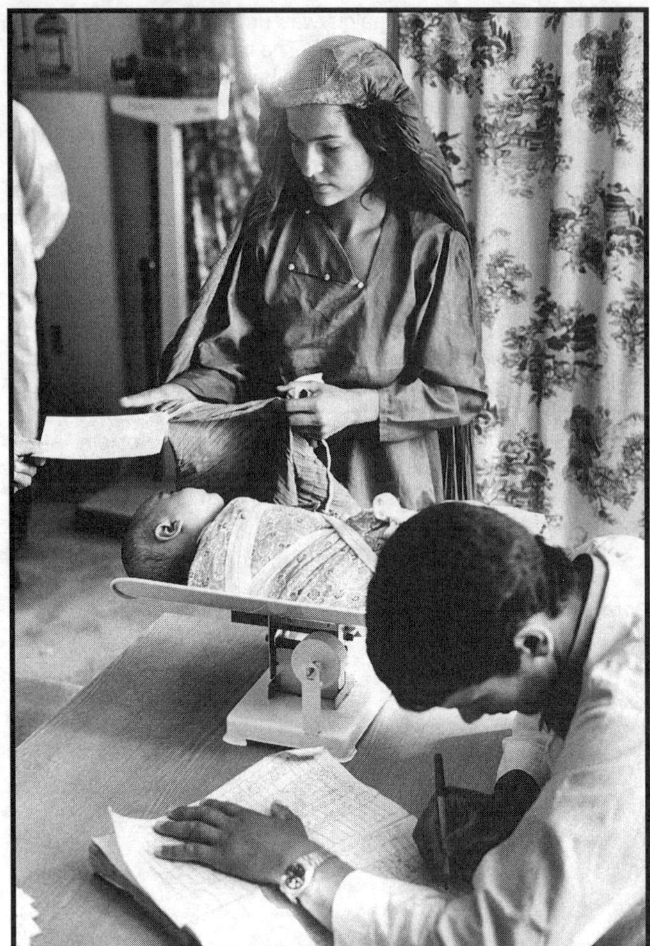

J. Hartley/UNICEF

AFGHANISTAN: Country data

Land:	
Area	**652,225 sq. km**
Borders	**China, Iran, Pakistan, Tajikistan, Turkmenistan, Uzbekistan**
Population:	
Population size	**20.9 million (UNFPA)**
(Other sources	***15-24.5 million)***
Population growth	**2.4% (USAID)** **1.6% (UNFPA)**
Languages:	
Pashto	**35%**
Afghan Persian (Dari)	**25%**
Turkic Languages (primarily Uzbek and Turkmen)	**11%**
30 minor languages (primarily Baluchi and Pashai)	**4%**
Much bi-lingualism *(Source: CIA)*	
Human Development Indicators:	
Under five mortality rate	**257/1,000**
(Developing World Average or DWA	***97/1,000)***
Infant mortality rate	**165/1,000** ***(DWA 66/1,000)***
Maternal mortality rate (1990)	**1,700/100,000** ***(DWA 470/100,000)***
Malnutrition	**affects up to 35% of children under five years old**
Deaths due to diarrhoeal diseases	**42%**
Crude birth rate (per 1,000)	**52** ***(DWA 26)***
Crude death rate (per 1,000)	**21** ***(DWA 9)***
Total fertility rate (per woman)	**6.9 children** ***(DWA 3.2)***
Contraceptive prevalence rate (1997)	**2%** ***(DWA 54%)***
Human development index rank	**169 (out of 174)**
Gender-related development rank	**135 (out of 137)**
GNP per capita	**1991 US$164**
(DWA, 1995 US$1,101)	**1984 US$222**

Editors' Note*: Figures are for 1996 unless otherwise stated. Reliable statistics, such as economic and industrial indicators, simply do not exist. Treat all statistics with caution.*

Life expectancy at birth (years):		
Male		43
Female		44
(DWA		*62)*
Population with access to:		
Health services (1985-95)	rural	17%
	urban	80% *(DWA 80%)*
Safe water (1990-96)	rural	5% *(DWA 61%)*
	urban	39% *(DWA 88%)*
Combined gross school enrolment:		
Female		9.2% *(DWA 51%)*
Male		26% *(DWA 60%)*
Total		13% *(DWA 47%)*
Adult literacy rate (1995):		
Female		15% *(DWA 62%)*
Male		47% *(DWA 79%)*
Total		32% *(DWA 71%)*
External refugees:		
Afghan returnees since 1989		3.9 million
Returnees in 1997		86,000
Afghan refugees in Pakistan		1.2 million
(Govt. of Pakistan estimate		*1.8 million)*
Afghan refugees in Iran		1.4 million
(Govt. of Iran estimate		*2 million)*
Aid flows (in US$1,000):		
1991		276,847
1993		249,104
1997		216,705
Climate:		
Average annual rainfall		13 inches/338mm
Kabul average temperatures	Jan.	–2.8°C
	July	24.4°C
Landmines (1997):		
Total high priority contaminated area remaining:		323.7 sq.km
Total contaminated area remaining:		725 sq.km
Opium (1997):		
Estimated number of farmers cultivating poppy		200,000
Amount of land used for poppy production		58,400 hectares
Total production of dry opium gum		2,800 metric tonnes
Average income per hectare	wheat	$558
	opium	$923

Sources: UNICEF State of the World's Children 1998, UNICEF/CIET MICS 1997, UNHCR 1997, UNDCP 1997, CIA World Factbook 1996, UNDP Human Development Report 1996; WHO Report "Hope" 1996, UNFPA World Population Prospects 1994 Revision

Afghanistan
provinces
KUNDUZ
TAKHAR
BADAKHSHAN
BALKH
SAMANGAN
BAGHLAN
FARYAB
JOWZJAN
KAPISA
KUNAR
LAGHMAN
BADGHIS
BAMIYAN
PARWAN
KABUL
WARDAK
NANGARHAR
LOGAR
HERAT
GHOR
URUZGAN
PAKTYA
GHAZNI
FARAH
PAKTIKA
ZABUL
NIMRUZ
HELMAND
KANDAHAR
N
W
E
S
Legend
Provinces
International borders
Provincial capitals
KM
0
100
200
300
400
Cartography: Yvan Boyjoo (Aid for Aid) 1998
Sources: United Nations & CROSSLINES Global Report

Agriculture

"Without our land, there is no food; without our water, there is no life; without our trees and flowers, there is no soul; and without our country, there is no poetry, no music...for then we are not Afghans."

– Tribal elder from Nangarhar province, 1989

Afghanistan's economy is based primarily on farming. And yet barely one-tenth of the country's land area is agricultural, half of which is rain-fed, the other half irrigated. According to pre-war figures, nearly 80% of Afghans live in rural areas and rely on farming for income or subsistence. During the decade-long Soviet occupation, much of Afghanistan's agricultural infrastructure was ruined. An estimated 22,000 villages in the country's 29 provinces were destroyed or severely damaged. In many areas, Soviet and Afghan government troops cut down vineyards, orchards, ornamental trees and shrubs for security reasons. The Soviets also destroyed some 3,000 ancient irrigation systems as a means of deliberately disabling the local economy, particularly in parts known to support the mujahideen. Afghanistan has suffered further destruction since the renewed civil war following the Red Army departure in 1989, but interfactional fighting has been responsible more for destroying Kabul and other urban areas than for destroying the countryside.

The mass exodus to Pakistan and Iran of one-third of the Afghan population – the majority from rural areas – also severely affected the agricultural situation. Whole regions, such as much of the Panjshair Valley or parts of Ghazni and Kandahar provinces, were almost completely depleted of their inhabitants. Most agricultural programmes and support services collapsed as trained professionals – from agricultural advisors to veterinary officers – left. Hundreds of thousands of cattle, camels, sheep and other livestock were killed in the bombing or from landmines; many, too, were stolen or sold off by their owners for survival. (SEE LIVESTOCK below). As a

KABUL

Poverty and food deficiency represent two of the most urgent problems for Kabul and other war-affected areas. In and around the Afghan capital, food-for-work programmes and other projects are being implemented to develop and recultivate farm areas which previously had been abandoned for lack of water and manpower. In one programme sponsored by the World Food Programme (WFP), local farmers dug wells and grew vegetables for distribution to city hospitals and homes. On completion of the project, the land was returned to its owners who have continued to farm.

result, once thriving farms, fields, fruit orchards and pastures were abandoned to the mercy of the wind, rain, snow and drought. Roughly half of the country's irrigation systems have been wrecked not only by direct war damage but also through lack of maintenance. (SEE IRRIGATION below) And as if this were not enough, countless agricultural areas have been rendered unusable by landmines; these will need to be cleared before they can again be put to the plough or returned to grazing. (SEE LANDMINES)

From self-sufficiency to collapse

Overall, the lack of cultivation and soil erosion has resulted in badly degraded agricultural land in many parts of the country. (SEE ENVIRONMENT) By the early 1990s, agricultural production had dropped by up to 70% (when compared to 1978 figures). Current humanitarian assistance efforts are therefore aimed at rehabilitating agriculture and restoring the national food supply.

To grasp the essentials of farming in Afghanistan, and the effects of war on the land, one needs to appreciate the enormous disparity that exists in the productive capacity among the various land types. Three-quarters of the country supports only sparse but extensive grazing in the mountains and deserts; a mere five percent of the land area, mainly in the irrigated valleys, produces 85% of overall agricultural output. Since the early 1950s, billions of dollars worth of international assistance – Soviet, American, German, French and other – has been spent in Afghanistan, much of it directed towards upgrading agriculture and increasing production through the development of large-scale infrastructure, and the expansion of forestry and natural resource management.

By 1978, the year anti-communist resistance first erupted, Afghanistan was largely self-sufficient in food. It was also a significant exporter of high quality fruit, silk, cotton and other products. Between 1978 and 1989, international assistance, mainly from the Soviet bloc, focused on bringing government-controlled land into

E. Girardet

production through large-scale development and state farms. However, many programmes totally collapsed with the war; numerous state farms, irrigation and forestry projects were either damaged or destroyed. Others were simply abandoned to the mujahideen by the former Soviet-backed regime. When the various guerrilla groups moved in, they frequently looted the facilities, gutted buildings and made off with any equipment that could be resold in Pakistan. Similarly, once magnificent forests, formerly managed by donor-funded programmes, have been ruthlessly cut down for timber by Afghan and Pakistani entrepreneurs, often with the connivance of Pakistani military and government officials who have made small fortunes from the trade. (SEE FORESTRY)

AGRICULTURE

Emerging from the war: an ability to adapt

Today, despite the overwhelming devastation, much of Afghanistan's basic production pattern remains both simple and robust. The system's simplicity – it has changed little over the past 2,000 years – has proved a major strength in the rapid re-establishment of agricultural production where fighting has stopped. Yet Afghan farmers, many of whom still work with beasts of burden, have shown a remarkable ability to adapt to sophisticated technology, such as high-yielding crop varieties, inorganic fertilizers and agricultural and veterinary chemicals.

The Food and Agriculture Organization (FAO), the leading UN agency for the rehabilitation of Afghanistan's agricultural sector, has helped ease the way for the return of nearly three million refugees to their homes since 1992. Village communities have been re-established, while abandoned land has been brought back into cultivation, providing food and employment for the returnees. Short-term rehabilitation efforts have involved removing landmines from access roads and farm land, distributing seed and planting materials to farmers, implementing disease and pest-control programmes, and restoring abandoned irrigation systems to some degree of functionality.

Implementing an effective strategy: a task of decades

Nevertheless, an effective, long-term rehabilitation, such as rebuilding irrigation systems, could take decades. The lack of reliable information is one hindering factor. The last official agricultural survey of Afghanistan was conducted in 1978; much of the information available is out of date and misleading. While various agricultural surveys have been attempted by select aid groups over the last 20 years, they have been limited to specific regions and often conducted under difficult conditions.

FAO has now developed an open-ended strategy (*Afghanistan Agricultural Strategy*, January 1997) aimed at fully developing the country's farming potential. Far more realistic than many past UN or donor-sponsored programmes, the FAO strategy seeks to operate as much as possible through NGOs supported by simple interventions at the local level.

The strategy has four principal objectives:

- to create national food security
- to increase economic and social development
- to raise the levels of skills and knowledge
- to protect scarce natural resources

Donor aid to Afghanistan over the past years has been largely humanitarian rather than economic. However, if and when peace returns, observers expect a shift from quick-impact activities to longer-term development. The FAO strategy may then emphasise working formally through regional or national structures. Further development assistance will then require increased economic justification. As the cash economy expands, observers note, pressures will grow for greater capital accumulation and investment.

According to the FAO strategy, increasing the overall food supply and creating saleable surpluses will provide the greatest potential access to food for all Afghans. Productivity, however, will need to support about 18 to 20 million people by the turn of the century. This will prove difficult, not only because of the effects of war, but also because Afghanistan must deal with a relatively narrow resource base.

As a primarily agricultural country, Afghanistan boasts a maximum of 3.5 million hectares of irrigated land and up to 4 million hectares of rain-fed land. Of the latter, only 1 million hectares can be used at any one time. Scattered farming communities, long distances and rugged terrain make the delivery of any form of services or transportation of crops problematic. Such drawbacks may encourage poor farmers in remote areas to focus on more easily-grown – and transported – narcotic crops, such as poppies for opium. (SEE DRUGS) While long periods in refugee camps have made many farmers aware of new technology, they often lack the capital and labour to raise productivity. Fertilizer production, for example, stands at 20% of pre-war levels, while agricultural product-processing has ceased completely.

Overall, the lack of government and internal security should not prevent the rehabilitation and development of agricultural production in many parts of the country. Indeed, the lack of government may even prove a good thing as it may stimulate greater local initiative. On the other hand, inefficient central government does not necessarily offer a favourable climate for developing internal and external markets. The uncertainty of continued conflict presents a major barrier to domestic and external investment in any sector of the economy. (SEE ECONOMICS)

For agriculture, this has resulted in an uneven availability, both in quality and quantity, of technical inputs such as fertilizers, chemicals and veterinary medicines. Much will depend on the ability of donors, aid agencies and private enterprise to provide local communities with support, including the improvement of basic infrastructure such as roads. Aid specialists often forget that Afghans are a resilient, mercatorial people capable of responding quickly to needs, whether in the form of transport services or selling agricultural equipment. In many areas, markets are working and inputs are available for those who can afford them. Programmes aimed at providing farmers with an increase in cash savings will accentuate their ability to buy quality seed and fertilizers, or to afford a tractor as a means of raising efficiency.

ESSENTIAL DATA

- **An estimated 22,000 villages in 29 provinces were destroyed or severely damaged during the Soviet war (1979-1989)**
- **Nearly 80% of Afghans lived in rural areas at the start of the Soviet war (1979)**
- **Soviet-Afghan security operations destroyed some 3,000 ancient irrigation systems during the Soviet war**
- **Agricultural production dropped by up to 70% from 1978 to the early 1990s**
- **Three-quarters of the country supports only sparse but extensive grazing in the mountains and deserts**
- **Five percent of the land area, mainly in the irrigated valleys, produces 85% of overall agricultural output**
- **Up to 3.5 million hectares of land is irrigated**
- **Up to 4 million hectares of land are rain-fed. Only 1 million hectares of this can be cultivated at any one time**

Sources: FAO, Swedish Committee for Afghanistan (SCA), UNDP

ESSENTIAL AGENCIES

ADA, CARE, DACAAR, FAO, MADERA, SCA, SOLIDARITES, UNDP

ESSENTIAL READING

Afghanistan Agricultural Strategy, FAO (Rome, 1997)
Afghanistan Poppy Survey, UNDCP (1997)
WFP briefing papers and situation reports on relief and rehabilitation in Afghanistan (1995, 1996 & 1997)
Afghanistan Rural Rehabilitation Programme, UNDP (Islamabad, 1994)
Afghanistan Rehabilitation Strategy, agriculture and irrigation, UNDP (Islamabad, 1993)
Afghanistan, Louis Dupree, Princeton University Press (2nd Edition, 1980; reprinted by Oxford University Press, 1997)

Irrigation

Agricultural irrigation in Afghanistan dates back more than 4,500 years with the oldest vestiges found in an ancient settlement near Kandahar. The establishment of permanent settlements and irrigation development went hand-in-hand as cultivation was largely impossible without some form of water conduit. Water and land allocation has been always closely linked to the customs of local populations. Maintenance work among irrigation systems, such as the regular cleaning of *karezes* (underground irrigation tunnels), remains a traditional activity in the farmers' seasonal calendar.

Nearly 85% of the country's water resources comes from the Hindu Kush mountains, whose winter snows provide a natural storage of water; spring and summer snowmelt support the perennial flow in all major rivers in Afghanistan. The remaining 15% comes from alluvial ground water aquifers and springs. Ground water from deep wells counts for less than 0.5%.

The bulk of the country's irrigation sources comes from three major river basins: the Amu Darya (Oxus) Basin to the north; the Desert Basin to the south and southwest; and the Indus Basin (including the Kabul River) to the east and southeast. Reliable data regarding water resources from rainfall and river flow are not available. All measuring stations operational in 1978 (over 140) have been destroyed or their equipment looted. Currently, none is working.

The war has had a devastating impact on irrigation. Some 3.5 million hectares of Afghanistan's farmland, producing nearly 80% of all wheat and 85% of other crops, were irrigated in 1978. Today, barely one-third (1.02 million hectares) of this area is being properly watered, resulting in a 30% national food deficit. The remaining 70% of irrigated lands suffers from poor water management, damage due to lack of maintenance and destruction as the direct result of war.

Irrigation can be divided into two main categories: traditional and modern. Traditional irrigation systems include the *arhad* (ground water lifted from shallow wells) and *karez* (a free flow of water from alluvial aquifers through specially-constructed underground tunnels). There are also small-, medium- and large-scale surface water systems supplied by nearby streams and rivers. Modern irrigation schemes involve formal surface water operations (often previously run by the government or state farms) such as dams and pumped water sprinkler systems from wells. As in many countries, the overall efficiency of such systems is poor, no more than 25% to 30% among both traditional and modern irrigation schemes. Labour shortages often mean poor canal maintenance and cleaning. In areas with high ground water tables, over-irrigation, bad drainage and water-logging often causes salination of the soil, forcing fields to lie fallow for one or two years.

Agricultural specialists believe that available water resources are capable of supporting the irrigation of up to 5.3 million hectares. Rehabilitation, however, can be a long process. Lack of maintenance, for example, can cause canals and *karezes* to become silted and blocked, often resulting in the river or water supply changing course. This can destroy existing farmland through flooding; erosion also removes thin layers of topsoil which can take decades to rectify, if ever.

Another problem is that the *mirab/vakil* system (traditional water rights distribution) has been seriously affected, if not abused, by local commanders and armed groups. In many areas, former mujahideen, warlords or Taliban fighters regulate water supplies at whim or based on contacts, bribes and corruption. This often results in chaos with some areas denied regular access to water.

Around 100 local and international NGOs as well as many UN agencies are involved one way or another in irrigation rehabilitation. Funding, nearly $20 million between 1989 and 1995, is provided mainly by the UN and the European Union (EU) but is unbalanced in its distribution. Food deficit areas such as Badakhshan, Bamiyan and Ghor are largely neglected.

According to the FAO, which has the mandate for overall irrigation planning in Afghanistan, the complete cost per hectare for rehabilitation comes to $300 for traditional schemes and $500 for modern ones. While 25% can be covered by locally organized food-for-work programmes, the remaining 75% must be raised in cash for the purchase of materials plus covering professional staff and operational costs.

While many NGOs have proved crucial in helping Afghans survive the impact of war and in the rehabilitation of the country's damaged infrastructure, most lack the professionalism and technical know-how to develop long-term hydraulic structures for irrigation purposes. This might be best left to specialized NGOs and the private sector.

Some observers warn that present progress in irrigation made by so-called "Quick Impact Projects" is unsatisfactory both in quality and quantity. Unless current financial resources ($3 million in 1997) are increased significantly, it will take 200 years for all existing rehabilitation schemes to return to full production. If sufficient funding were made available, some observers say, it would still require a whole generation to bring Afghanistan back to pre-war production levels.

ESSENTIAL DATA

Water resources

- **Nearly 85% of water resources originates from the Hindu Kush**
- **15% of water resources comes from alluvial ground water aquifers and springs**
- **Less than 0.5% of ground water comes from deep wells**

Irrigated land

3.5 million hectares of farm land were irrigated in 1978. Of this total in 1997:

- **40% (1.36 million hectares) remained damaged due to lack of maintenance**
- **30% (1.02 million hectares) was irrigated**
- **20% (0.68 million hectares) had poor on-farm water management**
- **10% (0.34 million hectares) remained destroyed or otherwise damaged by war**

Irrigation potential

- **Irrigation potential based on available water supplies: 5.3 million hectares**
- **Estimated rehabilitation period with current resources available in 1997: 200 years**

Source: FAO

ESSENTIAL AGENCIES

ADA, CARE, DACAAR, FAO, MADERA, SOLIDARITES

ESSENTIAL READING

Afghanistan Agricultural Strategy, FAO (Rome, 1997)

Livestock

Since the outbreak of fighting in mid-1978, the effect of Afghanistan's dragging war has had a devastating impact on much of the country's livestock, mainly cattle, sheep, goats, horses, donkeys and camels. While reliable figures regarding livestock populations do not exist, the 1991 *Agricultural Survey of Afghanistan* (ASA) by the Swedish Committee for Afghanistan estimates that losses amounted to as much as half of all draft oxen and two-thirds of sheep and goats.

Livestock populations suffered particularly heavy losses in Soviet bombing raids, ground assaults and other forms of military action. But landmines and scattered ordnance have affected animals since the early days of the war. (SEE LANDMINES) Not only have livestock been killed while grazing, but villagers often use them to walk through suspected minefields as a form of impromptu clearance. *Kuchi* nomads, who traditionally graze their animals on both sides of the frontier with Afghanistan and Pakistan, are believed to have suffered the most from landmines: by 1995 an estimated 35,000 of their animals had been killed by mines, with each household losing an average of nearly 25 animals (equivalent to about $3,000). This continuing scourge promises to kill and injure both humans and livestock for generations to come.

Numerous animals, too, succumbed as refugees made their way to Pakistan and Iran during the height of the fighting. Once in exile, many were forced to sell their animals for lack of grazing or for much-needed cash. Throughout the war, horses, donkeys, camels and mules were used by the mujahideen and aid agencies for supply caravans across the mountains and through the deserts, often with livestock casualties of 10% or more per trip. Farming too has suffered from the loss of livestock. For example, apart from milk and other dairy products, oxen are essential for the tilling of the soil.

Another problem provoked by the war was the collapse of veterinary services, the flight of trained personnel and the destruction of government facilities such as the state farms at Kabul, Jalalabad and Lashkar Gah. Exotic bulls used for crossbreeding, for example, were killed or removed as war booty. Apart from traditional medicines, livestock in many areas had little or no access to veterinary services, vaccination programmes and other drugs to combat anthrax, blackleg, sheep pox and enterotoxemia. This has been partially remedied by a relatively effective system of donor-sponsored Veterinary Field Units (VFUs) now operating in some 244 districts throughout the country.

There is also a growth in private extension services – a completely new concept for Afghanistan – although some are performed by unqualified individuals focusing only on the more lucrative forms of assistance. While some NGOs have brought in outside cattle for breeding, such as Swiss Brown bulls distributed by the Afghan Development Agency in Kandahar, Zabul and Uruzgan provinces, numerous returnees and merchants have brought in their own cattle, mainly Friesian or Friesian-type animals from Pakistan.

The VFUs, which will eventually be privatized, need to expand their activities. There is an urgent need for the creation of artificial insemination services for cows, sheep dips along the main migration routes and general control of parasites.

Given the shortage of trained professionals, a priority for aid organizations is to re-open veterinary and agricultural faculties to further rehabilitate and develop the livestock sector. Since women serve as integral players within the livestock production systems – the selling of eggs and dairy products provides them with cash income and increases their independence – aid projects should also ensure that they are included. A number of NGOs are already seeking to focus on women as crucial partners in the development of livestock production.

Despite the war's impact, however, headcounts since 1991 in nearly all the provinces suggest that livestock numbers, particularly cattle, are recovering. They may soon reach pre-war levels. Even the smallest and poorest farmers tend to keep at least one cow to cover basic sustenance requirements. Sheep and goat numbers are nearly back to normal. In the northern provinces, an estimated five million Karakul sheep once represented a major export for Astrakhan pelts. Although the war and low demands for pelts brought the industry into crisis, it now seems that Karakul flocks are returning to their former strength. Afghanistan is still among the biggest producers of Astrakhan pelts in the world.

Even if animal numbers prove somewhat overestimated, livestock production appears to be in relatively good shape. Further expansion, however, will depend on grazing and fodder crops, such as *lucerne* (*Medicago sativa), shaftal (Trifolium resupinatum)* and *berseem (Trifolium alexandrinum*). Fodder crops already represent five percent of arable land. Any further growth will have to depend on extra production or the increase of other field crops.

INFOBRIEFS

ESSENTIAL DATA

Livestock numbers	**1967**	**1991**
Cattle:	3,633,000	4,049,000
Sheep:	21,455,000	18,688,000
Goats:	3,187,000	N/A
Horses:	403,000	245,000
Donkeys:	1,328,000	1,131,000
Camels:	299,000	80,000

Livestock production (estimated figures in tonnes for 1996)

Cows milk:	680,000
Sheep and goat milk:	620,000
Total milk:	1,300,000
Beef:	43,750
Mutton:	104,000
Total meat:	146,750
Eggs:	350 million eggs
Wool:	33,000
Goat Hair:	4,465
Cashmere:	250
Astrakhan pelts	450,000

Source: Afghanistan Agricultural Survey, FAO (Rome, July 1996)

ESSENTIAL AGENCIES

ADA, AFGHANAID, DACAAR, FAO, MADERA, OXFAM, SCA, SOLIDARITES, UNHCR, UNICEF

ESSENTIAL READING

Afghanistan Agricultural Strategy, FAO (Rome, 1997)

British Medical Journal: Social cost of landmines in four countries: Afghanistan, Bosnia, Cambodia and Mozambique, BMJ (London, 16 September 1995)

A review of the livestock production systems of Afghanistan, N. Cossins, FAO (Rome, 1994)

Agricultural Survey of Afghanistan, Swedish Committee for Afghanistan (Peshawar, 1991)

Afghanistan, Louis Dupree, Princeton University Press (2nd Edition, 1980; reprinted by Oxford University Press, 1997)

Aid in the 1980s: reaping what you sow

For the first half decade of the Soviet occupation, the overwhelming proportion of outside humanitarian aid to Afghans was directed towards the estimated three million refugees based in Pakistan. Much of this was channelled through the Islamabad government and the Afghan resistance parties, despite considerable abuse of aid resources by both Pakistani officials and the Afghan parties in Peshawar. (Iran preferred to deal with its refugees on its own and did not allow outside agencies to assist). The Afghan parties, particularly those closely supported by the Pakistanis, also used aid as a means of influence over the refugees. As the war dragged on, control of outside military and humanitarian aid, as well as funding, became a crucial factor for trying to guarantee allegiance among the numerous resistance fronts inside Afghanistan. (Similar ploys can still be seen today with the Pakistanis, the Iranians and the Uzbek government and their clients inside the country).

For the estimated eight million Afghans living in the mainly resistance-controlled rural areas, healthcare and education systems had collapsed. Soviet efforts to root out the guerrillas meant a deliberate policy to destroy the economic infrastructure. Such tactics, among other things, resulted in a sharp decline of agricultural production and a consequent food deficit as shown in the first *Agricultural Survey Report* by the Swedish Committee for Afghanistan (SCA) in May 1988. (SEE AGRICULTURE)

Only an extremely limited amount of international relief, primarily medical, went to those Afghans seeking to survive in resistance-held areas. This was provided by a small handful of European, American and Muslim NGOs, most of whom transported their aid clandestinely by horse caravan across the mountains. Some, too, provided funding to needy civilians for the purchase of food, fertilizers and seed from government-controlled bazaars – a much cheaper form of aid than smuggling it inside.

For the hundreds of thousands of "internal refugees", who had fled to Kabul and other government-controlled towns, the relief situation was not much better than for many of those facing dire humanitarian predicaments in the countryside. Numerous victims were ignored by the communist government and the UN agencies still operating officially in Afghanistan. The only international aid (excluding the East bloc countries) that was available tended to be restricted to a few small health projects, such as those run by the World Health Organization (WHO) and UNICEF, plus some highly questionable UNESCO-supported education programmes. At the time, it was UN policy to operate only in government areas, thus limiting themselves to the capital and a few other large towns.

The crossborder NGOs, on the other hand, worked only in the rural areas controlled by the resistance and where the main part of the population lived. Organizations such as the Swedish Committee for Afghanistan (SCA), Médecins Sans Frontières, AFRANE, Afghanaid, Aide Médicale Internationale and a few others sought to alleviate the plight of civilians seeking to remain in the country, despite the risk of further military onslaught. Several European governments, while reluctant to acknowledge their involvement in crossborder relief, helped back some of these groups. Even the European Economic Community (as the European Union was then called) provided funds for small in-country projects.

Certain major aid agencies clearly were restricted by their mandates. The United Nations Commissioner for Refugees (UNHCR), for example, technically could deal only with refugees. On the other hand, some of the larger agencies had the means to assist civilians inside Afghanistan but consciously refrained from doing so for political and fund-raising reasons. They preferred to restrict their operations to 'official' sectors only. US-backed organizations, in particular, were expressly forbidden from dealing with any forms of crossborder humanitarian assistance. The US government, which was providing huge quantities of arms to the mujahideen but denying its involvement in the war, was terrified of having American nationals captured by the Soviet or Afghan government forces. As one American official working with CARE International noted at the time: "We are not into clandestine relief."

Such policies by both the UN and most donor countries actually may have contributed towards aggravating the refugee situation by placing such an enormous emphasis on humanitarian assistance outside Afghanistan. For their part, the Pakistanis did everything possible to assure that as much aid as possible passed through their own channels. Not only did international aid represent a *milch* cow of growing proportions every year, but also a means of promoting Pakistani policy inside Afghanistan – and Pakistan on the world stage.

From 1986 onwards, the international aid situation, particularly with regard to military assistance, began to change dramatically. Washington decided to support openly the mujahideen in their efforts to resist the Soviets. Over 600 million dollars a year worth of military and humanitarian aid began to pour in. Coordinated by the Central Intelligence Agency (CIA) and the US Agency for

International Development (USAID), this was distributed largely in collaboration with Pakistan's military intelligence organization, Inter Services Intelligence, or ISI. (SEE WAR WITHOUT BORDERS) Other aid sources, both official and private, ranging from the Saudi Arabians to the Chinese also became increasingly involved.

The rise in US aid resulted in a flood of NGOs, many of them desperately seeking projects for projects' sake. Even the UN was scavenging for projects to justify increased amounts of spending. Some NGOs, such as SCA, deliberately turned down USAID funding on the grounds that even if they wished, they could not spend much more money responsibly within the time constraints demanded by the American annual aid budget.

However, much of this humanitarian aid went astray. NGO coordinators and experienced observers estimated that no more than 20-30% of US aid actually reached intended beneficiaries inside Afghanistan. The rest ended up in the pockets of Pakistani government and Afghan party officials. This blatant corruption undermined the credibility amongst ordinary Afghans of the very people American policy was seeking to sustain – the exiled resistance leadership.

The failure of the USAID approach was largely the result of Washington's political efforts to establish an Afghan shadow government while remaining heavily dependent on the Pakistanis for implementing this policy, notably via the Peshawar parties. Many of the independent NGOs, however, preferred to cultivate direct links with the resistance fronts or "local authorities" inside Afghanistan. According to Anders Fänge of the Swedish Committee, whose organization was involved in crossborder relief since the early days of the war: "The most effective humanitarian aid given by the Americans was the Stinger [ground-to-air missile]. It meant that the gunships disappeared and the farmers could start cultivating their fields again. It also meant that the door was opened for more development-oriented activities [as compared to relief] in NGO and USAID programmes."

A significant proportion of international aid, both humanitarian and military, was directed by the Pakistanis towards the mainly Pashtun Afghan fundamentalist groups such as Hekmatyar Gulbuddin's Hezb-e-Islami faction. While relatively small amounts of aid did succeed in reaching non-Pashtun groups such as Commander Ahmed Shah Massoud's northern Jamiat-led alliance, the Americans ironically did much to arm the very extremists they later blamed for promoting international terrorism. Various Arab and other Muslim fundamentalist groups, such as the *Wahabi*, also stepped up their assistance both to the refugees and inside guerrilla fronts willing to accept their money and support.

On the military side, vast proportions of this military aid were stockpiled and later used against rival mujahed groups following the overthrow of the communist regime in Kabul in April 1992. Despite warnings by some international aid coordinators and journalists during the second half of the 1980s that US policy would only lead towards an even more disastrous Lebanon-style situation in the years ahead, American conservative elements preferred to continue with their support in order to "make the Russians bleed," as one US official noted. Or as another former US policy-maker under President Ronald Reagan added: "It was of no concern to us what would happen once the Soviets left." Today, some analysts directly attribute much of the bitter civil strife and post-Soviet devastation of Afghanistan to this extremely narrow-minded, myopic policy.

With the withdrawal of the Soviets in February 1989, attention was turned more intensely towards repatriation and reconstruction inside Afghanistan, with the UN assuming a more decisive role. The departure of the Soviets, however, meant a rapidly diminishing interest – and drop in funding – from the Americans. It became quickly apparent (as some observers had pointed out years earlier) that under the Reagan and Bush administrations, the plight of the Afghans themselves had never been the issue. What had mattered most of all was getting the Soviets out. By 1993, USAID had halted virtually all its funding for humanitarian and development projects. For Washington, Afghanistan was no longer on the radar screen.

Excluding its dismal activities earlier in the war, the UN started up its Afghanistan programmes in 1988, shortly after the Geneva accords. These were in full swing by the beginning of 1989. Many of the earlier approaches were plagued by poor coordination and misguided efforts to encourage the creation of Afghan NGOs. The UN also adopted a big brother attitude with a tendency not to listen to the international NGOs which had already been operating in-country for seven or eight years.

The UN's main problem was that Afghanistan was one of the first cases of a "complex political emergency" – also described as a "society in crisis and transition," i.e. a country in war and without a functioning central authority. During the 1990s, such crises became more common with the collapse of the Soviet Union and the end of the Cold War. As one leading independent aid coordinator recently noted: "The UN agencies have their tradition and experience in working with governments; they could never really understand what the absence of a government and a state administration actually meant for an aid programme. They still do not understand it, although they at least are aware of the problem today."

Children

"By not providing adequate care and services to their children, [these] societies endanger not only economic growth but also their chances for democracy and lasting peace. If the examples of armed conflict around the globe have taught us anything, it is that stability rarely endures in a climate of extreme want and inequality."

– Kofi Annan, United Nations Secretary-General, 1997

In the 40 or so armed conflicts and civil wars currently raging around the world, an estimated 80% to 90% of the victims are civilians, mainly women and children. Afghanistan is no exception, although the fact that the war has dragged on for nearly 20 years makes the situation worse. An entire generation of Afghan children have been traumatised, injured or killed by the war, and the ongoing nature of the conflict makes recovery and the chances of a 'normal' life desperately difficult.

Children's rights

In September 1990, world leaders assembled at the United Nations in New York to attend the World Summit for Children. A month earlier, the Convention on the Rights of the Child (CRC) had come into effect, and the summit built on this by adopting a Declaration on the Survival, Protection and Development of Children and a Plan of Action for implementing the Declaration in the 1990s. The Convention marks a change of emphasis in the approach to children. In UNICEF's words, "the idea that children have special needs has given way to the conviction that children have rights, the same full spectrum of rights as adults: civil and political, social, cultural and economic." The core of the Convention is to promote the right of every child to survival, to protection from exploitation and abuse, and to the fulfilment of his or her potential as a human being. Today the CRC is the most widely ratified human rights convention in history. Almost every country in the world has signed, including Afghanistan; only six have not, Switzerland and the United States among them. (SEE HUMAN RIGHTS)

Although Afghanistan has ratified the CRC, the Taliban does not recognise any UN Charters or Conventions ratified by previous governments. This, combined with the Taliban's rigid interpretation of Islamic *shari'a* law, has serious implications for the rights of Afghan children. In particular the severe restrictions on medical care and training for women is exacerbating the maternal mortality rate, currently the second highest in the world at 1,700 per 100,000 live births. This in turn threatens the right of children to survival (CRC, Article 6), and potentially their right to health (CRC, Article 24). The Taliban prohibition on both girls' education and female teachers clearly denies the right of all children to receive free primary education (CRC, Article 28), and makes judgement by sex, violating Article 2 of the Convention. In Kabul alone it is estimated that 150,000 boys and 104,000 girls are deprived of schooling. (SEE EDUCATION) Furthermore, the Taliban ban on women earning a living outside the home has a serious impact on the children of widow-headed households, forcing particularly those living in towns and cities onto the streets in search of money, food and firewood. This exposes them to the dangers of exploitation, abuse and even landmines, violating Articles 9,18 and 19 of the Convention.

ESSENTIAL DATA

- **Convention on the Rights of the Child: international law from 2 September 1990**
- **96% of the world's children live in states which have ratified the Convention**
- **Redirecting 25% of the developing world's military expenditure could pay for most of the Summits goals for the year 2000**
- **Afghanistan has ratified the Convention; Switzerland and the US have not**
- **The Taliban's refusal to recognise any UN Conventions ratified by previous governments and its strict interpretation of *shari'a* law have resulted in widespread abuses of children's rights to survival, protection and development**

ESSENTIAL READING

First Call for Children: World Declaration and Plan of Action from the World Summit for Children, Convention on the Rights of the Child, UNICEF (1990)
State of the World's Children 1997 & 1998, UNICEF
Report of the seminar on the Rights of the Child in Afghanistan, CCA (November, 1996)
State of Afghan Refugee Children in NWFP/Pakistan, CCA (June, 1996)

Child labour and street children

The ending of hazardous and exploitative child labour is the main focus of UNICEF's *State of the World's Children 1997* report. The report exposes ***four myths*** prevalent in discussions about this emotive issue:

- *Child labour is uniquely a problem of the developing world.* However, dangerous forms of child labour also exist in the so-called "first world."
- *Child labour will never be eliminated until poverty disappears.* Yet however poor or rich a society is, children can always be perceived as a cheaper and more exploitable form of labour.
- *Most child labourers work in the sweatshops of industries exporting cheap goods to the rich world's stores.* In fact most child labourers are found in the informal sector (streets, fields and homes); export industries account for probably less than five percent of child workers.
- *The only way to make headway against child labour is for consumers and governments to apply pressure through sanctions and boycotts.* But such sweeping measures only affect the export sector.

Not all work by children is unacceptable: at one extreme may be intolerable and exploitative work which threatens a child's health and safety; but at the other may be work which is highly beneficial and contributes to a child's development. Much child labour falls into the grey area between these extremes. The criteria against which to judge whether child labour is exploitative are those which apply to the physical survival and protection of the child, and its development, whether physical, cognitive, emotional, or social/moral.

Many hundreds of millions of child labourers work worldwide, half of them in Asia alone. There are many reasons for the existence of child labour. One of the most significant is the slashing of governments' social spending, often in response to austere structural adjustment regimes imposed by international financiers. Education in particular is undefended and in decline in exactly those developing world countries where schools could provide a meaningful alternative to exploitative child labour.

UNICEF defines seven broad types of child labour: domestic service, forced and bonded labour, commercial sexual exploitation, industrial and plantation work, street work, work for the family, and girls' work. Not all types of child labour are prevalent in Afghanistan. The shattered state of the Afghan industrial economy means that bonded child labour is on nothing like the scale of that seen in the carpet industries of, for example, Uttar Pradesh in northern India.

The strong family structures of tribal Afghan society, combined with Islam's inherent sexual conservatism, mean that commercial sexual exploitation of children is rare in Afghanistan. However, most other forms of child labour are widespread throughout the country. During harvest time in Hazarajat, for example, the entire family including children of all ages will work from dawn till dusk digging potatoes and storage pits to put them in.

Very little work has been done to assess the nationwide extent of child labour in Afghanistan. Save the Children Fund (UK) investigated child labour in the north, and in September 1997 published a Needs Assessment of Working Children in Mazar-e-Sharif. Between May and June 1996, the Swiss-based NGO Terre des Hommes (TdH), in collaboration with the United Nations High Commissioner for Refugees (UNHCR), conducted a ground-breaking survey of 28,000 child workers between the ages of 5 and 14 in Kabul. TdH admits that before the survey began they assumed most of the children would be orphans or street children. They were both surprised and heartened to find that in fact 98% of those surveyed lived at home with at least one parent or guardian. They attribute this to the strong sense of social responsibility fostered by Islam. Some 40% of the children surveyed were going to school as well as working on the streets; however, since the Taliban captured Kabul in September 1996 that figure is believed to have dropped considerably, thereby increasing the numbers of child street workers.

Typically, parents send their children out to polish shoes, burn incense for prayers, act as porters in the markets, wash cars, or simply beg for money – the UN and NGO quarters of Kabul providing particularly rich pickings. They also search wasteland and ruins for firewood, scraps of food, plastic, metal or paper – anything that can be used in the home or sold. In January 1997, AFP reported that Afghan children desperate to earn a few *Afghanis* were stealing human bones from graveyards, which were mixed with animal bones and exported to Pakistan to be turned into cooking oil, soap and chicken feed. The skeleton of an average Afghan can fetch up to 7,000 *Afghanis* (50 US cents at the time) the report said.

Many of the ruined buildings in and around Kabul and Afghanistan's other major towns still have not been cleared of mines or UXOs (Unexploded Ordnance), adding to the physical dangers street-working children face, and intensifying the trauma and guilt felt by parents of children injured while scavenging for their family. Undoubtedly, too, the Taliban restrictions on women working have increased the number of child workers since war-widows can no longer earn an income to support their hungry families.

In the absence of any government department formulating a coherent policy on child welfare, a number of international and indigenous agencies are working to alleviate the problems outlined above. In Kabul a child-focused working group of agencies meets on a regular basis to share information and coordinate action. ASCHIANA, an Afghan NGO supported by TdH, UNHCR, the International Committee of the Red Cross (ICRC), Médecins du Monde (MDM) and Pharmacins Sans Frontières (PSF), looks after up to 500 street-working children in day-care centres around Kabul, where it provides some formal and health education, vocational training, weekly medical attention, and two hot meals a day. The children are free to come and go as they wish and many combine time at the centre with a few hours work on the streets each day. Girls up to the age of seven are officially allowed to visit these centres, and female staff visit older girls in their homes.

The Taliban, with the help of UNICEF and the NGO Children in Crisis (CiC), run an orphanage for about 800 children in Kabul and aim to reunite children separated from their families by the conflict. However, those with no family to go to often remain at the orphanage after their eighteenth birthday because they are simply not prepared to face the outside world.

The Afghan Red Crescent Society (ARCS) runs *marastoons* in Kabul, Jalalabad, Mazar and Kandahar for the long-term homeless. Started in the 1930s by King Zahir Shah, they are open houses which provide food, clothing, soap and a bed, plus some handicraft training. Children are kept in a family compound with their parents or widows, separated from single men. WETCO, an Afghan NGO supported by UNHCR, runs a "school for orphans" in Kabul where about 120 boys and girls receive some non-formal education and vocational training.

ESSENTIAL READING

Needs Assessment of Working Children in Mazar-e-Sharif, SCF(UK) (September, 1997). Available from SCF offices in Islamabad, Mazar and London.
State of the World's Children 1997 & 1998, UNICEF

Child health

According to UNICEF's *State of the World's Children 1998*, the proportion of children who reach their fifth birthday is one of the most fundamental indicators of a country's concern for its people. Afghanistan's under-five mortality rate – the key indicator – was 257 per 1,000 live births in 1996, the fourth worst in the world and the highest outside Africa. By comparison, the rate in Sweden is 4 per 1,000, and the world average 88 per 1,000. Infant mortality is also more than double the average rate for developing countries: 165 children of every 1,000 born die each year before their first birthday. This means that over quarter of a million children die in Afghanistan before the age of five.

Nearly a half of them die from diarrhoeal diseases or acute respiratory infections; and a fifth of their deaths results from diseases which could be prevented through vaccination. One of the major health initiatives of the past few years in Afghanistan has been the Expanded Programme on Immunization (EPI) implemented by UNICEF and the World Health Organization (WHO) through the Ministry of Public Health (MoPH) and NGOs. Since 1994 there have been seven rounds of the polio campaign, reaching as many as 3.6 million children in 1997, and this has paved the way for immunizations across more than three-quarters of the country against BCG, DPT (diphtheria, pertussis/whooping cough and tetanus), measles and TT2. Detailed survey work is now underway to assess the actual impact of EPI nationwide, although UNICEF claims an average coverage of 40% for immunization against all six vaccine-preventable childhood diseases.

The control of diarrhoeal diseases (CDD) is a priority for UNICEF and health NGOs, with many basic health centres promoting the use of Oral Rehydration Therapy (ORT) or the preparation of home-made fluids, and improving standards of personal hygiene and sanitation in the home. In November 1996, Save the Children Fund-USA (SC-US) and the MoPH initiated an integrated public health programme in Kabul to reduce mortality and morbidity of children from acute respiratory infections and diarrhoeal diseases. The programme involved the training of NGO and MoPH staff, the treatment of over 25,000 children, distribution of essential drugs, and a homecare and visiting programme.

Latest survey data suggest that up to one-third of children under three are suffering from acute malnourishment. To combat this, agencies are providing K-Mix and BP-5 high protein rations for therapeutic and supplementary feeding of malnourished children. However, some agencies prefer to promote the use of local food in the home to create a more sustainable solution to the problem of malnourishment. (SEE HEALTH)

Children in conflict

The key issues of concern here are the vulnerability of children to injury or death due to landmines, the prevalence of war-related psychosocial trauma, and children either orphaned or forced to work because the conflict has killed or injured their parents.

In August 1997, a UNICEF team, led by Dr Leila Gupta, an independent consultant, completed the first-ever psychosocial assessment of children exposed to war-related violence in Kabul. More than 300 children aged between eight and 18 were interviewed about their experiences during battles for the city from 1992 to 1996. The results were far more shocking than even Dr Gupta expected: nearly three-quarters of all those interviewed had lost someone from their own family during that four-year period alone. Virtually all the children had seen violence during the fighting with their own eyes, and had heard the injured and dying screaming for help. Nearly half had actually witnessed people being killed during rocket and artillery strikes, and 90% had at some point believed that they too would be killed.

Dr Gupta has also worked on psychosocial trauma among Rwandan children and has drawn some telling comparisons. In Rwanda, the killing was more brutal, more person-to-person than

The global legacy of war *Christian Clark/UNICEF Somalia*

the shelling and rocketing typical of the Afghan war. But in Rwanda it was largely over in 100 days, whereas in Afghanistan the fighting has continued for nearly 20 years. The strongest emotion amongst Rwandan children at the time was, not surprisingly, one of fear. But one year after the genocide this emotion had become anger for 70% of those surveyed. While interviewing Kabuli children, however, Dr Gupta found that they were still more afraid than angry several years later, and still in a state of chronic trauma.

One of the best ways of coping with trauma is to avoid things which remind you of that original traumatic event. But this is impossible in Kabul: over half the city still lies in ruins, testimony to the destructive power of the war. Landmines within the city and throughout the countryside continue to maim and kill. Checkpoints, beatings and abductions by the Taliban in urban areas perpetuate a reign of fear. Thus Afghan children continue to be bombarded with sensory reminders of their past traumatic experiences and desperately lack the quiet space and loving care necessary for them to work through their grief, renew their trust in adults and restore their hope for the future.

In an effort to alleviate these problems, UNICEF is training health workers in ways to help children cope with their trauma and grief, and, in April 1996, SC-US launched a community-based psychosocial assistance and child-oriented landmine education programme. This has reached over 60,000 boys and girls in Kabul, and survived the Taliban educational restrictions by moving sessions to mosques, community buildings, hospitals and clinics. In order to provide mine-free areas in which children can play, SC-US has also built 17 playgrounds around Kabul city; if you visit them in the early evening, you may even catch a few fully-grown adults trying out the swings!

ESSENTIAL DATA

- **95% of Kabuli children interviewed had seen violence with their own eyes between 1992 and 1996**
- **72% had lost an immediate family member during the same period, 40% losing a mother or father**
- **90% believed they would be killed at some stage**

ESSENTIAL READING

Psychosocial assessment of children exposed to war-related violence in Kabul, Leila Gupta PhD., UNICEF (Kabul, 30 August 1997)
Promoting psychological wellbeing among children affected by armed conflict and displacement, International Save the Children Alliance (1996)

ESSENTIAL AGENCIES

ARCS, ASCHIANA, CCA, CiC, RBS, SCF-UK, SC-US, TdH, UNICEF, WETCO

Culture

> *"The sand of the desert is*
> *lightly blown away by a breath;*
> *still more lightly is the fortune*
> *of man destroyed."*
>
> *– Turkmen proverb*

Afghanistan, by virtue of its geographical position straddling the trade routes between Mediterranean Europe, the Middle East, the Indian subcontinent and China, has throughout its history been a cultural, ethnic and linguistic crossroads. A vast number of cultural influences – Persian, Sino-Siberian, Hellenistic, Roman, Indian, Turkish, Arab and Mongol – have all contributed to the material, literary and musical inheritance of Afghanistan.

However, nearly 20 years of war have shattered this precious cultural vessel: Kabul Museum was virtually destroyed by factional fighting and rocket attacks between 1992-1996, priceless Bagram ivories and Greco-Buddhist sculptures were looted and sold off to unscrupulous international dealers, the fifteenth century minarets and mausolea of Herat have been shelled, the colossal Bamiyan Buddhas have been threatened with destruction and the once highly decorated monks' cells carved out of the rockface there have been defaced with military graffiti and cooking fires. Only the mosques, it seems, are rising from the ashes.

Against enormous odds, the Society for the Preservation of Afghanistan's Cultural Heritage (SPACH), a largely voluntary organization started in 1994, is attempting to protect and preserve what remains by raising international awareness of this desperate situation and fostering links with the Afghan Ministry of Information and Culture, the United Nations Educational, Scientific and Cultural Organization (UNESCO), the

International Council of Museums (ICOM) and various other international donors and cultural institutions.

One of the best historical and cultural overviews is Nancy Hatch Dupree's book, *An Historical Guide to Afghanistan* (1977), available at the ACBAR Resource and Information Centre in Peshawar, and also from bookshops in Peshawar and Kabul. The following is a brief summary highlighting some of the most significant cultural remains and artefacts known to have existed before the war, covered in chronological order from Stone Age times to the modern era. For more details on individual sites and how to visit them, SEE REGIONS.

Prehistoric era (c.100,000-1,000 BC)

The Prehistoric era stretches from Stone Age times (c.100,000-2,000 BC) to the Bronze Age (c.5,000-1,000 BC). A number of key sites in Afghanistan have been revealed since the Second World War: Palaeolithic quartzite tools 100,000 years old were found west of Ghazni, and stone tools excavated from Neanderthal rock shelters in Badakhshan and Faryab are thought to be 50,000 years old.

However, it was in the caves of Aq Kupruk, beside the Balkh River in northern Afghanistan, that the most remarkable finds were made. As well as flint tools created so finely that their makers have been dubbed the "Michaelangelos of the Upper Palaeolithic", archaeologists found a human head sculpted, around 20,000 years ago, in light relief from a pebble – one of the oldest representations of man in the world. This pebble is currently missing, possibly stolen from Kabul Museum. At Neolithic sites (c.2,000 BC) in Darra-e-Kur, Badakhshan, pottery, stone vessels, shell ornaments and human burials were discovered, including goats' and childrens' skulls buried together.

The Bronze Age (c.5,000-1,000 BC) saw man move from mountain caves into village and urban communities and begin regional trading with Mesopotamia, Central Asia and the Indus Valley. The Tepe Fullol Hoard of five gold and 12 silver vessels, discovered east of Baghlan, dates from around 2,500 BC and includes a gold beaker with bull motif. Religious shrines discovered at the urban mound of Mundigak and at Deh Morasi, near Kandahar (c.2,000 BC) contained stunning figurines of pagan mother goddesses, at once sensual and demonically ugly.

At Shamshir Ghar some remarkable bone seals, one depicting a winged camel, were discovered dating from the second millennium BC. It was also around this time that lapis lazuli trading began in Badakhshan and Baghlan. Archaeological evidence suggests that Afghan lapis was used for decorative and medicinal purposes in the three great Bronze Age civilizations of Harappa on the Indus river, Mesopotamia, and beside the Nile in modern-day Egypt.

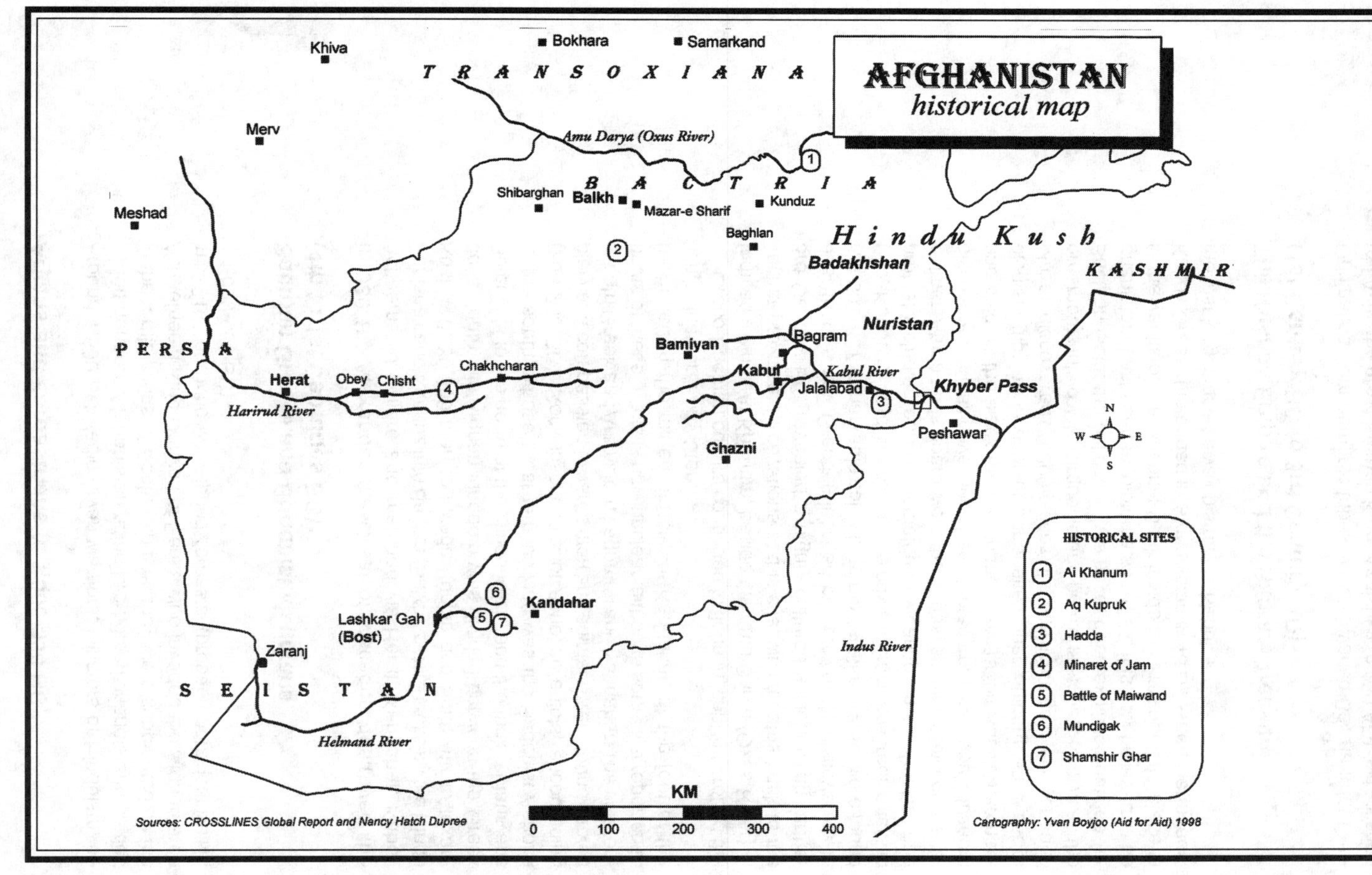

AFGHANISTAN
historical map
Bokhara
Samarkand
Khiva
TRANSOXIANA
Merv
Amu Darya (Oxus River)
BACTRIA
Meshad
Shibarghan
Balkh
Mazar-e Sharif
Kunduz
Baghlan
Hindu Kush
KASHMIR
Badakhshan
Nuristan
Bamiyan
Bagram
PERSIA
Herat
Obey
Chisht
Chakhcharan
Kabul
Kabul River
Jalalabad
Khyber Pass
Harirud River
Peshawar
Ghazni
N
W
E
S
HISTORICAL SITES
1 Ai Khanum
2 Aq Kupruk
3 Hadda
4 Minaret of Jam
5 Battle of Maiwand
6 Mundigak
7 Shamshir Ghar
Kandahar
Lashkar Gah
(Bost)
Indus River
Zaranj
SEISTAN
Helmand River
KM
0
100
200
300
400
Sources: CROSSLINES Global Report and Nancy Hatch Dupree
Cartography: Yvan Boyjoo (Aid for Aid) 1998

Aryans and Zoroastrians (c.1,500-330 BC)

Around 1,500 BC Vedic Aryan warriors, initiators of Hinduism, invaded northern Afghanistan riding two-horsed chariots and settled in the fertile plains of Bactria. In time they were supplanted by the Achaemenid King Darius I of Persia who invaded the Afghan area in 522 BC, and who worshipped Zoroaster (probably born near Balkh, c.1,000-600 BC).

Bactrian Greeks and Buddhist Mauryans (4th to 1st Centuries BC)

In 330 BC Alexander the Great of Macedon destroyed the Achaemenid empire and marched via Herat, Kandahar, Kabul, Panjshair and Kunduz into Bactria (Balkh), before crossing the Hindu Kush with 30,000 men to invade Punjab and Sind. After Alexander's death, his Afghan kingdom was divided between the Greek Seleucids to the north of the Hindu Kush, and the Indian Mauryans to the south, whose most famous king was the Buddhist Ashoka (268-233 BC). Rock inscriptions of Ashokan edicts, encouraging piety and compassion towards men and animals, were found carved in both Greek and Aramaic in Laghman and Kandahar. The whereabouts of these edicts is now unclear, although some are reported to be buried in the mined old city of Kandahar, at the foot of the 'Chihlzina,' or "Forty Steps."

Greco-Bactrian culture continued to flourish, centred around the fortified town of Ai Khanum, beside the Amu Darya (Oxus River) in Takhar province. Excavations at this site, which dates back to the 3rd Century BC, revealed a highly cultured society living further east than in any Greco-influenced city previously discovered. In Kunduz, 627 remarkable coins from the 1st Century BC were found (the "Kunduz Hoard") depicting the busts of Bactrian Greek rulers in profile, including one of Demetrius I wearing an elephant's head helmet. Among this hoard were the largest single Greek coins ever discovered, but all have since been looted from the Kabul Museum and sold on the black market. In the early 1980s Russian archaeologists digging in ancient burial sites near Shibarghan, west of Mazar, discovered 20,000 pieces of magnificent gold jewellery and ornaments inlaid with turquoise and precious stones. Known as the Bactrian Gold, the collection has never been exhibited outside Afghanistan. Last seen by diplomats in 1991, it is now believed to be in the vaults of the National Bank inside the Presidential Palace in Kabul. Greek rule ended in Afghanistan in 48 BC when Hermaeus, the last king, signed away his rule in Kabul.

The Kushan Empire and the Bagram Treasure (1st Century BC to 3rd Century AD)

Originating from nomadic tribes, which invaded Bactria from Central Asia, the great Kushan King, Kanishka (c.130 AD), established an empire which extended its influence from the Ganges Valley to the Gobi Desert. Centred in the summer on Kapisa, north of Kabul, and Peshawar in the winter, he promoted and hugely benefited from perhaps the richest trade of luxury goods the world has ever seen. Wines, ceramics and glass were avidly shipped east from Imperial Rome and Alexandria, in exchange for silks from the Han dynasty in China, and perfumes, spices and gems from India. In 1939 French archaeologists discovered a magnificent 2nd Century AD Kushan treasure trove at Kapisa. A leading scholar has suggested that this trove, known as the Bagram Treasure," represents, in capsule form, the extent and richness of the commercial activity along the Silk Route. Here are Chinese lacquers, Greco-Roman bronzes, plaster plaques, and vessels of porphyry and alabaster, Roman glassware and exquisite ivories from India. Together they form the most spectacular archaeological find of the twentieth century." (N. H. Dupree). The Bagram ivories (1st to 3rd Centuries AD) were used to decorate various objects, and depict mainly scantily-clad women and goddesses in a style typical of the art of the Indian subcontinent. The Hellenistic bronzes, which date no later than the 1st Century AD, include a statue of Hercules, a bust of Mars, and a mask of Silenus. Tragically many of the ivories have been looted from the Kabul Museum, broken up and sold on the international art market. (SEE KABUL MUSEUM)

Buddhism in Afghanistan (2nd to 8th Centuries AD)

King Kanishka also called a great council of Buddhist scholars in Kashmir, which decided to humanise Buddhism in order to gain popularity over militant Brahmanism. This new school of Mahayana Buddhism placed more emphasis on the miraculous life and compassionate personality of the Buddha. It promised all worshippers universal salvation with the help of enlightened individuals who returned from the brink of nirvana as *boddhisattvas*. This directly resulted in the artistic representation of the Buddha (and his *boddhisattvas*) in human form for the first time (previously he had been symbolised by devices such as a wheel, footprint or umbrella). Buddhist art flourished under the Kushans. Particularly remarkable was the Gandhara school, centred around Peshawar and Jalalabad, famous for its sculptures representing the Buddha with the physiognomy of a Greek god and the robes of a Roman emperor. Although Kanishka himself appears to have practised a more syncretic religion, during his reign the Buddhist resurgence swept rapidly along the Silk Route into China, Tibet and the Far East where it is far more widespread today than in the Buddha's native subcontinent.

Buddhist sites abound in all but far-western Afghanistan. The focal point of these sites are *stupas*, hemispherical domes containing burial relics. The *stupas,* originally surmounted by a series of umbrellas, were richly decorated with stone, stucco (lime, marble dust and sand) or mud sculptures depicting the life of the Buddha,

Large Buddha at Bamiyan *J. Walter*

to inspire the faithful as they walked around them in a clockwise direction. Hadda, near Jalalabad, was one of the most significant sites (2nd to 5th Century AD), featuring more than a thousand *stupas* and famous for remarkably expressive faces of visiting pilgrims, artists and merchants sculpted out of stucco. Tragically much of Hadda was destroyed by Russian bombs in the 1980s when the mujahideen were sheltering there, and its precious Gandharan sculptures were all looted from the Kabul Museum and sold off.

The most famous and perhaps best preserved of all Buddhist sites in Afghanistan is, of course, Bamiyan, home to the two colossal

Buddha statues, carved out of a rockface more than 1,600 years ago. (SEE HAZARAJAT) The Large Buddha towers 55 metres high (180 feet) and is the largest statue of its kind in the world. Hollowed out of the rockface are hundreds of monks' cells, their once magnificent wall paintings blackened by the cooking fires of nomads and defaced by military graffiti.

The earliest known examples (8th Century AD) of the cosmic *mandala* – which subsequently became the key symbol of tantric worship in the Buddhism of Tibet and Nepal – were discovered in the side valley of Kakrak. Other significant Buddhist remains include Tepe Maranjan and Guldara near Kabul; Shotorak near Bagram, famous for its rare imported-schist bas reliefs; Tepe Sardar in Ghazni; and Fondukistan in the Ghorband Valley, which in the 7th Century AD enjoyed the last, elegant blossoming of Buddhist art heavily influenced by the sensuous and languid Indian Gupta school.

The rise of Islam (7th to 12th Centuries)

Afghan history from the 3rd to 7th Centuries AD is a confusion of competing influences, unleashed upon the Kushan empire as it waned in the wake of Roman and Han decadence. Sasanians from Persia, followed by nomadic Hephthalites (White Huns) from Central Asia, descended on the region and for several centuries both Buddhism and Hinduism were practised in Afghanistan. However, in the mid-7th Century Arabs under the banner of Islam took Herat and, two centuries later, the Saffarids from Seistan (southwestern Afghanistan) spread Islam as far as Kabul and Balkh. Under the exuberant 9th Century Samanid dynasty from Bokhara, Balkh rose to prominence as an Islamic centre. The *No Gumbad* ("nine domes") mosque, remains of which still stand near Mazar, dates from this period.

However, under the formidable Sultan Mahmud, son of a slave-turned-general, Ghazni was to become one of the most glittering cities of the Islamic world. A great patron of the arts, Mahmud (998-1030) dominated Afghanistan and western Persia, and carried Islam into India, returning with fabulous booty with which to adorn his palaces in Ghazni and Bost (Lashkar Gah). Sadly, many of the splendid bronzes, marble reliefs, ceramics and frescoes from this period were looted or melted by a rocket attack on Kabul Museum in 1993. However, the two early 12th Century minarets, which stand on the outskirts of Ghazni, and the great arch and citadel at Bost, still testify to the power and sophistication of this empire.

The Ghaznavids were overwhelmed in the 12th Century when the Ghorid dynasty, led by Alauddin the "World Burner," gutted Ghazni and Bost. He then established his capital at Firozkoh and built victory towers out of Ghazni's soil, reportedly carried there "on the backs of captives whose blood served as mortar." Some historians believe that Firozkoh was situated at Jam in Ghor province where a magnificent minaret 65 metres high still stands. Leaning at a precarious angle towards the Harirud River, it is the highest minaret in the world after the Qutb Minar in Delhi, which was directly inspired by its Ghorid predecessor. The minaret's bold geometric designs and Persian-blue Kufic inscriptions are similar to those of the Ghorid portal of the great Friday mosque in Herat. Both structures are the only surviving creations of the late 12th Century Sultan Ghiyasuddin.

Mongol interlude (13th Century)

Genghis Khan, "sovereign of the sunrise," became offended when a goodwill gift of 500 camels laden with gold, silver, silks, furs and sable, which he sent to his neighbours in Balkh, went missing. He decided to pay the region a visit with 200,000 of his finest mounted troops, whom he likened to a "roaring ocean." By 1221 he had utterly devastated every town and murdered almost every living thing from Balkh and Herat to Ghazni and Bamiyan. So terrible was the destruction that the hilltop citadel of the Shansabani empire, near Bamiyan, is still known today as Shahr-e-Gholghola, or "City of Noise."

Timur and the Moghuls (14th to 17th Centuries)

Timur was next to arrive. Known to history as Tamerlane – meaning Timur-e-Lang or "Timur the Lame", because of an old war wound – he captured Balkh in 1369, Herat in 1381 and proclaimed himself emperor from Kabul to Samarkand (his home town) and the Aral Sea. Timur's youngest son, Shah Rukh, and the latter's amazing wife Gawhar Shad, inherited this huge kingdom in the 15th Century and under them the arts flourished. The five minarets and mausoleum of Gawhar Shad in Herat, described by British writer Robert Byron as "the most beautiful example in colour in architecture ever devised by man to the glory of his God and himself" still stand today, although now rather more battered than when he visited. The magnificently colourful and exuberant floral patterns of the tiles covering the Friday Mosque in Herat are largely a 20th Century restoration of the original Timurid decoration. In addition to this architectural heritage, philosophers, poets and the renowned miniaturist artist Bihzad also enjoyed lavish patronage in Herat. (SEE WESTERN REGION)

In 1504 Kabul fell to the Uzbek warrior Babur, descended from Genghis Khan and Tamerlane. Babur had been kicked out of his kingdom in Ferghana, east of Samarkand, and headed south in search of adventure. After taking Herat and Kandahar in 1507 he turned his attention in 1525 to Delhi and Agra where he founded the Moghul Empire and where he died in 1530. Kabul, however, had claimed a special place in his heart and he asked to be brought back to his favourite garden on the western slopes of Sher-e-Darwaza in Kabul to be buried. His tomb is still intact today although the terraced garden of flowerbeds, fountains and avenues of trees,

Friday Mosque in Herat *J. Walter*

which his successors laid out, was badly damaged during factional fighting and pillaging between 1992 and 1996. UNCHS (Habitat) is currently involved in bringing the gardens back to life.

For the 170 years following Babur's death, Afghanistan was the fulcrum between the two great empires of the Indian Moghuls, who controlled Kabul (and occasionally Kandahar) and the Persian Safavids who held sway in Herat. The main Moghul monument dating from this period is the *Chihlzina*, a stone chamber at the top of 40 steps carved out of a cliff on the western edge of Kandahar. Inside is a carved Persian inscription recording the conquests of Babur.

The emergence of Afghanistan as a nation (18th to 20th Centuries)

In 1709 a Ghilzai Pashtun called Mir Wais Hotak secured the independence of Kandahar from the Persians, but his successors were themselves superseded in 1738 by a Turkoman warrior who had taken the throne of Persia and titled himself Nadir Shah. Nadir continued into India and ravaged Delhi, thereby ending the Moghul Empire, but on his return in 1747 he was poisoned. An Abdali Pashtun who had led Nadir's personal bodyguard then assumed control of Kandahar, and was crowned Ahmed Shah Durrani.

By 1749 he had captured Kabul, Herat and Badakhshan, as well as Kashmir, Sind and Punjab. In creating the last genuine Afghan empire he became known as Ahmed Shah Baba, "Father of Afghanistan." His blue-domed mausoleum is still in perfect condition in Kandahar, and next to it is one of the holiest shrines in Afghanistan, the Shrine of the Cloak of the Prophet Mohammed. Ahmed Shah received the Prophet's cloak from the Amir of Bokhara in 1768 as part of a treaty to settle northern boundaries, and the shrine is covered in magnificent tile decorations above a foundation of green

NURISTAN

Nuristan is a remote – and in parts, still heavily forested – mountainous area of the Hindu Kush northeast of Jalalabad, whose people are famous for their spirit of independence. Alexander the Great and his men donned ivy-wreaths in the mountains there, drank the local homebrew and "lost their wits in true Bacchic frenzy." Tamerlane had a tougher time and had to be lowered down a cliff face in a basket, although history does not relate whether this was due to the moonshine or poor map-reading. Throughout the centuries the Nuristanis resisted all conquest and conversion. They became known as *Kafirs*, or Infidels, because they worshipped numerous nature and ancestor spirits. They left the bodies of their dead exposed to the elements for a year in wooden coffins, and then placed over the graves carved wooden effigies which the deceased spirits were believed to inhabit. A number of large carved wooden figures depicting fertility goddesses and ancestors were kept in the Kabul Museum, and have survived the war intact. It was not until 1896 that Amir Abdur Rahman succeeded in subduing the *Kafirs* and converting them by the sword to Islam; from then on he renamed their land Nuristan, "Land of Light." Among the first pre-Soviet, anti-communist revolts occurred in Nuristan in 1978 resulting in severe bombing of the region's main town, Kamdesh.

marble from Lashkar Gah. The cloak, which had not been seen in public since the 1930s, was taken out of its shrine by the Taliban Supreme Leader Mullah Omar in 1994 and shown to a crowd of several thousand *mullahs* to substantiate his claim to be Mullah Al-Momineen, or Leader of all Pious Muslims. (SEE SOUTHERN REGION)

The period following Ahmed Shah's death in 1772 is characterized by fratricidal and internecine struggles between the Pashtun Sadozai and Barakzai brothers, not helped by the fact that Ahmed Shah's son Timur left 23 sons and no appointed heir. The 19th Century saw the rise of British and Russian interference in the region and was generally inauspicious from a cultural point of view. In retribution for what they saw as Afghan treachery, the British demolished Kabul's famous covered bazaar in 1842 and then the Bala Hissar fortress in 1880. It was with British military advice that Amir Abdur Rahman razed to the ground most of the 15th Century buildings of Queen Gawhar Shad's *musalla* complex in Herat, for fear of a Russian attack in 1885.

Destruction, looting and preservation in the Twentieth Century

The late 20th Century has been disastrous for Afghanistan's culture. Many rural sites of great historical importance were damaged or destroyed during the Soviet war, and continue to be looted. The ensuing civil war since 1992 has shattered many cultural treasures in Kabul; and the avarice of the international art market is merely serving to encourage further pillaging of Afghanistan's treasures.

In 1982 UNESCO considered four locations in Afghanistan to be included on their list of World Heritage Sites: Bamiyan, Herat, the Minaret of Jam and Ai Khanum. However, no follow-up action was taken, and each of these highly significant sites continues to be under threat. In April 1997 a local Taliban commander provoked international outrage when he said he would "blow up" the Bamiyan Buddhas, which he presumably considered to be idols. Consequently Mullah Omar, the Taliban leader, stated that the Buddhas would not be touched since "the statues are not worshipped." However, woodsmoke, graffiti and sporadic bombing continue to threaten the survival of the statues, wall-paintings and cave-complexes of Bamiyan.

Latest reports from Ai Khanum suggest that it has been raked flat by bulldozers to facilitate the treasure-hunting of individual diggers. In Herat, repairs to the partially damaged 15th Century mausoleum of Gawhar Shad have been carried out with help from the World Food Programme (WFP) and the Danish Committee for Aid to Afghan Refugees (DACAAR). A number of international donors have recently pledged money to protect the Minaret of Jam from being undermined by the Harirud River, and to improve drainage and protection around the Big Buddha at Bamiyan.

Kabul Museum

The Kabul Museum, which opened in 1931, is situated at Darulaman six miles south of the city centre. As the only museum in the region devoted to the culture of Central Asia, covering 100,000 years of human history, its collection was unique. As a leading Pakistani academic and archaeologist, Professor Hasan Dani, said: "The collection of ivories, statues, paintings, coins, gold, pottery, armaments and dress from the prehistoric period to the Bactrian, Kushan and Gandhara civilizations, through to the Hindu, Buddhist and Muslim periods, was unimaginable."

From 1992 to 1996 it was on the frontline between warring factions and received two direct rocket hits, which destroyed many priceless artefacts. What remained was ruthlessly looted by successive waves of soldiers from whichever faction held Darulaman at the time. During the winter of 1993 UNCHS (Habitat) and SPACH worked with museum staff to weatherproof the building and secure doors and windows, but treasure-hunters continued to break in, shooting off padlocks and even trying to ram an armoured personnel carrier through the main entrance.

Only the highest quality pieces were removed from the museum, mostly in 1992-1993 when mujahed forces took control of Darulaman from government regime troops. This selective discrimination suggests that, in the words of Nancy Hatch Dupree, "the museum was not plundered by rampaging gangs of illiterate mujahideen" but by people working for middlemen who knew exactly what they were looking for. Najibullah Popal, curator of the Museum adds: "When the Kabul Museum was looted so many times, there must have been specialists showing the mujahideen which things to rob. There were thousands of books in the museum library. Most of the mujahideen can't read, yet all the books which had illustrations of the museum's best pieces were stolen."

Then in September 1996 museum staff, with support from SPACH, completed six months' work in registering what remained of the collection and removing it to the Kabul Hotel, a magnificent achievement under very difficult circumstances. To their credit the Taliban, after taking Kabul in the same month announced over Radio Shariat that "all people are called on to give back items from the Kabul Museum in their possession. It is illegal to have such items and Shariat law will apply to those who violate this rule."

Museum staff estimate that three-quarters of the collection has been lost, including 40,000 coins ranging from the 8th Century BC to the 19th Century, and the very valuable Bagram ivories – many of which have appeared on the international art market. In September 1995 General Babar, Pakistan's Federal Interior Minister, was quoted as saying that he had purchased one Bagram ivory for $100,000, and intended to give it back to Afghanistan when peace returned. A London antiquities dealer claimed to have been offered several dozen of the ivories in Peshawar for $10 million. Nevertheless more than 1,000 looted artefacts have been recovered through police confiscations, donations and purchases. Often SPACH cannot afford the exorbitant prices that Pakistani dealers demand for top quality objects, nor considers it morally right to pay such prices to looters. Forgeries are also appearing, even sporting Kabul Museum registration markings.

Art smuggling

> *"For centuries the Afghans have been smuggling. They love the challenge of it. It doesn't matter to them whether they're bringing in Bokhara rugs or AK-47s"*
>
> *– John Butt*

The ravaging of Afghanistan's cultural heritage must rank as one of this century's greatest artistic tragedies. An insidious combination of the immoral acquisitiveness of Western art collectors, the greed of local Afghan commanders and the corruption of diplomats, customs officials and academics is thriving off the chaos of war and stripping the country bare of internationally significant artefacts. Between 1993 and 1996 some 70% of the Kabul Museum's unique collection was looted; now it is the turn of rural areas.

During the Soviet war, numerous archaeological sites were exposed by indiscriminate Russian bombing of rural areas; but now the looting is more organized. Corrupt academics with a detailed knowledge of the location of key archaeological sites are directing local military commanders to the choicest sites. Tanks and landmines are used to keep out unwelcome guests. Bulldozers, pickaxes and shovels gouge into soil rich with historical remains. But the warlords are only interested in the most highly prized items: silver and gold, sculpture or coins.

Artefacts are smuggled through a complicated chain of middlemen before reaching the antiquities salerooms and private collectors of London, New York, Kuwait or Tokyo. Often the objects are first photographed and buried. Rich Western buyers or Pakistani dealers, prospecting in the bazaars of Peshawar, are then tempted into purchases by blurred photographs of looted items. The more experienced dealers disguise themselves as Pathan (or Pashtun) tribesmen and are driven up to inspect priceless antiquities kept under armed guard inside the fortified houses of warlords in the tribal territories towards the Khyber Pass. Once the deal is cut, falsified export permits are granted by corrupt Pakistani government officials, and the artworks are then smuggled back via Afghanistan through the porous borders of Central Asia and Russia into the markets of the West. Those implicated in the smuggling trade include Asif Ali Zadari, husband of Pakistan's deposed Prime Minister Benazir Bhutto, who has been accused of slipping Afghan antiquities into Britain under diplomatic immunity.

Art smuggling is now big business in Afghanistan and the North West Frontier Province of Pakistan. According to one senior Western diplomat, "the trade in Afghan antiquities has become the biggest money-earner after the heroin trade, and it is often the same mafias who are doing both." A Kushan coin from the time of Christ could fetch $20,000; a stone Buddha in the Gandharan style of the 1st to 5th Century AD three-quarters of a million dollars or more. Meanwhile the dealers justify their own greed and the acquisitiveness of their millionaire clients with arguments reminiscent of those of the 19th Century Lord Elgin when he pilfered the marble sculptures of the Parthenon in Athens for the British Museum: we are saving these objects from being destroyed by the war, they say. But whereas the treasure-hunters of the past at least put their booty on public display, today's thieves are concealing artworks of international significance in their penthouses and private collections, forever hidden from the gaze of professional art historians or curious passers-by alike.

Once the war is over...

> *"When the longed-for day comes when the fighting stops, the precious cultural heritage of Afghanistan will be one of the foundations on which a peaceful society can be constructed."*
>
> *– Federico Mayor, Director-General of UNESCO, September 1997*

Some people question whether it is right to waste valuable time and resources addressing cultural issues while war continues to tear the country apart, while millions of mines continue to maim and kill innocent civilians, and while thousands of children die each year from preventable diseases. By neglecting Afghan culture, however, one would fail to understand the complex series of forces which have shaped this troubled country's history and which will continue to shape its future course.

Furthermore, the ancient archaeological sites, the priceless artistic artefacts and the cultural monuments which continue to exist today, despite two decades of war, represent a unique and universal inheritance for the Afghan people. This legacy stands well beyond and above differences of race or tribe or politics. In a country where political and ethnic fragmentation threatens to shatter any sense of nationhood, this material cultural heritage common to all may yet prove to be emblematic of a national identity for future generations.

As Najibullah Popal, curator of the Kabul Museum, said after discovering that 70% of the museum's contents had been looted:

"The rest is gone. But if we have the Bactrian gold, we have something left to prove to the world that there was a time when we were not barbarians."

ESSENTIAL DATA

SPACH has a number of resources available for those interested in Afghan culture. A collection of books, articles and over 1,000 photographs and slides is kept in Peshawar, and the Society also has its own newsletter.
Membership of SPACH costs US$50 per calendar year. For further information please contact SPACH c/o:
ARIC, PO Box 1084, University Town, Peshawar, Pakistan.
TEL: + 92 (91) 40839, 44392
FAX: + 92 (91) 840471
E-mail: spach@undpafg.org.pk

ESSENTIAL READING:

A Catalogue of the Toponyms and Monuments of Timurid Herat, Terry Allen, Massachusetts Institute of Technology (Boston, 1981)
Music of Afghanistan: Professional musicians in the city of Herat, John Baily, Cambridge University Press (1988 – incls. Audio-cassettes)
The Road to Oxiana, Robert Byron, Macmillan (London, 1937; reprinted by Picador, 1981)
Afghanistan, Louis Dupree, Princeton University Press (2nd Edition, 1980; reprinted by Oxford University Press, 1997)
An Historical Guide to Afghanistan, Nancy Hatch Dupree (2nd Edition, Kabul 1977)
The National Museum of Afghanistan, a pictorial guide, Nancy Hatch Dupree (Kabul, 1974)
Bactrian Gold, Victor Sarianidi, Aurora Art Publishers (Leningrad, 1985)
Les Nouvelles d'Afghanistan (No. 41-42, Mars 1989) – contains numerous articles on Herat plus a bibliography of books, newspaper articles and video films.
Afghanistan Info, Swiss Committee for the Support of the People of Afghanistan (SCSPA), Neuchatel, Switzerland

ESSENTIAL AGENCIES

FONDATION BIBLIOTHEKA AFGHANICA, INTERPOL, SCSPA, SPACH, UNESCO, UNO, UNOCHA

Disability

When the word 'disability' is mentioned in connection with Afghanistan, most people automatically think of landmine victims and artificial limbs. Amputees, however, represent only about one-quarter of all disabled Afghans. About the same number again suffer restricted mobility through polio, and nearly half of the country's disabled are blind, deaf, mentally retarded, or multiply impaired.

No national survey has ever been conducted but observers work on a figure of around 700,000 people, or approximately three percent of the total population. Surprisingly this figure is lower than that for many industrialized countries, where an ageing population and higher standards of care for the disabled push the percentage up. However, although the total percentage may be lower in Afghanistan, the presence of impaired people affects the whole family, suggesting that disability influences in some way the lives of up to a tenth of the population. Furthermore, many of the disabled in Afghanistan die before they ever receive the care they need and so fail to become even a statistic.

The causes of disability are varied, but many are preventable. One solution is the ongoing Mine Action Programme, supervised by the United Nations Office for the Coordination of Humanitarian Assistance to Afghanistan (UNOCHA), which combines surveying, clearance and awareness training. (SEE LANDMINES) Immunization against polio, being spearheaded by UNICEF, the World Health Organization (WHO) and health sector NGOs, is another. But the "cold chain" (refrigeration), which is required to keep vaccines at the right temperature, presents considerable logistical problems.

Mental disability, such as cerebral palsy, is caused by oxygen starvation of a baby at birth, and undernourished pregnant women mean a high rate of birth complications. These could be significantly reduced by a greater presence of midwives and better Mother/ Child and prenatal healthcare. (SEE CHILDREN)

The Comprehensive Disabled Afghans' Programme (CDAP) which began in January 1995 is a joint UN agency programme involving some 12 UN and NGO agencies throughout the country. CDAP aims to facilitate the integration of disabled Afghans within

Afghan Para-Olympics

In July 1997, 23 disabled children and young adults from all over Afghanistan converged on Kabul to take part in the first-ever national disabled sports event. They came from as far afield as Herat, Kandahar and Jalalabad, flying in on ICRC and UNOCHA planes, or roughing it on local buses to participate in the two-day games. Wheelchair basketball, disabled cyclist races and volleyball all featured, but the biggest crowd-puller was the Herat vs. Jalalabad football match which 3,000 rapt spectators watched. The Afghan Minister of Sport presented certificates and the President of the National Olympic Committee talent-spotted. The games were organized by Keith Wise of ACBAR, Nick Clarke of Motivation, and the Afghanistan Olympic Committee.

Keith Wise is devoting all his spare time to promoting international sports events in landmine-afflicted countries such as Afghanistan, Angola, Cambodia and Vietnam. AARBRAR has its sights set on Sydney, after sending Afghan disabled cyclists to the Atlanta Para-Olympics and the Cycle-Messenger World Championships. Weekly disabled basketball clubs have sprung up in Herat and Kandahar, but Nick Clarke has his eye on a more cross-cultural mix...wheelchair *buzkashi!*

their own communities. It wants to see handicapped Afghans playing a full and constructive role in the programmes of mainstream services such as health, education, labour and community development. Its programme is therefore operated through a framework and policy of Community Based Rehabilitation (CBR), defined as a strategy within community development for the rehabilitation, equalization of opportunities, social participation and integration of all disabled people.

Amputees are more frequently seen than other disabled because they are the most mobile; but many other handicapped Afghans tend to be hidden from view, owing perhaps to a sense of cultural shame. Indeed even the words 'disabled' or 'handicapped' are in some senses considered pejorative: the 'disabled' person simply suffers from a physical or mental *impairment*, and is only *disabled* by society's prejudices against them. Hence much of CDAP's work focuses on the issue of impaired people's *rights* (and not simply their individual medical problems), on combating society's ignorance and prejudice and on mobilizing local communities to take responsibility for the rehabilitation and integration of impaired people.

In terms of the practical application of CBR principles, CDAP aims to achieve these tasks by mobilizing local resources through

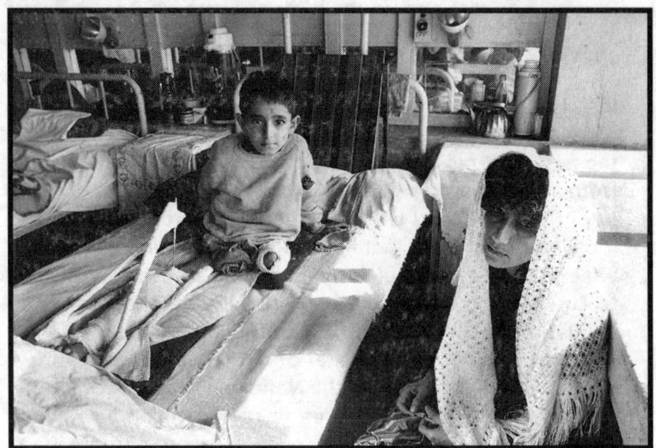

J. Hartley/UNICEF

field workers known as mid-level rehabilitation workers. Their responsibilities include: surveying the number of disabled people in their area; integrating handicapped children where possible into ordinary schools; developing home-based training in practical solutions with the families of the disabled; seeking out local craftsmen and women willing to take on impaired adults as apprentices for skills training; referring those who need it to health and other services; and support in creating local CBR committees and disabled people's organizations. Field workers in turn recruit and train volunteers, supply them with training materials, and thus create a cascade effect that maximizes access to local communities.

Revolving loans of $50-$100, repayable within a year, are also made available to enable disabled people to start their own businesses. One of the overriding aims is to avoid institutionalizing the disabled. By educating and involving family members in the training and integration process, entire communities become more aware of disabled people, their difficulties and the fact that they can act as contributing members of the community.

In April 1998, CDAP expanded its efforts to promote greater self-sufficiency and development in Afghan family life by starting a Vulnerable Women and Children (VWC) programme. Beginning in Badakhshan and Farah, the programme will provide vocational skills training and income-generation support for highly vulnerable women who look after their children and/or disabled husbands, and who are the only breadwinners of their families.

Funding for CDAP comes via the United Nations Development Programme (UNDP), which decides about programme strategy, but has delegated responsibility for coordination to the United Nations Office for Project Services (UNOPS). UNOPS in turn subcontracts NGOs to implement the programme in the field. Some NGOs are critical of this arrangement, arguing that two tiers of UN bureaucracy serve only to double administrative costs. The leading NGOs implementing CDAP include the Swedish Committee for Afghanistan (SCA) – which is currently responsible for three of the five CDAP programmes – Coordination for Humanitarian Assistance (CHA) and the Guardians. Radda Barnen (RBS) advises on CBR, gender and child rights issues. Contributions are made by the United Nations Educational, Scientific and Cultural Organization (UNESCO) (special education), the International Labour Organization (ILO) (employment support) and WHO (CBR, physiotherapy and orthopaedics).

Numerous orthopaedic centres exist in Afghanistan providing appropriate devices for the disabled, such as prosthetic limbs for amputees and braces (orthoses) for polio and tuberculosis victims. Sandy Gall's Afghanistan Appeal (SGAA) operates centres in Jalalabad and Kabul; the International Committee for the Red Cross (ICRC) run their own orthopaedic and physiotherapy centres in Jalalabad, Kabul, Mazar and Herat; and Handicap International (HI) are cooperating with an NGO, the Guardians, in running an orthopaedic centre in Kandahar. Physiotherapy training is provided nationwide by SGAA, the International Assistance Mission (IAM), and SERVE.

The Institute of Medical Education (part of the Afghan Ministry of Public Health) has also agreed on the curriculum for a two-year training course to qualify Afghan physiotherapists, spearheaded by SGAA and IAM, which will provide the beginnings of a career structure for Afghans in this field. Wheelchairs are manufactured by some of these agencies: in Jalalabad an international NGO called Motivation is producing excellent three-wheeler wheelchairs in various adjustable sizes, specifically designed for rough terrain and constructed entirely from locally-available materials. Also based in Jalalabad is the local NGO, Afghan Amputee Bicyclists for Rehabilitation and Recreation (AABRAR), which provides physical and educational rehabilitation to disabled Afghans.

Afghans impaired by deafness are cared for by SERVE, which runs a kindergarten in Jalalabad. They aim to teach deaf children sign language as soon as possible to counteract the social isolation which can quickly result when not even parents can communicate with their deaf children. Deaf adults are taught sign-language and vocational skills under local apprenticeships.

Reported cases of blindness and deafness among Afghans are on the increase. The causes are partly warfare (rocket, shell and mine explosions), partly insufficient basic healthcare, and partly the tradition of marrying close relatives. SERVE provides training for the blind in orientation, mobility and daily living skills, produces braille schoolbooks and tape-recorded books and stories, and encourages blind adults to set up their own businesses. IAM supports specialist eye hospitals in Mazar, Herat and Kabul, trains Afghans in ophthalmology and runs a lens factory in Kabul.

ESSENTIAL DATA

- **Amputees only represent one-quarter of Afghanistan's disabled; the remainder are impaired through polio, TB, blindness, deafness, mental retardation and cerebral palsy.**
- **Estimates suggest that around 700,000 Afghans are disabled, but one in ten of the population is affected in some way by having a handicapped family member.**

ESSENTIAL AGENCIES

CDAP programme coordinated by UNOPS and implemented by CHA, the Guardians, IAM, Motivation, RBS, SCA, SGAA, and WHO

ILO, UNDP and UNESCO support CDAP with funds and/or technical advice but are not present in the field

Other agencies include: ***AARBRAR, HI, ICRC and SERVE***

ESSENTIAL READING

Self care for spinally injured persons, Nick Clarke (available through Motivation)
Disability, Liberation and Development, Peter Coleridge, Oxfam (1993)
CDAP Annual Report and publicity material (available through UNOPS/CDAP)

Donor contributions

Total donor contributions in 1997

Country	US$	Country	US$
Australia	3,914,678	Netherlands	13,830,464
Austria	86,752	New Zealand	103,857
Belgium	438,993	Norway	9,864,144
Canada	13,096,784	Russia	67,000
China	362,000	Saudi Arabia	250,000
Denmark	1,954,851	Spain	4,186
EC*	45,399,080	South Korea	380,830
Egypt	44,500	Sweden	12,572,815
Finland	2,350,222	Switzerland	1,193,918
France	2,169,779	UK	13,782,773
Germany	4,465,617	USA**	15,690,648
Hong Kong	21,500	*Outside the Appeal*	
India	850,000	WFP	23,460,137
Ireland	382,539	ICRC	7,562,203
Italy	2,392,514	Other UN	291,606
Japan	11,013,912		
Liechtenstein	13,158	TOTAL	$188,638,623
Luxembourg	627,162	($56 million through the Appeal)	

Source: United Nations Consolidated Appeal for Afghanistan, 1998
** The European Community's figures for total humanitarian assistance to Afghanistan in 1996 (from DG 1B, DG VIII and ECHO) are ECU 77.5 million.*
*** The United States' own figures for total humanitarian assistance to Afghanistan in 1997 (from USAID, Department of State and Department of Defense) are $47.6 million.*
Editors' Note: *For more information on donor assistance, contact the relevant country's diplomatic mission in Islamabad.*

Drugs and drug trafficking

"Opium! Dread agent of unimaginable pleasure and pain!"

– Thomas de Quincey, 1821

Afghanistan is the world's leading supplier of illicit opium, recently overtaking Burma as the top producer. As part of the so-called "Golden Crescent" – including Pakistan, Iran and increasingly the other frontline former Soviet states – Afghanistan now (1997) generates over 2,800 metric tonnes of raw opium gum compared to just 200 tonnes in 1978. Some 80% of heroin seized in Western Europe is believed to originate from South West Asia, notably Afghanistan. The cultivation and production of products related to the drug trade involves up to one million Afghans.

The lawlessness that arose during the Soviet occupation and which continues under current civil war conditions has enabled mainly Peshawar- and Middle East-based drug trafficking rings to turn Afghanistan into the world's major producer of illicit and speculative opium. The years between 1990 and 1994 witnessed a relentless and unchecked annual increase in poppy cultivation.

According to the 1997 opium poppy survey by the United Nations International Drug Control Programme (UNDCP), the area under cultivation in Afghanistan ranged from 56,500-59,500 hectares. The 1995-1996 harvest produced a yield of between 2,200 and 2,300 metric tonnes of dry opium gum. The 1997 harvest rose by an additional 500 metric tonnes, nearly a 25% increase.

The higher yields are attributed to favourable weather, improved cultivation techniques and the shifting of some farmland (an additional 2.8%) to poppy cultivation. (SEE AGRICULTURE) Farmers, for example, are using urea fertilizer and new tractors from Pakistan to expand their production. The UN and other sources now estimate that Afghanistan produces nearly half the world's entire illicit opium production compared to Burma's 2,500 metric tonnes.

Opium poppies are cultivated in 10 out of 29 provinces in Afghanistan. An estimated three-quarters of the amount produced is grown in Helmand and Nangarhar provinces. The rest is grown in northern regions such as Badakhshan and Balkh, in the eastern mountain valleys of Kunar and in the areas around Kandahar to the south. At this time of writing, the Taliban controlled eight out of 10 of the opium-producing provinces with the remaining areas in the hands of the "Northern Alliance." White- and mauve-coloured poppies are openly grown along the main roads between Kabul and the Pakistan border.

Until the early 1990s, only a small proportion of the labs involved in heroin production operated out of Afghanistan, with full knowledge of the mujahideen. The poppy harvests were largely sold to the Peshawar-based trafficking groups (often operating in connivance with Pakistani military and government officials) with their own mobile production labs hidden among the tribal areas of the North West Frontier Province. In recent years, however, heroin-processing labs have become established in Afghanistan itself.

While reliable information is hard to come by, in-country processing operations are believed to be producing several hundred kilos of heroin daily. The heroin is then trafficked to Western Europe and the United States through Pakistan, India, Iran and the Central Asian states. A sizeable portion is also consumed by a growing population of users in Pakistan and India. Drug abuse is believed to be on the increase inside Afghanistan itself, mainly in the cities and particularly among young people. Heroin has been introduced largely by returnees from Pakistan.

Pashtun drug barons in the tribal areas on both sides of the Pakistan/Afghan frontier are heavily involved, as are former Afghan warlords who developed their fiefdoms during the days of the Red Army occupation (1979-1989). Some worked closely with the Afghan resistance or the Soviet-backed regime in Kabul, or with both. The Soviets are often alleged to have encouraged the drug trade as a means of undermining Pakistan and the West. Members of the Afghan resistance parties in Peshawar, including some of its leaders, have also been implicated in the trade. While publicly condemning drugs, some of the parties used poppy cultivation and opium production as a means of filling their coffers for the purchase of weapons and other supplies, as well as for personal enrichment. Peshawar's dramatic growth as a frontier city over the past two decades has been the result largely of international aid trickle down, overspill and corruption. But it has also benefited heavily from the drug trade. Both in Pakistan and increasingly Afghanistan, there are lavish houses and palatial compounds known to have been built by drug barons and often locally referred to as "the houses that drugs built."

Drug control efforts in Afghanistan have been particularly hampered by continuing civil strife and the lack of effective central and regional governments. The Taliban first banned the production of opium in late 1996 but took little or no action. Only in October 1997 did the Taliban formally agree to a more decisive ban of opium cultivation and production following considerable pressure from the UN, the Pakistanis, the Western Europeans and the Americans. Whether the Taliban will be able – or willing – to impose the ban is another question.

In return for taking firm action, the Taliban have been demanding appropriate international support and counter gestures such as the rehabilitation of the hydroelectric Kajakai Dam in the mountains northwest of Kandahar. However, the United States and many other countries have been keeping the Taliban at a distance because of the movement's continuing repressive policies. (SEE TALIBAN, WOMEN, EDUCATION). The US State Department also identifies Afghanistan as one of six countries not cooperating sufficiently in the international struggle against illegal drugs. The other countries are Colombia, Iran, Burma, Nigeria and Syria. International aid representatives and journalists travelling in Afghanistan have reported not only Taliban tolerance of opium production but evidence that officials are taxing it for much-needed revenue. Talib militiamen have been seen guarding opium warehouses as well as transporting the crop. Some drug lords are active supporters of the Taliban movement albeit, as some observers suggest, largely for opportunistic purposes.

The Taliban were quick to impose a ban on hashish – considered un-Islamic but smoked by numerous Afghans – soon after coming to power in September 1996. Enforcement, including severe punishment, has significantly reduced the trade in many areas. The Taliban, however, perceives opium production as a Western problem. Or as one farmer put it: "The West sends us weapons and bullets...We send the West the 'powder' with respect," he added, referring to heroin as the end product. The Taliban have been reluctant to crack down on the opium trade for fear of losing support in rural areas. As with many Afghans the Taliban have not forgotten that efforts by the Kabul regime in 1978 to enforce agricultural reform and other changes in rural areas, particularly tribal zones, helped spark the anti-Communist revolt.

For any ban to be effective, however, farmers will need to be offered a viable alternative – a must often emphasised by Afghanistan's Taliban-run Drug Control Commission. Many have benefited from the relative security provided by the Taliban to expand production. Even though farmers receive only a fraction of the opium's final worth – refined heroin fetches 50 times as much in London or New York – poppy cultivation offers far better and less backbreaking returns. Poppies are easier to grow, require less water and serve as an insurance against the failure of other crops. More importantly, they earn twice as much as wheat, while buyers are willing to pay cash advances to help purchase seeds and fertilizer. A small holder, for example, can easily produce 45 kilos of raw opium a year, earning $1,300, a small fortune. It will be hard for replacement crops to

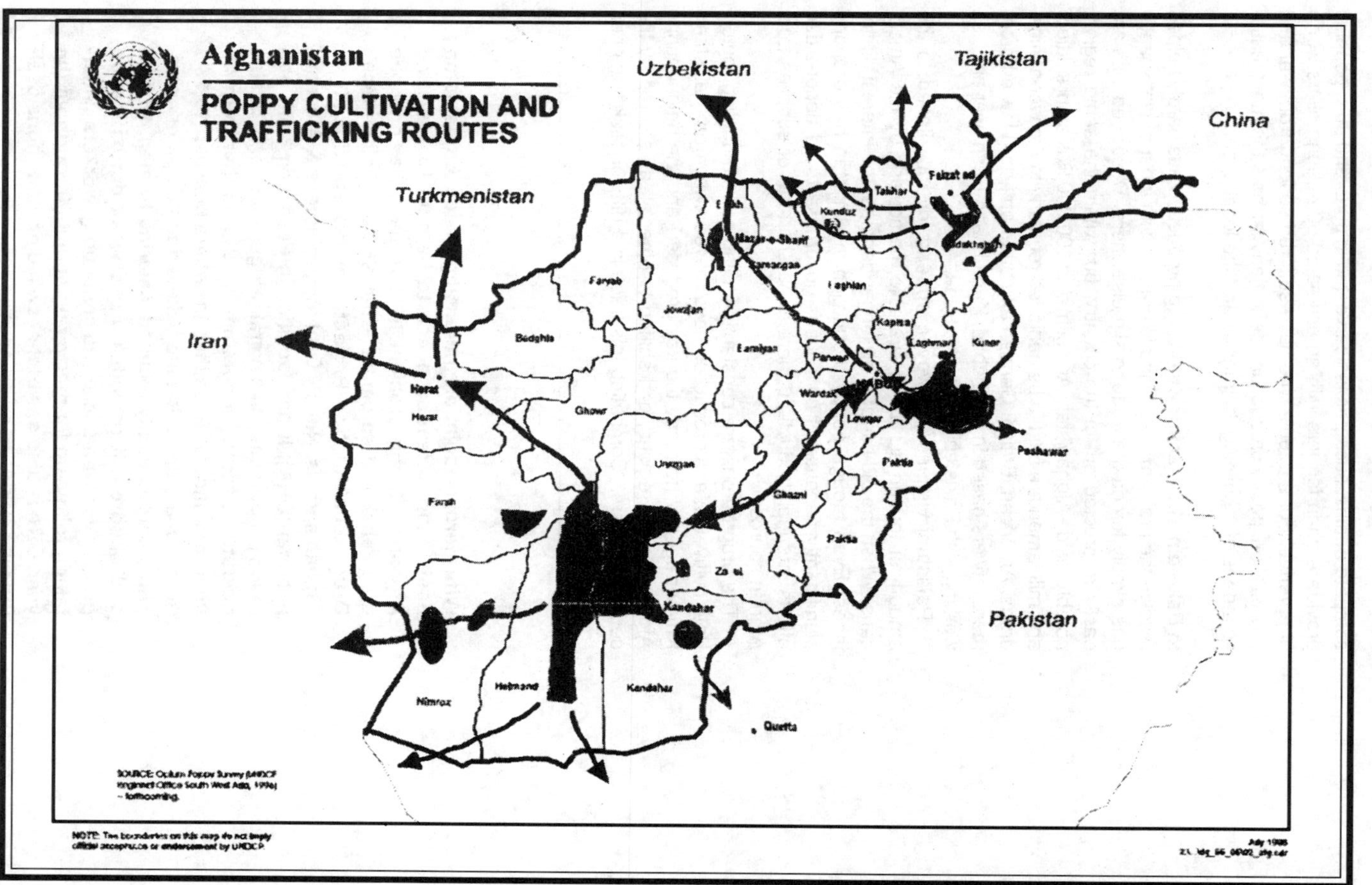
Afghanistan
POPPY CULTIVATION AND TRAFFICKING ROUTES
Uzbekistan
Tajikistan
China
Turkmenistan
Iran
Pakistan
Faizabad
Takhar
Kunduz
Mazar-e-Sharif
Samangan
Faryab
Jowzjan
Baghlan
Badghis
Bamiyan
Kapisa
Laghman
Kunar
Parwan
Herat
Ghowr
Wardak
Lowgar
Peshawar
Paktia
Uruzgan
Farah
Ghazni
Paktika
Zabul
Kandahar
Helmand
Nimroz
Quetta
SOURCE: Opium Poppy Survey (UNDCP Regional Office South West Asia, 1996) – forthcoming.
NOTE: The boundaries on this map do not imply official acceptance or endorsement by UNDCP.
July 1996

compete against such prices. Harvested in June and July, poppies provide Afghan farmers with an estimated 60 million dollars worth of revenue. For a people who have suffered so long from war and devastation, poppy production offers many farmers the most realistic means of rebuilding their farms and the local economy.

In Pakistan, the crackdown on drug production has hardly helped resolve the problem. Like trying to grapple with a bar of wet soap, it has simply forced the trade to slip elsewhere. Destroyed labs are easily re-erected out of the country, but within the same region, notably inside Afghanistan. An estimated 100,000 Pakistani soldiers and militiamen are said to be deployed regularly in the war against drugs. American, British, German and other anti-drug law enforcement officers based in Islamabad, Karachi and Peshawar are also working with Pakistan to curb the trade.

Pakistani vigilance, however, appears directly linked to the amount of foreign aid made available, particularly by the Americans. When the aid carrot is no longer dangled, the interest diminishes. Even though poppy production in Pakistan has dropped significantly because of continuous government and donor-aided efforts in supply reduction, there is no shortage of supplies from Afghan sources.

The drug barons are constantly finding new smuggling routes. Both cultivation and production have moved away from Pakistan's Khyber agency (formerly the key producer) and the neighbouring Afghan border regions, and shifted to other areas still run by the same traffickers. "Combating this trade is a difficult task that often

KICKING THE HABIT

With heroin addiction increasing inside Afghanistan itself, more attention needs to be paid to assisting Afghans with this problem. In 1997, there was only one drug rehabilitation centre – the NEJAT ('Deliverance') Drug Rehabilitation Project – aimed specifically at Afghan addicts. Run by Orphans, Refugees & Aid International (ORA), it has facilities in Peshawar, with outreach programmes to several refugee camps. ORA also operates a NEJAT programme in the northeastern Afghan province of Badakhshan, where between 10-25% of the local population are believed to be opium users. The centre is family-focused, catering to men, women and children. It provides a two-week detoxification programme with social and community workers undertaking follow-up for recovering addicts throughout the year. ORA is also one of the few aid organizations dealing with HIV/AIDS awareness.

barely scrapes the surface. Some of the Pakistanis we work with are themselves involved, receiving kickbacks, so we don't really get the ones who count. The traffickers also simply set up elsewhere," said one Western drug-enforcement agent.

Production has moved deeper inside Afghanistan to Helmand province, which has eclipsed Nangarhar as the country's leading producer. It is also increasingly moving to the frontier areas with the Central Asian Republics, where the traffickers encounter fewer restrictions. New production labs have appeared in Tajikistan and Uzbekistan with smuggling routes heading northwards to take advantage of growing markets in Russia and Eastern Europe.

Other trafficking routes include Iran and Turkey but also southwards through Baluchistan to the Indian Ocean along the Mekran coast where speed boats transfer the merchandise to waiting ships.

Organizations such as UNDCP, along with various donors and NGOs, are keen on helping farmers find equally lucrative alternative cash crops as a means of reducing poppy production. But there will have to be better coordination among the agencies themselves. It does not help when organizations such as the World Food Programme (WFP) dump 140,000 tonnes of wheat annually on the Afghan market, thus forcing prices to drop and undermining efforts to help farmers develop viable alternatives to replace poppies. Any strategy to combat poppy growing in Afghanistan as well as embracing law enforcement must not only take the needs of individual farmers into account, but also make the financial risks of growing poppy greater than any other cash crop, such as wheat, grapes, fruit trees and alfalfa.

The UN has drawn up a 25 million dollar a year plan to help enforce the 1997 Talib ban and encourage Afghan farmers to switch to other crops. Despite UN claims that it could eradicate heroin production in five or six years, however, such initiatives may have only a limited impact. As both aid coordinators and drug enforcement analysts point out, the basic elements of law enforcement need to be applied effectively and in combination with crop replacement programmes. But they also need to be developed on a regional basis. Otherwise, the production may simply move elsewhere. And as Pakistan has shown, even with the proper institutions in place, corruption, tribal rivalry and lack of political will may conspire to perpetuate the drug trade.

INFOBRIEFS

ESSENTIAL DATA

Illicit raw opium gum produced in Afghanistan

1978	200 metric tonnes
1996	2,200 metric tonnes
1997	2,800 metric tonnes

Provinces producing illicit opium in Afghanistan

10 out of 29

Total estimated area under cultivation in Afghanistan

1995	54,000 hectares
1996	55,000-58,000 hectares
1997	56,500-59,500 hectares

Total estimated area under cultivation in Pakistan

1995	4,709 hectares
1996	1,038 hectares

Control of areas under poppy cultivation in 1997

Under the Taliban	96%
Under Northern Alliance and others	4%

Origin

80% of the heroin seized in Western Europe originates from South West Asia, primarily Afghanistan

Refined heroin production (1996)

Global	220 metric tonnes
Afghanistan	88 metric tonnes (40%)

Refined heroin (estimated street value)

Karachi	$3,000 per kilo
New York	$50,000 per kilo

Sources: UNDCP, Western donor governments

ESSENTIAL AGENCIES

DEA, FAO, ORA, UNDCP, UNOPS

ESSENTIAL READING

UNDCP Updates (available from UNDCP, Islamabad)

Economics

"Our problem is our geographical location and our resources. For this reason, Afghanistan has always been at war."

– Ahmed Shah Massoud, ex-mujahed commander and former defence minister, 1997

Nearly 20 years of war since the outbreak of fighting against the communist regime of the People's Democratic Party of Afghanistan (PDPA) in Kabul in mid-1978 have had a shattering impact on the Afghan economy. Much lies completely destroyed. The Red Army occupation resulted in the devastation of many largely rural parts of the country coupled with the forced exodus of one third of the population. To the embarrassment and shame of many Afghans, however, it is the civil war of the 1990s that has inflicted the greatest damage on Kabul and other cities. Factional fighting has resulted in the systematic destruction and looting of numerous modern sector production facilities.

Prior to the Soviet invasion in December 1979, agriculture accounted for over half the nation's GDP. During the 1970s, modernization programmes under Presidents Mohammed Daoud and Nur Mohammed Taraki had begun to open up other economic areas. Financed largely through heavy borrowing and donor assistance, these initiatives sought not only to improve education and health services, at least in urban zones, but also to establish a large number of state-owned industries in sectors such as mining, energy, transport and communications. In addition, these programmes helped create more small and medium-sized consumer goods enterprises, particularly in and around the towns.

During the Red Army occupation (1979-1989), the Kabul regime – mainly with Soviet and East bloc funding – tried to expand the country's administrative infrastructure as well as promote further industrial and large-scale agricultural production. Increased mujahed resistance and general insecurity, however, soon brought many of these projects to a halt. This prompted a major economic decline. The Soviets, anxious to prove the positiveness of their presence, felt bound to prop up the PDPA government through heavily subsidised imports. Some of the crossborder international aid agencies seeking to support civilian populations in resistance-held areas were quick to latch on to this. It was often cheaper to assist local populations at the height of the war by buying wheat in nearby government-controlled towns than to bring it in by horse caravan from Pakistan. (SEE AID POLITICS)

At this time of writing, Kabul remains a gutted city strongly reminiscent of European cities devastated during World War II. The ruins of shell-ravaged office buildings, apartment blocks and residential houses look out onto rubble-lined streets, while cableless pylons and the torn remnants of trees pointedly remind one of the days when Kabul's urban population still enjoyed tree-lined avenues, trolley buses and regular electricity. In the countryside, whole villages have been eradicated, their walls now worn and crumbling from the rain and wind. Along the main roads, particularly near the towns and villages, stand the ghostlike vestiges of schools, factories, industrial depots and former customs posts.

Rebuilding from scratch

Little reliable data exists regarding the state of the country's economy. According to the *Agricultural Survey of Afghanistan* by the Swedish Committee (SCA), Afghanistan remains, in the conventional sense, "one of the least developed countries in the world." While certain parts of this landlocked country are being rehabilitated, or were never even touched by the direct effects of war, Afghanistan's most poignant long-term challenge will be the total rebuilding of its basic infrastructure. Many Afghans are experiencing extreme hardship with only limited resources to survive. It is perhaps even more desperate for those living in the cities. There are few jobs available and breadwinners must often support painfully large extended families. (SEE RELIEF & DEVELOPMENT)

As far as can be determined, much of the present economy is linked to international aid programmes and development, drug trafficking, and financial support for select political factions provided by foreign powers ranging from Iran and Pakistan to Saudi Arabia. The industrial sector is reported to be down to less than 20% of pre-war production. Only a small handful of manufacturing activities, such as handicrafts production, are still earning foreign currency. Many formerly significant (or growing) sectors, notably commodity exports, mining, cement production and agro-processing, have been wiped out or severely damaged.

Under present conditions, Afghans need to draw on as many sources as possible to ensure the continued survival of their families. While some members work the land, others seek jobs with aid projects. Or they work in the Gulf and Western countries such as Europe and North America, in order to send back remittances. Many, however, have little choice but to remain as refugees in Pakistan and Iran. (SEE REFUGEES)

According to aid agencies, such as CARE and the United Nations High Commissioner for Refugees (UNHCR) which have made studies of the issue, there appears to be a deliberate strategy of dispersion with refugee camps serving as principal labour reserves. From there, young men pursue highly mobile lifestyles travelling abroad for months, even years on end, wherever there is work. A 1997 study by the British Agencies Afghanistan Group, for example, noted that even with the growing number of returnees to Farah province in western Afghanistan, employment opportunities in Iran still serve as an important safety net for families. This is despite the continued risks of arrest, detention and deportation by the Iranian authorities. Many family members, including children, are involved in the small trading sector, selling anything from cigarettes to fresh fruit and medicines. Others seek to bring in supplies by bus or beast of burden, whether fuel from the countryside or basic essentials from Pakistan. Anything to keep the family going.

Breaking the subsistence yoke

Agriculture remains the country's principal economic sector with nearly four-fifths of the country's 17-22 million people living in rural areas. (SEE AGRICULTURE) As a result, the overwhelming majority of Afghans rely on farming as their principal – if not only – source of revenue. For the moment, the illicit cultivation and production of opium (up to one million Afghans depend on the drug trade for cash) represents the most lucrative form of agricultural production. (SEE DRUGS) Normal agricultural production has far to go before it can move beyond providing mere subsistence for people living in the countryside. At the same time, many Afghans, particularly young men or former mujahideen, are reluctant to work in agriculture; many have known the "bright lights" of the cities from their refugee days or experienced the power of "have gun, no work," during their time with the resistance or armed militia groups.

Dealing with shattered infrastructure is another formidable problem. In factories, power plants and manufacturing workshops, where vital machinery, fittings and vehicles were not wrecked in the fighting, equipment has been looted – often down to the last screw. This may have contributed to a lively and highly profitable scrap metal and spare parts trade, mainly with Pakistan, but it has left the country with little infrastructure. Most facilities will need to be completely recreated or overhauled.

Tourism, for example, a growing industry before the war, will not only require new hotels and travel services, including airports, but also basic support facilities. Known mountaineering, trekking, fishing and wildlife areas will need to be cleared of landmines. Another massive task requiring major international support will be the return of lost cultural treasures stolen during the fighting. (SEE CULTURE)

Most institutional facilities such as government offices, banks and university departments are barely functioning, if at all. Formal taxes have not been collected since the early 1990s. Many so-called regional or local governments exact checkpoint 'taxes' from the movement of goods and people inside Afghanistan and at the borders. Prior to the arrival of the Taliban, merchants and farmers were often 'taxed' at will – normally 10% of produce, usually in kind – by local commanders. Under the Taliban, taxes are lower with harsh *shari'a* punishment deterring a lot of impromptu revenue collection.

Afghanistan's thriving illicit economy

In Kabul and other Taliban-controlled towns, the economy is still functioning much as before. Prices tend to reflect costs with barter representing a significant portion of overall trade. Following rampant inflation during the 1990s, the Taliban are now seeking to impose price regulations. Street currency trading remains one of the country's few thriving licit economic sectors. The bulk of Afghanistan's 'real' economy, however, consists of the large-scale illicit trafficking of drugs, art treasures, duty free goods from Pakistan and Dubai, and – more recently – from Sinkiang in China, weapons. On occasion, the looted gains from aid agency compounds also provide a ready source of income. Some Afghan traders, a few closely linked with former warlords, have been making small fortunes out of smuggling. These smugglers have a strong vested interest in continued conflict.

Some donor governments and international organizations remain obsessive about the need for a country at peace with a firm, central administration. Only then, they feel, can any proper, long-term development be implemented, particularly in and around Kabul, Herat and Mazar. Many on-the-ground observers and aid practitioners, on the other hand, believe that such attitudes are restrictive and can only hamper Afghanistan's economic rehabilitation and development. As long as there are interested communities with concerned local leaders or decision-making institutions, they maintain, much can be achieved. Kabul's permission is not needed to rehabilitate irrigation schemes, construct clinics, open schools or establish agricultural extension services.

Afghans are a resilient people. The country's chaotic private sector seems to sprout up almost as soon as the echoes of mortar rounds and rockets recede in the distance. Transport services, *chaikhanas* (teashops) and shops selling the bare necessities suddenly appear among the ruins, or wherever business can made. Even at the height of the Soviet-Afghan war, certain perceptive aid agencies understood that peace or central government were not vital to working in regions not directly in the line of fire. As a result, they were able to help some areas implement limited forms of long-term development ranging from livestock projects to irrigation repair.

Commercial agreements and international aid: propping up a war economy?

In the same vein, continuing conflict has not prevented a growing list of companies from seeking business opportunities in Afghanistan. At least two oil consortia are pursuing agreements with the Taliban and other factions for the construction of a trans-Afghan natural gas and oil pipeline from neighbouring Turkmenistan to Pakistan and Iran. (SEE PIPE DREAMS) For their part, the Taliban has sent trade delegations to China, Japan, Indonesia, Malaysia and the USA to drum up foreign investment and win recognition for their government in Kabul. The Taliban's investment incentives are tantalisingly direct. According to the Afghan Ministry of Mines and Industries, the government will give land to anyone wishing to build a new factory. Companies, however, will have to build their own access roads, supply their own electricity and construct their own housing. The fact that there is "no real economy in the country, only real fighting," maintains the *Far Eastern Economic Review,* appears to make little difference to Taliban enthusiasm.

Currently, only limited amounts of government expenditure, whether by the Taliban or other authorities, are directed towards agriculture, health, education, water supply and sanitation. In many areas, the military clearly assumes priority over civilian needs. Aid organizations are widely seen as being the principal source of backing for the rehabilitation and running of social services, such as healthcare, drainage, and the building and repair of schools. While UN agencies and NGOs hasten to emphasise that they only seek to assist the needs of civilians, there is growing concern that aid programmes are in danger of replacing the government. As a result, the humanitarian agencies may themselves be partially – albeit inadvertently – responsible for helping prolong the fighting. The current humanitarian support system enables government leaders as well as war or drug lords to channel their resources towards bolstering their own military forces. Some observers place the number of people directly dependent on the civil war effort for their livelihood at up to half a million, so – for some – there is a strong interest in keeping the conflict going. (SEE AID POLITICS)

Plight of the cities

All of which does little to help Afghanistan deal with the real economic problems at hand. In fact, the situation in Kabul and other cities has worsened since the Taliban takeover. Roughly 80% of the population in Kabul is considered to be 'vulnerable', that is, not able to afford more than a basic diet of bread and tea. This includes people from all walks of life: doctors, civil servants, teachers, casual labourers... In addition, not only has the education of women been halted (with most female teachers fired from their jobs), but in a drive to cut expenses about a third of male government workers, many of them non-Pashtuns with links to the Opposition, have been dismissed. The effect on the economy of this massive decrease in the active workforce has proved substantial. Purchasing power has decreased, causing secondary industries to suffer.

The Taliban Finance Ministry in Kabul, however, has little direction to offer. Reportedly, the minister and his deputy both have *madrassa* (Koranic school) educations but there are no trained economists to speak of. Anyone with a more qualified education has long since left or has been forced out. Employees report to their offices but decision-making is merely symbolic and uninformed. There is little or no planning. Nor are there any financial resources to speak of. The only relevant administration capable of having an impact is related to security, including the control of frontiers and transport checkpoints. At the moment, *shari'a* law seems to be the only consistent mode of judiciary in most parts of Taliban-controlled Afghanistan. (SEE TALIBAN)

The Taliban economy: a mire of stagnation

In many respects, the fragmentation of Afghanistan's economy has been aggravated by the transfer of traditional village politics to the national scene. The running of the country is increasingly becoming a matter of inward-looking tribal and ethnic dominance for political and economic control with the mainly Pashtun Taliban seeking to assert themselves over non-Pashtun opposition groups such as the Tajiks, Hazaras and Uzbeks. And not unlike the clash for modernization versus cultural continuity under Daoud and later the Communists, Afghanistan under the Taliban is in the process of stagnating in a detrimental mire of ignorance and economic reversal. Both the communist Khalq and the Taliban seem to share similar degrees of self-righteous arrogance. Hardline policies and lack of regard for the population-at-large led to the downfall of the first; a similar fate may befall the second.

The prospect of continuing instability and war has not encouraged many donors to expend large sums of money on long-term projects. The same goes for private investment. While many small traders have not hesitated to start up businesses, theirs remain essentially mobile operations such as transport or consumer supply services. Few require any substantial infrastructure. Some Afghans and foreign traders, particularly those linked with smuggling, have had little compunction about building themselves more comfortable operational bases equipped with satellite dishes, refrigerators and electric generators. But most ordinary Afghans are wary of channelling too many of their meagre resources into projects which could go awry or which would remain susceptible to local security conditions, notably the return of conflict. This includes former mujahed commanders, who have done well out of the war but have little idea how to invest their wealth. Given the impact of high inflation, many Afghans are reluctant to invest in projects which do not have quick, high rates of return. Hence the understandable need to rely on smuggling as a significant source of income.

GEMS AND WILDLIFE

Precious and semi-precious stones such as lapis lazuli and emeralds have provided Afghans with an invaluable source of income, even during the height of the war with the Soviets. While weapons and other supplies were transported to mujahideen across the mountains from Pakistan on the backs of mules and horses during the 1980s, the same caravans returned loaded with semi-precious stones from ancient mines in the Panjshair Valley and Badakhshan. The revenue from such exports helped finance the armed resistance of commanders such as Ahmed Shah Massoud.

Nearly twenty years since the outbreak of fighting in mid-1978, the revenues produced by lapis lazuli extracted from the 6,000-year-old mines at Sar-e-Sang in the Hindu Kush – the world's only source of high grade lapis – are being used to finance the continuing war. But they are also being used to launder profits from the heroin trade. (SEE DRUGS) The deep blue lapis stones, often flecked with gold-like pyrite, are prized by American, Japanese and European jewellers as well as Arabs in the Middle East. While local miners (who also pilfer what they find for private profit) earn barely two dollars per 12-hour shift, the best polished stones can sell for up to $18,000 per kilo in Peshawar. Many lapis merchants are also involved in drug trafficking and use the stones as cover.

During one recent trip to northern Afghanistan, a British journalist encountered a caravan carrying precious stones and six Siberian hawks destined for the Saudi Arabian falconry market. Even more highly-prized than the peregrine falcon is the endangered *saker* falcon – individual specimens can fetch over $100,000.

While numerous villagers have begun rebuilding their homes and re-cultivating their farms in areas where peace has returned, some have seen their holdings destroyed once, twice or even more with renewed outbreaks of fighting. Following the mujahed takeover in Kabul in 1992, Afghans who could afford it began repairing their houses and businesses, even constructing new buildings. This in turn encouraged new trade such as the import and sale of construction materials as well as jobs for craftsmen. Many of these edifices were damaged again in the rocketing and interfactional conflict, particularly in January 1994, when some half a million people found themselves displaced by heavy fighting. When the Taliban took over in September 1996, numerous properties were looted. In some areas, such as Kandahar, Jalalabad and Herat, however, Taliban-imposed security has encouraged considerable construction, with mosques the first to be rebuilt. Yet many Afghans express concern that until a nationwide peace is established, renewed conflict could easily wrench them back to square one.

Tourism

The 1970s official tourist pamphlet boasts: "Say 'Afghanistan' – and you think of the friendliest country. Say 'Ariana' – and you've thought of the friendliest way of getting there." Despite the turmoil of war, many of the journalists and relief workers who have operated – often clandestinely – inside Afghanistan since the early days of the Soviet occupation still regard the country as one of the friendliest, if not in reality then certainly in their hearts. And while Ariana Afghan Airlines may have the right intentions, the few functional planes in its fleet based out of Delhi can only operate when it is safe to land. Current services include Boeing 727s carrying passengers and cargo to Delhi, Amritsar, Jeddah and Dubai with domestic services between Kandahar, Kabul and Jalalabad. (SEE TRAVEL)

There is little doubt that many of those who have experienced Afghanistan over the past two decades – as well as those who have lived and worked there before the war – will return, if and when peace gains the upper hand. The potential of developing tourism as a key industry is enormous. It is one that economic planners stress should be included in all sustainable development strategies for Afghanistan, particularly if they are to be linked to culture, environment, health, education and transport.

Many Afghans are now used to seeing foreigners from their refugee experiences. Many, too, have provided hospitality and other forms of assistance to journalists and relief workers inside the country. Even some of the most remote villages have had visitors sleep in their homes and mosques. According to one EFG editor, who has travelled thousands of miles by foot and by vehicle in the mountains and deserts, sleeping in countless villages along the way, one rarely encountered animosity except in areas strongly influenced by Arab and other mainly foreign Islamic extremist groups. Most villagers demonstrated a gracious sense of welcome albeit often mixed with curiosity, and sometimes suspicion. After all, Afghanistan was a country at war and the land was being assaulted by Soviet troops. Nor was there any shortage of government informers. So no one was really sure who was whom.

Renewed peace would enable Afghanistan to develop tourism from scratch. It would also enable Afghans do so in an intelligent manner. Careful management could ensure that Afghanistan does not become a tourist trash bin as has happened, for example, in parts of Nepal. As pointed out by some concerned planners, any form of tourist development will need to be culturally sensitive. It would need to be respectful of the country and its people, particularly given what Afghans have gone through during the war. In addition, much will depend on the attitudes of the authorities in power.

CURRENCY TRADING

Currency trading in Kabul and neighbouring Peshawar is big business. It represents the only large-scale financial activity in a country where the formal banking sector has collapsed. While governments have come and gone, currency trading has thrived, making handsome profits for some entrepreneurs, many of whom have employees working in other major towns and across the border in Pakistan. Access to hard currency is a crucial means of beating the country's current state of hyperinflation. While the *Afghani* has somewhat stabilized under the Taliban, local salaries, whether provided by the authorities or aid agencies, have largely failed to keep up with soaring inflation and plummeting devaluation against the dollar. At least ten Kabul merchants are officially renting satellite phones owned by the Ministry of Telecommunications (costing $700-$800 a month) for calling up international money markets.

The merchants, who need to provide $100,000 guarantees to set up their businesses, regularly call Peshawar to check the latest rates of US dollars, British pounds, Deutschmarks, *Afghanis*, Pakistani rupees and a dozen other currencies. During better days, the National Bank of Afghanistan provided the rates. Nowadays, the bank comes to them. The rates reflect everything from the support provided by various international donors to Afghanistan to opium prices and the amount of hard currency required by independent traders for the purchasing of outside goods. Some dealers will even trade ordinary cheques for European and American banks in return for cash.

The arrival of the Taliban in September 1996 somewhat stabilized the dollar rate, bringing it down to around 20,000 *Afghanis*. Dollar transports are sent up from Pakistan by road. Prior to the Taliban, however, the convoys were often robbed. An estimated $200,000 a day are sent up to the northern city of Mazar-e-Sharif, where the US dollar fetches around 60,000 so-called "Dostum *Afghanis*", locally-printed currency which is not legal tender elsewhere in the country. Official *Afghanis* are brought in by plane from Russia where they are printed.

While the majority of Afghans remain extraordinarily friendly, open and good-humoured, there is a great deal of largely imported religious self-righteousness and extremism that has soured much of Afghanistan's traditional hospitality. Photography, for example, is now virtually impossible in many areas because of the Taliban and other highly conservative Islamic groups. Both before and during the Soviet war, it was hard to find Afghans – apart from the women – who did *not* want their picture taken. (SEE PHOTOGRAPHY)

Numerous cultural treasures, monuments and other remarkable forms of heritage have been destroyed, severely damaged or looted. The Kabul Museum, for example, is believed to have lost as much as three-quarters of its collection. The Bala Hissar citadel overlooking the Afghan capital has been ruined even further by shelling since it was first wrecked in 1880 during the Second Anglo-Afghan War. The Gandhara Buddhist site of Hadda near Jalalabad was largely destroyed by the Soviets when the mujahideen took to sheltering there. The ancient city of Herat was badly bombed by the Soviets at the start of the war, and many ancient sites, including the minarets of the *Musalla* complex, have been damaged in the fighting, particularly in recent years. (SEE CULTURE)

Nevertheless, many of the former resistance and caravan routes could be re-established as tourist trekking trails by foot, horse or camel with villages providing stopover facilities, such as teashops. Significant ecosystems, such as the Ghazni wetlands, which serve as a renowned resting and feeding site for migrating birds, could be developed appropriately to attract bird watchers from all over the world. Paying volunteer programmes could help excavate or refurbish cultural and archaeological sites damaged by the war. It would also make sense to develop tourism on a regional basis to include neighbouring parts of Central Asia, Pakistan and Iran.

Fortunately for Afghanistan, there is already a vast human resource pool available for the development of a competitive and highly unusual tourist industry. Numerous Afghans have worked with international aid agencies or travelled with journalists inside the country. As a result, they already have experience working as guides, drivers, cooks and technicians. Many, too, speak or have a good command of one or more European language. With proper training in hotel and restaurant management and other forms of specialized tourism, thousands of jobs could be created.

Numerous private travel companies, both local and foreign, could be expected to cater to general and specialist forms of tourism such as trekking, mountaineering, fishing, hunting, bird-watching and cultural expeditions. Not only would local initiatives benefit, notably handicraft manufacturing and the arts, such as traditional music, dance and literature, but also overall development and investment. Part of the emphasis on tourism could be geared to making visitors aware of the need to rebuild the country and to preserve its cultural and natural heritage.

Pipe dreams

Despite the ongoing civil war, two international energy consortia are competing to run natural gas and oil pipelines from Central Asia through Afghanistan. The first 1,300 kilometre trans-Afghan pipeline scheme founded by the US oil company Unocal and its Saudi

Central Asian oil pipeline proposed by Unocal/Delta Oil

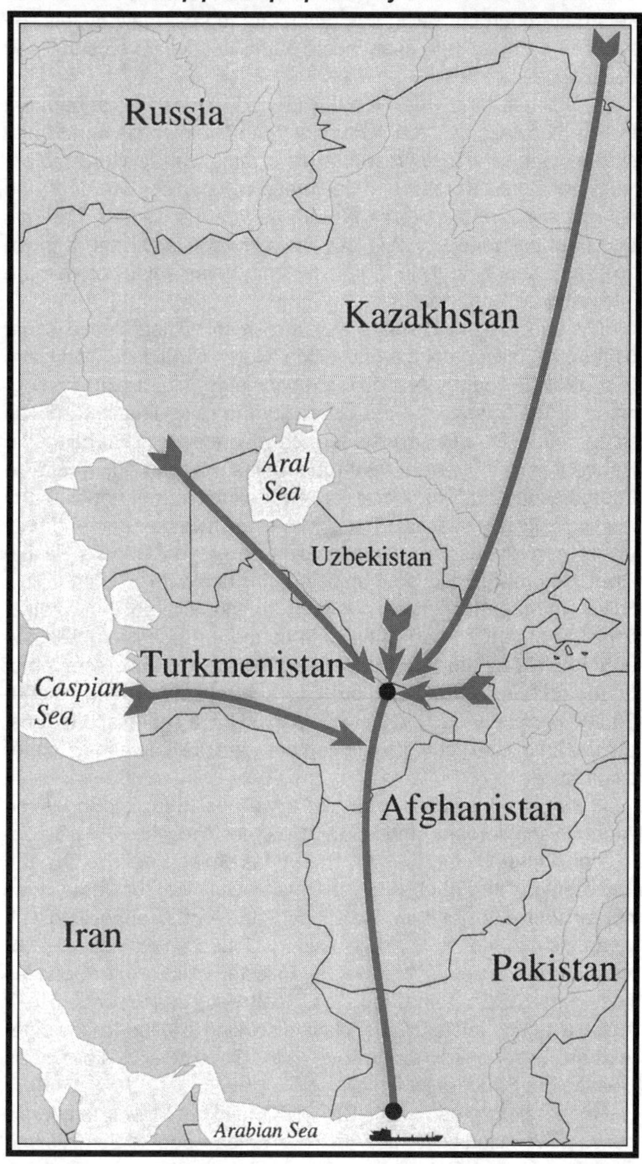

Arabian partner Delta Oil seeks to link the vast Dauletabad gas fields of Turkmenistan, potentially the third largest in the world, with Pakistan and possibly New Delhi, moving some 20 billion cubic metres of gas per year. A separate oil pipeline would run from Chardzhou through Afghanistan and Pakistan to the Indian Ocean, transporting roughly one million barrels of oil a day from different

Central Asian sources. Now that Turkmenistan's former Soviet markets have been cut back, it is desperate to seek new outlets. By late 1997, Unocal had spent some 50 million dollars on surveying the proposed routes.

In October 1997, the Taliban reportedly signed an agreement for the $2.5 billion Unocal-led project with Turkmenistan and Pakistan as well as with representatives of American, Saudi Arabian, Russian, South Korean and Japanese companies, who form the new consortium, the Central Asian Gas Pipeline Limited. The Taliban then announced that it had not agreed to any deal, a move seen as a negotiating ploy by the Islamic movement to obtain more international recognition.

The principal drawback for any agreement without peace is that neither the Taliban nor the opposition "Northern Alliance" can claim to control the country. Nor do the Taliban enjoy international recognition, a major snag for the consortium to raise finance, and an issue pointedly raised by the former government of Burhannudin Rabbani. Any agreement with the Taliban, it warned, would be treated as invalid. The World Bank, for example, will not lend any funding until it is satisfied that a "representative government" is in place. Nevertheless, such problems did not prevent General Rashid Dostum from signing a production-sharing deal with Diamond Oil, a British-managed offshore company headquartered in Mazar-e-Sharif, for the Kashkari oil fields in northern Afghanistan. Discovered in 1979 by the Soviets, the field has recoverable reserves of 50 million barrels and could produce at a rate of between 15,000-20,000 barrels per day. Other companies have expressed interest but the area is still being contested between the Taliban and opposition forces.

A rival pipeline consortium, TAP Pipelines set up by Bridas, an Argentinian company, and its Saudi partner, Ningharco, is also being considered by the Taliban. The Bridas project seeks to ship the Turkmen gas through Iran to the Persian Gulf. Iran, however, does not recognize the Taliban and supports the Afghan opposition with weapons and money. It also considers Unocal an extension of US influence in the region. Meanwhile, Pakistan military Inter Services Intelligence (ISI) provided logistics to both consortia to conduct their surveys in Afghanistan. Other players seeking to influence the pipelines project reportedly range from the US Government to key figures close to the Saudi royal family.

Unocal has hired former UN, NGO, diplomatic and academic consultants including former American ambassador to Somalia and Pakistan, Robert Oakley, and Gerald Boardman, ex-head of the US Agency for International Development (USAID) in Pakistan, to assist with its endeavours. Both Americans had played significant roles in supporting the mujahideen during the Soviet-Afghan war. Another American organization with close links to Afghanistan, the University of Nebraska at Omaha, which produced 12 million anti-Communist school text books during the 1980s, has been selected to train several thousand Afghan technicians in Kandahar in preparation for building the pipeline. While Bridas enjoys good Taliban contacts, it has not established such a broad support network of influence as Unocal. It also has problems with Turkmenistan over the forcible closure of certain Bridas oil and gas fields.

Some international aid representatives have strongly criticised the oil companies for what they consider to be the "privatization of war" even before peace is secured. One senior UN official described the oil company initiatives as a 'criminalization' process with the emergence of "warlord affiliated enterprises" adding nothing to the economy. Both Bridas and Unocal, however, maintain that building the pipelines will help bring peace to Afghanistan. Transit revenues alone are expected to provided over 50 million dollars a year. There are also indications that despite the rivalry the two companies may eventually be forced to work together.

ESSENTIAL READING

Return and reconstruction: economic coping strategies among farmers in Farah Province, Afghanistan, British Agencies Afghanistan Group/The Refugee Council (London, July 1997)
Understanding the Economy of Afghanistan, Kjell Öström, Swedish International Development Corporation (January, 1997)
Gemstones of Afghanistan, Gary Bowersox and Bonita E. Chamberlin, Geoscience Press (1997)

APPEAL FOR CORRECTIONS AND UPDATES

The editors would greatly appreciate if aid representatives, journalists and other readers could provide us with any changes and comments on information, statistical data and contact lists provided in this Essential Field Guide. Regular updates will be made available on the website of the International Centre for Humanitarian Reporting (http://www.ichr.org). New editions will include the corrected or updated material.

Education

"Afghanistan without educated women is like a bird with one wing"

– Female Afghan NGO worker in Peshawar, June 1997

The issue of education in Afghanistan provokes strong emotions these days, especially since the Taliban movement has closed virtually all girls' schools in the areas under its control. It has also attempted to prevent any form of female education whatsoever, for girls or women. Aid workers and journalists recently arrived in Kabul may be quick to condemn the Taliban for a gross violation of human rights. But complete responsibility does not lie with the Taliban.

The situations in Kabul and Herat are in some ways unique. Until the Taliban arrived, these were cosmopolitan towns where students enjoyed mixed classes and a liberal dress code. The Taliban may have changed all that, but the educational situation in rural areas, both in and out of Taliban hands, has been far less affected. Although up to half the country's boys may have been taught to read and write thanks to free primary education, many girls in rural Afghanistan were never allowed to go to school by often rigidly patriarchal and conservative villagers. Traditional rural resistance to westernized forms of education has a history going back many years. (SEE TALIBAN)

Soon after the April 1978 communist coup, the Khalq faction of the Marxist People's Democratic Party of Afghanistan (PDPA) began a mass literacy campaign which forced the tribal and mainly veiled Afghan women into classrooms with male teachers. The women's male relatives were furious and reacted by boycotting lessons and even destroying schools. Following the Red Army invasion of 1979, Afghan traditions and culture were once again swept aside by Soviet teachers who imported their communist ideology and syllabus wholesale and imposed Russian as a compulsory language. During the

REACH

One of the most innovative approaches to education in Afghanistan is being developed by the Radio Partnership of the International Centre for Humanitarian Reporting (ICHR) in cooperation with the BBC World Service. The Radio Partnership is a Geneva-based team which promotes the creative use of radio in development and peace building. REACH – Radio Education for Afghan Children – is a three-year project designed to bring basic schooling to the homes of Afghan children via the radio. It was developed in response to the Taliban ban on schooling for Afghan girls. Beginning at the end of 1998, the BBC Pashto and Persian service will broadcast half-hour distance education radio programmes focusing on numeracy, literature, ecology, history and "the world around us" six times a week. Special programmes to promote and encourage home educational 'facilitators' will also be aired weekly. The programmes will be produced by a 50-person team operating in conjunction with the BBC Afghan Education Drama (AED) project in Peshawar. The first year of REACH programming has been funded by UNDP, UNHCR, UNICEF, UNESCO and the British Department For International Development.

For more details contact BBC AED or ICHR.

Soviet war, around 2,000 schools were destroyed and over 15,000 teachers fled the country, many destined to become taxi drivers in Peshawar or New York. Numerous schools for Afghan refugee children were established in Pakistan's North West Frontier Province (NWFP) and Baluchistan. Supporters of the Afghan resistance were keen to bring up their children in the spirit of Islamic *jihad* and education once more became prey to political aspirations.

In the late 1990s one of the key problems, apart from that of equal opportunities for girls and boys to study, is that of developing an educational syllabus which is both relevant and politically neutral. Many schools still use textbooks with a heavily anti-communist bias developed by the University of Nebraska in Omaha (UNO) and funded by USAID. As many as 12 million books were printed during the Soviet war and, despite adjustments to their content, have never been fully replaced. One mathematics textbook poses the following problem: "If you have two dead Communists, and kill three more, how many dead Communists do you have?" Ironically, many Afghans who fought during the late 1970s and 1980s associate any form of western education with communism and the hateful Kabul-based Marxist intellectuals who set Afghanistan on the road to its present ruinous state with the Saur Revolution in 1978.

Taliban and women

The outlook for education in Taliban-controlled areas is currently extremely grim. Not only are all girls forbidden to attend school, but all females are banned from both teaching and teacher-training. This has a major impact on the education of boys as well. In Kabul alone, before the Taliban arrived in September 1996, around 250,000 children were either in full-time or 'shift' education. There were even 2,600 students studying at the Malalai Schools for Girls. But nearly three-quarters of Kabul's teachers were women. As a the result of current Taliban prohibitions, classroom sizes for boys have soared to as much as 200. The male teachers cannot cope. The boys who do go to school often learn virtually nothing. This is provoking growing discontent among Kabulis, who have always valued the importance of education. Quite apart from the devastating implications of a whole generation of under-educated children, educated Kabulis are worried about their very survival under such conditions. With only their education to sell, thousands of female teachers have either fled the capital or are reduced to begging on the streets in *burqas*. (SEE WOMEN)

The Taliban themselves give various reasons for their tough stand on the education of women. They argue that their first priority, in the wake of so much interfactional fighting between 1992 and 1996 is to save lives; once the security situation improves, then women will be educated. However, Kandahar has been secure in Taliban hands since 1994 but girls are still not allowed to go to school. The local Taliban argue that insufficient resources – most are spent on security – exist to transport girls and female teachers to school in separate vehicles; that their frontline fighters could not concentrate on the war if they knew their women were wandering the streets of

A teacher conducts a literacy class for women during a break in their carpet-weaving work. *UNICEF/5519/John Isaac*

ILLITERACY AND STATISTICS

American anthropologist Louis Dupree wrote in 1973 that Afghanistan is fundamentally a nation of poets. A glance at Afghanistan's literacy rates, however, suggests that it will take more than Pashto and Persian poetry to salvage Afghanistan from its present crisis. The literacy of both present and future generations, currently so threatened, will be crucial to the nation's development.

dangerous cities unescorted; that the local village mullahs in rural areas are against girls' education; they even argue that tens of thousands of women were trained as spies by the KGB during the 1980s and therefore cannot be trusted.

There may, however, be a more psychological explanation: many of the Taliban themselves are not well educated, at least in the Western sense, having been brought up in the all-male *madrassas* of Pakistan and Afghanistan where learning is limited to repeating the Koran by rote and studying the *shari'a*. Furthermore their strict interpretation of the role of women in Islamic society is underpinned by the traditionalist Pashtun tribal code, the *Pashtunwali*, which emphasises the function of women merely as objects of male pride. The Taliban, however, are not entirely consistent in their policies: an underground network of "home schools" has sprung up to give girls at least a basic education in a non-formal environment. The Radio Partnership of the ICHR is developing distance education programmes with the BBC, UNDP, the European Union, World Bank and other organizations aimed primarily at teaching literacy to girls by radio in home schools. (SEE REACH) The Taliban know this education exists but, as long as their fanatical religious police or frontline fighters are not too near, they often turn a blind eye.

Non-Taliban areas and universities

The situation is quite different in non-Taliban areas, at least in attitude if not in practice. Girls are free to go to school throughout regions controlled by "Northern Alliance" and Hazara forces, but more often the problem is simply one of a lack of school buildings, text books and teachers. The dropout rate is high, reflecting poor teaching, an irrelevant curriculum and continuing economic hardship which may force many boys to leave school and seek work.

Refugee Afghan children living in 140 camps in Pakistan's NWFP, however, are suffering from cutbacks in educational funding. These have resulted in the closure of almost all secondary schools and colleges. Many donors, such as the US government, are weary of supporting refugees who show no sign of returning to Afghanistan, and are focusing more on crossborder assistance. Primary schools continue to operate in refugee camps, but girls' attendance at these schools is still very poor.

A number of Afghan universities are struggling to continue against all odds. Kabul University, first founded as a medical faculty in 1932, was once home to 900 lecturers with links to other academic institutions around the world. After the fall of President Najibullah in 1992, it was virtually destroyed by interfactional fighting among the mujahideen. A group of devoted professors started from scratch to rebuild the place, collecting a library of quarter of a million books and increasing the student body to 10,000 including 4,000 women; then the Taliban arrived and it was once again closed down. Currently, a few courses are being run, but only for men with beards.

In Herat, a very active engineering faculty has been successfully transferred from Peshawar. Balkh University in Mazar, set up a decade ago, once boasted 6,000 students studying a range of subjects from medicine and English to law and Islamic studies; but it is struggling to survive at present. General Dostum, whose Jumbesh-e-Melli forces control the area, has paid for the construction of two faculties and a women's hostel. Universities abroad are helping out with the chronic shortage of books and journals. *Shi'a* Muslims study alongside their *Sunni* compatriots, and women, who at the end of 1996 accounted for two fifths of the Islamic faculty alone, are not forced to wear *burqas*. As Dr Sultanshar, dean of the Islamic faculty at Balkh University, says: "We observe Islamic law, but are open to new achievements. Women can drive cars if they want. We have a law saying both men and women have the right to work. The Prophet Mohammed's first wife was a business woman", he adds, "but why don't the Taliban know that? Because they are taught far from civilization. They are not living in the 20th Century."

Current agency activities and education statistics

Statistics on education are notoriously unreliable, and probably give an idea of the situation in urban areas only. At the time of the Soviet invasion, six percent of Afghanistan's adult women and a third of all men were considered literate. By 1995 that figure had risen to an estimated 15% for women, which is still one of the five lowest literacy rates in the world. Over half of all adult Afghan men were considered illiterate in 1995, and the figures for boys' and girls' primary school enrolment are about the same. These figures come from UNICEF's *State of the World's Children 1998.* Although UNICEF itself has scaled back much of its assistance for Afghan education in Taliban areas, it continues to support some home-schooling in rural areas and non-formal literacy and health training in internal refugee camps in the west of Afghanistan.

There are currently over 20 NGOs involved in the education sector in Afghanistan. One of the leading agencies is the Swedish Committee for Afghanistan (SCA), which supports some 650 primary schools in 17 provinces, supplying text books and school materials to over 160,000 students, and contributing to the salaries and training

"NEW HOME, NEW LIFE"

The BBC World Service first began broadcasting educational dramas in Persian and Pashto in the late 1980s. The success of these led to the formation of the BBC Afghan Education Drama Project (AED) and the launching in 1994 of its radio soap opera "New Home, New Life", which now enjoys an enormous listenership believed to be between 70-80% of the Afghan population.

Up to 80 themes ranging from landmine awareness, cultural heritage and drug production to personal hygiene, safe birthing practices and environmental issues are addressed through the medium of an entertaining radio drama. Topics are discussed at monthly consultations with aid agency representatives. Three episodes are broadcast a week, repeated three times, including an omnibus edition specially aimed at women and timed to coincide with Friday prayers when their husbands are at the mosque. The broadcasts are reinforced by a monthly cartoon magazine which includes a section entitled "Where there is no school", aimed at teaching basic reading and writing skills.

Field-based partnerships with local NGOs reinforce the messages of the radio drama by compiling topical individual storylines and producing educational songs. A listener from Khost wrote in to say: "We have learnt lessons from the drama. For example, if someone is killed, then giving a girl away to atone for the deed is wrong. Before, when we saw a mine we diffused it ourselves, but now we inform the demining office. If sometimes there is a dispute now we settle conflicts by discussion [*jirga*]." Throughout much of Afghanistan "New Home, New Life" has become compulsory listening, and provokes considerable village discussion and uncannily realistic reactions. When one of its most popular characters, Khair Mohammed, was killed by a stray bullet, people in Chaman held condolence meetings to mourn his death.

of nearly 6,000 teachers. Remarkably, independent surveys show that 13% of the SCA-supported students in rural Taliban areas are girls. This is mainly due to the advent of home-schooling outside the formal village school context in areas where communities are not so favourable towards female education. It also bears out what a number of NGOs have found: that when high-ranking Taliban authorities are confronted with a very principled and Westernised approach to female rights they will almost always refuse to cooperate;

J.Hartley/UNICEF

a more local and pragmatic approach negotiated at village and district level and coupled with imaginative solutions such as home-schooling, can often yield positive results. SCA runs women's education classes, including literacy training, basic health education, Koranic studies and vocational skills such as carpet weaving, gardening and candle and soap making.

The International Rescue Committee (IRC), which was responsible for printing 12 million anti-Communist UNO textbooks in the 1980s, has pulled out of the formal education sector in Taliban areas and now cooperates with CARE International in home-schooling, where access to both girls and female teachers is much higher. IRC also channels western donor money into leading Afghan NGOs such as the Afghan Development Association (ADA).

ADA is pioneering education, including schooling for girls, in many provinces such as Farah, Uruzgan, Zabul and Kandahar, which have been neglected by other agencies and have always had low levels of literacy. One of ADA's key aims is to integrate formal education with more practical training in health and sanitation, agricultural, veterinary and environmental issues.

In the Hazarajat of central Afghanistan, Oxfam is having some success in reaching girls in both formal and non-formal contexts; Terre des Hommes and ASCHIANA are using day-care centres in Kabul to reach girls and boys who work on the streets (SEE CHILDREN); Save the Children-USA (SC-US) runs landmine awareness education. In July 1997, for the first time since before the war, an attempt was made by the NGO Afghan German Basic Education (AG BAS-Ed) and UNESCO to promote interest in developing a new curriculum. Coordination for Humanitarian Assistance (CHA) teaches English language and computer skills in Herat, Farah and Kandahar; and ACBAR coordinates an Education Sub-Committee which negotiates with the Ministry of Education and Taliban authorities on key issues.

However, the vast majority of NGOs supporting education are only working in the eastern half of the country, and mostly in primary schools. This is a legacy of the old crossborder days when agencies were largely based in Peshawar and Quetta. Almost all of the western third of Afghanistan is currently being neglected by NGOs working in education. The lack of secondary and tertiary education poses serious questions about the capability of future generations to manage the transition of their country into the international community.

Agency approaches

The problem of women's access to education has split the humanitarian community. In a world where most donor governments and humanitarian agencies demand equal opportunities for men and women, the question of whether to support educational programmes in Taliban-controlled areas is a tricky one. Rigid Taliban policies discriminating against the education of girls and the employment of female teachers is in clear violation of the UN mandate requiring equal opportunities for both sexes.

As a result, UNICEF – as with several other agencies – has stopped its assistance to education programmes in those areas where girls are prohibited from attending school. From UNICEF's point of view, you cannot discriminate in education. Nor should a signal be sent to the Taliban that condones such policies. As Carol Bellamy, Executive Director of UNICEF, maintained in early 1997: "Together with many Islamic scholars, and UN agencies, and countries that have some influence with the Taliban, we must keep the pressure up until each and every girl and woman has her basic rights restored."

UNICEF's attitude has been heavily criticised by a number of NGOs. As one leading male Afghan educator remarked: "The UN are caught in their own words; the Western world only sees in black and white." By withholding support from Taliban areas, some observers feel, UNICEF is failing in its obligations to support schooling for boys, potentially jeopardising the education of half the children in any given area. Furthermore, they argue, given that Afghanistan is such a male-dominated society, it is crucially important to give boys a broad-based education so that when they grow up they may be more inclined than the present male generation to recognise the rights of women. However, as some educated Afghan women emphatically point out, such approaches do not particularly resolve the issue as they still deny girls access to education.

For many on-the-ground organizations, there is scepticism that agency pressure will succeed in changing the Taliban in its current policies, at least on a national level. According to one Talib official in Kandahar: "We will not change our policy if the UN care or do not care about women. The Taliban does not take notice." Faced with such intransigence at the centre of the movement, some agencies feel that a principled 'blanket' policy as applied by UNICEF will only encourage Taliban stubbornness. What is needed, they feel, is a more 'pragmatic' approach. Educational support should be negotiated on a case by case basis with the local authorities, whether Taliban or not. And it should include girls' education as part of the equation. As some agencies, such as SCA and ADA, have found, such pragmatism has met with qualified success.

ESSENTIAL DATA

Adult literacy rate (1995):		
Female	15%	
(Developing World Average/DWA	*62%)*	
Male	47% *(DWA 79%)*	
Combined gross school enrolment:		
Female	9.2% *(DWA 51%)*	
Male	26% *(DWA 60%)*	
Total	13% *(DWA 47%)*	
Secondary school enrolment in:	**Afghanistan**	**Pakistan (NWFP)**
No. of schools supported by NGOs	1,093	348
No. of boy students in these schools	213,334	67,408
No. of girl students in these schools	25,015 (10%)	20,712 (23%)
No. of male teachers:	7,856	1,902
No. of female teachers:	537 (6%)	882 (32%)

Sources: UNICEF State of the World's Children 1998, UNDP Human Development Report 1996, ACBAR School Database 1997

ESSENTIAL AGENCIES

ADA, AG BAS-Ed, BBC AED, BEFARe, CARE, CHA, IRC, ISRA, NAC, PSD, SCA, SC-US, UNESCO, UNICEF

ESSENTIAL READING

Initiatives in curriculum design and development, AG BAS-Ed & UNESCO (1997)
Basic Education Strategies (Afghanistan), UNESCO (1995)
The State of the World's Children 1997, UNICEF
ACBAR Education Sub-Committee reports
Report on a Survey on SCA Supported Girls' Education and SCA Built School Buildings in Afghanistan in Regions under Southern and Eastern SCA Regional Management, A. W. Najimi, Swedish Committee for Afghanistan (Peshawar, 29 August 1997)

Environment & conservation

"The environment is man's first right"

– the late Ken Saro-Wiwa,
Nigerian author and human
rights activist

Afghanistan boasts one the most spectacular and ruggedly beautiful landscapes in the world. And with it, a wild fauna and flora to match. As many a visitor can attest, there is a harsh, almost mystical beauty to this land. Even during the height of the war as refugees fled by foot across the high mountain passes of the Hindu Kush or rumbled through the shimmering steppelands of southern Afghanistan in overloaded trucks and tractors, it was hard not to be enthralled by a lone eagle soaring overhead or a light-footed gazelle sprinting along a dry river bed.

Today, however, much is being turned into a soulless terrain devoid of forests, wildlife, and even water. The direct and indirect damage to this country's environment by the war may represent Afghanistan's second-most crucial loss following that of its own people. Already during the early days of the war when the Soviets launched deliberate security operations against civilians in rural areas and refugees fled in growing numbers, it was evident that the destruction of Afghanistan's ecology and natural resources would have a profound impact for generations to come. But environmental considerations have been largely neglected by the international aid community.

As with numerous other current and former conflict zones worldwide – Angola, Cambodia, Mozambique, Somalia and the Gulf – the war has had a varying effect on the environment. Soviet bombing, often using phosphorous explosives to ensure burning, relentless cutting for firewood by refugees and the mujahideen, and uncontrolled lumbering by Afghans and Pakistanis alike have caused the devastation of thousands of hectares of forest since the early 1980s. (SEE FORESTRY) This has caused severe erosion and destruction of habitat in many parts of the country, particularly in the eastern provinces.

The proliferation of weapons has ensured the relentless hunting of wildlife in formerly remote regions ever since the mujahideen took to the hills to launch their attacks or to run supply convoys along former caravan routes. Similarly, hundreds of thousands of refugees, obliged to avoid the main government-held roads and crossing points, travelled through remote mountain areas to cross one of the 300-odd passes that led into Pakistan. Many brought with them cattle, camels and other livestock causing severe overuse of pasture lands. (SEE LIVESTOCK) Overgrazing has occurred around all the main farming centres and roads as fleeing civilians sought solace for their families and animals from the fighting.

Refugee influxes also precipitated heavy pollution of water supplies as well as the progressive destruction of woodlands in a desperate bid for fuel and shelter materials. Apart from limited wildlife surveys, it is not known what effect such additional pressures have had on the different species of fauna. Cheetah, lynx, otter and long-tailed marmot are all believed to be near extinction, or have sharply declined in the face of hunting and habitat degradation. The fur trade, however, does not appear to have been affected by the war as pelts of the more common – but also endangered – species continue to reach the international market.

Yet the war has left other aspects of Afghanistan's natural heritage intact. The depopulation of farms and villages as well as the presence of landmines and other unexploded ordnance in fields, woodlands and riverbeds has enabled certain species of fauna and flora

ENVIRONMENTAL AWARENESS

WWF-Pakistan and Sweden's Save the Children (Radda Barnen) are currently supporting an Environmental Education programme initiated by SAVE in Peshawar, Jalalabad and Kabul. Aimed at both refugees in Pakistan's North West Frontier Province (NWFP) and inside Afghanistan, it seeks to stimulate public awareness among local populations through the use of radio (Radio Kabul, BBC, etc.). The Female Education Programme of the International Rescue Committee in Peshawar has trained school teachers to initiate environmental awareness among some 5,000 pupils in NWFP. Environmental clubs have been created both in Pakistan and Afghanistan with the support of the Pakistan Environmental Protection Foundation, the NWFP Wildlife and Forest Department and other groups.

KABUL ZOO

One of the most pathetic symbols of destruction in the Afghan capital is Kabul Zoo. Badly shattered during various factional onslaughts since the departure of the Soviets in 1989, both the zoo and the German-built Natural History Museum have been badly ravaged by shelling and looting. Many of the original animals were killed in the fighting, starved to death, or were stolen. Now supported by small grants from the International Committee of the Red Cross and other aid groups to keep the animals fed, a number of tragic-looking inmates remain. These include a pair of lions, a brown and a black bear, several monkeys, a pair of wolves, a few vultures and some owls. All live in pitiful conditions and are often tormented by visitors. Given the occasional bad publicity by the foreign press coupled with admonishments from representatives of the international aid community, the local authorities are now seeking to improve facilities. Visitors pay a small entrance fee and zoo staff try to dissuade people from teasing the animals. WWF is seeking to rehabilitate the zoo as well as some of Kabul's children's parks to give the city a greener feel.

to proliferate in various former habitats, including along main roads such as between Kabul and Jalalabad. (SEE LANDMINES) According to conservation groups such as the Swiss-based World Conservation Union (IUCN) and the Society for Afghanistan's Volunteer Environmentalists (SAVE), a local Afghan NGO, most of the remote areas away from main towns and cities are believed to have retained their biodiversity. The abandonment of villages, particularly in the northeastern mountain regions including the Wakhan Corridor, as well as the lack of hunting and other forms of human encroachment, have allowed some forms of fauna ranging from snow leopard and brown bear to ibex, Marco Polo sheep and markhor to exist without interference. Some unsubstantiated reports even maintain that Caspian tigers continue to roam the more heavily forested, mountainous parts of eastern Afghanistan such as Paktya province.

Ironically, given the country's current devastation, the concept of biosphere reserves (protected habitats) reputedly originated in Afghanistan. The 5,000-year old city of Balkh, for example, boasted more than a million trees in the 17th Century. During this period, many other ancient Afghan cities made special efforts to ensure environmental protection. More recently, in 1973, Afghanistan became one of the first countries to become a party to the Man and

Biosphere Reserves programme. As a result, a number of areas in Afghanistan were declared Biosphere Reserves. However, with any notion of conservation management or protection eliminated by the lack of government and war since the early 1980s, these spheres were quickly relegated to little more than theoretical notions. Seven so-called 'protected' conservation areas still exist, but there is currently no proper management to guarantee their survival. Unless protection measures are implemented as soon as possible, conservationists fear that the situation could change drastically as refugees return home, landmines are cleared, and farming areas are once again put to the plough.

It is clear that Afghanistan's current conservation problems could have a direct impact not only on its own natural resources but on those of neighbouring countries. For example, illegal deforestation in Pakistan's North West Frontier Province is directly related to the route permits being issued by the Kabul authorities. The Siberian cranes which breed in Siberia but winter in India must pass through Afghanistan as part of their migratory flyway, sheltering in major wetland areas such as the Ghazni Marshlands, also a home and migratory stopover for some 250 other species ranging from flamingos to ducks and pelicans. The survival of endangered Marco Polo sheep in the Gojal area of Pakistan and in adjoining China is closely related to its protection in Pamir-e-Buzarg district of the

AIR QUALITY

The quality of air in most Afghan towns was generally good before the war. As with many Third World towns, however, outdoor air conditions have deteriorated as a result of rising population, dust, excessive coal and wood burning, and exhaust fumes from growing numbers of trucks, cars and motor-scooters. Many rural areas are also becoming affected.

Kabul may have a way to go before it becomes as bad as Bangkok or Jakarta, but it is getting there. The fact that Kabul exists in a broad, crater-like valley does not help air circulation. Walking outside during the day and early evening is becoming intolerable, not just in Afghan urban areas but also in Pakistani towns such as Peshawar and Quetta. Overcrowding, traffic jams and smog are all partly caused by the Afghan war.

Smoke from cooking and heating is the primary indoor air pollutant affecting health (respiratory and eye disorders), particularly that of women and children. And despite Islam frowning at tobacco, smoking is on the increase and is now considered a major indoor pollutant by health specialists.

Wakhan Corridor. The proper functioning of Pakistan's Warsak dam near Peshawar is dependent on water catchment along the upper Kabul River from Sarobi dam west of Jalalabad to its entry point into Pakistan.

Organizations such as the World Wide Fund for Nature (WWF), IUCN and SAVE are now pushing for the development of a conservation strategy for Afghanistan as part of any overall long-term rehabilitation and development programme. The continuation of the civil war will undoubtedly lead to a worsening of environmental problems. Yet even if the fighting persists, conservationists maintain, there is no reason why initial efforts should not be implemented towards assessing and improving the existing protected areas system in Afghanistan.

More immediate conservation efforts should include:

- Establishing baseline data of vulnerable and critically endangered species.
- Assessments of major ecosystems with a focus on forests, wetlands, and rangelands. Current available data are limited, out-of-date, or unreliable.
- Protection of natural resources shared with other countries such as water catchment areas from Jalalabad in Afghanistan to the Warsak dam in Pakistan. With target areas to extend 10 kilometres on both sides of the Kabul river, such protection would seek to provide drinking and irrigation water to local communities and their agricultural lands as well as to harbour local biodiversity and large populations of migratory birds. It would also help assure the longevity of Warsak dam.
- Surveys and research to identify and quantify available resources and existing problems.
- Conservation of major flyways of cranes, falcons and houbara bustards in the trans-boundary zone of Ghazni province in Afghanistan and Baluchistan province in Pakistan. Easy access across Afghanistan's borders, particularly for wealthy hunters from Saudi Arabia and the Gulf region, has brought increased pressure on such species. Rare falcons protected by the Convention on the International Trade in Endangered Species (CITES) can command prices of \$50,000 to \$100,000 – an absolute fortune for local Afghans and far more lucrative than drug trafficking.

ESSENTIAL DATA

- **Only one NGO – the Society for Afghanistan's Volunteer Environmentalists (SAVE) – is dedicated solely to conservation issues. Its 1996 budget was $96,000.**
- **From May 1998, SAVE began environmental impact assessment training for the UNOPS/P.E.A.C.E. programme to ensure community-led rehabilitation is more environmentally sensitive.**
- **The endangered *saker* falcon can fetch up to $100,000 per bird on the black market.**

ESSENTIAL AGENCIES

ADA, FAO, IUCN (including the TRAFFIC Network and The Wetlands Programme), MADERA, UNOPS, SAVE, SCA, UNDP, WWF-Pakistan

ESSENTIAL READING

An overview and assessment of Afghanistan's environment, Tareq A. Formoli, M. Afzal Rashid and James P. Du Bruille, Afghanistan Horizon/Afghan Development Association (September, 1994)
Opportunities for improved environmental management in Afghanistan, Nancy MacPherson, IUCN/UNOCA (Gland, Switzerland, May 1991)
Nature Reserves of the Himalaya and the Mountains of Central Asia, World Conservation Monitoring Centre, IUCN (Gland, Switzerland)
Armed Conflicts and Humanitarian Concerns: how attention to environmental scarcity can prevent human tragedies, Jeffrey A. McNeely, Chief Scientist, IUCN (Gland, June 1997)

Ethnic & tribal summary

PASHTUN

- Largest ethnic group in Afghanistan – around 7 million
- Dominant tribe from 1747 (Ahmed Shah Durrani) until 1978 (President Daoud)
- Predominately Pashtun political parties include the Taliban and Hezb-e-Islami led by Gulbuddin Hekmatyar
- Supported politically, financially and militarily by Pakistan
- *Location:* mainly eastern and southern Afghanistan, Kabul, Pakistan's North West Frontier Province
- *Language:* Pashto

TAJIK

- Second largest ethnic group in Afghanistan – around 3.5 million
- Main Tajik political party is Jamiat-e-Islami, based in Taloqan and led by Burhannudin Rabbani and Ahmed Shah Massoud
- Supported periodically by Tajikistan & Russia (and by France and Britain in the 1980s)
- *Location:* northeastern Afghanistan, Herat and Kabul
- *Language:* Dari (Persian)

HAZARA

- Largest *Shi'a* Muslim minority in Afghanistan – around 1.5 million
- Main political party is Hezb-e-Wahdat, based in Bamiyan and led by Karim Khalili
- Traditionally enjoy financial, political and military support from Iran
- *Location:* Hazarajat (Bamiyan and surrounding provinces), Kabul, Mazar-e-Sharif, Quetta & Baluchistan (Pakistan)
- *Language:* Dari dialect

UZBEK

- One of the largest ethnic minorities in Afghanistan – around 1.3 million
- Main political leader is General Dostum; main party Jumbesh-e-Melli
- Enjoy support of Uzbekistan and Russia
- *Location:* northern provinces of Jowzjan, Balkh, Baghlan and Kunduz between the Amu Darya (Oxus River) and the Hindu Kush range
- *Language:* Uzbeki (Turkic)

AIMAQ

- Turkic nomads and herders – numbering around 800,000
- *Location:* northwestern provinces
- *Language:* Dari

TURKMEN

- Semi-sedentary herders and farmers – numbering from 125,000 to 600,000
- *Location:* northern and northwestern provinces bordering Turkmenistan
- *Language:* Turkmeni – a Turkic language which is closely related to Uzbeki.

BALUCH AND BRAHUI

- Independent herders and smugglers – numbering around 300,000
- *Location:* southwest of country on border with Iran and Baluchistan/Pakistan
- *Language:* Baluchi, Pashto

NURISTANI

- Independent mountain people – numbering around 100,000
- Forcibly converted to Islam by Amir Abdur Rahman in 1896
- *Location:* Nuristan, eastern Afghanistan
- *Language:* Nuristani dialects

KUCHI

- Nomadic group, comprising mainly Pashtuns, with some Baluch and Kirghiz
- Estimated numbers range from 500,000 to three million
- *Location:* southwestern Afghanistan on borders with Iran and Pakistan

NOMADS IN NO-MANS LAND

"I was enjoying throwing the sugar-boxes on the fire. They exploded in the flames," explained a tall young Afghan to the crowd of avid listeners, "but then I trod on one. It was buried in the earth. I didn't see it." Bair Khan is a member of the *Kuchi*, a tribe of Pashtun nomads which has driven its sheep, goats and camels across the grasslands of the southern Hindu Kush since the beginning of time.

His family was nearing the end of a three-month march from the mountains of Zabul province down to the plains of Kandahar for the winter. When 19-year old Bair went on alone to prepare a camp for the night, an anti-personnel mine took his left leg off above the knee. He wrapped the bleeding stump in his turban and hobbled off in search of help. His family took him by truck to Quetta, over the border in Pakistan, where his leg was amputated. He was one of the lucky ones. Thousands of mine victims die from loss of blood or septicaemia before they make it to hospital.

I met Bair Khan in a *Kuchi* encampment east of Kandahar. He was taking part in an innovative community-based mine awareness programme started by the NGO Handicap International. As Nuri, the Afghan director of the project, explained, their aim is to build mine-awareness from the grassroots up. So his team advertises for community volunteers, trains them for two weeks, and sends them out on a motorbike and a full-time salary to run their own awareness sessions. Nuri makes random checks on his trainers and encourages them to form Mine Committees in the communities they visit. Sessions take place in mosques or, for the *Kuchis*, around a tent. "We train our trainers to tell stories, to act out the drama of an accident. They must involve the victims and learn the lessons," said Nuri.

About 50 nomads had gathered for the mine-awareness session, accompanied by half a dozen scruffy fat-bottomed sheep, a chicken and two donkeys. Waving models of mines, the trainer explained: "This one's a PMN-2. We call it the 'sugar-box.' And that's a 'butterfly' – it comes out of the sky." He tested the crowd. How do you recognise a minefield? What do you do if you see a mine? Or tread on one? Or see someone else tread on one?

Most of the nomads joined in enthusiastically, but there were dissenters too. "We don't care about mines," shouted one man, "we just want someone to feed us – we are hungry." He had a point: *Kuchis* have been the worst hit, losing about 35,000 animals to mines – or 25 beasts per household, with a market value of US$3,000. No wonder they are worried about what to eat. *JW*

Forestry & deforestation

The destruction of Afghanistan's forests since the start of the war in 1978 may prove to be the country's greatest environmental disaster. Conservationists warn that the deforestation process has now reached the stage where a total loss of Afghanistan's once magnificent woodlands may be imminent unless urgent, decisive measures are taken to protect this fast dwindling natural resource.

As a primarily semi-arid and desert country, less than 3% (the so-called 'legal' figure) of total land in Afghanistan is covered by forest, much of it in mountain areas such as Nuristan. But more realistic 'guestimates' allege that remaining forest cover is as little as 0.5%. Historical evidence suggests that large portions of Afghanistan were originally wooded. Over the millennia, the cutting of forests by human beings and browsing by domestic animals helped create the present grassland steppes. A 1997 report by the World Wide Fund For Nature (WWF) estimates that Afghanistan's forests are now being destroyed at the rate of 20,000 hectares a year. But reforestation and conservation initiatives rank low among aid agency priorities. Current deforestation practices now threaten to rapidly destroy what little remains in the foothills and mountains.

Afghanistan boasts two main types of forests: broad-leaved and needle-leaved. The first consists of oak and nut trees (pistachio) growing in highland areas from 1,300 to 2,200 metres. Serving as firewood, charcoal, fodder for livestock and food, these trees are considered vital for soil and water conservation. The second consists of conifers (cedar, pine, fir, juniper, spruce) in mountainous zones from 2,000 to 3,000 metres. These provide good quality wood for construction and furniture, and are effective for erosion control.

Significant deforestation started as government control over rural areas, particularly in the eastern provinces, deteriorated in the face of mujahed resistance. As villages emptied, any form of tree management dissipated. Shrubs growing in rangeland areas (70% of the country), and which play a vital role in soil and grassland conservation, have been increasingly uprooted and removed for fuel by refugees (including displaced persons), as well as by local and nomadic populations. Increased soil erosion in deforested or de-shrubbed areas in the mountains and lower rangelands is having an adverse effect on the land's ability to absorb water. So, wells are getting deeper and *karezes* are drying up. (SEE IRRIGATION)

During the height of the Soviet war, the Red Army regularly used phosphorous bombs in their efforts to curtail the mujahideen or to terrorise local villages. Such actions caused some large-scale burning of forests. The passage of hundreds of thousands of refugees every year to Pakistan caused further denuding of the trees. All state-controlled timber plantations, for example, were destroyed during the fighting.

The most poignant form of destruction, however, has been that of deliberate cutting by Afghans and Pakistanis alike, mainly for commercial purposes. In many cases, mujahideen, militia groups and local warlords have turned to lumber as a source of revenue, fuel and building materials. But timber traders from both sides of the border have profited massively from this practice, often with the connivance of Pakistani government and military officials. One EFG journalist remembers trekking through the thick forests of Paktya and Kunar provinces during the early days of the war only to return less than a decade later to find huge tracts turned into scarred, moon-like wastelands of withered stumps and rocks.

Current limitations on timber cutting in Pakistan's North West Frontier Province (NWFP) have encouraged the lumber *mafia* to turn its attention to Afghanistan; both as a source of timber and as a transit route for illegally harvested logs taken from Pakistan's Dir District and Bajaur Agency. Major deforestation has begun encroaching on many of Afghanistan's remaining forested areas, including Nuristan – a region that had remained relatively unscathed during much of the war. Some observers maintain that wealthy Pakistani

Extent of forests and woodlands (hectares)

	Estimated area (1979)	Remote Sensing (FAO, 1993)	Guestimate (FAO, 1996)
Evergreens (eastern and southeastern)	1.3 million	N/A	130,000
Non-fruit, deciduous (Nangarhar, Kunar, Paktya & Laghman)	130,000	N/A	13,000
Fruit bearing, deciduous (northern and western)	450,000	N/A	225,000
Closed-cover natural forest	N/A	942,000	368,000
Open-cover natural forest	N/A	258,000	N/A
Degraded forest high shrub	N/A	117,000	N/A
Total forest	1.88 m	1.32 m	368,000
Total percentage/land area	2.8%	2.0%	0.5%

Sources: 'Legal' estimates (1979); FAO (1993 remote sensing); 'Guestimates' for 1996 of closed cover forest based on 20% canopy, Report on forestry and agroforestry *by Dr Steven Newman (*Afghanistan Agricultural Survey*, FAO, Rome, November, 1996)*

timber traders, among them ex-government ministers and military, are heavily involved in the stripping of entire mountainsides of natural forest in exchange for dollars paid in cash to local residents.

Logs are now being transported from northeastern Afghanistan to Kabul. From here, they are taken via Ghazni and Kandahar to the border post of Chaman and into Pakistan's Baluchistan province – observers counted between 50-100 trucks a day along these roads in mid-1997. Despite having officially banned timber smuggling, the Taliban in Kandahar routinely levy taxes on all traffic. For fear of undermining local support, the Taliban are reluctant – and unable – to crack down on trade in mountainous, tribal areas. Nevertheless, to avoid taxes and detection, some entrepreneurs have taken to floating log rafts down the Kunar and Kabul rivers back into Pakistan. The Pakistani border authorities are happy to believe that all the timber transports originate from Afghanistan and not from North West Frontier Province.

As in many rural areas badly affected by nearly two decades of war, Kabul and other urban areas also have been depleted of trees and other greenery. Fighting and lack of irrigation have caused the destruction of countless trees, but so have fuel shortages. After food, energy represents the second most important requirement among local populations, particularly during harsh winters. Chopped stumps or withered trees and bushes are a common sight among the city's parks, gardens and streets. This has contributed to dust storms, poor health and an increasingly dry atmosphere. Kabul now faces a massive reforestation challenge. The local Afghan conservation group, the Society for Afghanistan's Volunteer Environmentalists (SAVE), is currently planting saplings as part of a World Food Programme (WFP) project to re-green the city's parks and other degraded sites. It also distributes trees for replanting among private gardens and for reforestation in the hills around Kabul to check landslides and soil erosion.

Reforestation

As Afghanistan suffers from a chronic wood deficit for building, furniture and other uses, and there is little or no control over timber trafficking, some observers believe that all natural forests could disappear by 2005, if not sooner. A policy of protection and reforestation needs to be implemented as soon as possible. However, given the country's lack of effective government and any form of forestry management, such approaches will need to be developed on a local and regional basis. Much of this responsibility will lie with the UN and various NGOs involved in agricultural and forestry rehabilitation.

The most relevant forestry and agroforestry programmes appear to be located in neighbouring Pakistan and China as well as India, where similar climatic and topographical conditions exist. Some aid coordinators suggest that donors should promote linkages with these countries to help formulate a practical reforestation and conservation strategy for Afghanistan. So far, however, no such strategy exists. The FAO's 1997 *Agricultural Strategy for Afghanistan,* for example, sent an environmentalist on its first mission but did not consider it worthwhile including him on its second; apparently there were "other priorities." Specialists strongly recommend that any proposed strategy should seek to increase the profitability of Afghan tree-based industries as a means of promoting economic development and social equity, notably programmes aimed at both men and women. Such approaches should be devised in a manner that contributes to the conservation of soil, water and biodiversity.

Obviously, the afforestation of areas destroyed in the war or ravaged by uncontrolled lumbering will need to be part of a long-term and comprehensive strategy. A number of aid programmes have begun planting saplings as a first step toward reforesting parts of the country but this is only a drop in the desert. MADERA, a French agency, has re-established a number of plantations to replace those destroyed in the fighting. In Nangarhar province, saplings have been distributed to school children for growing in schools and homes. A SAVE nursery will also begin providing saplings for the Darunta Watershed Management Scheme.

In the Janikhil areas of Khost province, where an estimated 30% of trees have been denuded by the war and commercial logging, aid groups are seeking to make local populations aware of the need to protect their forests. With German assistance, tree nurseries are being established as a source for future large-scale afforestation. Local populations, however, need to be convinced that forest products will contribute towards their income. Similar efforts are being made in other provinces (Kunar, Nuristan, Nangarhar, Laghman and Paktya) where uncontrolled deforestation is continuing.

Both agriculture and horticulture in Afghanistan have been developed traditionally in an agroforestry landscape. Poplars and mulberry trees are often planted in blocks or along the edges of fields and irrigation canals where they serve as boundaries, shade, or windbreaks. Fruit and nut orchards are used for so-called 'intercropping' with vegetables grown among the trees themselves. Some trees can dramatically improve crop yields, while others can serve as useful timber, animal fodder and fuel. As a result, farmers and returnees could play a significant role in afforestation approaches. The cash-cropping of trees for fruit and timber, for example, could serve to reduce a farmer's dependency on poppy cultivation as an alternative source of lucrative income. (SEE DRUGS)

ESSENTIAL READING

Afghanistan Agricultural Strategy, FAO (Rome, January 1997)

ESSENTIAL AGENCIES

FAO, IRC, IUCN, MADERA, SAVE, SERVE, WWF-International, WWF Pakistan

Health

Two decades of war have decimated Afghanistan's healthcare system. Thousands of facilities were destroyed, many of them deliberately by both the Soviets and the mujahideen. And as over five million Afghans fled the country as refugees, numerous trained health professionals were among them. In spite of the conflict, however, some Afghans enjoyed improved access to basic health care through the international aid agencies during the 1980s.

During much of the Soviet war, crossborder medical relief in resistance areas benefited relatively few Afghan civilians, with most international assistance focused on refugees in Pakistan. The first crossborder medical relief was initiated by a small handful of mainly French organizations, the so-called "French doctors" – Aide Médicale Internationale (AMI), Médecins Sans Frontières (MSF) and Médecins Du Monde (MDM). The greater part of their assistance, however, was concentrated in the eastern provinces bordering Pakistan, parts of Hazarajat and certain northern areas such as the Panjshair Valley and Badakhshan. Although the "French doctors" made the strongest impact media-wise throughout the 1980s, the Swedish Committee for Afghanistan (SCA) soon became the major provider of crossborder healthcare. By 1985, SCA was operating more healthcare activities – clinics, medicines, health personnel – inside Afghanistan than all three French groups together.

A significant difference in operational procedures marked the SCA and their French counterparts. The French preferred to send expatriate teams. This probably produced better quality medical assistance, but teams often encountered cultural and political difficulties. One 1984 survey indicated that the average lifespan of each 'French' clinic was roughly two years. The Swedes, on the other hand, focused on training and supporting existing Afghan personnel. This proved problematic during the early stages and did not produce particularly good quality medicine, but proved far more beneficial in the long-term.

From 1986 onwards, other organizations such as Norwegian Church Aid (NCA), International Medical Corps, Freedom Medicine, and MTA also came onto the scene. In addition, a number of local

Afghan NGOs became involved in crossborder health programmes. Some were little more than rip-off operators selling donated drugs on the black market or passing themselves off as 'doktors' and charging local Afghans for bogus care. But others performed good work, sometimes with extremely limited resources.

A very specific form of assistance inside the country for victims directly affected by the Soviet war was that provided by the International Committee for the Red Cross (ICRC). With ambulances ferrying war-wounded from the frontier to Peshawar or Quetta – the ones with thoracic or abdominal wounds rarely made it that far – the ICRC ran what were probably among the best surgical units for war injured in the world. These operations have since closed or relocated with most ICRC activities now based inside Afghanistan itself.

Today, over 80 international NGOs, UN agencies and Red Cross institutions are involved in supporting healthcare in Afghanistan. Assistance is mediated through the Afghan Ministry of Public Health (MoPH) and ranges from the provision of food, fuel and drugs for hospitals and clinics through to fully-equipped surgical teams and expatriate health professionals. Attempts at coordination by the MoPH, NGOs, donors and UN agencies resulted in the publication in May 1994 of a Minimum Primary Health Care Plan for Afghanistan. The Medical Sub-Committee of ACBAR, the NGO coordinating body, also seeks to improve coordination amongst NGOs. At this time of writing, however, there appears to be a serious breakdown of communication and trust between NGOs and the World Health Organization (WHO) in particular.

More than just a humanitarian crisis

The fragmentation of civil structures has further aggravated the material destruction of health facilities. But political, social, cultural and other factors have taken their toll by preventing the creation of an efficient healthcare system. Many of these weaknesses were fully apparent long before the emergence of the Taliban and even before the outbreak of war. As a result, some experienced aid professionals perceive Afghanistan's crisis to be more of an institutional than a humanitarian one. It is a crisis provoked by the collapse of a state.

A fundamental weakness in the overall situation is the way the international aid community has been operating in Afghanistan. There is much rhetoric about coordination and cooperation, but the situation remains very much a mess. In a country where there is no functioning central authority and administration, the aid community has inevitably found itself assuming a role as caretaker of health, public works and other social services normally carried out by the state. Currently, however, there is little of the coherent policy needed to realize this caretaker role effectively. The UN's attempts to build a common assistance strategy for Afghanistan may change this. (SEE UN STRATEGY)

Over the past five or six years, the main areas to have suffered an emergency medical crisis have been Kabul, the shifting frontlines, and – in February 1998 – the earthquake zone around Rustaq. In comparison, many rural areas have not been so badly off. Much attention focuses on the Afghan capital (the fact that the city produced and attracted such large numbers of refugees is one reason for this) which somewhat detracts from the situation in Afghanistan as a whole. It is dangerous and misleading to consider Kabul to be representative of the situation elsewhere in Afghanistan.

Much of Afghanistan's health crisis both in urban and rural areas revolves around the inability of the MoPH to pay even basic salaries to its employees or to purchase drugs and equipment. As more health professionals are forced to leave the country in order to survive and growing numbers of refugees returning from Pakistan and Iran overload the limited facilities that exist, the increased threat from communicable diseases only serves to put depleted resources under ever greater pressure.

According to ACBAR, Afghanistan's health programmes account for twice as much agency spending as any other assistance sector. Aid coordinators consider this a crucial humanitarian investment given that a healthy population is the *sine qua non* for any future socio-economic and cultural development. At the same time, virtually every other sector has an impact on the health of the Afghan people. In the agricultural sector, food production per capita is still substantially lower than pre-war (1979) levels, and livestock production has been seriously affected by conflict and disease. As a result many Afghans – especially children – are afflicted by chronic malnutrition and stunted growth. (SEE MALNUTRITION)

Water and sanitation are also crucial areas of concern. Only five percent of the rural and 39% of the urban populations are believed to have access to safe water, while poor sanitation throughout the country is the major underlying cause of morbidity and mortality in children. Afghanistan has among the highest rates of infant mortality (165 per 1,000 live births), child mortality (257 under five year olds out of every 1,000 born), and maternal mortality (1,700 per 100,000) in the world.

Recent Taliban restrictions in education are creating consequences which will be felt for generations to come: the lack of basic health and hygiene instruction for young boys and girls, and the prohibition of any women to undertake formal study or training in healthcare, is denying to millions of Afghans the right to healthy lives. Taliban attitudes towards the gender issue are furthermore seriously reducing access for Afghan women to hospitals, male doctors and timely treatment. The continuing impact of war on shelter and housing has left the country with more than a million homes to be rebuilt; meanwhile Afghans forced to dwell in ruined houses and temporary shelters are suffering from new health threats ranging from cholera and chloroquine-resistant malaria to skin diseases such as leishmaniasis and acute respiratory infections caused by the long cold winters. In addition, the UN Mine Action Programme estimates that the millions of landmines left in the country, or still being planted, kill or maim some 10 people a day.

Health care under the Taliban

As many aid agencies may hope, the Taliban – in its present form at least – could prove to be only a passing phenomenon. Nevertheless, since the Taliban swept into power in Kandahar in 1994 their rigid application of *shari'a* (Islamic law) to Afghan women has transformed the way international agencies have had to operate their healthcare programmes, primarily in Kabul and other cities. The most serious issue is that of the Taliban forbidding females from formal education and training in the healthcare sector. At the same time, access for sick women to male doctors is restricted. Female nurses and doctors are not even allowed to enter the same room as male patients, let alone treat them. (SEE WOMEN)

According to SCA and other agencies, however, Taliban restrictions have had little or no effect on the way clinics and other health institutions operate in many rural areas. Restrictions are very much as before. Male doctors can receive women patients, but are not allowed to touch or look when dealing with intimate diseases. They can only listen to female patients and then prescribe drugs or refer them to a female doctor if one is available, which is often not the case. Statistics from 203 SCA clinics in rural areas show that although only 10% of health workers are women, female patients represent the majority.

SOAP OPERA CLEANS UP

Effective health education programmes for the population in general, and for mothers and children in particular, can significantly reduce the incidence of medical conditions presented to clinics and hospitals. The BBC soap opera "New Home, New Life", to which as much as three-quarters of the population avidly listens, plays an important role in this respect. Issues such as the importance of young women receiving tetanus inoculations, personal health and hygiene, safe birthing practices, and the rational use of pharmaceutical drugs have all been addressed through the characters of the drama.

One BBC listener from Rabat village remarked: "Our Paktya people are uneducated. When children are born they take dirty knives from the kitchen and cut the cord. After cutting the cord they put henna, ashes or powder on the cord. But now after listening to the drama most people have stopped this, including my family."

Increasing Taliban restrictions are currently resulting in a grave shortage of qualified personnel. It is becoming increasingly difficult for female health workers to receive training, to report to male supervisors, or to travel from home to clinic. Such problems become worse the closer one is to the towns. Educational standards are expected to deteriorate significantly when the present generation of girls, denied the chance to study for the medical – or indeed any – professions, reach adulthood. There has been no institutional (university or college) training provided for female health workers since 1991.

At the same time, a few Taliban authorities in rural areas are remarkably 'liberal' and turn a blind eye to female-oriented NGO activities. Organizations such as SCA have managed to increase the number of girls in primary education in some provinces controlled by the Taliban. (SEE EDUCATION)

For a period of two months from August to October 1997, the Taliban authorities surpassed even their own usually draconian regulations by demanding that *all* women be moved from mixed hospitals in Kabul into one female-only 45-bed clinic, which was not properly equipped to deal with surgery or emergencies, and did not even have electricity. The demand was rescinded when it proved utterly unworkable. Nevertheless, the temporary ban inflicted lasting damage on a number of unfortunate women who had been turned away from emergency wards in mixed hospitals. Furthermore, government officials can enter hospitals and private clinics to supervise at will.

As far as international agencies are concerned, the issue is not so much one of segregation – many hospitals in the 'developed' world also segregate male and female patients – as one of equal access to the same quality of healthcare. The ban on women in Kabul attending any medical facility except the Central Polyclinic denied them access to the surgical and emergency care many of them needed, simply through a lack of space and facilities.

The Taliban have issued the following regulations (quoted verbatim) which apply to all hospitals and private clinics in areas under their control:

1. All the humanitarian assistance provided by the International Community should be given without any condition.
2. In the hospitals where women are hospitalized, male doctors and visitors should inform their entrance to their room in advance.
3. It is illegal and forbidden for women to use cosmetics and wear fashionable dress in the hospitals.
4. Wherever women are employed they should preserve their dignity and walk calmly. They should avoid creating noise by their foot steps.
5. It is forbidden for women to visit the hospitalized male patients in the case when there is somebody else in the room unless they are the blood relative.

WHO DOING WHAT?

The World Health Organization (WHO) Afghanistan is based in Jalalabad and has sub-offices in Kabul, Herat, Mazar, Kandahar, Faizabad, Kunduz, Ghazni and Bamiyan. As well as providing medical and surgical supplies, WHO trains doctors, nurses and traditional birth attendants (TBAs). It supports the vaccination of millions of children and pregnant mothers through the Extended Programme of Immunization (EPI). It rebuilds water supply networks and, through the Ministry of Public Health, rehabilitates hospitals and health facilities nationwide.

A number of NGOs have severely criticized WHO for what they perceive to be its tacit support for the Taliban. When the October 1997 ban on women from attending all clinics or hospitals except the Central Polyclinic was imposed in Kabul, all NGOs and UN agencies on the ground, bar one, complained in the strongest possible terms. The only agency not to voice dissent was WHO. With the approval of the Taliban, WHO is currently funding the rehabilitation of the Rabia Balkhi Hospital, intended eventually to accept women patients in its proposed new obstetrics & gynaecology ward.

In August 1997 Hiroshi Nakajima, director-general of WHO, said the World Health Organization wanted to cooperate closely with the Afghan national authorities and fully respected their local culture. He added that WHO was pursuing a policy of dialogue to influence the attitude of the Taliban. However, many NGOs feel that when the lives of ordinary Afghans, and women in particular, are put at risk by religious zealots, close cooperation with the authorities is not the most appropriate course of action. A joint donor/WHO fact-finding mission visited Afghanistan in November 1997 to look specifically at the issue of women's access to health services. The results were not available at this time of writing.

Another WHO practice, that of providing pre-packed kits of drugs to the MoPH, has been severely criticized by some NGOs who allege that WHO fails to evaluate requirements beforehand, fails to supply drugs with any consistency or regularity, and fails to check up on the use of drugs once provided. The result is that WHO has been found to supply medicines which are both out-of-date and inappropriate. WHO's press office in Geneva, considered by correspondents to be one of the worst information services within the United Nations system, is not particularly helpful either. Perhaps the new Director-General Mrs Brundtland will change all that.

6. All male and female patients and others have to pray at the proper time, except those who may have some legitimate and reasonable excuses.
7. All the personnel of hospitals should observe the Islamic Shari'a Law. They should be advised in case of a violation. In case he/she did not accept, a serious action should be taken against him by the hospital head or inform our department.
8. The women using office vehicles should not sit beside the driver.
9. No Afghan women is permitted to travel with expatriates in a vehicle.
10. Afghan women can not be appointed as senior staff in expatriates hospital.
11. Agencies working in health sector do not have the right to sent outside the country any Afghan women for any reasons. If there is any urgent need agencies should get approval of our department.

"The above mentioned eleven points are the directions under the Islamic Shari'a Law which should be respected. Nobody can disallow our supervisory teams who may control the hospitals at anytime."

More rules issued on 27 January, 1996 are as follows:

1. Female patients should be referred to female doctors, but if a male doctor is needed, the patient's Mahram (close male relative) should be present.
2. Female patients and male doctors have to respect Hejab (veil covering entire face and body of a woman) during examination.
3. Male doctor should neither look nor touch other parts of the woman except the affected site.
4. Female patients' attending place should be well covered and veiled.
5. In hospitals the person who arranges female patients' turn should be a woman.
6. In rooms where female patients are hospitalized, the doctors on night duty can go only if they are asked by the patient otherwise they are not allowed to enter in these rooms.
7. Chatting, sitting together between lady doctors-nurses and male doctors-nurses is prohibited, but if it is necessary to discuss about some points, they would discuss while observing well the Hejab.
8. Lady doctors should put on old dresses while going out and they should neither put on luxorious dress nor do other dress up or make up.
9. Lady workers and nurses are not allowed to go to rooms where men are hospitalized.

10. Hospital staffs have to pray in Jamahat (all together) at the required time, the person in charge of the hospital will appoint a Mullah and determine the place for praying (mosque).
11. Whenever government controllers go to hospitals and private clinics for controlling nobody can prevent them." (SEE TALI-*BANS*)

Health facilities and hospitals

Provincial hospitals are located throughout Afghanistan, in Balkh, Bamiyan, Farah, Ghazni, Helmand, Herat, Kandahar, Kapisa, Kunar, Laghman, Logar, Nangarhar, Paktya, Parwan, Wardak and Zabul *(Source: ACBAR)*. In addition to the above facilities, there are over 20 hospitals in Kabul alone (SEE TABLE next page) and 50 health clinics in the capital, specializing in tuberculosis, leprosy, malaria, leishmaniasis, Mother & Child Health (MCH), supplementary feeding, eye care, physiotherapy and the supply of medicines.

Mother and Child Health (MCH)

According to UNICEF, the proportion of children who reach their fifth birthday is one of the most fundamental indicators of a country's concern for its people. In their report *The State of the World's Children 1998,* the under-five mortality rate for Afghanistan in 1996 was 257 per 1,000 live births, the fourth worst in the world and the highest outside Africa. The rate in Sweden is four per 1,000 and the world average is 88 per 1,000. Infant mortality is also more than double the average rate for developing countries: 165 children out of every 1,000 born die each year before their first birthday.

Leading causes of mortality

ALL AGES

1. **Diarrhoeal diseases (42% of all deaths)**
2. **Malaria**
3. **Pulmonary tuberculosis**
4. **Measles**
5. **Acute cerebrovascular diseases**
6. **Bronchopneumonia**
7. **Peritonitis**
8. **Burns and accidents caused by firearms/missiles**
9. **Post-partum haemorrhage**

INFANTS

1. **Diarrhoeal diseases**
2. **Acute respiratory infections**
3. **Malnutrition**

Source: MEDAIR – Study of Health Provision and Needs in Kabul, *1997*

Hospitals in Kabul

NAME	SPECIALITIES	NO. OF BEDS	NO. OF DOCTORS	NO. OF NURSES	TOTAL NO. OF STAFF	AGENCY SUPPORT
MALALAI	Obs/Gyn	140	80 (mainly female)	16-20	380	AVICEN, UNICEF, PSF, WFP, ACTED
(RABIA BALKHI) until Sep 96	Obs/Gyn	30	69 (all female)	47	254	(PSF, ACTED) WHO rehabilitating
NAZOANO	Obs/Gyn	25	14 (mainly female)	4 (midwives)	42	ARF, UNICEF, ARCS, ACTED
INDIRA GANDHI	Paediatric	250	100	120	410	PSF, ACF, MSF, GAA, ICRC, WFP, SC-US, ACTED
ATATURK	Paediatric	80	25	20	130	PSF, ACF, SC-US, WFP, ACTED
MAIWAND	ENT, Plastic Surgery, Dermatology, Ophthalmology, Paediatrics	310	51	100	328	PSF, WHO, SC-US, MCA, ACF, IAM, ACTED
KHAIR KHANA "52-bed polyclinic"	Int.Med., Surgery, Obs/Gyn, Paediatric, ENT, Dental, Ophthalmology	50	53	57	240	PSF, SC-US, IAM, ACTED
(AVICENNA EMERGENCY) until Sep 96	Int.Med., Surgery	60	40	67	261	(PSF, WHO, ACTED)
AVICENNA CHEST	Heart & Lung, Cardiac Surgery	6	20	55	230	PSF, UNICEF, ACTED
ANTANI	Infectious Diseases	150	50	60	–	PSF, MSF, ACTED
ARCS	Int.Med., Surgery	48	9	12	48	IFRC, ICRC

KARTE SEH SURGICAL	Surgery	250	–	–	–	ICRC
KARTE SEH MATERNITY	Obstetrics	10	3	7	–	ICRC
KARTE SEH MEDICAL	Internal Medicine	50	20	–	–	MSF, WFP, ACTED
JAMHURIAT	Surgery, Int.Med., Burns Unit	250	100	100-120	400	MSF, PSF, WFP, ACTED, IAM
NEW ALIABAD	Surgery, Neurosurgery, Urology, Int.Med.	165	80	137	–	MDM, ICRC, PSF, IAM, ACTED
WAZIR AKBAR KHAN	Surgery, Orthopaedics, Internal Medicine	250	–	–	–	ICRC, PSF, GMS
MILITARY "400 BEDS"	Orthopaedics, Surgery, Internal Medicine	400	70?	–	–	Ministry of Defence, ICRC
(STATE SECURITY) closed	Surgery, Int.Med.	100	50	–	–	(Ministry of Security, ICRC)
POLICE	Surgery, Int.Med., ENT-Surgery	50	30	30	–	Ministry of Interior, ICRC
STOMATOLOGY	Dental, Facial & Neck Surgery	25	15	–	286	PSF, ACTED, ICRC
NOOR EYE HOSPITAL	Ophthalmology	50	–	–	–	IAM, ACTED
PSYCHIATRIC	Psychiatry	?	–	–	–	PSF, ACTED
QARABAGH	Surgery, Int.Med., Paediatrics	30	–	–	–	AVICEN

Note: The information on the number of staff has not been verified but was taken to be the approximate number of staff theoretically employed in the hospitals and definitely not the number of staff who would be present at their jobs on any one day. The table is not complete and may contain mistakes as each agency and MoPH have different lists and it was not possible in the time given to visit each hospital and to verify its existence.

Source: MEDAIR – Study of Health Provision & Needs in Kabul, Afghanistan 1997, *Appendix A*

Over a quarter of a million children are thought to die in Afghanistan before reaching the age of five. Nearly half die as a result of diarrhoeal diseases or acute respiratory infections; and 20% die from diseases which could be prevented through vaccination. Afghanistan's maternal mortality rate (1,700 deaths per 100,000 live births) is the highest in the world after Sierra Leone and equates to nearly one mother in 50 dying in childbirth. A number of factors contribute to this appalling figure: inadequate care during childbirth and a lack of midwives or traditional birth attendants (TBAs); malnutrition and stunting in young girls which later leads to small pelvic sizes and obstructed labour; and infections such as tetanus, resulting from low immunization levels. WHO estimates that 90-95% of all births in Afghanistan are home deliveries, with less than one in 10 deliveries attended by trained health personnel or TBAs.

Tuberculosis afflicts numerous Afghan women, with females representing 70% of reported sufferers. Drugs to treat the condition are available in the markets but with an effective course of medicine taking six to eight months to complete, a major problem is drug resistant tuberculosis caused by incomplete treatment. Second-line drugs are too expensive to use. WHO has recently implemented a strategy of "Directly Observed Treatment Shortcourse" (DOTS) to ensure that sufferers finish their treatment.

These disastrous levels of mother and child mortality are being tackled in a number of ways. One of the most ambitious MCH initiatives in Afghanistan is the Extended Programme of Immunization (see EPI below). UNICEF and various health NGOs have made the control of diarrhoeal diseases a priority. Many basic health centres promote the use of Oral Rehydration Therapy (ORT) or the preparation of home-made fluids, and aim to improve standards of personal hygiene and sanitation in the home. UNICEF is helping support primary health care and a safe motherhood initiative through local NGOs in five target provinces.

In November 1996, Save the Children Fund-USA (SC-US) collaborated with the Ministry of Public Health (MoPH) to initiate an integrated public health programme in Kabul designed to reduce mortality and morbidity of children from acute respiratory infections and diarrhoeal diseases. This involved the training of NGO and

MALARIA STATISTICS:	**1977**	**1997**
Annual incidence:	**80,000**	**3-4 million**
Lethal *P. Falciparum:*	**1%**	**20-30%**
No. of malaria centres:	**334**	**33**
Chloroquine resistance:	**none**	**50% of all cases in refugee camps**

Source: WHO 1997

MALARIA: MAKING A COMEBACK

Malaria is a disease of poverty and decay that flourishes in times of war. It has become a major health problem in Afghanistan owing to the breakdown of the country's public health system. Since the 1980s malaria has increased fivefold and *falciparum malaria* – the potentially lethal form more normally associated with Africa – has increased 100-fold. Yet before the war Afghanistan ran one of the most successful malaria control programmes in the world.

The pre-war control strategy was to spray houses with insecticides such as DDT to kill mosquitoes and break the malaria transmission cycle. UNHCR has adopted a similar strategy, using more modern insecticides, in Pakistan's refugee camps. This showed that spray campaigns can be very successful when properly managed. Cases of malaria among refugees were reduced from 180,000 to just 30,000 a year during the 1990s. But the problem with house spraying is the expense, and the need to respray annually. In Afghanistan it is no longer a viable strategy as the planning and organization required is impossible to achieve under current conditions.

An alternative strategy is needed: one that is cheap and simple to implement. Bednets are an old method of personal protection in South Asia but were rarely used by Afghans. Recent research has shown that when bednets are coated with the insecticide *permethrin,* mosquitoes are deterred from biting through the mesh and protection is much improved. A study in an Afghan refugee camp showed that 'treated' nets give 80% protection against malaria and given the right promotion are readily adopted by Afghans. In 1992 several health sector NGOs, led by HealthNET International, launched a project to sell subsidized bednets in eastern Afghanistan. To date, 200,000 family-size nets have been sold through NGO clinics and by mobile teams, protecting an estimated 700,000 Afghans. So far there is no sign of the market becoming saturated. It seems that Afghanistan is on its way to becoming a bednet-using culture.

What started as a simple project to promote self protection seems destined to become the country's primary malaria control strategy (with the beneficiaries rather than the state bearing most of the cost). As no effective government seems likely to evolve in the near future, the challenge now is to ensure a steady supply of nets and insecticide through the private sector, and to involve the community in the production and re-treatment of nets.

Mark Rowland, HealthNET International

MoPH staff, the treatment of over 25,000 children, distribution of essential drugs and a home care and visiting programme. The Swedish Committee for Afghanistan (SCA) trains community health workers, MCH trainers, health educators, TBAs and other cadres of health workers in rural Afghanistan. Terre des Hommes (TdH) has implemented a Home-Visiting Programme in Kabul for mothers and newborn babies. MEDAIR supports the TB Institute in Kabul and Médecins Sans Frontières (MSF) and Lepco treat TB in Ghazni and Mazar.

Despite considerable foreign support, however, most hospitals have very little or no medical or salary support. The majority of hospital sections are not even functional.

Extended Programme of Immunization (EPI)

One of the major health initiatives of the past few years in Afghanistan has been the Mass Immunization Campaign (MIC) which is conducted as part of the National Immunization Day (NID). This is a campaign carried out during a specific period and for a limited period of time. The Extended Programme of Immunization (EPI) is a longer-term initiative with routine and permanent immunization programmes. EPI functions all year round but expanded efforts with extra resources are organized as part of NID.

Immunization efforts are partly funded and coordinated by UNICEF and the World Health Organization (WHO) with the aim of significantly improving mother and child health. Actual immunization is implemented on the ground by the Ministry of Public Health (MoPH) and various NGOs.

It took the concerted efforts of the MoPH, WHO, UNICEF and the UN special envoy an entire year (1993-94), with the support of BBC World Service broadcasts, to persuade the different warring factions across Afghanistan to stop fighting for one week so that children and mothers nationwide could be immunized. Since 1994 there have been seven rounds of the polio campaign, reaching as many as 3.6 million children (over 80% of all Afghan under-fives) in 1997. This has paved the way for vaccinations across more than three-quarters of the country against tuberculosis (BCG);

Immunization coverage levels *(UNICEF, 1996-97)*

BCG (tuberculosis):	**47%**
DPT/OPV3:	**31%**
Measles:	**42%**
Polio:	**56% (80% of under-5s by 1997)**
TT2:	**37% (women of 15-45 years)**
Vitamin A supplement:	**13%**

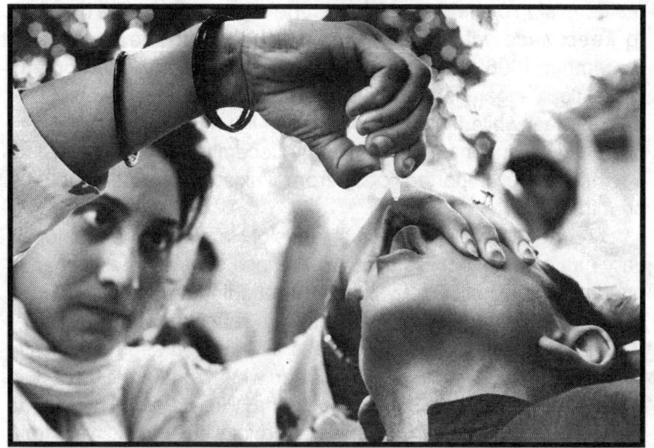

J. Hartley/UNICEF

diphtheria, pertussis/whooping cough and tetanus (DPT); measles and TT2.

The EPI initiative has been carried out under extremely difficult conditions. Access to much of the rural population has been restricted severely by the poor security situation and the deplorable state of roads across most of the country. This has stretched to the limit the cold chain required to keep vaccines at the correct temperature. As a result, not all beneficiaries have received the full course of vaccinations necessary to provide full protection. Currently detailed survey work is underway to assess the actual impact of the EPI nationwide. UNICEF, however, claims an average coverage for immunization against all six vaccine-preventable childhood diseases of 40%. Recent EPI work has concentrated on acceleration campaigns in low-performing districts, targeting those children under one-year-old and 15-45 year-old women who slipped through the net before. In addition, children between 6-23 months are receiving Vitamin A supplementation. NGOs taking the lead in implementing EPI are the Swedish Committee for Afghanistan (SCA) with 54 teams and the Norwegian Afghanistan Committee (NAC).

Malnutrition

Malnutrition, mostly in its mild and moderate forms, contributes to more than half of all child deaths worldwide. A 1997 survey carried out by CIETInternational for UNICEF (using the Multiple Indicator Cluster technique) suggests that malnutrition affects up to 35% of Afghan children under the age of five.

In Kabul, where the French NGO Action Contre la Faim (ACF) has carried out three nutritional surveys, the problem is not so much one of availability of foodstuffs as the astronomical increases in the cost of even the most staple foods. This has been aggravated by the devaluing of the local *Afghani* currency and the failure of wages to keep pace with inflation. In the 14 months leading up to December 1996, the cost of items such as *nan* (Afghan bread), wheat flour, sugar, potatoes and spinach went up by between 350%-500%. Meanwhile the *Afghani* slumped in value from a dollar rate of 4,600 in October 1995 to 23,000 by December 1996. This pushed up the cost of imported foods from Pakistan and neighbouring countries.

By contrast, in the central highlands of Hazarajat, the problem is very much one of access: the Taliban have consistently blockaded overland routes into Bamiyan and surrounding areas in an attempt to prevent food and other supplies from reaching enemy Hezb-e-Wahdat troops. As a result, the Hazaras have found great difficulty in finding markets for their potatoes and wheat, and are thus denied the means to buy-in essential foodstuffs. World Food Programme (WFP) attempts in 1997 to supply Hazarajat with food aid were frustrated by blockaded road routes, wholesale looting of wheat supplies from their warehouses in Mazar, and even targeting of their cargo aircraft on the ground by Taliban fighter-bombers.

Apart from the lack of nutritious food, other key factors contribute to malnutrition. The failure to breast-feed babies for at least the first six months is one. Low birth weight (which itself results from maternal malnutrition) is another. So is iodine deficiency. An estimated 1.5 million children a year could be saved worldwide if they were breast-fed exclusively for the first six months of their lives. Healthy growth and a strong immune system depend on this. Infant formula, the synthetic alternative to mothers' milk, is not only inferior but sometimes lethal when over-diluted with dirty water or served in unclean bottles.

Although no data on breast-feeding in Afghanistan is currently available, the concept of breast-feeding cannot be a new one:

> *"Mothers shall suckle their children two years*
> *completely, for such as desire to fulfil the suckling"*
>
> *Koran II.233*

UNICEF estimates that around one in five Afghan babies are born underweight, usually because their mothers are themselves malnourished. Such underweight children are much more vulnerable to seizures, blindness, deafness, cerebral palsy and mental retardation. As Afghanistan's rock salt – the source for much of the country's salt in rural areas – contains little or no iodine, the risk of iodine-deficient mothers giving birth to mentally-retarded children increases.

The December 1996 survey, carried out in Kabul by ACF, sought to determine the prevalence of both acute and chronic malnutrition in children aged 6-59 months as well as the prevalence of maternal malnutrition. A total of 1,325 children were surveyed in clusters covering all areas of the capital. One indicator of long-term or chronic malnutrition is stunting (low height for age) in children under the age of five. Stunting is caused by insufficient or poor quality food, poor feeding patterns, inadequate care of women and children, frequent infection and poverty. Not only does stunting weaken immunity and impair learning and working capacities, but it leads to a smaller pelvic size in girls, increasing the risk of obstructed labour and maternal mortality. And as if that were not bad enough, stunted parents are more likely to give birth to stunted children. The ACF report found that over half of the children surveyed in Kabul suffered from moderate or severe stunting.

Mid Upper Arm Circumference (MUAC) is the measurement used to determine the risk of mortality in children suffering from malnutrition. In Kabul 0.3% had a MUAC of less than 11cm (needing admission to a Therapeutic Feeding Centre or TFC); 4.2% measured 11-12cm (for admission to a Supplementary Feeding Centre or SFC); and 24.6% measured 12-13.4cm (at risk of malnutrition). At the TFC, severely malnourished children are given therapeutic milk and complimentary foods under 24 hour care in hospitals; they may also be released to day-care centres, with a dry ration given to them to take home in the evening. When the child's condition improves they are discharged and referred to a SFC which they attend once a week to be measured, to receive health education and to collect a weekly dry ration amounting to 1800 kcal per day.

ACF targets about 10,000 children in Kabul with feeding programmes run through hospitals and day-care centres (TFCs) and through MCH clinics (SFCs). The International Assistance Mission (IAM) cares for moderately malnourished children at Karte-Seh clinic, and Médecins Du Monde (MDM) treats both severely and moderately malnourished children at Pul-e-Sokhta clinic. UNICEF provides K-mix and BP-5 high protein rations for therapeutic and supplementary feeding, but is now promoting the use of local foods rather than BP-5 for treatment of malnourished children in their own homes. Other agencies involved in food aid include ARCS, CARE, GMS, ICRC, MEDAIR, UNHCR, and WFP/ACTED. (SEE RELIEF & DEVELOPMENT)

Training and education

The training of Afghan doctors, nurses and health workers is desperately necessary in a country where a whole generation of skills has been destroyed by war. Medical faculties exist at the Universities of Kabul and Jalalabad, but only for men. There is also a medical faculty in Mazar-e-Sharif. However, none of these faculties has systematic or regular training programmes. Nor do they have any proper lab training or teaching aids and materials. In addition, teachers often fail to receive salaries.

Although women's access to training in Taliban-held areas is severely limited, some instruction in nursing, midwifery and English is possible 'on-the-job'. The International Committee of the Red Cross (ICRC) and the Afghan Red Crescent Society (ARCS), for example, train both male and female Afghan health workers in the five hospitals they support in Kabul, Kandahar, Ghazni and Jalalabad.

Since 1980, Aide Médicale Internationale (AMI) has concentrated on the medical training of assistant doctors, lab technicians, X-ray technicians, dental students, Mother & Child Health (MCH) staff and Traditional Birth Attendants (TBAs). The Ministry of Public Health (MoPH) has agreed on a new two-year syllabus for training physiotherapists, promoted by the International Assistance Mission (IAM) and Sandy Gall's Afghanistan Appeal (SGAA). (SEE DISABILITY) IAM also seconds expatriate surgeons and nurses to train MoPH staff. The International Islamic Relief Organization (IIRO) runs a health institute in Peshawar which trains Afghans in X-ray, anaesthesia, laboratory and preventive medicine skills. Medical Emergency Relief International (MERLIN) trains surgical staff and TBAs as well as providing family planning education. Save the Children-USA provides health education and technical training in Kabul to reduce the morbidity and mortality of the under-five-year-olds suffering from respiratory infections and diarrhoea. The Swedish Committee for Afghanistan (SCA) provides training for doctors, mid-level health workers, TBAs and other paramedical staff. It also supports health education and preventive health care in 19 provinces of Afghanistan. SERVE runs a health education programme for school children and village women.

Agency support

The World Food Program (WFP) provides institutional feeding for a number of hospitals and food-for-work projects to rehabilitate clinics. Coal for heating hospitals is supplied by ACTED, a French NGO. Drugs and medicines are supplied to the Ministry of Public Health (MoPH) by the World Health Organization (WHO) and UNICEF. Pharmaciens Sans Frontières (PSF) supplies pharmaceuticals directly to the MoPH. PSF is also establishing the first biology laboratories at the six main hospitals in Kabul, Ghazni, Herat and Mazar. Help Germany runs annual plastic surgery clinics in Jalalabad. The International Assistance Mission (IAM) focuses on eye care at the Noor Eye Hospital in Kabul, and through mobile clinics and camps; it also supports Mother & Child Health care. The Japan Afghan Medical Service (JAMS) runs clinics specializing in acupuncture and the treatment of leprosy. The Islamic agencies Lajnat Al-Birr Al-Islamia (LBI) and Lajnat Al-Dawa Al-Islamia (LDI) support a number of hospitals in Pakistan's North West Frontier Province and the eastern provinces of Afghanistan.

Médecins Du Monde (MDM) has been in Afghanistan since 1980 (when it operated clandestinely) and is currently involved in rehabilitating hospitals in Herat and Farah provinces. The British medical agency MERLIN is supporting health clinics and training in

Farah, Badghis and Badakhshan. Médecins Sans Frontières (MSF) concentrates on Primary Health Care and the training of TBAs through Comprehensive Health Clinics (CHCs) in rural areas. HealthNet International is the 'development' agency which grew out of MSF, and specializes in the prevention and treatment of malaria and leishmaniasis. The Norwegian Afghanistan Committee (NAC) supports hospitals and clinics in Ghazni and Nuristan. Orphans, Refugees & Aid (ORA) focuses on drug rehabilitation

THE RED CROSS MOVEMENT

The International Committee of the Red Cross (ICRC) pursues its own agenda of caring for the war-wounded (both military and civilian) through operating ambulances and first aid posts on the frontline and surgical teams at five hospitals in Kabul, Kandahar, Jalalabad and Ghazni. Among the beneficiaries of Red Cross surgery is Mullah Omar, Supreme Leader of the Taliban, who was treated in an ICRC hospital in Quetta after losing an eye fighting for the mujahideen.

ICRCs original mandate to care only for those directly affected by the armed conflict has now been extended in Afghanistan to embrace all emergency surgical cases. The Red Cross-supported hospitals also receive medical and non-medical supplies, food for in-patients and staff on duty, maintenance and equipment, staff training and cash 'allowances' which are in effect the only salaries Ministry of Public Health (MoPH) staff actually receive. The ICRC is the only agency to provide basic healthcare for prisoners of war and political detainees. In collaboration with the Afghan Red Crescent Society (ARCS), it cares for 25,000 internal refugees, so-called Internally-Displaced Persons (IDPs), at camps in western Afghanistan. ICRC orthopaedic centres in Herat, Mazar, Kabul and Jalalabad provide prosthetic limbs, orthotic braces and physiotherapy for both physically- and mentally-impaired Afghans. (SEE DISABILITY)

The Geneva-based International Federation of Red Cross and Red Crescent Societies (IFRC) trains the ARCS to manage the response to natural disasters through a programme of Community Based First Aid (CBFA). IFRC provides drugs to 46 basic health care clinics under this scheme, with the aim of preventive rather than curative care along the lines of a General Practice. The Saudi and Kuwaiti Red Crescent Societies are also active in Afghanistan. (SEE RED CROSS)

through a treatment centre in Peshawar and in 1995 began HIV/AIDS awareness and counselling. The Swedish Committee for Afghanistan (SCA) runs a major primary health care programme through the support of over 200 Health Clinics in 19 provinces of Afghanistan.

ESSENTIAL DATA

Population:	**20.9 million**
Under five mortality per 1,000 :	**257 (4th worst in world, highest outside Africa)**
Infant mortality per 1,000 :	**165 (3rd worst in world, highest outside Africa)**
Maternal mortality per 100,000:	**1,700 (worst in world after Sierra Leone)**
Life expectancy at birth:	**45 years (3rd worst in world)**
Access to health services:	**29% of population (80% urban, 17% rural)**
Access to safe water:	**12% of population (39% urban, 5% rural)**
Access to adequate sanitation:	**38% of population (urban) 1% (rural)**
Low birth weight:	**20%**
Children under 5 with malnutrition	**35%**
Under fives who die from diarrhoea	**85,000 per year**
Deaths from tuberculosis	**12,000-13,000 per year (70% of cases are women)**

Sources: WHO Afghanistan, 1998; UNICEF State of the World's Children 1998; CIETInternational Multiple Indicator Cluster Survey 1997

Key players

The following potted biographies of key players in Afghanistan include both the quick and the dead. One feature of Afghan politics is that even when a player may disappear from the scene for a few months or years, he can never be ruled out from returning in force. A classic recent example is that of General Dostum, who supposedly "fled into exile" in Turkey after being ousted from Mazar in May 1997 by his one-time ally General Malik. However, Dostum returned four months later in a show of strength and took over military command of the "Northern Alliance" to hold Mazar against the Taliban assaults on the city in September 1997.

AKBARI, Mohammed

Leader of the smaller of the two Shi'a Hezb-e-Wahdat groups.

BIN LADIN, Osama

Described by the CIA as the financier of Islamic terrorism. Bin Ladin comes from a wealthy merchant family in Saudi Arabia. A vocal opponent of the Saudi Government, he has publicly stated his intention to rid Saudi Arabia of all US troops. Following the deaths of 19 American airmen in a truck-bomb attack on their barracks in the Saudi city of Dhahran he warned that the war between Muslims and the United States had begun. Arab and Western governments alike blame his gunmen for fomenting insurrections in Egypt, Algeria and Saudi Arabia.

During the 1980s, Bin Ladin supported the mujahideen and lost around 500 of his men. When the Soviets withdrew he became disillusioned with Afghan infighting and left for Sudan. Since May 1997 he has been based in Kandahar where the Taliban have offered him protection in return for his assistance during the war. Their condition however is that he does not speak out against the Saudi Government, which in June 1997 recognized the Taliban movement as the *de facto* government of Afghanistan. Bin Laden is suspected of involvement in terrorist attacks against US soldiers in Saudi Arabia and of organizing the 1993 bombing of the World Trade Centre in New York which killed seven people. The CIA is reported to have recruited around 1,000 Islamic mercenaries to seize Bin Ladin and abduct him to the US to face charges of terrorism.

DAOUD, Mohammed (1909-1978)

Former President of Afghanistan and arch-manipulator of the two Cold War superpowers. President of the Republic of Afghanistan from July 1973 until his assassination in April 1978 as a result of the Saur (April) Revolution which brought the Marxist People's Democratic Party of Afghanistan (PDPA) to power in Kabul.

Born in 1909 in Kabul, he followed a military career, which saw him become Commander of the Central Forces (1939-47) and Minister of Defence in 1946. As Prime Minister from 1953-63 he built up the military as a power base, encouraged social reforms and in 1959 permitted women to abandon the veil. He received considerable military and economic aid from the USSR (and some from the USA, prompting him to say "I light my American cigarettes with Russian matches"). However, by supporting the ambitions of Pakistan's NWFP to become an independent Pashtunistan he estranged both Pakistan and the USA; this pro-Pashtun ambition and his disregard for the King eventually led to his resignation in 1963.

In July 1973, with the support of the Army, the PDPA and the USSR, he staged a coup against his cousin King Zahir Shah, and proclaimed himself President of the new Republic of Afghanistan. He employed left wing elements in suppressing the nascent Islamist movement. His establishment in 1975 of the National Revolutionary Party, however, was aimed at limiting the power of the left. In order to force centralization and the extension of his personal power he assumed direct control over the Armed Forces and tried to promote nationalism in place of traditional ethnic allegiances. However Daoud's republic was plagued by economic inefficiencies and a lack of skilled personnel which led to an increasing economic, military and political dependence on the USSR. He attempted to reverse this total reliance by approaching the West and Pakistan, and by using finance from Iran and the Arab Gulf States to help reduce Soviet influence, but it was too late and he was overthrown by the PDPA coup of 27 April 1978.

DOSTUM, Abdul Rashid (1954-)

Northern warlord and former militia general under the Soviets. Leader of Jumbesh-e-Melli Islami (National Islamic Movement), Dostum is currently vice-president and military leader of the anti-Taliban "Northern Alliance," also known as the United Islamic Front for the Salvation of Afghanistan (UIFSA).

Born in 1954 in Jowzjan Province of a peasant Uzbek family, Dostum received only a few years of formal schooling and essentially taught himself to read and write. Dostum is a nickname he earned as a young man; *dost* means friend, and a *dostum* is everyone's friend. A product of the Soviet Union, he received military training in the USSR in 1980 and rose through the ranks of President Najibullah's communist regime army. Under Najibullah's regime he was entrusted with guarding the northern provinces of Jowzjan, Faryab and Sar-e-Pol. He was awarded the title of Hero of the Republic of Afghanistan and made a member of the central council of the Watan (formerly PDPA) Party. During the Soviet war, he emerged as a highly effective commander of both regular and militia pro-government forces.

By 1991, he was commander of the Jowzjani "Dostum Militia" numbering some 20,000 regular and militia soldiers, mostly Uzbek. However, he sensed the imminent downfall of Najibullah and in February 1992 switched sides to the mujahideen, thus precipitating the end of communist rule in Afghanistan. As he moved south through the Salang Pass towards Kabul with a column of armoured vehicles to claim his reward, his attempt to team up with Massoud against their mutual enemy Hekmatyar backfired. Dostum's troops were also involved in numerous incidents of murder, rape, and pillage against non-Uzbek Afghans earning themselves the nickname *gelim jam*, meaning "carpet-baggers."

On New Year's Day 1994 he switched sides again and joined Hekmatyar in a combined assault on Kabul which destroyed large areas of the capital and nearly succeeded in dislodging Massoud. Dostum then concentrated on building his own fiefdom in the northern city of Mazar-e-Sharif, complete with its own army, flag, currency and airline – Balkh Air.

After the battle with the Taliban for Mazar-e-Sharif in May 1997, Dostum was ousted by his one-time ally Abdul Malik and retired to Turkey to plot his comeback. In September he returned – allegedly, with American backing – to take control of Mazar and hold the city against further Taliban attacks. With the help of Hezb-e-Wahdat and Massoud's Jamiat forces, he beat back the Taliban and then directed his wrath against Malik whom he drove into exile.

The troops at his command are thought to number between 40,000-60,000 along with perhaps a thousand tanks and armoured vehicles, 20 or more bombers and several Scud missile launchers. Arms and money come reportedly from Uzbekistan and Russia, both keen to support the only man preventing a Taliban-inflamed Islamic fundamentalism from spreading throughout the Central Asian states of the CIS. Dostum is keen to exploit the oil and natural gas fields of northern Afghanistan and capitalize on potential trading routes to Central Asia from Iran.

As a whisky drinker and an Uzbek, Dostum is hated by the zealous Taliban; as an ex-Communist and political chameleon he is widely mistrusted by everyone else. No wonder he drives a black bullet-proof Cadillac.

GAYLANI, Pir Sayed Ahmed (1932-)

Traditionalist leader of the National Islamic Front of Afghanistan. Born into a prominent Sufi family which claims descent from the Prophet, Gaylani read theology at Kabul University before fleeing the country after the Saur Revolution. He founded the National Islamic Front of Afghanistan (NIFA), the best known of the three 'traditionalist' mujahideen parties, and one of the seven parties to form the Afghan Interim Government (AIG) in Peshawar in 1989. His party was often called the Gucci Front by its detractors because of the veneer of urban sophistication associated with Pir's sons and nephews.

Gaylani had a large religious following based mainly in Paktya, Kandahar and other eastern provinces, and by 1989 could claim to have around 20,000 supporters. He was never trusted by the fundamentalists because of his pro-monarchist tendencies. He has lost much of his influence and is currently living in Pakistan.

HAQ, Abdul (1958-)

Leading ex-commander of the mujahideen. One of the most effective and autonomous Hezb-e-Islami (Younis Khalis faction) commanders during the 1980s, Haq specialized in hitting Soviet targets in and around Kabul. During the Soviet war, he lost his foot in a landmine accident, an injury which severely curtailed his previous ability to act as a flying urban resistance commander. After the overthrow of the communist Najibullah regime in April 1992, Abdul Haq was made Security Minister in the new mujahed interim "Islamic Council." A favourite of many foreign correspondents seeking to cover the Soviet war in the Kabul region, he has been described by one reporter as "the English-speaking acceptable face of Islamic fundamentalism." He is now involved in business, operating, amongst other things, an air cargo company from the Gulf to Afghanistan.

HEKMATYAR, Gulbuddin(1947-)

Leader of the main faction of Hezb-e-Islami, one of the seven former mujahed parties based in Peshawar. A 'transplanted' Ghilzai Pashtun born in 1947 in Baghlan province, Hekmatyar studied engineering at Kabul University but fled to Pakistan after the Daoud coup of 1973. In 1975 he became a leader of Jamiat-e-Islami, the forerunner of Hezb-e-Islami, and launched attacks into Afghanistan with the covert assistance of the Bhutto Government. From December 1978, as leader of one of two Hezb factions, "Engineer Gulbuddin" as he was often referred to, gathered around him a group of mujahed commanders, some sharing his Islamic fervour, others his access to weapons, money and other resources. Hekmatyar enjoyed extensive support from Pakistani Inter Services Intelligence (ISI) and the US Central Intelligence Agency (CIA) despite the fact that many experienced journalists and aid workers

Gulbuddin Hekmatyar
by Nicola Jennings

in the field never considered his party a particularly effective force against the Soviet occupation.

An opportunistic man of few scruples, Hekmatyar has aroused violent antagonism over the years among many of his fellow compatriots. Moderate resistance leader Sibghatullah Mujaddedi once publicly accused Hekmatyar of killing more innocent Afghans than Soviet troops, describing him as a monster created and sustained by Pakistani military intelligence. Hekmatyar's Hezb has also been accused of killing various individuals not to his liking, including at least two BBC journalists and a leading Afghan poet and intellectual, Dr Sayed Burhannudin Madjruh. Hekmatyar endeavoured to weaken his fellow resistance rivals either through direct attack or by pulling out of anti-Soviet operations at the last minute in order to preserve his forces and ammunition. Hezb also made repeated threats against one EFG editor during his years as a foreign correspondent covering the war. Despite such an unsavoury reputation, he remained a favourite of the ISI and the CIA, who helped ensure that his Hezb faction remained one of the most highly-funded resistance parties in Peshawar.

By 1989 Hekmatyar's supporters were thought to number around 15,000, mainly Pashtuns, although Hekmatyar often claimed to have as many as 50,000 under his command. Hezb-e-Islami was considered one of the most ideological and radical of the Islamist groups before the emergence of the Taliban. Hekmatyar has ruthlessly sought to establish himself as the leader of an Afghan Islamic Republic to be governed under Islamic law. His alliance with the Khalqi General Shahnawaz Tanai to stage a coup – heavily backed by the Pakistani government – against the Kabul Government of Dr Najibullah was perhaps a typical example of opportunism rather than ideology in his bid to succeed at all costs. Unfortunately for him, the assault proved an utter failure.

For two months between April and June 1992, Hekmatyar's forces indiscriminately pounded the capital with artillery, mortar and rocket fire in a successful attempt to oust his enemy, the moderate Sibghatullah Mujadeddi, from power. From mid-1992 to late 1994, he served nominally as Prime Minister of the Islamic State of Afghanistan under President Rabbani. However, he avoided basing himself inside Kabul owing to fears (probably highly justified) for his own security, particularly from bitter rivals such as former resistance leader and defence minister, Ahmed Shah Massoud. During this period, Hekmatyar linked up with General Dostum's forces forming the Shura-e-Hamahangi alliance to fight against the Shura-e-Nezar alliance which included the Jamiat-e-Islami forces of Massoud. By mid-1995 Shura-e-Hamahangi, comprising Hekmatyar, Dostum and Hezb-e-Wahdat, controlled at least seven provinces in the north.

During the battle for Kabul between 1992-1996 it was Hekmatyar's troops, based in the southern parts of the city and on the slopes of Sher-e-Darwaza, who inflicted much of the damage on the capital. In June 1996, he formed an alliance with his old sworn enemy Rabbani to resist the Taliban, and once again became Prime Minister of Afghanistan. In an attempt to appear as zealous as the Taliban, he made himself very unpopular by banning music, cinema and football in Kabul.

However, even the Pakistanis have now dropped their one-time stooge in favour of the more effective Taliban movement which swept into southern Afghanistan in 1994. Currently dwelling in uneasy exile in Tehran, Hekmatyar is trying to persuade Pakistan to support him once more. However, his ruthless ambition and shameless opportunism have estranged him from many of his erstwhile allies.

KARMAL, Babrak (1929-1996)

Former President of Afghanistan under the Soviets from December 1979 to 1986. Born in 1929 in Kabul, the Persian-speaking son of an army general, Karmal became intoxicated by the left-wing ideas released into the liberal atmosphere of King Zahir Shah's rule of the 1950s. A founder member in 1965 of the Marxist-Leninist People's Democratic Party of Afghanistan (PDPA), he disputed leadership of the party with Nur Mohammed Taraki in 1965 and led the non-Pashtun Parcham ('Banner') faction until it reunited, through Soviet mediation, with Taraki's Pashtun Khalq ('Masses') faction in 1977.

On 27 April 1978 the PDPA with backing from the Army and massive Soviet support staged the violent coup known as the Saur Revolution which killed President Daoud and established Taraki as the first PDPA President of the Democratic Republic of Afghanistan. Karmal was made Deputy Prime Minister but in July 1978 he fell foul of the Khalqi faction and was stripped of party membership and all his governmental positions. However, following the murders of both Taraki and his deputy Hafizullah Amin in late 1979, the Soviets decided to support the Parcham faction in order to avoid the new Communist Government being overthrown by an Islamic government. As a result, Karmal was brought back from his Ambassadorship in Prague and appointed the new President of Afghanistan with effect from 27 December 1979, the official date of the Soviet invasion.

Karmal's Kabul regime proved to be a puppet government, instigated and dictated to by the Soviets. It never formed any clear policies of its own, but instead became obsessed with internecine infighting which eventually led to the replacement of Karmal as President by Dr Najibullah in 1986.

Considered a KGB agent and traitor, Karmal is condemned by many Afghans as the man put in power at the point of a Russian bayonet. He left Afghanistan for Moscow at the height of his countrymen's war with the USSR and died there of liver cancer in December 1996.

KHALILI, Karim

Hazara *Shi'a* leader. Khalili has led the *Shi'a* resistance group Hezb-e-Wahdat Islami (Unity Party) since March 1995, when the previous leader, Abdul Ali Mazari, died in Taliban custody. Hezb-e-Wahdat was formed in June 1990 in order to consolidate power among the eight previous Iran-backed *Shi'a* mujahed groups. Hezb-e-Wahdat, however, has split into two groups, the larger of which is controlled by Khalili. Based in Bamiyan, his Hezb-e-Wahdat faction has held the balance of power in Mazar throughout much of 1997. Although Khalili denies Iranian military support of his faction, large amounts of food aid, engineering supplies and technical expertise are flown in by air from Tehran to his Bamiyan stronghold in central Afghanistan.

Khalili is currently part of Rabbani's and Dostum's anti-Taliban "Northern Alliance", also known as the United Islamic Front for the Salvation of Afghanistan (UIFSA).

KHALIS, Mohammed Younis (1919-)

Pashtun leader of his own Hezb-e-Islami faction. Born in 1919 in Gandamak, and educated in Islamic law and theology, Khalis is a radical Islamist and anti-Communist. Forced to flee Afghanistan after the Soviet-backed Daoud coup of 1973, he joined Hezb-e-Islami with Hekmatyar, then seceded to form his own faction to fight the

Soviets, launching attacks from Pakistan. His commanders included Abdul Haq in the Kabul area, Amin Wardak in Wardak and Haji Qadir (Abdul Haq's brother and later governor of Nangarhar province). One of the few political leaders to have taken an active part in military operations, Khalis was known as the "Fighting Mullah." He is opposed to universal suffrage and the emancipation of women. In May 1991, while serving as interior minister in the Afghan Interim Government (AIG) in Peshawar, he resigned because of his opposition to *Shi'a* participation. Khalis is notorious for taking a teenage wife in his later years.

KHAN, Ismail (1947-)

Top former mujahed commander and one-time "Amir of Herat". Born into a modest Tajik family in Shindand, 100 km south of Herat, Ismail Khan made his name by leading the anti-communist mutiny of March 1979 when, as a captain in the PDPA army, he disobeyed orders to fire on a mob in the Herat bazaar. Instead, his troops massacred 350 of Herat's Soviet advisors and their families. Moscow retaliated by carpet-bombing Herat, shattering historic mosques and mausolea and killing anywhere between 5,000 and 25,000 people. The mutiny sparked open rebellion against the communists throughout the province, but Khan left Herat to join Rabbani's party Jamiat-e-Islami.

The mid-1980s saw him constantly on the move as one of Jamiat's key commanders. He established his reputation as a staunch nationalist and diehard Islamist with a healthy disrespect for Iranian and Arabian interference. In 1993 he was quoted as saying "Nobody, not even the Iranians, can impose their will on us." More recently, he has been highly critical of mujahed infighting and foreign interference which have conspired to deny Afghanistan the peace for which he fought for so long.

By the early 1990s, Ismail Khan had established himself as self-styled Amir of Herat, building himself on a hill overlooking the city a palace which is still clearly visible. As Governor of Herat he exercised power over five provinces in southwestern Afghanistan; but he failed to hold back the Taliban advance on his fiefdom in September 1995. In May 1997 on a trip to Faryab he was captured by Uzbek warlord General Abdul Malik and handed over to the Taliban who flew him to Kandahar. Reportedly denied access to radio and newspapers, and not even granted pen or paper with which to write his memoirs, he communicates from his Kandahar jail with his family in Meshad, Iran via Red Cross messages.

MALIK, Abdul

Uzbek warlord. One of the Uzbek Pahlawan brothers of Badghis province, Malik rose to become a general in Abdul Rashid Dostum's Jumbesh-e-Melli party in northern Afghanistan. In May 1997 he allowed Taliban forces into Mazar in what appeared to be an attempt to switch sides and oust General Dostum. Two days later Malik turned against the Taliban and joined Hezb-e-Wahdat forces in massacring several hundred Taliban soldiers. Dostum, who had left Afghanistan to plot his return from the safety of Turkey, reappeared in Mazar in September 1997 and shortly afterwards defeated Malik, forcing him into (temporary) exile.

MASSOUD, Ahmed Shah (1956-)

Leading Tajik commander. Often referred to during the Soviet war as the "Lion of Panjshair", but also the Che Guevara and even Tito of Afghanistan, Massoud is currently military commander of Jamiat-e-Islami, and part of the anti-Taliban "Northern Alliance."

Born an ethnic Tajik, Ahmed Shah Massoud is one of the most successful and publicised mujahed commanders. Based initially in the Panjshair (the valley of "five tigers" or "five lions", but also, depending on how you pronounce it, "five milks") of Parwan province northeast of Kabul, he now occupies headquarters in Taloqan to the north. Having survived numerous Red Army attacks Massoud reached a temporary truce with the Soviets in 1983, although he continued to carry out guerrilla assaults throughout the northern region.

Renowned for instilling discipline into his troops and teaching modern tactical warfare techniques, Massoud has engaged in a bloody internecine war against Gulbuddin Hekmatyar's Hezb-e-Islami. In October 1990 the two factions appeared to reach a truce, but in 1992 Massoud's Shura-e-Nezar Shomal (Supervisory Council

Ahmed Shah Massoud (left) *E. Girardet*

of the North) continued to clash with Dostum's and Hekmatyar's Shura-e-Hamahangi alliance.

Considered a devout Muslim but also a pragmatic modernist, Massoud has always been aware of the plight of civilians. On several occasions during the Soviet war, he ordered the Panjshair to be temporarily abandoned by its population so that he could undertake military operations against the Soviets unhindered by humanitarian concerns. One of the reasons why Massoud has reportedly hesitated from launching – at this time of writing – any direct attacks against the Taliban in Kabul is for fear of causing even greater civilian suffering and further destruction of the city. He has made it clear that any return to Kabul by his forces would include a rescinding of all Taliban decrees. "People hate the Taliban," he claimed in a recent interview, "Once our government returns to Kabul, we will restore rights for women 100 percent."

Despite Massoud's popularity among many Afghans during the Soviet war – he was a charismatic favourite of the French media – his reputation suffered badly when he moved to Kabul following the overthrow of the Najib regime. As defence minister in the Rabbani government, he was surrounded mainly by his Panjshairi clique, some of whom indulged in severe abuses of power and corruption.

Since being ousted from Kabul by the Taliban in 1996, Massoud began once again to demonstrate the courage and leadership qualities for which he has long been known. While a number of his commanders crossed over to the Taliban, largely, it is reported, in return for bribes, Massoud announced to his fighters that they could leave, or stay with him to help oust the Taliban in what would probably be a long and arduous struggle. Many chose to stay.

MAZARI, Abdul Ali (d. 1995)

Former leader of the Iran-backed *Shi'a* group Hezb-e-Wahdat (Unity Party). Mazari was killed while being held by the Taliban in March 1995.

MOHAMMEDI, Mohammed Nabi (1921-)

Traditionalist Pashtun leader of Harakat-e-Inqilab-e-Islami. Mohammedi was born in Logar and educated at the local *madrassa*, from which he graduated as a *Mawlawi*. In the 1950s he was one of the first religious leaders to campaign against communist influences in the Afghan educational system. Elected to parliament in 1964 during King Zahir Shah's experiment with democracy, he fled to Pakistan after the Saur Revolution and organized armed resistance to the Kabul regime through a network of other *Mawlawis*. In the 1980s he was leader of the so-called Islamic moderates and concentrated more on liberating his country than personal advancement. Early on in the war, his party, Harakat-e-Inqilab-e-Islami (Islamic Revolutionary Movement) was one of the more effective of the seven resistance forces based in Peshawar during the Soviet War, and enjoyed widespread support from Paktya in the east of Afghanistan to Farah province bordering Iran. Harakat was more of a clerical association than a political party, and stood between fundamentalists seeking an Islamic state and the more secular-minded royalists. However, as the war ground on, Mohammedi lost many supporters to the more radical Islamist parties of Sayyaf and Rabbani. Currently living in Pakistan.

MUJADDEDI, Professor Sibghatullah (1925-)

Afghanistan's interim President, April to June 1992. Born in 1925 in Kabul, Mujaddedi comes from an aristocratic Ghilzai Pashtun family in southern Afghanistan. Leaders of a prominent Sufi mystical order, the Mujaddedis have been fierce nationalists ever since one of the family led the Shor Bazaar uprising against the British in Kabul in the 19th Century. After studying at Cairo's prestigious al-Azhar Islamic University, he became professor of Islamic philosophy at Kabul University. A radical anti-communist, he was jailed from 1959-1964 for involvement in a purported plot to assassinate the Soviet premier Nikita Khrushchev. His protests against growing Soviet influence in the early 1970s forced him into exile, and at the time of the Saur Revolution he was head of the Islamic Centre in Copenhagen. When over 70 members of his clan were picked out by the communists and murdered, he returned to Pakistan to found and lead the armed resistance of the traditionalist and moderate National Liberation Front of Afghanistan, always the smallest of the seven Peshawar-based resistance parties.

Throughout the 1980s, his largely Pashtun guerrilla force was considered ineffective by Western arms suppliers, although he believes the ISI, Pakistan's military intelligence service, fabricated this myth to funnel more weapons towards their stooge, Gulbuddin Hekmatyar. In March 1989 he was first named President of the so-called Afghan Interim Government (AIG), a Peshawar-based rebel administration-in-exile. Many believed he was given the role precisely because he was the weakest of the seven mujahed leaders operating from Pakistan.

In April 1992 he swept into Kabul as the unlikely head of the new mujahed interim "Islamic Council", ending 14 years of communist rule in Afghanistan. "We are all Muslims", he said, "It is now time for us to join hands in unity and work for the reconstruction of our homeland." However, in a country filled with armed radicals, the tolerant Mujaddedi, who had even extended the olive branch to former collaborators of the communist regime, could not last. After two months of shelling from his hated enemy, the radical Islamist Gulbuddin Hekmatyar, he was ousted as President by Burhannudin Rabbani, and departed Kabul an embittered man.

As an Islamic moderate and an aristocrat, Mujaddedi makes no secret of his monarchist tendencies; he continues to play a role in peacemaking efforts. Currently living in Pakistan.

MUHSENI, Mohammed Asif (1935-)

Hazara leader of the Shi'a mujahed faction Harakat-e-Islami. Born in Kandahar and educated in the *Shi'a* universities of Iraq, Muhseni is called Ayatollah by his supporters. On returning to Afghanistan he founded the rural-based mujahed group Harakat-e-Islami (Islamic Movement of Afghanistan), and in 1980 was elected chairman of the "Afghan *Shi'a* Alliance," a mujahed umbrella group headquartered in Iran. In the 1980s, Harakat-e-Islami was the largest and most important of the eight Iran-backed *Shi'a* groups.

In June 1990 the *Shi'a* groups announced the formation a new organization called Hezb-e-Wahdat (Unity Party) in an attempt to consolidate *Shi'a* power. At this time of writing, Muhseni has not – so far – joined the coalition.

NAJIBULLAH, Mohammed (1947-1996)

Communist President of the Republic of Afghanistan 1986 to 1992, executed by the Taliban in September 1996. Born in 1947 in Kabul to Ghilzai Pashtun parents, Najibullah graduated from the College of Medicine at Kabul University in 1975. In 1965 he joined the Parcham faction of the PDPA, and was purged from government by Taraki along with other Parchamis in 1978. He remained abroad, but returned to Kabul with Babrak Karmal after the Soviet invasion in December 1979. Known as the 'ox,' he was president of KHAD, the secret police or State Information Service, from 1980-1986. In May 1986, Najib (another nickname) replaced Karmal as President of Afghanistan and Secretary-General of the PDPA.

Continuing friction between Parcham and Khalq factions led to further fragmentation of the PDPA into half a dozen or more splinter groups, encouraged by the Soviets who adopted this policy of divide and rule to ensure no one faction became too powerful or potentially anti-Soviet. Najib successfully headed off a Khalqi coup in March 1990, organized by his own defence minister Shahnawaz Tanai, although the Army was still very pro-Khalq. Under Najibullah the Army and all government ministries were dictated to by the USSR. Priority was given to education and the social services, all modelled on Soviet examples, and the media and all cultural institutions such as theatres and music were controlled by the Soviets.

Najibullah presided over the withdrawal of Soviet troops in February 1989, but increased armed conflict between his government and opposition mujahed forces resulted in the UN replacing him in April 1992 with a four-member council of the ruling Watan party (lit. 'Fatherland' party – previously the PDPA), followed soon afterwards by Mujaddedi then Rabbani as Presidents.

When the Taliban took Kabul in September 1996, Najibullah welcomed their arrival, but not for long. They dragged him out of his refuge in a UN compound, shot him dead and hanged his body by the neck from a lamp-post in the middle of Kabul, the symbolism of which did little to endear the Taliban movement to the West.

QADIR, Haji

Ex-Governor of Nangarhar province. Qadir, a former merchant with business links to (West) Germany, operated as a guerrilla commander during the Afghan-Soviet war, before assuming the governorship of Nangarhar following the mujahed takeover of Jalalabad. After the arrival of the Taliban, Qadir pulled back from the governorship. He is a brother of former guerrilla commander Abdul Haq.

RABBANI, Burhannudin (1940-)

President of the Islamic State of Afghanistan from June 1992 to September 1996. Born an ethnic Tajik in 1940 in Faizabad, Badakhshan province, and educated at Kabul and Cairo Universities in Islamic Studies, Rabbani was a founding father of the anti-communist Islamist movement from the late 1950s onwards. An inspirational Kabul campus leader in the mid 1960s, shortly after Afghanistan's Communist Party was founded, he attacked the relatively liberal regime of the King for its secular modernization and communist sympathies. In 1971 he was selected as leader of Jamiat-e-Islami (Islamic Society of Afghanistan) and in 1974 he fled from Daoud's regime into Pakistan, seeking government support there against left-wing influences in Afghanistan. In 1975 failed Jamiat raids into Afghanistan revealed policy differences between Rabbani and Hekmatyar which led to the latter forming his own Hezb-e-Islami party in 1976. Rabbani continued to lead the Jamiat after the Saur Revolution. Throughout the Soviet-Afghan war, Rabbani remained based in Peshawar before moving to Kabul in 1992.

Jamiat became one of the largest and best organized of the resistance groups during the Soviet War with an array of highly effective guerrilla "fronts of the interior" affiliated with the party in return for outside support, weapons and other supplies. By 1989 it had an estimated 20,000 followers, mainly Tajiks from northern and western Afghanistan, but including some Pashtuns. Rabbani's legendary senior military commander is Ahmed Shah Massoud. Another leading Tajik mujahed commander is Ismail Khan.

In June 1992 Rabbani took over power of the new mujahed interim "Islamic Council" from Sibghatullah Mujaddedi and declared the Islamic State of Afghanistan. In contrast to the moderate Mujaddedi, Rabbani called for the radical transformation of Afghan society on the basis of Islamic law and Koranic principles. He was elected President in December 1992 and Hekmatyar was appointed his Prime Minister. However, this fragile interim government was not destined to last. Vicious fighting over Kabul erupted in the first half of 1994 with President Rabbani's and Defence Minister Massoud's Shura-e-Nezar forces pitted against those of Dostum's and Hekmatyar's Shura-e-Hamangi forces.

The emergence of the Taliban in late 1994 and their capture of Kabul in September 1996 spelt the end of Rabbani's term of leadership. Based now in northern Afghanistan, Rabbani currently heads the anti-Taliban "Northern Alliance", also known as the United Islamic Front for the Salvation of Afghanistan (UIFSA).

SAYYAF, Abdul Rasul (1946-)

Leader of the radical fundamentalist Ittehad-e-Islami. After theological training at Kabul University and al-Azhar in Cairo, Sayyaf joined the Islamist movement under Rabbani. In 1980 he became the spokesman for the mujahideen alliance in Peshawar, and two years later formed his own group, Ittehad-e-Islami (Islamic Union for the Liberation of Afghanistan), which was the smallest of the *Sunni* fundamentalist factions. Sayyaf is an eloquent Arabic speaker and secured considerable financial support from Arabic Gulf states, especially the Saudi royal family. Ideologically close to Hekmatyar and Khalis, he was however accused of allying himself with Arab *Wahabi* groups.

Currently thought to be supporting the anti-Taliban Kunar uprising, Sayyaf himself is residing in Kunduz.

ZAHIR SHAH, Mohammed (1914-)

King of Afghanistan from 1933 to 1973. Zahir Shah was proclaimed monarch within hours of the assassination of his father, Nadir Shah. His cousin Mohammed Daoud was Prime Minister from 1953-1963, until Zahir Shah forced his resignation. In 1964 he introduced a new constitution which limited the role of the royal family in government and provided for free elections, a free press and the formation of political parties.

Kabul grew considerably through the flow of economic aid from both the East and the West, but many sectors of Afghan society did not benefit from this development. In 1973 while on a trip abroad the King was ousted in a coup by Mohammed Daoud who proclaimed Afghanistan a republic with himself as President. Zahir Shah abdicated shortly afterwards and has lived near Rome ever since.

During the late 1980s both the US and the Soviet Union were promoting the idea of Zahir Shah returning to Afghanistan not as King but as State President of a 'neutral' and coalition government. This administration could have held a "Loya Jirga" or National Council of tribal, resistance and religious leaders to form a consensus on the possibility of future elections.

Unlike their often misguided support of extremist Muslim fundamentalist factions, the Americans viewed the King as a moderate who would work to avert a bloody civil war for power among patriotic and extreme religious rivals in the wake of a Soviet withdrawal.

The monarchist cause was popular among other moderate leaders, such as Sibghatullah Mujaddedi who believed that the King was the only real symbol of national unity. This notion, however, was anathema to radical Islamists such as Gulbuddin Hekmatyar,

The Frontier Post 12 January 1992

who blamed the origin of Afghanistan's troubles on the King and his acquiescence to communist ambitions.

Zahir himself declined US proposals for a government-in-exile and later dismissed President Najibullah's offer to share power. "I have no ambition to restore the monarchy," he has repeated over and over again. "All I want is to restore the unity and prosperity of my country." Even now, some Afghans see the return of the King and the prospect of a "Loya Jirga" as the only hope for uniting their fragmented country. But at the age of 83 time is running out for Zahir Shah.

TALIBAN KEY PLAYERS

OMAR, Mullah Mohammed

Leader of the Taliban movement. Also known as Amir ul-Momineen (Prince of All Believers). Mullah Omar is Supreme Leader of the Taliban movement which swept to power through southern Afghanistan in 1994. He leads a reclusive life in Kandahar and refuses to meet foreign diplomats, journalists, aid agencies or UN officials. A former mujahed, he was wounded fighting the Russians, and had one eye removed at the Red Cross hospital in Quetta.

Officially aged 37, he was born into a poor family in Maiwand district near Kandahar. In the early 1990s he launched a movement from his local *madrassa* to combat the moral degradation to which he felt the mujahideen had succumbed. The main goal of the movement, whose membership is limited to *Taliban* (Islamic students) only, is to rid Afghanistan of "corrupt Western-oriented timeservers," and re-establish the rule of *shari'a*. Ironically for the leader of one of the most fundamentalist Islamic regimes in the world, he has, in the Governor of Kandahar's words, "not too much religious knowledge." Nevertheless his authority in all military operations and over the Taliban six-man ruling *shura* is absolute. Mullah Omar claims to support the possibility of peace negotiations, even with ex-communists such as General Dostum, and had this to say to the Pakistani newspaper *The News on Sunday* about female Afghans:

"As for women's rights, we are willing to talk about it and we feel Islam has given the most rights to women. We aren't opposed to girls' education but we have to decide about our priorities keeping in view our meagre resources. Islam supports education for both men and women and we have every intention of following Islamic teachings."

RABBANI, Mullah Mohammed

Head of Kabul Council and Deputy Leader of Taliban Movement

GHAOS, Haji Mullah Mohammed

Acting Minister of Foreign Affairs

HASSAN, Mullah Mohammed

Governor of Kandahar

MOTAQI, Mullah

Acting Minister of Information and Culture

TOURABI, Mullah

Notoriously hardline one-eyed, one-legged acting Justice Minister

Landmines summary

- **Total area contaminated by landmines: 725 sq.km**
- **Total high-priority contaminated area remaining: 324 sq.km**
- **Over 10 Afghans are killed or injured by mines & UXOs every day**
- **In 1997, five deminers from the UNOCHA Mine Action Programme were killed and nearly 70 injured in the course of duty**
- **In 1997, over 800,000 people received mine awareness training**
- **43.5 sq.km of new minefields have been laid since 1995**

Sources: UNOCHA, 1998, United Nations Consolidated Appeal for Afghanistan, January 1998

ESSENTIAL CONTACTS

ATC, DAFA, HALO Trust, HI, MAG, MCPA, MDC, OMAR, SC-US, UNOCHA
The United Nations demining database: http://www.un.org/Depts/Landmineswww.un.org/Depts/Landmines

ESSENTIAL READING

Living in a minefield: A report on the mine problem in Afghanistan, Médecins Sans Frontières (May 1997)
Landmines: Legacy of Conflict. A manual for development workers, Rae McGrath, Oxfam (1994)
Landmines: A Deadly Legacy, Human Rights Watch (1993)
Afghanistan Mine Clearance Programme, Workplan 1997, UNOCHA
Antipersonnel landmines, Facts and chronologies, Handicap International (2nd Edition, 1997)
Landmines: demining news from the UN – monthly

For practical advice on mine awareness and how to avoid mines while in Afghanistan SEE SECURITY TIPS

Language & poetry

The two main languages of Afghanistan are Dari (Afghan Persian/Farsi) and Pashto, both from the Iranian branch of the Indo-European family. Dari literally means "language of the court" and was the court language in Moghul India, just as it is the *lingua franca* of modern Afghanistan. Pashto, however, is officially the national language. Both languages use the Arabic script, written horizontally from right to left, but they are no more mutually intelligible than English is to German. Pashto is itself often divided into the softer 'Pushtu' of the Kandahar area, and the harder 'Pukhtu' of the North West Frontier Province.

The late American writer and archaeologist Louis Dupree makes the point that Afghanistan has a literate culture, but a non-literate society: "Most literate or non-literate Afghans, be they Persian-, Pashto-, or Turkic-speakers, consider themselves poets. Poetry, essentially a spoken, not a written, art, gives non-literates the same general opportunities for expression as the literates in a society. Afghanistan, therefore is fundamentally a nation of poets." (*Afghanistan, 1973*)

Poetry in Afghanistan flowered from the 9th to the 17th Centuries, climaxing in the cultural oasis of the court of Mahmud of Ghazni in the early 11th Century. In his court lived 900 scholars and 400 poets, probably the greatest of which was Firdausi, whose *Shah-Namah, Book of the Kings of Persia* had 60,000 couplets. Abdullah Ansari, the Pir of Herat (1005-1088 AD), was a Sufi leader who composed poetry to express his journey from orthodox religion to mysticism. Perhaps the greatest of the Pashto poets are the 17th Century Khushal Khan Khattak (1613-1690) and Rahman Baba. Khushal is the epitome of the Pashtun warrior-poet, the ideal Afghan character-type, who revelled as much in the beauty of man and nature as in waging war on neighbouring Moghuls or hostile Pashtuns. Rahman Baba, a contemporary of Khushal, was inspired by Sufism to turn more towards religious mysticism than to war.

The following is a selection of Afghan poetry, both Persian and Pashtun:

"If leadership rests inside the lion's jaw,
So be it. Go, snatch it from his jaw.
Your lot shall be greatness, prestige, honour and glory.
If all fails, face death like a man."

– Hanzala of Badghis, 9th Century AD
(trans. S. Shpoon)

"My beauty, I cannot exchange you for the cash of my life.
You are priceless. I will not sell you so cheap.
I hold your skirt with both my hands.
I may loosen my hold on my life, but not my hold on your skirt."

– Mahmud Warraq, 9th Century
(trans. S. Shpoon)

"From among all the good and bad things of the world,
Daqiqi has chosen four:
Ruby-red lips, the wail of the flute,
Blood-coloured wine, and the Zoroastrian religion."

– Daqiqi of Balkh, 10th Century
(trans. S. Shpoon)

"The Lasses of the Adam Khel,
As every lover knows,
Are delicately coloured – like
The petals of a rose;
My Love a snowy partridge is,
Who chooses winter time
To seek among the stony fells
A cloak of silver rime.
My Love, my Bird, remember that
A hawk, when he grows old,
Becomes more subtle in the chase,
His stoop becomes more bold:
Surrender then to me, for though
I seem no longer young,
The fervour of my love will taste
Like honey on your tongue."

Khushal Khan Khattak, 17th Century
(trans. Bowen)

"Your face is a rose and your eyes are candles:
Faith! I am lost. Should I become a butterfly or a moth?"

"My beloved returned unsuccessful from battle;
I regret the kiss I gave him last night."

"If you don't wield a sword, what else will you do?
You, who have suckled at the breast of an Afghan mother!"

– Traditional 'landay' or Pashto couplets

A Pathan Warrior's Farewell

"Beloved, on a parchment white
With my heart's blood to thee I write;
My pen a dagger, sharp and clean,
Inlaid with golden damascene,
Which I have used, and not in vain,
To keep my honour free from stain.
Now, when our house its mourning wears,
Do not thyself give way to tears:
Instruct our eldest son that I
Was ever anxious thus to die,
For when Death comes the brave are free –
So in thy dreams remember me."

– anon

Maps

A surprisingly large range of maps of Afghanistan and the region is available, although the accuracy of all but the latest sheets cannot be guaranteed. One EFG editor used a combination of tactical air pilotage charts, a CIA satellite map and a British 1893 map torn out of a book to travel through northeastern Afghanistan during the early 1980s. The aerial maps covered topography with a few select locations – some completely wrong – while the old map of the British Raj had more accurate names of villages and rivers albeit with curious spellings.

The most detailed work on mapping is currently being carried out by a partnership of the United Nations Development Program (UNDP) Islamabad, the Food and Agriculture Organization (FAO) of the UN in Rome, the French NGO ACTED and the Afghan Geodesy and Cartography Head Office. This partnership has produced a Land Cover Map of Afghanistan using recent satellite imagery, and is now updating a comprehensive database on Afghanistan for use in compiling more detailed maps in the future.

These latest maps are computerized. This enables a number of different layers to be built up, each with its accompanying database of information sitting 'behind' the visual image. The process is known as GIS (Geographic Information Systems), whereby existing maps are scanned into a computer in a digitized format and then linked to a database of information, ultimately enabling the map to be 'questioned.' The first layer is the baseline map detailing topography, roads and buildings; subsequent layers could cover anything from minefield locations to water resources. Layers are created by a combination of remote-sensed satellite imagery and ground reconnaissance.

In addition to the UNDP/FAO Land Use Map, the United Nations Centre for Human Settlements (UNCHS Habitat) has produced detailed GIS urban mapping for Kabul, Herat and Mazar. ACBAR Resource and Information Centre (ARIC) produces clear line-diagram street maps of Peshawar, Kabul and Jalalabad showing the locations of key agencies. ACBAR has also produced maps of NGO operations in Afghanistan by sector and by province.

Many NGOs and humanitarian agencies are now making their own maps using GIS programmes called MapMaker and MapMaker Pro which can be downloaded from the Internet. (See ESSENTIAL DATA below)

The ARIC Library in Peshawar stocks over 100 different map titles, ranging from US Defence Mapping Agency sheets to provincial maps and city street-plans. The library also offers a map photocopying service.

One of the most comprehensive mapping resources available on Afghanistan is the *National Atlas of the Democratic Republic of Afghanistan*, produced by GEOKART Poland in 1985. It comprises 63 colour maps illustrating all aspects of Afghanistan's physical and socio-economic geography. Based on data from 1975-1981, it is still available in bookshops in Kabul.

Probably the only available source for maps of smaller Afghan towns and cultural sites is Nancy Hatch Dupree's *An Historical Guide to Afghanistan* (2nd Edition, 1977) which can be found in bookshops in Peshawar and Kabul, or through ARIC Peshawar. In a wallet at the back of the book is a very clear but rather out of date street map of Kabul which is still useful for general orientation.

US military maps, produced from remote satellite imaging, of the entire region can be tracked down at Stanford's in London and the ARIC Library in Peshawar. Tactical Air Pilotage Charts (1:500,000) and Operational Navigational Charts (1:1,000,000) give detailed if somewhat out-of-date coverage of the whole country.

One of the largest private map collections in the world is held at the Royal Geographical Society in London. It contains 900,000 sheets of maps and charts, 2,500 atlases, 40 globes and 700 gazetteers. It has numerous maps of Afghanistan, and those out of copyright may be photocopied. The Map Room is freely open for consultation by any "serious enquirer" on weekdays from 1100 hrs to 1700 hrs.

The following maps of Afghanistan and the region are listed, by country and city, in order of publication, with the most recently published listed first. Actual map titles are in bold. Those maps dated before 1984 do not contain the 'new' provinces of Kunar and Paktika, and those dated before 1992 do not show the newly-independent Central Asian Republics.

AFGHANISTAN:

AFGHANISTAN, PAKISTAN

1:2 million
Geocenter UK Ltd.
1993/94
96x98cm
A striking shaded-relief map of these 2 countries which also stretches into the neighbouring states. Different grades of towns and roads are shown along with airports and time zone boundaries. Restricted areas, National Parks and sites of particular interest are also indicated.
Available from: Edward Stanford, UK (£5.99)

LAND COVER MAP: ISLAMIC STATE OF AFGHANISTAN

1:1.25 million + 1:250,000 sheets
FAO and Afghan Geodesy and Cartography Head Office
June 1997
Using US Land Satellite data from 1990 & 1993 for land cover information, and air photography from the late 1950s for topographical information, UNDP, FAO, ACTED, and the Afghan Geodesy and Cartography Head Office are cooperating on the production of up-to-date land cover 1:250,000 maps for all of Afghanistan.
Detail included in the Land Use sheet includes: Urban Areas, Agricultural Land, Forest and Rangeland, Barren Land, and Water Bodies/Other.
The next 2 years of project development will see the combination of USAID-funded database information from the early 1990s with remotely-sensed data to create the most accurate maps of the country ever. The results will be published in an atlas and on CD-Rom.
For more details contact:
Assistant Resident Representative, UNDP, Islamabad.
TEL: +92 (51) 211451-5
FAX: +92 (51) 211450

AFGHANISTAN

Scale: N/K
Map No. 3958 UNITED NATIONS
October 1996 (Colour)
Published by Department of Public Information – Cartographic Section
A three-colour map showing provinces, major towns and rivers, roads railways and airports, and surrounding countries.

AFGHANISTAN

1:1.5 million
Swedish Committee for Afghanistan
2nd edition 1991
100x70cm
This administrative and physical (colour relief-shaded) wall map includes 4 inserts: a 1:1 million scale map of the area around Kabul, a basic street plan of Kabul and economy and ethnography maps. An index booklet to place names and districts with supplementary population information accompanies the map.
Available from:
Edward Stanford, UK (£13.99);
Swedish Committee for Afghanistan,
GPO 689, Peshawar, Pakistan.
TEL: +92 (91) 840218
FAX: + 92 (91) 840519
E-mail: sca@Peshawr.psw.erum.com.pk

Svenska Afghanistankommitten
Essingeringen 90, S-112 6, Stockholm, Sweden.

AFGHANISTAN

1:1.5 million
Nelles (Maps)
68x50cm
This is a physical map with numerous spot heights. Roads are clear and are annotated with distances. Airstrips and places of interest are also shown. A simple plan of Kabul is inset, showing main street names and relative positions of monuments and public buildings.
Available:
Edward Stanford, UK (£5.95);
Bookshops in Islamabad and Peshawar;
Nelles Verlag,
Schleissheimer Str.371b,
D-80935 Munchen,
Germany.

MAP OF AFGHANISTAN
1:1.6 million
English and Arabic
Printed 1987
Includes 1981 population and land area in sq. km by province
Published by:
Gita Shenassi Institute, 1st Floor, 15 Arfa' St., Vali-ye-Asr Crossroad,
Inqilab Avenue, PO Box 14155-3441, Tehran, Iran
TEL: 679335 Telex: 213636D.5090

THE NATIONAL ATLAS OF THE DEMOCRATIC REPUBLIC OF AFGHANISTAN
63 colour maps on 36 pages
English and Dari
GEOKART Poland
Published 1985
Available: Some Kabul bookshops

ALPENVEREINSKARTE
Darrah-e-Issik-e-Bala (1:25,000 – 1978)
Koh-e-Pamir (1:50,000 – 1978)
Koh-e-Keshnikhan (1:25,000 – 1970)
Detailed mountaineering maps with contour-intervals of 20-40 metres
All available from: Edward Stanford, UK (£10.95)

POLITICAL MAP OF AFGHANISTAN
1:2 million
Published by the Afghan Cartographic and Cadastral Survey Institute, Kabul
2nd edition 1976
Colourful, but does not show new provinces of Kunar and Paktika.
Available: Most Kabul bookshops

KABUL:

UNDP/UNCHS Habitat:
Numerous GIS-generated maps of Kabul including the following:
Map of Kabul City
Kabul Water Reticulation Network Map
Mine Affected Areas of Kabul City
For more details contact:
Regional Programme Manager, UNCHS (Habitat), 5-B College Road,
F-7/3, Islamabad, Pakistan.
TEL: +92 (51) 272529
FAX: +92 (51) 274358

ACBAR/ARIC:
Clear line-diagram street plans, regularly updated and showing locations of key local and international agencies, as follows:
Shahr-e-Naw
Wazir Akbar Khan

KABUL
1:15,000
Feb 95/Jan 97
Colour map produced by Kabul Emergency Program Feb 95. The black and white version includes population estimates, and lists of hospitals as at Jan 97

KABUL CITY
1:25,000
Afghan Cartographic Institute 1972
In Nancy Dupree's *An Historical Guide to Kabul* (2nd Edition, 1972).

HERAT:

UNDP/UNCHS (Habitat):
Herat City Guide Map
Very detailed GIS-generated map showing key agency locations
January 1997

British NGO Shelter Project (BNSP):
Hand-drawn street plan
September 1993

JALALABAD:

ACBAR/ARIC:
Clear line-diagram street plan of Jalalabad showing locations of key local and international agencies

KANDAHAR:

Street-plan available from UNOCHA office, Kandahar.

PESHAWAR:

ACBAR/ARIC:
Clear line-diagram street plans, regularly updated, showing locations of key local and international agencies as follows:
University Town
Rahatabad, Nimat Mahal, Danishabad, Tajabad, Board, Nasir Bagh
Tahkal, Defence Colony, Kababian, Shami Road, Cantt., Dabgari
Hayatabad Town

See also maps in tourist guidebooks listed below.

ISLAMABAD:

UNWA:
The United Nations Women's Association (UNWA) has produced a guide to Islamabad and Rawalpindi entitled *Welcome to Pakistan* (1997). The following useful street maps are contained:
Super Market – Sector F-6
Jinnah Market – Sector F-7
Melody Market – Sector G-9
Aabpara Market
Blue Area
Rawalpindi Bazaars
Shifa Hospital

See also maps in tourist guidebooks listed below.

ESSENTIAL DATA

Map suppliers include:

- **MapMaker GIS programme details:**
Website: http://www.ibmpcug.co.uk/~MapMaker/-
Software: ftp://ftp.win-uk.net/pub/users/MapMaker/mm32zip.exe

- **Edward Stanford Ltd. (UK)**
12-14 Long Acre, Covent Garden
London WC2E 9LP, UK.
TEL: +44 (171) 836 1321 FAX: +44 (171) 836 0189

- **Karto Grafik**
Schonberger Weg 15-17, 6000 Frankfurt/Main 90
Germany.

- **East View Publications, Inc.**
3020 Harbour Lane North, Suite 110
Minneapolis, MN 55447, USA.
TEL: +1 (612) 550 0961 FAX: +1 (612) 559 2931
E-mail: eastview@eastview.com

- **Map Room, Royal Geographical Society**
(with The Institute of British Geographers)
1 Kensington Gore, London SW7 2AR, UK.
TEL: +44 (171) 591 3050 FAX: +44 (171) 591 3001
E-mail: maps@rgs.org

ESSENTIAL AGENCIES

ACTED, Aid for Aid (British company), ARIC, FAO, MapMaker Ltd., ResponseNet (part of Delorme mapping), RGS, SCA, UNCHS (Habitat), UNDP, Volunteers in Technical Assistance (VITA, German NGO)

ESSENTIAL READING

Historical Guide to Afghanistan, Nancy Hatch Dupree (2nd Edition, 1977): includes removable street map of Kabul and plans of many Afghan towns.

Pakistan Handbook, Isobel Shaw, The Guidebook Company (Hong Kong, 1996): includes maps of Islamabad, Peshawar and the North West Frontier Province.

Pakistan – a travel survival kit, John King & David St.Vincent, Lonely Planet (1995): includes maps of Islamabad, Peshawar and the North West Frontier Province.

Central Asia, Giles Whittell, Cadogan Guides (1996): includes maps of Turkmenistan, Uzbekistan, Tajikistan, Kirghizstan and Kazakhstan with street maps of major cities.

ARIC Shelf Check for Maps, ACBAR Peshawar (June 1996):
Lists over 100 map titles held by the ARIC Library and available for copying.

Refugees summary

1978: First refugees begin fleeing from midsummer onwards as fighting erupts in the wake of the Saur (April) Revolution.

1979: 600,000 refugees by the end of the year, fleeing to Pakistan (400,000) and Iran (200,000).

1980-83: Refugee exodus increases dramatically to 3.9 million as Soviet-Afghan military strikes against the resistance, including deliberate attacks on the civilian population in what some observers describe as "migratory genocide."

1987: Refugee populations in Pakistan, Iran and elsewhere reach 5.9 million.

1989: Red Army troops withdraw in February. Fighting in Afghanistan reverts to that of a civil war as mujahideen continue their battle against the communist PDPA Kabul regime. Refugee numbers continue to rise to 6.1 million despite some refugee returns.

1990: The Afghan exile population reaches a record 6.2 million, nearly half the world's total refugee population. An estimated 350,000 have returned to Afghanistan since 1988.

1992: Najibullah's communist government falls to the mujahideen in April. An estimated 1.6 million refugees return home.

1993-94: Factional fighting devastates much of Kabul with fighters often showing complete disregard for civilians. Up to one million internal refugees ("internally displaced persons" or IDPs) are now believed to have fled to other parts of the country. Another 1.3 million external refugees return to peaceful areas of the country. 3.4 million refugees still outside the country at the end of the year.

1994: Taliban forces capture Kandahar. Refugee numbers continue to fall slowly with returns.

1995: Taliban capture Herat in September. Repatriation of refugees from Iran comes to a halt. The Taliban reach the outskirts of Kabul. Refugee numbers stabilize at 2.7 million.

1996: Taliban capture Kabul in September. Fighting continues in northern and central Afghanistan.

1997: Refugee population in exile stands at 2.6 million.

Source: UNHCR

ESSENTIAL CONTACTS

BAAG, FRCS, ICRC, MSF, UNHCR, UNICEF, WFP

ESSENTIAL READING

Living in Exile: Report on a study of economic coping strategies among Afghan refugees in Pakistan, British Agencies Afghanistan Group (London, December 1996)
Exile and Return: Report on a study on coping strategies among Afghan refugees in Iran and returnees to Afghanistan, British Agencies Afghanistan Group (London, June 1996)
Going Home: a guidebook for refugees, International Federation of Red Cross and Red Crescent Societies (Sarajevo, 1997)
Tradition and Dynamism Among Afghan Refugees, International Labour Organisation
Disposable People? The Plight of Refugees, Judy Mayotte, Orbis Books
Left out in the Cold: The Perilous Homecoming of Afghan Refugees, Hiram A Ruiz, US Committee for Refugees
Long Years of Exile: Central Asian Refugees in Afghanistan and Pakistan, Dr Shalinsky, University Press of America
Refugees, II – 1997, Afghanistan: the unending crisis, UNHCR (Issue No. 108)
The State of the World's Refugees: A Humanitarian Agenda, UNHCR (1997)

Relief, rehabilitation & development

Most of the international aid operations in Afghanistan – in both Taliban and non-Taliban areas – are involved in emergency or basic rehabilitation programmes. To speak of development is too ambitious. Much of the country has been destroyed and it will take years for it to return to pre-1978 levels of infrastructure. It is difficult – and costly – to undertake any real long-term development on a nationwide basis as long as there is war. In addition, donors are reluctant to commit cash to lengthy development programmes in such unstable circumstances, making it difficult for many agencies to plan ahead.

This said, aid agencies are in the process of trying to move out of emergency assistance to more sustainable long-term projects. At the same time, it will prove no easy task to step away from the emergency level. The pressures of overcrowding, often aggravated by refugee returns (or refugee influxes in the case of renewed fighting) continue to stretch existing water and sanitation facilities, while landmine clearance is expected to dominate recovery for decades to come. What many people still need more than anything else is assistance to help alleviate chronic poverty through the provision of food aid, winter relief and basic health care.

UN and NGO involvement

The United Nations and other organizations involved in the rehabilitation process have been aware of such problems for quite some time. Following the departure of the Soviets in February 1989, the UN decided to direct much of its attention toward strengthening indigenous capacity within Afghanistan. UN officials believed that existing international and local NGOs lacked the means to meet most of the country's reconstruction needs. Nevertheless, up till then, a number of international humanitarian organizations, such as the Swedish Committee for Afghanistan (SCA), Médecins Sans Frontières (MSF) and MADERA had been providing humanitarian relief, including limited forms of rehabilitation, with considerable success despite the hazards of an ongoing conflict.

The UN, on the other hand, had restricted itself mainly to refugee programmes in Pakistan and a few activities in government-controlled areas of Afghanistan. The UN's failure to insist on providing more appropriate humanitarian assistance inside the country during the Soviet war may have actually contributed toward aggravating the refugee exodus. According to journalists and relief workers travelling clandestinely in these regions, many farmers might have remained inside Afghanistan had they received the means to repair the damage inflicted by Soviet assaults against civilian populations – means such as new seeds, tools or food to survive until the next harvest.

By finally involving itself more directly in Afghanistan in the 1990s, the UN encouraged the creation of new Afghan NGOs, most of which worked under contract with the UN. Other organizations, such as the United Nations High Commissioner for Refugees (UNHCR) sought to obtain further information on the places of origin of most refugees in order to assess their needs, if and when, they should return. By stimulating rehabilitation work in these areas to improve conditions, it was felt, the resettlement of some six million refugees would be facilitated.

To a degree, this approach has worked. According to UN sources, there has been a clear correlation between such rehabilitation activities and refugee returns. During the initial stages, however, most of these programmes operated in the largely Pashtun eastern provinces bordering Pakistan. This was mainly because of logistical access but also because of Pakistani pressure to relocate humanitarian operations near predominately Pashtun cities such as Jalalabad and Kandahar. This, the Pakistanis believed, would help firmly establish a mujahed 'government' presence inside Afghanistan, if possible under their own control. It was only with the fall of Kabul in April 1992 to the mujahideen that UN agencies and NGOs were able to operate on a similar scale in other mainly non-Pashtun areas, notably the west and the north.

Two decades of war have left Afghanistan's capacity to shelter and feed itself shattered. Despite numerous small-scale developmental initiatives which have been implemented in the quieter regions of the country, relief still plays a major role in acting as an humanitarian bridge between the desperate day-to-day situation of many Afghans and their uncertain future. In Kabul, where over half of all the city's homes have been destroyed, where government ministries are strangled by lack of cash and resources, where food supplies are out of reach because of war or inflation, emergency relief keeps literally hundreds of thousands of Afghans alive every winter.

In a city like Kabul, which suffers from chronic food shortages, bread is a more stable form of currency than cash. Nor is relief needed just in urban areas: Hazarajat, hidden away in the barren Hindu Kush mountains of Central Afghanistan, has been systematically blockaded by Taliban forces determined to starve out the rebel troops of Hezb-e-Wahdat. Tens of thousands of Hazaras are dependent on World Food Programme (WFP) food aid to see them through the long, cold winters.

Relief for the capital is mediated through the Kabul Relief Group, which is chaired by the UN Office for the Coordination of Humanitarian Assistance to Afghanistan (UNOCHA). NGO coordination is done by the Agency Coordinating Body for Afghan Relief (ACBAR) and comprises some 40 NGOs, plus the International Committee of the Red Cross (ICRC). The city is divided up between the key agencies into zones of responsibility. Beneficiaries are issued with Identity Cards featuring a coloured dot to indicate which agency is delegated to assist them. A working list of beneficiaries, around 50,000 families, has been drawn up by WFP and the French NGO, ACTED. Typically, most of these are low income with disabled or widowed members.

ACTED implements the WFP bakeries programme which provides up to quarter of a million loaves of subsidised bread a day in Kabul alone. The ability of ordinary Kabulis to buy basic food is deteriorating almost daily as government salaries remain unpaid and the *Afghani* currency continues to decrease in value. Currently, the subsidised loaves cost beneficiaries about a quarter of the market value. ACTED also mines coal in the Ghorband Valley, 130 km north of Kabul, which it donates to thousands of families in the capital and to all the main hospitals, clinics and orphanages as fuel for cooking, cleaning and heating. CARE Afghanistan distributes food to widows and vulnerable persons, while MEDAIR and Solidarités supply the same beneficiaries with non-food items. In Kabul, UNHCR provides non-food items to some 30,000 families during winter; these items include tarpaulins, winter clothes, lamps and thick quilts made by 1,600 widows. The widows are employed by UNHCR and earn 30,000 *Afghanis* ($1.40) per quilt, each of which takes two or three days to make.

The ICRC relief operation in Afghanistan is the largest of its kind in the world. Over one million Afghans benefit directly from its food and non-food assistance, not just in Kabul, but nationwide from Panjshair in the east to Helmand in the west to Pul-e-Khumri in the north. Food items (18,787 tonnes in 1996) include wheat flour, beans, rice and *ghee*; non-food items (2,373 tonnes in 1996) include coal, blankets, soap, candles, plastic sheeting and stoves. The Norwegian Afghanistan Committee (NAC) operates emergency aid projects in Ghazni, Badakhshan, Kabul and Jalalabad.

UNICEF has a relief component to its Afghanistan programme: it provides orphans with emergency shelters where needed, and has resources to cope with influxes of internally-displaced persons (IDPs), forced to leave their homes through flooding or fighting. WFP claims to spend more money than anyone else in Afghanistan. In Kabul alone in 1996, WFP spent $17 million on institutional feeding in hospitals and orphanages, on the 45 subsidised bakeries run for WFP by ACTED, and on water and sanitation. WFP food-for-work plays a major part in many assistance strategies, from embroidery training to recycling rubble into new building materials.

Refugees and IDPs

While the ICRC tries to avoid building refugee camps where possible, since the Ashgabad Conference in January 1997 it has been given overall responsibility for internal refugees, so-called "internally-displaced persons" (IDPs). The ICRC provides relief supplies to a number of IDP camps, notably in Herat. Mounting discontent between ICRC and the local Taliban authorities in the first half of 1997 over the question of whether relief supplies to the notorious Shahidahi 2 camp were finding their way to Taliban frontline fighters led to the ICRC delegate in Herat being forced to leave. However, ICRC's firm stance on fully checking IDPs' credentials before making handouts has been largely respected in the aid community.

Among the principal problems is the need to identify those who are the genuinely vulnerable, and then to rehabilitate camp-dwellers out of aid-dependency and back into self-sufficient communities. IDPs returning to Kabul seem to have developed better coping mechanisms. Most find shelter with relatives or friends. Relief for refugees is handled by UNHCR, although the agency still provides tents for some IDPs. Ironically, access to girls for education in Taliban-controlled areas has proved easier in IDP camps than in more settled environments. In the IDP camps of Herat, the International Assistance Mission (IAM) runs informal schooling for girls and boys together, as well as literacy and health education for women, vocational training and apprenticeship courses. This example shows how development can not only emerge out of an emergency situation, but even be enhanced by it. It also reveals how meaningless it is to try and categorize any area of assistance in Afghanistan as either one or the other.

The Frontier Post 4 March 1990

Relief or development?

One of the great frustrations which many NGOs face in Afghanistan is that of continually reapplying for emergency relief funding from donors on a yearly basis, while their programmes may need to run for three to five years to be truly effective. Most donors are unwilling to commit long-term funding to a country which has been at war for two decades and shows no sign of relenting. Bad experiences, such as the re-mining of the Shomali Valley soon after the HALO Trust had just de-mined it, do not exactly encourage donors to switch to a more developmental approach. However, many aid professionals believe that donors – and some inexperienced aid workers – fall victim to a number of ***incorrect assumptions***, such as:

- "The central government is unworkable and defiant of international human rights, so we cannot commit long-term funds until it changes."
- "Kabul is in the grip of a repressive regime where any form of long-term assistance is likely to be doomed."
- "In a country where the physical, political and economic infrastructures have been destroyed by 20 years of war, only emergency aid is possible."

Experienced observers are at pains to point out the fallacies inherent in these assumptions. While the Taliban "central government," which in early 1998 held sway over two-thirds of Afghanistan, may be obstructive to the aims and principles of international organizations, the movement comprises many tiers of influence, not all of which present the same front. The religious authorities in the urban areas of Kabul, Herat, Kandahar and Jalalabad are notoriously more extreme in their interpretation of Talib 'ideology' than the authorities in rural areas. Hence, many agencies have found that projects which would never be allowed in urban areas, such as home-schooling for girls or health and hygiene instruction for women, are perfectly possible in rural parts.

Often the local *mullah* or even provincial Talib governor may have a more progressive attitude towards development than the Ministers or Religious Police of Kabul and Kandahar. And while the destruction inflicted on Kabul may require a predominately emergency response, there are whole regions of Afghanistan where development is not only possible but desperately needed. This reasoning is probably behind the decisions of agencies such as Oxfam to work in Hazarajat, or UNDP to work in Farah.

One experienced donor representative in Kabul pointed out that what many people take to be development work is no more than the slow recovery from an emergency situation created by a conflict. Thus 'development' only starts when the country returns to the stage it had reached before the war began. This argument, however, may well seem rather academic in the eyes of many Afghans, for whom any move beyond reliance on food parcels and plastic sheeting would be development. The longer 'emergency' and 'development' are treated by donor agencies as mutually exclusive, the more damage will be inflicted on Afghanistan. For some observers, this approach ignores the essential and continuous transition from aid-dependency to self-sufficiency.

Much of Afghanistan is at peace, and many 'development' projects are running in tandem with the 'emergency' work of clearing mines and ensuring adequate food and shelter for the winter months. But the distinctions are blurred. In Azro District of Logar UNHCR is resettling returnees into villages provided with better educational, healthcare and agricultural opportunities than may have existed before. Is this emergency or development work? In a country where returnees are trying to start a new life, where local entrepreneurs are making money smuggling goods between Pakistan and Central Asia, and where much of the infrastructure is shattered, development has found fertile soil in which to take root. From the Community Forums of Mazar (SEE HOME-GROWN GOVERNMENT), to the reclamation of barren land through irrigation, to the creation of hundreds of thousands of new livelihoods proposed by the UN Strategic Framework Mission, it is clear what role development can play in partnership with the efforts of ordinary Afghans to improve their standards of living.

Some aid coordinators argue that peace is a necessary precondition for development. Yet it may, in fact, be quite the opposite: development may prove the best route towards peace. Given the means to make their own living and to craft their own futures, ordinary Afghans may feel they have something to lose and finally turn their backs on war.

Rehabilitation

Much of the rehabilitation aid currently delivered in the towns is in the form of small-scale water supply improvement and sanitation programmes. As health representatives point out, Afghanistan has one of the highest infant mortality rates in the world, and waterborne diseases are among the major causes. Health problems could be significantly reduced if more accessible clean drinking water and sanitation facilities were made available, and not only in the towns. Most Afghan communities are particularly vulnerable to water-related diseases whether they live in urban or rural areas.

Apart from peace itself, effective urban and rural rehabilitation remains a critical element to the successful reintegration of refugees. It is also vital to assist those Afghans who have stayed behind, but lost everything, to get back onto their feet. In many cases, refugees are better off than the poorest in the country. Yet numerous returnees have simply found conditions in Afghanistan too harsh. Other than charity or the sale of possessions, they have no other means of survival. For rehabilitation to succeed, it is crucial to provide some kind of safety net, both in rural and urban areas. Despite

The Frontier Post 16 November 1993

efforts by the UN, the World Food Programme (WFP) and the International Committee of the Red Cross (ICRC), many are still unable able to cope. As some aid coordinators have stressed repeatedly, the international community needs to ensure that the country's vulnerable people, whether refugees or not, do not go under, but have a chance to establish new lives.

At present, numerous Afghans must rely on family members working abroad for financial support. Others who tried returning to Afghanistan have found conditions too difficult and have resettled elsewhere. Or they have sent family members back to the camps. Some families, too, have deliberately remained in Pakistan because of the absence of adequate educational facilities in Afghanistan, particularly for girls. Another significant phenomenon is a growing trend toward urbanization, particularly among Afghans from rural areas who have experienced an urban environment in exile and now no longer wish to return to the agricultural sector.

On the whole, agencies now offer only material support and expertise while encouraging local communities to take part in the planning, implementation and maintenance of projects. Local populations, for example, are expected to provide their own forms of contribution, normally labour. Furthermore, aid groups have realised the importance of focusing on smaller areas for longer periods. Working in too large a region, it was found, only succeeded in provoking competition rather than cooperation among communities. All of which has strengthened the argument that greater coordination and more joint strategic planning among the aid agencies is vital if they are to avoid duplication and ensure that every region is covered.

According to the UN, this is what its Strategic Framework/Common Programme is hoping to achieve in the years to come. At present, however, there are still insufficient coordination efforts in many areas apart from those enforced by the donors. (SEE UN STRATEGY)

The involvement of local communities and particularly indigenous NGOs has not come without major problems. Many Afghans have come to depend on employment with the agencies as a means of survival. When the US Agency for International Development (US-AID) cut its operations inside Afghanistan in 1994, many projects were closed and a large number of people were put out of work. Schools had been built but there was no money to pay teachers' salaries. Similarly, when further funding for UN and other international organizations was reduced, local NGOs which had depended on UN contracts also went to the wall. International aid agency offices, such as the International Rescue Committee which acts as a clearing house for the European Union and other donors, are full of project proposals by Afghan NGOs desperately seeking funding. "This is always the problem with so-called 'humanitarian' operations," noted one experienced Western aid coordinator in Peshawar. "The reconstruction of Afghanistan requires a long-term commitment, not just projects which need to be renewed every year or two. Otherwise it's a sheer waste of money. It's also just not fair to the local communities."

Kabul – a city of survival

Kabul, more than any other city, has suffered terribly from the war, particularly since the mujahed takeover in 1992. An estimated 60% of all shelter in the capital has been reduced to rubble, far more than Beirut or Sarajevo. Other towns such as Kandahar, Ghazni, Herat and Jalalabad have been damaged to varying degrees. Mazar-e-Sharif, for example, now swollen to over 700,000 people, has suffered some physical destruction but much of the deterioration of infrastructure has been the result of lack of maintenance and population overload. Financial systems have collapsed, central government contacts have been cut, and the political process has been replaced by a military one. As in many other parts of the country, almost all available public expenditure is directed toward the security forces rather than reconstruction.

Separated from its traditional rural support, Kabul has had to rely largely on external forms of food, fuel, commodity supplies and humanitarian assistance. (SEE ECONOMICS) Continued fighting to the north of the capital and other areas coupled with the lack of municipal services, influxes of displaced people and general economic deterioration regularly hamper international efforts to adopt more long-term rehabilitation approaches instead of emergency assistance.

With more than 200,000 new refugees arriving from northern areas in late 1997, Kabul has been finding it increasingly difficult to deal with such pressures. An estimated half a million people are jobless. Despite traditional responsibilities towards extended families, growing numbers of residents are unable to support newly arrived members. Many are being forced to sell everything, such as furniture, simply to survive. Hence aid organizations like ICRC, the French agency Solidarités, the Norwegian Afghanistan Committee and CARE Afghanistan are obliged to distribute winter relief essentials ranging from charcoal and candles to soap and quilts to vulnerable groups.

Nevertheless, reconstruction efforts, albeit still limited, are continuing to expand beyond the provision of temporary shelter materials to war-affected communities. Among the principal organizations involved is UNCHS (Habitat), which, apart from seeking to improve water and sanitation is particularly active in helping to provide new housing for Kabul's homeless, in partnership with other UN agencies and NGOs.

As part of its operational procedure, Habitat first ensures that UNOCHA has cleared specific areas for reconstruction of mines. It then provides food-for-work programmes to recycle rubble into bricks, which are used as building materials. German Agro Action (GAA) provides timber doors, window frames and furniture from its factory in Kabul; and AREA makes cement roof beams to save on timber as an environmental measure to counteract deforestation. (SEE FORESTRY) If a family wants to reconstruct their house, they can apply for materials sufficient for two rooms: 60% of the cost is donated by international agencies, but the families must provide the rest themselves through free labour or cash. Over 2,000 houses have been rehabilitated in this way in Kabul alone. A similar project involving UNHCR and MEDAIR is being implemented to provide 1,000 houses in Kabul and Logar, except in this case Afghans are expected to provide 60% of the cost of rehabilitation themselves.

Water and sanitation in Kabul

Much of Kabul's mains water supply and sewerage has been destroyed by two decades of fighting, especially during the conflict between the mujahideen factions for the city from 1992-1996. Only around five percent of Kabul's population benefits from mains water supply at present, and until recently most people still drew their water from traditional shallow, open wells which were often polluted. A handful of international agencies, including CARE, GAA, UNCHS (Habitat) and Solidarités, have formed a Water and Sanitation Group which cooperates with the Ministry of Public Works to improve the situation.

Emergency stopgap work has concentrated on drilling wells and installing handpumps, which, by covering wellheads and preventing dirt from getting into the water, contribute towards better sanitation. Now agencies are also concentrating on rehabilitating Kabul's 27 major water networks which have the capacity to supply over 600,000 inhabitants. Pumping depended on mains electricity which has

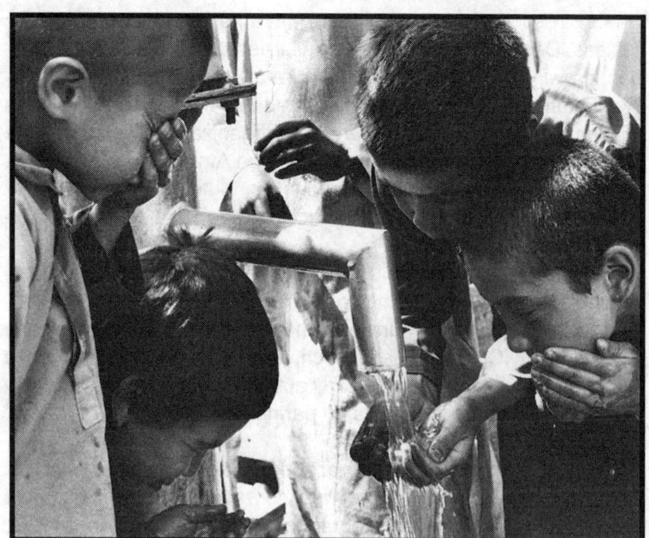

J. Hartley/UNICEF

largely been destroyed by the war, so now both imported and reconditioned Russian generators are being used.

Sanitation facilities in Kabul have also been seriously affected by the conflict. Many schools, hospitals and institutions have septic tanks overflowing. Only one modern sewage treatment centre existed in Kabul before the war – a Soviet-built system attached to some apartment blocks. It is currently being rehabilitated by Solidarités, along with the 15km Wazir Abad sewage canal. CARE and MEDAIR both integrate the rehabilitation of latrine and garbage facilities with basic health and hygiene education in Kabul. One problem facing emergency latrine construction is that Kabul has a very high water table and pits dug too deep leach waste in the city's water supply. ICRC has responded to this by modifying 8,000 latrines with higher steps and shallower pits. However these are temporary measures. Donors are not willing to commit funds for anything but emergency projects, so no progress has been made on the proper sewerage system which Kabul desperately needs.

Income generation

Income generation projects in Afghanistan concentrate both on teaching – or enhancing existing – skills, and providing capital to enable Afghans to begin making and marketing their own products. The provision of loans or credit has, however, proved very difficult in an Islamic culture which forbids usury. The Bangladeshi Grameen Bank, which has pioneered some extraordinarily successful micro-credit schemes all over the world, was banned from Taliban-controlled areas in July 1996 when divorced women were found to be benefiting from similar schemes in Bangladesh.

CARE gets round the problem by encouraging communities to save first into a fund and then spend later. In the north, beyond the Taliban's reach, it is a different story: Save the Children-USA operates a successful micro-credit scheme in Mazar and even charges interest. In Kabul, UNHCR operates an ingenious women's revolving fund programme in which groups of 10 women receive $500 to help them start capitalizing on their skills. While five women in the group receive $100 each and use it for one year, the other five monitor their colleagues to make sure no-one defaults. Then after one year, the five monitors receive the $500 back from the initial beneficiaries who then in turn become supervisors. The scheme thus becomes self-supporting, and repayment is to the group rather than to UNHCR. One of the dangers in micro-credit is that communities may feel enticed by the cash available to buy inappropriate technology, either through vanity or misguided enthusiasm. Nevertheless, when correctly handled, such schemes can create a genuine independence from aid handouts and foster great community motivation, self-sufficiency and pride.

Over 15 agencies are involved in income generation projects ranging from teaching carpentry and soap making skills to the production of handicrafts and handpumps. In Kabul CARE, in collaboration with local women's organizations, supports income generation for several thousand widows through skills training and food-for-work employment in tailoring, embroidery and knitting. Training centres around the homes of female Afghan trainers, and has the advantage of creating social networks for women who have lost the support of an extended family after years of war.

In Peshawar, DACAAR runs a sewing centre which develops both the creative and business skills of refugee Afghan women. After initial opposition from traditionalist Afghan men who did not want their wives to earn money, it is now a self-sustaining operation employing 1,500 women working in six different refugee camps. The DACAAR Sewing Project shop is located in Gul Mohar Lane, University Town, and is open for sales from 0900-1630 hrs Monday to Friday. German Agro Action (GAA) employs nearly 300 Afghans in its timber factories, and its furniture shop is now turning a healthy profit. A British NGO, the Ockenden Venture (OV), employs around 1,300 Afghan refugees in Pakistan's North West Frontier Province, producing over 450 different types of handicraft ranging from jewellery to knitted socks; 70% of these products are exported. OV also trains refugees in soap and shoe making, and runs a Goat Loan scheme for widows and needy families. Apprenticeship schemes are thin on the ground, partly because of the problems of Afghan women being restricted to the home in Taliban areas. However, Solidarite Afghanistan Belgium (SAB) has trained nearly 4,000 young refugee Afghans in 28 different apprenticeship-trades since 1985.

Rural areas

In rural areas, the majority of programmes have been directed towards agricultural production. They have focused on the repair of irrigation systems, flood protection structures, wells, erosion control, roads, bridges and culverts, but also the provision of improved seed, fertiliser and insecticides. Water pumps – including technical advice on how to use them – are being installed in villages. Horticultural rehabilitation and development projects including farming management and marketing workshops are being set up, and basic veterinary workers (BVWs) trained to operate self-sustaining and commercial extension services.

Some agencies are attempting to pursue genuine development initiatives. The Afghan Development Association (ADA), a local NGO, is implementing integrated rural development projects in southwest and central Afghanistan. These combine the rehabilitation of water supply, roads, bridges and horticulture with higher education in veterinary and agriculture, soil conservation and micro-hydropower.

In eastern Afghanistan, CARE is both rehabilitating irrigation, flood control and road infrastructures, and developing forestry as an income-generating initiative: three million poplar trees and mountain pines are planted and grown every year by farmers in Kunar, Khost and Paktya, from cuttings provided by CARE. The timber is used in construction and for export. DACAAR has moved towards a more developmental agenda in its integrated agricultural programme in eastern and western Afghanistan. They are adopting an area-based approach by grouping villages together and requiring both initial requests for assistance and 100% of the labour to come from the communities themselves. With DACAAR's technical help some villages have doubled their available agricultural land through proper water management.

Since 1991, Oxfam has been active in small-scale community development in the non-Taliban region of Hazarajat. Infrastructure, erosion control and food security projects are run in conjunction with community-based health education and veterinary training. Afghan girls and women, who previously may never have been to school, are free to attend a range of vocational, literacy and numeracy classes both in formal surroundings and in home schools during winter. Hazarajat is very remote from both the main lines of communication in Afghanistan and from the aid agencies based in Peshawar or Kabul. Except in some district centres, there have never been schools, health facilities, road maintenance or agricultural extension work in this region. Hence, any form of assistance in these areas could be regarded as development rather than rehabilitation.

The UNDP's P.E.A.C.E. initiative, standing for Poverty Eradication And Community Empowerment, is another attempt to move away from emergency responses to a more developmental approach, but has been criticised for both the randomness of the

OXFAM IN KABUL

Oxfam started on a huge urban supply water project aiming to rehabilitate networks supplying 40% of Kabul's water. They suspended work on this project in September 1996 when the Taliban prevented women's access to health education. As an aid agency, however, Oxfam remains in Afghanistan and is still working in areas not under Taliban control, notably Hazarajat and Mazar-e-Sharif.

While Oxfam says it is not using the projects as leverage against the Taliban they feel that their environmental health and hygiene programme is crucial for clean water to be effectively used. They have already spent $1.2 million on generators, pumps, pipes and compressors, and as much again is needed to complete it. At present, no one except Oxfam has the funding to do this. A major flaw in the programme is that $40,000 a month is needed to operate the fuel pumps once the system is up and running, but no one is willing to pay up as it is an open-ended commitment. On the distribution side, some 400 kilometres of underground piping – originally built in 1982 with support from the World Bank – remain to be checked. Capacity building at the Ministry of Public Works is urgently needed before the project can be handed over.

A number of NGOs interviewed were particularly critical of Oxfam's position in that such a large percentage of Kabul's population is dependent on this water. While Oxfam claims that it is not a matter of principle but practice which has caused the suspension of their programme, some observers feel that they are jeopardising the potential comfort and benefit which mains water would bring to hundreds of thousands of Kabulis.

target districts selected and for the ineffectiveness of the "representative committees" which it has formed in the communities where it works.

Home-grown government in Mazar-e-Sharif

Encouraging local communities to set up their own urban renewal agendas is one way of promoting sustainable development in Afghanistan. The following is based on a report by Samantha Reynolds of UNCHS (Habitat) who spent three years helping to establish urban rehabilitation programmes in the city.

Unlike Kabul, Mazar has been spared much of the physical destruction of war, but its infrastructure and financial, political and social institutions have collapsed. The military regime siphons all taxes and income off into the war effort. Public salaries, if paid at all, are frozen at old levels. Inflation has sent prices soaring. The UNCHS (Habitat) mandate was to "support and facilitate the indigenous process of urban repair and recovery" in a city of 700,000 people. But what exactly was the "indigenous process" Habitat was supposed to be supporting?

The UNCHS team first made surveys – forays into the land of mud and open sewage. They talked to people, trying to unravel the jumbled threads of social relations, formal and informal, traditional and customary, imported and imposed. It was a process that brought them closer to the people, but with one major problem: in all the meetings, Reynolds found herself to be the only woman. According to Reynolds, the caveat of "this is Afghanistan" was easy to fall back on, but what about progress? The men assured them that their women were too busy working at home to attend meetings; in any case one added, "what do they know that we have not already told you?" The much-vaunted mantra of "community participation" was beginning to sound hollow. Could a meeting – in which one sat with a motley crowd of men who, one felt, often had nothing better to do than be herded into yet another public gathering to nod heads at the shopping list of needs – really be considered "community participation"? Was there even a 'community', let alone 'participation'?

Reynolds and her team realized that the UN was part of the problem. After years of assistance, people had come to depend on the white jeeps to deliver public goods and services. Meetings had become merely an exchange of wish-lists and conditions. How move from this to a state of mature civic engagement, where people not only insist on their rights, but are ready to shoulder their social and community responsibilities?

After weeks of talking with men, the team suddenly had a breakthrough: a local *mullah* responded to Reynold's quiet insistence on involving women by agreeing to a meeting. As Reynolds describes it, "it was a cold winter morning...our breath hung in the air. Before long we heard the *muezzin* crackling into life over the frozen mudscape of domes. It was not a call to prayer, but a call to women to come to the mosque..." Dozens of them came, shrouded in traditional blue *burqas*: some were bright-eyed and curious, others sceptical and accusing. It was not the usual community meeting. There were no norms to be observed, no pecking orders, no predetermined agendas: it was a free-for-all. "Why do the people in white cars only talk to men?" challenged the women present, "why is the world not helping Afghanistan? Why is there no clinic here? Or school, or books, or teachers' salaries?"

For Reynolds, there were times when her work seemed like the opening of a Pandora's box. How could her team ever live up to the expectations being heaped on them? "Couldn't we just turn tail and tick off our survey boxes," she thought, "prioritize a solid piece of

FOREIGNERS BEWARE!

Rural Afghan society may be traditionally hospitable. But it also has a long tradition of suspicion towards any new-fangled ideas, especially if those introducing them come from the city or from a foreign land. Traditionalist resentment and rebellion at Kabul-led communist reforms in 1978-1979 precipitated the Soviet invasion. Taliban mistrust of Western values has led to the incarceration of thousands of Afghan women. For anyone from overseas attempting to employ alien means to achieve Western ends, it may be worth remembering what Olivier Roy has to say about such attempts:
"the proverbial hospitality of the Afghans is also a form of defensive screen. The guest, assigned to a precise place (the *hujra*) which he dares not leave without offending his host, is enmeshed in a formalism in which the ceremony of greetings and the ritual of the meal leaves little place for the exercise of authority or even simple investigation... The foreigner finds himself confronted by an endless series of evasions, procrastinations and side-stepping of the issue. The person who is responsible is always somewhere else, the horses are in the mountains and the truth is in the depths of the well."

Islam and Resistance in Afghanistan (2nd Edition, Cambridge University Press, 1990)

infrastructure, and pat ourselves on the back, saying we had consulted with the women?" But it sounded hollow and inadequate. Although they could do nothing immediately, they would continue to consult in order to develop a programme together. "In truth we had no fixed plan, but the women had real problems and needed real help," she added.

Habitat was faced with a humanitarian emergency which was the product or a symptom of a lack of civic order. At the same time, a system of civic order was needed to ensure that whatever aid was provided actually strengthened civic society and did not just prop up a military regime. There were instances in the same community of commanders misusing their influence to gain assistance for displaced people under their wing and then extract 'thanks' from the community for their services. But those donating were blind to these nuances, needing as they did some means by which to deliver.

What to do next? The Habitat team discovered that if the women were to continue consulting at all, they needed a place to meet. The women themselves expressed frustration at having skills they could not utilize for want of cash, markets or organization. So Habitat combined the two by granting some seed capital to the community to purchase tailoring and sewing equipment, and by establishing a revolving fund for materials and labour. Classic income-generating schemes of this nature sometimes founder, or fail to contribute to community progress, because they concentrate resources – and hence power – into the hands of a privileged few. To counteract this, the women decided that ownership of the assets would be kept with the community as a whole. They developed a profit-sharing system whereby workers would receive one-fifth of the profits, in addition to a salary, while four-fifths would go towards a community fund to be spent on running their Community Forums. In time, there was enough to pay for a local clinic, dispensary, literacy course, library and kindergartens.

According to Reynolds, there are currently eight Community Forums in different districts of Mazar. Gradually they have established their own systems of administration and management, and are building capacity towards taking on wider responsibilities related to public infrastructure. The women run them through a management committee and hold meetings every three weeks which the whole community may attend. The meetings aim to integrate the spiritual, administrative and social processes of life. They begin with a recitation from the Holy Koran, focusing on each participant's relationship with God. This is followed by the management committee's report on local district activities, cashflow, problems to be faced and decisions to be made. Most importantly the Forums are self-propagating, in that it is women from established Forums who support new ones. Male officials, elders and technical specialists are all invited to participate in sharing their concerns, skills and solutions.

Above all, these are Forums for civic engagement. Their governance of local affairs – through the authority vested in the management committee – matures by drawing regularly on the community's collective experience and engaging everyone in the rehabilitation process. Now the Community Forums of Mazar-e-Sharif are beginning to illustrate the key role economics has to play in the ordering of human affairs, and more especially the significant contribution women can make to the process, given the means.

ESSENTIAL AGENCIES

ACTED, ADA, AREA, CARE, DACAAR, GAA, ICRC, MADERA, MEDAIR, NAC, OV, Oxfam, SAB, SC-US, Solidarités, UNCHS (Habitat), UNDP, UNHCR, UNICEF, WFP

TALI-*BANS*

Sixteen verbatim decrees received from the office of Amr Bel Maruf wa Nai Az Munkar (Department for the Promotion of Virtue and the Prevention of Vice, also known as the Religious Police):

1. To prevent sedition and female uncovers
No drivers are allowed to pick up female who are using Iranian Burqa [*chador*]. In the case of violation the driver will be imprisoned. If such kind of female are observed in the street, their house will be found and their husbands punished.

2. To prevent music
In shops, hotels, vehicles and rickshaws cassettes and music are prohibited. If any music cassette found in a shop, the shopkeeper should be imprisoned and the shop locked.

3. To prevent beard shaving and its cutting
If anyone observed who has shaved and/or cut his beard, they should be arrested and imprisoned until their beard gets bushy.

4. To prevent not-praying and order gathering pray at the bazaar
Pray should be done on their due times in all districts. If young people are seen in the shops they will be immediately imprisoned. If five people guarantee [their good character], the person should be released otherwise the criminal will be imprisoned for ten days.

5. To prevent keeping pigeons and playing with birds
This habit/hobby should be stop. After ten days this matter should be monitored and the pigeons and any other playing birds should be killed.

6. To eradicate the use of addiction and its user
Addict should be imprisoned and investigation made to find the supplier and the shop. The shop should be locked and both criminals (the owner and the user) should be imprisoned and punished.

7. To prevent kite flying
Advise the people of its useless consequences such as betting, death of children and their deprivation from education. The kite shops in the city should be abolished.

8. To prevent idolatry
In the vehicle, shops, room, hotels and any other places, pictures/ portraits should be abolished. The monitors should tear up all pictures in the above places. The vehicle will be stopped if any idol is found in the vehicles.

9. To prevent gambling
The main centres should be found and the gamblers imprisoned for one month.

10. To prevent the British and American hair style
People with long hair should be arrested and taken to the Religious Police department to shave their hair. The criminal has to pay the barber.

11. To prevent interest charge on loans, charge on changing small denomination notes and charge on money orders
All money exchanger should be informed that the above three types of exchanging the money are prohibited in Islam. In the case of violation the criminal will be imprisoned for a long time.

12. To prevent washing cloth by young ladies along the water streams in the city
Violator ladies should be picked up with respectful Islamic manner taken to their houses and their husbands severely punished.

13. To prevent music and dances in wedding parties
The above two things should be prevented. In the case of violation the head of the family will be arrested and punished.

14. To prevent the playing of music drum
If anybody does this than the religious elders can decide about it.

15. To prevent sewing ladies cloth and taking female body measures by tailor
If women or fashion magazine are seen in the shop the tailor should be imprisoned.

16. To prevent sorcery
All the related books should be burnt and the magician should be imprisoned until his repentance.

(Translated by the Agency Coordinating Body for Afghan Relief (ACBAR) office on 6 January 1997)

More decrees...

The following were issued by the Department for the Promotion of Virtue and the Prevention of Vice:

"...One of the important commitments that our Department has to come up with is to adjust the society according to the Islamic Shari'a standards. These standards can guarantee the development of a society towards intellectualization, immaterialization and create a certain blockage against external devious making culture into our Islamic culture. Therefore, as an immediate step to apply virtual aims in our country we develop the two following regulations. These regulation have been prepared in accordance to the instruction of Shari'a law by our department."

For all international and national agencies

There must be a group of people amongst you to conduct the others towards goodness, welfare, virtues and prevent them from vices. The Islamic Shari'a law is completely valid in our country (Afghanistan). Therefore, all the Muslim citizens should observe and act accordingly.

All the expatriates who are living in Afghanistan should respect and observe the Islamic laws and rules. Based on the policy and working directions of this Department we communicate the following:

1. All the humanitarian assistance provided by the International Community should be given without any condition.
2. The Islamic Shari'a law of our country do not allow the employment of women in Government Departments or International Agencies. Women should not go outside their residence. This should be observed by all International Agencies and Afghan NGOs.
3. Women are allowed to work only in health sector at the hospitals and clinics. Agencies should not employ any Afghan women in any other sector.
4. Any local staff member of Agencies who do not observe the Islamic Shari'a law should be advised by the agency. Again in case of violation this department will have to take a serious action against the staff member.
5. Assistance to widows, poor women should be done through their blood relatives without employment of female surveyors.
6. Women are allowed to work in vocational sectors like embroidery, weaving etc., in the case they do not go out from their houses. Our department should be informed before hand through the blood relatives.
7. If the International Agencies of Afghan NGOs decide to employ or assist females, they should first obtain permission from our department.

8. To identify the real beneficiaries in surveys, the Mullah, Wakil and three elders of the district should be contacted.

Press releases from the Religious Police

November 1996: "We kindly request all our Afghan sisters to not apply for any job in foreign agencies and they also should not go there. Otherwise if they were chased, threatened and investigated by us, the responsibility will be on them. We declare to all foreign agencies to respect the issued regulation of Islamic State of Afghanistan and should strictly avoid employment of Afghan female staff."

14 January 1997: "Women, you should not step outside your residence, If you go outside the house you should not be like women who used to go with fashionable clothes wearing much cosmetics and appearing in front of every men before the coming of Islam.

"Islam as a rescuing religion has determined specific dignity for women. Islam has valuable instruction for women. Women should not create such opportunity to attract the attention of useless people who will not look at them with a good eye. Women have the responsibility as a teacher or coordinator for her family. Husband, brother, father have the responsibility for providing the family with the necessary life requirements (food, clothe etc.). In case women are required to go outside the residence for the purposes of education, social needs or social services they should cover themselves in accordance with Islamic Shari'a regulation. If women are going outside with fashionable, ornamental, tight and charming clothes to show themselves, they will be cursed by the Islamic Shari'a and should never expect to go to heaven.

The Frontier Post 16 July 1997

"All family elders and every Muslim have responsibility in the same respect. We request all family elders to keep tight control over their families and avoid these social problems. Otherwise those women will be threatened, investigated and severly punished as well as the family elders by the forces of the religious police.

"Religious police have the responsibility and duty to struggle against these social problems and will continue their effort until evil is finished."

4 February 1997: "Some of the Aid Agencies working in Kabul and provinces are using some pictures of people in their publications which is against the Islamic Shariat law and policy of the Islamic State."

11 March 1997: "Hereby we announce to all expatriates and national staff of Non Governmental Organizations to avoid carrying video, cassettes and alcoholic drinks to or from Afghanistan and respect the religious instructions of people of Afghanistan. Violators will be dealt according to the Islamic Shari'a law."

20 March 1997: "Men will not cut their beards but they will cut their hair."

5 October 1997: "All animal pictures and drawings of crosses hung in motor vehicles, houses or any other place shall be removed as from tomorrow. Painters decorating motor vehicles or houses with pictures shall rigorously refrain for painting the above kinds of pictures."

Quotes and headlines...

Mullah Hassan, Governor of Kandahar, on gay men: *"We have a dilemma on this. The difficulty is this: One group of scholars believes you should take these people to the top of the highest building in the city, and hurl them to their deaths. [The other group] believe in a different approach. They recommend you dig a pit near a wall somewhere, put these people in it, then topple the wall so that they are buried alive. A third group of scholars argue that homosexuals should be put on public display for a few hours with blackened faces."*

Mullah Hassan, Governor of Kandahar, on TV and cinema: *"Worshipping statues was forbidden by the Prophet Mohammed, and watching television is the same as seeing statues. Drawing pictures or looking at them is sinful. People have a right to entertainment, but instead of going to the cinema, they can go to the gardens and see the flowers. Then they will see the essence of Islam."*

(*The Guardian,* London 6 Jan 97)

Mullah Qalaamuddin, Deputy Head of the Religious Police, on how to administer a good beating: *"[He] said the only Islamically-acceptable instrument for administering beatings is a broad, two-foot long leather strap. He said he would resign if it was proven that steel cables had been used."*

(*BBC,* London 11 Oct 97)

Mawlawi Nezami, Head of Radio Shariat: *"We say the right things so we can be loved"*

Nur Mohammed, Governor of Herat: *"Women just aren't as smart as men. They don't have the intelligence. We categorically refuse to let women vote or participate in politics."*

(*The Sunday Times,* London 24 Mar 96)

Taliban justice

- Beating with whips and imprisonment for minor offences
- Amputation of hands for theft
- Execution for murder
- Death by stoning for adultery or "multiple intercourse" (sleeping with two men in one month) if witnessed by at least four people

Taliban contradictions

- The Ministry of Foreign Affairs in Kandahar issues permits for photography of buildings only and not of people. However, the same department requires a passport-size photo of all foreigners applying for visa extensions…
- Despite the ban on photography, the first secretary at the Taliban-staffed Afghan Embassy in Islamabad was himself photographed at the British High Commission on 3 September 1997 signing a Book of Condolence in front of a photograph of Princess Diana…
- Frontline Taliban fighters love to have their photographs taken despite the ban on pictures and idolatry…
- Men's hair must be cut short, but only on the fringe – shoulder-length bobs are permitted…
- Make-up is forbidden for women, but men often use black eyeliner…
- The Taliban employs former communists from the old Soviet-backed regime as mercenaries…

UN strategy: from strategic framework to common programming

In April last year, the UN's highest coordinating body, the innocuously-named Administrative Committee on Coordination (ACC) – chaired by the Secretary-General and including the Executive Heads of UN agencies as well as of the International Monetary Fund (IMF) and World Bank – met in Geneva for one of its regular six-monthly sessions. It took a decision to select Afghanistan as one of two countries to serve as a testing ground for a new approach by the international community to complex political emergencies. Sadako Ogata, the High Commissioner for Refugees, was said to have been instrumental in the choice.

This decision came as a welcome bolt from the blue to the aid community in Afghanistan. It complemented efforts that were already underway to review the way that assistance was being provided. Three months earlier, an extraordinary conference had been held in Ashgabad, Turkmenistan, which had brought together UN Member States, both from the region and major western donors, with the whole range of aid actors, including the Bretton Woods institutions, UN agencies, international and Afghan NGOs, the ICRC and the Red Cross and Crescent movement. It resulted in broad agreement to develop a holistic strategy for bringing sustainable peace to Afghanistan, recognising that "peace needs to be sought through political negotiation as well as built through support given to the population."

Both the Ashgabad meeting and the ACC decision took place against the backdrop of growing international alarm at developments within the country. The Taliban capture of Kabul in late 1996 had advertised both their own regressive policies and a number of ugly trends, including the country's growing importance as a source of "drugs and thugs" and of regional political instability. And by any social and humanitarian yardstick, Afghanistan merited an injection of international interest.

For then, as now, Afghanistan's unending nightmare continued. The fighting is in geographically limited areas, and could spread.

After nearly 20 years of war, the licit economy is in ruins, the environment degraded, infrastructure shattered. Land mines and unexploded ordnance litter the country. Up to a million people have been killed. There are still three million refugees and internally-displaced people. The country has some of the worst social development indicators in Asia, if not the world. Afghan authorities lack administrative resources, expertise and will. Abuses of human rights and humanitarian law abound. Women are denied the right to congregate and speak in public, have unequal access to health and education, and in urban areas are prevented from working. The psychological and physical suffering being endured by millions of people is incalculable.

In September 1997, a high level inter-agency mission arrived in the region led by Hugh Cholmondeley, the author of reports that had prompted the ACC decision to develop a strategic framework approach. The mission, which included representatives from the UN Development Programme (UNDP), the UN Department for Political Affairs (UNDPA), the UN Department for Humanitarian Affairs (UNDHA – now renamed the Office for the Coordination of Humanitarian Affairs), the World Bank and Oxfam, participated in a five-day workshop with all assistance 'stakeholders', made trips into Afghanistan and met with a wide range of actors before preparing a draft Strategic Framework document.

The document assessed the nature of the problem facing both Afghans and the international community, reviewed the assistance record, and assessed the international community's approach which, it said, had saved many lives, but lacked a unifying vision. It addressed the supply-driven nature of much aid planning and activity, the many overlaps and inconsistencies in programming, and the problem posed by absence of basic information about conditions on the ground to allow measurement of the impact of assistance efforts.

It proposed a new approach which is both radical and plain common sense. It suggested that immediate steps be taken to gain consensus among all those involved as to the nature of the political, economic, social and humanitarian problems. Principles should be identified to guide overall assistance efforts and the international community's relationship with the Afghans. And effective means should be found to develop a coherent and coordinated assistance effort in which the respective competencies of stakeholders – including countries in the region, donors, UN agencies, NGOs, Afghan authorities and communities – are recognised and their responsibilities made explicit.

The document was reviewed in early November by the Afghan Task Force, a small home-grown group consisting of donor, UN and NGO representatives, which meets regularly in Islamabad to provide a sounding board to the UN Resident/Humanitarian Coordinator, Alfredo Witschi-Cestari. It recommended that the Strategic Framework serve as the basis of an assistance strategy, and that this should be drawn up immediately to give greater operational flesh to the concepts in the Strategic Framework paper.

A draft Assistance Strategy was drafted and circulated in mid-November 1997, subjected to a large Review Meeting of donors and aid agencies in Islamabad – the Pakistani capital where most donors and UN agencies and a few NGOs dealing with Afghanistan are based – and presented to the Afghan Support Group (ASG) of donors at its second meeting in New York in early December. The ASG had been formed after the Ashgabad meeting on the initiative of Dutch Minister Jan Pronk. It consists of 14 countries plus the European Union – donors that between them account for the vast bulk of the response to Consolidated Appeals for Afghanistan.

The Assistance Strategy set out overall goals to inform the vision of sustainable peace in Afghanistan, notably that assistance must empower Afghans to build sustainable livelihoods. It proposed a number of principles to sustain international assistance efforts and suggested that means must be found to ensure the strategy supports, and be supported by, the international community's political efforts to seek a peaceful settlement.

The principles included upholding the UN Charter, the Universal Declaration of Human Rights and the Convention on the Elimination of all forms of Discrimination against Women. They also included presumption of the sovereignty of the Afghan state, transparency, respect for local traditions and customs, and commitment to securing Afghan involvement in and ownership of the strategy, while recognising that this would not be easy. It proposed that a common programme be formulated and that programme-wide, independent monitoring and evaluation be initiated. It also proposed a common fund. It set out steps for the revision of the Consolidated Appeal to allow it to serve as a management tool for donors and assistance actors alike.

The Assistance Strategy was warmly endorsed by donors in New York. One said that the only thing it had in common with other UN documents was the staple that held it together. It was seen as consistent with, if not animating, the Secretary-General's efforts to reform the UN. Praise was given to the process that had led to its creation, and for its essential recommendations, including the notion of a common programme. The only major reservation was regarding the common fund, on two grounds: that it might pose considerable bureaucratic problems for donors, and that it was premature. Donors committed themselves to communicating their support for the Assistance Strategy to the ACC and through the Executive Boards of UN agencies. Actors in the field are now faced with the challenge of translating the Assistance Strategy and the common programme into reality.

The 1998 Appeal for Afghanistan, issued on February 4th, elaborated steps that might be initiated to build a common programme, including proposals for revamping the Appeal itself. During the spring

"You will be glad to know that as part of the UN reform, it has been decided to cut down on meetings. I do of course realize that for some of you this announcement may have come a little too late."

UNHCR

of 1998, the UN Coordinator's office, both in Islamabad and through its five regional coordination offices within Afghanistan, systematically consulted all stakeholders on what common programming might consist of and how it could be sustained.

In late April 1998, a small group drawn from the UN, the World Bank and the NGO community drafted a document entitled *Making a Reality of Principled Common Programming* to take things forward. Its proposals are both radical and straightforward:

- assistance activities should, in future, be rooted in a thorough and shared understanding of what is going on in Afghanistan – politically and economically as well as socially
- overall needs should be agreed on the basis of that shared understanding and of the expressed needs of Afghans
- assistance actors should be realistic about their own capacities, as well as those of beneficiaries, before determining programme priorities.

Further, it proposes that in future, all projects should be attached to programmes (to avoid the "shopping list" syndrome whereby donors are presented with hundreds of seemingly stand-alone projects) and that programmes must demonstrate that they embody agreed principles and norms.

Regarding institutional arrangements, the proposal is that an Afghan Programming Board, which includes UN agencies, NGOs and donor governments (and on which ICRC, the Asian Development Bank and the World Bank will be invited to serve), take overall responsibility for common programming and for translating principles and operational guidelines into policies – for example, regarding gender mainstreaming, or home schooling. Debates and disagreements about principles have absorbed vast amounts of time and energy, generating more heat than light or clarity, and a mechanism is proposed whereby these issues can be debated and decisions taken. At the regional level, it is proposed that existing and nascent coordination arrangements be rationalized and consolidated in the creation of Regional Coordination Bodies – chaired by the local representative of the UN Coordinator and consisting of UN, NGO and (if, like the European Commission, they have a field presence) donors.

These proposals remain to be fully discussed by the Afghan Support Group and within the UN and NGO communities, but early indications are that donor governments are broadly supportive. Generally speaking, NGOs are positive while healthily sceptical, not least about the UN's own ability to join in and staff a truly coordinated, needs-driven, logical and collaboratively-programmed initiative. These doubts are shared by many in the UN itself.

At the time of writing, individual UN agencies' positions are uncertain. While the merits of common programming are recognised, there are concerns about its compatibility with the mandates and much-prized independence of UN agencies. No clear signal over what position to take has been given by UN agencies' headquarters, leaving the decision on what attitude to adopt to local Heads of Agencies and their field staff.

A key determining factor in the success of common programming will be whether the donors are sufficiently enthusiastic or determined to use their influence to encourage the UN agencies to support common programming. Cynics argue that, whatever the inherit merits of these proposals, many of which will require a leap of faith to work – and at the very minimum, a positive attitude by all involved – only donor pressure can provide the stick to move things forward.

Should the proposals that underpin common programming be broadly accepted, a major effort will be required to make them work, not least to equip the assistance community with the skills to reach consensus on key issues, whether operational, technical or programmatic, through Regional Coordination Bodies and the Afghanistan Programming Board.

Further issues that need to be addressed are how Afghans will be engaged and, eventually, assume overall responsibility for common programming, and what the consequences of a peace settlement – no matter how remote the prospect is currently – will be. Common programming is intended to be demand-driven, and is premised on a commitment to community participation in all aspects of programming. Realizing this commitment will not be easy; more widespread use of participatory needs-assessment will be required as will a much greater effort to communicate with and understand Afghan beneficiaries. A basis will also need to be found – possibly part of a broader Code of Conduct agreed with the authorities – on which local presumptive authorities can be involved in the work of the Regional Coordination Bodies and, eventually, the Afghanistan Programming Board.

While these proposals are chewed over, reality for most Afghans continues to deteriorate. There is greater activity on the international scene to find a political settlement, much of it catalysed by the Secretary-General's Special Envoy Lakhdar Brahimi. But there are few signs that the warring parties, particularly the Taliban, are prepared to come to terms with each other. A major earthquake in February 1998 in northern Afghanistan which killed thousands served as an abrupt reminder of the miserable circumstances endured by vast numbers of people.

The fate of the process – from Strategic Framework to common programming – is in the balance. If it succeeds, it may herald a new approach to complex political emergencies, one characterized by a new partnership between donors, aid actors and beneficiaries. If it fails, it could be condemned as yet another experiment inflicted upon the Afghans, an effort doomed by the intransigence of the international community towards reforming "business as usual." It represents a genuine attempt to improve collective efforts to build peace and save lives. As such, it deserves to succeed.

Editors' Note: *This piece is an updated and modified version of an essay provided by Michael Keating to the Overseas Development Institute, London.*

Women's rights

Calls for the end to Taliban policies which prohibit women from seeking employment and education have come from many Afghan civil rights groups. These include the Gender Advisory Group in Afghanistan, made up of men and women working for United Nations agencies and NGOs handling aid programmes in the country. In May 1997, the group called on the UN and member states to safeguard basic human rights in Afghanistan and urged them to take "careful account" of the Taliban's human rights record when considering their request for recognition or reconstruction aid in Afghanistan. The office of the UN Coordinator for Humanitarian Assistance to Afghanistan (UNOCHA) has set in place a framework for meetings with Taliban policy makers in Kandahar (this however may be in jeopardy following the UN's withdrawal of all its personnel from Kandahar in March 1998). It is also interesting to note that prior to naming the new resident representative of UNOCHA in 1996, the UN quietly decided not to appoint a woman to this position.

Afghan women's rights groups, notably the Revolutionary Association of the Women of Afghanistan (RAWA) and the Afghan Women's Council based in Peshawar, Pakistan have made regular appeals to the international community to protect women's rights in Afghanistan.

The Afghan Women's Network (AWN) has asked for a woman on every team negotiating with the Taliban, both on the political side with the Special Mission for peace in Afghanistan (UNSMA), and on the humanitarian side (UNOCHA), regarding requirements for the for the resumption of aid projects. The AWN has said it received verbal assurances from UN officials that there should be a woman on the Special Mission. (SEE HUMAN RIGHTS)

Widows

Kabul is a city of widows. There are an estimated 30,000 women who have lost their husbands in nearly 20 years of war and are now the sole providers for their families. Most of them are dependent on aid from various agencies and any attempt to prevent them from working and going out into the streets has a devastating effect on the city's population. CARE Afghanistan operates an emergency feeding programme for widow-headed households and is currently providing food assistance to 11,470 women. Food for widows is provided at sites in their districts. These may be old schools, government offices, or other open spaces. The agency employs an all-female distribution team to manage the registration and book keeping activities.

The Taliban are always present but tend not to interfere. Ever since the arrival of the Taliban in Kabul, managing projects to assist widows has been the most difficult and delicate of all CARE Afghanistan's undertakings. Staff have been beaten and threatened; edicts have been issued and then 'amended' which prohibited agencies from distributing relief goods to women or from employing them outside the health sector.

CARE has been able to manage the emergency feeding programme without serious interruption, although several adjustments to their operating procedures have been required in order to enhance the security of their female staff. The agency has had to hire a modest fleet of taxis to transport female staff because NGO buses are too high profile and attract the unwelcome attention of the Religious Police.

The Red Cross provides a similar relief programme for 20,000 widows in Kabul. A total of 300,000 people are assisted under the programme throughout the country.

A tradition of female defiance

The tradition of Malalai, the Afghan bride who in 1880 exhorted her battle-weary betrothed to die combating the British or live a life of shame, remains very much alive in Afghanistan. Many of today's traditionalist Afghan males often forget that high school girls played a crucial role in resisting the Soviets in Kabul. The so-called "children's revolts" inspired by high school girls in April 1980 on the second anniversary of the Saur Revolution resulted in the killing of some 50 students, 30 of them female. Thousands more were arrested and shunted off to police stations, army posts and the main prison at Pul-e-Charkhi east of Kabul.

On 21 April 1980, girls from Sourya High School launched a city-wide strike by marching on the university in protest against the Soviets and the hoisting of the new red flag of the Parcham PDPA regime. As they advanced, students from other schools joined them, but they were dispersed by government troops. On the second day, the girls marched again. This time, they confronted a group of taunting Parcham students backed by the security forces. Nahid, an 11th grade girl from the Rabia Balkhi High School, broke rank by stepping forward to berate the Parchamis for being little more than Soviet stooges. She then cried: "Liberty or death!" prompting the party militants to surge forward in an effort to grab her. Shooting broke

J. Isaac/UNICEF

out and Soviet helicopters flying overhead began firing on the crowd. Nahid was killed, as were dozens of other demonstrators. Amid wails of anguish and anti-communist abuse, the demonstrators were forced to retreat.

But protests continued. As girls from other high schools marched past armed soldiers and party militants, they flung off their veils, tossing them over the men's heads and shouting: "Here, these veils are for you. You are no men." Some of them threw stones at a jeep carrying Soviet advisors and their wives. The Soviets took cover firing several bursts at the protesters. Three girls were killed.

James Nachtwey/ICRC

Day after day, the demonstrations continued. The authorities tried to control the exits of the high schools to prevent pupils from leaving. Undaunted, the girls climbed over the walls, while boys from the Habiba High School near the Soviet embassy almost succeeded in reaching the compound. More firing erupted and at least six pupils fell dead or dying. On 28 April another major demonstration was held and students urging the Afghan police, as brothers, not to fire on them. When the gendarmes refused Parcham orders to do so, party militants started shooting, killing several more demonstrators. Hundreds of others were arrested. Many were held for weeks andmonths on end. Some were only finally released three years later. *EG*

The UN and the gender issue

On 3 June 1997, the Executive Committee on Humanitarian Affairs (ECHA – a consultation group established by the UN Secretary-General) made the following recommendations:

1. It is recommended that organizations of the UN system adopt a principle-centred approach to the gender issue in Afghanistan. This approach envisages continued engagement but also disengagement of UN Agencies from certain institutional assistance programmes which are not in conformity with the policies elaborated hereafter. This approach consists of the following elements.

(a) UN Agencies will continue to be engaged in life-sustaining humanitarian assistance activities for all Afghans in need, including male and female refugees, displaced persons and vulnerable populations.

(b) UN Agencies will engage in the rehabilitation of socio-economic infrastructure, rural and urban, so long as this benefits women and men equally in participation and results.

(c) UN Agencies will assist community-based rehabilitation activities as long as they benefit women and men equally in participation and results.

(d) UN Agencies will urge the Afghan authorities to guarantee the security of women and not use the "security conditions" as a reason for prohibiting women and girls from participating in, or benefiting from, such activities.

(e) UN Agencies will not engage in institution-building efforts of the Afghan authorities as long as their discriminatory practices continue.

(f) UN Agencies will maintain a dialogue with the Afghan authorities with a view to bringing about adherence to the principles enunciated by the Universal Declaration of Human Rights, so as to be able to engage in institution building efforts once peace has settled.

(g) UN Agencies will, however, be sensitive to the different approaches required when dealing with this issue in urban and rural areas.

(h) UN Agencies will strive to ensure that all staff, international and national, male and female, of the UN and other international agencies and their implementing partners, be allowed to work effectively and according to their specific expertise, in full security.

2. UN and implementing agencies will take a consistent approach and convey these principles in their interaction with the Afghan authorities. Heads of UN Agencies, funds and programmes will no longer make unilateral declarations on UN policies and practices relating to human rights observances in Afghanistan.

3. It is also recommended that:

(a) The UN should support and participate in the establishment of a Joint Technical Committee (JTC), proposed by the DHA Mission, particularly to provide the Afghan authorities with explanations on international standards as well as to facilitate the planning and implementation of UN assistance programmes.

(b) Ms. Angela King, Special Advisor to the Secretary-General on Gender Issues, should convene an ad-hoc meeting to review indicators and monitoring measures with detailed inputs from representatives of the UN organizations active in Afghanistan.

(c) A monitoring committee should be established under the chairmanship of the UN Coordinator to review compliance of agencies to the above-mentioned policies and guidelines, and report regularly to the Executive Committee on Humanitarian Affairs.

(d) A directive should be sent out to all agencies, informing them of the decisions of the Executive Committee and requesting them to fully participate in the implementation of the agreed-upon policies regarding the gender issue in Afghanistan, the creation of a monitoring committee and the Joint Technical Committee with the Afghan authorities.

(e) Regarding a possible return of UN agency country offices to Kabul, it was agreed that, among other requirements, employment of both national and international female staff was essential.

ESSENTIAL DATA

- **Afghan women have a life expectancy of 44 years**
- **89% of Afghan women aged between 15 and 24 years are illiterate compared to 54% of their male counterparts**
- **Illiteracy among women aged 25 years and over is 97%, compared to 77% of males of the same age range**
- **Before the arrival of the Taliban, 22% of university teachers were women**
- **The number of births (153/1,000) for women aged between 15 and 19 is one of the highest in the world**
- **Maternal mortality per 100,000 is 1,700 (the worst in the world after Sierra Leone)**
- **Of the estimated 12,000-13,000 deaths per year from tuberculosis, 70% of cases are women**
- **An Afghan woman will have an average of 6.9 children during her lifetime**
- **Abortion in Afghanistan is illegal**
- **Afghanistan has ratified the UN Convention on the Elimination of all forms of Discrimination against Women**

Sources: WHO Afghanistan, 1998, Women – Trends and Statistics (United Nations), The State of the World's Children 1998, UNICEF

ESSENTIAL CONTACTS

Afghan Women's Network (AWN)

International Working Group on Refugee Women (IWGRW)

Women's Commission for Refugee Women and Children (WCRWC)

The Revolutionary Association of the Women of Afghanistan (RAWA)

ICHR/ZANWEB: www.ichr.org/zanweb

ESSENTIAL READING

Women in Afghanistan: The violations continue, Amnesty International (London, June 1997)
Women in Afghanistan: A human rights catastrophe, Amnesty International (London, May 1995)
My Khyber Marriage, Morag Murray Abdullah, Arab World and Islamic Resources and School Services (AWAIR), Berkeley, CA
Three Women of Herat, Veronica Doubleday, Jonathan Cape (London, 1988)
Politics of Women and Development in Afghanistan, Hafizullah Emadi, Paragon House
Searching for Saleem: An Afghan Woman's Odyssey, Farooka Gauhari, University of Nebraska Press
The Performance of Emotion Among Pashtun Women: 'The Misfortunes Which Have Befallen Me', Benedicte Grima, University of Texas Press
Women in Afghanistan, Fahima Rahimi, Stiftung Bibliotheca Afghanica (Liestal, 1986)
Bartered Brides: Politics, Gender, and Marriage in an Afghan Tribal Society, Nancy Tapper, Cambridge University Press.

From New Trend Books, P.O. Box 356, Kingsville, MD 21087, USA:

The Struggle of Muslim Women, Dr Kaukab Siddique
Liberation of Women Through Islam, Dr Kaukab Siddique
Polygamy: Right or Remedy?, Dr Alauddin Shabaaz
Guardianship in Islam, Amin Abdullah

REGIONS

Restored Timurid tilework in Herat *J.Walter*

CENTRAL REGION

Central Afghanistan may be said to comprise of the provinces of Kabul, Kapisa, Parwan and Wardak, with the city of Kabul as its strategic crossroads. To the north lies the snowcapped Hindu Kush mountain range, soaring to over 5,000 metres and through which the Salang Tunnel blasts its way towards Mazar and the Uzbek border. To the east the main artery to Jalalabad and the subcontinent follows the course of the Kabul River, plunging through the spectacular Tangi Gharu and Silk Gorges before climbing through the Khyber Pass into Pakistan. The road towards Ghazni and Persia – for millennia the route of choice for successive conquerors of Kabul, Kandahar and beyond – escapes southwest through a cleft in the mountains. To the west and northwest lie difficult mountain passes into Hazarajat and central Afghanistan proper. (SEE HAZARAJAT REGION)

Kabul

The capital of Afghanistan – and its largest city – is situated at around 1,800 metres above sea-level. Its population is approximately 1.5 million, but this figure is very much an estimate and fluctuates according to the military situation. In 1978 the city had some 500,000 inhabitants.

Kabul's strategic location, in a fertile valley surrounded by high mountains and straddling major trade routes to the four corners of the compass, has made it the natural choice for a settlement since antiquity. It was known as Kubha in the Rigveda of c.1500 BC and as Kabura by Ptolemy (2nd Century AD). In the mid-7th Century AD Muslim Arabs captured the city, but its Hindu rulers were not ousted for another 200 years when the Saffarids finally established Islam in Kabul. As part of the Ghaznavid empire Kabul was attacked by Genghis Khan's hordes in the 13th Century and became the capital of a province of the Moghul empire, whose founder, Babur Shah (1483-1530), is buried on the eastern slope of the Sher Darwaza

The Frontier Post 12 August 1992

mountain. The Moghuls held Kabul until the mid-18th Century, when the Pashtun Ahmed Shah Durrani established the first Afghan Empire based on Kandahar in 1747.

From 1776 onwards Timur Shah, son of Ahmed Shah, made Kabul his capital, and for the next 40 years bitter infighting between Timur Shah's Sadozai brothers destabilized the capital. From 1819 right through to 1973 a rival Pashtun clan, the Mohammedzais, held sway, both as Amirs and as Kings. The "Great Amir" Dost Mohammed emerges as the key figure in mid-19th Century Kabuli politics, ruling the city from 1826-39 and again, after a brief and bloody British interlude, from 1843 until his death in 1863. Dost had provoked the British by making overtures to Russia and Persia, permitting a Russian agent, Vitkevich, to come to Kabul, and casting acquisitive eyes on Punjab territory captured by Ranjit Singh. The British backed Singh, invaded Afghanistan and sacked Kabul in July 1839. Thus began the First Afghan War.

The British installed a puppet ruler of Kabul, Shah Shuja, but he was so weak and unpopular that the British invading force became an army of occupation, complete with polo matches, ladies with parasols and thousands of Indian camp-followers. However, Afghan resentment was fired up and in November 1841 a mob attacked the British delegation, hacking to death the head of mission Sir Alexander Burnes in the process. During the subsequent and infamous retreat from Kabul the following January only a handful of the 16,000 British troops, wives and camp-followers survived, cut down in the passes between Kabul and Jalalabad by tribesmen who had treacherously offered them safe passage. Exacting vengeance, the British invaded a second time in 1842 torching the covered bazaar and plundering much of the city bare. Dost Mohammed returned to Kabul for 20 years during which time he brought Herat, Kandahar and the north under the sway of his capital. Meanwhile the British withdrew to lick their wounds and watch – a policy known in the diplomatic language of the day as "masterly inactivity."

However, Dost Mohammed's son Sher Ali, who became Amir on his father's death, provoked Britain into the Second Afghan War by inviting a Russian General into Kabul in 1878 to sign a treaty. Britain invaded and established a new mission in Kabul the following year, but after only six weeks mutinous troops murdered the hapless envoy and his staff. In 1880 Amir Abdur Rahman consolidated rule in Kabul and established the present day boundaries of Afghanistan. From his time onwards, the history of Kabul and that of Afghanistan as a nation become inseparable. (SEE HISTORY)

Today Kabul feels like an occupied city. Over half of the capital's buildings have been reduced to rubble, mainly during the devastating battle for power between rival mujahed factions from 1992-1996. The latest bitter twist in the tale for Kabul was the arrival in September 1996 of the Taliban, who started the way they meant to continue by smashing televisions and dangling audio and video tape from their checkpoints, by enforcing the wearing of untrimmed beards by men and the all-encompassing *burqa* veil by women. They provoked international outrage by dragging the communist former President Najibullah from his sanctuary in a United Nations compound, executing him and hanging him from a traffic policeman's tower in the middle of town. Many commentators feel that the Taliban view Kabul as their Sodom and Gomorrah – a place to be purged of any last vestiges of liberal anti-Islamic underculture...

Getting there

By air

Kabul has an international airport which continues to operate on the days it is not being shelled or rocketed by competing Afghan factions. The airfield is littered with the wrecks of old Soviet MiG fighters, helicopters and transport aircraft which were destroyed on the ground. Although pilots must negotiate a number of shell holes in the tarmac while taxiing, the actual runway is remarkably intact. As far as the terminal goes, your passports and visas will be checked (entry visa for arriving and exit visa for leaving) but Kabul International is not the place for duty-free shopping. Be prepared to have your bags searched: some people have had photos, films and cassette tapes confiscated by Taliban authorities. Smuggling alcohol in by air is not recommended.

The International Committee of the Red Cross (ICRC) operates two aircraft out of Peshawar which are scheduled to fly into Kabul every day of the week except Fridays. ICRC flights usually go via Herat on Saturdays and Tuesdays, via Kandahar on Sundays and Wednesdays, via Mazar on Saturdays, Tuesdays and Thursdays, and direct to Kabul on Mondays. ICRC flights are free for NGO staff but you may get "bumped off" your seat at any time by ICRC personnel. ICRC does not normally fly journalists, but you may be able to make special arrangements via their offices in Kabul or Peshawar. The United Nations (UNOCHA/UNDP) flies into Kabul from Islamabad; NGO staff pay ($190 one-way) but journalists go free, and once booked on you are unlikely to be "bumped off." UN flights to Kabul are scheduled for Sundays, Tuesdays and Thursdays, and sometimes go via Jalalabad. When fighting forces Kabul airport to close, planes divert to Gardez in Paktya province, two hours' drive south of the capital. (SEE TRAVEL)

Ariana Afghan Airlines, the national carrier, still operates three Boeing 727s based in Delhi which fly both international and domestic services via Kabul. Passenger flights between Kabul and Amritsar operate on Fridays, and between Kabul, Dubai and Jeddah on Saturdays. Domestic services are scheduled between Kabul and Jalalabad on Sundays and between Kabul and Kandahar on Fridays and Saturdays. One-way tickets for Jalalabad cost $20 for expatriates and 150,000 *Afghanis* for locals. For Kandahar the price is $63 for expatriates and 500,000 *Afghanis* for locals. Ariana also claims to operate a daily cargo service between Dubai, Kabul,

GARDEZ

Whenever Afghan factions decide to start lobbing shells and rockets at Kabul airport, ICRC and UN flights to the capital divert to Gardez in Paktya province. Otherwise the UN flies to Gardez on Mondays and Thursdays (on demand). The tarmac road from Gardez to Kabul is one of the best in Afghanistan, and the journey takes about two hours. If you need to spend the night here, the UNOCHA office has two guest rooms available at no charge, except for meals, laundry and tips for the cook. Situated at 2,900 metres, Gardez has a temperate summer climate (June-August) but harsh winters (December-February) when the thermometer can drop to minus 20 degrees Celsius. The security situation has been stable in recent years, but remember you are in a Taliban-controlled area. If you wish to visit any agencies in this region, make all necessary arrangements with field headquarters in Peshawar or Islamabad prior to arrival. There are no fax or mail services in Gardez. Recreation is limited to walking round an orchard called the Terra Garden, or jogging around the UN-NGO area. One locally-based aid official recommends that "women avoid jogging to avoid pandemonium."

Kandahar and Jalalabad. For more details contact Ariana's main office in Kabul, located in front of Zarnegar Park (TEL: 22372).

By road

Short of trekking in by foot disguised as a holy man or lurching in on a camel, the most interesting and atmospheric way to reach Kabul is by road; mind you, most people only do it once if they can help it…The eastern approach from Pakistan takes between seven to nine hours by car from Peshawar to Kabul, depending on how keen your driver is to shatter his suspension (and your vertebrae). On a good day the views are fantastic, ranging from spectacular rocky passes and snowcapped mountains to turquoise lakes and emerald green pastures fringing the Kabul River.

In the "bad old days" from '92-'96 you could be stopped at over 60 different checkpoints along this road, all manned by local commanders loaded with similar weapons but varying allegiances. Numerous aid workers and journalists have been held up at gunpoint and had their possessions – sometimes even their vehicles – stolen from in front of them. During the Soviet war the road was thick with Russian tanks, APCs and troop columns, so most journalists and adventurers entering or leaving Afghanistan from the east had to trek in by foot through the mountains to the north or south. Nowadays the Taliban have changed all that – for the better. The road is safer to travel along than at any time in the last twenty years. You can even catch a cab if the cash is right – anything from $80 to $200 depending on your bargaining skills.

To the north, the road from Baghlan through the Salang tunnel currently crosses the main frontline between Taliban and anti-Taliban forces, so negotiating a passage is tricky. Alexander the Great arrived in Kabul from the southwest, but the road is possibly worse now than it was then…the trip from Kandahar and Ghazni is a once-in-a-lifetime experience (never again!) for which you should allow two full days. Before the war a central route from Herat to Kabul taking at least four days via Chakhcharan and Bamiyan was possible, but currently the Taliban/Hazara frontline somewhere in Ghor province makes this difficult. For more details on this and other routes, refer to Nancy Dupree's *An Historical Guide to Afghanistan* (Second Edition, 1977).

From Peshawar to Kabul overland

Heading west from Peshawar, the road takes you through the semi-autonomous tribal agencies of the North West Frontier Province, which for centuries has been home to smugglers, arms dealers and, more recently, drug barons. (SEE PESHAWAR) You must get a special tribal agencies permit in advance to travel through this area. (SEE VISAS) If you are coming from Afghanistan a permit is not necessary, but the border post will issue you with an armed guard to escort you free of charge. The route then winds up into the Khyber

WARNING

KABUL IS ONE OF THE MOST HEAVILY MINED CITIES IN THE WORLD — STICK TO THE TRODDEN PATH OR TRAVEL WITH A GUIDE !

Pass before reaching the border crossing at Torkham after about one and a half hours by car. The frontier closes between 1200 hrs and 1400 hrs and Pakistan is half an hour ahead of Afghanistan so make sure you arrive at the border before 1130 hrs Afghan time if you are driving to Peshawar. The Pakistanis close their side of the border at 1800 hrs but may still be persuaded to let you through later.

From the forts and picket posts of the Khyber you descend into the Nangarhar valley. Before the war, this area boasted several hundred thousand acres of irrigated citrus fruit and olive farms created under a joint Afghan-Soviet scheme to reclaim the desert. Tall poplars planted as windbreaks continue to sway elegantly in the breeze, but most of the cash-crops have been ripped up during two decades of fighting. The mujahideen gave the farms their *coup de grace* by completely trashing and looting them, hard on the heels of the government forces in 1989. The odd fir and cypress tree herald your arrival in Jalalabad (one and a half hours from Torkham), a town founded by the Moghuls who were among the first to make this route via the Khyber popular. The military garrison at Jalalabad was the distant sanctuary towards which a British army of 4,500 soldiers and 12,000 camp-followers was desperately retreating after an ignominious departure from Kabul in January 1842. Apart from a few prisoners who strayed back months later, only one Englishman, Dr Brydon, completed the retreat; the remainder were cut to pieces in the passes which lie between here and Kabul.

West of Jalalabad the road joins the Kabul River on the other side of which Buddhist caves are carved into the cliff-face. Over one thousand Buddhist sites and *stupas* are scattered across the Jalalabad valley, the most famous of which is Hadda. Some date back as far as 200 AD but many have now been badly looted. (SEE CULTURE) The road continues past the turquoise Darunta Reservoir, built in the 1960s and once home to four types of Chinese carp, and across a flat plain punctuated with typical fortified *qala* (Pashtun houses) and *chaikhana* (teahouses). Despite the Taliban restrictions, it is common to hear music emanating from these *chaikhana* and women in the fields or by the road seldom wear the all-encompassing *burqa*.

The worst section of road is from the Darunta dam to Sarobi – scenes of heavy fighting during the Soviet war. From here, it degenerates into a dirt track; old men and young children sweat away filling potholes with stones, eagerly awaiting the flutter of bank notes in the dusty wake left behind by passing vehicles. Before Sarobi you pass through Tangi Abreshom, the Silk Gorge, which was the scene of one of the most spectacular mujahed ambushes of the war: several hundred Soviet soldiers are believed to have perished when their armoured column was fired on. Some of their vehicles remain, as still as headstones, in mute testimony to a misguided war.

From Sarobi the route passes high to the south of the stunning Naglu Reservoir before plunging between the sheer rock faces of the Tangi Gharu gorge, considerably more impressive than the Khyber Pass. Once spat out onto the Kabul Plateau, the capital is within sight. Almost immediately on your left, you can see the massive edifice of Pul-e-Charkhi, the notorious East German-built prison used by the communist government for detaining thousands of political and military opponents during the 1980s. From Jalalabad the trip to Kabul should take no more than four or five hours by car.

If you do not have access to your own vehicle, ask around either in Peshawar or Kabul – aid agencies are often happy to carry an extra passenger, but you may need to break the journey in Jalalabad. Buses run but take twice as long; taxis will take you from Kabul to Torkham (US$100), but you must change to a Pakistani vehicle to reach Peshawar. World Food Programme (WFP) food convoys sometimes offer lifts to freelancers, but take two days to reach Kabul from Peshawar. Check with the logistics department of WFP in Islamabad.

Orientation

Kabul is bisected by the Kabul River which flows through the centre of town from the southwest to the northeast. Almost all the international agencies operating in Kabul are based north of the Kabul River in Shahr-e-Naw (meaning "new town" and begun in 1935) and the adjoining Wazir Akbar Khan (named after Amir Dost Mohammed's son who murdered the British Garrison Commander in 1842). In the centre of the new-town stands the Arg, a citadel and walled palace built in 1888 by Amir Abdur Rahman to replace the old Bala Hissar fortress.

The airport lies five kilometres northeast of Shahr-e-Naw. To the northwest lies the Kolola Pushta or Round Fort, and the Intercontinental Hotel perches on a spur of rock four kilometres to the west. The mountains to the southwest of Shahr-e-Naw through which the Kabul River squeezes are the Koh-e-Asmai and Koh-e-Sher Darwaza.

The road running west through this rocky cleft leads to Kabul University and Karte Seh. South of the Kabul River lies the old town

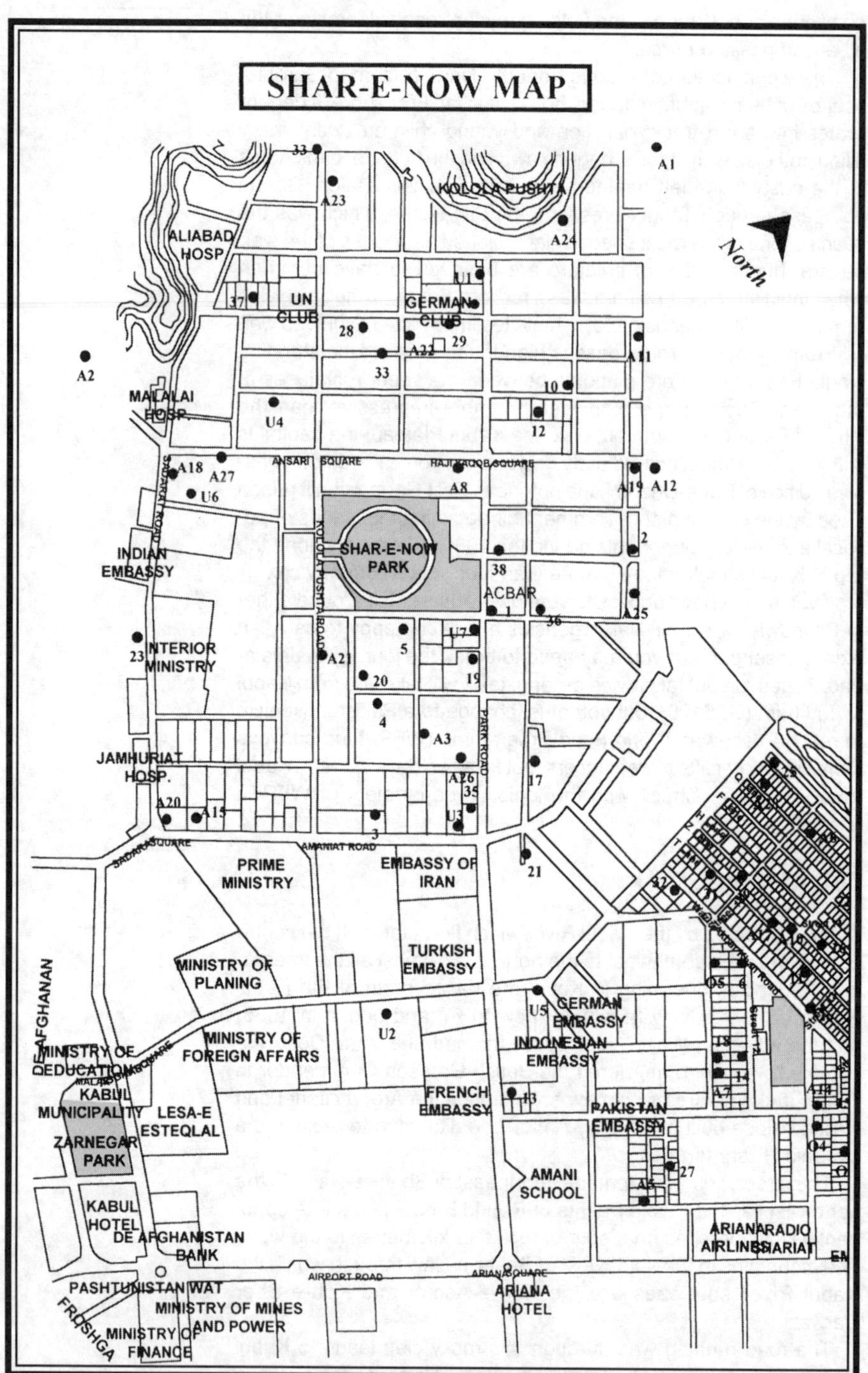

SHAR-E-NOW MAP
North
KOLOLA PUSHTA
ALIABAD HOSP
UN CLUB
GERMAN CLUB
MALALAI HOSP.
ANSARI SQUARE
HAJI YAQOB SQUARE
SHAR-E-NOW PARK
KOLOLA PUSHTA ROAD
PARK ROAD
ACBAR
INDIAN EMBASSY
INTERIOR MINISTRY
JAMHURIAT HOSP.
SADARAT ROAD
SADARAT SQUARE
AMANIAT ROAD
PRIME MINISTRY
EMBASSY OF IRAN
TURKISH EMBASSY
MINISTRY OF PLANING
MINISTRY OF FOREIGN AFFAIRS
GERMAN EMBASSY
INDONESIAN EMBASSY
FRENCH EMBASSY
PAKISTAN EMBASSY
DE AFGHANAN
MINISTRY OF EDUCATION
KABUL MUNICIPALITY
LESA-E ESTEQLAL
ZARNEGAR PARK
KABUL HOTEL
DE AFGHANISTAN BANK
PASHTUNISTAN WAT
MINISTRY OF MINES AND POWER
MINISTRY OF FINANCE
FROSHGA
AMANI SCHOOL
AIRPORT ROAD
ARIANA SQUARE
ARIANA HOTEL
ARIANA AIRLINES
RADIO

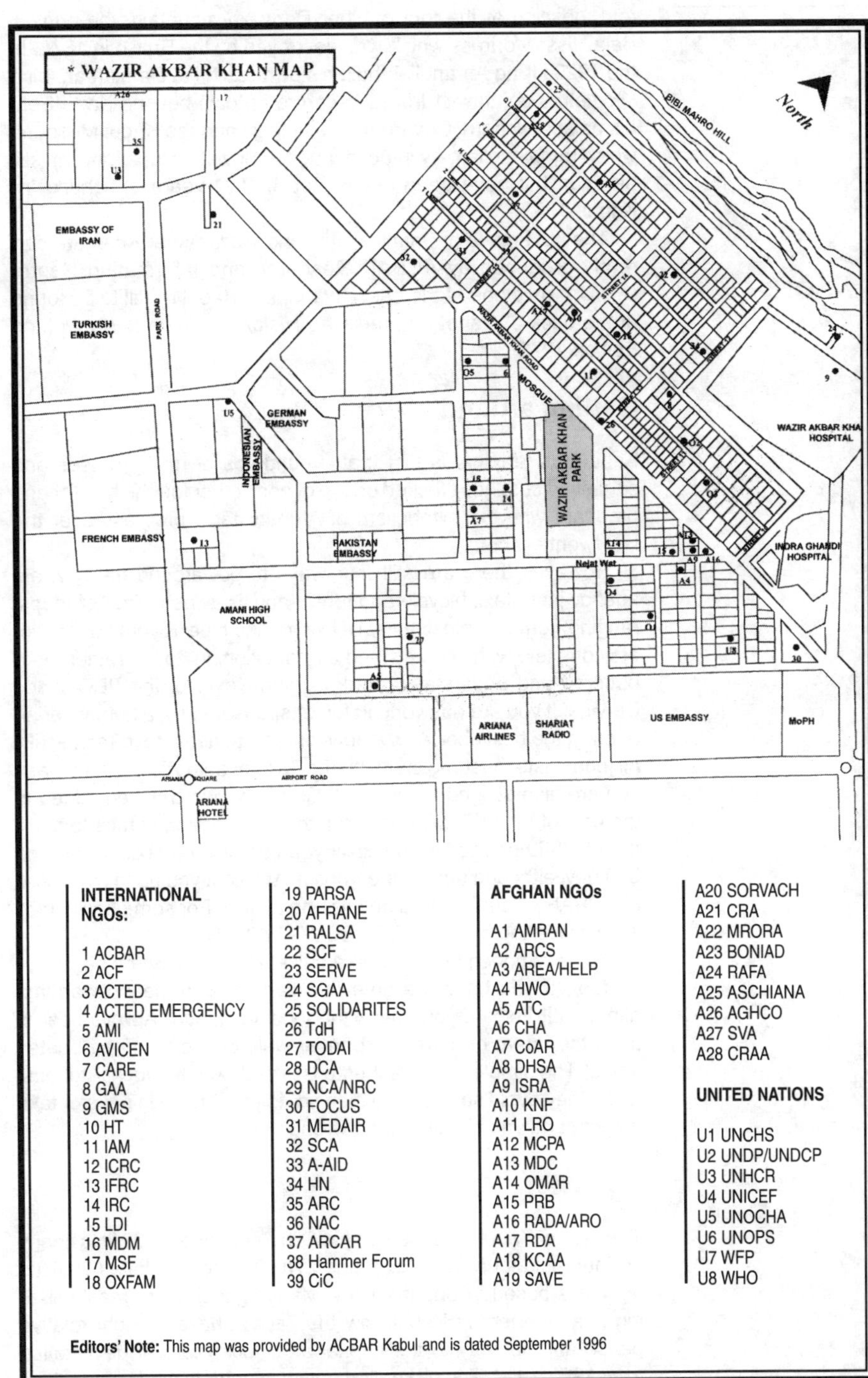

Editors' Note: This map was provided by ACBAR Kabul and is dated September 1996

and, nestling at the foot of Sher Darwaza mountain, the original Bala Hissar fortress which was destroyed by the British in 1878. In the 1920s King Amanullah built his own capital at Darulaman, nine kilometres southwest from the centre of town beyond Karte Seh: his palace, various Government buildings and the Kabul Museum, which remained largely intact during the Soviet occupation, can still be seen but have been devastated by five years of fighting in Kabul.

The best maps of Shahr-e-Naw and Wazir Akbar Khan are currently produced by ACBAR Resource and Information Centre (ARIC), while one of the best city maps of Kabul is still to be found at the back of Nancy Dupree's *An Historical Guide to Kabul* (2nd Edition 1972).

Getting around

Kabul bus terminal is just that – hundreds of rusting buses and squashed coaches stacked on top of each other four high – a scene pregnant with the symbolism of Afghanistan's progress over the last twenty years.

However, there are still four ways to get around the city: aid agency jeep, taxi, bicycle and foot. Kabul is awash with 4x4 jeeps, ranging from the latest shiny UN white and blue Toyota Landcruisers complete with snorkels and air-conditioning, to the rather more battered and understated Mark II Land Rover of the BBC World Service. If you are not working for, or sponsored by, a humanitarian agency, the best choice as a newcomer is to hire a taxi. Technically all journalists must register with the Taliban authorities; this means you are also obliged to hire an 'official' taxi, which when added to the cost of the 'official' (and obligatory) interpreter, comes to more than US$60 per day. Unofficially you can pick up taxis for around $20/day, although trips to the frontline will cost you up to $100. Ask at ACBAR Kabul for more details and advice. For some basic rules when travelling by car (SEE SECURITY TIPS).

Some experienced aid workers like to get around by bicycle or on foot. If you have the time this can be extremely rewarding, although it helps if you speak the local language. Always bear in mind the threat of mines and never walk or cycle "off the beaten track." The simplest rule of thumb is: check with the local Afghans, and if they avoid somewhere then so do you. Travel in pairs or take a guide and you should not go wrong.

Agencies

The map of Kabul produced by ARIC in September 1997 lists nearly 40 international NGOs, 30 Afghan NGOs and 10 United Nations agencies based in Shahr-e-Naw. Many agencies are reestablishing headquarters in Kabul now the Taliban have brought relative peace and security to the capital after four years of devastation from 1992-1996. The UN pulled out its expatriate staff when things

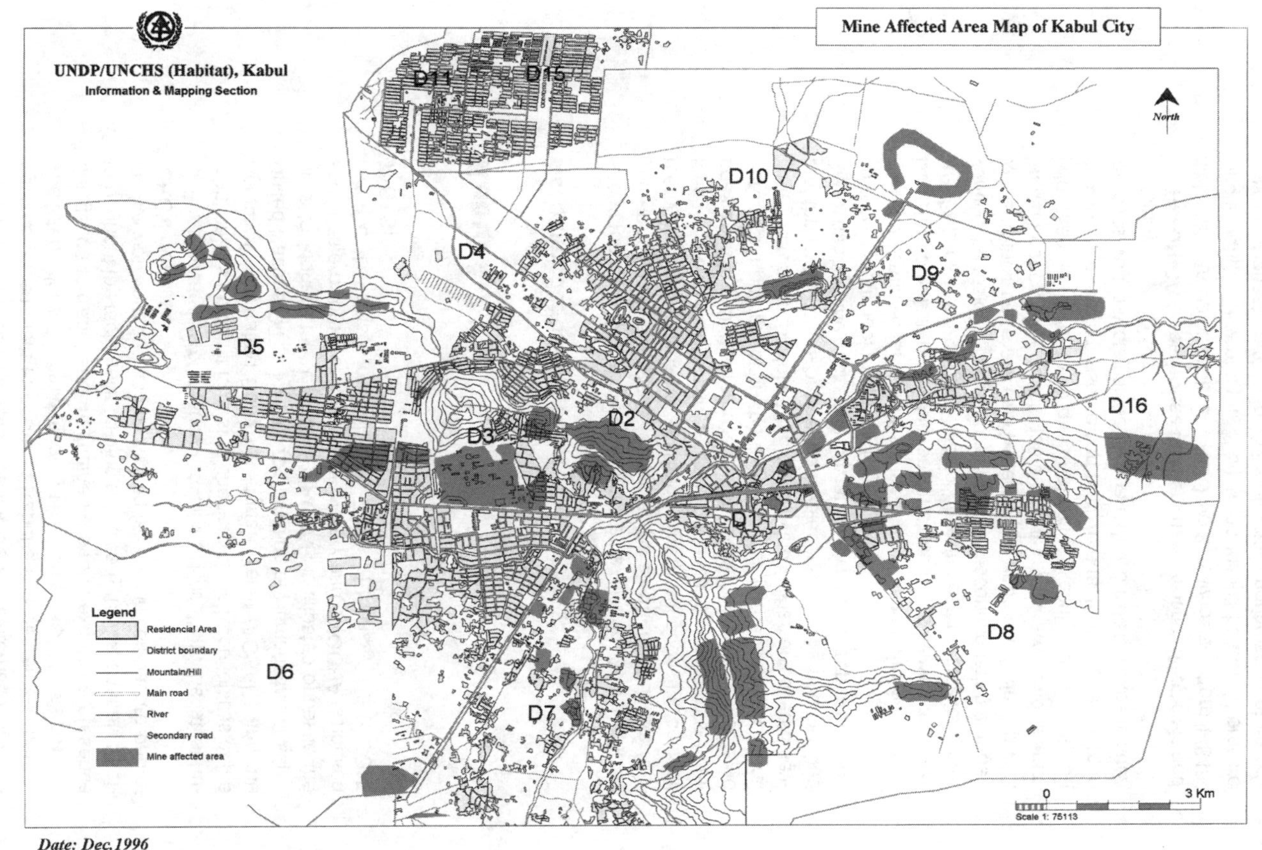

Date: Dec.1996

got difficult, and most of the UN agencies are now based in Islamabad. While expatriate staff have returned, UN agency-heads are unlikely to come back to Kabul until there is an internationally recognized government in power in Kabul and a guaranteed peace. The International Committee for the Red Cross (ICRC) has its main delegation in Kabul and maintained a strong expatriate presence throughout the factional infighting of the early 1990s; after all, treating the war wounded and promoting fair play in combat are part of ICRC's mandate.

For an overview of agency activities in Kabul and the latest humanitarian situation it is best to check in at the Kabul offices of the Agency Coordinating Body for Afghan Relief (ACBAR) and the United Nations Office for the Coordination of Humanitarian Assistance to Afghanistan (UNOCHA). ACBAR is situated opposite the southeastern corner of Shahr-e-Naw Park and UNOCHA is housed in the UNDP offices opposite the Turkish Embassy. (SEE CONTACTS)

Kabul A-Z

Accommodation and Food

Accommodation in Kabul is currently rather limited. As a journalist you are officially supposed to stay at the **Continental Hotel** (formerly the Intercontinental – US$65/night), although the cocktail lounges, heated swimming pool and beauty parlour which the hotel boasted in the 1970s are no longer available. Some expatriates go here to eat out, although the experience is perhaps more cultural than gastronomic. In late 1996 the arriving Taliban discovered several thousand bottles of beer concealed in the cellar and crushed the lot beneath the tracks of a Soviet tank, while a group of parched correspondents looked on longingly.

The alternative for journalists is not to come to Kabul as journalists. But do not automatically assume you can stay with the *AFP, AP, BBC* or *Reuters*. The Taliban have imposed restrictions preventing the resident correspondents from accommodating any visitors and their spies are everywhere. One approach is link up with an aid agency, either back home or out in Peshawar and Islamabad. Many of them have guesthouses in Kabul and may let you stay there in return for some sort of coverage. If you are a German journalist you may stay at the German Club, but do not expect much company.

The UNICA Guesthouse is where most visiting UN officials and diplomats stay, along with any NGO workers who can afford it ($40/single/night; $60/twin/night; $55/person for full board). There are only eight guestrooms and UN staff take priority, so book in advance through UNOCHA/UNDP in Islamabad. Rooms come with *en suite* bath and a desk. There is one local telephone, plus a CTOR radio for contacting the UN in Islamabad, but no satphone facilities are available for residents. Journalists have not been allowed to spend the night here since the arrival of the Taliban. The building has been a guesthouse since 1945 and used to belong to King Zahir Shah's sister-in-law. Located at the northwestern end of Kolola Pushta road in Shahr-e-Naw and known locally as the "UN Club" it is the main focus for Kabul's expatriate socializing, drinking and gossiping. Thursday night through to Sunday night is the time to visit, but get here early – the party is over by half eight in the evening because of the curfew. Western-style lunch and dinner are available for $6, along with cheaper bar snacks. Visitors must pay $2 entrance fee at the door and the dress code (once inside) is relaxed. Unfortunately Afghans are not allowed to enter the Club.

The German Club (TEL: 31505), located near the foot of the Kolola Pushta fort in Shahr-e-Naw, has a dozen or more guestrooms with *en suite* bathrooms which stand empty most of the time. Previously the International Club, it has definitely seen better days. A waiter who worked here for 40 years remembered hundreds of guests before 1992 and a thriving amateur dramatic scene. Now its bar is dry and its facilities dusty from disuse. Although it does not belong to the German government, only Germans may stay here overnight, including German journalists. Food can be provided but order early – they need a day's warning.

The Herat Restaurant is an excellent local café in Shahr-e-Naw where you can savour a more indigenous menu. The decor, however, is far from indigenous: a tropical fish tank sits beneath a poster of Newcastle-upon-Tyne in England, complete with English caption ("Liberty is the only thing you cannot have / Unless you are willing to give it to others"). Black-turbaned Pashtun soldiers of the Taliban walk blithely past it, unaware of the irony, and sit cross-legged on a raised dais at the end of the room, their kalashnikovs resting beside their bowls of rice. Private dining rooms are available, and an excellent lunch of *qabuli, maast & chai sabz* (rice & mutton, yoghurt and green tea) will cost little more than a dollar. *Afghanis*, dollars and Pakistani rupees are all accepted.

Books

Kabul is surprisingly well-served by bookshops, considering over half the city has been reduced to rubble. There are several good ones at the end of Chicken Street where you can still pick up 1970s guidebooks, maps and tourist brochures. The Shah M. Book Co. has two shops, one at the Intercontinental Hotel and one downtown in Chahrai Saddarat. Their prices are often two or three times higher than the shops in Chicken Street but they do stock some new titles. For more information on Kabul read the following:

An Historical Guide to Kabul, Nancy Hatch Dupree (Kabul, 2nd Edition, 1972)

An Historical Guide to Afghanistan, Nancy Hatch Dupree (Kabul, 2nd Edition, 1977)

Cabool in 1836-37 and 8, Being the Personal Narrative of a Journey to, and Residence in, that City, Sir Alexander Burnes, (London, 1842; reprinted by Ferozsons, Lahore, 1964 and by Akademische Druk-u. Verlagsanstalt, Graz, 1973). Despite the author's knowledge of the city, he was hacked to death by a frenzied mob in 1841.

An Account of the Kingdom of Caubul, Mountstuart Elphinstone, John Murray (London, 1815; reprinted by Akademische Druk-u. Verlagsanstalt, Graz, 1969 and by Oxford University Press, Karachi, 1972)

Signal Catastrophe; The Retreat from Kabul, 1842, Patrick Macrory, Hodder and Stoughton (London, 1966).

Other guidebooks exist, but virtually all are out of print. There are libraries of books in English and European languages at the UNICA Guesthouse and the German Club.

Embassies & Visas

In the 1970s there were 25 diplomatic missions in town, but since 1989 most expatriates have left; now only a handful are manned, such as the Pakistani and Turkish embassies. The Russian embassy lies in ruins; the American legation is deserted apart from a caretaker team; and the magnificent British mission – home to the "best housed man in Asia" and guarded until 1994 by a team of Gurkhas armed with little more than *kukris* – was handed back to Pakistan and promptly shelled. It is best to check with ACBAR or UNOCHA in Kabul to find out which embassies are currently operating.

Visas may be renewed at the Ministry of Foreign Affairs (MFA) in Kabul, and if you are leaving Kabul by air you must get an "exit visa" from the MFA otherwise you will not be allowed on the plane. If you are driving out via Torkham to Peshawar an exit visa is not necessarily demanded, but check the situation on the ground. For getting visas to visit Afghanistan SEE VISAS.

Emergencies

If you find yourself in Kabul when the opposition forces are shelling or rocketing the city, the only thing to do is lie low and wait for an opportunity to leave if things get too hot for your liking. (So bring along a good book and your shortwave radio). There is a 16-man bunker under the UNICA club in Shahr-e-Naw if you are desperate, otherwise take shelter in the cellar of your house or under the stairs. It may sound obvious, but try and resist the temptation to go outside if there is shooting: what goes up must come down and many people have been killed or injured by falling bullets and shrapnel.

In an emergency both the ICRC and the UN will try to evacuate their own staff and everyone else (in that order) either by vehicle or by air, so keep in touch with them. (SEE SECURITY TIPS)

Information

For more information about United Nations activities, contact the Regional Representative for UNOCHA at the UNDP office in Kabul. UNOCHA should be able to give you a briefing on the latest security and landmine situation. Make sure you receive some kind of landmine awareness briefing, preferably from UNOCHA in Islamabad before travelling to Afghanistan.

For more details on NGO activities contact ACBAR in Shahr-e-Naw. (SEE CONTACTS) The best way to meet aid agency workers and resident journalists is to turn up for a drink at the UNICA Guesthouse on a Thursday, Friday or Saturday night between six and eight-thirty in the evening.

Local Rules

Kabul is in many ways an unique city, and quite different from the rest of Afghanistan. A once western-oriented and sophisticated urban population has not taken kindly to Taliban repression, leading to heavy-handed tactics on the part of the authorities. The Taliban are more nervous and uncertain of themselves in Kabul than in the more homogenous Pashtun cities of Kandahar or Jalalabad. As a result anyone visiting or working in Kabul has to take special care not to incur Taliban wrath or endanger the lives of the Afghans that he or she may be with. (SEE SECURITY TIPS)

Medical

Access to health care in Kabul may well be better than in most western cities. There are dozens of agencies specializing in the medical sector and over 20 hospitals in the capital. (SEE HEALTH) If you are suffering it is probably best to arrange to see a health NGO through ACBAR – most agencies are more than willing to help out. One EFG Editor on a recent trip to Kabul received physiotherapy and ultrasound treatment free-of-charge from an Afghan working for an international NGO.

The ICRC runs surgical units at Karte Seh and Wazir Akbar Khan hospitals and will operate on all emergency cases. (SEE PERSONAL HEALTH)

Money

There are no functioning banks in Kabul and noone takes credit cards, so make sure you bring enough cash; US Dollars or Pakistani Rupees are the best. Ask around for the current exchange rate and the best place to change money. Some dealers (if they trust you) take personal cheques for European and North American banks. The market is open rather than black, but take a strong, large bag to carry your loot off in: at today's rates you will walk away with a million *Afghanis* in return for forty bucks. (SEE MONEY)

Darulaman Palace, damaged by mujahed infighting from 1992-1996 *J. Walter*

Post & Telecommunications

Before coming to Kabul spend a bit of time saying goodbye to your loved ones, because letters take months to reach the outside world (if at all) and satphones clock in at between five to ten dollars a minute. The local telephone network functions adequately and most agency offices and guesthouses are hooked up. If you are a journalist operating through a humanitarian agency you may be able to use their satphone; otherwise try approaching UNOCHA or the ICRC. The owner of the German Club runs a public satphone downtown – ask at the German Club for details. ACBAR will send messages by radio telex to their office in Peshawar for onward transmission by e-mail to international addresses. A local courier, Ariana News Agency (TEL: 25974) will collect your mail-pouch and drive it to Peshawar for onward distribution the next day. Individual letters can be sent this way via ACBAR. (SEE RADIO & TELECOMMUNICATIONS)

Recreation

Roller-blading around Kabul may attract unwelcome attention in the present climate, but a surprising amount of recreational possibilities do exist. The UNICA Guesthouse is the best place to start. The club boasts a squash court (racquets available, bring your own balls), a swimming pool (closed October-April), a grass volleyball court, table tennis and even two pool tables for diehard fitness freaks. Sometimes there are step-aerobics and circuit-training sessions, depending on who in town is motivated enough to organize them. Couch-potatoes can sunbathe by the pool or watch satellite TV.

Membership of the UN Club is $2 per day, $15 per month or $90 per year, after which all facilities are free.

The German Club has three clay tennis courts in good condition, and a swimming pool which sadly lies empty at present. Tennis racquets and balls are available, as well as changing and washing facilities. Volleyball, bowling, billiards and bingo are all on offer, as is a theatre fully equipped with stage curtain and lighting. Membership is $3 per day or $90 per year.

Bear in mind Islamic restrictions on dress before taking exercise in Kabul. Always change at the club and never wander around Kabul in shorts. Joggers can stretch their legs running around the garden of the Turkish Embassy, but do not try running around suburban Kabul because you will most likely either get arrested or tread on a mine. If you must undress, do it beside the pool in the UN Club, not on the roof of your guesthouse. For the more adventurous, there is good swimming (but not much shade) up at Kargha Lake, 10 km to the west of the city.

Shopping

Shopping in Kabul took a turn for the worse after the British Army torched the famous covered bazaar 120 years ago. The Afghans however, never ones to miss out on a quick buck, have bounced back and now import numerous western goods from Dubai. If *qabuli, maast & chai sabz* are not your style, then the 'supermarkets' of Flower Street will sell you Pringles, baked beans and even decaffeinated coffee, at a price. For trophy hunters and ethnic collectors, Chicken Street is still lined with stalls desperate to do business. Turcoman carpets, lapis jewellery, *Kuchi* bedspreads, and fake Lee Enfield pistols are all on sale. Flying visits from UN functionaries have pushed prices up, but with large amounts of banter and green tea you should be able to knock between a third and two thirds off the asking price, depending on how ruthless you are feeling.

Sights

Sightseeing may not be the first thing which comes to mind on a visit to Kabul, but there are still a number of places well worth visiting if you have the time. The best sources of information on the subject remain the two guidebooks written in the 1970s by Nancy Dupree. What follows is a modest update.

Kabul Museum. Before the war this was one of the most important collections of archaeology and ethnography in Central Asia. The Hellenistic, Greco-Buddhist, Ghaznavid and subsequent periods were all represented. Its neoclassical home, constructed by King Amanullah in Darulaman, 10 km from the centre of town, was shattered by factional fighting between 1992-1996, and much of the collection was looted or destroyed. What remains of the collection was moved in 1996 to the Kabul Hotel for safekeeping. (SEE CULTURE)

Kabul University. Kabul University was founded in 1932 with the establishment of the school of medicine, followed by faculties of law and political science, natural sciences, economics, home economics, education, engineering and pharmacy. A new campus was built in 1964 and affiliations with American, French, German and Egyptian universities were established. The University reached a peak of 8,500 students and 800 teachers in 1976, but following the Saur Revolution the curriculum became more Soviet-orientated. Twenty years of war have shattered the university both physically and intellectually. (SEE EDUCATION)

Mausoleum of Amir Abdur Rahman. Located in the centre of town, just north of the river, the mausoleum stands in Zarnegar (lit. "adorned with gold") Park, although neither gold nor park is much in evidence today. Originally built by the Amir (1880-1901) as a private pleasure pavilion, his son Amir Habibullah laid him to rest here. Nowadays the mausoleum is a popular place for graffiti artists and heroin addicts to hang out. The nearby tomb of King Amanullah's brother Hayatullah is used for drying laundry.

Minaret of Maiwand. Only the stump of this unremarkable monument remains; but it signified a remarkable Afghan victory over the British near Kandahar in 1880. The Afghans were about to give up when out rushed a young Pashtun bride named Malalai, ripped off her veil and raised it over her head as a battle standard with the cry, "My love, if you do not fall today in the battle of Maiwand, by Allah you will be saved as a symbol of shame!" What would the Taliban have made of her?

Pul-e-Khisti Mosque. A large blue dome rising above the markets just across the river from Zarnegar is that of Kabul's largest mosque, originally built at the end of the 18th Century. It stands next to the Pul-e-Khisti (lit. "Bridge of Bricks") in what was the centre of Kabul from the 17th-19th Centuries. Damaged during recent fighting, it is now one of the very few historical buildings in Kabul being restored.

Shah-Do Shamshira Mosque. This yellow two-storey mosque is probably the best preserved in Kabul and sits picturesquely beside the Kabul River in the centre of town. Built in the reign of King Amanullah, its name means the Mosque of the King of Two Swords.

Weather

At an altitude of 1,800 metres, Kabul is the highest of Afghanistan's main cities, so pack warm clothes for all times of year. Average temperatures for the capital are: January, minus 2.8°C; July, 24.4°C.

NORTHERN REGION

Northern Afghanistan may be defined as the region of the country lying to the north of the Hindu Kush mountain range. Both geographically and culturally it is an area more closely related to Central Asia than to Persia or the Indian subcontinent. Its ethnic mix of Tajiks, Uzbeks and Turkmens reflects the nationalities of those living over the border of the Amu Darya (Oxus River) to the north.

Although the largest city in northern Afghanistan is now Mazar-e-Sharif, the region was dominated for nearly three millennia by the city of Balkh. Zoroaster preached fire-worship here around 1000-600 BC. Alexander the Great based his army here for two years in 329 BC. And in the first centuries after Christ, Buddhist pilgrims flocked to temples which thrived under the Kushan dynasty. In 663 the Chinese adventurer Hsuan-tsang remarked that Balkh had three of the most beautiful buildings in the world. With the advent of Islam in the 8th to 9th Centuries, Balkh became known as the "Mother of Cities", so numerous were its mosques and so rich its intellectual, poetical and spiritual culture. However, the destructive habits of Genghis Khan put an end to this glorious city in 1220, and even one hundred years later the famous traveller Ibn Battuta found the entire area "in ruins."

With Balkh and northern Afghanistan straddling the important trade routes to Central Asia, the city made a brief recovery in the 15th Century under the patronage of the Timurid ruler of Herat, Shah Rukh. Then for several centuries Kabul and Bokhara competed for influence over the northern territories, until Ahmed Shah Durrani, "Father of Afghanistan", finally established the frontier of his kingdom along the line of the Amu Darya in 1768. Balkh was then made the capital of Afghan Turkestan, but for health reasons the city was abandoned in 1866 in favour of a small village by the name of Mazar-e-Sharif. From the lengthy perspective of Afghan history, therefore, Mazar is rather a gatecrasher to the party. For many centuries famous only for its shrine to the cousin of the Prophet Mohammed, it has prospered over the last century at Balkh's expense.

Before the Soviet war Mazar had become a centre of militant Muslim youth, along with Panjshair, Baghlan and Badakhshan. In the early 1980s, the influence of Rabbani's party Jamiat-e-Islami spread throughout the north of Afghanistan, closely linked to the local reputation of three commanders. Mazar was the base for Zabiullah, who was killed in 1984, while Ismail Khan held sway in Herat to the west, and Ahmed Shah Massoud operated throughout the northeast. Jamiat took root in the north partly because of the political and military astuteness of its leaders, but also because this area of Afghanistan was far less tribal than the Pashtun south, and hence more amenable to military organization across a whole region.

The significance of northern Afghanistan did not escape the Russians either. In the words of the French Central Asian specialist, Olivier Roy, "that part of Afghanistan which is of strategic importance is shaped somewhat like an hourglass in which the Salang Pass is the neck." To the north are the plains from Shibarghan to Kunduz and the land route to Termez and Central Asia. To the south lies the strategically crucial crossing of the Hindu Kush range through the Salang tunnel, and the route via Kabul and Jalalabad to India. The area encompassed is rich and well-populated, with the added attraction of the country's main natural resources: the gas and oil fields of Shibarghan, and the copper mines at Any in Logar. This of course was also the route of the Soviet invasion in 1979, mounted from Termez and mobilized through the Salang Pass to Kabul.

From February 1992, when General Dostum mutinied against the communist regime of President Najibullah, until May 1997, when the Taliban launched their ill-fated assault on the city, Mazar-e-Sharif was an island of peace. For five years Dostum controlled an independent militia force numbering an estimated 40,000 to 60,000 soldiers. On the strength of this private army, he created his personal fiefdom in Mazar, complete with its own flag, currency and airline – Balkh Air. Many educated Afghans fled the factional fighting which rocked Kabul from 1992-1996 and settled in Mazar. More have joined them since the arrival in Kabul of the ultra-conservative Taliban. Thus Mazar became an alternative capital, with a more liberal environment where women and children had greater access to education and work than in Taliban-controlled areas.

General Dostum enjoys the financial and military support of Uzbekistan and Russia who see him as the one man capable of preventing a Taliban-inspired Islamic fundamentalism from spreading north into their territories. At present Mazar remains at the centre of Dostum's and ousted President Rabbani's anti-Taliban Northern Alliance. However, Khalili's Hazara party Hezb-e-Wahdat is also very influential within the city. Jamiat-e-Islami keeps a small presence in Mazar, but is concentrating more on consolidating its position in Kunduz to the east. (SEE KEY PLAYERS)

As a gateway for Afghanistan north to the Central Asian Republics of the CIS and west to Iran, Mazar became economically prosperous; and it could still stand to benefit from the untapped oil and natural gas fields nearby. However, the Taliban assaults in May and September 1997 – involving the shelling of both the airport and the city – have sent shock waves through this once quiet haven. Stories of mass graves and mutilations have further increased ethnic tensions across the region.

Mazar-e-Sharif

Owing to fighting in and around Mazar for much of 1997, EFG Editors were not able to check up personally on the facts contained in this chapter. For the practical details contained about the city we are indebted to Shon Campbell of Save the Children Fund (UK) and UNICEF's Mazar office.

Getting there

By air

When Mazar airport is not being shelled or rocketed by Afghan factions, it can receive over six regular services a week from Pakistan. Although Mazar is not under Taliban control, you are not allowed to bring in cassettes, videos or alcohol on these flights.

The UN flies two to three times per week from Islamabad, scheduled for Mondays, Tuesdays and Thursdays. The Monday flights sometimes go via Bamiyan, the Tuesday flights via Faizabad, and the Thursday flights tend to be direct. The cost is US$300 one-way for NGO staff, but free for journalists. Tickets should be arranged through UNOCHA Islamabad or Mazar. The UN provides road transport for the 20 km drive from the airport to the UNOCHA office in Mazar.

ICRC provides passenger flights up to three times per week from Peshawar, usually on Saturdays, Tuesdays and Thursdays. Flights are often via Kabul and Herat on Saturdays and Tuesdays, and via Kabul only on Thursdays. There is no charge for the service but you may be "bumped off" your booking by any member of ICRC at any time. Irregular cargo flights also bring in medical stocks and supplies, so you may be able to hitch a lift out on the empty plane. Transport is provided from the airport to the ICRC office, located about three km from the city centre.

Balkh Airlines, operated by the anti-Taliban "Northern Alliance", also flies to Mazar from Pakistan.

Both the UN and ICRC fly to Faizabad on demand. The UN flights are normally scheduled for a Tuesday.

By road

The Uzbek border lies one hour's drive away to the north of Mazar at Hairaton. After crossing the Amu Darya (Oxus River), the road continues to Termez. Leave Mazar early to cross the border as the Uzbeks are notoriously slow with formalities, and both border posts close at different times for lunch breaks. The bridge-crossing is quite long if you are on foot so keep the luggage as light as possible.

Owing to instability in the region the border remained closed for most of 1997. Check with UNOCHA or on the ground for the latest situation.

The journey from Bamiyan to Mazar takes about one and a half days by four-wheel drive jeep; the roads via Jabal-us Seraj and Doshi are both passable. The route from the south via the Salang Pass is difficult as long as the frontline between Taliban forces and the "Northern Alliance" straddles the road north of Kabul.

Before travelling into or out of Mazar, check on the security situation prior to departure, since there are sometimes problems between the various ethnic groups and commanders controlling segments of the roads in all directions. White UN and NGO vehicles normally pass unhindered through the numerous checkpoints, but local taxis and buses are often stopped and sometimes robbed along the way. On several occasions, however, armed opportunists have left foreigners' wallets untouched at the request of other Afghan passengers, since they were seen as 'guests.' The local authorities are keen to punish Afghans who make problems for foreigners, but in times of instability anyone is fair game unless accompanied by the vassal of someone more powerful than the attacker.

Between June and October it is possible to drive from Chitral in Pakistan to Faizabad by road.

Orientation and getting around

Mazar is named after the Shrine of Hazrat Ali, which dominates the Central Square of the city, and is a useful reference point for getting around. The curfew in Mazar from 2200 hrs to 0400 hrs is rigorously respected by foreigners and locals alike. Passing a checkpoint too close to the 2200 hrs witching hour may result in the unpleasant sight of a rocket-propelled grenade aimed at the car window! There are no mines in the immediate vicinity of Mazar, but check with UNOCHA if you are planning to visit areas further afield.

Agencies

The fighting of May and September 1997 seriously affected the work of international organizations in Mazar. Compounds and warehouses were looted of vehicles, food supplies and much more besides. Expatriate personnel spent in some cases over a week sheltering in underground bunkers before being airlifted to safety. But for most Afghan staff and inhabitants, evacuation is not an option.

ACBAR lists about 20 NGOs which had a presence in Mazar in spring 1997, although check with their international headquarters to find out if projects are actually going ahead on the ground.

Among the lead agencies operating in the region are the UK and US Save the Children Funds. Both have been working in Mazar, in primary schools, child-to-child health education, and the rights of children. SCF (UK) has published a Needs Assessment of Working Children in Mazar-e-Sharif, dated September 1997 and available from SCF offices in Islamabad, Mazar and London. Save the Children Fund-US has pioneered micro-credit schemes to support local enterprises, and UNCHS Habitat has been building the capacity of Community Forums to promote urban rehabilitation. (SEE RELIEF & DEVELOPMENT)

Mazar A-Z

Accommodation and Food

Accommodation possibilities in Mazar are limited. The new UNICA Guesthouse is located some distance from the centre of town, but has the twin attractions of a large garden and a cash bar. As elsewhere the cost is $40 for the room per night, or $55 for full board. Mazar Hotel (the local Hilton) is centrally located, and costs around $50 per night for journalists and $25 for NGO staff. However, prices can jump by as much as $20 in times of crisis. Nearby you may be able to find accommodation with Oxfam for between $20-30 per night. Alternatively try the renovated Bharat Hotel, located on the northeast corner of the central square directly opposite the telephone exchange.

Eating out in Mazar is limited to several *kebab-khanas* on the west side of the Hazrat Ali Shrine in the centre of town, or at the expensive UNICA Guesthouse. To the south of the shrine are some side-streets with markets selling fruit and vegetables. If you are visiting from Pakistan, any luxury items such as chocolate, cheese, tea or coffee would be enthusiastically received by your hosts!

Embassies & Visas

Although much of northern Afghanistan is controlled by the anti-Taliban "Northern Alliance", it is reported that Afghan visas from Taliban-controlled embassies and consulates are still valid. Check this again before departure. On arrival in Mazar, update this as soon as possible with an "exit visa" from the Ministry of Foreign Affairs since no border crossing or airport departure is allowed without this.

A number of foreign consulates are located in Mazar, including the missions of Iran, Uzbekistan and Turkmenistan. The Uzbeks are making it difficult to get a visa: applications must be made to Tashkent via UNOCHA and take anything from two weeks to six months to be processed. The Pakistani and Turkish consulates are currently closed.

Emergencies

Do not leave the town during insecure periods without appropriate authorization. Leaving Mazar at such times is both difficult and – since UN/NGO departures can be seen as a signal of loss of control

– may be opposed by the local authorities. In May and September 1997 lawless factions looted the compounds of UN and NGO agencies whose personnel had left. Quick retrieval of stolen property is, however, a priority for local authorities in order to regain the confidence of the international community.

As long as the Uzbek blockade of the border bridge over the Am'u Darya continues, a road evacuation via this route is virtually impossible. Evacuation overland to the west is also tricky, given the likelihood of factional fighting around Balkh, Shibarghan and Andkhoi. Both the UN and ICRC have organized airlifts to evacuate key personnel, but this is dependent on negotiating a ceasefire with local commanders to enable the planes to land. If you decide to try your luck with the UN or ICRC in an emergency situation, make sure you obey orders, because UN evacuation convoys in the past have been kept waiting by journalists keen to get one last shot. Any large collection of expatriates and expensive jeeps is a conspicuous target, so it is best not to hang around or force other people to. (SEE SECURITY TIPS)

Information

Call in at the United Nations Office for the Coordination of Humanitarian Assistance to Afghanistan (UNOCHA) for the latest security information, and to arrange interpreters. The UN/NGO office at the Department of Foreign Affairs is the first stop for information on work permits, exit visas and security problems. For specific technical information it is possible to get an introduction to other government departments.

Local Rules

Although Mazar and much of northern Afghanistan is not under Taliban control, the dress code is still conservative, especially for foreign women. Loose clothing covering most of the body, and a light shawl to cover the head and chest are recommended. Foreign women are given more concessions than local women when it comes to dress and behaviour, but dressing appropriately goes a long way towards avoiding problems. Do not try and stare down the men staring at you – it only makes them more interested; and do not walk around alone at night. On Wednesday mornings ladies only can visit the Hazrat Ali Shrine to see local women picnicking with their relatives. As a foreign man in northern Afghanistan, there are less restrictions, but remember not to wear shorts or look at local women. (SEE CLOTHING & KIT)

Medical

The main health risk is from water-borne bugs leading to diarrhoea, hepatitis and typhoid. It is also wise to take precautions against malaria and leishmaniasis-carrying sandflies. Numerous local pharmacies stock a variety of medicines, and medical NGOs provide backup for most problems. However, any serious treatment should be carried out in Pakistan. The dusty environment may be irritable to contact lens wearers, so bring plenty of cleaning solution – none is available in Mazar. (SEE PERSONAL HEALTH)

Money

A huge three-story money market, known as the Kefayat, is located on the west side of the Hazrat Ali Shrine in the centre of Mazar. Deals are done for US dollars and "Dostum *Afghanis*" but the latter are not valid in Taliban-controlled areas. Exchange rates can fluctuate remarkably quickly, depending on military gains or losses which may impact on the local economy, so do not change too much at a time. The current going rate is around 60,000 Dostum *Afghanis* for one US dollar. (SEE MONEY & BARGAINING)

BUZKASHI

***Buzkashi*, which literally means "grabbing the goat", is Afghanistan's fearsomely aggressive national sport in which dozens of horsemen compete to wrench the carcass of a headless goat out of their opponents' hands. Banned in Taliban-controlled areas as non-Islamic, *buzkashi* is still played in Mazar and the northern provinces. It was often played in Peshawar at the height of the Soviet war by mainly northern Afghan refugees and mujahideen on R&R. Pakistan-based games are more sporadic today. Originally introduced by the Mongol hordes of Central Asia, the eminent historian Louis Dupree writes that these nomads "used prisoners of war instead of goats, dismembering the hapless creatures and reducing them to masses of hominid jelly during the play." The use of a headless goat is therefore presumably a sop to modern sensibilities.**

The aim of the game is to grab the goat's carcass by one leg, gallop off down the 400 metre long pitch, round a flag, and dump it in a chalked-out ring, before collecting your prize-money. But it's not quite that easy. The dead calf can weigh up to 50 kilos and is covered in slime after being marinated for a few days. Then you have a hundred other horsemen careering towards you, intent on ripping the goat out of your hands. Whips are allowed, but guns and knives are considered bad form. If the English character could be defined by a genteel game of cricket (and the Swiss by curling), then *buzkashi* must embody the warrior-blood of the Afghan people. *JW*

Post & Telecommunications

Mail is sent by UN and ICRC flights to and from Pakistan. A satphone can be used at the public phone office, located next to the Department of Foreign Affairs at the northeast corner of the Hazrat Ali Shrine. International connections cost around US$4 per minute, but avoid early mornings when the money-changers are checking out regional market prices. Check with UNOCHA and NGOs for the latest available telecommunication facilities. Visits to agencies in Mazar are best arranged via their Pakistan-based or international offices. (SEE RADIO & TELECOMMUNICATIONS)

Recreation

Apart from volleyball at the UNICA Guesthouse, there is not much sport in Mazar, unless you fancy your hand at some *buzkashi*. Some people jog in the WFP compound. Walking through the bazaar or possibly through the desert to the north of the city are more sedate options. The desert and hill area to the south of the city is unsafe.

Shopping

You can find carpets and handicrafts on the west side of the Hazrat Ali Shrine, but they are usually overpriced so bargain hard. As well as traditional Turcoman and Baluch carpets, you should be able to find Uzbek *gelim* which are woven rugs rather than knotted carpets. Stop by the *mandawi* (the vegetable market) and see how the vast majority of locals pick over vegetables that foreigners would probably not even consider edible. The cost of living has gone up 50% in the last year, so remember that bargaining for non-luxury items may be denying locals the few cents benefit they desperately need. The local second-hand bazaar is full of very cheap clothes in various sizes. The traditional long-sleeved coat worn by the men of Mazar is known as the *chapan* and comes in both single-weight summer and quilted winter variants.

Sights

Shrine of Hazrat Ali. This magnificent shrine, which gave rise to the name Mazar-e-Sharif – "Tomb of the Exalted" – still stands in the Central Square, relatively unscathed after 20 years of war. The faithful believe that Hazrat Ali – cousin and son-in-law of the Prophet Mohammed, and the fourth orthodox Caliph of Islam – lies buried here. Thousands of worshippers used to converge on the shrine during the elaborate festival of Nawroz in March to celebrate the coming of spring and a new year of hoped-for prosperity.

Although Hazrat Ali was murdered in 661 AD and buried near Baghdad, local tradition relates that his followers feared the body would be desecrated by his enemies. So they mounted the Caliph's mortal remains on a white female camel. After many weeks of wandering she collapsed exhausted and the body was buried here, where she fell. Genghis Khan destroyed the original shrine, and the present building dates from the 15th Century, although most of the stunning decoration is the result of modern restoration.

Balkh. Balkh has several buildings well worth visiting, although access may be problematic, and the condition of the sites has not been confirmed. Check with the UNOCHA office in Mazar for the latest security and mine clearance information. Sites include the 15th Century Timurid Shrine of Khwaja Abu Nasr Parsa; the Bala Hissar and city walls of ancient Balkh; the tomb of the ill-fated poetess Rabia Balkhi; and the Masjid-e-No Gumbad, which dates from the early 9th Century, making it the earliest Islamic monument yet identified in Afghanistan.

Weather

From December to March Mazar is very cold (toothpaste freezes in the tube), and the only heating is by 'bukhari' – simple diesel stoves which make everyone in the vicinity smell the same after a few days. Little snow falls in the city, but the mountains to the south are snow-capped most of the winter. Spring brings rain and mud, but summer is usually very hot and dusty, with temperatures reaching 40 degrees Celsius in July and August.

EASTERN REGION

The eastern region of Afghanistan consists of the area neighbouring the North West Frontier Province of Pakistan, namely the provinces of Kunar, Laghman, Nangarhar, Logar, Paktya and Paktika. It is a mountainous region traditionally dominated by various competing Pashtun tribes. The largest town in the area, and the capital of Nangarhar province, is Jalalabad which sits astride the strategically significant route from Kabul via the Khyber Pass to the Indian subcontinent.

During the early 1990s Nangarhar province was the prime region for cultivation of the opium poppy and has only recently been overtaken in volume by Helmand province in the far west of the country. One reporter is quoted by Barnett Rubin as saying in May 1992: “For miles around Jalalabad, 80 percent of the arable land produces nothing but poppies, UN officials say. And the farmers like it that way. Today opium brings the farmer 10 times more money than wheat – and there is plenty of cheap bread for sale in town, thanks to the flow of free flour [from USAID].”

Jalalabad

Situated at an altitude of 569 metres in a fertile plain irrigated by the Kabul and Kunar rivers, and flanked by the mountains of the Hindu Kush to the north and the Spinghar to the south, Jalalabad is an oasis compared to most Afghan towns. Traditionally a warm winter retreat for royalty and wealthy urbanites, it is famous for its springtime orange-blooms, which still blossom around the Mausoleum of Amir Habibullah in the centre of town. Before the war Jalalabad thrived on its orchards of citrus fruit, watered and powered by the hydroelectric dam at Darunta to the northwest of the city. However, most of these mechanized farms built by the Soviets were looted and destroyed by mujahed factions in 1989 and are only now beginning to be replanted. More recently, the city has become a foothold for many aid agencies keen to expand their operations cross-border into Afghanistan from nearby Peshawar.

In 329 BC Alexander the Great passed this way with 30,000 troops *en route* to his conquest of India. From the 2nd to 7th Centuries AD over a thousand Buddhist *stupas* in nearby Hadda and Basawal echoed to the chants and incantations of meditating monks, and Nangarhar was one of the most important pilgrimage sites in the Buddhist world. The region was also at the centre of the remarkable Gandhara school of sculpture which represented the Buddha for the first time in human form, with a Grecian profile and Roman robes. Indeed the Buddha himself is said to have visited the valley in order to slay the demon dragon Gopala, and Chinese pilgrims have written of the sacred relics once housed in Hadda's shrines: a fragment of the Buddha's skull entirely covered in gold-leaf, a tooth, some hair – there was even a *stupa* erected where he had clipped his fingernails.

The name Jalalabad means Abode of Splendour, and is said to descend from Jalaluddin Akbar, Moghul Emperor of India, who founded the city in 1570. It was the Moghuls who established the Khyber Pass as the main route through to India. For many years the town was in the margins of history, but reappears in the drama of the retreat from Kabul of the 16,000 strong column of British troops and camp followers in January 1842. They were desperately seeking sanctuary in the British garrison at Jalalabad, but only the legendary Dr Brydon made it, while the remainder were hacked to death and a lucky few taken prisoner. In 1919 Amir Habibullah was murdered while hunting near Jalalabad and his mausoleum still stands in the centre of town.

For most of the Soviet war Jalalabad was a bastion of the communist government regime supported by Red Army forces. The airport was used for numerous Soviet offensives against guerrilla positions in the nearby Safed Koh region to the south and the Hindu Kush to the north.

Throughout the 1980s, the mujahideen made repeated – but not particularly effective – attacks against government positions deliberately located on the outskirts of the city to draw fire. In March 1989, in the aftermath of the Soviet withdrawal, Jalalabad became the focus of an ill-conceived guerrilla assault, but government forces held off the rebels. The plan was thrust upon the resistance alliance of Peshawar-based parties by the Americans and Pakistan's Inter Services Intelligence agency (ISI) in an attempt to force a swift mujahed victory over the communists in Kabul. But the attack failed due to a lack of broad-based resistance support.

After the fall of the Najibullah regime in April 1992, Jalalabad was ruled as a semi-autonomous province by the "Nangarhar Shura." Representatives of mujahed parties, which were fighting each other in Kabul, would hold meetings together in Jalalabad. From 1992-1996 dozens of different local commanders controlled sections of the road between Jalalabad, Kabul and the Pakistan border, and each extorted tax or loot from passing vehicles. But since the city was taken by the Taliban in 1996, without a shot being fired, the

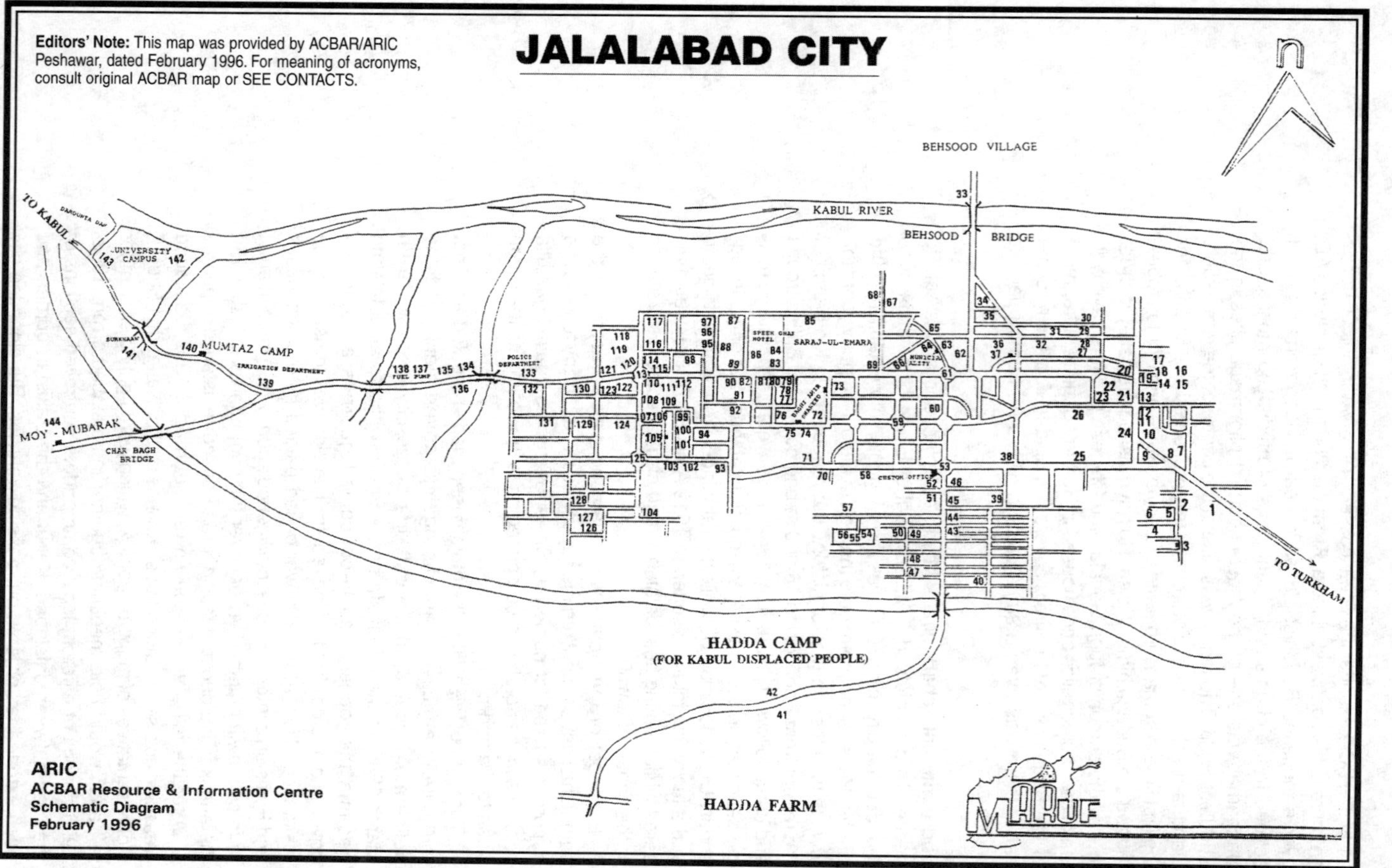
JALALABAD CITY
Editors' Note: This map was provided by ACBAR/ARIC Peshawar, dated February 1996. For meaning of acronyms, consult original ACBAR map or SEE CONTACTS.
BEHSOOD VILLAGE
KABUL RIVER
BEHSOOD
BRIDGE
TO KABUL
UNIVERSITY CAMPUS
MUMTAZ CAMP
IRRIGATION DEPARTMENT
FUEL PUMP
POLICE DEPARTMENT
MOY - MUBARAK
CHAR BAGH BRIDGE
SPEEN GHAR HOTEL
SARAJ-UL-EMARA
CUSTOM OFFICE
TO TURKHAM
HADDA CAMP
(FOR KABUL DISPLACED PEOPLE)
HADDA FARM
ARIC
ACBAR Resource & Information Centre
Schematic Diagram
February 1996

40 AGHCO, Angoor Bagh Bus Stop Tel. 3416
109 AGHCO Children's Hospital, Char Rahi Marastoon Tel. 2213
91 AGHCO Guest House, opp. University Hospital Tel. 2821
126 ATC, Samt-e-She, Mamuriat-e-Makruyan
120 ADA, Kabul-Jal Highway, Char Rahi Sehat-e-Aama
130 AAEA, Char Rahi Sehat-e-Aama
75 AOGH, Chowk/Gulahi Araba Tel. 2615
26 APWO, H#4, St#2, Power Station, Godam-e-Sangi Rd
50 GTZ-BEFARe, Reig Shah Mard Khan Tel. 2277
99 ACLU, Kabul-Jal Highway, opp. Dar-ul-Malemeen Masjid Tel. 2258
107 AABRAR, Public Health Sch, Char Rahi Marastoon Tel. 2913
48 ARDA, Angoor Bagh Tel. 3422
7 AREA, H#2, Qasaba St, Torkham Hadda
38 Agriculture Department Tel. 3183
51 ASYA, behind Spinghar Cinema Tel. 2230
20 Ariana Afghan Airlines, Mustufiat Konah Tel. 2180
8 Assoc. of Emergency Relief & Reconstruction in Afghanistan
96 ARC, Kabul-Jal Highway, next to Hazratan Masjid
54 ARC Eye Clinic, Kandak-e-Khad-e-Sabaqa
123 AVICEN, Kabul-Jal Highway, Char Rahi Sehat-e-Aama
72 Bagh-e-Amir Shaheed
140 Bagh-e-Mumtaz
2 BDA, Saranwali Kohna
65 Bank, Zone 1, opp. Masjid-e-Imam tel. 2597, 2898
105 BCURA, Char Rahi Marastoon, next to Sehat-e-Aama Tel. 2388
19 CARITAS, Front of Tribes Presidency Tel. 2689
125 Char Rahi Marastoon
113 Char Rahi Sehat-e-Aama
61 Chowk-e-Mukhaberat
53 Chowk-e-Talashi
21 Cometa-e-Walayati Tel. 2255
23 Culture & Information Dept. Tel. 3448
137 DACAAR, Cheknawry, Tangi Teel, Fabricah Qand
112 Dar-ul-Malemeen, Zone 3 Tel. 2717
143 Darunta Dam
101 Darul Imamal-Bukhari for Orphans (IIRO) Tel. 2818
46 Dental Clinic for Afghan Refugees, Chowk-e-Gumruk
22 Dalaki Baba
11 Education Department Tel. 2332, 4494
74 ERU, behind Bagh-e-Amir Shaheed, Gulahi Araba
76 ERU (Guest House), next to AOGH hospital Tel. 3449
132 FAO Veterinary, next to Alikhil Masjid Tel. 2760
41 Farm-e-Hadda
94 GAA, Gulahi Araba Tel. 2027
52 Gumruk (Customs) Tel. 3358
42 Hadda Camp
71 Hadda-e-Laghman (Now)
70 Hadda-e-Laghman (Sabeqa)

60 Hawz-e-Khushk
88 HAF, next to University Hospital
27 HAF Residence, St#23, Zone B, Hadda Rd
28 HELP Germany, Bank Rd Tel. 2233
14 Hostel
134 Hotel-e-Zeba
92 ICRC, University Area 3, H#2 Tel. 2803
106 ICRC Orthopaedic Centre, Char Rahi Marastoon
9 ICRC/ARCS, next to Medical Faculty Tel. 2737
116 IHSAN, Arbaban, opp. Teacher Training Ctr Tel. 2108
95 Imam Hanifah Talimi Markaz Tel. 2602
138 Inhesarat (Monopoly) Tel. 2209, 3224
44 IRC, H#1, St#3, Chaparhar Rd Tel. 2591
90 IRC Printing Press, opp. University Hospital
98 International Orphan Care, Chowk-e-Hazratan
87 IIRO, next to University Hospital Tel. 2107
18 IIWC, Front of Tribes Presidency Tel. 2212
39 ISRA, Chaparhar Hadda Tel. 2996
24 Jail Tel. 2583
36 Kohi Noor Foundation, Felwan St Tel. 2807
16 Kunar Shura Office
15 Laghman Shura Office
128 Lycee-e-Cheknawry Tel. 3190
131 Lycee-e-Naswan (Girls' High School)
121-2 MADERA, Char Rahi Sehat-e-Aama Tel. 2825, 2565, 3421
127 Mamuriat-e-She
124 Marastoon
104 Masjid (Mosque)
93 Masjid-e-Araban
59 Masjid-e-Bazazi
97 Masjid-e-Hazratan
10 Medical College Tel. 2592
25 MSF, Torkham Rd, near Godam-e-Sangi Tel. 2063
30 MSF/HealthNet International, Bank Rd
64 MCI, next to Nangarhar Sharwali
135 MDC, Hotel-e-Zeba
34 MCPA, Pul-e-Behsud, opp. Faaid-e-Aama
144 Muhi Mubarak
62 Mukhabarat (Communication Dept.) Tel. 3333
81 MARUF, opp. Spinghar Hotel
12 Mustufiat (Finance Dept.), Qasabe Area, behind Jail Tel. 2958
49 MUWAFAQ Foundation, Reig Shah Mard Khan Tel. 2420
80 NDCDU, opp. Spinghar Hotel Tel. 2218
69 Nangarhar Restaurant
115 NPO/RRAA, opp. Dar-ul-Malemeen
73 OSGAP, opp. Spinghar Hotel Tel. 2203
43 OMAR, Farm Hadda, Cheplahar Hadda Tel. 2591
102 Pakistan Consulate, Char Rahi Marastoon Tel. 2010

5 Peace Home Union Aid for Afghan Refugees Tel. 3379
33 Pul-e-Behsud
141 Pul-e-Surkhaw
136 Pul-e-Zandarma
129 Qabrestan (Graveyard)
67 Qasr (Palace) Tel. 2057
17 Qasr-e-Number 2 (Bagh-e-Zakheera)
133 Qumandani Amnia (Police HQ) Tel. 2123, 2121
55 Reconstruction Surgery for Afghans, Kandak-e-Khad-e-Sabaqa
119 RSSA, Char Rahi Sehat-e-Aama
118 RAFA, Char Rahi Sehat-e-Aama, Baborain
117 RAH, H#203, St#2, A-2, Zone 3, opp. Dar-ul-Malemeen Tel. 2439
83 RDA, Spinghar Hotel Tel. 2376
139 Ryasat-e-Kanal (Irrigation Dept)
13 Ryasat-e-Qabael Tel. 2381
114 SAFA, St#C9, Char Rahi Sehat-e-Aama Tel. 2612
111 SGAA, Char Rahi Sehat-e-Aama Tel. 2510
47 SJAWO, Angoor Bagh, Zakhirah Teel Tel. 3152
110 Sehat-e-Aama Nursing School, Char Rahi Marastoon Tel. 2510, 1112
85 Seraj-ul-Emorat
4 SERVE, Torkham Hadda, towards Saranwali, St#4 Tel. 2427
89 Shafa Khana-e-Atfal (Children's Hospital) Tel. 2025
63 Sharwaa (Municipality) Tel. 2695, 2677
100 SHEFA, opp. Dar-ul-Malemeen Masjid Tel. 2380
82 SAVE, opp. Spinghar Hotel
58 Spinghar Cinema
84 Spinghar Hotel Tel. 2376
86 SRO, next to Spinghar Hotel
37 SCA, Chowk-e-Mukhaberat, near Ganbazi Masjid Tel. 2164
29 SCA Guest House, Bank Rd Tel. 2860
31 SCA Store, Bank Rd Tel. 2860
103 SCA Store, Char Rahi Marastoon
1 Torkham Hadda
66 TV Centre, Sayed Jamaluddin Chowk Tel. 2969
35 UNHCR, Hadda-e-Behsud, Khorma Bagh Tel. 3326
78 UNDP, opp. Spinghar Hotel
3 UNICEF, Raig Shah Mard Khan Road, Zone 4 Tel. 3162
57 Union Aid for Afghanistan, Joay 7
45 UMCA, opp. Electricity Dept, St#1 Tel. 3251
6 UNOPS, Sarak-e-Saranwali, Torkham Hadda Tel. 3119
142 University Campus
32 UNOCHA, Bank Rd, opp. Governor's House Tel. 2633
68 Waliyat (Governor's Office) Tel. 3167
79 WFP, opp. Spinghar Hotel
41 WFP Store
56 WHO Main Office, Kandak-e-Khad-e-Sabaqa
77 WHO, opp. Spinghar Hotel
108 WHO Public Health, Char Rahi Sehat-e-Aama Tel. 2318

security situation both in and around the city has improved. Jalalabad and the surrounding area are predominately Pashtun so there is less anti-Taliban resentment and tension here than in Kabul or Herat.

Getting there

By air

Jalalabad airport is situated three or four kilometres east of town. It is served by ICRC flights from Peshawar and UN flights from Islamabad. The UN flights are scheduled for Sundays and Thursdays, and usually connect with Kabul or Gardez. ICRC flights depart two to three times a week on an irregular basis: contact flight operations in Peshawar for more details. Ariana Afghan Airlines flies from Kabul to Jalalabad on Sundays; the cost one-way is $20 for expatriates and 150,000 *Afghanis* for locals. Ariana also claims to operate daily cargo flights into Jalalabad from Dubai via other Afghan towns. (SEE TRAVEL)

By road

Jalalabad is the first major Afghan town over the border from Pakistan. As such, it is an important logistical staging post for convoys of food and supplies. If you are travelling independently you may be able to hitch a lift on a WFP food convoy. They take a day to reach Jalalabad from Peshawar. In a car the drive from Peshawar to the border is about one and a half hours, and the same again on to Jalalabad. Remember that the border at Torkham is shut between 1200 hrs and 1400 hrs and Pakistan is half an hour ahead of Afghanistan so make sure you arrive at the border before 1130 hrs Afghan time if you are driving to Peshawar. The Pakistanis close their side at 1800 hrs A tribal areas permit is needed if you are driving from Peshawar to Jalalabad, but it is not required for travel in the other direction. From the west, Jalalabad is about four or five hours' car or jeep ride from Kabul. For more details of this journey, SEE CENTRAL.

Orientation & getting around

Jalalabad is laid out on a grid plan, with the Kabul river and the Hindu Kush to the north and the Spinghar mountains to the south. The main road runs east-west, and the Spinghar Hotel is centrally positioned, with the UNDP office directly opposite. Three-wheeled tuk-tuks are available if you do not have access to a jeep. The ACBAR Resource and Information Centre (ARIC) has produced a schematic diagram of Jalalabad showing the locations of most agencies and key offices.

Agencies

ACBAR registers the presence of over 70 NGOs in Jalalabad, in addition to which the International Committee of the Red Cross (ICRC) and numerous UN agencies are also active. For more information on agency activities visit the UNOCHA office located opposite the Governor's house at the east end of town or contact ACBAR in Peshawar.

The World Health Organization (WHO) has its headquarters here and ICRC supports the public hospital which is the main health facility for the whole of the eastern region of Afghanistan. For agency telephone numbers see the chart below.

Jalalabad A-Z

Accommodation and Food

UNICEF has a guesthouse in Jalalabad; ask at their Peshawar office for more details. Alternatively arrange accommodation with an aid agency. Otherwise the Spinghar Hotel (TEL: 2367) is the best place to stay. Located opposite UNDP in the centre of town, it is rather a forlorn place now, but its luxuriant gardens speak of a more peaceful past. A double room with *en suite* European bathroom costs $25 per night. The restaurant serves adequate Afghan food for both residents and nonresidents.

Embassies & Visas

The Pakistan Consulate (TEL: 2010) issues single, double and multiple entry visas; it is located at Char Rah Marastun, four blocks southwest of the Spinghar Hotel.

Medical

The ICRC supports the Jalalabad Public Hospital with a surgical unit, and will treat any emergency surgical cases. (SEE PERSONAL HEALTH)

Post & Telecommunications

In addition to agency radio communications, Jalalabad has a local telephone network. Agency and office telephone numbers – as compiled by ACBAR in February 1996 – are found below.

Sights

Jalalabad has few sights to visit. The Buddhist stupas at **Hadda** provided an underground haven for the mujahideen, but were largely

SERIAL	AGENCY	TEL. NO.
1	AARBRAR	2913
2	ACLU	2258
3	Afghan Obs & Gyn Hospital	2615
4	AGHCO	3416, 2821
5	AGHCO Children's Hospital	2213
6	AGHCO Guest House	2821
7	Agriculture Department	3183
8	ARC	–
9	ARDA	3422
10	AREA	–
11	Ariana Afghan Airlines	2180
12	ASYA	2230
13	AVICEN	–
14	Bank, Zone 1	2597, 2898
15	BCURA	2388
16	CARITAS	2689
17	*Cometa-e-Walayati*	2255
18	Culture & Information Dept.	3448
19	DACAAR	–
20	*Dar-ul Mualemeen*	2717
21	Education Department	2332, 4494
22	ERU (Guest House)	3449
23	FAO Veterinary	2760
24	GAA	2027
25	*Gumruk* (Customs)	3358
26	GTZ-BEFARe	2277
27	HAF	–
28	HELP Germany	2233
29	ICRC	2803
30	ICRC/ARCS	2737
31	IHSAN	2108
32	IIRO	2107, 2818
33	IIWC	2212
34	*Imam Hanifah Talimi Markaz*	2602
35	*Inhesarat* (Monopoly)	2209, 3224
36	IRC	2591
37	ISRA	2996
38	Jail	2583
39	Kohi Noor Foundation	2807
40	*Lycee-e-Cheknawry*	3190
41	MADERA	2825, 2565, 3421

SERIAL	AGENCY	TEL. NO.
42	MCI	–
43	MCPA	–
44	MDC	–
45	Medical College	2592
46	MSF	2063
47	*Mukhabarat* (Communication Dept.)	3333
48	*Mustufiat* (Finance Dept.)	2958
49	MUWAFAQ Foundation	2420
50	NDCDU	2218
51	NPO/RRAA	–
52	OMAR	2591
53	OSGAP	2203
54	Pakistan Consulate	2010
55	Peace Home Union Aid for Afghan Refugees	3379
56	*Qasr* (Palace)	2057
57	*Qumandani Amnia* (Police HQ)	2123, 2121
58	RAH	2439
59	RDA	2376
60	*Ryasat-e-Qabael*	2381
61	SAFA	2612
62	SGAA	2510
63	SJAWO	3152
64	*Sehat-e-Aama* Nursing School	2510, 1112
65	SERVE	2427
66	*Shafa Khana-e-Atfal* (Children's Hospital)	2025
67	*Sharwaa* (Municipality)	2695, 2677
68	SHEFA	2380
69	SAVE	–
70	Spinghar Hotel	2376
71	SCA	2164
72	SCA Store & Guest House	2860
73	TV Centre	2969
74	UNHCR	3326
75	UNDP	–
76	UNICEF	3162
77	UMCA	3251
78	UNOPS	3119
79	UNOCHA	2633
80	*Waliyat* (Governor's Office)	3167
81	WFP	–
82	WHO	2318

destroyed by Soviet bombing during the 1980s. The **Seraj-ul Emorat** is a palace built by Amir Habibullah around 1910. Set in pleasant gardens, just to the east of the Spinghar Hotel, the building was sacked during tribal revolts in 1928. The **Mausoleum of Amir Habibullah,** down a lane opposite the Seraj-ul Emorat, is a rather gaudy-coloured neoclassical creation complete with dome and porticos. The Amir ruled from 1901 until 1919 when an unknown assassin killed him near Jalalabad, probably because his political stance was not sufficiently pro-Islamic/anti-British. His two sons and successors, Amanullah (*ruled* 1919-1929) and Enayatullah (*ruled* 14-17 January 1929) are also buried here. The mausoleum is set in a garden of orange trees. The Moghul garden at **Nimla** lies about 40 km west of Jalalabad towards Kabul. Said to have been laid out by the beautiful wife of Emperor Jahangir (1605-1627), it is the only remaining Moghul garden in Afghanistan, and has recently been restored by FAO. The foundations of an old British fort may be seen at **Gandamak**, 11 km from Nimla, where, in January 1842, British infantry soldiers made one desperate last stand against the marauding Afghans – they were killed to a man.

Weather

Jalalabad is 1100 metres lower in elevation than Kabul and enjoys a much milder climate in winter. Palm trees grow beside the Kabul river and some geographers have referred to the Jalalabad valley as sub-tropical. Spring (March-April) is an excellent time to visit, but summers are very hot and dusty with temperatures reaching over 40 degrees Celsius.

SOUTHERN REGION

Southern Afghanistan stretches from the foothills of the Hindu Kush down to the deserts of Seistan and the Baluch border. Geographically it is a region dominated by the Helmand River which rises in Hazarajat and flows southwest for 1,300 km through Uruzgan, Helmand and Nimruz provinces before vanishing into the marshes that stretch across into Iran. Ethnically, the south is heavily Pashtun, with pockets of Baluch and Brahui in the sparsely inhabited deserts on the borders of Iran and Pakistan. As Baluch are also found in Iran and Pakistan, there is a strong sense of a single (albeit not unified) Baluch identity in all three countries.

The main city of the south is Kandahar, which was the centre of the Pashtun kingdom formed in the mid-18th Century by the so-called "Father of Afghanistan" Ahmed Shah Durrani. Kandahar however has not always been the preeminent city in this region. From the 9th to 12th Centuries the cities of Zaranj in Seistan (modern-day Nimruz) and Bost (modern-day Lashkar Gah) were thriving, such that "once there were so many fine buildings and palaces that one could easily walk from Bost to Zaranj on the rooftops without once touching the ground" (quoted by Dupree), and medieval historians referred to the area as the "garden of Asia" and the "granary of the East." But today these ancient cities are all but consumed by the shifting sands of the *Dasht-e-Margo* (Desert of Death) and the *Dasht-e-Jehanum* (Desert of Hell), and the riverside pleasure palaces of Bost lie in ruins.

Kandahar

For many centuries Kandahar has been of great historical and strategic significance. Located at the intersection of three key roads to Herat, Kabul and Quetta over the border in Pakistan, it has found itself astride the main route of adventurers and empire-builders from Alexander the Great to the Taliban. Situated at around 1000 metres it has been settled since antiquity. Alexander rebuilt the city in 329 BC and the name Kandahar may derive from his Eastern name

'Sikander' or 'Iskandar.' From the 7th Century onwards it was absorbed into various Islamic kingdoms; and during the 11th and 12th Centuries it was very much eclipsed in significance by the Ghaznavid winter capital of Bost. In the 1150s Bost was destroyed by the Ghorid ruler Alauddin the "World Burner", and in the 1380s Timur razed Zaranj to the ground, after which Kandahar rose in prominence. From the 16th to 18th Centuries Persian Safavids and Indian Moghuls argued over it; and the famous *Chihlzina*, a rock chamber at the top of "Forty Steps" hewn out of a rock face outside the city, contains a Persian inscription recording the conquests of the Moghul emperor Babur.

Safavid influence however gained the upper hand in Kandahar, until in the early 1700s Mir Wais Hotak, the Ghilzai Pashtun chief of the city, rebelled against the decadent Persians by murdering one of their envoys during a picnic. Mir Wais died in 1715, but as Afghanistan's first great nationalist he had set in train the process which resulted in Ahmed Shah Durrani forming the last great Afghan empire in 1747. Ahmed Shah Baba – "Father of Afghanistan" as he is popularly known – made Kandahar his capital until his death in 1772, extending his influence as far as Kashmir and Delhi. Internecine struggles forced his second son and successor Timur Shah to move his capital to Kabul in 1776. In the 19th Century, British forces occupied Kandahar in the first two Afghan Wars and suffered one of their heavier defeats nearby at Maiwand in 1880, when the famous bride Malalai ripped off her veil and, waving it aloft as a battle standard, fired up the Afghans to claim victory. General Roberts was sent from Kabul immediately to avenge the defeat, marching his force of 10,000 men on foot for 324 miles to Kandahar in the searing heat of August, covering the distance in just 23 days. While this appears an astonishing feat to a modern reader, it seems no big deal for the average Victorian soldier; as Major Ashe writes: "…our march up to the present time has been a veritable picnic, not unaccompanied by a rubber of whist in the afternoon, and not divested of that little duck and quail slaughter which in measure consoles our youngsters for their banishment from Hurlingham…" (quoted in Dupree). The British defeated the Afghans the day after arriving in Kandahar, but departed after eight months and left Amir Abdur Rahman to fight his cousins for control of the city.

Apart from Red Army occupation during the 1980s Kandahar has been controlled by Pashtuns ever since the British departed. Owing to its strategically significant situation, the city became one of the key points of the Soviet "Security Ring" after the 1979 invasion. The American-built airport, which was supposed to serve as a fuelling stop for long distance aircraft from Europe to India but lost out with the arrival of the Jumbo 747, was transformed into a major base for anti-resistance operations. The Soviets launched regular MiG and helicopter gunship assaults against mujahed positions throughout the region. While the Soviets occupied the centre of the city, the mujahideen controlled the surrounding area right up to the district of Dand on the southern fringe of Kandahar. This district

Kandahari boys playing near mined ruins *J. Walter*

was heavily defended and bombed, and as a result remains largely ruins and minefields today.

Following the Red Army withdrawal, Afghan infighting only added to the destruction. From 1989-1992 the mujahideen fought the Communist regime troops of President Najibullah; and from 1992-1994 five different mujahideen factions all competed with each other for control. When the Taliban took Kandahar (without a shot fired) in September 1994, they found the city virtually deserted, heavily mined, and with most of its citizens living as refugees in Pakistan. Through disarming the mujahideen and skilful negotiations with local commanders they managed to bring peace and security to the area for the first time since 1980.

Kandahar is the most conservative and Pashtun of Afghanistan's major cities. As a result the Taliban movement prefers to base itself here rather than in the more ethnically mixed and cosmopolitan Kabul. Many of the Taliban's strict interpretations of *Shari'a* Law, such as untrimmed beards for men and *purdah* for women (which prevents them from working away from home or even leaving the house unattended by a male relative), derive from the traditional southern Pashtun customs of this region of Afghanistan. Huge numbers of refugees have returned since the Taliban brought stability to the city; with population estimates ranging from 150,000 to 500,000 inhabitants, Kandahar is the second largest city in Afghanistan.

Although some reconstruction is visible – notably a new palace for the Saudi terrorist Osama Bin Laden – the city's infrastructure has been devastated by war, and the damage caused by mines and the shelling of irrigation systems has badly affected local agricultural capacity. Opium poppy, however, which needs less water than wheat or cotton, is thriving, especially in Helmand where more poppy is grown than in any other province in Afghanistan. Since the Taliban took Herat in September 1995, the opening of the main road from Central Asia to Pakistan via Kandahar has boosted the city's economic trade in both legal and smuggled goods. Taxes on this trade keep the Taliban war chest topped-up, while the international agencies are left to look after the city's rehabilitation.

Getting there

By air

Both ICRC and the UN operate flights into Kandahar from Peshawar and Islamabad respectively. Currently both ICRC and UN flights are scheduled for Sundays and Wednesdays. ICRC flights often interconnect with Kabul en route, and UN flights often interconnect with Herat en route. Costs for one-way tickets with the UN are $640 for UN staff and $400 for NGO staff. A special charter flight would set you back $6,400.

Ariana Afghan Airlines runs a passenger Boeing 727 from Kabul to Kandahar on Saturdays and in the other direction on Fridays. The cost is $63 for foreigners and 500,000 *Afghanis* for locals. Ariana also operates cargo flights between Kandahar and Dubai. (SEE TRAVEL)

By road

TRAVELLERS BEWARE! **The southern region of Afghanistan is the most heavily mined in the country, with numerous unmarked anti-tank minefields near main roads. When driving always remember to avoid verges or short cuts – stick to the beaten track if you want to stay alive!**

Kandahar is easily accessible by road from Pakistan. From Quetta to the border at Chaman is around 120 km, and Kandahar lies a further 110 km to the northwest. The total journey takes between six and seven hours by car. The road from Herat is well worth travelling, once at least, as it skirts some fascinating scenery between the last remnants of the Hindu Kush mountains and the deserts to the southwest. Allow 13-14 hours to drive the 565 km from Herat to Kandahar in a sturdy car or jeep, or two days by bus.

The road to Kandahar from Kabul via Ghazni and Qalat-e-Ghilzai is for enthusiasts only; at times the 'corrugations' make travelling it feel more like being adrift in a heavy sea than in a landlocked country. At least two bridges are down which may make winter or spring passages tricky with rain and snowmelt.

From Kabul to Ghazni is about five or six hours by jeep or taxi; from Ghazni to Kandahar is 12-14 hours, and a four-wheel drive vehicle is recommended. For the whole journey of 488 km allow two full days by jeep.

Orientation

The original town laid out by Ahmed Shah Durrani in the 1760s still exists in the form of the *Char Suq* and its various bazaars laid out in a quartered rectangular plan. To the east of this Old Town lies the airport and the road to Kabul; to the west lies the New Town, the road to Herat, and the jagged crests of some low mountains.

Most of the international agencies are located in the New Town, while to the south much of the city is still rubble and minefields. Most of the "tourist sites" worth seeing are located in the Old Town, except for the Chihlzina which is to the west of town on the way to Herat.

There are no good street maps of Kandahar available currently. A very clear but out-of-date street plan is contained in Nancy Dupree's book *An Historical Guide to Afghanistan* (2nd Edition, 1977), but the local UNOCHA office may be able to supply you with one that is more up to date.

Getting around

Call in at the United Nations Office for the Coordination of Humanitarian Assistance to Afghanistan (UNOCHA) to receive a briefing on the latest mine clearance situation. Avoid using the verges of roads, where anti-tank mines are sometimes found, and never wander into uninhabited areas or off the beaten track. There have been a number of tragic accidents involving both local and international aid personnel in the region. There may be a chance of hitching a lift around town in a UN or aid agency vehicle.

Apart from aid agency jeeps the best way to get around is by three-wheeled *tuk-tuk*, or taxi if you have long legs. Always agree on a price before getting in. Local guides and interpreters can be hired through UNOCHA.

Agencies

STOP PRESS!

UN OPERATIONS IN SOUTHERN AFGHANISTAN WERE SUSPENDED IN APRIL 1998 UNTIL FURTHER NOTICE

Around 15-20 UN agencies and NGOs are currently working in or out of Kandahar. For an overview of agency activities in the region and the latest humanitarian situation it is best to check in at the Kandahar office of UNOCHA. The local Afghan NGO coordinating body is called SWABAC but seems to be fairly ineffectual at present.

Médecins Sans Frontières works in Primary Health Care in Uruzgan province; UNOCHA coordinates UN agency activities, operates planes and radio communications, and runs one of the largest mine clearance operations in the country.

Agriculture and irrigation

Many of the urban and canal systems were mined during the war in order to prevent the enemy using them as trenches. Clearance of these canals from mines and silt is one of the most crucial tasks facing aid agencies in the region. DACAAR is sinking boreholes and installing handpumps. FAO is working to improve crop yields, poultry and fish farming. UNDCP is attempting to control the cultivation of opium poppy without many results so far. (SEE AGRICULTURE)

Community development

In five districts around Kandahar, UNDP's P.E.A.C.E. initiative is attempting to mobilize village development committees in order to eradicate poverty and promote community empowerment. Partner agencies include UNOPS (rural rehabilitation), FAO Livestock and Crops, UNDCP, and UNCHS Habitat (urban rehabilitation). The project is aiming to establish accountable systems of local governance which will bind Afghans together in the development of their communities. Improvements will include work on agricultural infrastructures, building link roads from farmers to markets, irrigation works, and urban water and sanitation.

Detention

The largest jail in Afghanistan is located in Kandahar: it currently houses around 2,000 prisoners of war from the forces of the anti-Taliban "Northern Alliance." ICRC visits the prison to ensure that sufficient food, water and sanitation are provided, to check for possible human rights abuse, and to exchange Red Cross messages.

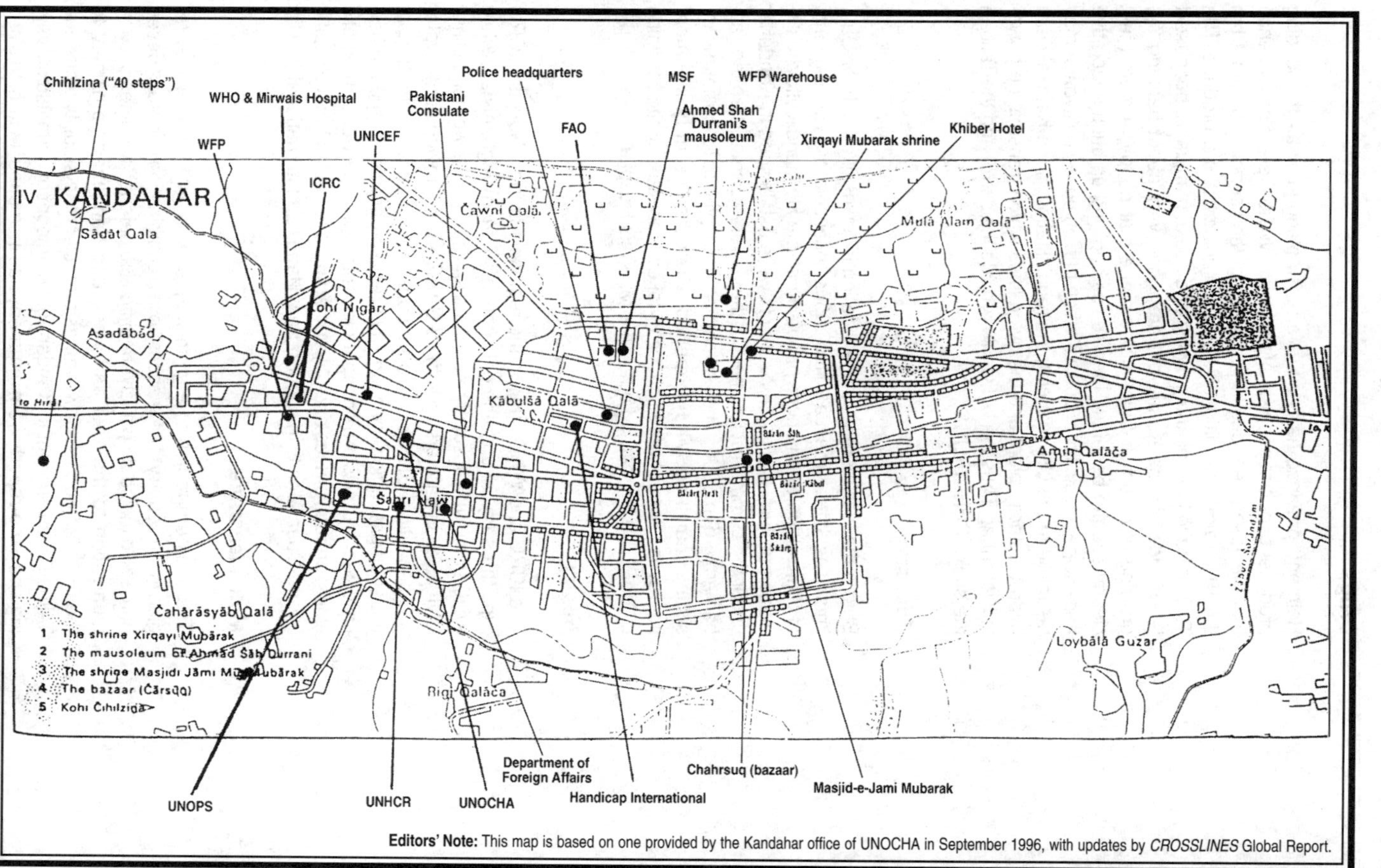

Editors' Note: This map is based on one provided by the Kandahar office of UNOCHA in September 1996, with updates by *CROSSLINES* Global Report.

Drugs

Helmand province has now overtaken Nangarhar as the leading producer of opium poppy in Afghanistan. While there is no evidence that the Taliban are dealing in the drug, they certainly benefit from the 10% *zakat* or traditional Islamic tax on agricultural produce. The Taliban have banned the growing and use of marijuana, because it is forbidden in the Koran, but are more wary about banning the growing of opium outright. They argue that poppy farmers must clearly see the benefit to themselves of giving up such a lucrative trade. One possibility is that a Taliban ban on poppy cultivation may be linked to the UN financing the rehabilitation of the Kajakai Dam hydroelectricity plant and the pylon lines which transmit the power to Kandahar. Thus the UN would provide the carrot and the Taliban the stick. (SEE DRUGS)

Education

Before the war there was coeducation in towns like Lashkar Gah, known as "Little America" in the 1950s because of the vast amounts of State Department money poured into the Helmand Valley reclamation project. Some girls' schools were established in Kandahar under the communist regime, but these were all shut when the Taliban arrived in 1994. They remain shut despite Taliban rhetoric insisting that they will be opened when the "security situation" improves. Some home-schooling takes place and limited training of MoPH staff is carried out at the Mir Wais Hospital.

Health

The ICRC and WHO support the regional Mir Wais Hospital. ICRC runs the surgical unit, the only one in southern Afghanistan, while WHO and UNICEF supply medicines and support the women's clinic. UNICEF – in partnership with DACAAR – is improving urban water and sanitation. UNICEF also supports health education throughout the southern region via shortwave radio programmes and mother-child health clinics. An orthopaedic centre which provides prosthetic limbs, orthotic braces and physiotherapy is run at Mir Wais Hospital by the Guardians with support from Handicap International (HI).

Mine clearance

The southern region of Afghanistan is the most heavily mined region in the country. The reasons lie in a combination of porous desert borders to the south (which are difficult to defend), key lines of communication to the east and west, and Kandahar's proximity to the Pakistan border. However, as a result of the stability which the Taliban have brought to Kandahar, the amount of minefield surveying and mine-reports from returnees has increased. In turn, this has led to the total area of high priority land which needs to be cleared rising to 118 sq.km. Hence half of all the high priority mine clearance areas of Afghanistan lie in this region.

Ironically it is the Afghans' own minefields which provide more of a problem to clear than Russian ones. The Russians usually marked or mapped their minefields, whereas the mujahideen scattered anti-tank mines in 'nuisance' fields without any pattern or record of where they were laid.

Of the 180 minefields discovered within Kandahar city, 67 had been cleared by September 1997. Most of these minefields are in the south of the city, but anti-tank mines have been found as close as one metre from the edge of the tarmac road leading from Kandahar airport to the centre of town.

Within the UNOCHA mine action programme are both international agencies such as Handicap International (HI) and Afghan agencies such as the Mine Detection Dog Centre (MDC), Afghan Technical Consultants (ATC), Demining Agency for

GREEN DESERTS

In the mountains northwest of Kandahar, the waters of one of Afghanistan's largest rivers, the Helmand, are arrested by the Kajakai Dam. Completed in 1953 it is the largest earth-filled dam in the world, and at 91 metres high is the highest dam in Afghanistan. Its hydro-electricity plant — currently non-operational — has the potential to produce 350 megawatts of power. The Taliban elite in nearby Kandahar are desperate to get the plant going again. UNOCHA mine dogs have been demining the land around the bases of the enormous power pylons which still march over the mountains from the lake to the plains.

Some observers believe that UN rehabilitation of the dam may be linked to a deal with the Taliban to outlaw the growing of poppy which is rife in the region. The Kajakai Dam, along with the nearby Boghra Canal and Arghandab dam, feed the irrigation works of the immense Helmand Valley reclamation project which the US initiated in the early 1950s to transform 350,000 hectares of semi-desert into fertile farmland. The project — funded by the US State Department — benefited the US engineers involved but left Afghanistan's Agricultural Development Bank with huge debts which it could never pay off. Now heavily silted up, it stands out as an example of a failed attempt to apply Tennessee River Authority principles in a third-world context. **(SEE IRRIGATION)**

Afghanistan (DAFA) and the Organisation for Mine Clearance and Afghan Rehabilitation (OMAR). Mine dogs are particularly useful for detecting plastic anti-tank mines which metal detectors miss.

The accident toll even for these professionals is high: nationwide, there are around 50 mine clearance casualties every year. HI conducts an innovative Community Based Mine Awareness programme among *Kuchi* nomads in the region. While active male adults between the ages of 18-40 years are considered the group most at risk, HI's project also reaches women and children through non-formal awareness sessions conducted by locally-trained Afghans out in *Kuchi* encampments. (SEE NOMADS IN NO-MANS-LAND)

Refugees and IDPs

UNHCR is dealing with returnees from Baluchistan, where it is reported that around 100,000 are waiting to return. ICRC and UNICEF provide blankets and shelter for several thousand internal refugees, also known as internally displaced persons (IDPs). There are no IDP camps in or around Kandahar. However, CRC operates a small *marastoon* in Kandahar which houses the homeless. (SEE REFUGEES)

Kandahar A-Z

Accommodation and Food

The UNICA Guesthouse is the most obvious first port of call. As elsewhere UNICA costs $55 per night full board, or $40 just for the room. Payment is by cash or ANZ Grindlays Pakistan Bank cheque. Facilities include satellite television and satphone, air-conditioned rooms, and a wide selection of drinks available most nights of the week.

If you visit UNICA for a drink on a Thursday or Friday evening you may be able to negotiate a bed in the guesthouse of an international aid agency. Alternatively you can find local accommodation and food at the Khiber Hotel located opposite the Id Gah gateway at the northern end of the Old Town.

Embassies and Visas

You can extend your Afghan visa at the Police Headquarters or the Ministry of Foreign Affairs. A one month exit visa currently costs $10, two months is $20 and so on. Passport photos are required. The Pakistani Consulate in the New Town also issues single, double and multiple entry visas. Allow two or three days for a Pakistani visa to be issued. (SEE VISAS)

WARNING

THERE ARE STILL OVER 100 UNCLEARED MINEFIELDS WITHIN THE CITY OF KANDAHAR — NEVER GO ANYWHERE WITHOUT A GUIDE !

Emergencies

There are two small underground bunkers at the UNOCHA office for use in emergencies. Medical emergencies are best evacuated to Islamabad or Karachi by ICRC or UN aircraft. The hospital in Quetta is reportedly no better than the ICRC-supported Mir Wais hospital in Kandahar. (SEE SECURITY TIPS)

Information

For more information about United Nations activities, and for a security briefing, contact the Regional Representative for UNOCHA in the UNICA Guesthouse compound. Make sure you receive some kind of landmine awareness briefing, preferably from UNOCHA in Islamabad before travelling to Afghanistan.

The UNOCHA office in Kandahar should be able to find you an interpreter. For more details on NGO activities in Kandahar contact ACBAR in Kabul or Peshawar. The best way to meet aid agency workers and resident journalists is to turn up for a drink at the UNICA Guesthouse on a Thursday night between six and eight-thirty in the evening.

Local Rules

Photography in Kandahar is tricky. In this most conservative corner of Afghanistan it is best to get a permit from the Department of Foreign Affairs which allows you to take buildings but not living creatures. The permit is free and should be written out while you wait. Try to make a show of getting people out of the frame, although a wide-angle lens may still squeeze some in. (SEE PHOTOGRAPHY)

Currently it is very difficult for western women to go into the bazaar, after an incident involving expatriate staff from one of the aid agencies here. However, the situation changes constantly, so ask around.

Be careful while travelling through tribal agency areas if travelling by road between Kandahar and Quetta in Pakistan. Take a local

Afghan guide or colleague who speaks Pashto, Dari and Urdu to smooth the way.

Medical

Take precautions against mosquitoes and sandflies: they carry malaria and leishmaniasis. The latter is a particularly unpleasant disfiguring disease which causes open lesions on the face and body. Hepatitis, cholera and typhoid vaccines are also recommended. At least two western journalists and aid workers known to the EFG editors have died from hepatitis while working in the region. Diarrhoea is a major problem in Kandahar, so boil your drinking water for 10 minutes or use a good-quality filter. For medical emergencies there is always the Mir Wais hospital at the western end of the New Town which has an ICRC surgical unit. (SEE PERSONAL HEALTH)

Money

Bring US dollars for the UNICA Guesthouse and Pakistani Rupees or dollars to change downtown. (SEE MONEY & BARGAINING)

Post and Telecommunications

Post is best sent through the UN or ICRC system. All local telecommunication between aid agencies is by radio. International calls are made either by satellite phone; visitors may use the satphone at the UNICA Guesthouse, or try at the ICRC. A public microwave phone system is also available in the city which relays international calls via Quetta. (SEE RADIO & TELECOMMUNICATIONS)

Recreation

Bring plenty of books. There are no libraries or sporting facilities in Kandahar.

Shopping

Baluch handicrafts are available in the bazaars of the Old Town. Kandahar is also famous for its fabulous pomegranates, peaches, figs, grapes and extremely juicy melons.

Sights

The most comprehensive guidebook available on the historical sights of Kandahar remains Nancy Dupree's *An Historical Guide to Afghanistan* (2nd Edition, 1977) available through ACBAR or at various bookshops in Peshawar and Kabul.

Many of the sights worth seeing are located in the Old Town. Laid out by Ahmed Shah Durrani in the 1760s this rectangular city

The Shrine of the Cloak of the Prophet Mohammed *J. Walter*

was once surrounded by walls up to 30 feet thick, punctuated by six huge gateways. These fortifications were largely demolished in the 1940s.

Mausoleum of Ahmed Shah Durrani. This colourful octagonal building is dedicated to the memory of Ahmed Shah Baba, the "Father of Afghanistan", who inaugurated and ruled over the first great Pashtun Afghan dynasty from 1747-1772. It is located in the north-west quarter of the Old Town near the Id Gah gateway.

The Shrine of the Cloak of the Prophet Mohammed. Known locally as *Da Kherqa Sherif Ziarat*, the shrine is located next to Ahmed Shah's mausoleum and is one of the most holy shrines in Afghanistan. The exterior decoration of the shrine is magnificent: foundations of green Lashkar Gah marble, sparkling tilework over every surface and gilded archways make the nearby mausoleum of the city's founder look somewhat pedestrian.

The cloak itself cannot be seen. It was handed over to Ahmed Shah by the Amir of Bokhara in 1768 to consolidate a treaty over territories to the north. Traditionally the cloak is only brought out during times of national crisis. It had not been seen in public since the 1930s, when in 1994 when Mullah Omar, the Supreme Leader of the Taliban, removed the cloak from its shrine and held it before a crowd of several thousand clerics and Kandaharis, claiming it as a visible symbol of his role as Mullah Al-Momineen, Leader of All Pious Muslims.

The Mosque of the Hair of the Prophet. Known locally as the *Jame Mui Mobarak*, you will find the entrance to this mosque off the covered bazaar just to the east of the *Chahr Suq,* where the four bazaars of the Old Town converge. The Hair came from the Amir of Bokhara at the same time as the cloak, and is kept in a golden sheath in a casket under mountains of holy blankets and banners.

The local *mullah* or caretaker will let you into the side chapel where the Hair is enshrined. The mosque itself was built in the 19th Century and a water canal flows through the spacious shady courtyard, attracting travellers and the destitute.

Chihlzina ("Forty Steps"). About four km west of Kandahar, high above the plains on a rocky outcrop, is a cave carved out of the mountain. Known as the *Chihlzina*, forty steps lead to this chamber, inside which is an inscription relating the conquests of the Moghul emperor Babur and his son Humayun. After Babur's death in 1530, the struggle for succession drove his son into temporary exile in Persia. Humayun staged his return to Delhi by first occupying Kandahar in 1545 with the help of the Persians. After his own death in 1556 the city fell within the Persian sphere of influence. One of the most important battles in Afghanistan's history was fought at the foot of the *Chihlzina*. Here in 1881 Amir Abdur Rahman conquered the forces of his rebellious cousin Ayub Khan, making way for him to establish not just Kabul as his kingdom, but the whole nation of Afghanistan.

Zor Shahr ("Old City"). ***Check with the UNOCHA office and local Afghans about possible minefields before exploring this site.*** The original "Old City" of Kandahar – destroyed by Nadir Shah of Persia in 1738 – lies at the foot of the cliffs into which the *Chihlzina* is cut. Earlier this century archaeologists found Buddhist, Greek and Islamic treasures here, including two edicts of the Emperor Ashoka carved into blocks of stone in Greek and Aramaic. Dating from the 3rd Century BC, the familiar themes of piety and humility are ones which modern-day players on the Afghan stage would do well to note:

> *"Those who praise themselves and denigrate their neighbours are self-seekers, wishing to shine in comparison with the others but in fact hurting themselves. It behoves to respect one another and to accept one another's lessons." (trans. Wheeler)*

Weather

Temperatures range from around freezing point in winter (December to February) up to 35-40 degrees Celsius in summer (June to August). Spring (March to May) and Autumn (September to November) are the most pleasant times to visit.

WESTERN REGION

Western Afghanistan is a land which looks more towards Persia than the Indian subcontinent for its inspiration and its history. Lying at the eastern fringe of the great Iranian plateau, its parched earth is baked for months on end by fifty degrees of sun and blasted by a wind which blows nonstop for one hundred and twenty days. This land is a world away from the glacial mountains of the Hindu Kush, whose remnants barely penetrate the west of the country, trailing away into low, craggy ridgelines like the tip of a crocodile's tail. The wide plains which characterize this region make it difficult to defend, and for much of its history Herat and western Afghanistan have been invaded and liberated by competing Russian, Persian, British and Afghan forces keen to maintain a buffer between their spheres of influence and hostile neighbours.

Herat

"Here at last is Asia without an inferiority complex"

– Robert Byron, on arrival in Herat in 1933

Of all the cities of Central Asia, Herat must rank as one of the richest not only in terms of its history and strategic importance, but in the whole cultural spectrum of architecture, painting, poetry and music. Capital of the province of Herat and the largest city in western Afghanistan, Herat borders both Iran and Turkmenistan, and the city's prominent merchants make the most of border-trade and smuggling opportunities. Situated at an altitude of 950 metres, Herat used to be famous for grapes, fruit and cotton crops grown with the aid of extensive irrigation. Before the Soviet war its population was around 160,000, comprising mainly Persian-speaking, non-Pashtun *Sunni* Muslims, with a large minority of *Shi'as*. With Kabul over a thousand kilometres away by road, Herat established a reputation for being independent, both strategically and culturally. Today the city remains restless under the yoke of Taliban occupation.

Cultural Herat reached its height in the Timurid Renaissance of the 15th Century, under the rule of a dynasty of Uzbek princes who have been described as the Oriental Medici. While the artistic climax of the Timurid Empire may have been in the delicate tile-mosaics and painted miniatures for which Herat is justly famous, the Empire was conceived in more violent circumstances.

In the 13th Century Herat was governed by a local Persian dynasty known as the Karts – the bronze cauldron in the Friday Mosque is all that remains of their stay here. However an Uzbek adventurer by the name of Timur rallied the northern tribes to his cause, took control of Balkh and then destroyed Herat in 1381. An old war wound in his right leg caused him to limp and gave rise to his nickname Timur-e-Lang, otherwise known to western historians as "Timur the Lame" or Tamerlane. Timur's death in 1405 precipitated a series of bloody intrigues out of which his youngest son Shah Rukh emerged victorious to rule an empire stretching from Mesopotamia to the borders of China. His generous patronage of the arts, and that of his remarkable Queen, Gawhar Shad, led to a cultural renaissance which saw the flourishing of Bihzad the miniaturist and Jami the poet, not to mention countless other court artists, architects and philosophers. From the portraits of these Timurid princes of pleasure we can, in Byron's words, detect:

> *"a personal idiosyncrasy about them which tells of that rare phenomenon in Mohammedan history, an age of humanism. Judged by European standards, it was humanism within limits. The Timurid Renascence, like ours, took place in the fifteenth century, owed its course to the patronage of princes, and preceded the emergence of nationalist states. But in one respect the two movements differed. While the European was largely a reaction against faith in favour of reason, the Timurid coincided with a new consolidation of the power of faith. The Turks of Central Asia had already lost contact with Chinese materialism; and it was Timur who led them to the acceptance of Islam, not merely as a religion, for that was already accomplished, but as a basis of social institutions."*

Despite Shah Rukh's death in 1447 and his Queen's murder a decade later, Herat continued to blossom in a golden age under the rule of their successor Sultan Husain Baiqara (1468-1506). However, decadence and personal ambition conspired to bring about the end of the Timurid Renaissance. In 1507 Herat fell to another Uzbek invader, Babur, who went on to found the Moghul Empire in

India. But Herat must have made an impact on him for he did not destroy the city. Quite the opposite in fact. The towering *iwan* portals of the Friday Mosque and the Shrine of Ansari near Herat – surmounted by arcaded galleries and twin lantern-turrets – are architectural motifs which reappear again and again in the now world-famous mosques and mausolea which Babur and his successors created in Delhi and Agra.

Babur died in 1530. Herat soon fell under the sway of the Persian Safavid empire for two centuries. During most of the 18th and 19th Centuries Herat was a semi-autonomous state occupied by a succession of Pashtun princes who alternately fought off Persian advances on their city and attempted to advance their control over Kabul. In 1828 the Russians defeated Persia and began to entertain ambitions eastwards towards India. Their support for the Persian siege on Herat from November 1837 to September 1838, along with Amir Dost Mohammed's Russophile leanings, were to provoke the ill-fated British invasion of Afghanistan in 1839. Herat survived the siege, was spared either Russian or British occupation, and remained independent until Amir Dost Mohammed completed his unification of Afghanistan by seizing the city in 1863. He died a month after taking Herat and lies buried at Gazargah, five kilometres to the east of the city. Turbulent years of succession followed, with Amir Abdur Rahman struggling to wrest Herat from a rebellious cousin in 1881 and making himself unpopular by resettling Pashtun southerners up in Badghis.

From 1887-1888 the northern and western boundaries of Afghanistan were formally established by a joint Russian-British Boundary Commission, but Britain remained exceptionally touchy about western Afghanistan in general, and Herat in particular, because of its highly strategic role as a buffer between British India and Persian and Russian ambitions. The so-called "Panjdeh Incident" in 1885, when Russian troops seized the Afghan fort of Panjdeh north of Herat, led to British officers advising on the defence of Herat – advice which led to the destruction of the fabulous Timurid *musalla* complex in order to deny an army advancing on the citadel any cover from fire.

Herat has maintained its independent reputation for much of the 20th Century. In the 1960s the city was a stronghold for the new Islamist movement. The communist reforms of 1978-1979 sparked off widespread rebellion across the country, and the first organized revolt against the People's Democratic Party of Afghanistan (PDPA) was in Herat in March 1979. The Herat revolt was unique in being a carefully planned cooperation of militant Islamists from the Jamiat party, local *mawlawi* clergy and a mutinous army garrison led by Captain Ismail Khan. Hundreds of communist officers, teachers, Russian advisors and their families were killed in Herat and the surrounding villages. A week later government troops with air support from the USSR retook the town and killed between 5,000 and 25,000 of Herat's population in the process. This was the first instance of direct Soviet military intervention into Afghanistan prior to the invasion of December 1979.

For most of the 1980s Ismail Khan extended his influence over Herat and northwest Afghanistan as far as Maimana, and the region became predominately supporters of Rabbani's *Sunni* party Jamiat-e-Islami. Along the border between Afghanistan and Iran pockets of *Shi'a* resistance fighters appeared but to little military effect. The Soviets stationed a large number of troops 150 kilometres south of Herat at Shindand where a major airbase directly threatened the Persian Gulf. Three divisions of Russian military and airborne troops were based between Herat and Kandahar throughout the early 1980s, but their role was as much to contain Iranian territorial ambitions as to dislodge the Afghan resistance. Thus western Afghanistan once again became a strategic buffer zone.

Following the withdrawal of Russian troops in 1989, Ismail Khan established himself as the virtual Amir of Herat, ruling over a semi-autonomous region of the country. He captured tanks, fighter aircraft, helicopters and transport planes from the retreating Russians. He played host to delegations from Pakistan and Saudi Arabia who were afraid that Iran might take Herat in the absence of a strong government in Kabul. Apart from the fact that they considered the Iranian *Shi'a* Muslims to be heretics, both the Pakistanis and the Saudis had their eyes on the possibility of oil – either the exploration for it in northern Afghanistan, or the piping of it from Turkmenistan via Herat to Pakistan and the Arabian Sea. Iran stepped up the pressure by imposing a trade blockade, and supplies had to come through Turkmenistan. Over a million Afghan refugees had fled into Iran during the Soviet war. From 1993-1994 Iran tried to destabilize Herat by forcing as many as 1,500 of these refugees a day back into western Afghanistan. However, by 1995 the flow of returnees had reduced to a trickle as the Taliban movement flexed its muscles in the region.

The Taliban made several attempts to take Herat in 1995, but were beaten back twice at Girishk and Shindand by forces loyal to Ismail Khan and Ahmed Shah Massoud, who had sent troops over specially from Panjshair to help his Jamiat ally. However, in September of that year Khan's forces collapsed and the Taliban took the city.

Since then the city's inhabitants – who had grown used to an independent and relatively liberal lifestyle – have periodically rebelled against Taliban prohibitions. In January 1997, several hundred women clad in *burqas* marched through the city to protest against the closure of the *hamams* (public baths) – they were hosed down and beaten by Taliban troops. An effigy of Mullah Omar, the Taliban supreme leader, appeared with a hand-grenade dangling round his neck. A cassette-player attached to a bicycle parked in the middle of Herat blared out anti-Taliban propaganda until the tape ran out – no-one dared stop it for fear that it might be booby-trapped. Men have been rounded up and locked in cells until their beards grow to the required length; women have been prevented

WARNING

THERE ARE STILL MINEFIELDS IN THE VICINITY OF HERAT — NEVER GO ANYWHERE WITHOUT A GUIDE !

from working for international agencies except in the health sector. Girls are not allowed to go to school, but the local people will not be cowed – they have organized "home-schooling" for their daughters in secret locations.

Getting there

By air

The most convenient and least exciting way into Herat is by air. The wrecks of half a dozen Soviet MiG fighters lying on the ground greet your arrival. If you are travelling independently, arrange beforehand for someone from UNOCHA to meet you at the airport. The flight from Islamabad or Peshawar takes a little over two hours. Both the ICRC and UN operate planes into the city on a regular basis: ICRC flights leave from Peshawar on Tuesdays and Saturdays, and often interconnect with Kabul and Mazar en route. UN flights leave from Islamabad on Sundays and Wednesdays, and often interconnect with Kandahar en route. Currently the ICRC flights are free and the UN charges $390 for a one-way ticket. It is also possible to fly commercially into Mary (Turkmenistan) or Meshad (Iran) and then take public transport to Herat. The UN flies into Farah on Sundays (on demand). (SEE TRAVEL)

By road

Four overland routes converge on Herat from each point of the compass. The roads from Meshad in Iran and Mary in Turkmenistan arrive from the west and the north respectively. These routes are now major arteries for smuggled goods as well as possible entry points into Afghanistan for the more intrepid overland traveller. An eastern approach to Herat used to be possible from Kabul via Bamiyan and Chakhcharan; the attraction of this route for those with four or five days to spare is that it passes through magnificent mountain scenery, visiting the colossal Buddhas of Bamiyan and the turquoise lakes of Band-e-Amir *en route*.

Currently however, the route crosses a frontline between Taliban and Hazara forces, and the area between Obey and Chisht-e-Sharif is reported to be mined. The route to the south arrives from Kandahar via Shindand, and has reverberated to the sounds of countless conquerors through history, from the marching step of Alexander's army to the mechanical roar of Taliban tanks. The road threads a delicate path between the mountains of the Hindu Kush and the shifting sands of *Dasht-e-Margo* – the Desert of Death. Its arrival in Herat is heralded by thirty-two thousand jack-pines planted in the 1940s on either side of the road by one of the city's more enlightened governors (most have now been cut down). Allow 13-14 hours to drive from Kandahar to Herat in a jeep, or two days by bus.

Orientation

Herat lies in a long fertile plain which spreads east and west between the Paropamisus mountains five kilometres to the north, and the Harirud river as far again to the south. The Harirud, which rises in the highlands of Bamiyan and flows west into Iran, is Herat's lifeline; you will cross it while driving into the city from the airport. The Old City is divided into four quarters containing the Citadel, Friday Mosque and covered bazaar. To the north and east of the Citadel lies the Shahr-e-Naw (New Town) where most of the UN and NGO offices are located. To the northwest lies the *musalla* complex.

Maps of Herat are hard to come by. UNCHS (Habitat) has produced a very detailed GIS-generated City Guide Map dated January 1997 with the locations of UN agencies and NGOs on it. UNOCHA Herat can provide you with a much simpler diagrammatic map made by the British NGO Shelter Project (BNSP) dated September 1993.

Getting around

Call in at the UNOCHA office (located in the compound of the UNICA Guesthouse) to receive a briefing on the latest mine clearance situation. There may be a chance of hitching a lift around town in a UN or aid agency vehicle. Apart from aid agency jeeps the best way to get around is by taxi. Taxis can be hired at the corner of the street 100 metres south of the UNICA Guesthouse. They charge between $5-$10 for a morning's work.

Agencies

Around 20 UN agencies and NGOs are currently working in or out of Herat. For an overview of agency activities in the region and the latest humanitarian situation it is best to check in at the Herat offices of the Agency Coordinating Body for Afghan Relief (ACBAR) and the United Nations Office for the Coordination of Humanitarian Assistance to Afghanistan (UNOCHA).

For agency telephone numbers see ***Post & Telecommunications*** below.

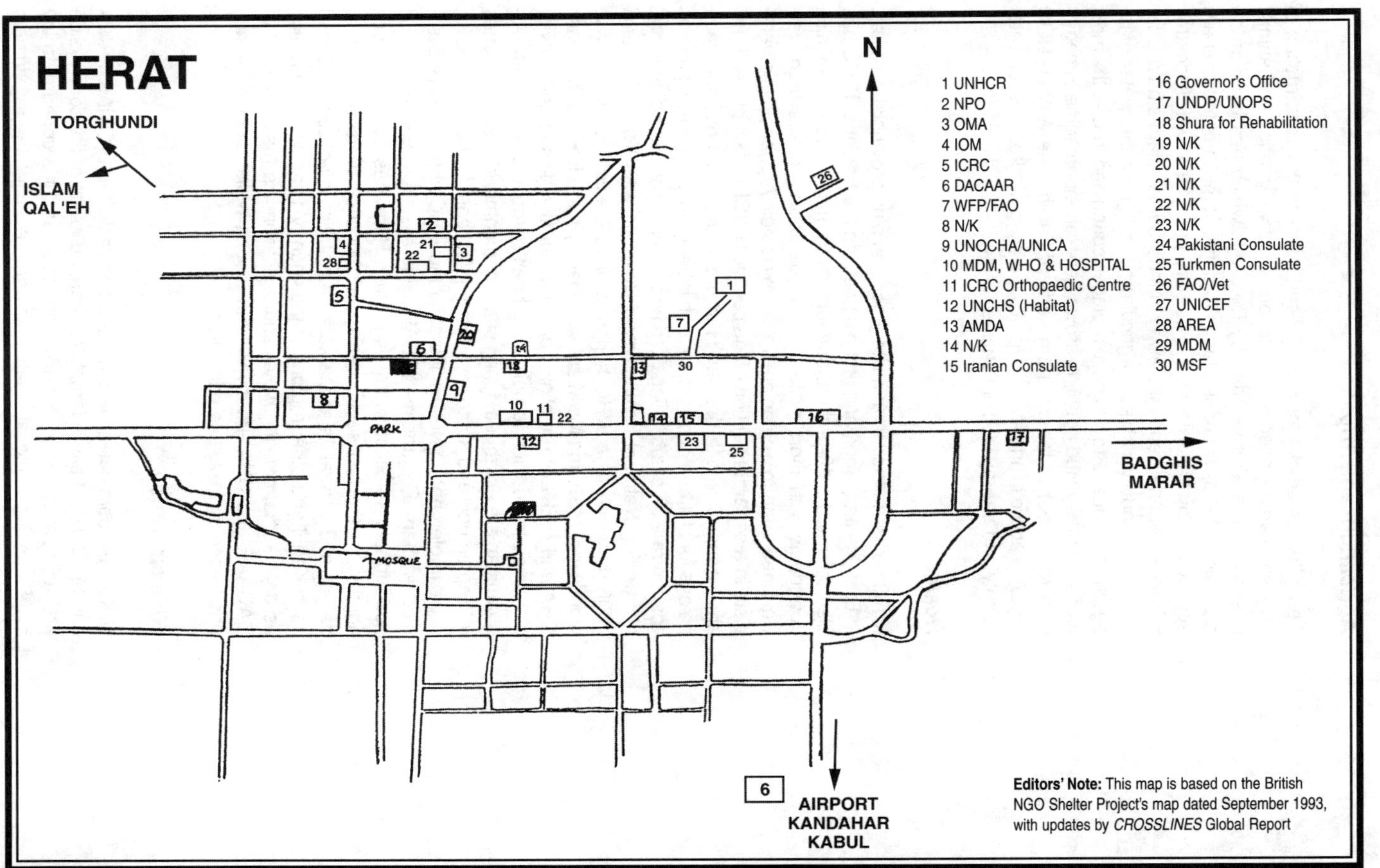
HERAT
TORGHUNDI
ISLAM QAL'EH
N
1 UNHCR
2 NPO
3 OMA
4 IOM
5 ICRC
6 DACAAR
7 WFP/FAO
8 N/K
9 UNOCHA/UNICA
10 MDM, WHO & HOSPITAL
11 ICRC Orthopaedic Centre
12 UNCHS (Habitat)
13 AMDA
14 N/K
15 Iranian Consulate
16 Governor's Office
17 UNDP/UNOPS
18 Shura for Rehabilitation
19 N/K
20 N/K
21 N/K
22 N/K
23 N/K
24 Pakistani Consulate
25 Turkmen Consulate
26 FAO/Vet
27 UNICEF
28 AREA
29 MDM
30 MSF
PARK
MOSQUE
BADGHIS
MARAR
AIRPORT
KANDAHAR
KABUL
Editors' Note: This map is based on the British NGO Shelter Project's map dated September 1993, with updates by *CROSSLINES* Global Report

Agriculture and irrigation

Agriculture is crucial for Herat's economy, and the construction of irrigation canals, seed multiplication, soil conservation and animal husbandry are all supported by DACAAR which has been in the area since 1993. Water shortages throughout much of the year are aggravated by flash floods in February and March which destroy irrigation channels and take away topsoil. Some villages have doubled their land available for agriculture through proper water management. Wheat and rice have replaced cotton and fruit as the main crops, but very little poppy is grown here, although some is beginning to appear in the southern parts of Farah. The Afghan NGO AREA is active in and around Herat pioneering wind-pumps for water supply and energy-efficient stoves.

Health

ICRC supports the Herat military hospital plus provincial hospitals in Badghis and Ghor, and first aid posts on the frontline. ICRC has also operated a 40-bed orthopaedic centre here since 1993 which now deals with more polio, TB and paraplegic cases than war-wounded. Afghan women are treated by female Afghan physiotherapists in a separate section of the centre. UNICEF distributes drugs and cooperates with the MoPH in organizing immunization campaigns for children and women of childbearing age. Current projects concentrate on establishing fixed health centres in each district and on running National Immunization Days for polio from 1997 until 2000 by which time WHO hopes to have eradicated the disease worldwide. MSF and MDM are vaccinating in the IDP camps, while CHA and MERLIN run clinics on a community, district and provincial level. In addition to polio, key health problems in western Afghanistan are diarrhoea during summer months, cholera from June to September, and acute respiratory infections during winter. CHA is the implementing NGO in Herat for the UN Comprehensive Disabled Afghans Programme (CDAP), and assists in vocational and non-formal rehabilitation training. Since Herat has not seen much fighting for the last seven years, and because of its proximity to Iranian and Central Asian markets, malnutrition is not such as threat as in Kabul and other regions of the country. However, in a region as dry as this, drinking water and sanitation are major problems. DACAAR and CHA are involved in sinking wells, digging latrines and health and hygiene education.

Mine clearance

UNOCHA coordinates the mine clearance activities of OMAR, MCPA and MDC. Herat city is largely cleared, but parts of the countryside are still heavily mined. Frontline forces in Badghis continue to lay mines, driving out local inhabitants and preventing the repatriation of returnees.

Refugees and IDPs

In 1993 the number of Afghan refugees returning from Iran peaked at over 600,000 persons, many of whom settled in Herat province *(Source: UNHCR 1997)*. But by 1997 this had reduced to a mere 834, largely because of the Taliban presence in western Afghanistan. Many would-be returnees have been put off by reports of 'ethnic-cleansing' on the border, where Taliban troops seize Tajik, Hazara and *Shi'a* men they suspect of being hostile and lock them up. Herat's four prisons are visited regularly by ICRC delegates to ensure adequate standards of health and hygiene. UNHCR and ICRC are currently assisting the Ministry of Repatriation in taking care of 30,000 internal refugees or internally-displaced persons (IDPs) in camps outside the city.

Many IDPs have fled the fighting in Badghis, Faryab and Jowzjan provinces between the Taliban and Dostum's Jumbesh forces. ICRC removed their support for one IDP camp (Shahidahi 2) when they suspected that frontline fighters were benefiting from high levels of humanitarian aid supplied to local families posing as IDPs. IAM, with support from UNICEF, is able to run non-formal education for boys and girls in these camps. Homeless children inside the city are supported by WFP food-for-work programmes and UNICEF shelters. However, the WFP food-for-work policy has not been popular with NGOs because it is seen as undermining the value of both local wheat and local labour, thus perpetuating a state of dependence and preventing the development of self-sufficient communities.

Herat A-Z

Accommodation and Food

Agonising over where to stay in Herat is a predicament unlikely to confront any visitors to this city. The only practical choice is the UNICA Guesthouse, located in a walled compound just to the northeast of the Old Town. As elsewhere in Afghanistan, the charge is $40 per night or $55 if you want three meals a day thrown in. If this is too expensive – or booked up – you may be able to stay in the guesthouse of an aid agency based in Herat, but this is very much on an *ad hoc* basis. Ask around in Islamabad, Peshawar and Kabul before arriving, or else go to the UN Club for a drink on a Thursday or Friday night and check out the lie of the land. There is one alternative: the Afghan Hotel (formerly known as the Minarets Hotel) is a rather dusty hostelry where a room with shower and Asian lavatory will set you back $10 per night, including breakfast. It is located opposite the ICRC office. As for dining out, most expatriates eat in their own houses or at the UN Club, although some go down to the bazaar in the Old Town for kebabs occasionally.

Books

Bookshops are pretty nonexistent in Herat so bring all your reading with you. For more local information read the following:
A Catalogue of the Toponyms and Monuments of Timurid Herat, Terry Allen, Massachusetts Institute of Technology (1981)
Music of Afghanistan: Professional musicians in the city of Herat, John Baily, Cambridge University Press (1988 – incls. Audio-cassette)
The Road to Oxiana, Robert Byron, Macmillan (London, 1937; reprinted by Picador, 1981)
Three Women of Herat, Veronica Doubleday, Jonathan Cape (London, 1988)
An Historical Guide to Afghanistan, Nancy Hatch Dupree, (2nd Edition, Kabul, 1977)
Les Nouvelles d'Afghanistan (No. 41-42, Mars 1989) – contains numerous articles on Herat plus a bibliography of books, newspaper articles and video films.
There is a small library at the UNICA Guesthouse.

Embassies & Visas

Both Pakistan visas and extensions for your Afghan visa can be obtained in Herat. There are also Consulates representing Iran and Turkmenistan; ask at UNOCHA for more details. (SEE VISAS)

Emergencies

There is a UN bunker underneath the UNICA Guesthouse which doubles up as a bar and disco when the city is not under siege. The UNOCHA/UNDP representative is also the Area Security Coordinator (ASC). Anyone wishing to benefit from UN security facilities and evacuations must abide by the ASCs instructions. For a medical emergency, the best course is evacuation to Pakistan. Going to Meshad is difficult from a visa point of view, and there are very few expatriate doctors in Herat. If you cannot get out to Pakistan, try contacting ICRC or MSF. The advantage of being evacuated by the Red Cross is that they may provide medical staff to accompany you in the air. (SEE SECURITY TIPS)

Information

For more information about United Nations activities, contact the Regional Representative for UNOCHA in the UNICA Guesthouse compound. UNOCHA should be able to give you a briefing on the latest security and landmine situation. Make sure you receive some kind of landmine awareness briefing, preferably from UNOCHA in Islamabad before travelling to Afghanistan. The UNOCHA office in Herat should be able to find you an interpreter. For more details on NGO activities in Herat contact ACBAR. The best way to meet aid agency workers and resident journalists is to turn up for a drink at the UNICA Guesthouse on a Thursday or Friday night between six and eight-thirty in the evening.

Medical

Apart from the odd cholera epidemic, Herat is reasonably safe from nasty diseases; although preventive measures for malaria and hepatitis are recommended. Well-water is safe to drink, but boil and/or treat anything coming out of a tap. (SEE PERSONAL HEALTH)

Money

There are no banks in Herat – all money-changing is done on the open market. Bring US Dollars or Pakistani Rupees. (SEE MONEY & BARGAINING)

Post & Telecommunications

Many NGOs send their post with the ICRC aeroplane to Peshawar. Herat does have a functioning local telephone service, but for international calls you need a satphone or CTOR radio. ICRC, MDM and UNHCR have satphones, or ask at UNOCHA. Local telephone numbers are overleaf.

Recreation

The UNICA Guesthouse has a volleyball pitch and a hard tennis court. Go down on a Friday or Saturday and you are bound to find a game of some sort going on. There are two satellite TVs as well – remember international news comes on at half past the hour in Afghanistan. For liquid recreation, "international night" for nonresidents is on a Thursday from six or seven in the evening onwards. There is a swimming pool in the ICRC compound.

Shopping

Herat is most famous for its blue glass which is still made locally. It comes in three colours – green, turquoise and royal blue – and any number of shapes, from wine goblets and decanters to candlesticks and tumblers. One local entrepreneur, who calls himself "Haji Dollar," has recently developed a line in blue glass champagne flutes which seems a little ambitious under present circumstances. The quality is rather poor, although the odd pieces of straw or dung which find their way into the glass lend it a certain rustic authenticity.

There is a line of shops opposite the northeastern corner of the Friday Mosque crammed full of blue glass and numerous other *objets d'art* of dubious provenance. The going rate for a glass goblet is no more than a dollar. Lapis jewellery, Greek coins and Buddhist earthenware will all be proffered in your direction as well – but look out

SER.	ORGANIZATION	TEL. NO.
1	ADA	2851
2	AHDAA	2075
3	ARAA	3425
4	AREA	3169
5	CHA	3178
6	DACAAR	2849
7	DCA	2444
8	FAO	3221
9	GAF	2410
10	IAM	3321
11	ICRC	2236
12	IIRO	2453
13	IOM	3362
14	MDC	2752
15	MDM	3569
16	NHC	2152
17	NPO	2629
18	OMAR	3024
19	OV	2272
20	UNCHS	2348
21	UNHCR	3362
22	UNICA Guesthouse	3180
23	UNICEF	3209
24	UNOCHA	3488
25	UNOPS	2125
26	VAF	2483
27	WFP	3035
28	WHO	2123
29	AIRPORT	2111, 2622
30	IRAN CONSULATE	2820-1, 2830
31	PAKISTAN CONSULATE	2051
32	TURKMEN CONSULATE	3534

for fakes. You can still buy Baluch rugs and Turcoman carpets in the rug bazaar located at the southwestern corner of the *Chahr Suq* in the Old Town. One local workshop, supported by CHA, trains local people in vocational skills – they will sell you hand-knotted carpets which have been made to old Turcoman patterns and coloured with natural dyes.

Sights

Herat is one of the most rewarding cities in Afghanistan for sightseeing. Despite the ravages of over a century of modern explosives, a great deal remains which is worth seeing. Some sights, like the Friday Mosque, are actually more spectacular now after restoration than they were earlier this century.

Citadel *(Qala-e-Ikhtiyaruddin)*. The Citadel perches atop a rocky bluff at the northern end of the Old Town and dominates the bazaar and the low plain to the north. Built in 1305 by a Kart governor, it was attacked by both Genghis Khan and Timur before becoming the centre of the Timurid Empire for the whole of the 15th Century. Timur's son Shah Rukh repaired the fortress and decorated some of its towers with blue tiles, but once the sun had set on the Timurid Renaissance in 1507 Herat and its citadel were subjected to waves of Persian and Uzbek attacks. In 1838 a British Army officer, Lieutenant Eldred Pottinger, occupied the citadel and organized its defences against the siege of a Russian-backed Persian army. In the 1980s UNESCO restored some of the citadel's walls and Timurid decoration. Today, the citadel is occupied by Taliban forces and is closed to visitors.

Friday Mosque *(Masjid-e-Jami)*. The Friday Mosque in Herat is undoubtedly one of the finest examples of Islamic art and architecture to be found anywhere in Afghanistan, even in all Central Asia. Yet as recently as the 1930s it was described as having "no colour; only whitewash, bad brick, and broken bits of mosaic" (Byron). Almost all of the magnificent tilework which can still be seen today was recreated according to original Timurid designs under a remarkable restoration programme which started in 1943. This work continues despite the unrest in other parts of the country. WFP provides boys with food in return for learning how to make the tiles and working to complete the restoration.

The mosque was laid out in 1200 by the Ghorid Sultan Ghiyas-ud-Din who established his capital at Herat after the collapse of the Ghaznavid Empire. All that remains of the Ghorid decoration is one portal to the south of the main entrance carved with floral motifs, geometric patterns and bright turquoise-blue Kufic script in high relief. Entrance to the mosque is permitted for men only, through a passageway in the eastern portal. Inside is a splendidly shining marble courtyard nearly 100 metres long, surrounded on four sides by arcaded walls in the centres of which are four *iwans,* or vaulted open-fronted halls, all covered with exuberant Timurid-style tilework. A large bronze cauldron dating from the 14th Century sits in the courtyard; once it contained *sherbat,* a sweet drink supplied to the faithful on feast-days, but now it acts as a large donation box. The best time to visit the mosque is in the early morning, before crowds of curious Afghans appear and the intense sun bleaches the walls of colour. But try to avoid visiting during Friday morning prayers between 12 and two o'clock. If you want to take photographs, check first with your guide, make sure no-one is in the picture and do it

Musalla complex, Herat *J. Walter*

quickly before black-turbaned Taliban zealots catch you with a camera dangling around your neck.

The Musalla Complex. Were you to look north from the ramparts of the Citadel of Herat at dusk you would catch sight of five strange towers rising from the gloom like the chimneys of a brick factory or the legs of an upturned table. These minarets and a badly damaged mausoleum are all that remain of Queen Gawhar Shad's *musalla* (place of worship), which once comprised "the most glorious productions of Mohammedan architecture in the fifteenth century" (Byron). The complex survived the collapse of the Timurid Empire and successive assaults by Uzbeks and Persians, but was largely destroyed in 1885 on the advice of British Army officers who were keen to help Amir Abdur Rahman defend the westernmost outpost of Afghanistan against Russian advances from the north. Two earthquakes and the Soviet War inflicted more damage and today only five of the original thirty minarets survive, lurching at dangerous angles and pockmarked with rocket and small-arms fire. The *musalla* represented the climax of Timurid decorative art – tile-mosaics of ever more intense colour and intricate design which had developed from the coloured brick patterns of the 12th Century Seljuks and the geometric terracotta mouldings of the Ghorids. Today only tantalising traces remain.

The complex originally comprised of a mosque to the north and a *madrassa* or theological college to the south. Queen Gawhar Shad, wife of Shah Rukh and daughter-in-law of Timur, commissioned the madrassa in 1417 and, after being murdered 40 years later, she was buried in a mausoleum within its walls. She was a remarkable woman, not only on account of her inspired artistic taste and patronage, but also because of her religious tolerance: as a *Sunni* queen she was responsible for the construction of the *Shi'a* Imam Reza mosque of Meshad in modern-day Iran, then under her sway.

The Queen's mausoleum still stands, and by climbing up to the base of its Persian-blue ribbed dome you can look out over the whole of Herat – from the Citadel in the south towards Gazargah in the east – from the Paropamisus mountains in the north towards the setting sun. The lone leaning minaret to the east of the mausoleum was one of a pair marking the entrance to the *madrassa,* and by all accounts its decoration was plainer than that of the college itself. The surface of the shaft is adorned with robust diamonds of royal blue tile-mosaic filled with flowers. Within the tower local boys dare each other to scramble up the spiral staircase and wave from the top balcony where the muezzin used to cry the call to prayer for the faithful 120 feet below.

To the north of the mausoleum stand four minarets dating from the reign of Sultan Husain Baiqara (1468-1506), last of Herat's Timurid rulers. Originally marking the four corners of another *madrassa,* their delicate lacy decoration speaks eloquently of the decadence of empire. In 1507 Herat fell to the Uzbek adventurer Babur, the founder of the Moghul Empire. Of Baiqara's reign he writes: "what happened with his sons, the soldiers and the town was that everyone pursued vice and pleasure to excess."

Gazargah. "Everyone goes to Gazar Gah," wrote Byron in the 1930s, "Babur went. Humayun went." Today it is hardly crowded with tourists, but it is still a popular retreat for Heratis on holiday. Situated under a stand of umbrella-pines on a low hill five kilometres east of Herat, Gazargah is the Shrine of Khwaja Abdullah Ansari, a famous Sufi poet and mystic philosopher who lived in Herat during the 11th Century. His shrine was rebuilt by Shah Rukh in 1428 and consists of a large rectangular walled courtyard filled with graves, a sacred well and a royal picnic pavilion. Of Ansari himself Byron had this to say:

> *"Khoja Abdullah Ansari died in the year 1088 at the age of eighty-four, because some boys threw stones at him while he was at penance. One sympathises with those boys: even among saints he was a prodigious bore. He spoke in the cradle; he began to preach at fourteen; during his life he held intercourse with 1,000 sheikhs, learnt 100,000 verses by heart (some say 1,200,000) and composed as many more. He doted on cats."*

Within the main courtyard is a splendid 30 metre high *iwan* whose Timurid decoration reveals Chinese influence, testimony perhaps to the diplomatic and cultural missions which Shah Rukh exchanged with the Chinese Emperor during the first half of the 15th Century. The tomb of the saint is enclosed in a blue cage and beside it are a superbly carved marble pillar five metres high and a holy ilex tree. Rather like Roman Catholic saints in rural Europe it seems that Ansari is believed to possess magical powers, and specifically power to cure barrenness. Women who cannot conceive choose a stone from near the saint's tomb to represent the child for which they long; they then wrap it in its cradle of linen, dangle it from a branch of the sacred ilex tree and say a prayer for their baby to Ansari.

The courtyard is full of tombs. Amir Dost Mohammed, the bane of the British for much of the 19th Century, is buried here in a white marble tomb behind a balustrade. Inside a small chamber set into the north wall of the courtyard is the *Haft Kalam* ("seven pens"), a stunningly carved late 15th Century sarcophagus of black marble. You may need to ask the caretaker to unlock the chamber.

To the south of the main shrine is the *Khana Zarnegar* ("Pavilion adorned with Gold") whose interior used to be painted in gold and lapis lazuli; it is currently locked. Just to the north of the shrine is the early 15th Century *Hauz-e-Zamzam*, a small covered reservoir whose crystal clear contents were said to have been purified by several goatskins of water from the sacred well of *Zamzam* in Mecca. Beneath the pine trees is the 17th Century picnic pavilion known as the *Namakdan* or 'Saltcellar' because of its manysided shape. From here you can enjoy a good view of Herat, its distant minarets and the Paropamisus mountains.

Outside Herat. About 12 kilometres south of the city is the Pul-e-Malan ("Bridge of Riches") which was a tourist attraction 500 years ago when the Moghul Emperor Babur paid it a special visit. The road east along the Harirud valley from Herat to Obey and Chisht-e-Sharif is meant to be delightful. Obey (107 km from Herat) used to be famous for its hot springs and wooded gorge; Chisht (173 km from Herat) was well-known for its two 12th Century *gumbad* or domes, and for being the home of the Chishtiya Sufi brotherhood. Continuing along this road you will reach the 800 year-old Minaret of Jam (313 km from Herat), a spectacular tower 65 metres high, tottering on the banks of the Harirud river in a remote mountain valley. Reportedly not 'discovered' by western archaeologists until 1957, it is the second highest minaret in the world after the Qutb Minar in Delhi. As the only surviving architectural monument from the Ghorid period, it is of enormous cultural and historic significance. However, there are reports that the route to Jam from Herat is mined, so ask around in Herat before embarking on this journey. This "central route" is described in some detail in Nancy Dupree's guide to Afghanistan. Continuing east, Chakhcharan (capital of Ghor) lies 113 km from Jam, and from there Kabul is a further 575 km away via Bamiyan. The route used to take five days or more to complete by jeep – with a frontline and numerous unbridged rivers to cross, it could now take much longer.

Weather

The weather in Herat is dry and hot in summer, with temperatures reaching over 30 degrees Celsius and 120 days of ripping winds from May to August. In January the thermometer can drop to freezing, and from February to April the rains often cause flash flooding. Best times to visit are from September to October and April to May.

HAZARAJAT

Hazarajat is a remote and mountainous region in central Afghanistan which covers the three provinces of Bamiyan, Uruzgan and Ghor, plus parts of neighbouring provinces. It is one of the poorest areas of the country, and for much of the 20th Century was oppressed by hostile Pashtun rulers. This oppression conspired with harsh geography to make Hazarajat one of the least developed corners of Afghanistan.

Dominated by the snowcapped Hindu Kush range, known here as the Koh-e-Baba – rising to over 5,000 metres – it is nevertheless a region of striking natural beauty. Emerald-green valleys thread thin as ribbons through barren rocky gorges, and at harvest time the blazing autumnal tints compete with brightly-clad farmers and their families in a festival of colour. The Hazaras who traditionally inhabit this area are, according to one recent writer, probably the second largest ethnic group in Afghanistan, yet one of the least known. They are distinguishable from other Afghans both by their faces, which appear Mongolian, and their religion, which is largely *Shi'a* Muslim. Although many Hazara men sought work in Afghanistan's towns as casual labourers, the majority still live in Hazarajat.

Traditionally Hazarajat has resisted any attempt at rule from a central Afghan power. But in the 1890s, the Hazaras clashed with an invasion force of Pashtun troops sent in by Amir Abdur Rahman, and many Hazaras were scattered as far afield as Iran and Pakistan. The traditional tribal system of those who remained was seriously undermined by Pashtun immigrant settlers. In this century the Hazaras openly rebelled against the communists in late 1978 and 1979, and from the start of the Soviet war Hazarajat was independent of communist influence, largely remaining so for the duration of the war. This was mainly because of the region's geography which made it both inaccessible and strategically irrelevant. The only communist government post in the whole of Hazarajat was at Bamiyan, and the Soviets stopped their military operations in the region in 1981. Resistance to the Soviets centred around two competing factions, the *shura* of Sayed Beheshti, and the Nasr, a party formed by followers of Iran's Ayatollah Khomeiny. But in the 1980s, despite internal divisions, the Hazaras succeeded – with Iranian support – in winning autonomy for their region from the Pashtun-dominated centre for the first time in a century.

In June 1990 Iran put pressure on the eight separate Hazara mujahed groups to form one Unity Party, the Hezb-e-Wahdat, in order to consolidate the power of Iran-backed *Shi'as* in Afghanistan. It was led by Abdul Ali Mazari until March 1995, when he was killed while in Taliban custody. Hezb-e-Wahdat has now split into two groups, the smaller led by Mohammed Akbari, and the larger controlled by Karim Khalili. Based in Bamiyan, Khalili's Hezb-e-Wahdat party held the balance of power in Mazar-e-Sharif throughout much of 1997.

Although Khalili denies Iranian military support for his faction, large amounts of food aid, engineering supplies and technical expertise are flown in by air from Tehran to his Bamiyan stronghold in central Afghanistan. However, resentment in Hazarajat against Tehran grew in 1995 after thousands of Hazara refugees were forcibly repatriated from Iran. Currently Khalili is part of Rabbani's and Dostum's anti-Taliban "Northern Alliance."

Bamiyan

Most famous for its 1,700-year-old colossal Buddha statues, and for the turquoise waters of Band-e-Amir, Bamiyan has for many years been neglected by Peshawar-based aid organizations. However, a small number of agencies are now establishing themselves in this remote region of Afghanistan.

Getting there

By air

The UN and ICRC operate flights (on demand) into Bamiyan and Yakawlang. Before flying into Hazarajat, however, flight operations staff have to contact Hezb-e-Wahdat forces stationed in Bamiyan to warn them not to shoot at the incoming aircraft. The peace of the Bamiyan valley is often shattered by Hazara anti-aircraft positions opening up on any Taliban aircraft which fly overhead. However, in late December 1997 two UN planes, one a WFP-chartered plane carrying badly-needed supplies of wheat, and one a UN passenger plane carrying an investigation team, were targeted by Taliban bombs while on the ground at Bamiyan airport. Halfway down the dirt airstrip at Bamiyan lie the remains of the aircraft which crashed on 21 August 1997 while carrying Abdul Rahim Ghaforzai. Ghaforzai, an ethnic Pashtun who had been Afghanistan's ambassador to the UN and a leading light in the anti-Taliban "Northern Alliance", was killed along with most of the other passengers.

UN flights from Islamabad are usually scheduled for Mondays, calling at both Yakawlang and Bamiyan, and sometimes going via Mazar. Contact ICRC flight operations in Peshawar for details of their service. (SEE TRAVEL)

By road

Bamiyan is one-and-a-half days' drive by four-wheel drive jeep from both Kabul and Mazar. The route from Mazar is via Doshi or Jabal-us Seraj. From Kabul, there are two routes: a southern route via the Hajigak Pass (177 km) and a northern route via the Shibar Pass (237 km). The northern route passes through Charikar and the Ghorband Valley, but is difficult while the frontline remains just north of Kabul. The southern route leads northwest off the main Kabul-Ghazni road at Maidan Shar. From November until May the roads may be impassable due to snow and flooding from rain and snow-melt. Roads are also often closed by Taliban forces trying to block-ade Hazarajat and limit supplies reaching Hezb-e-Wahdat troops. Yakawlang and Band-e-Amir are both about four to five hours drive west of Bamiyan.

Orientation

Bamiyan lies in the broad valley of the Bamiyan river which flows here from west to east. To the north of the river rises the rocky ridge into which the colossal Buddhas and monks' caves are carved; to the south on a raised plateau lie Khalili's headquarters and farm-land stretching up into the Koh-e-Baba mountains.

Getting around

Check with locally-based agencies about the mine-clearance situa-tion; most of Bamiyan is not affected, but the hilltop fort of Shahr-e-Gholghola is thought to be mined still. Getting around in Bamiyan can be difficult. One or two UN agencies have their own jeeps which you may be able to hitch a ride on; otherwise the Afghan Red Cres-cent Society hires out its jeep with a driver for around $150 per day. Roads throughout the region are very poor however, and for half the year may be unusable due to snow or flooding.

Agencies

Although Hazarajat has not suffered from the military assaults of Soviets, mujahideen or Taliban in the way that many other areas of Afghanistan have, its isolation from the rest of the country has re-duced economic activity to very low levels. Previously Hazaras earned money through unskilled labour in Kabul and other towns, but the increased urban warfare and ethnic tension of the 1990s has forced many of them to return home. This places greater pressure on already overstretched agricultural resources, leading

Hazara girls, Bamiyan *J. Walter*

to erosion and food shortages. Access to markets has been seriously restricted in recent years by Taliban blockades of Hazarajat, limiting farmers' ability to generate income through selling livestock or potatoes. Hence in recent winters tens of thousands of Hazaras have been at risk of starvation, while agencies' attempts to solve the problem have only been partially successful. Standards of healthcare and education are extremely low: there are no government clinics or hospitals in the region, and no government schools outside district centres. Local government is virtually nonexistent, and the two factions of Hezb-e-Wahdat which wield power in the region provide few social services.

ACBAR lists around half a dozen agencies operating in Bamiyan province. The only health facilities in the region are those run by NGOs such as the Iranian Red Crescent hospital in Yakawlang, the MSF clinic/hospital in Panjao, and the Lepco leprosy and TB clinic in Lal (Ghor province).

Oxfam is working through village *shuras* in Lal, Panjao and Yakawlang to improve agricultural yields, health and sanitation, animal production and education. Schooling in 60 villages for both girls and boys, literacy training and health education for women take place during the long winters, when travel and agricultural work are not possible.

UNCHS (Habitat) is embarking on a programme of urban rehabilitation in and around Bamiyan town, involving the construction of improved water and sanitation systems, new schools, and latrines for the 4,000 IDPs living in caves beside the colossal Buddhas. UNHCR has an office in Yakawlang, although since the influx of returnees from Iran from 1992-1995 there has been little movement of refugees. WFP's efforts to fly in much-needed supplies of wheat and food-aid to Bamiyan during winter 1997 were frustrated by the

Taliban's refusal to allow what they perceived as indirect support for rebel Hezb-e-Wahdat troops. Taliban forces have bombed both the airport and the market at Bamiyan in an attempt to sabotage WFP food-aid efforts. WHO has an office in Bamiyan which coordinates UN flights and radio traffic.

Bamiyan A-Z

Accommodation and Food

If you can arrange an introduction to Karim Khalili then he has a very comfortable guesthouse perched above the Bamiyan river with an excellent view of the Buddhas. The Afghan Red Crescent Society runs a guesthouse with four bedrooms. The charge for full board is eight dollars per night. They also hire out their landcruiser for $150 per day.

Books

The Valley of Bamiyan, Nancy Hatch Dupree, Afghan Tourist Association (2nd Edition, Kabul, 1967)
The Hazaras of Afghanistan – An Historical, Cultural, Economic and Political Study, Dr Sayed Askar Mousavi, Curzon Press Ltd. (London, 1997)

Embassies & Visas

There are no consulates in Hazarajat

Local Rules

In terms of working and living in Bamiyan, access to both women and men is easier. The Hazaras are a very friendly, hospitable and approachable people. Dress for women should be modest and loose-fitting, but a *chador* is not necessary. Nevertheless, local women often wear *burqas* when away from their homes or fields.

Medical

There are no government medical facilities in the region, so if you get ill try to contact one of the international medical aid agencies or fly out to Pakistan.

Post & Telecommunications

There are no telephones in the region and few organizations have radios.

HAJI CULTURE

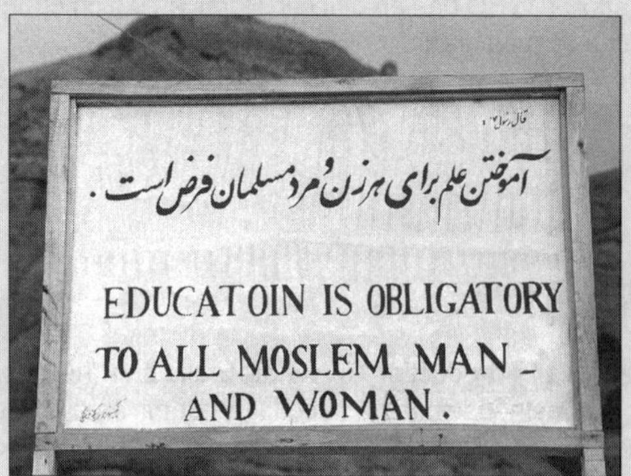

J. Walter

So the sign read, written boldly in English and Farsi, which stood outside the Office of the Director of Culture for Bamiyan Province. I ventured inside to see if I could get a permit to visit the colossal Buddhas for which Bamiyan is so famous. After knocking gingerly on the nearest door, an elegant voice from within said something incomprehensible. I opened the door and walked in. On the floor sat a rotund figure, cross-legged and looking rather like a buddha himself. The man — who was wearing a smart *shalwar kameez*, double-breasted grey jacket, grey *karakul* hat and a neatly trimmed beard — rose and introduced himself: "Haji Safwat, or Haji Culture if you prefer. May I be of assistance?" I explained that I wanted to see the Buddhas, and he duly wrote out a ticket for me. Spying my camera and a good opportunity, he asked if I could take his photo standing at the feet of the Large Buddha.

As we walked out of his office together I asked him about the sign I had seen at the entrance. "You can teach all your family and guests there is no difference between men and women in Hazarajat," he said, adding mischievously, "The women who cannot work under Taliban — they are welcome to work for me in Bamiyan!" His small piercing eyes gleamed and he chuckled quietly to himself. "Twenty years before," he said, returning to his theme, "the school children here have very good contact with foreigners — they learn many things — we want this again." On top of his job as Director of Culture, Haji Safwat teaches a handful of students sociology at Bamiyan University, but they are desperately short of funds and resources. And a region which once benefited from a steady stream of tourists and visitors has seen virtually none for two decades.

We arrived at the feet of the Large Buddha which towered 180 feet above us, a vast bulk of a body, standing — in the words of Bruce Chatwin — "upright in his niche like a whale in a dry dock". His face had been sawn off and his legs and arms broken by Persian iconoclasts two and a half centuries ago, but his huge feet, robed torso, impassive mouth and pendulous earlobes remained largely intact. I took Haji Safwat's photo as he stood dwarfed by the great statue's big toe, and asked:

"Is it just *Sunni* Muslims who believe that the picture of the human face is wrong or do *Shi'as* think the same thing?"

"It is not the *Shi'a* or the *Sunni* who think this," he replied gravely, "It is the Taliban who do not like the face and the Pakistan who want to destroy our culture."

"But the faces of the Buddhas and the wall-paintings were destroyed long before the Taliban came," I said.

"Yes, but the people did not destroy the faces because of their religion but because the faces were made with gold and covered with precious stones," explained the Director.

This talk of gold and jewels brought Haji Safwat onto the sticky subject of the money needed to preserve Bamiyan's heritage (he had given me the ticket to view the Buddhas free of charge). "I'm afraid I'm not really your man for this one" I said defensively, "but I'll ask the Red Cross if they could sort out some artificial limbs for the Big Buddha." His eyes gleamed and another chuckle emanated from his motionless mouth. Then he launched into a wish-list which left me feeling distinctly awkward:

"We need money for repairs. We must build a wall to protect the Buddhas. Drainage to prevent erosion. Archaeologists to advise. Chairs and table for my office. New offices. Salaries for me and my staff. New jeeps for me and my staff. A museum. Salaries for the museum staff. A guesthouse for tourists and visitors. Salaries for..."

"But he only asked me to take his photo," I thought to myself rather miserably, as his list grew ever longer and more ambitious. Fortunately for me, a donor fact-finding mission led by the Society for the Preservation of Afghanistan's Cultural Heritage (SPACH) visited Bamiyan a few weeks later. Then in December 1997 the Norwegian donor NORAD pledged $50,000 to SPACH for emergency work on the Buddhas as well as on the Minaret of Jam in Ghor province to the west.

For Haji Culture's sake and sanity, as well as for the sake of Afghanistan and her people, let us hope that the money keeps on coming. *JW*

Weather

Bamiyan town is situated at an altitude of 2,500 metres so pack some warm clothes whatever time of year you are visiting. Winters are harsh and the entire region is often snowbound for months at a time from November onwards. Spring brings flooding caused by snowmelt and rains, making road travel difficult. Summer and autumn are when most of the agricultural work is done. In October the valleys are a blaze of colour with autumnal tints firing the hillsides gold and brightly-clad families out in the fields for the harvest.

Sights

Before visiting any of the following sights, pay a visit to the Office of the Director of Culture for Bamiyan Province, situated just to the southwest of the Large Buddha. You may need to pay for permits or receive letters of introduction from the Director.

The Large and Small Buddhas. The colossal Buddhas of Bamiyan are one of Afghanistan's most impressive cultural sites and, towering to heights of 38 and 55 metres, are among the largest images of the Buddha ever created. Carved out of a sheer rockface overlooking the Bamiyan river, they continue to dominate a valley which has been Muslim for over a thousand years.

Dating from the 3rd to 4th Centuries AD, these colossal statues represent the culmination of a Buddhist culture inspired by the religious vision and business acumen of the Kushan King Kanishka who ruled the Afghan area in around 130 AD Bamiyan was a staging post for the Silk Route whose luxurious caravans linked the fabulous jewel and spice markets of China and India with the wealth and avarice of Imperial Rome.

A council of Buddhist leaders which met in Kashmir at Kanishka's behest were the catalyst for a new interpretation of Buddhism, known as Mahayana or the "Great Vehicle". This sees the Buddha as a compassionate demigod surrounded by cohorts of *boddhisattvas*, rather like the saints of the Roman Catholic tradition. Unlike the earlier Theravada/Hinayana tradition which concentrates on meditation as the route to *nirvana*, Mahayana Buddhists pray to their lord and saints for assistance in their spiritual quest.

As part of this personalising of their religion, the Buddha came to be represented for the first time in human form. The colossal statues of Bamiyan are thus cousins of the first human images of the Buddha created from the 2nd Century onwards by the Gandhara school of art centred around what is now Peshawar.

As Nancy Dupree, author of a guide to the valley in 1962, wrote:

"Here, as the embodiment of cosmic man, the Buddha stands not so much as a god but as an extraordinary man, one who participates in human experiences but exists above them because of his oneness with moral precepts."

The statues occupy large niches cut into the cliff-face about quarter of a mile apart. They were roughly hewn out of the sandstone cliffs and their features then modelled in an applied mixture of mud and wheat straw. This was covered in a fine plaster which was painted: the Large Buddha was clothed in a red cloak, the smaller one in blue. Both their faces were gilded. The niches above the statues' heads are filled with wall-paintings which you can examine at close quarters by climbing onto the heads of the statues (via a sandstone staircase carved out of the cliff). Over the Small Buddha can just be deciphered the figure of a Sun-God riding his chariot through a dark blue sky. This links the Bamiyan Buddhas with the sun-god traditions of Greece (Helios and Apollo), Sasanian Persia (Mithra) and India (Surya). The wall-paintings above the Large Buddha's head are in better condition: the Buddha is seated with his *boddhisattvas* and surrounded rather incongruously by scantily-clad ladies playing musical instruments. These latter figures are thought to be inspired by the sensual Indian Gupta tradition of the 7th Century AD.

The two colossal Buddhas of Bamiyan did not, however, impress the eccentric English traveller Robert Byron when he visited them in 1934. He had this to say:

"Neither has any artistic value. But one could bear that; it is their negation of sense, the lack of any pride in their monstrous flaccid bulk, that sickens."

And yet the "negation of sense" is a central tenet of Buddhism, which teaches its disciples that through releasing themselves from the suffering caused by clinging to the senses, they may reach *nirvana*. But what about the bare-breasted girls dancing above the head of the Large Buddha's "flaccid bulk" ? Or the 7th Century account of the Chinese traveller Hsuan-tsang, who wrote of the Large Buddha: "The golden hues sparkle on every side, and its precious ornaments dazzle the eye by their brightness." The Buddhist complex of Bamiyan – in its celebration of both sheer physical bulk and sparkling superficial beauty – embodies the central paradox of the Mahayanan tradition. The Buddha rejected the metaphysics of Hindu gods and human souls in favour of a physician's philosophy to cure the ills of the world. He preached a doctrine of detachment from the pain of a transient, physical existence. Yet he is represented here, vast and resplendent in the (once) glittering robes of a demigod.

Today the statues are showing their age: the Persian Nadir Shah chopped off the legs of the Large Buddha about 250 years ago, and

Muslim iconoclasts also sawed off both the Buddhas' faces. More recently, mujahed fighters have been taking pot shots at the 1,700 year-old wall paintings with their kalashnikovs and selling off the fragments. In April 1997 a Talib commander caused an international outcry when he threatened to blow up the statues if he ever made it into the Bamiyan valley. Most of the monks' cells which pepper the cliff-face between the two Buddhas have been defaced with graffiti and woodsmoke, and many are occupied by about 4,000 so-called "internally-displaced" refugees. But hope is in sight: at the end of 1997, NORAD and a number of other international donors pledged cash for emergency repairs to stabilize the condition of the Buddhas. The work will include building a protective wall around the base of the statues and improving the drainage on the mountainside above the site to minimise damage from water erosion.

Kakrak Buddha. A third statue of the Buddha, standing 6.5 metres high, has been carved out of a cave in the Kakrak valley to the east of Bamiyan town. Wall-paintings, which were removed from the site before the war, depicted a central Buddha surrounded by concentric rings of smaller seated Buddhas.

These diagrams are thought to be the first examples of the cosmic *mandalas* which subsequently gained great popularity in the art and worship of Nepalese and Tibetan Buddhism. The paintings probably date from the 8th to 9th Centuries AD, the end of the Buddhist period in Bamiyan. The Kakrak valley lies 20-30 minutes drive east of town; 4x4 transport is recommended as the route crosses a small river.

Shahr-e-Gholghola ("City of Screams"). This rocky hilltop citadel towers above the south bank of the river about two kilometres east of Bamiyan. Once the centre of the 12th Century Islamic Shansabani dynasty, the citadel now lies deserted, its ghostly stones bleached as white as bone.

For two centuries the Buddhist culture of Bamiyan was subjected to the proselytising efforts of Abbasids and Saffarids, until the later 10th Century when the valley finally succumbed to the rule of Islam. Two centuries later, the brother of Ghorid King Alauddin the "World Burner" (so-called for razing Ghazni to the ground in 1151) presided over his magnificent capital from this rocky stronghold. Then in 1221 Genghis Khan arrived, and his utter destruction of every living thing in the valley gave rise to the name *Shahr-e-Gholghola* which means, literally, "City of Screams."

Shahr-e-Zohak ("The Red City"). This magnificent pile of ruins occupies a highly strategic mountain spur 17 km east of Bamiyan, at the confluence of the Bamiyan and Kalu rivers. For two millennia the fertile valleys to the west have been defended by fortresses built atop this crimson-coloured cliff. The present fortifications date from the reign of the Shansabani kings during the 12th to 13th Centuries, and it was here that Genghis Khan's favourite grandson was

WARNING

THE AREA OF SHAHR-E-GHOLGHOLA IS STILL MINED — DO NOT ATTEMPT TO CLIMB THE HILL WITHOUT A GUIDE !

mortally wounded while leading an attack in 1221. His grandfather's revenge on the valley of Bamiyan and its inhabitants was murderous and merciless.

The entrance to the fortress is via a ramp on the east side of the spur which zig-zags up the cliff-face between decorated defensive towers. If you look up you will notice that every step is covered by firing positions from at least two of these towers. Furthermore the towers had no doors, so to reach the parapets the defenders clambered up ladders, pulling them up afterwards so as to make the fortress even more impregnable. The view from the summit of the "Red City" is well-worth the climb: snowcapped mountains and jagged pinnacles of rock rise all around, looking especially fantastic at sunset.

You need a permit from the Director of Culture in Bamiyan to visit Shahr-e-Zohak, as well as a letter from him to the local Hezb-e-Wahdat commander on the ground to authorise your passage. If the soldiers are not too busy shooting at Taliban aircraft they will accompany you up to the fortress. The drive to Shahr-e-Zohak takes about one hour, but allow at least four hours for a round trip from Bamiyan, to leave time for exploring the site and having tea with local commanders *en route.*

Band-e-Amir. These fabled turquoise lakes lie deep in the arid ochre mountains of the Koh-e-Baba range, 75 km west of Bamiyan town. The name means "Dam of the King", and refers to the sulphurous mineral deposits which have created natural dams, some up to 12 metres high, behind which five lakes have formed. The miraculous presence of these glittering lakes in such a desolate land is attributed to the superhuman powers of Hazrat Ali, who not only made the dams but also killed the dragon of Bamiyan, all in one day.

The four to five hour drive to Band-e-Amir, via the village of Shahidan, is magnificent but only to be attempted in summer months by four-wheel drive vehicle. The lakes are situated at an altitude of over 2,900 metres, so swimming is a bracing experience. There is no accommodation at the lakes and precious little vegetation, so take a tent, warm clothing and cooking fuel with you.

ISLAMABAD

If you take a taxi up to the viewpoint of Daman-e-Koh in the Margalla Hills just to the north of Islamabad, you will see that the city has been laid out with the imagination of an accountant. In 1958 the President decided that Karachi was too hot and crowded to be the country's capital, so a new, somewhat cooler, more hospitable and open site was selected near the former British garrison town of Rawalpindi in northern Pakistan.

Three years later, the spacious and leafy Islamabad began to emerge. It conforms to a gridded masterplan devised by Greek architects, with separate enclaves designated for administrative, diplomatic, recreational, educational, industrial and residential purposes. Rather than name these districts, they are referred to simply by a letter (referring to North-South position) and a number (East-West position); the district F-16 always amuses Pakistani plane-spotters.

Islamabad has been the headquarters-in-exile for most of the United Nations agencies operating along the Afghan periphery since the early 1980s. The fact that it has been possible to work inside Afghanistan since the early 1990s has not induced the UN to move its base of operations (the International Committee of the Red Cross has its main delegation in Kabul). If you need to meet UN heads of agency or diplomats, Islamabad is the place to find them. However, most NGOs are based either in-country or in Peshawar. UN flights into Afghanistan use Islamabad as their hub.

Getting there

By air

Pakistan International Airways (PIA) has two flights a week to Islamabad from New York, one via Frankfurt, one via Amsterdam. Both PIA and British Airways (BA) fly twice a week to Islamabad from London. Emirates flies from Dubai to Islamabad on Tuesdays, Wednesdays, Fridays and Sundays. Royal Saudi Airlines also flies direct to Islamabad.

Daily PIA services operate from Islamabad to Peshawar at 0730 (arriving at 0905) and 1745 (arriving at 1830). From Peshawar to Islamabad there are daily services at 1200 and 1845. A daily service flies from Islamabad to Quetta at 1330 (arriving at 1455). From Quetta flights leave daily at 1105 and 1655.

Airline contact numbers are as follows:

PIA Islamabad:	TEL: +92 (51) 816051-56 (domestic) +92 (51) 815041 (general enquiries)
BA Islamabad:	TEL: +92 (51) 274070, 274080, 273081-3 FAX: +92 (51) 274078
Royal Saudi Airlines:	TEL: +92 (51) 270131
Uzbekistan Airways:	TEL: +92 (51) 828331/4
Aero Asia:	TEL: +92 (51) 823072, 823645

For more information on flights in and out of Islamabad and Afghanistan SEE TRAVEL.

By road

The Grand Trunk (GT) Road which runs between Lahore and Peshawar passes 14 km to the southwest of Islamabad. This is the Pakistani equivalent of the Nairobi-Mombasa highway, and just as dangerous. Careering trucks and buses are determined to dominate and show little mercy to cautious drivers. While the GT road was a relatively pleasant drive during the early 1980s, it is now a definite health hazard as traffic, casualty rates and pollution increase by the year.

The best time to do the journey is at the weekend. Avoid travelling at night (beware of roaming camels and donkeys, but also stoned Pakistanis) and drive defensively by day. Most hotel drivers drive relatively well; hold on to a good one if you find one. The trip from Peshawar takes two to three hours. Taxis are as quick as flying, but more expensive than a one-way air ticket. Plenty of buses make the journey day and night. Along the route lie the Margalla Pass (defined by the historian Sir Olaf Caroe as the real boundary between the Indian subcontinent and Central Asia) and Taxila, once a centre of the Buddhist Gandhara Kingdom.

For more information on driving into Afghanistan from Islamabad/Peshawar SEE CENTRAL.

Orientation

Islamabad is sandwiched between the wooded Margalla Hills (still alive with jackals, mongooses and the occasional leopard) which rise from the city's northern edge, and the noisy bazaar town of Rawalpindi, 15 km to the south. The international airport is on the way to Rawalpindi. There are good views of the city from both the Margalla range and from Shakarparian Park to the south. To the east lie the Presidential Palace and Diplomatic Enclave, to the west lies the Grand Trunk road to Peshawar. The centre of town is dominated by the dual-carriageway of the so-called "Blue Area" which contains most of the modern shops and office blocks. 'F' districts lie to the north of the Blue Area, and 'G' districts to the south.

See maps in guidebooks listed below.

Getting around

If you cannot get a lift in an agency vehicle, taxis can be hired by the day. You can arrange one through your guesthouse/hotel or flag one down in the street. Daily rates are around PakRupees 800, but agree on the price before getting in. Motorscooter rickshaws and some horse-drawn *tongas* are also available in Rawalpindi.

Agencies

Most of the UN agencies have their headquarters in Islamabad, including the **United Nations Office for the Coordination of Humanitarian Assistance to Afghanistan (UNOCHA)** which is now co-located with the United Nations Development Programme (UNDP). For more information on UN agencies, contact:
UNOCHA, House 292, Street 55,
F-10/4, Islamabad.
TEL: +92 (51) 211451-5 FAX: +92 (51) 211450
E-mail: unocha@undpafg.org.pk

Some international NGOs have Islamabad offices. For more details, SEE CONTACTS or call on the **Agency Coordinating Body for Afghan Relief (ACBAR)** in Peshawar at the following address:
2 Rehman Baba Road, University Town
(UPO Box 1084), Peshawar
TEL: +92 (91) 44392, 40839, 45316, 45347
FAX: +92 (91) 840471
E-mail: acbaar@radio.psh.brain.net.pk

Islamabad A-Z:

Accommodation and Food

Islamabad has several international standard hotels and some excellent guesthouses. Hotel rooms range from PakRupees 5,000-40,000 per night. Guesthouses charge between PakRupees 1,200-2,000 per double room, and some take credit cards. Most provide *en suite* 'western' bathrooms, satellite TV in your room and international phone/fax facilities at reception. Here is a small selection:

Marriott Hotel (formerly the Holiday Inn):
Aga Khan Road, Shalimar 5
PO Box 1251, Islamabad
TEL: +92 (51) 111 22 33 44 FAX: +92 (51) 201071, 825113
E-mail: guest@isb.marriott.infolink.net.pk Telex: 5612 & 5740 HISD
Double rooms from PakRupees 8,000 per night
Centrally-located luxury five-star hotel at the northeastern end of the Blue Area. Facilities include swimming pool, tennis courts, health club, international direct dialling (IDD) from your room, and business centre with computer, fax and e-mail.

Holiday Inn (Islamabad Hotel)
Municipal Road, Islamabad
TEL: +92 (51) 827311 FAX: +92 (51) 273273, 824021
E-mail: holiday@isb.comsats.net.pk Telex: 5643 IHI PK
Double rooms from PakRupees 6,000 per night
Modern downtown hotel located near administrative enclave. Facilities include IDD from your room and e-mail. UN and NGO agency personnel, and accredited journalists get a 30% discount on room rates.

Continental Guest House
94, Nazimuddin Road
F-8/4. Islamabad
TEL: +92 (51) 256670-1, 853343 FAX: +92 (51) 262144, 852753
Luxury guesthouse with international phone and fax facilities, satellite TV and "round the clock coffee bar."

Chez Soi
6 Kohsar Road, F-7/3 TEL: +92 (51) 276821

Jacaranda Inn
17 College Road, F-7/3 TEL: +92 (51) 2731834

International Guesthouse
House 12, 7th Avenue
Islamabad
TEL: +92 (51) 827098-9 FAX: +92 (51) 827562

For politically incorrect MacDonald-Fraser enthusiasts, there is also **Flashman's Hotel** in downtown Rawalpindi, but it does not quite live up to its name.

Books

Welcome to Pakistan: Islamabad, Rawalpindi (United Nations Women's Association 1997). This excellent 100-page guidebook contains the most up-to-date and comprehensive information available on Islamabad, and is aimed mainly at those moving out here to live. Chapters contain details on geography & history, language, customs, religion, health, housing, schooling, cars & driving, pets, leisure & charitable activities, gardening, sightseeing, and a practical guide to everything from carpet cleaning and Christmas trees to hairdressers and handymen. It also contains useful maps of the markets and bazaars of both cities. The book costs PakRupees 200 (sales support a home for retarded children) and is available from:

UN Community Liaison Officer,
2nd Floor, Saudi Pak Tower, 61-A Jinnah Avenue, Islamabad.
TEL: +92 (51) 279165 FAX: +92 (51) 279080-83

Culture Shock! Pakistan: A Guide to Customs & Etiquette, Karin Mittman & Zafar Ihsan, Kuperard (1991)
Pakistan Handbook, Ivan Mannheim & Dave Winter, Trade & Travel Handbooks (1996)
Pakistan Handbook, Isobel Shaw, The Guidebook Company (Hong Kong, 1996), includes maps of Peshawar and the North West Frontier Province.
Pakistan - a travel survival kit, John King & David St.Vincent, Lonely Planet (1995), includes maps of Peshawar and the North West Frontier Province.
Good bookshops include **Book Fair** (Jinnah Market, F-7), **London Book Co.** (Khosar Market, F-6/3), **Mr Books** (Super Market, F-6), and **Vanguard Books** (Super Market, F-6). There are also bookshops in Rawalpindi.

Good **libraries** include the following:

The American Centre
60 Jinnah Avenue, F-6/4
TEL: +92 (51) 824051
A library of books, periodicals, videos and US Information Service material.

The British Council Library
14 Civic Centre. Melody Market, G-6/3
TEL: +92 (51) 111 424 424 FAX: +92 (51) 276683
This English-language library stocks some titles on Afghanistan, along with international newspapers, periodicals and videos.

French Cultural Centre
House 15, Street 18. F-7/2

Embassies & Visas

For Pakistan. Three types of visa are available for Pakistan: single and double entry for tourists and multiple entry for foreigners working in the country. In order to get a multiple entry visa, you need a letter from a company or agency in Pakistan to vouch for you. For a list of Pakistan embassies worldwide and foreign missions based in Islamabad, SEE CONTACTS.

For the Khyber Pass. SEE PESHAWAR

For Afghanistan. Try to arrange an Afghan visa in your home country if possible. Otherwise the Afghan Embassy in Islamabad issues visas, but the procedure for 'newcomers' can take up to a week even for accredited journalists and aid workers. Start your application process early in the week and remember that Friday afternoon, Saturday and Sunday are holidays. Visas cost $30 and you will need two passport-size photos (there are studios in Super Market). If you are a regular visitor to Afghanistan and sponsored by the UN or a major aid agency you may be able to get a visa in as little as one day. The Embassy will only issue single-entry visas which are literally valid for *entry* only. In order to leave Afghanistan you will have to get a special *exit* visa in-country. (SEE VISAS, JOURNALISM)

The address of the **Afghanistan Embassy in Islamabad** is:
House 17, Street 28, F-6/1-21, Islamabad
TEL: +92 (51) 824505 FAX: +92 (51) 824504

Information

For general information, contact the UN Community Liaison Officer, 2nd Floor, Saudi Pak Tower, 61-A Jinnah Avenue (TEL: +92 (51) 279165; FAX: +92 (51) 279080-83), or the Community Liaison Officer at the US Embassy (TEL: +92 (51) 826161). For more information on agency activities, SEE AGENCIES above.

The following are some useful Telephone numbers in Islamabad:

Directory Enquiries:	**17**
Police (Emergency):	**15, 922 2566**
Shifa International Hospital:	**446801, 446830**
UN Club:	**279313**

Medical

Make sure your vaccinations are up to date for polio, typhoid, tetanus, rabies and hepatitis A and B, as vaccine quality in Pakistan cannot be guaranteed. Islamabad is not considered to be a malarial zone, but take precautions to be safe.. If you get sick, consult your embassy for advice. Otherwise the Shifa Hospital, H-8, is one of the best in town. There are also some good dentists registered with various embassies. (SEE PERSONAL HEALTH)

Money

If you are bringing cash, US dollars are the most widely accepted. The newer and crisper the notes the better, and avoid any pre-1993

$100 notes because of local fakes. You will get a better rate for big denomination bills. American Express Bank and Bank of America (TEL: +92 (51) 815035) have branches in the Blue Area; ANZ Grindlay's Bank is in the Diplomatic Enclave. VISA cards are also used in certain shops and even in the bazaars.

Post & Telecommunications

The General Post Office is located on Post Office Road, G-6/2 (TEL: +92 (51) 825957), and the Telegraph and Telephone Office is situated behind the Marriott Hotel on Ataturk Avenue, F-5. Long-distance telephone, fax and telex facilities are available but you may have to wait. E-mail is available from both the Marriott and Holiday Inn Hotels, but not from guesthouses.

Mobile telephones can be rented or bought from a number of companies based in Islamabad. While local calls cost more, international calls by mobile phone are up to three times cheaper than calling from a hotel. (SEE RADIO & TELECOMMUNCIATIONS)

Recreation

UNISRAP (United Nations International Staff Recreation Association in Pakistan), House 3, Street 2, F-7/3. TEL: +92 (51) 279313 E-mail: club@unisrap.isb.erum.com.pk

Known more simply as the UN Club, it sports a bar and restaurant, table tennis, satellite TV and a grassy garden containing a swimming pool. International (open) nights are on Fridays from 1930-0030 hrs, and Saturday brunch (which can keep you going all weekend) is also open to visitors from 1200-1530 hrs.

The **Marriott Hotel** has probably the best sports facilities in town, including a 50 metre swimming pool, health club with sauna, weights room and jogging machines. You can also arrange to play squash, tennis and golf at the Islamabad Club through the Marriott.

The **Islamabad Club** is on Murree Road and can be contacted direct on +92 (51) 829005 – horse-riding is one of the sports on offer.

Other clubs include the **American Club** (TEL: +92 (51) 826161), **British Club** (TEL: +92 (51) 822131), **Canadian Club** (TEL: +92 (51) 249100) and **French Club** (TEL: +92 (51) 821093). "Hash-house harrier" races are organized by the British and Australian missions.

For less clubby types, there are some wonderful walks in the **Margalla Hills** just to the north of Islamabad, with particularly good bird-watching for ornithologists. For more details read *Hiking in the Margallas* published by the **Asian Study Group** (ASG). The ASG is located in the Malik Complex, 80W. Jinnah Ave., Blue Area (TEL: +92 (51) 815891 – open 1500-1700 hrs) and holds lectures and film evenings on Pakistani culture etc. An arboretum on top of **Shakaparian Hill** to the south of the city affords good views. It is filled with trees planted by visiting politicians: a magnolia from Kurt Waldheim nestles near chir pines from Nicolae Ceaucescu and Burhannudin Rabbani…Mullah Omar next?

Shopping

The best bazaar in Islamabad is the **Sunday Market** (previously the Friday market), held all day every Sunday between Municipal Road and Garden Road, south of the Holiday Inn Hotel. There is an **Afghan Market** here which deals in carpets, *gelims*, lapis jewellery and blue glass from Herat. Prices are often better than Peshawar.

The bazaars of Rawalpindi are also very colourful places to shop. Bara Bazaar is good for imported Japanese and English electrical goods, kitchen things and Chinese silks; Moti Bazaar specializes in women's clothing and jewellery; Raja Bazaar is in the old part of Rawalpindi where you will find everything from vegetables to false teeth; Saddar Bazaar specializes in handicrafts, car parts and fish; and Sarafa Bazaar is the place to find silver and gold.

Weather

Islamabad is situated 518 metres above sea-level (higher than Peshawar) and enjoys cool weather from October to March (lowest temperature around 3 degrees Celsius). May and June can be very hot (up to 48 degrees), prior to the monsoon rains which sweep through from July to September. The Margalla Hills rise up to 2,500 metres so there is always somewhere to escape to if things get sticky.

Peshawar

Ever since the first refugees began trickling into the North West Frontier Province of Pakistan in mid-1978, Peshawar has served as an exile headquarters for guerrilla factions and an operations base for numerous aid agencies. As the war developed, this dusty provincial capital of drug smugglers and arms traffickers 35 km from the Khyber Pass began to establish itself as a principal humanitarian centre and launching pad for journalists seeking to cover the Afghan story. With its crowded bazaars and smoke-filled tea shops, Peshawar still retained, during the late 1970s and early 1980s, some of the exhilarating frontier flavour of Kipling's India.

By March 1980, well over 20 resistance groups had set up shop in Peshawar, many with sub-offices in Quetta in Baluchistan province to the southwest. The international press corps had descended *en masse,* while hundreds of thousands of refugees were flocking to the camps on the outskirts of town or up and down the frontier. Peshawar exuded the atmosphere of a den of spies. Diplomats, reporters, intelligence agents, war junkies, smugglers, drug enforcement officials and various travellers were constantly drifting through this romantic Casablanca of the East to check on the Afghans, the opium trafficking scene, and whatever plots one cared to unearth. Everyone seemed to have an agenda.

During the early years of the war, Peshawar remained a modest town with relatively little traffic and pollution. It was easy to travel from the Cantonment (where most of the visiting foreign correspondents stayed) out to University Town (where the aid agencies began to establish themselves) or to the Old Town bazaar area by *tuk-tuk* (motor scooter rickshaw) or even *tonga,* a horse-drawn trap.

For numerous reporters and aid workers, Peshawar represented one of the most exciting towns in the world. Apart from the hundreds (later several thousand) expat relief workers operating in the region, the city emerged as a crucial transit centre for countless reporters, camera teams and crossborder relief workers seeking to "go inside." The nights were often rocked by gunshots (usually bravado firing into the air) but occasionally rockets or bombs that killed and injured people. There was definite frontline atmosphere that appealed to the romantic notions of many.

But as massive international aid poured in, Pakistani government and Afghan resistance leaders became even more corrupt, and the drug and weapons trafficking industry grew, this once alluring provincial capital on the razor's edge of conflict developed into a veritable nightmare. The war, refugees, aid and drugs completely changed the city. By the late 1980s, some 200 international agencies and NGOs had established operations bases in the town. The Pakistani and Afghan population more than tripled, while the streets became clogged with brand-new vehicles and whole new residential areas sprang up with shops, villas, garages and satellite-dishes. Even worse, a pall of dust, filth and fumes hung perpetually over the city. The frontier romanticism had gone.

With the return of many of the refugees and the transfer of numerous aid agencies into Afghanistan, Peshawar has become a somewhat more quiet, even manageable town. The war, drugs and aid have definitely helped develop various new industries that would not have existed otherwise. It is now the residence of quite a few traffickers who benefited sumptuously from international aid and drug rake-offs.

In many respects, Peshawar will remain a Pakistani-Afghan commercial centre, whether for licit or illicit trade. Many Afghans with jobs are reluctant to return home, and may never do so, even if the fighting stops. And if they do, it is certain that they will retain commercial links in order to exploit the Indian subcontinental market. For journalists, but also aid coordinators, the town remains a useful stopping-off point for contacts, research, background briefings and interviews before heading off into Afghanistan. In addition, there are now a number of comfortable and well-equipped guesthouses with international phone lines and fax machines that did not exist before. But as many old hands will tell you, Peshawar just ain't the same when compared to the more tense but scintillating heyday of humanitarian relief and crossborder journalism during the early and mid-1980s.

Getting there

By air

Many Peshawar-based aid workers and journalists fly from Europe/ North America to Dubai and connect direct to Peshawar, using Pakistan International Airlines (PIA). PIA flights from Dubai to Peshawar leave at 0100 hrs on Mondays, Tuesdays and Fridays, arriving at 0450 hrs.

The PIA regional service between Pakistan and Central Asia flies between Peshawar and Tashkent on Mondays. Daily PIA services operate from Islamabad to Peshawar at 0730 hrs (arriving at 0905 hrs) and 1745 hrs (arriving at 1830 hrs). From Peshawar to Islamabad there are daily services at 1200 hrs and 1845 hrs.

Pakistan International Airways (PIA) contact numbers:

Peshawar:	TEL: +92 (91) 273081-9 (main office) 279162-6 (reservations) 270035-9 (airport)
Islamabad:	TEL: +92 (51) 816051-56 (domestic) 815041 (general enquiries)

Aero Asia also provides regional services: call +92 (91) 258272, 277289, 275237 (office) or 277656-8 (airport). For more information on flights in and out of Afghanistan SEE TRAVEL.

By road

The Grand Trunk (GT) Road runs between Lahore and Peshawar, passing within 14 kms of Islamabad. To reach Peshawar from Islamabad, head west from Zero Point and turn right when you meet the GT road. The trip takes two to three hours. Taxis are as quick as flying, but more expensive than a single air ticket. Plenty of buses make the journey day and night. Along the route lie the Margalla Pass (defined by the historian Sir Olaf Caroe as the real boundary between the Indian subcontinent and Central Asia) and Taxila, once a centre of the Gandhara Kingdom.

For more information on driving into Afghanistan from Peshawar SEE CENTRAL.

Orientation

The majority of aid agencies are based in University Town which lies a couple of kilometres west of the airport, down Jamrud Road. The Cantonment, Saddar Bazaar and the Old City lie to the east of the airport.

The **Agency Coordinating Body for Afghan Relief (ACBAR)** produces the following line-diagram street plans of Peshawar showing locations of key local and international agencies as follows:

- University Town
- Rahatabad, Nimat Mahal, Danishabad, Tajabad, Board, Nasir Bagh
- Tahkal, Defence Colony, Kababian, Shami Road, Cantt., Dabgari
- Hayatabad Town

See also maps in tourist guidebooks listed below.

Getting around

Even up to the mid-1980s, the best form of travel around Peshawar was the *tonga* – a horse-drawn trap. Some people still use them, but Peshawar is now awash with agency jeeps, minibuses and that scourge of third-world cities, *tuk-tuk* motor-rickshaws. Taxis can be hired by the day – flag one down in the street or arrange one through your guesthouse or the American Club. Daily rates are around PakRupees 500, but agree on the price before getting in.

Agencies

ACBAR lists around 120 NGOs and UN agencies based in University Town alone. (SEE CONTACTS) For more information on international NGOs contact **ACBAR** at the following address:
2 Rehman Baba Road, University Town
(UPO Box 1084), Peshawar.
TEL: +92 (91) 44392, 40839, 45316, 45347 FAX: +92 (91) 840471
E-mail: acbaar@radio.psh.brain.net.pk

For more information on Afghan NGOs contact the **Afghan NGOs Coordination Bureau (ANCB)** at the following address:
25 Chinar Road, University Town, Peshawar.
TEL: +92 (91) 43476

For more information on UN agencies, contact the **United Nations Office for the Coordination of Humanitarian Assistance to Afghanistan (UNOCHA)** at the following address:
20 D/A Circular Road, University Town, Peshawar.
TEL: +92 (91) 41131 FAX: +92 (91) 840316
Mob: +92 (351) 263107

PESHAWAR A-Z

Accommodation and Food

There is no shortage of places to eat and sleep in Peshawar, but if you need to visit international agencies then the most convenient place to stay is University Town. Here are some ideas:

Old Town

Pearl-Continental Hotel
Khyber Road
TEL: +92 (91) 276361
FAX: +92 (91) 276465
Telex: 52389 PEARL PK.
Around PakRupees 3500 per double room
If you need to off-load some excess dollars then this is the place for you. The most luxurious hotel in Peshawar, it is situated several kilometres east of University Town near the Old Fort. Facilities include a good restaurant for body-building breakfasts, the 'gulbar' for imported drinks, swimming pool, health club and access to an 18-hole golf course. You can make international direct-dial telephone

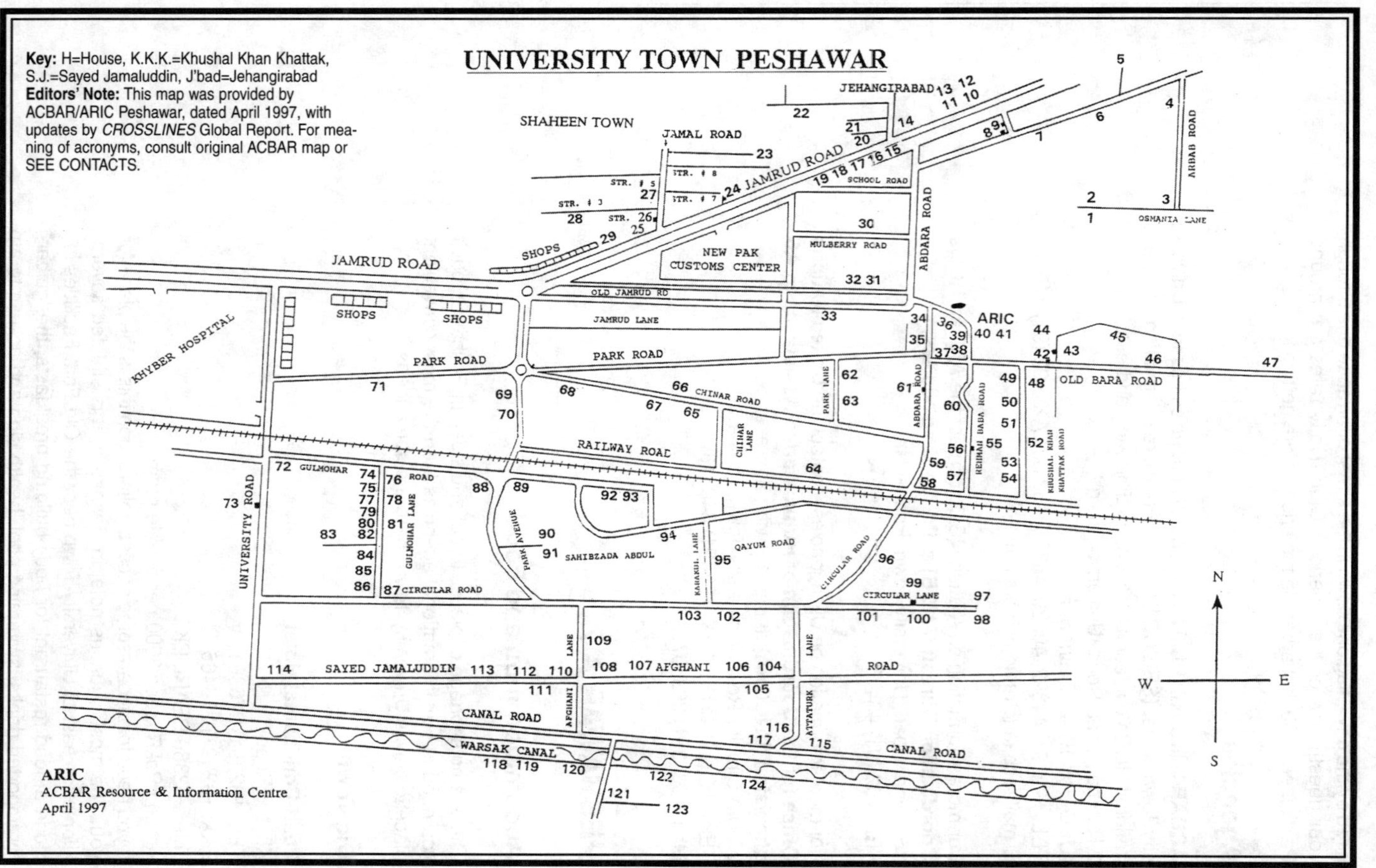
UNIVERSITY TOWN PESHAWAR
Key: H=House, K.K.K.=Khushal Khan Khattak, S.J.=Sayed Jamaluddin, J'bad=Jehangirabad
Editors' Note: This map was provided by ACBAR/ARIC Peshawar, dated April 1997, with updates by CROSSLINES Global Report. For meaning of acronyms, consult original ACBAR map or SEE CONTACTS.
SHAHEEN TOWN
JEHANGIRABAD
JAMAL ROAD
JAMRUD ROAD
SCHOOL ROAD
ARBAB ROAD
OSMANIA LANE
ABDARA ROAD
MULBERRY ROAD
NEW PAK CUSTOMS CENTER
SHOPS
OLD JAMRUD RD
JAMRUD LANE
PARK ROAD
KHYBER HOSPITAL
ARIC
OLD BARA ROAD
CHINAR ROAD
PARK LANE
CHINAR LANE
REHMAN BABA ROAD
KHUSHAL KHAN KHATTAK ROAD
RAILWAY ROAD
UNIVERSITY ROAD
GULMOHAR ROAD
GULMOHAR LANE
CIRCULAR ROAD
PARK AVENUE
SAHIBZADA ABDUL
QAYUM ROAD
KAHAKUL LANE
CIRCULAR LANE
SAYED JAMALUDDIN
AFGHANI ROAD
AFGHANI LANE
ATTATURK LANE
CANAL ROAD
WARSAK CANAL
N
S
W
E
ARIC
ACBAR Resource & Information Centre
April 1997

40 ACBAR, 2 Rehman Baba Rd Tel. 40839, 44392
48 ACBAR Survey Unit, 34-F K.K.K. Rd Tel. 842286
41 ARIC, 2 Rehman Baba Rd Tel. 44392
18 AAEA, Flat 30, Spinzar Plaza, J'bad Tel. 842378
92 A-AID, 5-B Gulmohar Rd Tel. 841083, 42030
50 ACF, 17-F K.K.K. Rd Tel. 43227
56 ACRD, 25-B Rehman Baba Rd Tel. 43335
90 ACTED, H#800-T, 10 Park Avenue Tel. 842878
47 ADA, 43 Old Bara Rd Tel. 45333
82 Afghan Consulate, 17-B/C Gulmohar Lane Tel. 842486
51 AFRANE, 17-F/A1 K.K.K. Rd Tel. 41492
20 AG BAS-Ed, H#1, St 1, J'bad Tel. 843063
57 AGTTP, 25-B/2 Rehman Baba Rd Tel. 45372
43 AHSAO, 1426-T Old Bara Rd Tel. 45577
105 AIC, 18-E S.J. Afghani Rd Tel. 40953
9 AICC, H#3, Abdara Chowk Tel. 44995
53 AITM, 15-F/B K.K.K. Rd Tel. 44312
120 Al Bader Hospital, Canal Lane Tel. 842698
78 AMA, 53-C Gulmohar Lane Tel. 43283
2 Amani High School, Osmania Lane, Arbab Rd
91 AMI, 800-T, 10 Park Ave Tel. 43631
122 AMRC, 2 Canal Bank Rd Tel. 41691
66 ANCB, 25 Chinar Rd Tel. 43476
119 AOGH, H#1048, Canal Bank Rd Tel. 41381
100 ARC, 9 Circular Lane Tel. 840592
17 ARCAR, Flat B-18, Spinzar Plaza, J'bad Tel. 44986
121 ARDA, H#184, Upper Canal Rd Tel. 842189
35 AREA, 17-E Abdara Rd Tel. 41993, 45417
12 ATA-AFG, Flat 4, 1st Fl, Khyber Plaza Tel. 840126
31 ATC, 45-D/4 Old Jamrud Road Tel. 840122
114 AVICEN, 55-D/B S.J. Afghani Rd Tel. 45279
1 AWRC, Osmania Lane, Arbab Rd Tel. 841552
83 BBC AED, 17-B/C Gulmohar Lane Tel. 842320
44 BONIAD, H#44, 16-C Old Bara Rd Tel. 840771
68 British Council, 17-C Chinar Rd Tel. 42818
19 BRP, Flat #32, 3rd Fl, Spinzar Plaza Tel. 43821
62 CARE Int, 6 Park Lane Tel. 40328, 40614
98 CBR, 37-D/1 Circular Lane Tel. 842193
55 CDAP-UNOPS, 20-F Rehman Baba Rd Tel. 41667
24 CRFA, Alfarooq St, Shaheen Town Tel. 43281
84 DACAAR, 10 Gulmohar Lane Tel. 843078, 44237
85 DACAAR Sewing Project, 18 Gulmohar Lane Tel. 842530
65 DCA, 22-C Chinar Rd Tel. 40871, 840414
28 ECAR-ENT, St. #3, off Jamal Rd, Shaheen Town Tel. 841454
97 EDS, 37-D/1, Circular Lane Tel. 842793
70 ELP, 53-III/B Park Ave Tel. 40290
14 ESO, 7-B 3rd Fl, Zaraq Plaza el. 45583
59 EU, 5-C/II Abdara Rd Tel. 843003, 43574
86 FAO, 19 A/C/93 Gulmohar Lane Tel. 845088
80 GAO, 17-B Gulmohar Lane Tel. 42613
76 GSMCS PSU, 2 Gulmohar Lane Tel. 842277
109 GTZ-NSP, 39-D/3 S.J. Afghani Lane Tel. 841601
63 HAF, 10-B Park Lane Tel. 840621
69 HAFO, 53-B Park Ave Tel. 44677
108 HCI, 39-D/2 S.J. Afghani Rd Tel. 840524
96 HealthNet Int, 4 Karakul Lane Tel. 42551, 44027
64 HELP, H#9 Railway Rd Tel. 840776
22 Hezb-e-Wahdat, St #2, nr. Faiz Sons Flats, J'bad Tel. 45509
99 IAM, 8-D/1 Circular Lane Tel. 842634
107 IBNSINA, 39-D/1 S.J. Afghani Rd Tel. 45279
77 ICD, 3-C Gulmohar Lane Tel. 41496
11 ICRC, 40 S.J. Afghani Rd Tel. 42071, 41673
124 ICRC Car Workshop, Canal Rd Tel. 41511
110 IFRC, 43-D S.J. Afghani Rd Tel. 843116
37 IRC, Main Office, 80-E Old Bara Rd Tel. 41274, 41845
103 IRC, Female Educn., 26-B Circular Rd Tel. 841723
94 IRC, Health Education Resource Centre (HERC),
40-C Sahibzada Abdul Qayum Rd Tel. 41341
103 IRC, Kodakistan Educn., 26-B Circular Rd Tel. 43227
104 ISRA, 68-D/2 S.J. Afghani Rd Tel. 42245
73 JAMS, 58-C UNIVERSITY Rd Tel. 44350
36 JIFF Physiotherapy, I Rehman Baba Rd Tel. 41278
29 KELC, 1st Fl, Orukzai Plaza Tel. 843755
8 KELC/WS, New Arbab Colony, Arbab Rd Tel. 841656
11 KNF, Flat 6, 2nd Fl, Khyber View Plaza, Jamrud Rd Tel. 843303
13 KRCS, Jamrud Rd Tel. 41508
123 LBI, 3304-5 Canal Rd Tel. 41485, 840249
4 LDI, 1 Arbab Rd Tel. 840021, 42595
72 Leprosy Services, 11 Gulmohar Rd Tel. 41093
96 Lycée Esteqlal, 2 Circular Rd Tel. 40721
81 MADERA, 53-C/II Gulmohar Lane Tel. 840546
116 Mahad-Albar-Asnahi, 62-E Canal Rd Tel. 43713
16 MARUF, Flat B-18, Spinzar Plaza, J'bad Tel. 44986
79 Mercy Int., 17-C Gulmohar Lane Tel. 843471
89 MERLIN, 7-A Gulmohar Rd Tel. 42534
106 MSF (Holland), 25 S.J. Afghani Rd Tel. 42400
5 Mulana Jamee High Sch, Arbab Rd Tel. 42676
58 Muslim World League, 6 Railway Rd Tel. 844180
21 Muslim Women Soc., H#1, St #2, J'bad Tel. 41141
49 NAC, 20-F K.K.K. Rd Tel. 43717, 41346
27 Naheed Shahed Primary Sch, Jamal Rd, Shaheen Town Tel. 840552
60 NCA, 84-E Rehman Baba Rd Tel. 45267, 41226
33 NPO/RRAA, 15-B Old Jamrud Rd Tel. 41129
2 ORA, 27-F K.K.K. Rd Tel. 841280
32 OV, 43-D/2 Old Jamrud Rd Tel. 40410
15 PCFA, C 27-29 Spinzar Plaza, J'bad
39 PRB, 77-E Rehman Baba Rd Tel. 41641
112 PSD, 43-B, S.J. Afghani Rd Tel. 844019
25 RADA, Jamal Rd, Shaheen Town Tel. 43358
113 RAFA, 43-D S.J. Afghani Rd Tel. 40893
118 RBS, H#1, South Canal Bank Rd Tel. 840987
3 Rehabilitation Centre for Disabled Afghan Refugees
T-875 Arbab Colony, Arbab Rd Tel. 844387
26 ROAOW, Jamal Road, Shaheen Town Tel. 43358
10 RSSA, Flat 6, 2nd Fl, Khyber View Plaza Tel. 842617
6 Saydah Ame Salimah High Sch, New Arbab Colony Tel. 844743
67 SCA, 24-D/E Chinar Rd Tel. 840218, 840257
87 SCA Workshop, 41 Circular Rd Tel. 840530
30 SERVE, 7 Mulberry Rd Tel. 840292, 41706
101 SGAA, 5-A Circular Lane Tel. 843028
117 SNI, 60-E Canal Rd Tel. 41130
46 SOLIDARITES, Hujra Hse, Old Bara Rd Tel. 840228
63 SRCS, 2 Gulmohar Rd Tel. 840213
88 START, 51-C/1 Park Ave Tel. 41081
54 Supreme Coordination Council of Islamic Revolution
of Afghanistan, 15-F K.K.K. Rd Tel. 844185
42 Taliban Movement, 1426-T Old Bara Rd Tel. 844331
74 UNHCR, 1 Gulmohar Lane Tel. 41152
61 UNHCR in NWFP, 13 Abdara Rd Tel. 844305
34 UNICEF, 17-B/4 Abdara Rd Tel. 43669, 840496
115 Union Aid for Afghan Refugees, 64-E Ataturk Lane Tel. 43609
45 UNO, 56-C Old Bara Rd Tel. 44536
102 UNOCHA, 20-D/A Circular Rd Tel. 41131, 840316
23 VSB, St 11, Jamal Rd, Shaheen Town Tel. 843618
7 WELP, New Arbab Colony, Arbab Rd Tel. 41674
71 WRC, 38-B Park Rd Tel. 42237
38 WUFA, 38-E Rehman Baba Rd Tel. 840318
5 Zarghunah High Sch, Arbab Rd Tel. 42676

calls from your room, and a business centre provides fax, telex and photocopying services.

Khan Klub
No.2225, K, New Rampura Gate
Nevay Darwaza
TEL: +92 (91) 214802, 2567156 FAX: +92 (91) 2561156
From PakRupees 1,500-3,500 per suite
For an authentic 'frontier' feel the Khan Klub is hard to beat. The 200 year-old traditional *haveli* has been beautifully restored to create a restaurant and eight luxurious suites. Both local and international food is served to the strains of classical eastern music while diners sit cross-legged on cushions.

Cantonment

Dean's Hotel
Islamia Road
TEL: +92 (91) 276483-4, 279781-2
FAX: +92 (91) 279783
From PakRupees 1,950-2,700 per double room

Green's Hotel
Saddar Road
TEL: +92 (91) 276035-7 FAX: +92 (91) 276088

University Town

Apart from the American Club, all the guesthouses listed below should charge between PakRupees 1000-1500 per double room, and some take credit cards. Tax is charged on top. Most provide *en suite* 'Western' bathrooms, satellite TV in your room and international phone/fax facilities at reception.

The American Club
24-D Circular Road
TEL: +92 (91) 41321 FAX: +92 (91) 843967
If you want to meet aid workers and journalists, the American Club is one of the best places to stay or hang out. Liquid refreshment in the form of a swimming pool and a bar make this a particularly popular venue for expats at weekends and on Friday and Saturday nights. Other facilities include tennis courts, a pool table, restaurant and satellite TV. Four or five double rooms provide accommodation for $35 per person per night. Officially known as the United States Government Employees' Association (USGEA), membership must be arranged through the US Consulate (TEL: +92 (91) 279801-2, FAX: +92 (91) 276712). Full members may sign in guests (for a $2 fee), but temporary membership is available free of charge if you provide the Consulate with a letter of introduction from your office or sponsoring agency.

The Executive's Guesthouse
71-E Abdara Road
TEL: +92 (91) 842593-4, 41454 FAX: +92 (91) 842595

The Regent House
34-C Circular Road
TEL: +92 (91) 844661 FAX: +92 (91) 844088
and
44-D/A Old Jamrud Road
TEL: +92 (91) 840670-1 FAX: +92 (91) 840082

Shalimar Guesthouse
12-D/B Circular Road
TEL: +92 (91) 42885 FAX: +92 (91) 43642

VIP House
Old Bara Road
TEL: +92 (91) 842806, 42378 FAX: +92 (91) 843392

Food

For western-style and Chinese food the **Pearl-Continental** restaurants are very good. The food at the **American Club** is adequate, although the menu has hardly changed over the last 10 years. A number of Pakistani-run "fast food" outlets have opened up just across Jamrud Road from University Town. For something oriental try the **Hong Kong Chinese Restaurant** (TEL: 274504) on The Mall in the Cantonment. Other local favourites include **Shiraz** and **Usmania** restaurants on Jamrud Road near the airport.

For traditional "frontier food" and musical accompaniment, the **Khan Klub** (see above) is one of the best places to eat out, although it is about 20-30 minutes drive from University Town. If mad-cow disease appeals to you, then try **Khyber Bazaar** in the Old Town where you can sit outside on *charpoys* and tuck into hunks of dead meat and slabs of *naan* the size of snowshoes.

Books

The **ACBAR Resource and Information Centre (ARIC)** provides probably the best reference library on Afghanistan in the region. Located at 2 Rehman Baba Road, University Town, it is open from 0800-1630 hrs on Mondays to Thursdays, and from 0800-1230 hrs on Fridays. It is closed on Saturdays and Sundays. It contains nearly 4,000 books, agency reports, maps, journals and videos on every conceivable sector of interest in Afghanistan. Photocopying for documents and maps is available for a small fee. A number of Nancy Hatch Dupree's books are for sale at ARIC. The *CROSSLINES Essential Field Guide to Afghanistan* is also available here.

The **Afghan Media Resource Centre (AMRC)** has an enormous collection of photographs, video and film footage, newspapers and magazines at its offices in 2 Canal Bank Road, University Town (TEL: +92 (91) 41691, 45256). Funded in the 1980s by the US State Department to train Afghan photographers and cameramen, the majority of its work concentrated on documenting the war against the Russians.

Saddar Bazaar in the Cantonment has two of the best bookshops in Pakistan: the **London Book Co.** on Arbab Road (TEL: 272722) and **Saheed Bookbank**. They sell a good selection of titles on Afghanistan as well as Persian and Pashto dictionaries.

Peshawar, Historic City of the Frontier, A. H. Dani, Khyber Mail Press (1969)
Pakistan Handbook, Isobel Shaw, The Guidebook Company (Hong Kong, 1996), includes maps of Peshawar and the North West Frontier Province.
Pakistan – a travel survival kit, John King & David St.Vincent, Lonely Planet (1995), includes maps of Peshawar and the North West Frontier Province.

Embassies & Visas

For Pakistan. SEE ISLAMABAD and VISAS

For the Khyber Pass. All expats travelling from Peshawar by road up to Landi Kotal, the border at Torkham and on through the Khyber Pass into Afghanistan need to get a Tribal Areas Permit from the Government of the North West Frontier Province. A written application must be made to the Home and Tribal Affairs Department, located at the civil secretariat next to the Governor's House. The application should be accompanied by photocopies of your passport and relevant Pakistani and Afghan visas. The permit can take up to four days to be issued so plan ahead. Once you receive the permit, report to the office of the Political Agent of the Khyber Agency before 0900 hrs on the day of departure in order to join the daily border convoy. The Political Agent's office is on Bara Road near Qayum Stadium in Saddar Bazaar. Coming back from Afghanistan by road through the Khyber Pass, you do not need a Tribal Areas permit – the local militia will give you an armed escort.

For Afghanistan. Try to arrange an Afghan visa in your home country if possible. (SEE VISAS) Otherwise the Afghan Consulate in Peshawar issues visas, but the procedure for 'newcomers' can take up to a week even for accredited journalists and aid workers. Start your application process early in the week and remember that Friday afternoon, Saturday and Sunday are holidays. Visas cost $30 and you will need two passport-size photos (there are studios in Saddar Bazaar). If you are a regular visitor to Afghanistan and sponsored by the UN or a major aid agency you may be able to get a visa in as little as one day. The Consulate will only issue single-entry visas which are literally valid for *entry* only. In order to leave

Afghanistan you will have to get a special *exit visa* in-country. The address of the Afghan mission is as follows:

Consulate General of the Islamic State of Afghanistan
Gul Mohar Lane, University Town
(GPO Box 119), Peshawar.
TEL: +92 (91) 842486 Mob: +92 (351) 290133

Information

For more information on agency activities, SEE AGENCIES above. The following is a list of useful telephone numbers in Peshawar:

Ambulance:	**214575**
Church:	**276519**
Combined Military Hospital:	**2016168-9**
Fire Brigade:	**279074**
Ministry of Information:	**276145, 275230**
Museum:	**271310**
Police:	**213222, 212222**
Pakistan Television Corporation:	**279102-9**
Railway:	**274437 (enquiries)**
	211555, 214165 (reservations)
Sehrai Travels and Tours:	**TEL: 272084-5 FAX: 276088**

Local Rules

Despite its "rebel-stronghold" reputation, Peshawar is nevertheless a predominately Muslim town and you should respect the local dress code. Both expatriate men and women should cover their legs and wear reasonably loose-fitting clothes, but there is no need to wear *shalwar kameez* around town. If you must take your kit off, the pool at the American Club is the best place to do it.

If as a woman you are touched-up in the bazaar, do not keep quiet otherwise the offender may think you quite like it! Make a scene, shout, even scream. By reacting strongly you will probably shame him into stopping or running off. An EFG editor sent one assailant of a female colleague into the gutter to the hearty congratulations of numerous bazaar-goers.

Medical

Make sure your vaccinations are up to date for polio, typhoid, tetanus, rabies and hepatitis A and B as vaccine quality in Pakistan cannot be guaranteed. Take precautions against malaria and diarrhoea. If you get sick, consult a medical NGO or call the American Club for a list of doctors who could refer you to the Combined Military Hospital. (SEE PERSONAL HEALTH)

Money

If you are bringing cash, US dollars are the most widely accepted. The newer and crisper the notes the better, and avoid any pre-1993 $100 dollars bills because of local fakes. You will get a better rate for big denomination bills. Most of the money-changers are down at Khyber Bazaar in the Old Town or at Saddar Bazaar in the Cantonment. Check what the official bank rate is before street-dealing on the "open market". Travellers' cheques are only accepted at the major banks. Personal cheques on US and UK banks are also accepted if the dealer knows you.

ANZ Bank, located in the Cantonment at 35 The Mall (TEL: +92 (91) 274246, 272646; FAX: +92 (91) 275367), provides modern banking facilities. Opening hours are Monday to Friday 0900-1330 hrs and 1500-1700 hrs, with a break for Friday prayers from 1230-1500 hrs. There is also Saturday banking from 0900-1330 hrs. For cash advances of PakRupees on a credit card the charge is PakRupees 300. (SEE MONEY)

Post & Telecommunications

There are some reports of mail being opened at the GPO in University Town, so it may be better to send your letters from the post office in Saddar Bazaar. For important documents or cash, try to find someone flying out of the country who can post it for you. A courier service operates between Peshawar and Kabul. Ask at ACBAR for more details.

Mobile telephones can be rented or bought from a number of companies based in Islamabad. While local calls cost more, international calls by mobile phone are up to three times cheaper than calling from a hotel. (SEE RADIO & TELECOMMUNCIATIONS)

Many agencies based in Pakistan use e-mail on a routine basis. A number of networks are currently available: BRAINnet serves Peshawar; Comsats has a 56.6 bts server for Karachi, Islamabad, and Peshawar (coming soon); and Compuserve has a (slow) Karachi server. For short-term visitors and those without access to e-mail facilities, ACBAR Peshawar office offers an e-mail service: give them your text on a floppy disc and they will send it for one dollar a page.

Contact:
BRAINnet Digitware Systems, 43 Park Road,
University Town, Peshawar
TEL: +92 (91) 844309 FAX: +92 (91) 844310
E-mail: info@psh.brain.net.pk
Compuserve, Karachi server: TEL: 021 567 2141

Recreation

For couch-potatoes and sun-worshippers the **American Club** is the best place to relax: swimming with poolside waiter service is laid on, plus satellite TV and a video library. A pool table is upstairs and tennis is over the road. There is a **squash and tennis club on Park Road**, University Town, which costs PakRupees 200 per month to join.

The **Pearl-Continental Hotel** has a swimming pool, badminton, health club and golf course. There is also squash and tennis available on temporary membership basis at the rather sleepy **Peshawar Club**, a throwback from the British Raj. It used to be one of the most imperious clubs in India, but went virtually broke when Pakistan introduced prohibition for Muslims and the establishment lost one of its best sources of revenue.

For the more adventurous, there is **trekking** up in the Swat, Chitral and Gilgit valleys to the north. Call Green Tours at Green's Hotel for more details. The **Khyber Steam Safari** is a novel way to visit the Afghan border. The British built the railway from Peshawar up to Landi Kotal on the Khyber Pass in the 1920s. A must for train-spotters, the route takes in 34 tunnels, crosses 92 bridges and culverts and the 42 km journey takes about four and a half hours up and three hours back. By road the trip to the border takes about an hour.

For more details of steam railway tours call the Railway or a local travel agency such as Sehrai Travels and Tours (SEE INFORMATION above).

Shopping

Peshawar is a shopper's paradise – you can buy anything from rubber bands to rocket-propelled grenades if you know where to look. The Old City is full of bazaars (including **Khyber Bazaar**) crammed full of carpets, clothes stalls, teashops, brassware, jewellers, leather goods, fruit, vegetables and pyramids of spices bright as powder-paint.

Saddar Bazaar in the Cantonment is the place for off-the-peg clothes, books and other modern kit. Peshawar is a good place to have clothes tailor-made, and there are outfitters on The Mall and down the Jamrud Road.

For contraband and electrical goods, **Smugglers' Bazaar** is where things fall off the backs of lorries. Known locally as the Karkhanai Bazaar, it lies near the Kachagari refugee camp on Jamrud Road. For counterfeit British guns, drive to **Darra Adam Khel**, 40 minutes south of Peshawar on the road to Kohat. The Pathan tribes have made arms here since 1897, when the British tolerated the trade in return for unmolested travel along frontier roads. Check locally to find out if foreigners are still allowed to visit.

Weather

Weather in Peshawar is hot and sticky most of the year, although relatively pleasant from October to February, and hotter and stickier from June to August. Bring loose-fitting cotton clothes, a sunhat and plenty of patience.

ESSENTIAL A-Z

E. Girardet

Clothing & kit

During the Soviet-Afghan war, most reporters and aid workers operating on a cross-border basis would dress up in *shalwar kameez* with a *pakul* (woollen blanket) slung over their shoulders while wearing turbans (mainly in Pashtun areas) or *kolas* (woollen hats) for the northern regions. Often such garb was simply the best way to slip by the Pakistani control posts and to avoid informers inside Afghanistan, but was not necessarily needed inside resistance-held areas.

By the mid and late 1980s, US and European army surplus gear made its appearance among many mujahideen – and foreigners. Once inside the country, it was often easier to wear a pair of jeans or trousers, particularly if trekking through the Hindu Kush. There is nothing worse than trying to negotiate rocky terrain with a pair of loose flowing *shalwars.*

Nevertheless, for many foreigners during the 1980s, it became *de rigeur* to sport the Afghan 'clandestine' look. Some did it very well too, particularly the French photographers and visiting Paris intellectuals with their *causes celebres.* They managed to make their Afghan garb look thoroughly *romantique* and *Rimbaudesque* (the poet, not the macho hunk) with a silk scarf flung haphazardly – but carefully – around their necks. It looked good in *Paris Match*. The Brits, some of whom were ex-military, tended to be more down-to-earth by combining the best of SAS equipment (night-sights, bivvy bags and survival belts) with solid trekking gear from mountaineering outfitters. The Americans often arrived with the latest but not necessarily most practical gear (computers, water filters, and ABC airline guides); but they made sure they picked up the best-looking Afghan costumes for their rugged "reporters-at-the-front" on-camera presentations. One blond-haired Dutch journalist insisted on wearing the 'Soviet look,' a khaki *shalwar kameez* topped by a khaki Red Army hat, which did not exactly endear him with his colleagues, particularly when travelling in resistance-held areas.

Perhaps the most popular – and useful – import, quickly copied by the bazaar tailors and increasingly worn by image-conscious mujahideen, was the Banana Republic photo-vest with all its pockets.

Shepherd-boy in Paghman *J. Walter*

Perhaps what mattered most of all then – and now – if working in the field was a solid pair of boots.

Dress for non-combatant Afghans has always been traditional, except pre-war in some of the larger cities. The mini-skirts and sleeveless tops which some Afghan women wore in Kabul in the 1970s were very much the exception, not the rule. The all-covering tent-like *burqa* has been worn by mainly rural women since long before the Taliban arrived. Until the war and their exposure to crowded refugee camps, however, rural women remained unveiled in their villages or while working in fields. Only when strange males were present or when visiting towns did they cover up. The Taliban have now made it an across-the-board rule.

However, most visitors to Afghanistan nowadays do not try, or need, to disguise themselves as native Afghans. From the point of view of personal security as well as identification, it is best to look recognisably 'western.' Although some concessions have to be made to Muslim customs – especially by western women – it is important to "be who you are" and be straightforward about your work so as not to arouse suspicion.

The following are some general suggestions for suitable clothing for western visitors. See the relevant regional chapter for advice on local rules and climate at different times of year.

Women

In general, ordinary loose-fitting western dresses and below-the-knee skirts can be worn, with loose trousers on underneath to cover the legs, calves and ankles. Wear blouses with long sleeves and avoid low bust-lines or figure-hugging outfits. When you are in public, cover your head with a shoulder-length scarf or *chador*. In more conservative areas, *shalwar kameez* may be more appropriate, and in more liberal areas you may not need to wear a *chador* at all. Be careful when sitting on the floor in the presence of Afghan men to cover your knees and feet.

Men

Long trousers and long-sleeved shirts are fine. Shorts should not be worn in public except when playing sports within NGO or UN compounds. Jeans or khaki trousers with bush jackets or other forms of 'rugged' dress are fine if travelling or operating in the field. When visiting government officials or educated people, jackets and ties are appropriate, if the weather is not too hot. Clean, presentable clothes are a sign of respect for your Afghan hosts or colleagues. There is no need for western men to grow beards or wear head-dress.

Clothing for the frontline

If your work takes you into the line of fire, you must wear the right kit to protect yourself. Flak jackets are essential to safeguard you against the threat of flying shrapnel and stray bullets. Make sure the jacket has removable ceramic plates front and rear to protect your heart. Each plate should weigh around five kilos to be at all effective, and should be fitted when there is a threat of gunfire. Practise wearing the jacket with plates fitted to get used to the weight before going to the frontline. Combat helmets are also essential and have saved the lives of a number of journalists working in Afghanistan. Good walking boots – already worn in – are essential. Wear a survival belt containing a first aid kit, shell dressing, Swiss army knife, string, space blanket, poncho, pen, notebook and your personal documents. If you lose everything else, you have at least got this. An essential item for all travel in Afghanistan is a portable shortwave radio to catch the latest on the *BBC, VOA* or *Deutsche Welle*, particularly in times of crisis.

ESSENTIAL READING

The SAS Survival Handbook, John Wiseman, Harvill Publishers, 77/85 Fulham Palace Road, Hammersmith, London W6 8JB, UK. (1986, reprinted, 1994) £12.99. A useful book if travelling in difficult terrain or war zones.
Medicine for Mountaineering, Edited by James E. Wilkerson, MD, The Mountaineers, 715 Pike Street, Seattle, WA 98101, USA (2nd Edition, 1975). For backcountry and mountain trekking.

Festivals & holidays

Festivities in Afghanistan have taken something of a downer since the Taliban poured cold water on music, kite flying and anything allegedly un-Islamic. Friday is still the weekly holiday, unlike Pakistan which recently switched to a Western-style weekend. This can make liaison between agencies in both countries difficult for half the week from Thursday afternoon to Monday morning. Traditionally the following holidays *used* to be observed:

21 March: New Year's Day, also known as Farmers' Day. Agricultural fairs and *buzkashi,* the Afghan version of polo.

27 May: Independence Day. Celebrating freedom from the British in 1919.

17 July: Republic Day. Marked the founding of the Republic of Afghanistan in 1973.

31 August: Pashtunistan Day.

9 September: National Assembly Day.

15 October: Deliverance Day. Commemorated the victory of King Nadir Shah over Bacha Saqao in 1929.

24 October: United Nations Day

Islamic religious holidays are set according to the lunar calendar and hence, from a Western point of view, vary in timing from year to year. The main festivals are as follows:

Ashura: 10th day of *Moharram,* otherwise known as Martyrs' Day, anniversary of the death of Husain, cousin and son-in-law of the Prophet.

Mawlud-e-Sharif:	The Prophet's Birthday
Ramazan:	(also *Ram'zan* or *Ramadan*) the month of fasting
Id ul-Fitr:	three day feast at the end of *Ramazan*
Id-e-Qurban (Azha):	a day of sacrifice during the month of the *Hajj* (pilgrimage to Mecca)

Insurance

As Afghanistan is considered a conflict area, most of the insurance companies we contacted said they would not cover groups and individuals operating in the region. One large Swiss group proudly declared that it did not take "risks with risks." The London-based Private Patient Plan (PPP), however, told us that they were prepared to insure relief workers, journalists and others while in Afghanistan, but only for sickness, accidents and other 'normal' liabilities. Travellers must also be part of PPP regular annual health-care programmes. War-related incidents could not be covered. It was not clear whether this would include 'accidental' incidents with landmines. The only brokers we found who were prepared to insure against loss of limb through landmine injury were Crispin Speers & Partners of London.

The United Nations and other organizations have their own coverage – often forbidding their employees to remain in any conflict-prone area if the security situation deteriorates. The International Committee of the Red Cross, which operates in most war zones around the world, has its own arrangements with Lloyds. A number of travel companies, such as Cooks also have their own insurances, but not for war zones.

We have checked around and come up with the following companies willing to provide general cover for the region as well as for Afghanistan itself. Prices and sums insured vary widely starting from $250 for four months of basic war risk cover, so it is worth shopping around.

ESSENTIAL CONTACTS

CRISPIN SPEERS & PARTNERS
International Insurance and Reinsurance Brokers
18 London Street, London, EC3R 7JP, UK.
TEL: +44 (171) 480 5083 FAX: +44 (171) 702 9276
Provides variable proforma cover including war risks, injury from landmines, baggage and money losses, plus personal liability. The best we could find.

Other contacts for general coverage in Afghanistan but not specific war risks include:

Private Patient Plan Healthcare
Phillips House, Crescent Road
Tunbridge Wells, Kent, TN1 2PL, UK.
TEL: +44 (1892) 503856
FAX: +44 (1892) 503189

International Health Insurance - Danmark a/s
Palaegade 8, DK-1261, Copenhagen K, Denmark.
TEL: +45 (33) 15 3099
FAX: +45 (33) 32 2560
E-mail: ihidk@ibm.net
Website: www.ihi.dk

The Swiss member-supported medical air service REGA, can fly you out of war zones and back to Europe if injured or sick.
REGA
GAC, PO Box 1414, 8058 Zurich Airport, Switzerland.
TEL: +41 (1) 654 3222
FAX: +41 (1) 654 3590
Website: www.rega.ch

Journalism & reporting in the field

During the Soviet-Afghan war, it was in many respects far easier to report the situation in Afghanistan than it is today. This, despite the fact that journalists were often required to travel by foot with the mujahideen for days or weeks at a time prior to filing their reports. The portable satphone remained just a dream. (SEE MEDIA) Each of the guerrilla factions sought to project its own very partisan view of the war, but journalists usually had choice over how, where and what they sought to cover. There was a degree of healthy competition among the various mujahed parties to attract those reporters with the most influential access to the outside world (e.g. US television networks) as a means of raising their own profiles. Some guerrilla groups were better than others, and journalists tended to focus on those with proven track records. The 'when,' however, was always a bit unpredictable as planning in Afghanistan was often on an *ad hoc* basis.

When the mujahideen took Kabul in 1992, the new Minister of Defence, former guerrilla commander Ahmed Shah Massoud, continued with his tradition of media openness to foreign journalists. There was little interference and his aides were usually on hand to explain the party line and to protect reporters from the excesses of less disciplined fighters (such as confiscating camera equipment). On the other hand, Massoud's arch rival Gulbuddin Hekmatyar did little to encourage good press relations: the murder in 1994 by his men of a BBC radio correspondent was hardly considered a good public relations move.

Today, all the factions involved in the fighting continue to peddle highly partisan views of the war. There are few independent sources of information or analysis. Journalists are forced to rely for much of the time on information they are given by the factions and the evidence they can gather on their own. Aid workers are reluctant to speak out on political questions. Even purely humanitarian issues seem to have a political dimension.

Sources: Tim Johnston/Reuters, BBC, CROSSLINES Global Report, UNOCHA.

As before, Kabul remains the centre of media attention. All four organizations representing the permanent foreign press corps *(BBC, Reuters,* the *Associated Press* and *Agence France Presse)* are based there, making infrequent trips to provincial centres such as Mazar-e-Sharif, Herat and Kandahar. But their proximity helps them to be on the spot when needed. They were filing on the Rustaq earthquake in February 1998 well before the international humanitarian community got its act together. In fact, even outside journalists were already reporting on the ground before the first aid supplies got through.

Until the Taliban captured Kabul in September 1996, the attention of foreign editors was generally limited to human interest stories. These focused primarily on the hardships of the people of Kabul who lived under an almost constant barrage of rockets and artillery. The Taliban takeover sparked a media frenzy: the International Committee of the Red Cross (ICRC) flew 120 journalists into the city in a matter of weeks. Many reports gave the impression that Kabul had changed overnight into a version of Phnom Penh at Year Zero.

Since then, the dominant themes have been the Taliban's treatment of women and some of the more extreme edicts they have promulgated in their drive to establish the world's purist Islamic state. (SEE TALIBAN) The Taliban have put a number of important restrictions on reporters, some ideological, others stemming from practical concerns. For many observers, such policies are turning Afghanistan into a 'closed' conflict more than ever before, at least in Taliban-controlled areas.

The Taliban have banned photography and filming of living animals, including humans, on the grounds that the depiction of living creatures is banned in Islam. (SEE PHOTOGRAPHY) They have banned reporters from talking to women, although it is unclear if this ban extends to female journalists. The Taliban maintain that Afghan women should have no contact with males outside their immediate family. (SEE WOMEN)

Theoretically, reporters visiting Kabul must stay at the Continental Hotel – the former Intercontinental – and hire Taliban-approved drivers and translators. The Taliban unabashedly admit that this is to help the state-owned hotel make money. Some enterprising journalists, however, manage to operate on their own without the Taliban knowing. The orders are less strictly enforced outside Kabul. The dogmatic imposition of rules and regulations in the Afghan capital is more a reflection of the fact that the Taliban regards the cosmopolitan city as a den of corruption and loose morals.

But it is crucial for journalists to seek a broader perspective on Afghanistan than can be found in Kabul. The urban-rural divide is almost as important as the military split. As in the past, this leads to much press coverage giving a misleading impression of the way Afghans regard the factions, particularly the Taliban. Much of the country's population is rural and uneducated. The small remaining educated urban elite with whom Westerners spend most of their time tend to be those who have lost most under the Taliban. They are the most critical of Talib rule. However, it would be a mistake to assume that these views are representative of the Afghan population as a whole.

The rural population in Talib-controlled areas – two-thirds of the country – has always proved conservative, both in religion and custom. Their lifestyles have changed little under the new rulers. It is mainly southern rural Pashtuns who enabled the Talib crusade to spread so fast. Both rural Pashtun men and women have traditionally represented one of the most conservative influences in Afghanistan. The only recent major change in lifestyle has been the security that the Taliban have managed to bring in place of the brutal and arbitrary rule of the warlords who proceeded them.

Nevertheless, two-decades of war as well as years of refugee exile have had an effect on rural Afghans that has yet to be gauged. Prior to the Soviet-Afghan war, for example, rural women only wore veils in urban areas such as market places and wherever strangers were present. They did not necessarily cover themselves when in their villages or fields. Under the Taliban, they are required to wear the *burqa* whenever outside. There is also strong evidence that many women, both urban and rural, in Herat and other northern areas bitterly resent Talib restrictions.

Within their rules, the Taliban are willing to help correspondents. They understand the power of the foreign press, not in terms of international perception – about which they care little – but because of domestic impact. All the local media, such as Radio Shariat, are discredited as propaganda tools of the various factions. As a result, the overwhelming majority of Afghans listen to shortwave radio services such as the *BBC, VOA* and *Deutsche Welle* (all of which broadcast in Pashto and Dari) as their principal sources of information.

In the frontline areas, Talib fighters are less inclined to restrict foreign reporters. (Many smoke cigarettes and listen to music which are frowned upon by the movement). They are generally better informed and more willing to provide information than their spokesmen in Kabul. But in time-honoured Afghan fashion, they tend to exaggerate military gains. The Taliban have sometimes restricted access to the frontlines in the wake of a military defeat when emotions are running high, saying they are trying to guarantee the safety of foreigners.

For reporting purposes, the picture is different in the north. Non-Pashtun traditions and Islamic interpretation are often in direct conflict with the Taliban. To describe northerners as more liberal is perhaps an overstatement but they are less dogmatic. In general, journalists have little problem in travelling or reporting.

While both camps are sensitive to the international media, they do not seem to expect uncritical coverage. They will call in a correspondent if they are unhappy with a report, but will generally accept it if the reporter can show that it is the truth. There have been few documented cases of systematic harassment of visiting journalists by the factional leaderships. Most trouble is directed at the permanent correspondents. Local commanders have been a source of trouble, but mostly for reasons of financial gain rather than ideology.

The frontlines are generally less dangerous than often imagined. Fighters of all factions are truly reluctant to let foreigners take foolish risks. Sometimes, however, this serves as a deterrent from visiting areas where the news might prove less flattering. Most Afghans, irrespective of their allegiances, are happy to see foreigners and to discuss the situation in their country. Afghanistan today is not Algeria. Nor is it Beirut at the height of its conflict. Westerners are mostly a welcome diversion and an excuse to show the splendid traditions of hospitality that have survived despite the war. What follows are some practical tips for getting into Afghanistan and reporting from the field:

Communications

There are no regular international communications links between Afghanistan and the outside world. Journalists best carry their own satellite communications equipment if they are intending to cover breaking news. In Kabul there is a – monitored – satellite link in the main post office. They only take fax and voice. It is not possible to receive calls. NGOs and permanent correspondents in Kabul are officially forbidden from allowing other journalists to use their communications equipment. NGOs in the north will sometimes allow visiting journalists access to their equipment. (SEE RADIO & TELECOMMUNICATIONS)

Press cards

The **International Centre for Humanitarian Reporting** in Geneva issues press cards to ICHR members who are *bona fide* journalists covering humanitarian and conflict issues. These are designed to help members in the field and may be of assistance when approaching aid organizations and government offices. (SEE ICHR)

Rules & regulations

Both the Taliban and the opposition of the north insist that journalists register with their authorities. The rules are less strict outside Kabul and Mazar. In Kabul, journalists should go to the Press Department of the Ministry of Foreign Affairs with two photographs for registration. You will be told to stay in the Continental Hotel and assigned a registered translator. You will only be allowed to use a taxi-driver registered with the hotel. Assume that any Taliban-registered interpreters or drivers may inform on you to the authorities. German nationals can stay at the German Club. In Herat, Jalalabad and Kandahar, journalists may stay at the UN guesthouses. In Mazar, local accommodation is generally available. (SEE REGIONS)

Exceptions are made for journalists who are sponsored by one of the registered foreign aid agencies in Kabul, including NGOs.

The official conditions for this are that journalists must solely cover the activities of the organization. Employees of the four registered news organizations *(AFP, AP, BBC, Reuters*) can stay at their respective offices, but resident correspondents in Kabul are expressly forbidden from accommodating visiting freelancers. Do not stay with local families in Kabul; your presence may put them at risk.

In the north, journalists should register at the Department of Foreign Affairs opposite the Bharat Hotel in Mazar. There are no official restrictions on the movement of journalists. (SEE PHOTOGRAPHY, NORTHERN REGION). *Editors' note: Afghanistan is a divided country. Regulations vary from region to region.*

Taliban restrictions

Photography and filming of living beings are forbidden in Taliban-held parts of Afghanistan. (SEE PHOTOGRAPHY) It is wise to get specific permission for any filming in public in Kabul. It is also forbidden to interview women. It is officially illegal to import/export video or audio tapes from Taliban areas. Restrictions are looser outside the cities, but it is still prudent to check. There are no restrictions on filming or photography in the north, except at airports.

Mullah Omar, the Supreme Leader of the Taliban Movement, based in Kandahar, has never spoken to a non-Muslim journalist, and Mullah Rabbani, his deputy in Kabul, rarely gives interviews. Most of the other Taliban leaders can be seen, given time and patience. Mullah Qalaamuddin, the deputy head of the Religious Police (the Department for the Promotion of Virtue and the Prevention of Vice) is particularly recommended for quotes on the Taliban's policy towards women. Sher Mohammed Stanakzai, deputy Foreign Minister, gives a relatively inoffensive version of Taliban policy in good English. Women journalists may have problems meeting Taliban officials, and should keep their head covered at all times in public. It is not wise for foreign women to talk alone in the streets of Kabul. They are not, however, required to wear the *burqa*.

Travelling to Afghanistan

Most journalists travel into Afghanistan from Pakistan although some occasionally enter from the north or west. There is a relatively trouble-free road from Peshawar to Jalalabad and Kabul. Travellers will need to get permits from the Khyber Tribal Agency office in Peshawar Cantonment to transit the tribal areas *en route* to the border. (SEE PESHAWAR, CENTRAL REGION)

The **United Nations** will fly *bona fide* journalists free into Kabul, but insist on a letter of commission/employment from a recognised news organization and a valid visa. The United Nations does not give precedence to journalists. The **International Committee of the Red Cross** will not usually fly journalists into Taliban areas but will take them into the opposition-held north under certain circumstances. Both organizations ban video and music cassettes, and pictures from being taken on their flights in line with Taliban restrictions. Ariana Afghan Airlines flies irregularly from the Gulf. (SEE TRAVEL)

Travel inside Afghanistan

Taxis are generally safe and good value, but be careful what you say in front of your driver. There are curfews throughout the country, but times vary. Do not attempt to travel after curfew, especially in Kabul and Mazar. Taxis are also available for long trips, as are buses. It is sometimes possible to travel within Afghanistan on UN or ICRC planes. Do not travel in the north after dark; the roads are unsafe outside the cities because of banditry. Some Taliban governors are less than welcoming to the press; Ghazni and Herat are particularly bad. (SEE TRAVEL and SECURITY TIPS)

United Nations support for journalists visiting Afghanistan

Free flights. The United Nations will transport journalists free-of-charge on its light aircraft in and out of Afghanistan providing:

- There is space available.
- They can show a letter signed by an editor/bureau chief vouching for their authenticity. Freelancers must be able to show documentation from a commissioning organization. Letters of accreditation should be faxed to Flight Operations (see below) well in advance.

- They have a valid double-entry visa for Pakistan and an entry visa for Afghanistan.

Generally speaking, the UN flies to Kabul, Mazar and Herat three times a week; and to Jalalabad and Kandahar twice a week. Flights to Bamiyan, Farah, Faizabad and Gardez are once weekly, on demand. Flights tend to leave early in the morning. Passengers are required to check in at Flight Operations two hours prior to departure. Baggage is restricted to 20 kg per person. Excess baggage may be carried at a cost of five dollars per kg, so long as the plane is not carrying a lot of cargo. TV crews are advised to bring the minimum amount of equipment. Journalists should direct all flight enquiries to:

Flight Operations
UNOCHA/UNDP Islamabad
TEL: +92 (51) 211451-5 FAX: +92 (51) 211450
E-mail: unocha@undpafg.org.pk

Pre-visit briefings. Before travelling to Afghanistan, journalists can call UNOCHA/UNDP to arrange a briefing by the Public Affairs Officer, who can also put you in touch with other Public Affairs Officers from UN agencies working in Afghanistan, and can help plan itineraries.

What you can expect inside Afghanistan. UN officials in Afghanistan are happy to help journalists – within reason. They will readily demonstrate the work they are doing and talk about it. Many of them have considerable experience in Afghanistan and are very knowledgeable, but will not talk on record about other issues. They can advise you on how to get the permits you need, but will not be able to do this for you.

Visas

The Taliban administration is recognised by only three countries: Pakistan, Saudi Arabia and the United Arab Emirates. The Taliban will generally not accept visas issued by opposition embassies, such as those in London or Paris. The Taliban Embassy in Islamabad and the Consulate in Peshawar (manned largely by the same officials of previous regimes, including the former PDPA government) have to clear journalist visas with the Ministry of Foreign Affairs in Kabul, a process that can take time. Ensure that you have an exit visa on departure at Kabul airport. (SEE VISAS)

Opposition visas can be obtained in opposition embassies (e.g. London, Paris and Geneva). "Northern Alliance" officials will also accept Taliban visas for entry, although they insist on issuing a new visa on arrival.

It is possible to obtain a Pakistani visa in Kabul, Herat and Kandahar, but not in the north. Reporters should make sure that they have at least a double entry Pakistani visa if travelling to the north.

Money & bargaining

Afghanistan has no functioning banks and noone takes credit cards, so make sure you bring enough cash. US Dollars or Pakistani Rupees are the best. Make sure your dollars are post-1993 notes (because of fakes), and not damaged or creased. Larger denomination notes will fetch better rates of exchange. The market in Afghanistan is open rather than black, and currency trading is one of the few 'industries' thriving in the country. (SEE ECONOMICS)

Changing money

Ask around for the current exchange rate and the best places to change money. Some dealers (if they trust you) take personal cheques from European and North American banks.

The local currency is known as the *Afghani*, and there are two versions – one Taliban and one "Northern Alliance" (known as the "Dostum Dollar"). Neither currency is valid in "enemy territory." At early 1998 rates of exchange, one dollar will buy you around 20,000-25,000 Taliban *Afghanis*, and around 60,000 Dostum *Afghanis*. Currency rates can rise or fall according to military victories and defeats, regional power politics or the price of opium. So rather than doing big deals, change small amounts often so as not to fall victim to fluctuating exchange rates, and bring a large bag to carry away your loot.

If you are travelling via Pakistan, there are international banks in Peshawar and Islamabad which can give you PakRupees in exchange for travellers' cheques or credit card cash advances. Bear in mind that if you intend to stay in UNICA Guesthouses while in Afghanistan, they will only accept cash payments in dollars.

Bargaining

As a foreigner, it is worth bargaining over luxury items such as carpets, glass or jewellery. Try the usual tricks – initial enthusiasm, mock horror at the exorbitant price, feigned disinterest, walkout and reluctant return, large amounts of green tea and good humour –

and you should be able to knock between a third and two thirds off the asking price, depending how ruthless you are feeling.

However, the *Afghani* has been devalued by 40,000% since the beginning of the war, and the cost of living has soared for most ordinary Afghans. So when it comes to buying non-luxury goods, be generous and pay the asking price rather than arguing over a few cents which local traders need far more than you do.

Begging

The giving of alms to beggars is an acceptable and necessary facet of the Muslim faith. However, the combination of urban drift, unemployment, disability and poverty which arose from two decades of war has given rise to many more beggars on the streets. This is aggravated in cities such as Kabul and Herat where Taliban authorities have forbidden Afghan women from working, resulting in often well-qualified professionals begging for money in *burqas*. Lack of work and poor schooling force mothers to send their children out onto the streets to beg, especially in the NGO and UN quarters of town, such as Wazir Akbar Khan in Kabul. Some children will make an effort to sell you something or perform a service, such as shoe-cleaning or guarding your vehicle, in return for a few *Afghanis*. Prostitution is reportedly on the rise. (SEE CHILDREN)

Whether you should or should not give money to beggars is a desperately difficult question, for which each visitor must make a personal decision. Some feel that to give money only encourages dependency on handouts – precisely the situation that most aid agencies are trying to get away from in their programmes. They say that Westerners who hand out cash only encourage more and more aggressive begging. Others argue that a few thousand *Afghanis* mean nothing to an expatriate but a great deal to an Afghan, although this itself sounds patronising. One solution is to give money to women, but not to children who may be more likely to squander it. Some experienced aid workers, however, have suggested that time and attention are more important than money. If the coast is clear, speak to the women who beg and let them know that you understand their plight. Remind them why you are there and what you are doing to help. Banter and joke with the children who beg, and they will often forget about asking you for money. You can probably help these people more by persuading donors and aid agencies to pressure the Taliban into allowing women to work or by providing more assistance for children. Job-creation and food-for-work programmes can help alleviate begging and aid dependency.

Baksheesh

As in many Third World countries, *baksheesh* can be regarded as a tip to a hotel porter or a taxi driver. But in Afghanistan, *baksheesh* is also the word for bribery (or extortion) to people in positions of influence such as a government official or a fighter cradling a kalashnikov. It is not advisable to palm Taliban officials (extortion is forbidden) although many are certainly not averse to receiving some *Afghanis* or dollars in return for services rendered. *Baksheesh* is definitely current in many areas. It's up to you, but *baksheesh* as a form of bribery certainly is not necessary. It can even be insulting to people with a deep tradition of hospitality. You may be able to get round a stubborn or obstructive official by reminding him that you are a *guest* in their country! Patience, banter and studied ignorance of what is being suggested are often the best ways of getting things done. Numerous experienced journalists and aid workers who have worked in Afghanistan since the early days of the war have never been obliged to pay bribes, despite often determined demands by various corrupt individuals. More often than not, the matter was turned into a joke (amid slight embarrassment) when it was realized that no bribes would be forthcoming.

Of course, there are always bad eggs, usually the higher up the ladder you go. The Peshawar-based resistance parties during the Soviet-Afghan war were notoriously corrupt as were many commanders, Pakistani government officials and others benefiting from the aid bandwagon. Even the humanitarian agencies were sometimes forced to pay for the honour of dispatching relief caravans into Afghanistan. Prior to the Taliban, numerous *ad hoc* checkpoints demanding 'tolls' (normally not from foreigners) used to abound along the main roads leading to Kabul and other main towns. These have come to an end under the Taliban in their zones of control. Now the Taliban seek to impose the traditional Islamic *zakat* (10% tax) but in a more official manner. Checkpoints still exist in urban areas and in the north.

Having said all this…the fatal mistake the British made, prior to their disastrous retreat from Kabul in January 1842, was to stop paying off the local tribal commanders between the capital and the British garrison at Jalalabad. Is there a difference between a payment for loyalty and a bribe? Best bear in mind the old adage: "You can always rent an Afghan but you can never buy one."

Personal health

"When you're wounded
and left on Afghanistan's plains,
An' the women come out to cut up what remains,
Jest roll to your rifle an' blow out your brains,
An' go to your Gawd like a soldier."

Rudyard Kipling, Barrack-room Ballads (1892)

The main threats to personal health in Afghanistan – other than rocket-fire and landmines – are malaria and infections caused by dirty food and drink. None of these can be prevented by injections, so be aware of the dangers at all times, take the necessary precautions and you should be able to avoid the Kipling option. Carry a basic first aid kit on you to cope with malaria, diarrhoea, headaches, animal bites, small cuts etc., plus sterilized needles and syringes for emergencies. Ticks and bedbugs can also be a problem, particularly when staying in rural areas with cattle in the vicinity.

Immunization

Make sure you visit your doctor or a specialist travel clinic at least a month before travelling to the region in case you need additional vaccines. Pakistani immigration officials sometimes check for proof of cholera and yellow fever immunizations from visitors arriving from areas infected with those diseases. The quality of vaccines available in Pakistan cannot be guaranteed, so make sure you arrive with all the necessary immunizations. You must be up to date on polio (10-year vaccine), tetanus (10-year vaccine) and typhoid (mostly three-year vaccines). In addition, get protection against hepatitis A (the more effective *havrix* vaccine has replaced the old

In compiling this section, the EFG editors are grateful for the help of the London Hospital for Tropical Diseases, Dr Antony van der Bunt of Help the Afghans Foundation, and Mark Rowland of HealthNET International.

gamma globulin one), hepatitis B and rabies. Take advice from your doctor on coverage against Japanese encephalitis and meningitis, but at present these are not considered necessary. The vaccine for cholera is ineffective and the condition can in any case be easily treated.

Malaria

According to the Hospital for Tropical Diseases in London, malaria kills more British tourists than any other tropical disease. Malaria exists all year round in Pakistan and much of Afghanistan at altitudes of less than 2,000 metres. It is present in both urban and rural areas and there is no vaccination available to prevent it. The recommended prophylaxes are a weekly dose of two chloroquine tablets (trade names include: *Nivaquine and Avloclor*) and a daily dose of one or two proguanil tablets (trade names include: *Paludrine*). These must be started one week prior to arrival in the region, taken without a break while in-country, and continued until one month after departure from the region. The potentially deadly *falciparum* malaria is chloroquine-resistant, but this is to some extent overcome by combining the daily *Paludrine* dose with your weekly chloroquine. It is not *Larium*-resistant, but *Mefloquine/Larium* drugs can have some disturbing psychological side effects. Chloroquine and *Paludrine* may affect your eyesight if taken for several months or more. Bring enough pills with you for the whole stay: chloroquine and *Paludrine* are not available in Pakistan.

The best way to avoid getting malaria is to avoid getting bitten by mosquitoes in the first place. This is the solution many people living in the region for more than a few months adopt, rather than popping pills. Wear long-sleeved shirts, socks and long trousers, especially from early evening onwards when the mosquitoes come out. Also, use mosquito repellent (containing 35% or more of the active agent DEET), smoke coils or electronic "King Mats", and impregnated bednets. For more details, see malaria box opposite.

Stomach Upsets

Diarrhoea is caused by careless eating and drinking. Most visitors to this region suffer from it sometime during their stay. It is said that the chances of getting diarrhoea can be reduced by one third simply by washing your hands with soap and water before handling and eating food. Never drink tap water – always boil it (for 20 minutes) or add iodine, and use purified water or green tea (it will have been boiled) for brushing your teeth. Activated charcoal filters are OK as long as you clean them regularly. Check bottles of "mineral water" for intact seals. Avoid ice in drinks, ice-cream, unpasteurised milk, salads, raw vegetables and seafood (unlikely in Afghanistan!). Yoghurt (*maast*) is a popular side dish with many Afghan meals and should be fine to eat, but make sure that it has not been watered down. In restaurants, avoid cold meats and sauces and

PROTECTION AGAINST MALARIA

Two types of malaria are found in Afghanistan and Pakistan: 75% is due to *vivax* malaria, the non-lethal type, while 25% is due to *falciparum* malaria which causes more severe symptoms and even death if left undiagnosed or untreated. Visitors should take precautions against malaria, particularly if intending to stay overnight in rural areas during the main transmission season from June to November.

Malaria is rarely transmitted in the major cities of Pakistan or Afghanistan, although visitors may be troubled by 'nuisance' mosquitoes in urban environments. The exceptions to this rule are Jalalabad in eastern Afghanistan and Kandahar in southern Afghanistan where agricultural and residential areas overlap and malaria-bearing mosquitoes are abundant.

Kabul lies at too high an altitude for malaria transmission; the risk in that city is from cutaneous leishmaniasis, a disease transmitted by biting sandflies, in which ulcerous lesions occur on the face and limbs around the site of the bite. Malaria is rare in Herat and Mazar-e-Sharif but is common in rice-growing areas in the northern provinces of Kunduz and Baghlan, in the eastern provinces of Nangarhar, Kunar, Laghman and Khost, and in the southern provinces of Kandahar and Helmand.

Ideally, visitors should travel with a *permethrin*-treated bednet, obtainable from many shops in Europe and North America specializing in outdoor recreation. Prophylaxis with chloroquine (two tablets weekly) and Paludrine (two tablets daily) should give adequate protection against both forms of malaria.

However, no prophylaxis is perfect, so if you develop a fever (38 degrees Celsius or higher) visit a competent laboratory or health NGO and have a blood smear examined for malarial parasites. Other symptoms of malaria include periodic shivering, headache, body ache and possible bouts of diarrhoea. Vomiting can be a symptom of the potentially deadly *falciparum* malaria.

For adults, curative treatment of *falciparum* malaria requires a single dose of three Fansidar tablets (available in Pakistan), that of *vivax* malaria requires 10 tablets of chloroquine taken over three days. Follow dosage instructions exactly.

Contributed by Mark Rowland,
HealthNET International

THE FIVE Fs OF DYSENTRY

Dysentry (bloody diarrhoea) is usually caused by infections picked up from one or more of the following 'carriers':

FOOD

FINGERS

FAECES

FLIES

FOAMITES (ANTS)

You can reduce the chances of getting diarrhoea by one third simply by washing your hands before eating!

make sure any meat you eat has been well-cooked. Drink tea rather than Pepsi (often locally bottled) or blended fruit juice. A good general rule is: ***Cook it, Peel it, or Leave it.***

If you get diarrhoea you must rehydrate with large amounts of purified water and oral rehydration salts (ORS). ORS can taste pretty grim so try and buy flavoured ones and drink with cold water. Don't stop eating, but stick to simple, dry food and try to avoid bunging yourself up with pills (e.g. Imodium, Lomotil) except when travelling.

Emergencies

In a medical emergency the best course of action is to go to the office of the nearest international NGO specializing in health, or find a hospital supported by the International Committee for the Red Cross (ICRC). The ICRC runs surgical units in Kabul (Karte Seh and Wazir Akbar Khan hospitals), Kandahar, Herat and Ghazni, and will operate on all emergency cases. The ICRC can arrange emergency air evacuations if necessary. The American Club in Peshawar has a list of current doctors in town, who are able to refer cases to the Combined Military Hospital.

Some travellers carry a set of sterilized needles and syringes to guard against possible infection by HIV or hepatitis B. Make sure your travel insurance covers you for emergency medical repatriation, as well as protecting you in the event of "war and kindred risks." (SEE INSURANCE)

ESSENTIAL CONTACTS

The London Hospital for Tropical Diseases:
TEL:
+44 (171) 530 3500 (general enquiries)
+44 (171) 388 9600 (Healthline Travel Clinic)
+44 (1839) 337733 (vaccinations hotline)

Medical Advisory Services for Travellers Abroad (MASTA):
UK-based 24-hour travel healthline which also provides tailored 'healthbriefs' and health supplies by post
TEL: +44 (1891) 224100

International Traveler's Hotline:
US-based healthline, Monday-Friday 0800-1630 (EST)
TEL: +1 (404) 332 4559

Centre for Disease Control
Website: www.cdc.gov.

Travellers' and Migration Medical Unit
Policlinique de Médecine (Asia Dept.)
Hôpital Cantonal Universitaire
25, rue Micheli-du-Crest
1211 Geneva 14
Switzerland.
TEL: +41 (22) 372 9603

Water Filters

Filopur AG
Seestrasse 83
8700 Küsnacht
Switzerland.

Katadyn Produkte AG
Birkenweg 4
8304 Wallisellen
Switzerland.

ESSENTIAL READING

Where There is No Doctor, David Werner, Hesperian Foundation

Staying Healthy in Asia, Africa and Latin America, Moon Publications, 722 Wall St, Chico, CA 95928 USA.

Health and Medical Information Booklet, American Embassy, Islamabad 1997 (available at the American Club, Peshawar)

Traveller's Medical Companion, E. Graber & P.M. Sieger, Fielding's (New York, 1990)

Photography & filming

Taking photographs or filming in Afghanistan has never proved the easiest of tasks, but that is no reason to be put off. The arrival of the Taliban has made matters far more difficult but not impossible, while in non-Taliban areas, such as the north, little has changed. As before, working with a camera requires a combination of persistence, wit, imagination and inordinate amounts of patience. (SEE JOURNALISM, MEDIA)

An extraordinary array of photo-essays and television documentaries have emerged over the past twenty years, many of them produced under extremely hazardous conditions, and not just in frontline war zones. Afghan males enjoy their vanity and we have encountered few, particularly among the fighters (including the Taliban) who dislike having their photographs taken. "Ax, ax" ("picture, picture") is often the most common request when a camera is produced, particularly if there is a gun to show off.

Since their arrival on the scene in 1994, the Taliban have banned films and television, and forbidden the photographing of living creatures including humans. Film teams encountered similar obstacles during the 1980s and early 1990s in areas where fundamentalist groups operated, such as those backed by Hekmatyar Gulbuddin's Hezb-e-Islami or Arab *Wahabi.* Journalists have been threatened, shot at and, in at least once instance, murdered because of their efforts to film. Photographers have also encountered problems in Hazara areas in the central highlands, where Iranian *Shi'a* influences are strong. However, if you travel with one of their people, such as Hazara guide, they can be extremely friendly and hospitable. Arriving with an aid vehicle accompanied by a Tajik or Pashtun guide may cause suspicion.

Yet most photographers and cameramen interviewed say filming is only a problem in certain Taliban areas, such as Kabul, Herat and Kandahar. And even then, this has not prevented some news organizations, such as the BBC, from filming in Talib areas. As one leading journalist noted, while the Taliban may be difficult, they are not invariably hostile. Nor are their rules always hard and fast; out of the capital, one can always find some reasonable individuals

E. Girardet

among their ranks. But many Talibs are rural Pashtun fighters from the south, and when they reach Kabul they tend to be more sensitive to foreign influences. Often it is a matter of saving face. If they feel under threat with a photographer flaunting his or her camera, they will react by clamping down. In Kandahar, where the Taliban are very much at home, some photographers have found them to be less strict; but experiences vary widely (see below). It helps to have local contacts, such as respected aid agencies, to break the ice. Many organizations have established their own friendly relations with officials who are ready to help or who realize the importance of some good television footage over the international airwaves. But even then, it doesn't always quite work that way.

In Kandahar, one EFG editor received a photo permit specifically granting him permission to photograph anything but living creatures. But when he tried to photograph a local shrine, Taliban still prevented him from shooting, despite the official document. (SEE BOX below) In another encounter with a British journalist, a Taliban official explained that the notion of creating an idolatrous graven image related only to the face. If one pictured him down to the waist, this would not constitute a "graven image."

One possible rule of thumb is that it is often easier to film in the non-Pashtun areas, such as among Tajiks and Uzbeks in the north, than in the eastern border zones with Pakistan, where Pashtun tribesmen dominate. Another is that the further away one is from Taliban centres of authority, the less obstreperous they are with regard to depicting "graven images." It all depends on your relations with the people you are with. Photographing agricultural projects or clinics in rural areas may prove relatively easy given that many Afghans are proud of what they have achieved. They are all the more delighted to show them off. And if a zealous Islamist appears on the scene, as they inevitably do, wait till he leaves or get someone to distract him. Nevertheless, even in Mazar it is not necessarily that easy. There is still a strong legacy of the Soviet period. The local government requires all journalists to report to the Department of Foreign Affairs on arrival. This is also the only way that a journalist will obtain an exit visa to leave.

Once out of the immediate glare of the Taliban, however, Afghan men and children seem quite happy to have their photographs taken. During one recent tea stop at a *chaikhana* along the road from Kabul to Jalalabad, patrons enthusiastically asked for their photographs to be taken as music (also theoretically banned by the Taliban) blared in the background. As one veteran cameraman, who has filmed in most parts of the country, noted: "You just play it by ear. If they look hostile, then you talk with them and explain what you're doing. Usually they're quite sympathetic. But then the problem is that they all want to be filmed." It also helps to address rural Pashtuns in Pashto rather than Dari. The latter may suggest affiliation with the opposition.

Perhaps one of the biggest frustrations is filming where children are present, such as in refugee camps or villages. Hordes of shouting, squealing youngsters will suddenly appear out of nowhere jostling for position in front of the camera lens. More often than not, it becomes impossible to work. Good luck to anyone trying to hold them back. Usually the best approach is simply to photograph as quickly and as surreptitiously as you can. One camera team filming in Kabul during the fighting in 1994 had armed soldiers keep the children back so that the cameraman could film normal "life under siege" in the bazaar. Unfortunately, when the shopkeepers saw armed men chasing the children, they thought a new attack was in the offing and immediately closed their shops producing instantly abandoned streets.

Women and photography

It is a different situation among Afghan women. It is best to avoid openly photographing women as this may be considered highly offensive and un-Islamic, particularly in the more conservative Pashtun areas. Usually, it is the men who object the most. If you fail to ask their consent and try filming women working in the fields or gliding through the bazaars in their *chadors*, they will immediately berate you and an ugly situation could ensue. Filming women is particularly difficult at close quarters for male cameramen. In 1994 one EFG editor had little problem, as a male journalist, in photographing widows in Kabul and Pakistani refugee camps, once permission had been obtained. Sadly, this reflects their status within Afghan society, particularly under the Taliban.

Over the years, a number of foreign women photographers and filmmakers have managed to produce some excellent footage of Afghan women and their surroundings. To do so, they infiltrated circles of Afghan women and obtained their trust. Female aid

PHOTOGRAPHY IN KANDAHAR

"Photography is impossible in this city", assured the Kandahar field director of Médecins Sans Frontières, and with the roads awash with black-turbaned Taliban I could understand his point. But I was only here once and why should it matter if I just stuck to inanimate objects like mosques and mausoleums? My local Afghan guide recommended that we visit the Department of Foreign Affairs to get a permit. I needed to renew my visa anyway so I agreed to go along. We were ushered into a small office where a delicate young Taliban official sat behind a desk, beside a much older, burlier man. The former dealt with photo permits, the latter with visas. The Taliban wore a shimmering white *shalwar kameez* with gold trimming and an embroidered waistcoat. Beneath a neat little cap peeped a carefully coiffured bob-style haircut, and he was sporting both wispy beard and black eyeliner. He looked more like an *haute couture* fashion model than a fundamentalist fighter. But his indoctrination shone through as he signed and stamped the permit: "Make sure you do not snap any living creatures," he said vacantly. Meanwhile the burly Afghan – obviously an official who had worked in the office long before the Taliban movement was ever heard of – looked on with a mixture of disdain and disbelief. "For your visa renewal," he barked, "we require two passport size photographs." I looked astonished, but couldn't resist a quick smirk in the direction of the *talib*. He grinned back at me the grin of a man on whom logic has only the most tenuous hold. "You may have your photo taken here in Kandahar," added the burly one, "there are plenty of studios in the bazaar." *JW*

workers, too, have succeeded in photographing women while working with them out of the direct glare of Afghan men. It is often easier to film women in 'humanitarian' surroundings such as clinics or food distribution centres, where they become part of the overall story and are not considered principal subjects. Some camera teams have also relied on hidden cameras although usually with the connivance of the Afghan women with whom they are working.

Nevertheless, discretion is crucial and asking permission helps. One CNN crew visiting Kabul in September 1997 barged into a female hospital ward and began filming without permission. This was sheer stupidity and caused an entire delegation of visiting journalists and aid representatives, including the European Union's Commissioner for Humanitarian Affairs, Emma Bonino, to be detained at gunpoint for three hours. A more experienced crew might have got away with it by being somewhat less obtrusive. At the same time, however, even discretion may achieve little or nothing, so it's your call. But remember that heavy-handed behaviour often results in the Afghans accompanying you being more severely treated (and even beaten) than the Westerners. It also makes life for the resident correspondents and aid workers much more difficult after the offending journalists have gone home.

Advice for photographers in Afghanistan:

- Use common sense and discretion when photographing. Try and gauge what the mood is.
- If you can't be discreet (or surreptitious as the case may be), ask the permission of people you would like to photograph. Get them into conversation first and explain what you are doing. Then see if it is alright to take photographs.
- Avoid photographing military installations and potential targets (airports, bridges, government buildings etc.) unless you are accompanied by Afghans who know the area and are aware of what is or is not acceptable. In Pakistan, for example, it is strictly forbidden to photograph anything strategic, be it a hydroelectric dam or an historic Moghul fort. Ancient fortresses may be documented in full detail in the museums, but they still seem to be considered military secrets.
- Don't photograph out of UN or ICRC aircraft without permission. You may be forbidden from flying with them again.
- Learn to shoot from the hip if you can't point your camera directly at what you want. Or pretend to be doing something else.
- Cover your red recording light if filming clandestinely. Many Afghans, particularly in towns, are aware of how video-cams work.
- If you are with a fellow journalist or companion, have one of you do all the talking while the other quietly gets on with filming or taking photographs.
- Carry a polaroid camera to give away instant photographs. This is the best way of breaking down barriers. Even the most hardened, anti-camera Talib may soften if he can see his portrait instantly.

Radio & telecommunications

The United Nations Office for the Coordination of Humanitarian Assistance to Afghanistan (UNOCHA) operates a system of radio communications in all the principal towns of Afghanistan for the benefit of both UN and NGO agencies. A 24-hour listening watch is maintained at UNOCHA radio rooms in Kabul and Islamabad. In Kabul, the Agency Coordinating Body for Afghan Relief (ACBAR) operates a nightly radio check at 2100 hrs to ensure that all NGO staff are safely home before curfew. In areas where there is no local telephone network (most of the country), radio provides not only a lifeline in emergencies but the only means of day-to-day routine communication.

Long-distance communication is usually by High Frequency (HF) radios. The range of these radios is hundreds, sometimes thousands, of kilometres. Typical brands are the CODAN and CTOR systems.

Short-distance communication is usually by Very High Frequency (VHF) radios, typically in the form of hand-held walkie-talkies. Their range is very short unless used with a frequency 'repeater' which extends the range to 40-50 km.

Radios are not like telephones. There are a limited number of channels available which have to be shared between everyone. Hence radio traffic and conversations should be kept to a minimum.

Rules for radio use

- Keep your radio switched on and in the battery charger at night to enable emergency contact.
- Before calling anyone else, listen first to check that the channel is free.
- Most duty stations have a VHF stand-by channel to make initial contact, and another channel to which you switch to continue talking.
- Press the 'call' switch firmly and hold down for half a second before speaking, to ensure that all of your message is transmitted.

- For security reasons, refer to each other by call-sign not by name, and where possible refer to "your location" or "my location" rather than specifying place names.
- Never mention UN or ICRC flight times over the radio.
- Never mention the movement or payment of money over the radio.
- Keep your conversations brief. Radios are not telephones.
- Where possible always travel with some form of radio: VHF walkie-talkie for short distances, or HF radio for longer distances.
- Report all your general movements to your base station.

Radio security

If you are in an emergency, use the phrase "BREAK, BREAK, BREAK, THIS IS…" in order to alert users that you wish to send an urgent message. If you hear this phrase it means that someone is in trouble! Stop your call, listen to the emergency message, and then respond as appropriate.

Radio communication is not secure. Anyone with a radio can listen in, so never mention confidential information while "on air."

Phonetic Alphabet

The phonetic alphabet is an international system used by civil, military, marine, aviation and ground organizations. It is a standard system which allows for clear communications, and should be used on all UN radio nets.

A – ALPHA	**N – NOVEMBER**
B – BRAVO	**O – OSCAR**
C – CHARLIE	**P – PAPA**
D – DELTA	**Q – QUEBEC**
E – ECHO	**R – ROMEO**
F – FOXTROT	**S – SIERRA**
G – GOLF	**T – TANGO**
H – HOTEL	**U – UNIFORM**
I – INDIA	**V – VICTOR**
J – JULIET	**W – WHISKEY**
K – KILO	**X – X-RAY**
L – LIMA	**Y – YANKEE**
M – MIKE	**Z – ZULU**

Radio broadcasters

Both the International Committee of the Red Cross (ICRC) and ACBAR provide a printed daily digest of radio news for general consumption. The stations monitored are *BBC, VOA, Voice of Shariat* and *Radio Iran.*

British Broadcasting Corporation

BBC World Service, Bush House, Strand, London WC2B 4PH, UK
TEL: +44 (171) 240 3456 FAX: +44 (171) 257 8258
E-Mail: worldservice.letters@bbc.co.uk
Website: www.bbc.co.uk/worldservice

English language service. News is broadcast every hour on the half hour in Afghanistan, and half an hour later in Pakistan. BBC World Service short wave frequencies in Khz and local times for Afghanistan are as follows:

0630-0715:	1413 Khz	1430-1830:	1760 Khz
0630-0800:	9410 Khz	1930-2330:	12095 Khz
0730-0830:	1413 Khz	2130-2300:	6090 Khz
0730-1345:	11760 Khz	2200-0030:	9410 Khz
0830-1030:	15575 Khz	2215-2300:	1413 Khz
1030-1930:	15565Khz	2330-0030:	5975 Khz
	(Sat/Sun)	2330-0130:	1413 Khz

Persian and Pashto language services. In addition to daily news summaries, the popular soap opera *New Home, New Life* is broadcast three times a week in Persian on Saturdays, Sundays and Mondays and repeated in Pashto on Tuesdays, Wednesdays and Thursdays. On Fridays is broadcast the omnibus edition of the drama plus Afghan music. (SEE EDUCATION for more information on *New Home, New Life*). Special features on issues such as refugees, deforestation or drugs are also run. Short wave frequencies in Khz and local times for Afghanistan are as follows:

Persian service
0700-0730: 720, 1251, 1413, 6095, 7235, 15380 Khz
1415-1655: (Thu/Fri) 12030, 15585 Khz
1915-2000: 648 (from 1930), 1251, 11885, 15380 Khz
2045-2130: 1413, 6090, 6195, 11960, 15380 Khz
2300-2330: 720 (Sat/Sun), 1413, 5975, 7210, 9510 Khz

Pashto service
0630-0700: 648, 5875, 6095, 7235, 15380 Khz
1245-1415: (Fri) 12030, 15585 Khz
2000-2045: 648, 6195, 11960, 15380 Khz
2015-2045: 1413 Khz
Publication: *BBC On Air* (monthly)
TEL: +44(171)257 2211 FAX: +44(171)240 4899
E-Mail: on.air.magazine@bbc.co.uk

Voice of America (VOA)

300 Independence Ave. SW, Washington DC 20547, USA.
FAX: +1 (202)619 0211 E-Mail: letters@voa.gov

English language service. English language news is broadcast daily by VOA to South Asia on the following Khz frequencies (all times local to Afghanistan – Pakistan is half an hour later):
0530 and 0630: 7115, 7205, 9740, 9850 Khz
1830, 1930, 2030 and 2130: 6110, 7125, 7215, 9575/9645 Khz

Persian and Pashto language services. VOA broadcasts local language news to Central Asia on the following Khz frequencies (all times local to Afghanistan – Pakistan is half an hour later):

Dari (Persian) service
0630-0645: 7265, 9535, 9805 Khz
1945-2030: 7235, 9770, 15435, 17870 Khz

Pashto service
0600-0615: 6025, 9505, 9650 Khz
1900-1945: 9705, 11725, 11760 Khz
Publication: *VOA GUIDE* (monthly)

SUGGESTIONS FOR IMPROVED RECEPTION

Shortwave reception conditions change from day-to-day and sometimes from hour-to-hour, so try all available frequencies to get the best reception. Short wave signals travel thousands of kilometres, and a simple external aerial can help improve reception. This can be a few metres of any wire (insulated or un-insulated) clamped to or coiled round your radio's whip antenna. Extend the wire aerial near to or outside a window. Be careful not to dangle the aerial above or below electric power lines, and disconnect it from your radio during electric storms. You can also improve frequency by holding your transistor at different angles or stepping outside into the open away from any engine or other interference.

Sources: BBC, VOA

Frequency conversion chart

SHORT WAVE		MEDIUM WAVE	
Frequency range		*Frequency range*	
Khz	Metres	Khz	Metres
25670-26100	**11**	**1413**	**212**
21450-21850	**13**	**1323**	**227**
17550-17900	**16**	**1296**	**231**
15100-15600	**19**	**1197**	**251**
13600-13800	**21**	**930**	**323**
11650-12100	**25**	**792**	**379**
9400-9915	**31**	**720**	**417**
7105-7325	**41**	**702**	**427**
5875-6200	**49**	**648**	**463**
		576	**521**

Deutsche Welle radio

50588 Cologne, North Rhein Westphalia (NRW), Germany
TEL: +49 (221) 389 2500 FAX: +49 (221) 389 2510
E-Mail: online@dwelle.de Website: www.dwelle.de/

German language service. German language news is broadcast daily by Deutsche Welle radio to South Asia on the following Khz frequencies (all times local to Afghanistan – Pakistan is half an hour later):

0630-0720: 1548, 6035, 7160, 7285, 7355, 9515, 9615 Khz
2030-2115: 1548, 6170, 7225, 7305, 9585 Khz

Persian and Pashto language services. Local language news is broadcast daily to Central Asia on the following Khz frequencies (all times local to Afghanistan – Pakistan is half an hour later):

Dari (Persian) service
1825-1850: 15525, 17825 Khz

Pashto service
1800-1825: 15525, 17825 Khz

Publication: *DW-plus* (monthly)

Voice of Shariat

This has replaced Radio Kabul and acts as the Taliban propaganda channel. News is broadcast daily at 0700 hrs and 2000 hrs local time.

Telephones

There are no international telephone lines serving Afghanistan, so most agencies use HF radio, radio-telex or satellite phones to communicate out of the country. Commercial satphone services are available in Kabul, Mazar and Kandahar. (SEE REGIONS) Satphone rates vary, but expect to pay from four to 10 dollars per minute. Some satellite links can send faxes and e-mail as well. In the early 1990s satphones were the size of suitcases; now they can come as small as a laptop computer. Most Afghan factional commanders have their own satphone numbers as well. Resident journalists in Afghanistan guard their satphones jealously so if you are a free-lancer do not assume you can make use of their facilities – best bring your own.

Some international satphone manufacturers are as follows:

Global Telephone and Telecommunication (GT&T)
10 rue Lenoir, B-1348 Louvain-La-Neuve, Belgium.
TEL: +32 (10) 457975 FAX: +32 (10) 457979
GT&T produce the Global Microsat which weighs 2.4kg, costs $3,500 and offers a call price of $2.40 per minute anywhere in the world.

Thrane & Thrane
Tobaksvejen 23, DK-2860 Soborg, Denmark.
TEL: +45 (39) 558800 FAX: +45 (39) 558888
Telex: 19298 thranedk
Thrane & Thrane make the Standard C microwave telex system which can send messages to other fax machines without being affected by atmospheric conditions.

NERA
20 Imperial Way, Croydon, Surrey, CR0 4RR, UK.
TEL: +44 (181) 686 5701 FAX: +44 (181) 686 6811
NERA make the Mini-M satphone which costs around £2,500 and weighs 2.5 kg. It can send fax and e-mail messages.

Mobile phones in Pakistan

Many agencies and journalists based in Pakistan are using mobile phones for both domestic and international calls. Two systems are available, one analogue and one digital. All major towns in the country can be reached. The digital service currently offered in Pakistan is GSM (Global System for Mobile Communications). GSM users can make international calls in countries with GSM agreements by using a special 'SIM' card.

Pakistan is in the process of signing up to the GSM network, which in due course will allow users access to "international roaming"

without the need to change their mobile telephone number. However, a new communications venture called Iridium is due to be launched at the end of 1998 in which 77 low-orbiting satellites will provide mobile telephone coverage for all non-GSM areas. If you have the right PCMCIA card, then sending fax and e-mail by mobile phone is also possible.

Mobile telephones can be rented or bought from any of the three companies based in Islamabad, listed below. You will need to provide passport and credit card details in order to get hooked up, and have to produce a letter of reference from your organization or sponsor in Pakistan for the government's benefit. While local calls cost more, international calls by mobile phone are up to three times cheaper than calling from a hotel. Companies in Islamabad offering mobile telephones are:

Mobilink
Pakistan Mobile Communications (Pvt) Ltd., 12th Floor,
UBL Building, Jinnah Avenue, Blue Area, Islamabad.
UAN: +92 (51) 111 300 300 TEL: +92 (51) 273984-89
FAX: +92 (51) 273982-3 Mobile: +92 (300) 597575
E-mail: Farhat@isb.mobilink.infolink.net.pk

Paktel Ltd
Paktel Centre, 68-E Jinnah Avenue, F-7/G-7, Islamabad.
UAN: +92 (51) 111 222 111 TEL: +92 (51) 271100
FAX: +92 (51) 271118 Mobile: +92 (351) 7375 555

Instaphone
Pakcom Ltd., Instaphone Centre, 75 East Blue Area, Fazal-ul-Haq Road, PO Box 1681, Islamabad.
UAN: +92 (51) 111 500 500 TEL: +92 (51) 274175-8
FAX: +92 (51) 273555 Mobile: +92 (351) 264010

E-mail

Many agencies based in Pakistan use e-mail on a routine basis. A number of networks are currently available: BRAINnet serves Peshawar; Comsats has 56.6 bts servers for Karachi, Islamabad and Peshawar; and Compuserve has a Karachi server. For short-term visitors and those without access to e-mail facilities, ACBAR Peshawar office offers an e-mail service: give them your text on a floppy disc and they will send it for one dollar a page. E-mail is available at the Marriott and Holiday Inn hotels in Islamabad, but currently the charges are as high as for sending a fax.

For a fee, ACBAR Kabul office can send your electronic messages out of Afghanistan via HF radio to ACBAR Peshawar and thence by e-mail to international addressees. Local e-mail service providers are:

BRAINnet Digitware Systems
43 Park Road, University Town, Peshawar.
TEL: +92 (91) 844309 FAX: +92 (91) 844310
E-mail: info@psh.brain.net.pk

BRAINnet Islamabad
TEL: +92 (51) 566026 FAX: +92 (51) 524432
E-mail: info@ibrain.brain.net.pk

BRAINnet Quetta
TEL: +92 (81) 836055 E-mail: info@qta.brain.net.pk

Compuserve
Karachi server: TEL: (021) 567 2141

Security tips

Afghanistan is clearly a dangerous country to visit, but, unlike many war zones, it is rare to feel personally threatened. While some visitors may feel uneasy about so-called Muslim fundamentalism and "tribal conflict," the strict Islamic discipline of the Taliban movement has actually improved the security situation in many areas under their control, although at the price of personal liberty. Furthermore the great importance Afghans attach to hospitality and the protection of guests enhances the personal security of travellers and visitors – as long as you are friends with the right side! If you can learn a few words and greetings in Dari and Pashto, and pick up some of the local gestures and ways of behaving, you will feel much more secure around Afghans. (SEE DARI & PASHTO PHRASEBOOK and TRADITIONS & CUSTOMS)

However, Afghanistan is the last country in which to be complacent about personal security. In a war that has lasted nearly two decades, vicious factional fighting – such as that which tore apart Kabul from 1992-1996, and which erupted in Mazar in May and September 1997 – can threaten everyone. Another deadly legacy of the war is the presence in Afghan soil of millions of landmines. These show no respect for faction, nationality or religious denomination. Twice, while on assignment in Afghanistan, EFG editor Edward Girardet travelled with groups where one individual inadvertently left the path only to step on a mine. What may look like an idyllic pastoral scene with gurgling irrigation canals, green pastures, and fruit-laden orchards may in fact be a minefield!

The following security tips are based on the personal experience of EFG editors, interviews with journalists and NGO staff, and advice provided by United Nations security manuals.

Before entering Afghanistan:

- Make sure you receive the correct **inoculations** prior to visiting Afghanistan. Maintain any antimalarial regime, and always carry oral rehydration salts (ORS) in your bag.

- Make up a **survival belt** containing a basic first aid kit, shell dressing, penknife, string, space blanket, poncho, biro, notebook and your personal documents. If you lose everything else, you have at least got this.
- Ensure you are sufficiently **insured** before travelling out to Afghanistan. Check with insurers that the threat of "war and kindred risks" does not invalidate your policy. Make sure you are covered for possible loss of limb or life through landmine damage. (SEE INSURANCE)
- Arrange a **security briefing** with the United Nations Office for the Coordination of Humanitarian Assistance to Afghanistan (UNOCHA) headquarters in Islamabad.
- Attend a **landmine awareness** briefing (through UNOCHA). Become familiar with the different types of mines laid, what potentially mine-laid areas look like, and what to do in a mine-casualty situation.

On arrival in-country

- Stay constantly alert to the threat of landmines. Do not step off main roads onto verges or into fields, either in towns or rural areas. Do not take "short-cuts" when travelling by road.
- Do not walk off the road into the bushes for a leak!
- Never walk alone through unknown city/village streets. Find a local guide or driver.
- Minimise your time spent in bazaars and crowded areas.
- Be aware of the curfew time in each destination you visit.
- Dress and behave in a way sensitive to the local culture and religion (SEE CLOTHING & KIT and TRADITIONS & CUSTOMS).
- Avoid asking indiscreet questions or discussing religion and politics in public.
- Avoid wearing or carrying valuable items in public, e.g. gold chains, cameras etc.
- Always carry a torch (flashlight), personal identification and a minimal amount of money on you at all times.
- If an incident occurs while you are away from your office or residence, radio your headquarters and move immediately to the nearest international agency building. Where possible, inform the UN Area Security Coordinator (ASC) of the situation. (SEE RADIO & TELECOMMUNICATIONS)
- If you are hijacked or robbed, do not resist. Stay calm, act confidently and cooperate (within reason).
- Remain constantly alert to any changes in the situation where you are working.
- Do not take alcohol on any mission at any time.
- Do not promise local people anything you cannot deliver.
- Do not handle or fire weapons of any sort.
- Do not use or carry illicit drugs.
- Do not buy any obviously looted historical items which may be offered to you, unless you intend to hand them over to

REMEMBER:
SECURITY IS A STATE OF MIND

Keep well informed of events and raise your level of security awareness accordingly. Over 50% of security incidents occur during travel and most occur after dark. So prepare and plan your work accordingly.

SPACH (Society for the Preservation of Afghanistan's Cultural Heritage).

- Ensure you travel with your passport and necessary visas on you at all times.
- Be aware of the location of the nearest hospitals and medical posts.
- Always stay well-informed. Accurate information can enhance your safety, as long as you increase your security awareness accordingly.

In Taliban-controlled areas

While you may be safer from the threat of war in Taliban-controlled areas, you are nevertheless more likely – as an Afghan or expatriate – to be harassed if the Religious Police catch you breaking the strict rules they have laid down. Most of the problems which expatriates have got into are of their own making: when European Union Humanitarian Commissioner Emma Bonino and her party were arrested in Kabul in September 1997, the journalists with them had clearly been contravening rules forbidding the filming of Afghan women. When two expatriates working for the French NGO Action Contre la Faim (ACF) were imprisoned for a month in February 1997 and then deported, they had been involved with a private party to which over 50 veiled Afghan women had been invited.

While virtually no aid agency personnel would condone the rigid policies of the Taliban in cities such as Kabul, Kandahar and Herat, they nevertheless respect the existence of rules within which they must discreetly work. Short-term visitors who come in with a provocative or complacent attitude succeed only in getting themselves into trouble, endangering the lives of any Afghans who may be with them, and souring the atmosphere for those who are working in the area long-term. Here are some security tips for those visiting or working in Taliban-controlled areas:

- Be very careful about what you say in front of people you do not know, especially 'official' interpreters and drivers. There are informers everywhere, so remember: "careless talk costs lives!"

- Do not bring 'official' interpreters into private houses or offices if at all possible.
- Avoid visiting Afghans at their homes, even if you are invited. There are cases of Afghans being beaten by the Religious Police after such visits. It is, however, normally acceptable to attend Afghan weddings and funerals.
- Avoid asking large numbers of Afghans to visit your house. Keep visits low-key, and ask guests to arrive and leave at different times so as not to attract attention.
- Be very careful where you speak to Afghan women, and take the advice of experienced agency workers.
- Be discreet. Do not openly photograph Afghans in public. Even if you get away with it, they may get beaten or disciplined if caught. (SEE PHOTOGRAPHY)
- Be careful to conceal any cassettes and photos you may have.
- It is best to stay in single-sex accommodation.
- If you are watching television or listening to music, close the windows and keep the curtains shut.
- Do not climb onto roofs or you may be accused of spying on people next door.
- Make sure your living quarters are not visible from neighbouring rooftops.

Road travel

One of the most routine events while travelling by road is to be stopped at checkpoints. It is important here to defuse any tension in the situation as soon as possible. Do not be arrogant or insistent about your "rights of passage," and do not force the guard to lose face. Listen before speaking. Try to find common ground. Bring in some humour – practise your Dari or Pashto. Although you should generally stay inside your vehicle, smile and, if you have to get out, shake hands or touch the guard gently on the shoulder – Afghan men are very tactile, especially in Kandahar!

When travelling by car there are some basic rules to remember:

- Never drive off-road onto verges or along short-cuts – they may be mined.
- Never drive alone. Use a local driver.
- When travelling by road, take two vehicles, especially at night.
- Take an HF or VHF radio to inform your headquarters of your departure, proposed route and arrival.
- Avoid poking your camera out of the window.
- Keep cameras, cassettes and other valuable items hidden from view at checkpoints.
- Keep the windows wound up and the doors locked, especially after dark.
- Never jump a checkpoint: slow down, turn on the cabin lights (if you are travelling at night), chat to the guard, and always be patient and cooperative if searched.

- Never raise your voice or get into an argument at a checkpoint.
- Let your Afghan colleagues or driver talk with checkpoint guards first.
- Do not get out of your vehicle at checkpoints and keep the doors locked.
- Never stay out after curfew (2100 hrs or 2200 hrs depending on the situation – check).
- Avoid driving after dark in rural areas.
- Log in any long journeys with the local UN/ACBAR office.
- Vary your routes to and from the office/residence as much as possible.
- Do not leave vehicles unattended.
- Keep your fuel tanks full at all times.
- Carry basic spare parts, tools, tyres, torches, fire extinguishers, water and first-aid kit in your vehicle at all times.
- Reverse your vehicle into your compound at night in case you need to make a quick exit.
- Take advice on where you may need armed escorts or unarmed guides.
- If you are being hijacked, try to radio your base station without the hijackers noticing.
- Do not attempt to rescue vehicles or goods from bandits.
- If driving from Peshawar to the Afghan border at Torkham remember to get a tribal agencies permit. On the return journey pick up an armed escort at the Pakistani border post.
- Be careful of what you say in front of any Afghan drivers or passengers.

Walking and cycling

Some experienced aid workers like to get around by bicycle or on foot. If you have the time this can be extremely rewarding, although it helps if you speak the local language. Always bear in mind the threat of mines and adhere to the following basic rules:

- Never walk or cycle "off the beaten track."
- Check with the local Afghans, and if they avoid somewhere then so should you.
- Travel in pairs and/or take a local guide.
- If as a women you are "touched-up", or worse still beaten, in the bazaar or on the street, then make a scene by shouting or screaming. Often the offending persons will take fright if other passers-by start noticing.

Emergencies

There have been a number of emergencies involving international aid agency personnel, most notoriously the evacuations from Mazar-e-Sharif during the fighting in May and September 1997. In the May situation, a BBC team of journalists and cameramen came under heavy criticism from the UN for keeping an evacuation convoy

The Frontier Post 22 April 1992

waiting while they were out getting last-minute footage for their report. The UN in turn was criticised for assembling such a large and obvious convoy of expensive white vehicles and international staff together in a public place, while armed factions were on the loose. In the September evacuation, many NGO personnel decided to entrust themselves to the International Committee of the Red Cross (ICRC) instead of the UN. Some journalists argue that the best course of action in an emergency is to seek out the local Afghan commander who – if he takes you in as his guest – will offer you protection as a matter of honour. The point is that whatever course of action you decide on, you should make your decision early and stick by it. The UN and ICRC have different phases of emergency, involving increasingly drastic action such as the evacuation of all non-essential personnel. If you want UN or ICRC protection then you must inform them in good time and play by their rules. Do not expect to be able to jump on the evacuation bandwagon at the last minute.

Some basic rules for emergency situations are as follows:

- In a potential emergency, check your information is accurate and do not overreact.
- Consult with both the ICRC Delegate and UN Regional Representative for evacuation plans in an emergency. Once you have committed yourself to the care of the UN or ICRC, obey orders.
- The UN has protective bunkers at Kabul, Herat, Jalalabad and Kandahar, designed to provide protection against rockets and artillery shelling. Non-UN personnel may use them in time of emergency, subject to space. Contact the local UN Area Security Coordinator for details.

- If your location is being shelled or rocketed and you cannot reach a UN bunker, take shelter under the staircase or in the basement of your house, and stay away from windows.
- If in an active war zone, sleep with your boots on and keep a small emergency pack by your side at all times with extra clothes, a space blanket, some rations, a first aid kit, and if possible, a shortwave transistor radio. You need to be able to leave on the spur of the moment.
- Do not go outside while there is shooting – what goes up must come down. Many people have been injured or killed by stray bullets and flying shrapnel.
- In a medical emergency, go straight to the nearest ICRC, medical NGO or UN office. There are ICRC-supported hospitals with surgical units in Kabul (Karte Seh and Wazir Akbar Khan hospitals), Jalalabad, Ghazni and Kandahar (Mirwais hospital). The ICRC treats all medical emergency cases regardless of nationality.
- Remember: there are no armed UN personnel or peacekeepers in Afghanistan to protect you.

Loss of personal possessions

- If moving to Afghanistan to live, ensure that you provide your main office with a detailed inventory of personal possessions to facilitate reimbursement in case of loss or destruction.
- If you are robbed of your passport or any possessions, report the incident immediately to UNOCHA or ACBAR.

Kidnapping

Kidnapping has been widespread throughout many areas of Afghanistan over the past few years, although these incidents have rarely involved international staff. To minimise the threat of kidnapping:

- Make sure that your presence in-country is known by the regional UNOCHA office, ACBAR, an NGO office or media organization, so that if you go missing someone will notice.
- Keep a low profile, especially after normal working hours.
- When entering and leaving your house and office, keep an eye out for suspicious vehicles or individuals. Potential kidnappers will often watch a house for several days to check up on your movements. If in doubt, stay at home or drive past the house, and report anything suspicious to the UNOCHA office.
- Alternate your routes between home and office when possible.
- Watch out for any vehicles which may be following you. If you think you are being followed drive to the nearest UN/NGO office, checkpost or village (if on mission). Do not let the other vehicle overtake you.
- Avoid driving or walking alone. Lone people are the easiest targets. Travel in pairs or take a guide, and always carry a hand-held radio with you.

- Take advice on what sort of dress is appropriate for the location. Do not try to disguise yourself as an Afghan, but try not to be too distinctive either.
- When answering the door or gate to your house, check who the caller is *before you open the door.* Look from an upstairs room if no windows are near the door/gate.
- If in the worst case kidnappers try to abduct you at gunpoint, do not resist – they may shoot you!

Suggestions if you are abducted:

- Cooperate with your captors (to the minimum extent), but do not volunteer money, information or other assistance.
- Avoid staring directly at your captors, but try to get a good mental picture of their faces and other physical attributes.
- Do not try to escape unless you are certain of success. If recaptured, your situation will be much worse.
- Observe your kidnap location and routes to it, if possible.
- Talk to your captors, if appropriate. Human contact sometimes reduces the risk of violence, but do not be too friendly or submissive as this may only provoke them.
- Try to appear strong and impassive, even if you are feeling terrified. Do not display your emotions or react to your captors' provocations.
- Eat and drink as much as possible, even if stress takes away your appetite. You need to maintain strength in these situations.
- Stay mentally alert by getting as much sleep as permitted, and use "mental exercises" to take your mind off the immediate situation.

Remember: *Kidnappers are often ruthless and desperate people, but they have usually planned the abduction well. In the majority of cases they will try for 'soft' or easy targets first. Your personal awareness and habits can reduce the likelihood of your being considered a 'soft' target for kidnapping.*

Landmine awareness

This section is adapted from advice contained in the UN Summary of Security Procedures in Afghanistan (SSP) 1997

Afghanistan is one of the most heavily mined countries in the world. Millions of landmines and unexploded ammunition lie concealed in fields, road verges, water canals and the rubble of ruined buildings. The best personal defence against this threat is to be able to recognise which areas are likely to be mined, and to avoid taking unnecessary risks.

WARNING!

Mines are laid to be invisible...

Types of exploding devices

Landmines come in two types: anti-personnel and anti-tank mines. Anti-personnel mines are designed to maim rather than to kill. Typical injuries are the loss of one or more limbs either below or above the knee/elbow. Anti-tank mines are designed to destroy a fully-armoured battle tank and are therefore enormously dangerous: there are numerous stories of trucks and minibuses which have been blown up by these mines while driving 'off-road,' with all occupants on board being killed. In 1997 UN mine clearance workers found an anti-tank mine buried just one metre from the edge of the tarmac main road leading from Kandahar airport to the city.

Unexploded Ordnance (UXOs) are any explosive devices which have not detonated, such as rockets, grenades, bombs and booby-traps. UXOs are found all over Afghanistan in rural and urban areas and can be even more dangerous than mines.

Mines and UXOs come in all shapes and sizes, some are metal and some are plastic, some lie buried while others sit on the surface. Previously, mine awareness briefings concentrated on what these weapons looked like and what their technical specifications were. But since mines are designed and laid not to be seen, this approach is impractical – far better identify areas where mines are likely to be laid and avoid them.

Mines and UXOs can be found almost anywhere. UNCHS (Habitat) has produced a map of the mined areas of Kabul, and the UNOCHA Mine Action Programme constantly updates its maps of mined and cleared areas.

Mines are normally used to defend a specific area, deny access to a position, or are randomly placed as a deadly form of harassment. UXOs can land anywhere – even in your back yard! Steer clear of the following areas:

- Unused footpaths, tracks and short-cuts.
- Verges of vehicle tracks and roads.
- Vehicle turnaround points.
- In and around culverts and bridge abutments.
- Alongside walls, especially those of damaged buildings.
- In the doorways and room corners of deserted houses.
- In and around wells and water access points.
- In irrigation and drainage canals.
- Around abandoned military posts and destroyed vehicles.
- In low-lying or hidden areas of cover where an enemy could hide from view.

Telltale signs

The UNOCHA Mine Action Programme paints rocks with RED paint to signify dangerous areas and known minefields. After an area is cleared the rocks are repainted WHITE. In unmarked areas you can look for these 'telltale' signs:

- Skeletons and dead animals (e.g. donkeys, cows, goats or dogs).
- Small, round but regularly spaced potholes (mine detonation points).
- Uncultivated ground in otherwise cultivated areas.
- Ammunition cases or containers (fighting and mines go together).
- Tin cans (food cans from soldiers or tin from bounding mines).
- Deserted buildings in a populated area.
- Pieces of wire and small wooden stakes (POMZ mines).
- 'Bypasses' lying on the ground (they can look like pens).
- Small piles of rocks, crossed sticks, or rocks across a track, may be used to indicate that mines or UXOs are nearby.

DOs and DON'Ts

- DO NOT touch or move interesting or unknown objects.
- DO NOT pull or cut unknown wires.
- DO NOT leave well-worn paths or tracks – even for calls of nature!
- DO NOT throw rocks at unknown devices.
- DO NOT think it is safe to jump from rock to rock in mined areas.
- DO NOT let drivers leave the main road or track for overtaking.
- DO NOT rush to an accident victim unless the track to them is cleared of mines.
- DO NOT walk or drive in unknown areas without a local guide.
- DO seek information on local mine problems before starting work in an area.
- DO ask local people about mine problems and take a local guide when you travel.
- DO retrace your steps out of suspect areas whenever possible.
- DO send drivers and new staff on a mine awareness course.
- DO mark, photograph (from a distance) and report suspicious devices.
- DO always stay alert to the telltale signs for mines and UXOs.
- DO trust your own judgement and don't follow others blindly.

What do you do if you see a mine or UXO?

- STOP, STAY CALM, THINK!
- Shout a warning to anyone with you.
- Turn around and retrace your steps slowly and *exactly.*
- Once on safe ground, mark the danger area with a line of rocks.
- Report it to the nearest UNOCHA representative or demining NGO office immediately.

ESSENTIAL READING

UN Summary of Security Procedures in Afghanistan (SSP) 1997 27pp, available from Field Security Officer, UNOCHA, Islamabad

Security Awareness – an aide memoire, UNHCR (Geneva, 1995)

Security Guidelines for Women, UN Security Coordination Office (New York, 1995)

The SAS Survival Handbook, John Wiseman, Harvill Publishers (London, 1986; reprinted 1994)

Traditions & customs

Success in your work and travels in Afghanistan will depend to a large extent on how well you get on with Afghans, to what extent you respect their traditions and customs, and how well you adapt your way of behaving to be in tune with your environment. From dealing with bored guards at roadblocks to stubborn government officials to tribal elders or women's groups, your understanding of the different aspects of the Afghan character will be critically important, and possibly life-saving. (SEE SECURITY TIPS) It is crucial to remember that drinking tea is not just a means of quenching one's thirst, but also a sign of respect, hospitality and, in some cases, political astuteness. Even if you are not thirsty, or cannot bear the thought of yet another cup of tea, it may be best not to refuse too often.

Nancy Dupree summarises the importance to Afghans of correct behaviour as follows:

> *"By disregarding social niceties, a person brings discredit upon himself and thereby diminishes the reputation of both his immediate family as well as his extended family or group. Conversely, individuals gain respect, maintain status and enhance their standing in the community through polite behaviour. Much of etiquette, therefore, is designed to preserve* zat, *honour. As a consequence, Afghan society places much emphasis on correct behaviour."*

Traditionally the elder women of the Afghan household are responsible for teaching etiquette, while the male elders ensure its enforcement. However increased migration into urban areas in the 1960s, coupled with the concurrent rise of Communism in the 1960s and 1970s undermined traditional social values. Nevertheless, the disrespect which young Afghan intellectuals – fired with Marxist zeal – showed towards village elders and their wives and daughters during the attempted land and education reforms of 1978 led to widespread revolt across the entire country. Much of Afghanistan's history in the 20th Century has been characterized by this conflict between the more westernized intellectuals of the urban centres and the more traditional rural inhabitants. King Amanullah was forced out of office because his reforms of the 1920s – including abolishing the veil for women – were considered too radical. The backlash against 'modernizing' Afghan communists in 1978-1979 led to the invasion of the country by the Soviet Union.

Even the Taliban movement can be seen as a traditionalist response to the perceived moral corruption and lawlessness of western-backed mujahed factions. The conservative customs of rural Afghanistan should not be underestimated. On the vexed issue of girls' education, for example, in many agricultural communities – long before the Taliban was ever heard of – girls were never permitted to go to school by their parents. It simply was not the tradition. One of the most contentious questions facing Western assistance efforts is the extent to which these traditions should be respected, especially when they come into conflict with principles passionately-held by the so-called "developed world." The BBC soap opera *New Home, New Life* has pioneered programmes aimed at gently changing social attitudes and traditions, such as the time-honoured Afghan treatment for the wound left after cutting a child's umbilical cord: rubbing in cow-dung. But how decide where to draw the line between traditions and bad habits?

Day-to-day manners

In terms of manners, Westerners often appear crude and unpolished compared to Afghans. The Western way of business is brisk, no-nonsense, and 'up-front.' But for Afghans it is extremely rude to launch straight into business without proper greetings and a good banter over a glass or two of tea. The advantage of the Afghan way is its civility and relaxing effect; the disadvantage is that meetings can drag on for hours and hours without reaching a definite conclusion. Efforts to shortcut traditional greetings with a quick 'hello' will be considered rude or indifferent. Most Westerners find a balance, but just remember to observe how your hosts and colleagues behave before launching in yourself.

"It is a matter of gauging the situation and not offending your hosts," noted one veteran journalist. "Newcomers who are in a hurry often don't understand this. For Afghans, hospitality is part of their dignity. Even if they are very poor and have almost nothing to offer, it allows them to retain their own self-respect." At the same time, however, one must know when to decline. If someone in the bazaar or in a *chaikhana* offers you their food, gratefully decline, several times if necessary. They are simply being polite. If they still insist on sharing their meal, then sit down and eat a little with them lest they become offended. (Be careful, however, not to take the choice bits of the food.) Don't forget, they also wish to know who you are and it is their country. When you feel that you have done your bit for decorum, then place your right hand against your heart to indicate that you have had your fill and thank them.

On one occasion early during the Soviet war, an EFG editor had to indulge in at least half a dozen lunches in the Baluch region of the Chagai Hills in Helmand province as each village or camp on the way back to Pakistan was waiting with a specially prepared meal for a group of journalists who were passing through the area that morning. The situation nearly erupted into a *crise d'état*, when two reporters in the group – anxious to get back to Quetta to file their stories – refused to stop. Only when it was made clear to them that insult might very quickly develop into injury did they agree to ceremoniously accept a few bites from each meal. Overall, the best advice is to play it by ear and to be sensitive to your hosts.

As regards Afghan women, it is best for Western men not to acknowledge them in the street or in rural areas, particularly those under Taliban control. This is for the women's own protection. In the words (verbatim) of one local EFG source: "Do not look repeatedly to a girl or a women even if she is old. Be careful no to twinkle and avoid using other kinds of signs." In private, however, it is acceptable for Western men to acknowledge Afghan women with a smile, and if they are 'educated' or you know them, then you can shake hands and talk with them where appropriate. In general, Western women enjoy better access to Afghan women than do Western men.

Here are some basic rules:

First meeting:

- Stand up when any Afghan – and especially an elder – enters the room.
- Exchange greetings whenever meeting friends or strangers. For men this involves crossing your heart with your right hand, shaking hands and sometimes even a 'bear-hug', if you are good friends. Afghans go through this whole procedure many times a day, often with the same people.
- Never interrupt Afghans while they are praying or deep in conversation.
- The most common verbal greeting is *A-salaam a-laykum* ("Peace be upon you"), to which the reply is *w-laykum o a-salaam* ("And upon you be peace"). (SEE DARI & PASHTO PHRASEBOOK)
- It is best to show respect for elders and superiors by referring to them by their title rather than first name. The word for 'father' is *baba*, 'mother' is *madar*, and someone who has been on pilgrimage to Mecca is *haji*.
- Before embarking on any business talk, you should ask after your host's/visitor's health, life, family etc. However, men should not inquire about Afghans' wives or daughters unless you are very close friends.

E. Girardet

- Western men should not look at, point at or shake hands with Afghan women in the streets or in rural areas.
- As a Western woman it is best not to offer your hand to an Afghan man to shake. Wait for him to offer you his hand first.
- Men and women, even married couples, should not touch each other in public.
- Never use the left hand for passing or touching anything or anyone.

As a guest in an Afghan home or at a meal:

Afghans across the country are renowned for their generous hospitality, and Pashtuns in particular regard the comfort and security of their guests as a matter of great honour. Even unexpected guests must be welcomed, regardless of how inconvenient their arrival may be. As a journalist covering the Soviet war, EFG editor Edward Girardet was almost always offered the most congenial hospitality in numerous villages and refugee camps. Only on two or three occasions did villagers refuse to offer tea or provide a place in the mosque or a house to sleep. When this happened, they tended to be Afghans associated with Arab or other foreign Islamic groups. Afghans travelling with Girardet sought to explain this embarrassment by saying that such people did not understand what Islam and Afghan traditions were about.

On greeting a guest to his house or tent, the host will usually offer tea and then wait for the visitor to explain why he is there. Guests are never turned away, nor asked how long they may be staying. Some basic rules to observe in this situation are as follows:

- Do not visit someone's house without getting prior permission from the head of the household.

- Afghans will often ask you to share a meal with them when they cannot afford it, so let them ask you several times to make sure they really mean it.
- A gift for your hosts, such as a small bag of sweets, is appropriate.
- Never enter a room or home without knocking or coughing to announce your presence. On entering, greet everyone with "*A-salaam a-laykum*" or "*salaam alek*," even if you have only been absent from the room for a few moments.
- Remove your shoes before entering the guest room. (A good tip is to wear a pair of shoes you can slip on and off easily – laced-up boots are bad news! Or keep a pair of sandals in your pack).
- Never walk on prayer mats.
- Men and women are often entertained separately. It is best to go along with this custom unless you are confident of behaving otherwise.
- If you are guest of honour you will be seated at the top of the room (although still on the floor) away from the entrance. Seating is usually by precedence, with those of lowest status seated nearest the door.
- Sit cross-legged – never stretch your legs out towards others or stick your feet up on tables or desks.
- Only serve, touch and eat food with the right hand.
- Afghans take pride in offering large amounts of food to their guests. Take less than you can eat at first so that you have room for the second and third helpings which will be offered to you.
- Eat slowly; when you as a guest finish eating then your hosts will too.
- Do not shout, laugh too loudly or sing during meal times.
- Do not interrupt others in conversation.
- Never blow your nose in public – if you have to, go outside or into a bathroom.
- Always ask before lighting up a cigarette

.

For more information on beggars and baksheesh SEE MONEY; for more on dress SEE CLOTHING & KIT.

Travel

In the days of the "Great Game" – that vast strategic game of chess played across Central Asia between the foreign ministries of Britain and Russia throughout the 19th and early 20th Centuries – you would travel to Afghanistan in disguise. Slipping away from your regiment or colonial office on the pretext of "shooting leave," you would head for the frontier clad in the garb of a Muslim holy man or Baluch carpet dealer, with nothing but your wits and a few gold sovereigns between you and an anonymous death in a dark dungeon or dank defile.

Today, travelling into Afghanistan is more prosaic and less risky than a hundred years ago or during the Soviet war. But it is not without its share of danger. Crossborder infiltration is still possible, although there is not much point now that you can fly or drive into most of Afghanistan's major towns without much risk.

Both the United Nations Office for the Coordination of Humanitarian Assistance to Afghanistan (UNOCHA) and the International Committee of the Red Cross (ICRC) operate flights into Afghanistan from Pakistan. The International Assistance Mission (IAM) is considering offering an aviation service at a reduced charge for NGOs in the near future. Ariana Afghan Airlines offers both domestic and international services, and in the north of Afghanistan, Balkh Air has been resurrected. Fighting regularly affects scheduled services, with both Mazar and Kabul airports closed for extended periods during 1997. While UN and ICRC planes are not normally targeted by Afghan factions, there have been isolated incidents – in particular in Bamiyan – when bomb-attacks have nearly hit UN aircraft on the ground. Flight operations staff are constantly having to negotiate with different factions to allow their planes into hostile airspace without being subjected to anti-aircraft fire.

Road travel inside Afghanistan is safer in Taliban-controlled regions than it has been for two decades. While Taliban checkpoints still operate in these areas, there is not the profusion of different factional roadblocks and the threat of looting or hijacking which there was in the early 1990s. Since September 1996 when the Taliban took Jalalabad and Kabul, the drive from Peshawar to Kabul has been safe and straightforward. (There used to be over 60 checkpoints along this road, operated by different local commanders each exacting their local 'tax'). The main road from Turkmenistan via Herat and Kandahar to Quetta and Pakistan is the other main overland artery, both for smuggling and legitimate trading. The road route from Uzbekistan to Mazar and northern Afghanistan, via the "friendship bridge" across the Amu Darya (Oxus River) south of Termez, has been blocked since May 1997 when the Central Asian Republics took fright at the Taliban advance north.

For more details on road and air travel to specific regions within Afghanistan, SEE REGIONS.

Internal flights

The United Nations Office for the Coordination of Humanitarian Assistance to Afghanistan (UNOCHA). UNOCHA operates one Beach King Air 200 aircraft which seats 10 persons, and one Beach King 1900C which seats 19 persons, flying regularly between Islamabad and all major Afghan cities.

Both UN and NGO staff are charged for the flights, but journalists can travel free of charge if there is enough space, and if approved by their respective embassies. (SEE JOURNALISTS) Ambassadors and Pakistanis also travel free.

Flight schedules

A monthly flight schedule is issued during the last week of each month for the following month. Copies are available from all UN agencies or at the UNOCHA Flight Operations Office in Islamabad. The provisional flight schedule is as follows, leaving Islamabad and returning the same day:

Destination	Day	Price o/w US$		
		UN	NGO	Charter
Kabul*	Sun, Tue, Thu	300	190	3,000
Herat	Sun, Mon, Wed	630	390	6,300
Jalalabad	Sun, Thu			
Kandahar	Sun, Wed	640	400	6,400
Mazar-e-Sharif	Mon, Tue, Thu	480	300	4,800
Faizabad	Tue (on demand)			
Khost/Gardez	Mon, Thu (on demand)			
Farah	Sun (on demand)			
Bamiyan/Yakawlang	Mon (on demand)			

**When Kabul airport is closed due to fighting, the service is diverted to Gardez, which is two hours' drive south of the capital.*

UN flights do not normally operate on Fridays and Saturdays. Special charter flights can be arranged to different destinations in Afghanistan, CIS countries, Meshad, and Tehran. Charter costs are around 10 times the single fare charge.

STOP PRESS! UN AIRFARES INTO AFGHANISTAN ARE REDUCED BY 50% FOR THE WHOLE OF 1998, THANKS TO A UK GOVERNMENT CONTRIBUTION TO UNOCHA FLIGHT OPERATIONS.

Booking and travelling

Bookings must be made (preferably by agencies not individuals) with the Flight Operations Office at the point of departure at least 48 hours before the flight.

The booking request forms are:

Pink:	For UN International Staff
Green:	For Afghan National Staff of UN Agencies
White:	For Non-UN personnel sponsored by UN agencies or NGOs
Red:	For chartering an aircraft

- When booking, agencies must certify that the passenger has a valid passport and visa for the destination and departure points.
- Return bookings should be made by agency staff in the city from which the return flight originates, and must be reconfirmed by the passenger immediately on arrival there.
- Bookings made by NGOs are provisional up to 24 hours before the flight. NGO passengers whose seats are confirmed 24 hours before the flight take precedence over UN passengers who book less than 24 hours before the flight.
- Agencies whose passengers fail to check in for departure without cancelling will be charged 50% of the fare.
- Requests for charters should be made as early as possible, so that the flight can be listed in the monthly schedule. This enables other agencies to take advantage of space available, thereby reducing the cost to the agency requesting the charter.
- Check-in time for flights out of Islamabad is two hours prior to departure at the UNOCHA Flight Operations Office. Check-in for flights out of Afghanistan is through the Regional UNOCHA office, from which transport to the airport will be provided. Personal baggage entitlement is strictly 20 kgs, and cargo must be booked in at least 48 hours before departure. Agency mail and pouches up to five kgs may be booked in until 1500 hrs on the day before the flight.

Contact: **Manager Aircraft Operations**
UNOCHA, Street 55, F-10/4, Islamabad
TEL: +92 (51) 211451-5 FAX: +92 (51) 211450
Telex: 54553 UNOCA PK

The International Committee of the Red Cross (ICRC). The ICRC currently operates two light passenger aircraft out of Peshawar to the major cities in Afghanistan. The advantage of ICRC flights is that they are free for NGO workers; the disadvantage is that ICRC delegates can bump you off the flight at a moment's notice. ICRC does not normally fly journalists into Afghanistan, but you may be able to make special arrangements via their offices in Kabul or Peshawar.

Flight schedules

Kabul	Saturday, Sunday, Monday, Tuesday, Wednesday, Thursday
Herat	Saturday, Tuesday
Kandahar	Sunday, Wednesday
Mazar-e-Sharif	Saturday, Tuesday, Thursday
Jalalabad	Two to three times per week on demand

ICRC does not usually operate flights on a Friday. There are flights to Bamiyan and Faizabad on demand, but bookings cannot be guaranteed. Contact ICRC Air Operations in Peshawar for more details.

Booking and travelling

- All requests for outward and return journeys should be submitted in writing on an ICRC Travel Request Form, bearing the official stamp of your organization, by 1200 hrs on the Tuesday prior to the week of departure (Saturday being the first day of the week).
- In Peshawar requests may be submitted by mail or by fax; in Afghanistan requests must be submitted to the ICRC delegation in Kabul.
- Passengers must call the relevant ICRC delegation the day before the flight between 1400 hrs-1700 hrs to confirm their booking and check-in time. Check-in will be at the relevant ICRC delegation from which transport to the airport will be provided. Personal baggage allowance is strictly 20 kgs.
- Cancellations can be made by phone but written confirmation is also required, and no later than 1200 hrs on the day before the flight. Any passengers failing to cancel or to show up will not be granted reservations in the future.
- All passengers must be in possession of a passport valid for six months and valid visas for Afghanistan and Pakistan, including any necessary exit visas for leaving Afghanistan, without which you will not be permitted to board the plane.
- Currently it is prohibited to import or export through Afghanistan any video or audio tapes, CDs, fashion magazines, alcohol or pictures of living creatures. Export of electronic devices out of Pakistan requires an export permit.
- It is forbidden to take pictures at any airports in Afghanistan or Pakistan, or from any ICRC aircraft.

"ONE LUMP OR TWO?"

As I peered through the window, eight US-made Pakistani F-16 fighter aircraft landed, refuelled and took off again, their wings weighed heavy with weapons of war. Once the last of the jets had vanished in a haze of airfuel, our slim white aircraft, emblazoned with the protective red crosses of the ICRC, taxied to the end of the runway. We were flying into Kabul from Peshawar Airport – the Pakistan Air Force's closest airfield to the frontline.

It was my first time into Afghanistan. I was expecting to rough it – tossed in the back of a Hercules military transport plane perhaps, surrounded by sacks of food-aid or boxes of medicine. I had some US Army boots on, khaki trousers and a rather mangey beard (which an old Afghan hand had advised me to grow). But on boarding the plane I found all the male passengers were clean-shaven, sporting neatly-pressed chinos and shiny loafers. The women wore elegant long summer dresses and shawls. Inside , the aircraft was cleaner than a dentist's waiting room. The deep-upholstered seats even had white "anti-macassars" folded over the headrests (originally introduced by 19th Century English hostesses to protect their antique furniture from the exotic gentlemen's hair oil which it was fashionable to import from the Celebes at that time). And we were flying into a war-zone?

As we waited for clearance from air-traffic control, the pilot gave us a security briefing. Here we go, I thought, heart racing: Action in the event of mid-air interception? Tactics to avoid anti-aircraft fire? A calm, clipped South African accent crackled over the intercom. "Good morning ladies and gentlemen, this is your captain speaking. Our flight time to Kabul will be approximately one hour. Coffee is in the flasks at the front of the cabin, but take care to use two cups – it's very hot." Was this the hottest it got?

Flying over the mountains flanking the Khyber Pass, ridge after ridge of rock thrust skywards like shark's teeth. To the north lay the snowcapped mountains of the Hindu Kush. Westwards the land became drier and more parched, with only the thin emerald ribbon of the Kabul river for relief. As we dipped and landed, the airport was littered with wrecked Soviet aircraft and pockmarked with the potholes of past rocket attacks. Despite the smashed windows and scarred walls of the terminal building, there was an Afghan official checking everyone's visas. As we waited in the queue, one of the passengers whispered to me: "You'd better shave that goatee off. It makes you look like a Tajik – they're the enemy around here!" *JW*

- Journalists are not currently permitted to travel on ICRC aircraft, unless they are specifically covering ICRC stories. Call the ICRC delegation in Peshawar or Kabul for more details. (SEE JOURNALISTS)
- Cargo (20-100 kgs) may be carried in exceptional circumstances. Call for details.

Contact: **ICRC Air Operations**
Charrahi Haji Yaqub, Shahr-e-Naw, Kabul
TEL: Kabul 35247
40 Jamalud-Din Afghani Road, University Town, PO Box 418, Peshawar.
TEL: +92 (91) 43723, 41371, 41673 FAX: +92 (91) 840413
Telex: 52328 ICRC P PK

Ariana Afghan Airlines

Ariana Afghan Airlines, the national carrier, still operates three Boeing 727s based in Delhi which fly both international and domestic services via Kabul. Passenger flights between Kabul and Amritsar operate on Fridays, and between Kabul, Dubai and Jeddah on Saturdays. Domestic services are scheduled between Kabul and Jalalabad on Sundays and between Kabul and Kandahar on Fridays and Saturdays. One-way tickets for Jalalabad cost $20 for expatriates and 150,000 *Afghanis* for locals; and for Kandahar the price is $63 for expatriates and 500,000 *Afghanis* for locals. Ariana also claims to operate a daily cargo service between Dubai, Kabul, Kandahar and Jalalabad. For more details contact Ariana's main office in Kabul, located in front of Zarnegar Park (TEL: Kabul 22372).

Balkh Air

In 1996, a controversial British businessman-*cum*-arms-dealer was reported to have supplied a second-hand 80-seater BAC 1-11 aircraft to the anti-Taliban General Abdul Rashid Dostum. Dostum's airline, Balkh Air, operates out of the northern city of Mazar-e-Sharif and claims to carry passengers between Afghanistan, Pakistan, Iran and Moscow. The plane had been destined for the knacker's yard, and British authorities had only given permission for it to fly one-way to Ostend to be scrapped. It was considered so dangerous the authorities stipulated that the plane be flown at low altitude with its landing-gear down. However, far from scrapping it, the unscrupulous Brit repaired it and flew it to Afghanistan…happy flying!

International air connections

There are numerous services into the region, principally via Dubai and Pakistan. One of the most popular routings for Peshawar-based personnel is to fly from Europe/North America to Dubai and connect direct to Peshawar, using Pakistan International Airlines (PIA). PIA flights from Dubai to Peshawar leave at 0100 hrs on

Mondays, Tuesdays and Fridays, arriving at 0450 hrs. PIA operates flights to Islamabad from 60 cities around the world, including most European and North American capitals, but not from Australasia. PIA has two flights a week to Islamabad from New York, one via Frankfurt, one via Amsterdam. Both PIA and British Airways (BA) fly twice a week to Islamabad from London. Emirates flies from Dubai to Islamabad on Wednesdays, Fridays and Sundays. Check airlines for other connections to Pakistan via Moscow, Delhi, and elsewhere.

Regional air connections

The **PIA** regional service between Pakistan and Central Asia is as follows:

Monday	Karachi-Peshawar-Tashkent
Tuesday	Karachi-Lahore-Tashkent-Almaty
Saturday	Karachi-Islamabad-Almaty-Tashkent
	Karachi-Tehran
Sunday	Karachi-Ashgabad-Baku

Uzbekistan Airways operates services from Tashkent to Karachi, as well as London, Amsterdam, Frankfurt, Istanbul, Tel Aviv, Sharjah, Jeddah, Bangkok, Kuala Lumpur and Beijing. **Turkmenistan Airways** and **Kyrgyz Airways** also operate flights from Europe to their regional capitals. Call CIS Travel (see below) for more details.

Pakistan domestic air connections

PIA domestic services are as follows:

Islamabad/Peshawar: Daily services operate from Islamabad to Peshawar at 0730 hrs (arriving at 0905 hrs) and 1745 hrs (arriving at 1830 hrs). From Peshawar to Islamabad there are daily services at 1200 hrs and 1845 hrs.

Islamabad/Quetta: A daily service flies from Islamabad to Quetta at 1330 hrs (arriving at 1455 hrs). From Quetta flights leave daily at 1105 hrs and 1655 hrs.

Contacts:

Pakistan International Airways

Amsterdam:	TEL: +31 (20) 626 4710-15 FAX: +31 (20) 620 3779
Brussels:	TEL: +32 (2) 511 5777, 511 6142
London:	TEL: +44 (181) 741 8066 FAX: +44 (181) 741 9376

New York:	TEL: +1 (212) 370 9150/55 FAX: +1 (212) 808 4695 (continued)
Zurich:	TEL: +41 (1) 811 2737-39 FAX: +41 (1) 811 2741
Islamabad:	TEL: +92 (51) 816051-56 (domestic) TEL: +92 (51) 815041 (general enquiries)
Peshawar:	TEL: +92 (91) 273081/89, 279162/66

British Airways:

London:	TEL: +44 (1345) 222111
Islamabad:	TEL: +92 (51) 274070, 274080, 273081-3 FAX: +92 (51) 274078
Peshawar:	TEL: +92 (91) 276035-37, 273252

Emirates Airlines:

Amsterdam:	TEL: +31 (20) 316 4222
Dubai:	TEL: +971 (4) 800 4444
London:	TEL: +44 (171) 808 0808
New York:	TEL: +1 (212) 800 777 3999
Zurich:	TEL: +41 (1) 307 1111

Uzbekistan Airways:

Amsterdam:	TEL: +31 (20) 653 5200
Frankfurt:	TEL: +49 (69) 2710 0265
London:	TEL: +44 (171) 935 1899
Islamabad:	TEL: +92 (51) 828331/4

Specialist travel agents

A number of specialist and bucket shop travel agents operate out of New York, London, Paris, Amsterdam, and Berlin. The following travel agents specialize in air travel to the region and have been helpful to EFG editors:

Key Travel
92-96 Eversholt Street,
London NW1 1BP, UK.
TEL: +44 (171) 387 4933
FAX: +44 (171) 387 1090

CIS Travel
7 Buckingham Gate,
London SW1E 6JP, UK.
TEL: +44 (171) 828 7613
FAX: +44 (171) 630 8302

Steppes East
Central Asia specialists. Good on visas.
TEL: +44 (1285) 810267
E-mail: sales@steppeseast.co.uk

ARTOU Travel & Travel Books
Asian travel plus good selection of French and English language travel books and maps.
8 Rue de Rive, Geneva, Switzerland.
TEL: +41 (22) 818 0202
FAX: +41 (22) 818 0229

RAPTIM Travel
Special fares for journalists and aid workers.
31, route de l'aeroport, 1215 Geneva, Switzerland.
TEL: +41 (22) 799 2140
FAX: +41 (22) 799 2144

Visas

During the heady days of the Soviet War, many freelance journalists entered Afghanistan clandestinely, trudging over some remote frontier mountain pass at the dead of night, accompanied by armed mujahideen. Nowadays, however, it is essential to obtain a visa before going into the country. Foreigners attract a great deal of attention, not just because of their colour but also because of their access to money and international media. You will be noticed, and if you do not have a visa, you will probably end up in jail, or at least detained at some police or militia post. This in turn will make you a burden to overstretched Red Cross, UN or NGO workers who will be involved in extricating you. You have two choices: get a visa in your country of origin, or wait until you arrive in Pakistan or Iran and sort it out on the spot. The only visas currently available are single-entry, for which you must provide around $30 and two passport-size photos. In order to leave Afghanistan again you will need to get a separate *exit visa*.

For those of you travelling without the support of an official agency or organization, one intrepid traveller recently had this advice: "I got a journalist visa from the Afghan embassy in Abu Dhabi based on a Khao San [ie. fake] Bangkok press card and a letter from a friend who runs a small Middle Eastern culture-type tabloid. The application was referred to Kabul and approved within two weeks. The visa cost US$30."

Entering from Pakistan

For accredited aid workers and journalists, Afghan visas are not especially difficult to obtain. In the past you could get a visa in a day or two, and this is still the case for people travelling with established UN agencies, NGOs or the Red Cross. However, since mid-1997 all applications from 'new' or unrecognised media or relief/development agencies have been referred to Kabul. This means the process can take up to a week. Also bear in mind that not much work is done from Thursday afternoon through to Monday morning, so start your application early in the week. The Afghan missions in

Islamabad, Peshawar and Quetta are all currently staffed by Taliban officials, which means that visas issued from these missions may not be valid in non-Taliban areas. However, one of our Mazar sources adds: “Although much of northern Afghanistan is controlled by the anti-Taliban Northern Alliance, it is reported that Afghan visas from Taliban-controlled embassies and consulates are still valid. Check this again before departure. On arrival in Mazar, update this as soon as possible with an “exit visa” from the Department of Foreign Affairs since no border crossing or airport departure is allowed without this.”

For more details on North West Frontier regulations for driving into and out of Afghanistan from Peshawar, *SEE PESHAWAR.*

Addresses of Afghan missions in Pakistan are:

Embassy in Islamabad
House 17, Street 28, F-6/1-21, Islamabad
TEL: +92 (51) 824505 FAX: +92 (51) 824504

Consulate in Peshawar
Gul Mohar Lane, University Town, GPO Box 119, Peshawar
TEL: +92 (91) 842486 Mob: +92 (351) 290133

Entering from outside the region

If you do not want to hang around in Pakistan, try and get a visa through one of the Afghan missions listed below. However, Afghan embassies staffed by non-Taliban officials (e.g. in London and Paris) may issue visas which are not acceptable in Taliban-controlled areas (see below on non-Taliban visas issued in Meshad). Nevertheless it is better to arrive in the region with at least some kind of visa rather than none at all, and then play it by ear.

Addresses of international Afghan missions are:

France
32 avenue Raffael, 75016 Paris.
TEL: +33 (1) 45 25 05 29 FAX: +33 (1) 45 24 26 87

Switzerland
63 rue de Lausanne, CH-1202 Geneva.
TEL: +41 (22) 731 1616

United Kingdom
31 Prince’s Gate, London SW7 1QQ.
TEL: +44 (171) 589 8891 FAX: +44 (171) 581 3452

United States of America
2341 Wyoming Avenue, NW, Washington, DC 20008.
TEL: +1(202) 234 3770-1 FAX: +1(202) 328 3516

Entering from Iran

In June 1997, an independent traveller was issued a tourist visa for Afghanistan by the consulate in Meshad, eastern Iran. It only took three hours to obtain and cost $30 along with two photos. He adds: "Apparently, travellers who arrive at an Afghan border controlled by the Taliban (e.g. Islam Qala) with a visa issued by a non-Taliban controlled diplomatic post (e.g. the Afghan consulate in Meshad, Iran) are supposed to be given a letter by the immigration authorities (in *lieu* of an entry stamp in their passport). This letter allows one to travel to the nearest foreign ministry office (e.g. Herat), where the payment of a nominal sum (I was told one dollar for each day of the length of the visa) will allow travellers to receive a passport stamp, which will officially convert a non-Taliban tourist visa into a Taliban tourist visa.

Travellers should note that not all Taliban immigration authorities are aware of these procedures. If (as happened to me), a traveller simply receives an entry stamp upon crossing into a Taliban controlled area of Afghanistan with a visa issued by a non-Taliban diplomatic post, he or she may well be denied the right to exit the country." So: make sure you 'Talibanize' your tourist visa where appropriate.

Renewing visas in Afghanistan

This is no problem and can normally be done while you wait. Bank on $10 per month of extension plus two passport photos – even in Taliban areas where photographs of "living things" are supposed to be forbidden. For local rules SEE REGIONS.

Leaving Afghanistan

The Afghans define a single-entry visa as one which allows the holder in but *not out!* You will be turned back from boarding an aeroplane leaving the country if you do not possess an ***exit visa.*** These are obtained from the Ministry/Department of Foreign Affairs in the city of your departure. There are a few exceptions: Bamiyan, where no-one seems to check, and Torkham where travellers leaving overland for Pakistan are also generally allowed through without an exit visa.

Taliban restrictions on women

Since March 1998, a number of female Muslims working for international agencies have been refused Afghan visas because they were travelling alone. The Afghan Embassy in Islamabad requires them to travel with a close male family member. UNOCHA is negotiating to have this restriction lifted.

Weather

Afghanistan has a mainly dry continental climate, with considerable variation in climate and temperature both diurnally and annually. Hot, dry summers – reaching over 50 degrees Celsius in the deserts of the southwest – are complemented by bitter winters – with temperatures plunging to minus 40 or 50 degrees in the mountains of the Hindu Kush.

Nevertheless, between these extremes, Afghanistan, like Europe, has four distinct seasons. From November to March, the snow-line creeps down to around 1,800 metres and snow blankets Kabul most winters. The rains last from January onwards into spring, but increase the higher up you go. Average annual rainfall across the country is 13 inches/338mm. From March to May the warmer weather encourages fruit blossoms, wild flowers, carpets of grass and rivers full of rainfall and snowmelt. The summer months from June to August are extremely hot and dusty unless you are in the mountains. From September to November, the fresh mornings, warm days and spectacular autumnal tints make these probably the best months to travel in Afghanistan.

There is great regional variation in weather across Afghanistan. Out of the five main cities, Kabul (situated at 1,800 metres) is the highest in elevation, so pack warm clothes for all times of year. Average temperatures for the capital are: January, minus 2.8°C; July, 24.4°C. However, the thermometer can drop to freezing in Mazar, Kandahar and Herat as well during winter. In summer, temperatures in these cities can reach 35-40 degrees Celsius. In Herat the heat is relieved by 120 days of tearing winds from May to August.

The baking heat in many arid or semi-arid regions also makes overland travel difficult for ill-equipped travellers, so always take water. Breakdowns are no fun. Jalalabad (elevation 700 metres) enjoys a subtropical climate and is much milder in winter than Kabul, but extremely hot in summer. The Jalalabad plains are frost-free all year, enabling the cultivation of orange and olive groves within view of the snow-covered Safed Koh and Hindu Kush ranges. Bamiyan, situated at 2,500 metres, is often blocked by snow for several months of the year.

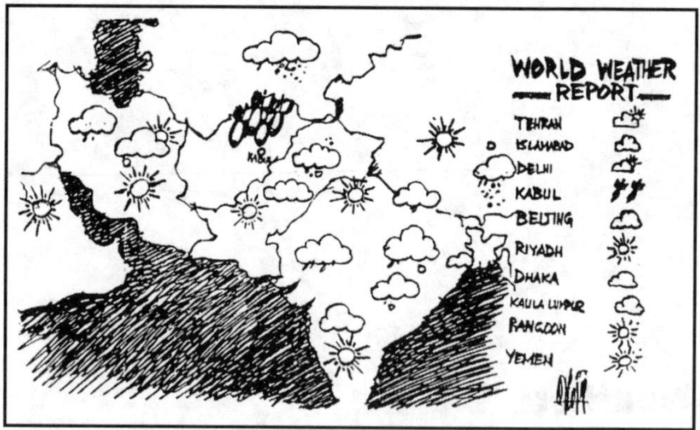

The Muslim 13 January 1994

During the 1980s, numerous refugees, particularly children and the aged (as well as their animals) died from exposure, bitterly cold blizzards and from flash-floods as they sought to cross the Hindu Kush into Pakistan. Heavy snows and mud from spring thaws seriously hampered humanitarian relief operations in northern Afghanistan, following the earthquake near Rustaq in February 1998. Spring floods also take a heavy toll on both people and agricultural land every year, often devastating the plains in the southwest of the country.

Advice for women

Afghanistan may sound like a nightmare for any Western woman to visit, let alone to work in. Yet female aid workers and journalists generally enjoy better access to ordinary Afghans than do Western men. This is for the simple reason that foreign men cannot meet Afghan women as easily as foreign women can meet both Afghan men and women. This aspect of "gender privilege" is something often overlooked by people who assume that being female in Afghanistan is automatically bad news. In addition, as many French and other female medical aid workers found while working inside Afghanistan during the Soviet war, women were often made 'honorary' men (or 'neutered' as one French doctor preferred to describe it) by the Afghans. This meant that they could sit, eat, drink tea and even sleep (that is, in the same room) with Afghan men without any problem. Only strictly fundamentalist or extremely conservative Afghan men would refuse to acknowledge foreign women or even shake hands with them. This acceptance of foreign women still exists, even among the Taliban, but many men are now reluctant to shake hands for fear of retribution.

Dress is one of the most obviously limiting factors for women working in Afghanistan. Even in non-Taliban areas the dress code is conservative. One of our contributors had this to add: "Foreign women are given more concessions than local women when it comes to dress and behaviour, but dressing appropriately goes a long way towards avoiding problems." Some basic guidelines are as follows:

- Do not try to look too 'Afghan' or you may be treated accordingly. Dress conservatively but look recognisably 'Western.'
- Avoid wearing figure-hugging or revealing clothes.
- Ordinary loose-fitting western dresses and below-the-knee skirts can be worn, with loose trousers on underneath to cover the legs, calves and ankles.

EFG Editors would like to acknowledge the help of Annie Sewell, Angela Kearney and Shon Campbell in compiling this section.

J. Hartley/UNICEF

- Do not walk off the road to find a bush to spring a leak behind – you may walk into a minefield. Long, baggy dresses/skirts provide good cover for answering calls of nature while on the road.
- Wear blouses with long sleeves and avoid low bust-lines.
- In more conservative areas, *shalwar kameez* may be more appropriate.
- In public, cover your head and chest with a long shawl or *chador*.
- In more liberal areas you may not need to wear a *chador* at all, but check first.
- Pack your best underwear at the top of your bag. It puts the Taliban off searching deeper!
  (SEE CLOTHING & KIT)

Security is something to be aware of but not paranoid about. It is very rare for Western women to be threatened by Afghans; in fact, many women working or travelling in Afghanistan say that sexual harassment is far worse in Pakistan. If you are harassed in a public place, it is best to make as much of a scene as possible so as to shame whoever the culprit is. In 1997 a foreign woman working for an international aid agency was beaten by Taliban soldiers in Herat, despite wearing a *chador*. Reportedly it was not until she started screaming that the soldiers ran off. However, this type of incident is very much the exception, and Taliban authorities later apologised for the mistake. Unless recognized as foreigners, Western women wearing *chadors* have been roughed up by Pakistani frontier scouts at the border (or even thwacked with a baton, as recently happened to one EFG contributor), on the assumption that they are 'only' Afghan women.

Many experienced female expatriates continue life nearly as normal in Afghanistan: they drive vehicles, walk or cycle through the bazaar and play very much an equal role with their male colleagues. In Kabul particularly, there is a strong community of female aid workers to give you support. However, some towns – such as Kandahar – are more conservative than others. So if you are a new arrival, check out the situation with someone experienced before wandering around on your own.

In order not to attract unwanted attention or provoke the wrath of the Religious Police, bear in mind some basic ground rules:

- As a western woman it is best not to offer your hand to an Afghan man to shake – wait for him to offer you his hand first.
- Avoid sitting near Afghan men (choose your own small chair)
- Keep your conversations off the streets and behind closed doors.
- Women and men (even married couples) should not touch each other in public.
- Be careful, when sitting on the floor in the presence of Afghan men, to cover your knees and feet.
- Do not try and stare down the men staring at you – it only makes them more interested.
- Do not walk alone at night.

(SEE PERSONAL SECURITY and TRADITIONS & CUSTOMS)

ESSENTIAL READING

Security Guidelines for Women, UN Security Coordination Office (New York, 1995)

For more essential data and agency contacts SEE WOMEN, WOMEN'S RIGHTS and WEBSITES

APPEAL FOR CORRECTIONS AND UPDATES

The editors would greatly appreciate if aid representatives, journalists and other readers could provide us with any changes and comments on information, statistical data and contact lists provided in this Essential Field Guide. Regular updates will be made available on the website of the International Centre for Humanitarian Reporting (http://www.ichr.org). New editions will include the corrected or updated material.

CONTACTS

J. Hartley/UNICEF

Coordinating agencies

AGENCY COORDINATING BODY FOR AFGHAN RELIEF (ACBAR)

ACBAR was established in 1988. It currently has a membership of some 76 NGOs, both international and Afghan agencies. The main aim of ACBAR is to provide a framework within which those agencies and organizations, providing assistance to Afghans, can exchange information and share expertise in order to enable a more coordinated, efficient and effective use of resources.
Work focuses on four priority areas:

A. Management & policy –
The ACBAR Secretariat undertakes to represent its members in discussions on key policy issues, as well as issues involving liaison with the United Nations agencies, donors and the Pakistan, Iranian and Afghan Authorities.

B. Information & database –
ACBAR acts as the focal point for general information. Two annual publications are produced – the "Database of NGO Activities" and the "Directory of Humanitarian Agencies Working for Afghans." Maps are also prepared electronically and manually on NGO activities by sector and province on an *ad hoc* basis. In March 1998, ACBAR took over the Health and Education Resource Centre (HERC), previously operated by IRC to produce silkscreen-printed educational and public health materials.

C. Coordination –
Through a series of regional and sectoral sub-committees information is shared, and guidelines are produced on recommended standards and modes of operation in the field.

D. Resource and Information Centre (ARIC) –
Comprising a library and mapping service, the aim is to gather, organize and disseminate information within the aid community. The library has an expanding range of books, journals, NGO reports, etc. on Afghanistan.

BUDGET: $408,000 PERSONNEL: 81
ADDRESSES:
2 Rehman Baba Road, UPO Box 1084, University Town, Peshawar.
TEL: + 92 (91) 44392, 40839, 45347 FAX: + 92 (91) 840471
E-Mail: acbaar@radio.psh.brain.net.pk
House 4, Street 6, Farukhi Wat, Shahr-e-Naw, Kabul.
TEL: Kabul 35673, 30509, 33684

Editors' Note: *Contact lists have been compiled from the ACBAR Directory of Humanitarian Agencies Working for Afghans (May 1997) ACBAR updates (March 98), the UN Consolidated Appeal for Afghanistan 1998, agency reports and returned EFG questionnaires. Agencies listed are those with an annual operating budget over US$500,000, or with a specialist focus. These lists are not exhaustive and are bound to contain some errors. Please help us keep up to date by sending your changes and corrections to the Editors at the following address:*

CROSSLINES Essential Field Guide to Afghanistan
International Centre for Humanitarian Reporting (ICHR)
Villa de Grand-Montfleury, 1290 Versoix, Geneva, Switzerland
FAX: +41 (22) 950 0752 E-mail: info.ichr@itu.ch

AFGHAN NGOs COORDINATION BUREAU (ANCB)

ANCB was established in 1991 in response to a need for an agency to coordinate the activities of Afghan NGOs. The aim of ANCB is to stimulate activities aimed at improving the quality of life of Afghans and to encourage their voluntary return to their home country.

ANCB objectives:

- To coordinate in the development and welfare of activities run by Afghan NGOs;
- To provide technical support in planning and upgrading their activities and performance;
- To facilitate the relationship of Afghan NGOs with the government, *shuras*, donors and international agencies;
- To promote volunteerism in Afghan groups.

BUDGET: $28,850 PERSONNEL: 18
ADDRESS: 25 Chinar Road, University Town, Peshawar.
TEL: +92 (91) 43476 FAX: +92 (91) 41081

BRITISH AGENCIES AFGHANISTAN GROUP (BAAG)

Coordinating body for British NGOs working in Afghanistan. BAAG produces a monthly news update on the political and military situation for its members, and publishes occasional reports on the refugee situation both in Afghanistan and in the NWFP.
ADDRESS: BAAG, c/o British Refugee Council, Bondway House, 3/9 Bondway, London SW8 1SJ, UK.
TEL: +44 (171) 582 6922, 820 3098 FAX: +44 (171) 582 9929

ISLAMIC COORDINATION COUNCIL (ICC)

ICC is a body coordinating humanitarian organizations working to save the Afghans at places of refuge as well as inside Afghanistan. The Council reflects the concern of the Muslim *umma* for distressed Afghan people. A total of 16 Muslim organizations are members of ICC.

ICC objectives:

The goal of ICC is to provide a forum in which member organizations can discuss their concerns, design policy guidelines for delivering assistance, resource management and other operational issues with the ultimate purpose of improving coordination in refugee assistance in NWFP and elsewhere, as well as for the repatriation and resettlement of Afghan refugees. Any Muslim organization working for Afghans and committed to the regulations of the Council can be a member of the ICC (a written commitment is needed).
BUDGET: $93,800 (1994) PERSONNEL: 13
ADDRESS: 3 Gul Mohar Road, University Town, PO Box 991, Peshawar.
TEL: +92 (91) 54506

SOUTHERN/WESTERN AFGHANISTAN AND BALUCHISTAN ASSOCIATION FOR COORDINATION (SWABAC)

SWABAC was formed in Quetta in August 1988, by NGOs undertaking relief and rehabilitation assistance in those geographical areas.
SWABAC, like ACBAR, provides a forum in which member organizations can discuss their concerns regarding policy guidelines for delivering assistance, resource management and other operational issues – with the ultimate purpose of improving coordination in refugee assistance in Baluchistan, as well as in the repatriation and resettlement of Afghan refugees.
BUDGET: $52,000 (1995), $none (1996) PERSONNEL: 12
ADDRESS: House 187/J Block 5, Satellite Town, Quetta.
TEL: +92 (81) 440265, 440662 FAX: +92 (81) 440265

UNITED NATIONS OFFICE FOR THE COORDINATION OF HUMANITARIAN ASSISTANCE TO AFGHANISTAN (UNOCHA)

SEE UN AGENCIES

NGOs active in the region

AFGHANAID (A-AID)

Founded in 1991 much of the work of Afghanaid is in the fields of engineering and agriculture. Afghanaid focuses its efforts on securing basic needs for rural communities including: nutritious food, adequate shelter and clothing, safe drinking water. It is currently starting small activities in community health. Projects include:

- **Engineering:** construction of roads, bridges, irrigation and housing;
- **Agriculture:** forestry, seed multiplication, fruit and vegetable production;
- **Income generation:** bee-keeping and poultry.

BUDGET: $3,840,000 (1997) PERSONNEL: 184
ADDRESSES:
Local: 5B Gul Mohar Road, University Town, Peshawar.
TEL: +92 (91) 42030, 841083, Kabul: 32268 FAX: +92 (91) 840322
E-mail: Grader@Afghanaid.psh.brain.com.pk
International: 2nd Floor, 16 Mortimer Street, London W1N 7RD, UK
TEL: +44 (171) 255 3355 FAX: +44 (171) 255 3344

AFGHAN AMPUTEE BICYCLISTS FOR REHABILITATION AND RECREATION (AABRAR)

AABRAR was founded in 1992, based in Peshawar, with a centre providing rehabilitation and physical therapy for disabled Afghans in Jalalabad. AABRAR's main areas of operations are:

- **Physical therapy** for men, women and children;
- **Rehabilitation** course for lower limb disabled men and boys, including classes in literacy, first aid, bicycling for rehabilitation;
- **Jalalabad screening clinic** provides free referral to the re-constructive plastic surgery unit at Peshawar's Dar us Salaam hospital.
- **Outpatient clinic** service to general population in Nangarhar province.

BUDGET: $95,000 PERSONNEL: 36
ADDRESS: 106, Gul Haji Plaza, Jamrud Road, Peshawar.
TEL: +92 (91) 42417, Jalalabad 2913

ACTION CONTRE LA FAIM (ACF)

Founded in 1979 to fight famine and hunger around the world. Since 1995 ACF Afghanistan has been involved in:

- **Nutrition assessment** in Kabul, in order to establish facts on malnutrition before wintertime;
- **Providing tools**, methodology and protocols for nutrition activities;
- **Water potability test** analysis in MCH centres and clinics.

BUDGET: $670,000 PERSONNEL: 50
ADDRESSES:
Local: Charahi Feez Mohammed Khan, Shahr-e-Naw, Kabul.
TEL: Kabul 33104 SATPHONE: +873 682 041195
International: 9, rue Dareau, 75014 Paris, France.
TEL: +33 (1) 53 80 88 88 FAX: +33 (1) 45 65 92 50

ACTED

Agence d'Aide a la Cooperation Technique Et au Developpement (ACTED) is a French NGO based in Kabul and active in the following sectors:

- **Bakeries:** since 1994 ACTED has been the implementing partner for the WFP bakeries programme, which provides around 200,000 loaves of subsidised bread per day to 50,000 families in Kabul;
- **Coalmining:** extracts coal from a mine in the Ghorband Valley, north of Kabul, to supply the capital's hospitals, clinics and orphanages with power and heat. Also mines coal near Pul-e-Khumri for supply to Mazar-e-Sharif;
- **Urban rehabilitation:** builds timber doors and window frames, repairs latrines;
- **Mapping:** implementing partner in UNDP/FAO mapping and database project.

BUDGET: FFr 7,498,939 (1995) PERSONNEL: 31
ADDRESSES:
Local: Gul Frushy, Shahr-e-Naw, Kabul. TEL: Kabul 33119
International: 33 rue Godot de Mauroy, 75009 Paris, France.
TEL: +33 (1) 42 65 33 33 FAX: +33 (1) 42 65 33 46 E-Mail: acted@worldnet.fr

AFGHAN DEVELOPMENT ASSOCIATION (ADA)

ADA was created in 1990 with the aim of implementing rehabilitation and development projects. ADA aims to integrate agricultural and environmental training into its education programme (both for students and teachers) to promote more sustainable development and future peace in Afghanistan. ADA's areas of operations include:

- **Education:** school construction, financial support for schools and teacher training, vocational training;
- **Agriculture/Horticulture:** farm mechanized stations and nurseries, distribution of fruit trees to farmers, veterinary vaccinations;
- **Environmental issues:** soil conservation, flood control, afforestation, micro-hydro electricity;
- **Infrastructure:** canal rehabilitation and development; road and bridge repair.

BUDGET: $1,824,000 (1997) PERSONNEL: 332
ADDRESSES:
Local: House 432, Old Bara Road, University Town, UPO Box 922, Peshawar.
TEL: +92 (91) 45333, Kabul: 33104 FAX: +92 (91) 42230
International: 1225, 8th Street, Suite 430, Sacramento, CA 95814, USA.
TEL/FAX: +1 (916) 446 0806

AMITIE FRANCO-AFGHANE AIDE HUMANITARIE ET INFORMATION (AFRANE)

From its foundation in 1979 until 1986, AFRANE concentrated on humanitarian help and information, through a periodical review called *Les Nouvelles d'Afghanistan* (quarterly, FFr150/year) and in collaboration with the Center de Recherches et d'Etudes Documentaires sur l'Afghanistan (CEREDAF). From 1986 onwards the agency has focused on rural development, and in partnership with CoAR created the Afghan Agriculture Experimental Centre in 1991. AFRANE is also involved in emergency aid in Kabul.
BUDGET: $100,000 (1997) PERSONNEL: 94
ADDRESS: 84E, Rehman Baba Road, University Town, Peshawar.
TEL: +92 (91) 41492 FAX: +92 (91) 44122
CEREDAF: 16 passage de la Main d'Or, 75011 Paris, France.
TEL: +33 (1) 43 55 63 50

AFGHAN GERMAN BASIC EDUCATION (AG BAS-Ed)

Created in 1996 as a follow-up agency for the GTZ-funded Basic Education for Afghan Refugees project (BEFARe), AG BAS-Ed is working in eastern Afghanistan in the fields of formal and non-formal education, and in mother and child health training. Worked with UNESCO and Afghan Ministry of Education in 1997 to develop a new curriculum to replace past communist and mujahideen propaganda.
BUDGET: $147,000 (1997) PERSONNEL: 35
ADDRESSES:
GPO Box 1270, Peshawar Cantt.
TEL: +92 (91) 843063 FAX: +92 (91) 842693
Nangarhar Office, Next to SCA Office, Kama Hada, Near Chowk-e-Mukhabirat, Jalalabad. TEL: Jalalabad 2133

AFGHAN/GERMAN HELP COORDINATION OFFICE (AGHCO)

AGHCO was founded in 1983 through the joint venture of German and Afghan doctors. With the support of CARE Germany, AGHCO has provided one and two year nursing courses. More than 600 male and female students have graduated. **The medical services and facilities of AGHCO include:**

- 25-bed hospital in Kunar;
- 80-bed hospital and polyclinic in Jalalabad;
- Three Primary Health Units in Nangarhar, Paktya and Kunar provinces;
- Polyclinic and training centre in Kandahar.

BUDGET: $512,950 (1996) $57,000 (1997) PERSONNEL: 146
ADDRESS: Danishabad, Canal Road, University Town, PO Box 679, Peshawar.
TEL: +92 (91) 840491, Jalalabad 2213 FAX: +92 (91) 840707

AIDE MEDICALE INTERNATIONAL (AMI)

AMI is a French humanitarian agency based in Paris. In 1980 AMI sent its first medical team inside Afghanistan to assist in an emergency mission. AMI focuses on medical training. Since 1985, AMI has trained more than 104 assistant doctors, and 26 laboratory, x-ray and dental technicians. Other projects include:

- **Installation of a 40-bed district hospital** in Bakari, Logar;
- **Basic health clinic**, established in 1993 in Kamdesh, Nuristan;
- **Kabul sub-office**, opened in June 1995, to begin the rehabilitation of 10 MCH clinics within Kabul city.

BUDGET: $1,320,000 (1997) PERSONNEL: 70
ADDRESSES:
Local: 10 Park Avenue, University Town, Peshawar.
TEL: +92 (91) 43631, Kabul 33574 FAX: +92 (91) 840419
International: 119, rue des Amandiers, 75020 Paris, France.
TEL: +33 (1) 46 36 04 04 FAX: +33 (1) 46 36 66 10

AGENCY FOR REHABILITATION AND ENERGY-CONSERVATION IN AFGHANISTAN (AREA)

AREA is the continuation of a GTZ project called Domestic Energy Saving Project (DESP) established in 1984. AREA designs and implements projects which directly or indirectly contribute towards wood saving, energy conservation and environmental protection. Projects include:

- **Agriculture:** seed multiplication, forestry, ram pumps;
- **Alternative technology:** fuel-efficient stoves, biogas, wind-pumps, micro-hydro power;
- **Bakeries:** 900 bakeries in refugee camps of the NWFP and eastern Afghanistan;
- **Shelter:** concrete roofing beams, brick-kilns – community-based.

BUDGET: $641,000 (1997) PERSONNEL: 551
ADDRESS: 17E Abdara Road, PO Box 709, University Town, Peshawar.
TEL: +92 (91) 41993, 45417, Herat 3169 FAX +92 (91) 41993

AFGHAN TECHNICAL CONSULTANTS (ATC)

ATC was created in 1989 as an implementing agency working on mine clearance. ATC has 22 manual **demining teams**, two mechanical demining teams and three Battle Area Clearance (BAC) teams, each consisting of 30 men and one Explosive Ordnance Disposal Team (EOD). The three BAC teams and EOD section are carrying out explosive ordnance disposal in Kabul city, while the other 22 teams are working in eastern and central Afghanistan. ATC to date has cleared mines in sixteen provinces of Afghanistan.
BUDGET: $4,935,000 (1997) PERSONNEL: 1204
ADDRESS: 45/D-4, Old Jamrud Road, University Town, GPO Box 1149, Peshawar. TEL: +92 (91) 840122, 40412 FAX: +92 (91) 44780

AFGHANISTAN VACCINATION AND IMMUNIZATION CENTER (AVICEN/IBNSINA)

AVICEN used to run an orphanage in Kabul, but was thrown out by the Taliban because of suspected links with opposition parties. AVICEN was involved in the Expanded Programme of Immunization (EPI), but has now handed over operations to IBNSINA, an Afghan NGO.
BUDGET: $1,279,000 PERSONNEL: 492
ADDRESS: 39 D-1S, SJ Afghani Road, University Town, UPO Box 922, Peshawar.
TEL: +92 (91) 45279, Kabul 62612 FAX: +92 (91) 840493

BBC AFGHAN EDUCATION DRAMA (BBC AED)

The BBC World Service first began broadcasting educational dramas in Persian and Pashto in the late 1980s. The success of these led to the formation of BBC AED and the launching in 1994 of its **radio soap opera "New Home, New Life"**, which now enjoys an enormous listenership believed to be between 70-80% of the Afghan population. For more details, SEE EDUCATION.
ADDRESS: 8 Abdara Road, PO Box 946, University Town, Peshawar.
TEL: +92 (91) 842320, 42765-7 FAX: +92 (91) 842319
E-Mail: (name)@bbcaed.pwr.sdnpk.undp.org

BASIC EDUCATION FOR AFGHAN REFUGEES (BEFARe)

BEFARe is a bilateral project between the governments of Pakistan and Germany, and supports education of Afghan refugees in over 250 schools in Pakistan's North West Frontier Province (NWFP). BEFARe supports a second NGO, AG BAS-Ed, which works in the education sector inside Afghanistan. BEFARe carries out activities in three areas:

- **Primary education:** The project trains teacher trainers, headmasters, teachers and supervisors; 64,000 primary students and 1,608 teachers are supported with books, guides and teaching aids.
- **Basic health education for females:** Covering the main aspects of mother and child health;
- **Literacy for females and males:** Over 580 male and 250 female instructors have received a week's training in each literacy level (Primer, Reader, Arithmetic).

BUDGET: $570,000 (1997) PERSONNEL: 264
ADDRESSES:
Local: 8 Tatara Road, Rahatabad, PO Box 1481, Peshawar.
TEL: +92 (91) 840631, 42955 FAX: +92 (91) 841047
E-mail: gtz@befare.psw.erum.com.pk
International: Postfach 5180, D-65726 Eschborn, Germany.
FAX: +49 (6196) 797299

COOPERATION CENTRE FOR AFGHANISTAN (CCA)

Operational in Afghanistan since 1990, CCA specializes in the promotion of human rights and sustainable development. CCA seeks the full application of international human rights standards in Afghanistan by educating the public in **human rights and monitoring** the improvement of the human rights situation in the country. CCA has offices in Kabul, Mazar and Bamiyan.
BUDGET: $250,000 (1997) PERSONNEL: 56
ADDRESS: House 420, Street 13, Phase 1, Hayatabad, Peshawar.
TEL: +92 (91) 810116 FAX: +92 (91) 810116

COORDINATION OF HUMANITARIAN ASSISTANCE (CHA)

CHA was established in 1988 and is involved in:

- **Agriculture:** improved seeds and fertilizer;
- **Irrigation and infrastructure:** cleaning & repair of *karezes* & roads;
- **Health and vocational**: vaccination projects, vocational training for war widows, auto workshop.

BUDGET: $1,083,000 (1997) PERSONNEL: 261
ADDRESS: 84E Rehman Baba Road, University Town, Peshawar.
TEL: +92 (91) 41188, 41492, Herat 3178 FAX: +92 (91) 44122

CARE INTERNATIONAL (CI)

CARE International, founded in 1945, is an international relief and development organization. CARE was involved in Afghanistan from 1960-1979, providing health care and medical training. The agency initiated the Afghan Village Assistance Programme in 1988 to create conditions conducive to sustained repatriation of refugees. CARE's operations in Afghanistan include:

- **Emergency response:** winter food parcels for 35,000 war widows and their children in Kabul;
- **Water and sanitation:** both urban and rural water supply, delivery and drainage, supporting 17,000 households; also latrine construction and health and hygiene education;
- **Rural rehabilitation:** irrigation, flood/erosion control, road construction from village to market, tree planting (poplars for construction and fruit trees), agricultural extension;
- **Education:** pioneering home schools for around 1,700 pupils, teacher training and provision of teaching materials; *(continued)*

- **Income generation:** 'credit' schemes whereby the community is encouraged to save first and spend later; home-based food-for-work (quilts, clothes, candles), widows' skills training.

BUDGET: $5,307,000 (1997) PERSONNEL: 243
ADDRESSES:
Local: House No. 6, Park Lane, Park Road, University Town, UPO Box 926, Peshawar.
TEL: +92 (91) 40328, 45317, Kabul 32621 FAX: +92 (91) 841826
E-mail: care@afghan.psw.erum.com.pk
International:
CARE USA
151 Ellis St. NE, Atlanta, GA 30303-2439, USA.
TEL: +1 (404) 681 2552 FAX: +1 (404) 577 9418
E-mail: (name)@care.org Website: www.care.org
CARE UK
Tower House, 36 Southampton St., London WC2E 7HE, UK.
TEL: +44 (171) 379 5247 FAX: +44 (171) 379 0543

CIET INTERNATIONAL

A New York-based **survey and research** consultancy; CIET stands for Community Information and Epidemiological Technologies. Specialists in researching data for emergency situations, CIET uses a pioneering Multiple Indicators Cluster Survey method (MICS) aimed at eliminating random error. A typical cluster will comprise of 120 households and 600-700 people; every house is visited in order to achieve a representative cross-section of the cluster or so-called "sentinel site." In 1997, CIET carried out research for UNICEF and the UNOCHA Mine Action Programme, using 131 separate clusters, established across every province in Afghanistan.
ADDRESS: 847A 2nd Avenue, Suite 387, New York 10017, USA
TEL/FAX: +1 (212) 308 8633
E-Mail: CEWCIET@156.COMSATS.NET.COM

COORDINATION OF AFGHAN RELIEF (CoAR)

CoAR was created on the initiative of a group of Afghans in 1989, in order to contribute to the rehabilitation process of Afghanistan. During the last six years CoAR has extended its rehabilitation and development, actively promoting partnerships with other development and rehabilitation agencies. Projects include:

- **Agricultural rehabilitation**: wheat seed multiplication, horticulture, veterinary;
- **Engineering:** canal cleaning and water supply, construction of schools and bridges;
- **Emergency:** carpentry, shelter and bakery;
- **Welfare:** education and teacher training, health clinics and widows' vocational training.

BUDGET: $681,000 (1997) PERSONNEL: 211
ADDRESSES:
House 93, Street 4, N 3, Phase 4, Hayatabad, UPO Box 1013, Peshawar.
TEL: +92 (91) 813299, 818165 FAX: +92 (91) 813299
House No. 151, Street 7, Road 15, Wazir Akbar Khan, Kabul.
TEL: Kabul 62702

DANISH COMMITTEE FOR AID TO AFGHAN REFUGEES (DACAAR)

DACAAR is a consortium of four Danish NGOs operational in Pakistan since 1984 and in Afghanistan since 1988. DACAAR's long-term objective is to move from rehabilitation towards development assistance. Sectors of operation are:
Pakistan:

- **Sewing project:** an income-generating project employing around 1,500 Afghan refugee women in high-quality tailoring and embroidery for local and export sales. Shop hours are Monday-Friday 0900-1630 hrs (TEL: +92 (91) 842530);
- **Hand pump factory:** employs over 100 people and produces the Kabul Hand Pump, and the Indus Hand Pump for deeper wells. In 1994 a total of 4,700 pumps were produced.
- **Water supply** for refugee camps in Pakistan: started in 1986, it includes improvement and maintenance of shallow wells and the installation of hand pumps. *(continued)*

Afghanistan (in both eastern and western provinces):

- **Agriculture:** irrigation systems, seed multiplication, soil conservation, flood control, animal husbandry;
- **Water and sanitation:** provision of baths and latrines, health and hygiene education;
- **Repair and rehabilitation** of public and community buildings, and public roads;
- **Emergency** work on an *ad hoc* basis.

BUDGET: $7,971,000 (1997) PERSONNEL: 708
ADDRESSES:
Local: 10 Gul Mohar Lane, PO Box 855, University Town, Peshawar.
TEL: +92 (91) 843078, 44237, 40731, Herat 2849 FAX: +92 (91) 840516
TELEX: 52307 DACAAR PK.
E-mail: director@dacaar.psh.brain.com.pk
International: PO Box 53, Borgergade 10, DK-1002, Copenhagen, Denmark.
TEL: +45 (33) 912700 FAX: +45 (33) 328448
E-Mail: drc@drc.dk

DEMINING AGENCY FOR AFGHANISTAN (DAFA)

DAFA was established by UNOCHA in 1990 with the long-term aim to clear all high priority mined areas in **southwestern Afghanistan.** DAFA currently has 12 demining teams. Priorities for demining, set by the UNOCHA Mine Action Programme, are: residential areas, roads, public pathways, irrigation systems, agricultural and grazing land, NGO project sites and areas where refugees are planning to return.
BUDGET: $3,007,000 PERSONNEL: 583
ADDRESS: 139/F Block 4, Satellite Town, PO Box 548, Quetta.
TEL: +92 (81) 442056, 448309 FAX: +92 (81) 447206

DUTCH COMMITTEE FOR AFGHANISTAN VETERINARY PROGRAMMES (DCA-VET)

DCA-VET began crossborder operations into the Panjshair Valley in 1985, and established the Veterinary Training and Support Centre (VTSC) in 1988 which trains around 45 'para-vets' a year. DCA also operates Veterinary Field Units (VFUs) at district level, and five Veterinary Support Centres in-country.
BUDGET: $1,904,000 (1997) PERSONNEL: 121
ADDRESS: 819 Jamrud Road, GPO Box 792, Peshawar.
TEL: +92 (91) 40871, 44731 FAX: +92 (91) 840258

EMERGENCY RELIEF UNIT (ERU)

ERU was established in 1994 to assist "internally-displaced persons" newly arrived in Jalalabad from Kabul. ERU has undertaken the following programmes:

- **Sanitation:** Detailed plan to clean up Jalalabad, including repair of all culverts, establishment of city waste dumps and ongoing city waste removal.
- **Community health workers:** Survey of the displaced in Jalalabad which led to the implementation of systematic health education programmes.
- **Income generation:** Aiming for self-sufficiency among the Sarshahi women. The programme will start with small-scale training in soap making.

BUDGET: $500,000 PERSONNEL: 509
ADDRESS: House No 2, Street C9/2, Zone 2, Jalalabad.
TEL: +92 (91) 43912

GERMAN AGRO ACTION (GAA)

GAA works globally to improve the food situation and rural living conditions in the Third World. In Afghanistan GAA works in the following sectors:

- **Urban reconstruction:** GAA operates a carpentry factory in Kabul making doors and window frames, and a separate profit-making furniture shop;
- **Sanitation:** manufacture and rehabilitation of latrines and septic tanks;
- **Agriculture:** seed multiplication, installation of hand pumps, rehabilitation of roads, wells and irrigation systems;
- **Food for work:** to vulnerable groups in Kabul and eastern Afghanistan.

BUDGET: $3,000,000 PERSONNEL: 34
ADDRESS: "Office behind ICRC", Jalalabad.
TEL: Jalalabad 2027
Kabul: SATPHONE: +873 682 623 845 SATFAX: +873 682 623 846

HELP THE AFGHANS FOUNDATION (HAF)

HAF was established 1984 in The Hague, The Netherlands, as a relief agency for refugees from the Afghanistan war, in particular for women, children and the disabled. HAF concentrates on **medical assistance** to refugee camps, hospitals and clinics in and around Peshawar and Jalalabad, including the funding and managing of the Paediatric Unit of the University Hospital in Jalalabad.
BUDGET: $233,000 (1997) PERSONNEL: 8
ADDRESSES:
Local: 10B Park Lane, PO Box 819,
University Town, Peshawar.
TEL: +92 (91) 840621 FAX: +92 (91) 840621
International: Binckhorstlaan 309, 2516 BC,
The Hague, Holland.
TEL: +31 (70) 383 6641

HELP GERMANY (HG)

HELP was founded in 1981 as a fund raising agency to help Afghan refugees. It now operates the following projects inside Afghanistan:

- **Interplast surgery** for Afghans: Based in Jalalabad, a team of plastic-, hand- and micro-surgeons comes to operate on patients suffering from war injuries, deformities of face and limbs, scars from burns, and congenital malformations.
- **Shelter:** Concrete girder production in Kabul.
- **Community-based rehabilitation:** 18 programmes, mainly irrigation.

BUDGET: $1,000,000 (1997) PERSONNEL: 41
ADDRESS:
9 Railway Road, University Town, GPO Box 912, Peshawar.
TEL: +92 (91) 840776, Kabul 33934

HANDICAP INTERNATIONAL (HI)

Began work in 1985 in Baluchistan among disabled Afghan refugees. Since 1995 HI has moved most of its services into Afghanistan and opened an office in Kandahar. Sectors of intervention include:

- **Training local staff:** technicians to manufacture orthopaedic devices, physiotherapy assistants, complementary training on plastic technology;
- **Community-based mine awareness:** based in Kandahar, this involves direct training and employment of community trainers who in turn train local communities in mine awareness; also lobbying through "mine action month" activities.
- **Quetta:** Mobile teams of local physiotherapy assistants and outreach workers make monthly field trips into Baluchistan.

BUDGET: $1,124,000 (1997) PERSONNEL: 64
ADDRESSES:
Local: Handicap International, PAK/AFG, PO Box 477, Quetta.
TEL: +92 (81) 440142 FAX: +92 (81) 444793
International: 14, avenue Berthhelot, 69007 Lyon, France.
TEL: +33 (7) 869 7979 FAX: +33 (7) 869 7994

HEALTHNET INTERNATIONAL (HN)

HN was originally part of Médecins Sans Frontières (MSF) Holland, but formed a separate organization in 1993 to concentrate on healthcare and sustainable development in the aftermath of crisis. HN's operations in Afghanistan concentrate on:

- **Malaria and leishmaniasis control programmes:** research and implementation, technical lab support to other agencies;
- **District healthcare support:** capacity-building at Ministry of Public Health level in Jalalabad, through the main provincial hospital and satellite clinics in Nangarhar province; community health worker training.

BUDGET: $1,350,000 (1997) PERSONNEL: 300
ADDRESS:
4 Karakul Lane, PO Box 889,
University Town, Peshawar.
TEL: +92 (91) 42551, 44027 FAX: +92 (91) 840379
E-mail: malaria@msfhni.psh.erum.com.pk

HALO TRUST (HT)

HT established its office Kabul in 1988 and concentrates on **mine clearance**. Four teams are involved in demining and two doctors per team provide treatment for injured deminers and local people. A specialist bomb disposal team operates in the Kabul area. HT also operates in the medical sector, with dispensaries in Kabul, Jabul-us Seraj and Pul-e-Khumri, and clinics in Kabul treating malnourished children and pregnant women.
BUDGET: $1,310,000 PERSONNEL: 1,000
ADDRESSES:
Local: Shahr-e-Naw, KRC Street, Kabul.
TEL: Kabul 32934 SATPHONE: +873 682 340467
SATFAX: +873 682 340468
International: 804 Drake House, Dolphin Square,
London SW1V 3NW.
TEL: +44 (171) 821 9244 FAX: +44 (171) 834 0198

INTERNATIONAL ASSISTANCE MISSION (IAM)

IAM was founded in 1966 and has worked continuously in Afghanistan since then. All expatriate personnel are unpaid volunteers seconded from member agencies, and all go on a four-month Dari language course on arrival in-country. IAM offers both Dari and English language courses to non-IAM personnel by prior arrangement. With operations in Kabul, Herat and Mazar-e-Sharif, IAM's main projects are:

- **Health and eye care:** Noor Eye Hospital (Kabul), ophthalmic centres (Mazar & Herat) and mobile eye clinics and camps; MCH clinics (Kabul & Mazar); secondment of expatriate surgeons and nurses to train/assist government doctors (Kabul & Mazar);
- **Education and rehabilitation:** Physiotherapy School of Kabul; education and rehabilitation for the visually impaired; vocational rehabilitation unit for people with disabilities; community health education; teaching English as a Foreign Language (EFL); IDP education and apprenticeships (Herat).
- **Economic development:** solar-water heating, micro-hydro power and smokeless oven projects in Kabul/Charikar; community-based development programmes in Herat and Mazar.

BUDGET: $1,300,000 PERSONNEL: 175
ADDRESSES:
Local: Wazir Akbar Khan, Lane 1, Street 15, PO Box 625, Kabul.
TEL: Kabul 25723, Herat 3321 SATFAX: +873 682 340252
PO Box 1167, Peshawar.
TEL: +92 (91) 842634
International: Partnership House, 157 Waterloo Road,
London, SE1 UU, UK.
TEL: +44 (171) 928 8681 FAX: +44 (171) 401 3215

IBNSINA: SEEAVICEN

INTERNATIONAL ISLAMIC RELIEF ORGANIZATION (IIRO)

IIRO is based in Saudi Arabia and has been working for Afghan refugees in Pakistan, Iran and inside Afghanistan for several years. Sectors of work are:

- **Health institute** run in Peshawar, which trains approximately 75 Afghans in X-ray, anaesthesia, laboratory and preventative medicine;
- **Four hospitals for Afghan refugees** in Pakistan (Miranshah, Peshawar, Quetta);
- **Three hospitals in Afghanistan** (Khost, Parwan, Jowzjan);
- **Orphan support programme** through which more than 11,000 Afghan orphans and 300 widows are given monthly financial assistance;
- **Education:** higher education institute in Peshawar for BA and MSc degrees; 24 schools and 45 Koranic centres in different refugee camps and provinces of Afghanistan.

BUDGET: $5,200,000 PERSONNEL: 643
ADDRESS: F-10/4, 13 Nazimuddin Road,
GPO Box 1850, Islamabad.
TEL: +92 (51) 281594, 290581 FAX: +92 (51) 282138

INTERNATIONAL RESCUE COMMITTEE-PAKISTAN (IRC)

IRC was founded in the United States in 1933 at the request of Albert Einstein to assist opponents of the Nazi regime. IRC is a non-sectarian voluntary organization providing relief to refugees and the dispossessed worldwide. IRC has worked in Pakistan since 1980, and began crossborder rehabilitation in 1988. Up until 1992, IRC was heavily funded by USAID and printed the 12 million notoriously anti-communist textbooks developed by the University of Nebraska at Omaha. IRC also acts as a clearing house for funding from international donors to Afghan NGOs. IRC attention is moving away from refugees in NWFP towards returnees in eastern Afghanistan. Sectors of operations are:

- **Rural rehabilitation:** agriculture, irrigation, nursery and sustainable food security programmes;
- **Education:** IRC has pulled out of formal schooling in Afghanistan because of Taliban restrictions; some primary education in refugee settlements and home schooling crossborder;
- **Health:** Medical programme for refugees in NWFP;
- **Income generation:** Vocational training, small business training, credit-scheme and income generation programmes;
- **Water and sanitation:** water supply, EPI and sanitation programmes;

BUDGET: $4,450,000 (1997) PERSONNEL: 1,317
ADDRESSES:
Local: 80E Old Bara Road,
University Town, Peshawar.
TEL: +92 (91) 41274, 43242 FAX: +92 (91) 840283
International: 122 East 42nd Street, 12th Floor,
New York, NY 10168-1289, USA.
TEL: +1 (212) 551 3000 FAX: +1 (212) 551 3185

ISLAMIC RELIEF AGENCY (ISRA)

ISRA is an international NGO which offers aid, irrespective of creed or race, to victims of natural disaster and foreign aggression. Its work for Afghan refugees began in 1984. ISRA has four main areas of operation:

- **Social welfare:** Two centres for orphans in NWFP and seven more inside Afghanistan: 7,000 orphans have been registered so far;
- **Health:** Six clinics in Afghanistan and one in Peshawar; two drop-in centres for vulnerable children (orphans, disabled, destitute and street-working children), providing hygiene, basic education and vocational training to approximately 1,000 children; donation of medicines and equipment to Afghan hospitals;
- **Education:** Primary schools and vocational training have moved crossborder into eastern Afghanistan; women's education currently suspended;
- **Rural development:** 10 nurseries in Kabul and eastern Afghanistan, seed production and processing projects in Kunar, farmer training in improved techniques for sulphur drying and packing, pest control and powdery mildew control programmes.

BUDGET: $1,000,000 (1997) PERSONNEL: 111
ADDRESS: House 68/D-2, SJ Afghani Road,
GPO Box 1019, University Town, Peshawar.
TEL: +92 (91) 42245, 840365 FAX: +92 (91) 840429

JAPAN AFGHAN MEDICAL SERVICE (JAMS)

JAMS was founded in 1986 as an Afghan Leprosy Service for refugees in the NWFP of Pakistan. Since 1988 JAMS has expanded to cover other common diseases, minor and reconstructive surgery. Projects include:

- **45-bed hospital** and outreach camps; local capacity enhanced by expatriate doctors;
- **Tropical disease training** for Afghan doctors;
- **Three clinics** in eastern Afghanistan, equipped with labs and pharmacies;
- **Leprosy and dermatology** mobile health clinics in Kunar;
- **Pain clinic (acupuncture)** which helps patients without medicines, including a stomatology unit.

BUDGET: $505,600 PERSONNEL: 116
ADDRESS: 3-C II, Circular Road, University Town, Peshawar.
TEL: +92 (91) 44350 FAX: +92 (91) 841167

LAJNAT AL-BIRR AL-ISLAMIAH (LBI)

LBI is part of the World Assembly of Muslim Youth based in Saudi Arabia. LBI started work for Afghanistan in 1988. Fields of operation in eastern Afghanistan include:

- **Education:** teacher training institute located in Peshawar;
- **Rural development:** irrigation, nurseries, reforestation, farm mechanization, seed multiplication;
- **Health:** Al-Birr Hospital in Paktya (70 beds) and a Primary Health Care programme for women and children;
- **Social welfare:** Over 4,500 orphans are provided with financial support, and 225 are housed in an orphanage in Kunar;
- **Emergency relief packages:** Food and clothes donations to refugees;
- **Human resource development:** Vocational skills training courses.

BUDGET: $785,000   PERSONNEL: 220
ADDRESS: 3304/5 Safaid Dheri, GPO Box 1055, Peshawar.
TEL: +92 (91) 840249, 41485   FAX: +92 (91) 840385

LAJNAT AL-DAWA AL-ISLAMIAH (LDI)

LDI is an Islamic charity working in the fields of health, education and relief for refugees in both Pakistan and Afghanistan:

- **Health:** 200-bed hospital in Peshawar, three hospitals and several clinics in NWFP and eastern Afghanistan;
- **Education:** support for 10 secondary and two primary schools, and a teacher training institute in Pakistan; four Koranic centres; training for electricians; publication services to translate and print literature into Farsi and Pashto;
- **Relief:** includes a drinking water programme, which builds tube-wells in refugee camps.

BUDGET: $1,541,200   PERSONNEL: 610
ADDRESS: 1 Arbab Road, University Town, GPO Box 906, Peshawar.
TEL: +92 (91) 840021, 42595   FAX: +92 (91) 840533

MADERA

MADERA (Mission d'Aide au Developpement des Economies Rurales en Afghanistan) is a European NGO founded in 1988. MADERA works through 26 permanent centres in eastern and central Afghanistan, and aims to link present rehabilitation concerns with a long-term development perspective. Sectors of operation include:

- **Integrated refugee return:** working in partnership with NGOs in the fields of health, education, drinking water and community building;
- **Rural rehabilitation:** afforestation, agricultural land clearance, seed supply, canal repair, flood control, livestock, extension work.

BUDGET: $3,300,000 (1997)   PERSONNEL: 412
ADDRESSES:
Local: 53C-II Gul Mohar Lane, UPO Box 1464, University Town, Peshawar.
TEL: +92 (91) 840546, Jalalabad 2825, 2565   FAX: +92 (91) 840234
E-mail: Office@madera.psw.erum.com.pk
International: 3 rue Roubo, 75011 Paris, France.
TEL: +33 (1) 43 70 60 07   FAX: +33 (1) 43 70 60 07

MERCY CORPS INTERNATIONAL (MCI)

MCI began implementing its medical work for war-wounded and refugees in Quetta in 1986 and its agriculture projects to rehabilitate southwestern Afghanistan in July 1988. Projects include:

- **Health:** One-year courses for advanced medical assistants with three months in a specialized field, e.g. Mother/Child Health training; 44 clinics with refresher and supervision missions conducted by training doctors.
- **Agriculture:** irrigation, sanitation, road repair, agronomy, animal husbandry, rebuilding houses and public buildings, discretionary funds for survival assistance.

BUDGET: $801,000   PERSONNEL: 236
ADDRESSES:
Local: House No. 10, Arbab Karam Khan Road, GPO Box 314, Quetta.
TEL: +92 (81) 442863   FAX: +92 (81) 449473
E-mail: mail@mci-qat.sdnpk.undp.org
International: 3030 SW First Avenue, Portland, Oregon, 97201-4796, USA.
TEL: +1 (503) 242 1032   FAX: +1 (503) 796 6844

MINE CLEARANCE PLANNING AGENCY (MCPA)

MCPA is an Afghan NGO set up in early 1990. MCPA has its headquarters in Islamabad with sub-offices in Peshawar, Quetta and Kabul. MCPA acts as the coordinating agency for the Afghan Campaign to Ban Landmines (ACBL).
Sectors of operation:

- **Technical survey** of mined areas in Afghanistan and their identification;
- **Preparation and provision of minefield maps** and updated information about mined and cleared areas;
- **Training** of deminers and surveyors;
- **Database** where data about the UNOCHA Mine Action Programme is stored and analysed for planning and management purposes;
- **Advance operational planning** of demining activities in consultation with UNOCHA and other mine clearance agencies.

BUDGET: $956,000 (1997) PERSONNEL: 243
ADDRESS: House 13,
Street 19, F-8/2, Islamabad.
TEL: +92 (51) 855939 FAX: +92 (51) 282617

MINE DETECTION DOG CENTER (MDC)

MDC was established by the United States Agency for International Development (USAID) to take part in demining operations in Afghanistan. In 1989 MDC started to train dogs which were then deployed to work with demining agencies operating in Afghanistan. Dogs are particularly useful in detecting plastic-cased mines which metal-detectors miss. MDC has now started its own Mine Dog Groups and a dog-breeding programme which has proved very successful. To date 140 dogs have been trained.
BUDGET: $3,156,000 (1997) PERSONNEL: 425
ADDRESS: Jamal Food Industry,
Mumriz Chowk, GPO Box 857,
Pabbi, Peshawar.
TEL: +92 (91) 229236 FAX: +92 (91) 229179

MÉDECINS DU MONDE (MDM)

MDM has been in Afghanistan since early 1980. Operations include:

- **Support for the regional hospital in Herat** (300 beds), including rehabilitation of the operation theatre and surgical supplies;
- **Three dispensaries for camps** of internally displaced persons and returnees;
- **Rehabilitation** of hospitals in Qala-e-Naw and Farah;
- Focus on **mother and child healthcare.**

BUDGET: $1,000,000 PERSONNEL: 78
ADDRESSES:
Local: Lane Z, Street 13,
Wazir Akbar Khan, Kabul.
TEL: Kabul 61162
International: 62, Rue Marcadet,
75020 Paris, France.
TEL: +33 (1) 44 92 14 14 FAX: +33 (1) 44 92 14 55

MEDAIR

Swiss-based NGO working in Afghanistan since 1996. Operations focus on immediate relief and rehabilitation and include:

- **Health:** TB treatment through the national TB institute in Kabul; support for Khair Khana hospital in Kabul;
- **Relief:** winter distribution of non-food items for 10,000 widows in Kabul;
- **Shelter:** manufacture of roof beams and window frames for returnees in partnership with UNHCR;
- **Sanitation:** urban canal clearance, latrine and waste disposal rehabilitation, health and hygiene education;
- **M-Link:** pilot scheme to act as facilitator between international donors and Afghan NGOs.

BUDGET: $2,000,000
ADDRESSES:
Local: House 68, T Lane,
Wazir Akbar Khan, Kabul.
TEL: Kabul 24730
International: Chemin de la Fauvette, 98, CH-1012,
Lausanne, Switzerland.

MEDICAL EMERGENCY RELIEF INTERNATIONAL (MERLIN)

MERLIN is a British-based emergency medical NGO which began working in Afghanistan in February 1995. Operations in Kandahar, Farah, Badghis and Badakhshan provinces include:

- **Drug and medical equipment** distribution;
- **Physical rehabilitation** of district clinics and hospitals;
- **Medical training** and supervision of Traditional Birth Attendants;
- **Health surveillance;**
- **Medical emergency preparedness** along the Iranian border for large influxes of returning refugees.

BUDGET: $1,000,000 (1997) PERSONNEL: 271
ADDRESSES:
Local: 7-A Gul Mohar Road, GPO Box 727, University Town, Peshawar.
TEL: +92 (91) 42534 FAX: +92 (91) 842572
E-mail: merlin@gmr.pwr.sdnpk.undp.org
International: 14 David Mews, Porter Street, London, W1M 1HN, UK.
TEL: +44 (171) 487 2505 FAX: +44 (171) 487 4042
E-mail: hq@merlin.org.uk

MOTIVATION

A British NGO established in 1990 to assist landmine victims in Cambodia, Bosnia and Afghanistan. Motivation specializes in **custom-built wheelchairs** for the disabled and seating for children with cerebral palsy. Its Jalalabad workshop produces three-wheeler wheelchairs made from local materials, adjustable for spine height and balance, and designed to cope with the rough outdoor conditions encountered in Afghanistan. Motivation also makes crutches, prostheses and orthoses.
ADDRESS:
Brockley Academy, Brockley Lane, Backwell, Bristol, BS19 3AQ, UK
TEL: +44 (1275) 464012 FAX: +44 (1275) 464019
E-mail: motivation@motivation.org.uk Website: www.motivation.org.uk

MÉDECINS SANS FRONTIÈRES (MSF)

MSF was established in 1971 as a non-profit, non-political international organization by doctors determined to offer emergency assistance wherever wars and man-made disasters occur in the world. Dependent on volunteer health professionals, MSF is committed to publicly denouncing any violations of basic humanitarian principles to which its members bear witness. Three separate MSF sections are working in Afghanistan: MSF (Belgium) operates in the north and Bamiyan, based out of Mazar; MSF (Holland) operates in Herat and Uruzgan, with a head office in Peshawar; MSF (France) operates in Kabul, Ghazni and Gardez. The programmes in Afghanistan cover the following:

- **Primary health care:** rehabilitation and support of hospitals, comprehensive health clinics and rural health posts nationwide;
- **Mother/child health:** including training of Traditional Birth Attendants (TBAs);
- **Water and sanitation:** including public health assistance to refugees, returnees and internally-displaced persons;
- **Emergency preparedness:** containing outbreaks of cholera and TB; ready to intervene in cases of acute healthcare emergency in all parts of Afghanistan.

BUDGET: $6,006,700 PERSONNEL: 684
ADDRESSES:
Local: 25 SJ Afghani Road, GPO Box 889, University Town, Peshawar.
TEL: +92 (91) 42400 FAX: +92 (91) 843154
Kabul: Behind Cinema Zinah, Shahr-e-Naw, Kabul.
TEL: Kabul 30511 SATPHONE: +873 382 040112
SATFAX: +873 382 040117
MSF Belgium: 39, rue de la Tourelle, 1040 Brussels, Belgium.
TEL: +32 (2) 280 1881 FAX: +32 (2) 280 0173
MSF France: 8, rue St Sabine, 75011 Paris, France.
TEL: +33 (1) 40 21 29 29 FAX: +33 (1) 48 06 68 68
E-mail: Office@paris.msf.org
MSF Holland: Max Euweplein 40, PO Box 10014, 1001 EA Amsterdam, The Netherlands.
TEL: +31 (20) 52 08 705 FAX: +31 (20) 62 05 170
E-mail: (name)@amsterdam.msf.org

NORWEGIAN AFGHANISTAN COMMITTEE (NAC)

NAC was founded in 1979 in response to the Soviet invasion, initially working in medical support and cash-for-food programmes. Working out of Ghazni and Badakhshan, current sectors of assistance include:

- **Emergency aid**: in Ghazni, Badakhshan, Kabul and Jalalabad;
- **Health:** Support for local health systems, midwife pilot projects, vaccination programmes, hospitals and clinics in Ghazni and Nuristan;
- **Education:** Direct support to 43 schools; funding for mine awareness and environmental education;
- **Reconstruction:** Irrigation system rehabilitation; school, hospital and health clinic reconstruction;
- **Agriculture:** Wheat trials, seed multiplication, vegetable production, crop protection and forest protection;

BUDGET: $2,002,000 (1997) PERSONNEL: 105
ADDRESS: 21F/A, Khushhal Khan Khattak Road,
GPO Box 993, University Town, Peshawar.
TEL: +92 (91) 43717, 41346, Kabul 33684 FAX: +92 (91) 840517

NORWEGIAN PROJECT OFFICE/RURAL REHABILITATION ASSOCIATION FOR AFGHANISTAN (NPO/RRAA)

NPO/RRAA was originally established in Peshawar in 1990, and was supervised by NCA until 1994 when it became an independent Afghan NGO. In 1992 the agency established offices in Jalalabad, Gardez, Mazar and Herat. Only a limited number of projects remain in Pakistan to serve the neediest refugees. The key sectors of NPO/RRAA's activities are: **income generation** and **skills training; construction; agriculture; water supply; relief supply; education.**
BUDGET: $786,000 (1997) PERSONNEL: 232
ADDRESS: 15-B Old Jamrud Road,
University Town, Peshawar.
TEL: +92 (91) 41129, 45210 FAX: +92 (91) 840107

GERMAN AGENCY FOR TECHNICAL COOPERATION (NSP/GTZ)

NSP is a GTZ project working through NGOs in Afghanistan. GTZ is the main implementing agency for **technical assistance from the German government.** NSP was originally set up in Germany in 1994 and moved to Pakistan in 1995. NSP cooperates with 15 NGOs in the fields of vocational training, basic education, health and infrastructure.
BUDGET: $920,000 (1997) PERSONNEL: 16
ADDRESS: 39 D/3, SJ Afghani Road,
University Town, Peshawar.
TEL: +92 (91) 841601 FAX: +92 (91) 840986

ORGANIZATION FOR MINE CLEARANCE AND AFGHAN REHABILITATION (OMAR)

OMAR is an Afghan NGO established in 1990 and offers different types of mine awareness courses, training aids and publications on mine awareness. By the end of 1991, OMAR completed its **mine awareness training** in the refugee camps of Pakistan (NWFP and Baluchistan) and now operates courses and campaigns inside Afghanistan. Eight **mine clearance** teams concentrate their demining efforts in western Afghanistan (Herat, Farah, Badghis).
BUDGET: $630,300 PERSONNEL: 490
ADDRESS: 21, Street 2, G-2, Phase 2, Hayatabad, PO Box 1433, Peshawar.
TEL: +92 (91) 812919, 812084, Kabul 2591 FAX: +92 (91) 812085

ORPHANS, REFUGEES & AID (ORA INTERNATIONAL)

ORA is a German-based organization, founded in 1981 to assist vulnerable groups worldwide. ORA began assisting Afghan refugees in 1983. Since 1991 the agency has concentrated on **drug rehabilitation** in Peshawar and Badakhshan, and **HIV/AIDS awareness** and support.
BUDGET: $403,000 (1997) PERSONNEL: 77
ADDRESSES:
Local: F-27 K.K.K. Road,
University Town, Peshawar.
TEL: +92 (91) 841280 FAX: +92 (91) 841089
E-mail: ora@ora.psh.brain.net.pk
International: Am Rothbusch 26, D-34497 Korbach, Germany.
TEL: +49 (5631) 63011/4 FAX: +49 (5631) 63015

OCKENDEN VENTURE (OV)

Founded in England in 1960, OV established a Pakistan office in 1984 and works in the following sectors:

- **Handicrafts**: the largest producer of Afghan handicrafts in Pakistan, marketing the products of eight other agencies, and exporting 70% of production;
- **Construction:** construction and maintenance of schools, warehouses, BHUs, roads and bridges, and employs 2,500 refugee men on construction projects;
- **Training:** tailoring courses, soap making, embroidery, shoe-making and handicraft apprenticeships;
- **Agriculture:** a Goat Loan Scheme for widows and needy families.

BUDGET: $486,000 (1997) PERSONNEL: 96
ADDRESSES:
Local: 43/D-2, Old Jamrud Road,
University Town, Peshawar.
TEL: +92 (91) 40410 FAX: +92 (91) 841219
E-mail: ajpk@ockende.psh
International: Constitution Hill, Woking,
Surrey, GU22 7UU, UK.
TEL: +44 (1483) 772012 FAX: +44 (1483) 750774

OXFAM

OXFAM is a British NGO established in 1942 for the relief of poverty and suffering worldwide. OXFAM's projects in Afghanistan include:

- **Hazarajat:** Rural Development Programme initiated in 1991 in Bamiyan and Ghor provinces; implements projects in agriculture, veterinary, health education, literacy and numeracy, community development and small-scale infrastructure;
- **North:** working in Balkh and Baghlan provinces on rural reconstruction, water supply, school rebuilding;
- **Kabul:** major infrastructure project in piped water supply, suspended in September 1996 because of Taliban restrictions on health education for local women; Kabul office pursuing programme of advocacy to improve the situation.

BUDGET: $300,000 (1997) PERSONNEL: 98
ADDRESSES:
Local: House 149, Street 7B,
Wazir Akbar Khan, Kabul.
SATPHONE: +873 662 660140, +873 682 341014
SATFAX: +873 662 660141, +873 682 341015
Liaison Office, House 179, Street 73,
G-9/3, Islamabad.
TEL: +92 (51) 261883 FAX: +92 (51) 261889
International: 274 Banbury Road,
Oxford, OX2 7DZ, UK.
TEL: +44 (1865) 311311 FAX: +44 (1865) 313780
E-mail: (name)@oxfam.org.uk

PHARMACIENS SANS FRONTIÈRES (PSF)

PSF is a French medical NGO which began work in Afghanistan in 1995. Projects are implemented out of Kabul, Herat and Mazar as follows:

- **Supply of medicines**, medical equipment and hygiene items;
- **Pharmacies** rehabilitation and monitoring in medical establishments (including training for control of pharmaceutical stock);
- **Biological laboratories** located in six hospitals in Kabul, Ghazni, Herat and Mazar.

BUDGET: $975,000 PERSONNEL: 11
ADDRESSES:
Local: Street 13, Lane F, House No. 270,
Wazir Akbar Khan, Kabul.
TEL: Kabul 62039 SATPHONE: +873 682 080955
SATFAX: +873 682 080958
International: 4 voie Militaire des Gravanches,
63100 Clermand Ferrand, France.
TEL: +33 (4) 73 98 24 98

RÄDDA BARNEN (RBS)

RBS, the Swedish "Save the Children," was founded in Stockholm in 1919. It is a child rights organization. RBS opened its Peshawar office in 1989, but does not implement projects. The agency supports the following projects with funding and training:

- **CDAP** (Comprehensive Disabled Afghans Project) being implemented by UNOPS;
- **Mine awareness** and education, including funding the Afghan Campaign to Ban Landmines (ACBL);
- **Refugee** programmes, aimed at initiating self help activities to meet the needs of the most vulnerable refugee children and the disabled;
- **Health** and social services among Afghans in Peshawar;
- **Internally-displaced persons:** assistance in and around Jalalabad.

BUDGET: $397,000 (1997) PERSONNEL: 44
ADDRESSES:
Local: 228, Gulhaji Plaza,
UPO Box 1424, Peshawar.
TEL: +92 (91) 44784, 840987 FAX: +92 (91) 840349
International: Grensesvingen 7,
0661, Oslo 6, Norway.
TEL: +47 (22) 570080 FAX: +47 (22) 688547

SOLIDARITE AFGHANISTAN BELGIUM (SAB)

SAB began assistance to Afghan refugees in Pakistan in 1985 and crossed into eastern Afghanistan in 1991. It is involved in two sectors:

- **Education:** primary schools and teacher training in Afghanistan and in refugee camps in Pakistan;
- **Vocational training/Income generation:** apprenticeship scheme in 28 trades; tool-kits are supplied to master craftsmen for each apprentice placed; graduates also receive a standard tool-kit; credit facilities for micro-enterprises; beneficiaries are Afghans aged 15-20 years (25% are from vulnerable groups, e.g. widows, orphans and disabled aged 15-45 years).

BUDGET: $1,015,000 (1997) PERSONNEL: 102
ADDRESS: ITC: 3-1, Phase 5, Hayatabad,
PO Box 799, Peshawar.
TEL: +92 (91) 812456-7 FAX: +92 (91) 810307

SOCIETY OF AFGHANISTAN'S VOLUNTEER ENVIRONMENTALISTS (SAVE)

SAVE was founded in August 1993 to work for the environmental wellbeing, rehabilitation and sustainable development of Afghanistan. The agency is an Afghan-managed foundation dedicated to campaigning, study and research, and implementing intervention projects. From May 1998, SAVE began environmental impact assessment training for the UNOPS/P.E.A.C.E. programme to ensure community-led rehabilitation is more environmentally sensitive. Sectors of operation are:

- **Forestry:** reforestation and the promotion of agroforestry by establishing forest and orchard nurseries; research of suitable varieties of trees and bushes for future reforestation;
- **Education:** awareness programmes on the environment among school children and people in forested areas;
- **Income generation:** SAVE campaigns for funds to assist destitute families and individuals to enable them to participate in income generation programmes.
- **Resource Centre:** contains books, reports and pamphlets on the environment; the monthly newsletter *SAVE* focuses on the ecological problems and the pace of rehabilitation in Afghanistan.

BUDGET: $96,000 PERSONNEL: 29
ADDRESS: House 514, Street 15,
E2 Phase 1, Hayatabad, Peshawar.
TEL: +92 (91) 813838

SWEDISH COMMITTEE FOR AFGHANISTAN (SCA)

SCA was founded in 1980 to work for the withdrawal of the Soviets and to assist in the Afghan people's struggle for independence. SCA established a permanent office in Peshawar in 1982, and is one of the leading NGOs working in education and rural infrastructure in Afghanistan. Operations include:

- **Primary health care**: support and monitoring for about 200 clinics and 1,300 health workers; supply of medicines and equipment; training of Traditional Birth Attendants (TBAs) and Mother/Child Health (MCH) workers; implementing partner in the Comprehensive Disabled Afghans Project (CDAP) and Expanded Programme of Immunization (EPI); water supply and sanitation;
- **Education:** support for over 650 rural primary schools and home-schooling, covering 4,250 teachers and over 162,000 students (including 30,000 girls); teacher-training courses at the three regional offices (Ghazni, Nangarhar, Takhar); basic education courses for around 650 women;
- **Rural development:** seed testing and multiplication in six different climatic zones; surveys and extension services to Afghan farmers; training for both SCA and other extension workers; women's agriculture project; micro-loans for women;
- **Rural engineering:** construction of 900 shallow water wells, 24 primary schools, seven basic health clinics, several irrigation and latrine projects.

BUDGET: $8,407,100 (1997) PERSONNEL: 593
ADDRESSES:
Local: 24-D/E Chinar Road, University Town, GPO Box 689, Peshawar.
TEL: +92 (91) 840218, 840257, 43279 FAX: +92 (91) 840519
E-mail: sca@peshawar.psw.erum.com.pk
International: Sturegatan 16, S-114 36 Stockholm, Sweden.
TEL: +46 (8) 660 8550, 660 7320 FAX: +46 (8) 660 8548
E-mail: sca-sak@algonet.se

SAVE THE CHILDREN UK (SCF-UK)

SCF-UK has been working in Afghanistan since 1994 in the fields of health and education. In March 1996 SCF-UK suspended its programme in Herat after the Taliban closed girls' schools and forbade women from working outside the home. The agency continues to work out of Mazar in the following:

- **Lower primary formal education;**
- **Child-to-child health education;**
- **Working children and children's rights**

BUDGET: $290,000 (1997) PERSONNEL: 17
ADDRESSES:
Local: 194-A College Road, F-7/3, Islamabad.
TEL: +92 (51) 279214-5 FAX: +92 (51) 279216
E-mail: scf.uk@infolink.net.pk
Karte Mamoreen, Mazar-e-Sharif, TEL: Mazar 2173
International: 17 Grove Lane, London SE5 8RD, UK.
TEL: +44 (171) 703 5400 FAX: +44 (171) 703 2278

SAVE THE CHILDREN-US (SC-US)

Save the Children (USA) was founded in 1932 and operates in 41 developing nations. The agency began working in Afghanistan in 1988 and runs programmes out of Kabul, Mazar and Andkhoi, focusing on:

- **Primary health care:** integrated public health respiratory infection and diarrhoea control programme providing health education, technical training and materials support to partner hospitals in Kabul;
- **Education:** non-formal education through communities, hospitals and clinics;
- **Economic opportunities** via affordable credit programmes and vocational training for vulnerable women and men with disabilities;
- **Children and war:** a programme initiated in Kabul in 1995, involving community-based psychosocial assistance and landmine education, targeting over 60,000 children; construction of 16 playgrounds/safe play areas in Kabul.

BUDGET: $2,451,000 (1997) PERSONNEL: 300
ADDRESSES:
Local: 14-B, Street 61, F-7/4, PO Box 1952, Islamabad.
TEL: +92 (91) 821829, 279212 FAX: +92 (91) 824902, 279210
E-mail: Scjuh@net.pk
International: 54 Wilton Road, Westport, Connecticut, 06880, USA.
TEL: +1 (203) 221 4000, 221 4200 FAX: +1 (203) 221 4210, 227 5667

SERVING EMERGENCY RELIEF AND VOCATIONAL ENTERPRISES (SERVE)

SERVE began operations in 1980 in Peshawar, and specializes in the following sectors:

- **Health:** basic health education for children and first aid for village women; repair of canals and provision of clean water in northern Afghanistan;
- **Disability:** Braille printing, orientation & mobility training and daily living skills are taught to the visually impaired; visually impaired children are integrated into local schools with the aid of braille books; signs used by deaf Afghans are documented and hearing aids provided; Afghans are trained in basic physiotherapy procedures and an orthotics workshop supplies splints, canes and artificial limbs; part of the Comprehensive Disabled Afghans Project (CDAP).
- **Environment:** Solar oven technology to help stop deforestation by reducing the need for fuel wood (over 30,000 solar ovens have been made and sold in Afghanistan); forestry project to train Afghan farmers in horticulture and agroforestry skills; re-establishing of fruit trees to combat opium poppy production and provide an income;
- **Relief:** Communities are helped through food for work programmes and mass emergency relief distributions.

BUDGET: $587,000 (1997) PERSONNEL: 275
ADDRESS: 7 Mulberry Road, PO Box 477,
University Town, Peshawar.
TEL: +92 (91) 840292, 41706 FAX: +92 (91) 840422
E-mail: adminp@serve.psh.brain.net.pk

SANDY GALLS'S AFGHANISTAN APPEAL (SGAA)

SGAA is a British NGO set up in 1986 specifically to provide assistance for disabled Afghans. Based in Kabul and Jalalabad, SGAA is part of the Comprehensive Disabled Afghans Project (CDAP). Operations include:

- **Orthopaedic workshops:** Afghan orthopaedic technicians are trained to make and fit artificial limbs, splints and callipers;
- **Physiotherapy departments:** Afghan physiotherapy technicians are trained to treat patients using mainly manual physiotherapy techniques; a two year training curriculum is being developed; once technicians have graduated, they are established in independent workshops, clinics or hospitals in conjunction with the local health authorities.

BUDGET: $738,000 (1997) PERSONNEL: 127
ADDRESS: 5A Circular Lane,
University Town, Peshawar.
TEL: +92 (91) 843028 FAX: +92 (91) 843028

SOLIDARITÉS (SOLID)

During the Soviet occupation of Afghanistan, SOLIDARITÉS (under a different name) gave emergency aid in the form of food or cash, along with more long-range development programmes in education and agriculture. Emphasis was given to re-establishment of physical and social infrastructure. Operating out of Kabul, Bamiyan and Wardak, current projects include:

- **Urban water and sanitation:** Collection and disposal of human waste from housing estates, schools and hospitals; rehabilitation of waste water treatment plant serving 170,000 Kabulis; drilling of 1,000 wells and handpumps; rehabilitating existing water supply networks using local resources
- **Rural rehabilitation:** Technical and financial support in irrigation projects (canals, *karezes*, dams) and development programmes (mechanization, seeds and fertilizers, agricultural training and extension); assistance in rebuilding physical infrastructure (roads, bridges, dams, soap and brick factories).
- **Winter relief:** Non-food items for 30,000 families in Kabul.

BUDGET: $5,807,000 (1997) PERSONNEL: 1222
ADDRESSES:
Local: Hujra House, Old Bara Road,
University Town, Peshawar.
TEL: +92 (91) 840228 FAX: +92 (91) 844745
International: 19, rue Daviel, 75013 Paris, France.
TEL: +33 (1) 45 88 33 22 FAX: +33 (1) 45 89 74 78

SOCIETY FOR THE PRESERVATION OF AFGHANISTAN'S CULTURAL HERITAGE (SPACH)

Established in 1994 in response to a growing awareness of the vulnerability of the cultural heritage of Afghanistan, SPACH aims primarily to share information about the state of collections, historic monuments and archaeological sites among local and international cultural institutions and individuals in order to limit the destruction caused by the ongoing war. Activities have included:

- **Assistance in salvaging** 1,500 objects from the Kabul Museum and moving to a more secure location; help in preparing a photo inventory of what remains in order to determine which objects may be lost or retrievable;
- **Support for assessment missions and emergency repairs** to the Bamiyan Buddhas, Minaret of Jam and other important sites;
- **Preparation of photo catalogue** of historic sites, using both pre-war scholarship and material from recent site visits;
- **Raising international awareness** of the richness and vulnerability of Afghanistan's cultural heritage, through a newsletter, exhibitions and lectures, and cooperation with the Afghan Ministry of Information and Culture, UNOCHA, UNESCO, the International Council of Museums and other cultural institutions worldwide.

ADDRESSES:
Local: SPACH, c/o ARIC, PO Box 1084,
University Town, Peshawar.
TEL: +92 (91) 840387, 40839 FAX: +92 (91) 840471
E-mail: spach@undpafg.org.pk
International: SPACH, c/o UNOCHA,
16 avenue Jean Trembley, Petit Saconnex,
CH-1211, Geneva 10, Switzerland.
FAX: +41 (22) 788 2204

TERRE DES HOMMES (TdH)

Terre des Hommes is a Swiss-based NGO committed to helping children in distress, by providing emergency relief, primary healthcare, training and protection to children and their families around the world. TdH began work in Afghanistan in 1995, to assist in projects for street children in Kabul. Operations include:

- **Child day-care:** following a needs assessment of children working and living in the streets of Kabul (1996), TdH supports two child day-care centres run by the Afghan NGO, Aschiana; children receive literacy, numeracy and health education, behaviour training, handicraft training, and their own hygiene supplies.
- **Mother and child home-visiting**: teams of midwives visit new mothers and babies in their homes during the first six weeks after birth; early identification of risk factors may reduce mother and child morbidity and mortality in Kabul.

BUDGET: $450,000 PERSONNEL: 30
ADDRESSES:
Local: House 51, Street 13, Wazir Akbar Khan, Kabul.
TEL: Kabul 62520
International: Case Postale 912, Lausanne -1000, Switzerland.
TEL: +41 (21) 653 6666 FAX: +41 (21) 653 6677

UNIVERSITY OF NEBRASKA AT OMAHA/EDUCATION PROJECT FOR AFGHANISTAN (UNO/EPA)

UNO was the contractor for the USAID Higher Education Project at Kabul University from 1974 to 1978. Throughout the Soviet War, UNO produced more than 12 million textbooks (notoriously anti-communist) for Afghan primary schools, and provided literacy training to 48,000 mujahideen in their winter camps. UNO's spending totalled around $45 million, but slumped after the withdrawal of USAID support from Afghanistan in 1994. UNO is currently involved in developing a **technical training package on behalf of the US oil company Unocal.** Their aim is to train up several thousand Afghans around Kandahar as a future workforce to construct the Central Asian oil and gas pipelines planned to transit Afghanistan *en route* to Pakistan.
BUDGET: $200,000 (1997) PERSONNEL: 16
ADDRESS: 56-C, Old Bara Road, University Town, Peshawar.
TEL: +92 (91) 44536 FAX: +92 (91) 840492

WRITERS UNION OF FREE AFGHANISTAN (WUFA)

WUFA is an independent, non-profit organization of Afghan writers, professionals and specialists established in Peshawar in 1985. It focuses on pluralism, participation, democracy, human rights and the reconstruction of Afghanistan. Its objectives are to **oppose dictatorship, discrimination, foreign surrogates and foreign interference** in any form. The organization has published two journals and has held international seminars and conferences on different aspects of Afghan society. WUFA currently maintains a library of 3,000 books, journals and newspapers in English, Dari, Pashto and German languages going back to 1984.
BUDGET: $48,000 PERSONNEL: 22
ADDRESS: 78E Rehman Baba Road, University Town, Peshawar.
TEL: +92 (91) 840318 FAX: +92 (91) 840288

WORLD WIDE FUND FOR NATURE (WWF-PAKISTAN)

WWF-Pakistan believes in linking the environmental problems of Afghanistan into a region-wide approach to conservation. Deforestation in eastern Afghanistan affects Pakistan's NWFP; the protection of the Marco Polo sheep in Khunjerab National Park must be linked to conservation of Afghanistan's Wakhan Corridor; a catchment area policy for the Kabul River must be created as the river flows into Pakistan's NWFP; wetlands west of Kabul and south of Ghazni need to be protected in order to maintain the flyways for cranes and other rare birds towards the Chitral River and Baluchistan. Pakistan is used as a route for timber, snow leopard and falcon smuggling, adding to the **urgency for a region-wide approach to conservation.** WWF-Pakistan has established links with the Afghan Ministries of Environment and Planning, has offered to help train Kabul-based forestry students, and has provided some funding to rehabilitate Kabul Zoo.
ADDRESS: 42-C, Sahibzada Abdul Qayyum Road, UPO Box 1439, University Town, Peshawar.
TEL: +92 (91) 841593, 842096 FAX: +92 (91) 841594
E-mail: ashiq@wwf.psh.brain.net.pk

APPEAL FOR CORRECTIONS AND UPDATES

The editors would greatly appreciate if aid representatives, journalists and other readers could provide us with any changes and comments on information, statistical data and contact lists provided in this Essential Field Guide. Regular updates will be made available on the website of the International Centre for Humanitarian Reporting (http://www.ichr.org). New editions will include the corrected or updated material.

United Nations agencies

Editors' Note: This information is compiled from the 1998 Consolidated Appeal for Afghanistan, individual agency publications, and returned EFG questionnaires. Budget figures are calculated as the total of secured funds for 1998, plus additional requirements through the 1998 Appeal.

United Nations Office for the Coordination of Humanitarian Assistance to Afghanistan (UNOCHA)

UNOCHA operates under the overall responsibility of the UN Office for the Coordination of Humanitarian Affairs. It provides coordination of logistical support for programmes of both the UN system and NGOs in Afghanistan, through the following initiatives:

- **Single UN Coordinator:** also acts as UNDP Resident Representative, appointed for humanitarian and development activities inside Afghanistan.
- **Consolidated Appeal:** compiled by UNOCHA in partnership with other UN agencies, NGOs and donors. In 1997 donors provided $56 million via the Appeal (42% of the total requested), although total assistance to Afghanistan in 1997 totalled $217 million. The 1998 Consolidated Appeal is requesting $157 million, with an increased emphasis on longer-term projects such as education, and rural and urban rehabilitation.
- **Common Assistance Strategy:** broadly accepted by donors and the external assistance community, this approach was initiated at the Ashgabad Conference in January 1997 and developed through the Strategic Framework process.
- **Afghanistan Support Group (ASG):** an active body of major donors, based outside the region but contributing to the assistance strategy.
- **Afghanistan Task Force:** an informal advisory group of donor, UN and NGO representatives, based in the region, which works with the UN Resident/Humanitarian Coordinator.
- **UN Regional Coordination Officers:** senior field-based coordinators in Kabul, Jalalabad, Herat, Kandahar and Mazar (tbc).

In the field, UNOCHA manages the following operational projects:

- **Mine Action Programme:** responsible for the strategic planning, operations management, coordination and fund-raising of all mine action activities in Afghanistan. In partnership with NGOs, activities include: **mine awareness**, implemented by Ansar Relief Institute (Iran), BBC AED, HI, OMAR; SC-US; ARCS; **mine clearance** implemented by ATC; DAFA; OMAR, HALO Trust, MDC; **mine survey** and high risk area marking, implemented by MCPA; and **monitoring**, evaluation and training. For more information on landmines, see UNDPKO below.
- **Aircraft Operations:** UNOCHA operates two passenger aircraft based out of Islamabad, with regular flights into all Afghanistan's major cities and towns. For more details SEE TRAVEL.
- **Radio network:** UNOCHA coordinates HF voice and radio-telex facilities for UN agencies and NGOs, and maintains 24-hour radio rooms in Kabul and Islamabad. For more details SEE RADIO & TELECOMMUNICATIONS.
- **Humanitarian projects:** voluntary repatriation and assistance to internally-displaced persons; food aid; water supply and sanitation; agriculture; emergency support for health and community-based basic education.

UNOCHA/UNDP BUDGET: $41,550,750
ADDRESSES:
Islamabad: House 292, Street 55, Sector F-10/4, Islamabad.
Mail: PO Box 1809, Islamabad, Pakistan.
TEL: +92 (51) 211451-5 FAX: +92 (51) 211450
E-mail: unocha@undpafg.org.pk
Peshawar: 20D/A, Circular Road, University Town, Peshawar.
TEL: +92 (91) 41131 FAX: +92 (91) 840316
International: 16 avenue Jean Trembley, Petit Saconnex, CH-1211, Geneva 10, Switzerland.
TEL: +41 (22) 788 2215, 788 2230 FAX: +41 (22) 788 2204
Publications: *Weekly Update* on events in Afghanistan, *Consolidated Appeal for Afghanistan*, *Consolidated Annual Report on Humanitarian Assistance*, annual *Mine Action Programme Workplan* and *Report*, *Aina* quarterly magazine, *Paigham* (Dari/Pashto monthly magazine)

Office for the Coordination of Humanitarian Affairs (OCHA):

Formerly the Department of Humanitarian Affairs (DHA), the restructured OCHA will concentrate on its three core functions: **policy development, advocacy of humanitarian issues** and **coordination of humanitarian emergency response**, including negotiating the use of military resources in humanitarian emergencies through the Military and Civil Defence Unit (MCDU).
ADDRESSES:
United Nations, New York, NY10017, USA.
TEL: +1 (212) 963 9072 FAX: +1 (212) 963 3630
Palais des Nations, CH-1211, Geneva 10, Switzerland.
TEL: +41 (22) 788 7020 FAX: +41 (22) 788 6389
Website: www.reliefweb.int/dha_ol/index.html

Food & Agriculture Organization of the United Nations (FAO)

FAO has a mandate to raise levels of nutrition and standards of living as well as to improve agricultural productivity. FAO is the leading UN agency for the rehabilitation of Afghanistan's agricultural sector, and has helped ease the way for the return of nearly three million refugees to their homes since 1992. FAO has now developed an open-ended strategy (*Afghanistan Agricultural Strategy*, January 1997) aimed at fully developing the country's farming potential. The strategy seeks to operate as much as possible through NGOs and has four principal objectives: to create national **food security**, to increase **economic and social development**, to raise the levels of **skills** and knowledge and to protect scarce **natural resources**. In addition, FAO is operational in the following sectors:

- **Crop and food supply** assistance mission: in cooperation with WFP;
- **FAO Crops:** sustainable crop production for food security through seed supply, pest control, irrigation, soil fertility, income generation; part of UNDP's P.E.A.C.E. programme.
- **FAO Livestock:** livestock development for food security through training veterinary staff, micro-credit, improved fodder and nutrition, animal feed manufacture, poultry breeding; part of UNDP's P.E.A.C.E. programme.

FAO CROPS BUDGET: $14,834,097 FAO LIVESTOCK BUDGET: $4,872,500
ADDRESSES:
Peshawar: 19A-C, 3 Gul Mohar Lane, University Town, Peshawar.
International: Division of Information, Viale delle Terme do Caracalla, 00100 Rome, Italy.
TEL: +39 (6) 57051 FAX: +39 (6) 57052-3
Website: www.fao.org
Publications: *Afghanistan Agricultural Strategy* (January 1997), *Food Outlook*, *Ceres Magazine, The State of the World's Food and Agriculture.*

United Nations Centre For Human Settlements (Habitat)

UNCHS Habitat focuses on providing active support to rehabilitation initiatives in both rural and urban communities in Afghanistan. The aim is to support community-driven processes of urban recovery and strengthen traditional systems of community participation and management. Habitat has offices in Kabul, Mazar, Herat, Kandahar, Farah, Wardak, Taloqan and Bamiyan, and produces **GIS-generated maps** of many Afghan towns. In March 1998, Habitat launched an informal development forum to promote discussion of field experiences relating to development. Habitat is also rehabilitating Babur's Garden in Kabul, and as part of the UNDP P.E.A.C.E. programme, concentrates on:

- **water and sanitation:** urban water supply, drainage and waste removal;
- **community development**: rebuilding urban communities through promoting local structures of governance;
- **shelter;**
- **employment generation;**
- **energy production**, using appropriate technology.

BUDGET: $7,357,000
ADDRESSES:
Islamabad: 5-B College Road, F-7/3, Islamabad.
TEL: +92 (51) 272529, 261025 FAX: +92 (51) 274358
E-mail: joxidental@hab.infolink.net.pk
Kabul: Charahi Haji Yacoub, Shahr-e-Naw, Kabul. TEL: Kabul 30717, 30808
International: PO Box 30030, Nairobi, Kenya.
TEL: +254 (2) 621244 FAX: +254 (2) 624266, 624267

United Nations International Drug Control Programme (UNDCP)

UNDCP works with states to tackle the global drug problem and its consequences. UNDCP started implementing a new four-year $16.4 million Afghanistan Drug Control Programme in 1997. UNDCP has chosen a "positive conditionality" approach whereby the communities, districts and provincial authorities agree to the progressive implementation of a poppy ban in target areas in exchange for a package of development assistance (defined in participation with beneficiaries, but typically involving agriculture, irrigation, rural infrastructure and education projects). During 1997, UNDCP started work in Kandahar and Nangarhar provinces. The programme is composed of the following modules:

- **Capacity building for drug control;**
- **Drug control monitoring system;**
- **Poppy crop reduction:** the most crucial module of the programme, aiming to create alternative sustainable livelihoods for farmers currently engaged in opium poppy cultivation;
- **Demand reduction support;**
- **Law enforcement** (to be added when the necessary conditions exist).

BUDGET: $16.4 million (over four years)
ADDRESSES:
Regional Office for Southwest Asia: 11th Floor, Saudi Pak Tower, 61A Jinnah Avenue, Blue Area, PO Box 1051, Islamabad.
TEL: +92 (51) 279087-8 FAX: +92 (51) 279085
E-mail: undcppakistan@undcp.un.or.at
International: Vienna International Centre, PO Box 500, A-1400 Vienna, Austria.
TEL: +43 (1) 213450
E-mail: undcp_hq@undcp.un.or.at Website: www.undcp.org
Publications: *World Drug Report, UNDCP Update on Afghanistan*

United Nations Development Programme (UNDP)

UNDP is the world's largest multilateral source of grants and technical assistance for sustainable human development, as well as being the primary coordinating organization for all UN development activities worldwide. In May 1997, UNDP launched a multi-year integrated development programme for Afghanistan, entitled Poverty Eradication And Community Empowerment (P.E.A.C.E.), and funded for an initial two-year period with $34 million of UNDP core funds. The overall objective of the P.E.A.C.E. initiative is to contribute to the restoration of peace in Afghanistan through poverty alleviation, good governance building and community empowerment in both rural and urban areas. Approximately 23 rural districts and six urban centres have been selected for initial programme work. Future cooperation is planned with UNDCP, UNHCR and NGOs; in 1997 implementation was through:

- **FAO Crops:** sustainable crop production for food security through seed supply, pest control, irrigation, soil fertility, income generation;
- **FAO Livestock:** livestock development for food security through training veterinary staff, micro-credit, improved fodder and nutrition, animal feed manufacture, poultry breeding;
- **UNCHS (Habitat):** rebuilding urban communities through promoting local structures, water supply, sanitation and shelter, employment generation, energy production;
- **UNOPS:** strengthening rural communities through credit and employment support, skills development, water supply and irrigation, energy development, rural access roads.

- **UNOPS/CDAP:** the Comprehensive Disabled Afghans Programme, training field rehabilitation workers, mobilizing local communities, enhancing awareness of disabled people's needs, capacity building.

BUDGET: $14,394,000 (not including UNOCHA and implementing agencies)
ADDRESSES:
Islamabad: House 292, Street 55, Sector F-10/4, (PO Box 1809) Islamabad.
TEL: +92 (51) 211451-5 FAX: +92 (51) 211450
E-mail: (name)@undpafg.org.pk
Kabul: TEL: 26051, 24824
International: One UN Plaza, New York, NY 10017, USA.
TEL: +1 (212) 906 5558 FAX: +1 (212) 906 6365
E-mail: (name)@undp.org Website: www.undp.org
Publications: *see UNOCHA above; in addition, the various UNDP programmes put out their own newsletters and factsheets.*

United Nations Department of Peace-Keeping Operations (UNDPKO)

UNDPKO is the umbrella agency for all UN Mine Action Programmes worldwide. UNDPKO recognizes that humanitarian mine action is not about mines, but about people and their interactions with a mine-contaminated environment. The aim of a mine action programme is to create an environment in which people can live more safely and in which economic and social development can occur free from the constraints imposed by landmine contamination. As a result, UNDPKO is promoting the following:

- **Integrated mine action** – not just mine clearance;
- **Complementarity** – not competition between UN and NGO agencies;
- **Coordination** – rather than direct implementation.

ADDRESS:
Mine Action Service, United Nations, DC1-1584, New York, NY10017, USA.
TEL: +1 (212) 963 1875 FAX: +1 (212) 963 1040
E-mail: cassidy@un.org
Websites: www.un.org/Depts/Landmine/ and www.un.org/Depts/dpko/homepage.htm
Publications: *Landmines: demining news from the United Nations*

United Nations Education, Scientific and Cultural Organization (UNESCO)

UNESCO has been working in Afghanistan on and off since 1948, in the sectors of education and culture. However, with the advent of the Taliban, most UNESCO activities in Afghanistan appear to be greatly reduced. UNESCO's education objectives for 1998 are:

- To provide education facilities to all refugee returnees;
- To develop a model on learning under stress to be replicated elsewhere;
- To assist in the development of a policy on education.

UNESCO's cultural programmes to date have included:

- Assistance to SPACH and Kabul Museum;
- Cultural exhibitions to increase awareness of artistic heritage;
- Assessment of damage to national monuments.

BUDGET: $350,000
ADDRESSES:
Islamabad: Saudi Pak Tower, PO Box 2034, Islamabad.
TEL: +92 (51) 829452 FAX: +92 (51) 825341
E-mail: unesco@isb.compol.com
Website: www.unesco.org
International: 7 place de Fontenoy, 75352, Paris, France.
TEL: +33 (1) 45 68 10 00 FAX: +33 (1) 45 67 16 90
Publications: *UNESCO Courier*, *Basic Education Strategies: Afghanistan (1995), Modules on management of primary schools under stress (1996), UNESCO quarterly bulletin, Museum International, Nature and Resources.*

United Nations Population Fund (UNFPA)

UNFPA assists in providing population assistance to developing countries, through improving reproductive health and contraception services and formulating population policies. A key principle is the focus on individual male and female choice, not on achieving demographic targets. Half of UNFPA assistance is targeted at reproductive health including maternal and child healthcare and family planning. A further 15% of UNFPA assistance goes into projects carried out by NGOs. UNFPA's programme in Afghanistan has been suspended since 1992 due to the political situation in the country. *(continued)*

ADDRESS: 220 East 42nd Street, New York, NY 10017, USA.
TEL: +1 (212) 297 5020, 297 5087 FAX: +1 (212) 557 6416
E-mail: (name)@unfpa.org
Publications: *State of the World's Population.*

United Nations High Commissioner for Refugees (UNHCR)

UNHCR's two main objectives are to provide international protection to refugees and to find durable solutions to their problems. Since April 1992, a record 3.9 million refugees have returned to Afghanistan. Yet Afghans still represent UNHCR's largest single refugee caseload, and have done for the past 17 years. Currently 2.6 million Afghan refugees remain in Pakistan and Iran. More recently, UNHCR has also been called on to provide assistance to internally-displaced persons (IDPs) who, while not crossing an international border, exist in a refugee-like situation inside their own country. UNHCR works in cooperation with the ICRC, other UN agencies and many NGOs, and its involvement in Afghanistan is as follows:

- **Integrated approach to repatriation:** identifying obstacles to repatriation with refugees and working to solve them; voluntary repatriation assistance includes repatriation grant packages and transport assistance for those returning, and support for the communities in Afghanistan to which returnees are moving back;
- **Quick Impact Projects (QIPs):** over 300 small-scale and seven large-scale regional projects concentrate on the provision of safe drinking water, improvement of irrigation systems, reconstruction of homes, creation of income opportunities, repair of roads, and rehabilitation of health and education facilities.
- **Assistance to women:** skills training, income generation, micro-credit group-guaranteed loans;
- **Observed voluntary repatriation:** dropped from a record 1.4 million in 1992 to 86,000 in 1997; monitoring the rights and welfare of returnees.

BUDGET: $21,423,585
ADDRESSES:
Islamabad: House 24, Street 89, G-6/3, PO Box 1263, Islamabad.
TEL: +92 (51) 820877, 821683, 827663
International: PO Box 2500, CH-1211, Geneva 2, Switzerland.
TEL: +41 (22) 739 8502 FAX: +41 (22) 739 7377
E-mail: HQP100@unhcr.ch Website: www.unhcr.ch
Publication: *Refugees* magazine and *The State of the World's Refugees.*

United Nations Information Centre (UNIC)

UNIC is mandated by the United Nations to provide information about UN activities to all concerned including the general public. UNIC is tasked with assisting the press and broadcast media in producing news, press conferences and panel discussions on UN issues. UNIC is also a source of official documents and public information materials such as maps, photographs, UN archive footage, and statistics on economic and social development.
ADDRESSES:
Islamabad:
House 26, Street 88, G-6/3, PO Box 1107, Islamabad.
TEL: +92 (51) 270610, 823976 FAX: +92 (51) 271856
E-mail: unic@paknet2.ptc.pk
International: Information Centres Service, Department of Public Information, United Nations Secretariat, Room 1060F, New York, NY10017, USA.
TEL: +1 (212) 963 0106 FAX: +1 (212) 963 7330

United Nations Children's Fund (UNICEF)

UNICEF's primary goal is to realize the rights of all children and women, enabling even the most disadvantaged of them to fulfil their basic needs, to receive protection from harm and abuse and to develop their full potential as human beings. These rights to protection, survival and development lie at the heart of the Convention on the Rights of the Child, the most widely accepted human rights treaty in history. UNICEF carries out programmes in 138 countries worldwide. UNICEF maintains an information section in its Peshawar office to provide information to visiting journalists. Through its offices in Herat, Mazar-e-Sharif, Kandahar and Jalalabad, UNICEF implements the following programmes:

- **Health:** Expanded Programme on Immunization (EPI); primary health care and safe motherhood initiative; control of diarrhoeal diseases (CDD);

- **Nutrition:** therapeutic/supplementary feeding for malnourished children; screening and growth monitoring; promotion of local foods;
- **Water, environment and sanitation:** provision of safe water, sanitation facilities and hygiene knowledge to 300,000 beneficiaries;
- **Education:** The Taliban's closure of girls' schools in Herat in September 1995 led to UNICEF's suspension of support to education programmes in those areas where girls are not allowed to go to school. Since October 1996 this suspension has been nationwide, except for regions under control of the "Northern Alliance;"
- **Women-specific programmes:** skills training; income generation for the vulnerable and widows; social credit for rural women's development;
- **Children in conflict/anti-war agenda:** support for SC-US's children's landmine education project in Kabul; commissioning of survey of psychosocial trauma among children in Kabul; orphanage support;

BUDGET: $13,795,600
ADDRESSES:
Peshawar: 17-B(4) Abdara Road, PO Box 1078, University Town, Peshawar.
TEL: +92 (91) 43669, 45261, 840496 FAX: +92 (91) 840437
E-mail: (name)@uncfapo.erum.com.pk
International: 3 United Nations Plaza, H-9F, New York, NY10017, USA.
E-mail: pubdoc@unicef.org Website: www.unicef.org
Publications: *State of the World's Children, Progress of Nations, Annual Report, First Call for Children.*

United Nations Special Mission For Afghanistan (UNSMA)

UNSMA's ostensible role is to search for a peaceful political solution to the ongoing war in Afghanistan. During 1997, however, UNSMA's failure to make much progress was underlined by the upstaging of Norbert Holl, UNSMA's boss, by a visit to Afghanistan of Ambassador Lakhdar Brahimi, the Special Envoy of the Secretary-General, on a peace/fact-finding mission. Brahimi has emphasised the need for a strict embargo on arms entering Afghanistan, and the responsibility of Iran and Pakistan to ensure that this is enforced. He favours efforts to bring together *ulema* (Islamic scholars) from both warring sides as a first step towards peace talks, and he has drawn attention to the need for an improvement in human rights, particularly with regard to women.
ADDRESS:
Islamabad: 14, Nazimuddin Road, F-8/1, PO Box 1428, Islamabad.
TEL: +92 (51) 853363, 253647 FAX: +92 (51) 261233
E-mail: DPKO-UNMOGIP@un.org

World Food Programme (WFP)

To help combat world hunger, WFP provides food aid to developing countries to promote economic and social development and to help meet emergency needs in the wake of natural or man-made disasters. WFP claims to spend more money per year in Afghanistan than any other agency: its 120,000 tonnes of annual food aid alone are worth over $50 million. In 1997, over 1.14 million Afghans in 23 provinces benefited from WFP's relief and life-sustaining rehabilitation assistance. WFP welcomes visits by journalists, and sometimes provides transport to freelancers by overland food convoy into Afghanistan. Principal sectors of operations within the Afghanistan programme include:

- **Urban bakeries:** in Kabul, Mazar, Jalalabad, Kandahar and Faizabad, benefiting up to 800,000 Afghans during winter months; include widows' bakeries operated by and for widows;
- **Food for training:** income-generating skills, e.g. textile and carpet production, poultry projects, health training, carpentry, masonry, tile-making (Herat mosque); benefiting nearly 9,000 women;
- **Food for seeds:** provides wheat to over 4,700 farmers in exchange for improved seeds, distributed at a subsidy to small farmers;
- **Food for work:** employment for over 24,000 Afghans working on: rehabilitation of health clinics and schools (where women/girls have access); drinking water schemes; sanitation; flood control and protection in disaster prone areas; shelter reconstruction assistance;
- **Emergency feeding** for victims of natural disasters;
- **Feeding of internally-displaced persons** in camps inside Afghanistan;
- **Repatriation assistance** through food aid to returning refugees from Pakistan and Iran;
- **Institutional feeding** of hospitals' in-patients and out-patients, and orphanages;
- **Logistical services** to UN agencies and NGOs inside Afghanistan.

BUDGET: $55 million
ADDRESSES:
WFP Afghanistan: House 38, Street 86, G-6/3, PO Box 2507, Islamabad.
TEL: +92 (51) 826710, 828874, 828934 FAX: +92 (51) 278046
E-mail: kabul@wfpafg.sdnpk.undp.org (continued)
WFP APT (Afghanistan, Pakistan, Tajikistan): Saudi Pak Tower, 61A Jinnah Avenue, Blue Area, Islamabad 44000.
TEL: +92 (51) 827150, 278045 FAX: +92 (51) 827149
E-mail: (name)@wfpisb.sdnpk.undp.org
WFP International: Via Cristoforo Colombo 426, 00145 Rome, Italy.
TEL: +39 (6) 522821 FAX: +39 (6) 522828/48 Website: www.wfp.org

World Health Organization (WHO)

WHO is one of the leading UN agencies working in the field of health. Headquartered in Jalalabad, WHO has sub-offices in Kabul, Herat, Mazar, Kandahar, Faizabad, Kunduz, Ghazni, Bamiyan and Islamabad. Major programmes in Afghanistan include:

- **Disease prevention:** control and treatment of tetanus, measles, diphtheria, pertussis, polio, TB, acute respiratory infections, diarrhoeal diseases, malaria, leishmaniasis, rabies, malnutrition;
- **Supplies:** provision of medical/surgical supplies to Ministry of Public Health, hospitals and clinics;
- **Training** of doctors, nurses, public health workers, TBAs;
- **Vaccination** of children against preventable childhood diseases, and pregnant mothers against tetanus; seven rounds of the Mass Immunization Campaign in partnership with UNICEF and NGOs since 1994;
- **Water supply:** provision of safe drinking water supplies; rehabilitation of networks in Kandahar, Ghazni, Jalalabad, Kunduz and Badakhshan.
- **Rehabilitation** of hospitals and medical facilities.

BUDGET: $7,261,000
ADDRESSES:
WHO Main Office: WHO Compound, Jalalabad.
WHO Support Office: PO Box 1936, Islamabad.
TEL: +92 (51) 251645, 252272 FAX: +92 (51) 280830
E-mail: WR@who-afg1.sdnpk.undp.org
WHO International: Ave Appia 20, CH-1211, Geneva, Switzerland.
TEL: +41 (22) 791 2111 FAX: +41 (22) 791 4844
Publications: *"Hope"* (Report on Afghanistan, December 1996), *World Health*

Other governmental agencies

International Organization for Migration (IOM)

IOM is a *non-UN* intergovernmental body with 60 member states and 50 observer states. It has been working with victims of the Afghan conflict since 1979 in the fields of medical treatment, resettlement of refugees to third countries and repatriation, the latter in collaboration with UNHCR. IOM has offices in Kabul, Kandahar and Herat, and is also active in Jalalabad. An additional office in Meshad (Iran) works under an agreement with UNHCR. IOM is currently implementing two programmes, both targeting the return of qualified Afghans in order to contribute to the country's reconstruction:

- **Return of selected NGOs** to Afghanistan, through the provision of transport and reintegration assistance for staff and families; supply of necessary professional equipment; help in project development and implementation;
- **Return of 30 Afghan medical doctors** and other healthcare professionals and their families, of whom at least 10 are women; they will be matched with priority vacancies in healthcare institutions in remote areas; and provided with basic professional equipment and reintegration assistance.

BUDGET (1998-99): $1,400,000
ADDRESSES:
Islamabad: House 6, Main Embassy Road, G-6/4, Islamabad.
TEL: +92 (51) 819248 FAX: +92 (51) 822968 E-mail: mission@iom-isb.sdnpk.undp.org
International: 17 route des Morillons, CH-1211, Geneva 19, Switzerland.
TEL: +41 (22) 717 9111 FAX: +41 (22) 798 6150
E-mail: hq@iom.int Website: www.iom.int

The Red Cross movement

INTERNATIONAL COMMITTEE OF THE RED CROSS (ICRC)

The ICRC's permanent presence in Afghanistan dates from 1986. Prior to that, the ICRC made periodic trips to Kabul and other parts of Afghanistan to visit prisoners or negotiate the exchange of Soviet POWs. Its principal medical operations consist of support for five major hospitals treating war-wounded and emergency cases inside Afghanistan (previously ICRC ran hospitals in Quetta and Peshawar). Currently there are over 100 expatriate and nearly 1,000 local staff in Afghanistan, with the main delegation in Kabul and sub-delegations in Kandahar, Herat, Jalalabad and Mazar-e-Sharif. The ICRC operates a fleet of 100 vehicles in-country and two aircraft based in Peshawar to facilitate operations. (SEE TRAVEL) The Committee has been made the focal point through which all assistance to internally-displaced persons (IDPs) is mediated. All factions in the conflict recognise the ICRC's specific humanitarian mandate based on neutrality and impartiality, and enshrined in Article 3 of the Geneva Convention. Operations are as follows:

Relief Assistance (SFr 31 million):

- Largest ICRC relief program in the world, implemented in 20 provinces;
- Emergency relief for Afghans displaced by fighting, floods and earthquakes: basic food, shelter, medical care, safe drinking water, waste disposal;
- In Kabul 40,000 vulnerable families (around 280,000 people) receive regular nutritional and non-food assistance;
- The Afghan Red Crescent Society (ARCS) targets 5,000 other very destitute families (35,000 people) throughout Afghanistan under ICRC monitoring;
- Food-for-work and cash-for-work programmes avoid creating aid dependency and encourage rehabilitation projects in irrigation, agriculture, sanitation and reconstruction;

Health Assistance (SFr 17 million):

- Full support for five hospitals in Afghanistan: Wazir Akbar Khan and Karte Seh hospitals in Kabul, Mirwais hospital in Kandahar, Jalalabad Public Health hospital and Ghazni hospital; treating war victims and all emergency surgical cases;
- Expatriate work concentrates on teaching and training local staff in the management of war-wounded;
- Over 40 ARCS medical establishments receive support;
- First aid facilities in the Panjshair Valley and Bamiyan province, and ambulance teams on the frontlines;
- Prosthetic/Orthotic centres in Kabul, Jalalabad, Herat and Mazar; treatment for landmine victims and the disabled; training for local physiotherapists and technicians; 195 local workers are employed, of whom 60% are disabled former patients;
- Water and Sanitation: upgrading traditional latrines, collecting night soil, and providing access to safe water; improved sanitary conditions for IDPs and prison populations.

Protection-Detention (SFr 10 million):

- Since June 1994 nearly 7,000 detainees from every faction have been registered and repeatedly visited by ICRC delegates in around 90 different detention centres across the country;
- Constantly reminding authorities to treat detainees with respect and to improve conditions of detention; upgrading sanitary and medical facilities;
- Detainees can talk in private to delegates, send and receive Red Cross messages, and receive medical treatment, clothes and blankets in winter;
- Permanent office opened in the Panjshair Valley in June 1997;
- Trouble visiting Taliban prisoners held by Jumbesh forces in Mazar;
- Emergency rehabilitation of Pul-e-Charki prison in Kabul and Sarpoza prison in Kandahar;
- Tracing of family members via Red Cross message, through provincial offices of the ARCS.

Cooperation with ARCS (SFr 5.7 million):

- Through institutional and material support the ICRC aims to strengthen the ARCS's ability to respond to the needs of the most vulnerable and poor Afghans through a nationwide network of offices in every province.

Dissemination/Information (SFr 1 million):

- Dissemination of the work and principles of the ICRC and International Humanitarian Law is conducted through lectures and briefings at every sub-delegation; two-pronged approach in Taliban and non-Taliban areas:
- Taliban areas: training ARCS staff; specially prepared radio programmes on Radio Shariat; field trip dissemination;
- Non-Taliban areas (the north): dissemination via television and radio programmes, including the BBC's "New Home, New Life" soap opera; brochures, leaflets and comics;
- ARCS mine-awareness teams also promote humanitarian principles.

Press:

- Despite Taliban restrictions on journalists' activities, the ICRC Press Office meets correspondents from AFP, BBC, Reuters and VOA on a daily basis;
- Information about ICRC programmes is translated into Pashto and distributed once a week to the local media;
- The Press Office in Kabul produces the following reports: *News in Afghanistan* (daily digest of radio reports from Voice of Shariat, BBC, VOA and Radio Iran); *ICRC News* (short reports on current activities); *Media Kit* (monthly report with photos about human interest stories); *Overview of ICRC Activities* (quarterly general report – no photos); *Factsheets* (briefs on different sectors of assistance).

Sub-delegation in Peshawar:

- Logistic and administrative support for ICRC operations in Afghanistan;
- Maintains contact with Afghan factions based in Peshawar;
- Operates flights (free for aid workers) from Peshawar to various destinations within Afghanistan. (SEE TRAVEL & JOURNALISTS)

Publications & Videos:

ICRC in Afghanistan (12pp, unbound)
Getting to know the ICRC (27pp, October 1996)
ICRC: Answers to your questions (42pp, October 1996)
ICRC: The Fundamental Principles of the Red Cross and Red Crescent (35pp, July 1996)
The ICRC headquarters in Geneva has an extensive photo & video library.

BUDGET (1998): SFr 72,780,301 (approx. $50 million)
PERSONNEL: 1,100

ADDRESSES:
Kabul: Charrahi Haji Yaqub, Shahr-e-Naw, Kabul.
TEL: Kabul 35247
Peshawar: 40 Jamalud-Din Afghani Road, University Town, GPO Box 418, Peshawar.
TEL: +92 (91) 42071, 41673, 41371 FAX: +92 (91) 840413
Headquarters: 19, Avenue de la Paix, CH-1202, Geneva, Switzerland.
TEL: +41 (22) 734 6001 FAX: +41 (22) 733 2057
E-mail: asia.gva@gwn.icrc.org
Website: www.icrc.org

INTERNATIONAL FEDERATION OF RED CROSS AND RED CRESCENT SOCIETIES (IFRC)

IFRC works to alleviate suffering caused by natural disasters (ICRC deals mainly with war and conflict situations) and directly supports national societies. Since 1989, IFRC has supported the Afghan Red Crescent Society (ARCS) in its health and relief programmes, and has reinforced ARCS's organizational structure nationwide. As the only indigenous, nationwide humanitarian organization able to work with all ethnic groups and to reach women through its services, ARCS is uniquely placed to assist the most vulnerable Afghans. IFRC, through ARCS, assists up to 1.5 million beneficiaries in 31 provinces in the following fields:

- **Basic health services and training:** through 46 clinics nationwide; health education courses to link curative and preventive health; health training for teachers from targeted schools;

- **Community-based first aid:** Includes translation of first aid manual into Dari and Pashto;

- **Rehabilitation/welfare**: *Marastoons* (homes for the homeless) programmes for the handicapped and disadvantaged;

- **Relief:** Non-food emergency supplies for the most vulnerable; disaster preparedness plan (supervised by ICRC in conflict areas);

- **Coordination:** at city and field level, between IFRC, ICRC and ARCS to avoid duplication of effort.

BUDGET: $11,006,254
PERSONNEL: 163

ADDRESSES:

Local: 43D, SJ Afghani Road, University Town, Peshawar.
TEL: +92 (91) 843116 FAX: + 92 (91) 843116
TEL: Kabul 21193

International: 17 Chemin des Crets, case postale 372, Petit-Saconnex, CH-1211, Geneva, Switzerland.
TEL: +41 (22) 730 4222 FAX: +41 (22) 733 0395
E-mail: (name)@ifrc.org
Website: www.ifrc.org

AFGHAN RED CRESCENT SOCIETY (ARCS)

Founded in 1934, ARCS operates in four main areas: **health, relief** (ARCS has developed a system of listing and identifying those families facing severe hardship), ***Marastoons*** (homes for the homeless), and **voluntary self-help.** ARCS is a member of the International Federation of Red Cross and Red Crescent Societies (IFRC) and has re-established active branches in 31 of Afghanistan's 32 provinces. ARCS is funded 100% by IFRC and ICRC.
BUDGET: $900,000
ADDRESS: Shafa Khana Qwai Markaz, Kabul.
TEL: Kabul 44916

SAUDI RED CRESCENT SOCIETY IN PAKISTAN (SRCS)

SRCS started its activities for Afghan refugees in Pakistan in the health and relief sectors in 1979. Operations around Peshawar and Quetta include:

- **Health:** BHUs provide comprehensive health cover; three hospitals for Afghan refugees; mobile units visit nine orphan centres; eight mobile operation theatres visit the distant areas of NWFP and Baluchistan; three field referral labs; physiotherapy centre and artificial prosthesis programme; dental unit; training courses; and a number of hospitals and clinics inside Afghanistan receive medical supplies;
- **Income generation:** quilt-making by widows at Nasir Bagh camp; training in shoe-making, tailoring for disabled Afghans, carpentry and blacksmith work; blanket and tent factories.

BUDGET : $2,500,000 PERSONNEL: 117
ADDRESS: 2 Gul Mohar Lane, University Town, PO Box 397, Peshawar.
TEL: +92 (91) 840213, 840207

Resident donors

EUROPEAN COMMISSION (EC)

Funding from the EC for Afghanistan comes from the European Community Humanitarian Office (ECHO), and from Directorates General (DG) 1B and VIII. In 1997, EC grants for humanitarian aid totalled $45,399,080 (*Source: UNOCHA)*, making it the largest donor to Afghanistan. (According to EC sources, total humanitarian assistance to Afghanistan in 1996 was ECU 77.5 million). Partners in Afghanistan include CARE, Halo Trust, Médecins Sans Frontières, UNOCHA, Handicap International and ICRC. Funds are used for:

- **Refugee reintegration** (DG 1B): supporting priority areas (demining, food security, rural rehabilitation, water supply, education and health) that promote durable resettlement.
- **Food aid** (DG VIII): relief (vulnerable populations, displaced persons, returning refugees) and food security projects are supported through WFP, ICRC and European NGOs.
- **Emergency aid** (ECHO): medical support, water supply, sanitation, shelter and relief items for citizens affected or displaced by fighting.

ADDRESSES:
Local: Delegation of the European Commission to Pakistan (Peshawar Office), Refugee and Humanitarian Aid for Afghanistan, 5C-2 Abdara Road, UPO Box 975, University Town, Peshawar.
TEL: +92 (91) 843003, 43574 FAX: +92 (91) 843003
International: European Community Humanitarian Office (ECHO), 200 rue de la Loi, B-1049, Brussels, Belgium.
TEL: +32 (2) 295 4400 FAX: +32 (2) 295 4572 E-mail: echo@echo.cec.be

NORWEGIAN CHURCH AID (NCA)

NCA is a donor agency working with implementing partner agencies for the rehabilitation and development of Afghanistan and to assist refugees and the internally displaced. NCA aims to support partner agencies in developing long-term (3 year) plans based on participatory principles and finances projects in various sectors such as: health, irrigation, agriculture, water, sanitation, rehabilitation, income generation, education, energy, environment and emergency relief. NCA's main implementing partners are the Norwegian Project Office/Rural Rehabilitation Association for Afghanistan (NPO/RRAA), CoAR and ADA. NCA has a special interest in building peace and reconciliation through greater awareness of human rights among NGO and UN staff. An all-Afghan network called Cooperation for Peace and Unity (CPAU) has been set up, and seminars held on the implications of aid on the lives of ordinary Afghans.

BUDGET: $3,212, 000 (1997) PERSONNEL: 32
ADDRESSES:
Local: 84-E Rehman Baba Road, University Town, Peshawar.
TEL: +92 (91) 45267, 41226 FAX: +92 (91) 840304
E-mail: <nca@afghan.psh.brain.net.pk
Opposite the German Club, Shahr-e-Naw, Kabul.
TEL: Kabul 32980, 30737 SATPHONE: +873 682 420515
International: NRC, Pilestredet 15B, PO Box 6758, St Olav's Plass, 0130 Oslo, Norway. TEL: +47 (23) 109800 FAX: +47 (23) 109801

Diplomatic missions

Embassies and consulates in Islamabad and Peshawar

Afghanistan Embassy
House 17, Street 28, F-6/1, Islamabad.
TEL: +92 (51) 824505 FAX: +92 (51) 824504

Afghanistan Consulate
Gul Mohar Lane, University Town,
GPO Box 119, Peshawar.
TEL: +92 (91) 842486 Mob: +92 (351) 290133

Australian High Commission
PO Box 1046, Islamabad.
TEL: +92 (51) 824345 FAX: +92 (51) 820112

British High Commission
Diplomatic Enclave, PO Box 1122,
Ramna 5, Islamabad.
TEL: +92 (51) 822131-5 FAX: +92 (51) 823439

Canadian High Commission
Diplomatic Enclave, G-5, Islamabad.
TEL: +92 (51) 279100 FAX: +92 (51) 279110

Chinese Embassy
House 11, F-8/2, Islamabad.
TEL: +92 (51) 252426 FAX: +92 (51) 256887

Danish Embassy
House 9, Street 90, G-6/3, Islamabad.
TEL :+92 (51) 214210-2 FAX: +92 (51) 823483

Embassy of France
Diplomatic Enclave, GPO Box 1068, Islamabad.
TEL: +92 (51) 213981 FAX: +92 (51) 822583

German Embassy
PO Box 1227, Diplomatic Enclave, G-5, Islamabad.
TEL: +92 (51) 279430 FAX: +92 (51) 279436

Indian High Commission
Diplomatic Enclave, Islamabad.
TEL: +92 (51) 814371 FAX: +92 (51) 820742

Iranian Consulate

Street 2, G-5/1, Islamabad.
TEL: +92 (51) 212694 FAX: +92 (51) 213791

Italian Embassy

54 Margalla Road, F-6/3, Islamabad.
TEL: +92 (51) 210091-2 FAX: +92 (51) 829026

Royal Netherlands Embassy

2nd Floor, PIA Building, Blue Area, PO Box 1065, Islamabad.
TEL: +92 (51) 279510-3 FAX: +92 (51) 277058, 206576

Norwegian Embassy

House 25, Street 19, F-6/2, Islamabad.
TEL: +92 (51) 279720-4 FAX: +92 (51) 279726

Embassy of Sweden

Diplomatic Enclave, Islamabad.
TEL: +92 (51) 828712 FAX: +92 (51) 822 5284

Embassy of the United States of America

Diplomatic Enclave, Islamabad.
TEL: +92 (51) 826161 FAX: +92 (51) 214222

Consulate of the United States of America

11 Hospital Road, Peshawar Cantt., NWFP.
TEL: +92 (91) 279801-2 FAX: +92 (91) 276712

Pakistani embassies worldwide

Afghanistan:

Embassy of Pakistan, Shahr-e-Naw, Kabul.
TEL: Kabul 21374
Consulate, Kheyabun-e-Herat, Kandahar.
TEL: Kandahar 2452

Australia and New Zealand:

Embassy of Pakistan, 59 Franklin Street, PO Box 198, Manuka, Canberra, ACT 2603.
TEL: +61 (6) 950 021-2
Consulate, 500 George Street, 11th floor, Sydney, NSW 2000.
TEL: +61 (2) 267 7250

Canada:

Embassy of Pakistan, 151 Slater Street, Suite 608, Ottawa K1P 5H3.
TEL: +1 (613) 238 7881
Consulate, 3421 Peel Street, Montreal H3A 1W7.
TEL: +1 (514) 845 2297
Consulate, 4881 Yonge Street, Suite 810, Willowdale, Toronto, M2N 5X3.
TEL: +1 (416) 250 1255

China:

Embassy of Pakistan, 1 Dongzhimenwai Dajie, Sanlitun Compound, Beijing.
TEL: +86 (1) 532 2504, 532 2581

European Community:

Permanent Mission of Pakistan, 25 Ave Delleur 57, Boitsfort 1170, Brussels, Belgium.
TEL: +32 (2) 733 9783

Hong Kong:

Consulate of Pakistan, Suite 3806, China Resources Building,
26 Harbour Road, Wanchai.
TEL: + 852 827 0681

India:

Embassy of Pakistan, 2/50-G Shantipath, Chanakyapuri, New Delhi.

Iran:

Embassy of Pakistan, Kheyabun-e-Doktor Fatemi, 1 Kheyabun-e-Shahid Sarhang Ahmad, E'temad Zade, Tehran.
TEL: +98 (21) 934 331-2

Ireland:

Honorary Consulate of Pakistan, 8 Millbrook Court, Millbrook, Dublin 6.
TEL: +353 (1) 800103

United Kingdom:

Embassy of Pakistan, 35 Lowndes Square, London SW1Z 9JN.
TEL: +44 (171) 235 2044
Consulate, Fraternal House, 45 Cheapside, Bradford BD1 4HP.
TEL: +44 (1274) 721921

United States of America:

Embassy of Pakistan, 2315 Massachusetts Avenue NW, Washington DC.
TEL: +1 (202) 939 6200
Consulate, 12 East 65th Street, New York, NY 10021.
TEL: +1 (212) 879 5800

Media & photographic organizations

International Agencies:

Agence France-Presse (AFP)

Kabul: Street 5, Wazir Akbar Khan.
SATPHONE/FAX: +873 382 081 542
Islamabad: House 3, Street 56, F-6/4, PO Box 1276.
TEL: +92 (51) 822485, 822738 FAX: +92 (51) 822203

AlertNet

The Reuter Foundation, 85 Fleet Street, London EC4P 4AJ, UK.
TEL: +44 (171) 542 2431 FAX: +44 (171) 278 9345
E-mail: john.owen-davies@reuters.com

Associated Press (AP)

House 6A, Street 25, F-8/2, Islamabad.
TEL: +92 (51) 260957, 252566 FAX: +92 (51) 256176, 251640
Mob: +92 (351) 265109, 266235
E-mail: (name)@ap.org

Australian Broadcasting Corporation

A-11 Westend Colony, New Delhi 110 021, India.
TEL: +91 (11) 687 2153 FAX: +91 (11) 687 2153

The Australian

1st Floor, 42 Jorbagh, New Delhi 110 003, India.
TEL: +91 (11) 464 5538 FAX: +91 (11) 464 0931

British Broadcasting Corporation World Service (BBC)

Kabul: SATPHONE/FAX: +873 682 344 317
Islamabad: House 6, Street 8, F-7/3.
TEL: +92 (51) 826026, 826076 FAX: +92 (51) 270420
Mob: +92 (351) 265109
Peshawar: TEL: +92 (91) 842320, 42767 FAX: +92 (91) 842319
Afghan Education Drama (AED): 8 Abdara Road, PO Box 946, University Town, Peshawar.
TEL: +92 (91) 842320, 42765-7 FAX: +92 (91) 842319
E-mail: (name)@bbcaed.pwr.sdnpk.undp.org
Persian and Pashto Service: Bush House, Strand, London WC2B 4PH, UK
TEL: +44 (171) 240 3456 FAX: +44 (171) 379 6785 (direct)
E-mail: (name)@bbc.co.uk
English Service: Bush House, Strand, London WC2B 4PH, UK
TEL: +44 (171) 485 8063

Deutsche Welle
House 8, Street 32/1, F-8/1, Islamabad.
TEL: +92 (51) 280213 FAX: +92 (51) 256506

DPA (German Press Agency)
Block 18, 2nd Floor, Supermarket, F-6 Markaz, Islamabad.
TEL: +92 (51) 826042 FAX: +92 (51) 821997

European Community Humanitarian Office (ECHO)
Press and Information, Rue de la Loi 200,
B-1049 Brussels, Belgium.
TEL: +32 (2) 295 2627 FAX: +32 (2) 295 4572
E-mail: (name)@echo.cec.be

Far Eastern Economic Review
108/10 Tufail Road, Lahore Cantt., Pakistan.
TEL: +92 (42) 372072 FAX: +92 (42) 666 2895

Financial Times
222 Khadim Hussain Road, Rawalpindi, Pakistan.
TEL: +92 (51) 581005 FAX: +92 (51) 586421
Mob: +92 (351) 370970

Frankfurter Rundschau
D-433 Defence Colony, New Delhi 110 003, India.
TEL: +33 (11) 464 9367 FAX: +91 (11) 464 9367

German Radio (ARD) South Asia
148 Golf Links, New Delhi 110 003, India.
TEL: +91 (11) 462 3022 FAX: +91 (11) 460 2771

The Guardian
2 Nizamuddin East, New Delhi 110 013, India.
TEL: +91 (11) 469 7985 FAX: +91 (11) 464 7613

Kyodo (Japanese Press Agency)
House 31, Street 28, F-10/1, Islamabad.
TEL: +92 (51) 291577 FAX: +92 (51) 297031

The New York Times
56 Janpath, New Delhi 110 001, India.
TEL: +91 (11) 332 1965, 332 2853 FAX: +91 (11) 371 2237

REUTERS
Kabul: House 125, Street 15, Wazir Akbar Khan.
TEL: 23187 SATPHONE/FAX: +873 171 6412
Islamabad: House 4, Street 2, F-6/3, PO Box 1069.
TEL: +92 (51) 274757-8 FAX: +92 (51) 274759
Mob: +92 (351) 375144
Karachi: TEL: +92 (21) 568192
London: 85 Fleet Street, London EC4P 4AJ, UK.
TEL: +44 (171) 250 1122 E-mail: (name)@reuters.com

Time
House 5B, Street 18, F-8/2, Islamabad.
TEL: +92 (51) 261440 FAX: +92 (51) 260331

The Times
New Delhi
FAX: +91 (11) 643 1527

United Nations Children's Fund (UNICEF)

Information/Communications Officer
17-B Abdara Road, PO Box 1078,
University Town, Peshawar.
TEL: +92 (91) 840496, 43669 FAX: +92 (91) 840437
E-mail: (name)@unicef.org

United Nations Office for the Coordination of Humanitarian Assistance to Afghanistan (UNOCHA)

Press Liaison Officer
Street 55, F-10/4, Islamabad.
TEL: +92 (51) 211451-5 FAX: +92 (51) 211450
E-mail: unocha@undpafg.org.pk

Voice of America (VOA)

Islamabad:
TEL: +92 (51) 278784, 277344 FAX: +92 (51) 277349
Mob: +92 (351) 370273
Dari Service, Washington:
TEL: +1 (202) 619 0340 FAX: +1 (202) 619 2400

The Washington Post

B-56 Paschim Marg, Vasant Vihar,
New Delhi 110057, India.
TEL: +91 (11) 611 1368 FAX: +91 (11) 611 1368

Local/Regional Agencies:

Afghan Media Resource Centre (AMRC)

2 Canal Bank Road, UPO Box 909,
University Town, Peshawar.
TEL: +92 (91) 41691, 45256

Asia Times

House 7B, Street 43, F-8/1, Islamabad.
TEL: +92 (51) 263185 FAX: +92 (51) 263215

APP (Associated Press of Pakistan)

Zeropoint, Islamabad.
TEL: +92 (51) 819983-4 FAX: +92 (51) 819986-7

Dawn

Islamabad:
TEL: +92 111 444 777
FAX: +92 (51) 202710

The Economic Daily, China

House 1, Street 16, F-6/3, Islamabad.
TEL: +92 (51) 821337 FAX: +92 (51) 223625

The Frontier Post

Islamabad:
FAX: +92 (51) 819841

Iran Radio/TV

Islamabad:
FAX: +92 (51) 255536

IRNA (Iranian Press Agency)

Islamabad:
TEL: +92 (51) 827954 FAX: +92 (51) 282778

Jang
Islamabad:
TEL: +92 (51) 556223

Middle East Broadcasting
House 301, Street 49, G-10/3, Islamabad.
TEL: +92 (51) 252151 FAX: +92 (51) 282778

The Muslim
Islamabad:
FAX: +92 (51) 277485

The Nation
Peshawar:
FAX: +92 (91) 211127

The News
Peshawar:
TEL: +92 (91) 271612 FAX: +92 (91) 555371

Pakistan Observer
Islamabad:
FAX: +92 (51) 262258

Pakistan Times
Islamabad:
TEL: +92 (51) 251216, 829297 FAX: +92 (51) 510779

Pakistan TV
Islamabad:
TEL: +92 (51) 920 2194 FAX: +92 (51) 920 8655

PPI (Pakistan Press Institute)
Islamabad:
TEL: +92 (51) 816747 FAX: +92 (51) 810435

Russian Press Agency
Islamabad:
FAX: +92 (51) 278023

Wadat
Peshawar:
TEL: +92 (91) 214034, 212425 FAX: +92 (91) 214321

Wafa
Peshawar:
TEL: +92 (91) 840318 FAX: +92 (91) 840288

Xinhua News Agency
House 12A, Street 31, F-8/1, Islamabad.
TEL: +92 (51) 252779 FAX: +92 (51) 281490

Humanitarian photography contacts

Editors' Note: *the following agencies have active photographic departments or are interested in approaches from freelance photographers. Where no specific address is indicated, apply to the Press and Public Information department at the agency's headquarters.*

Aga Khan Development Network

The Aga Khan Development Network includes programmes for economic development and culture. Sectors of work: Islam, Tourism, Education, Architecture, Urban Planning, Health.
ADDRESS: Aiglemont, 60270 Gouvieux, France.
Publications: *Development Network*

Canadian International Development Agency (CIDA)

CIDA is a provider of international development assistance to developing and emerging countries.
ADDRESS: Media Relations Office, 200 Promenade de Portage Hull, Quebec, K1A OG4 Canada.
TEL: +1 (819) 953 6534 FAX: +1 (819) 997 7397
E-mail: Christine_Skaladany@acdi-cida.gc.ca Website: www.acdi-cida.gc.ca
Publications: *CIDA update*

CARE International (SEE NGOs)

CARE International is a confederation of ten CARE agencies which delivers relief assistance to people in need and long-term solutions to global poverty.
ADDRESS: International Secretariat, Boulevard du Regent, 58/10, B-1000, Brussels, Belgium.
TEL: +32 (2) 502 4333 FAX: +32 (2) 502 8202
E-mail:careci2@ibm.net Website: www.care.org

European Community Humanitarian Office (ECHO)

SEE RESIDENT DONORS

Food and Agriculture Organization of United Nations (FAO)

SEE UN AGENCIES

The International Red Cross and Red Crescent Movement

Combines the 171 National Red Cross and Red Crescent Societies, the ICRC and IFRC. Most National Societies have publications and are usually in need of photographers, volunteer or otherwise.
ADDRESS: International Federation of Red Cross and Red Crescent Societies (IFRC), Photo Service: Francoise Borst-Vermont, PO Box 372, CH-1211 Geneva, Switzerland.
TEL: +41 (22) 730 4222 FAX: +41 (22) 733 0395
E-mail: borst@ifrc.org Website: www.ifrc.org

International Organization for Migration (IOM)

SEE PAGE 470

Magnum Photos

A cooperative of photojournalists and documentary photographers founded in 1947 with a unique selection of humanitarian and conflict coverage worldwide. Offices in Paris, London, New York and Tokyo.
ADDRESS: Magnum Paris, 5 Passage Piver, 75001 Paris, France.
TEL: +33 (1) 5336 8888 FAX: +33 (1) 5336 8887
E-mail: 100412.1021@compuserve.com
Website: www.magnumphotos.capgemini.co.uk

Médecins Sans Frontières (MSF)

SEE NGOs

OXFAM

SEE NGOs

PANOS Institute

PANOS promotes development which is socially, environmentally and economically sustainable. It has offices in London, Paris and Washington DC.
ADDRESS: 9, White Lion Street, London N1 9PD, UK.
TEL: +44 (171) 278 1111 FAX: +44 (171) 278 0345
E-mail: panoslondon@gn.apc.org Website: www.oneworld.org/panos

Save The Children UK (SCF)

SEE NGOs

United Nations (UN)

Subjects mainly on United Nations issues, such as international conferences, peacekeeping initiatives, etc.
ADDRESS: Phototheque, Palais des Nations, CH-1211 Geneva, Switzerland.
TEL: +41 (22) 917 3317 FAX: +41 (22) 917 0073
Website: www.un.org

United Nations Children's Fund (UNICEF)

Subjects extremely varied, including coverage of children's issues in war and humanitarian situations.
ADDRESS: Press & Information, Photo Library, Palais des Nations, CH-1211 Geneva 10, Switzerland.
TEL: +41 (22) 909 5519 FAX: +41 (22) 909 5907
E-mail: hmartin@unicef.ch Website: www.unicef.org
Publications: *State of the Worlds Children, Progress of Nations, Annual Report and First Call for Children.*

United Nations Development Programme (UNDP)

SEE UN AGENCIES

United Nations Educational, Scientific and Cultural Organization (UNESCO)

SEE UN AGENCIES

United Nations Population Fund (UNFPA)

SEE UN AGENCIES

United Nations High Commissioner for Refugees (UNHCR)

Subjects: Refugee issues worldwide with excellent coverage of Somalia, Rwanda, Afghanistan, South East Asia and other regions.
ADDRESS: Attention: Photo Archives, Palais des Nations,
Case Postale 2500, CH-1211, Geneva, Switzerland.
TEL: +41 (22) 739 8513 FAX: +41 (22) 739 7314
E-mail: hollmann@unhcr.ch Website: www.unhcr.org
Publications include: *Refugees* magazine and *State of the World's Refugees.*

US Agency for International Development (USAID)

320 21st Street, NW, 21st & C building, SA-18, Room 308e,
Washington DC, 20523-0004, USA.
TEL: +1 (703) 875 5810 FAX: +1 (703) 875 4866

World Food Programme (WFP)

SEE UN AGENCIES

World Health Organization (WHO)

SEE UN AGENCIES

Human rights groups

AMNESTY INTERNATIONAL (AI)

AI is a London-based international advocacy organization which campaigns against human rights abuses worldwide. AI has published several papers on the human rights situation in Afghanistan, including: *Women in Afghanistan, a human rights catastrophe* (May 1995), and *Women in Afghanistan: The violations continue* (June 1997).
ADDRESS: International Secretariat, 1 Easton Street,
London WC1X 8DJ, UK.
TEL: +44 (171) 413 5500 FAX: +44 (171) 956 1157
TEL: Geneva: +41 (22) 798 2500
E-mail: amnesty@gn.apc.org Website: www.amnesty.org

HUMAN RIGHTS WATCH

350 Fifth Avenue, 3rd Floor, New York, NY 10018, USA
TEL: +1 (212) 290 4700 FAX: +1 (212) 736 1300
E-mail: hri@hrw.org

LAWYERS' COMMITTEE FOR HUMAN RIGHTS

330 Seventh Avenue, 7th Floor, New York, NY 10001, USA
TEL: +1 (212) 629 6170 FAX: +1 (212) 967 0916
E-mail: nyc@lchr.org

PHYSICIANS FOR HUMAN RIGHTS

100 Boylston Street, Suite 702, Boston, MA 02116, USA
TEL: +1 (617) 695 0041 FAX: + (617) 695 0307

ROBERT F. KENNEDY CENTER FOR HUMAN RIGHTS

1367 Connecticut Avenue NW, Suite 200,
Washington DC 20036, USA
TEL: +1 (202) 463 7575

SCHELL CENTER FOR HUMAN RIGHTS

Yale Law School, New Haven, Connecticut 06520, USA
TEL: +1 (203) 432 7129

Women-focused agencies

AFGHAN WOMEN'S NETWORK (AWN)

A group of Afghan women living in Pakistan and Afghanistan – active in Peshawar, Islamabad, Mazar-e-Sharif and Kabul. Many of the women previously worked in Afghanistan as lawyers, engineers, professors and doctors. They now work with NGOs, UN agencies and in schools. "Although Afghanistan had no official delegation to the Fourth World Conference on Women in Beijing, a few of us attended the NGO Forum and were inspired to start the Afghan Women's Network in September l996." – *AWN*
ADDRESS: Contact via ACBAR or UNOCHA.

INTERNATIONAL WORKING GROUP ON REFUGEE WOMEN (IWGRW)

A Swiss-based NGO, forming part of the Special Committee of International NGOs on Human Rights (Geneva). IWGRW is active within the Afghan diaspora in western Europe, and is currently initiating a project entitled: *Chadars of Peace: Women Promoting Reconciliation in Afghanistan.*
ADDRESS: 37-39 Rue de Vermont, PO Box 96,
CH-1211, Geneva 20, Switzerland.
TEL: +41 (22) 733 4150 FAX: +41 (22) 734 7929

THE REVOLUTIONARY ASSOCIATION OF THE WOMEN OF AFGHANISTAN (RAWA)

RAWA has been active since the mid-1980s, and is a left-of-centre group which does not advocate violence. RAWA campaigns for women's rights and provides education and health facilities for women and children. It has set up a number of programmes in Afghanistan but has had to scale down these operations because of the threats it receives. Most of its operations are based in Afghan refugee areas in Pakistan. These include several schools in Peshawar and Quetta and a health centre in Quetta. RAWA publishes an occasional journal entitled, *The Burst of the 'Islamic Government' Bubble in Afghanistan.*
ADDRESS: PO Box 374, Quetta, Pakistan.

WOMEN'S COMMISSION FOR REFUGEE WOMEN AND CHILDREN (WCRWC)

122 East 42nd Street, 12th Floor, New York, NY 10168-1289
TEL: +1 (212) 551 3111 FAX: +1 (212) 551 3180
E-mail: wcrwc@intrescom.org
Website: www.hypernet.com/wcrwc.html

Policy & research institutes

Strategic and Defence Studies Centre – Australian National University (SDSC)
GPO Box 41, Canberra, ACT 2601, Australia.
TEL: +61 (2) 49 21 77 FAX: +61 (2) 57 18 93

International Institute for Strategic Studies
23 Tavistock Street, London, WC2E 7NQ, UK.
TEL: +44 (171) 379 7676 FAX: +44 (171) 836 3108

Nizhni Novogrod State University – Centre for Peace and Conflict Resolution Research
Ulianov Street 2, Nizhni Novogrod, 603005, Russian Federation.
TEL: +7 (831) 239 0249

Centre for South Asian Studies – Jawaharlal Nehru University
School of International Studies, New Mehranli Road, New Delhi, 110 067, India.

Center for International Security and Arms Control – Stanford University
320 Galvez Street, Stanford, CA 94305-6165, USA.
TEL: +1 (415) 723 9625 FAX: +1 (415) 723 0089

The Carter Centre International Negotiation Network
c/o Conflict Resolution Programme, The Carter Centre, 453 Freedom Parkway, Atlanta, GA 30307, USA.
TEL: +1 (404) 420 5185 FAX: +1 (404) 420 5196

Mersham Center – Ohio State University
199 West, 10th Avenue, Columbus, OH 43210 2399, USA.
TEL +1 (614) 292 1618 FAX: +1 (614) 292 2407

Radcliffe College, The Mary Ingraham Bunting Institute
34 Concord Avenue, Cambridge, MA 021 138, USA.
TEL: +1 (617) 495 8136 FAX: +1 (617) 495 8136

Centre for Peace Studies
Global Rea House, 20 Pembroke Park, Dublin 4, Ireland.
TEL: +353 (1) 684914

Deutches Orient Institut
Mittelweg 150, Hamburg, D-20148, Germany.
TEL: +49 (40) 441481 FAX: +49 (40) 418214

Nederlands Institut voor International Betrekkingen Clingendael
PO Box 93080, The Hague, 2509 AB, The Netherlands.
TEL: +31 (70) 24 53 84 FAX: +31 (70) 328 2002

Panteios University of Social & Political Sciences
Institute of International Relations, 136 Syggrou Ave, GR-176 71, Athens, Greece. TEL: + (1) 922 0031 FAX: +(1) 922 8429

Commercial contacts

The only international commercial organization of any size currently operating in Afghanistan is the US oil company Unocal. For telecommunications companies operating in Pakistan, SEE RADIO & TELECOMMUNICATIONS.

UNOCAL

Unocal Central Asia Ltd. is wholly owned by Unocal Corporation (USA), a high technology, energy resources company established in 1890. Unocal is active in 32 countries worldwide and produces crude oil, natural gas, and geothermal resources in eight countries. Unocal operates over 26,000 km of pipelines in the US, North Sea, and South East Asia, and manages marine terminals with over 20 million barrels of storage. Unocal leads an international consortium (including Delta Oil Company of Saudi Arabia) which is proposing to construct two oil and natural gas pipelines from Turkmenistan through western Afghanistan to Pakistan. (SEE PIPE DREAMS)

ADDRESSES:

Local:

Unocal Pakistan Ltd., House 9, Street 29, 8th Avenue, F-7/1, Islamabad.
TEL: +92 (51) 278995-6 FAX: +92 (51) 278994

International:

The Central Asian Oil Pipeline Project Team, Unocal Central Asia Ltd.,
14141 Southwest Freeway, Sugar Land, Texas 77478, USA.
TEL: +1 (713) 491 7600 FAX: +1 (713) 287 5145

INFORESOURCES

J. Hartley/UNICEF

Getting the news

News clippings

Daily:

"News From Afghanistan"

Compiled by Bernt Glatzer, University of Heidelberg, Germany. Taken from international English language print and broadcast media.
Available (free of charge) from:
ARIC library, ACBAR, 2 Rehman Baba Road,
PO Box 1084, Peshawar, Pakistan.
TEL: + 92 (91) 44392, 40839 FAX: + 92 (91) 840471
E-mail: acbaar@radio.psh.brain.net.pk
or
E-mail: bernt.glatzer@urz.uni-heidelberg.de

Monthly:

"Afghanistan News Bulletin"

Compiled by Afghanistan News Clipping Services. Cut from Pakistani English language newspapers, and broken down into the following sectors: Afghanistan General; Afghan Government in Kabul; Refugees; Leaders/Parties; Foreign Interest; Photos; Cartoons
Available from: Afghanistan News Clipping Services,
Peshawar, Pakistan.
TEL: +92 (91) 841083
Price: PakRupees 400; US$20; Abroad US$30

Bi-monthly:

Pressklipp om Afghanistan

Compiled by Svenska Afghanistankommitten (SAK) and Afghanistankomiteen i Norge (AiN). Cut from wide range of international English and Nordic language newspapers and magazines.
Available from: Svenska Afghanistankommitten, "Pressklipp om Afghanistan",
Sturegatan 16, 114 36 Stockholm, Sweden.
TEL: +46 (8) 64 23 90-9
Price: 250 kronor per year

News digests

Daily radio monitoring:

Both ICRC and ACBAR provide a printed daily digest of radio news for general consumption. The stations monitored are BBC, VOA, Voice of Shariat and Radio Iran. Digests are available through ICRC and ACBAR offices in Peshawar and Kabul.

Weekly:

"United Nations Assistance for Afghanistan: Weekly Update"

UNOCHA weekly update on political and humanitarian situation, and on the latest UN agencies' assistance in all regions of Afghanistan.
Available from UNOCHA Islamabad or Geneva:
UNOCHA Islamabad, House 292, Street 55, Sector F-10/4, PO Box 1809, Islamabad, Pakisan.
TEL: +92 (51) 211451-5 FAX: +92 (51) 211450
E-mail: unocha@undpafg.org.pk
UNOCHA Geneva, 16 avenue Jean Trembley, Petit Saconnex, CH-1211, Geneva 10, Switzerland.
TEL: +41 (22) 788 2215 FAX: +41 (22) 788 2204

Monthly:

British Agencies Afghanistan Group: "Afghanistan Update"

A monthly bulletin covering political and humanitarian developments in Afghanistan and the region.
Available from: Information Coordinator, British Agencies Afghanistan Group (BAAG), 3/9 Bondway, London SW8 1SJ, UK.
TEL: +44 (171) 582 6922 FAX: +44 (171) 582 9929

Annually:

ACBAR: "News Summary on Afghanistan"

An annual review of the previous year's developments. Includes political, military, economic and security matters.
Available from: ACBAR (see above for address)

News on the Web

http://www.alertnet.org
Reuter Foundation's AlertNet – the latest humanitarian news worldwide.

http://wwwnotes.reliefweb.int/emergency/afghan/format
Information from the United Nations Office for the Coordination of Humanitarian Affairs' ReliefWeb.

http://www.unicef.org/newsline/97pr43.ht
News items on Afghanistan from UNICEF.

http://www.afghani.com/media.htm
News on Afghanistan.

http://www.sx.culture.afghanistan
News group.

http://www.un.org/News/
General news on UN activities.

http://www.sabawoon.com/news/fri.htm
News and information on Afghanistan

Websites

General:

http://www.oneworld.org
OneWorld Online is an umbrella website for over 100 international and local human rights and sustainable development organizations. For more information, contact OneWorld Online:
Email: justice@oneworld.org
TEL: +44 (1494) 481629 FAX: +44 (1494) 481751

http://www.afghan-web.com/facts.html
General facts on Afghanistan.

http://frankenstein.worldweb.net/afghan/
Online Afghan Downtown Community

http://www.gl.umbc.edu/hqurba1/.info/
CIA's fact sheet on Afghanistan.

http://www.clearlight.com/octagon/index.shtml
Octagon Bookshop, London – specialist Afghan books.

http://www.unsystem.org/index7.html
Official locator for UN Agency websites.

http://www.cfcsc.dnd.ca/links/wars/afg.html
War, peace and security guide for Afghanistan.

http://www.nrc-no/idp.htm
Global IDP survey website

Women's issues and human rights:

http://www.afghans.com/anaisf
Afghan Women's Association International.

http://www.afghan.web.com/woman/
http://www.afghan.web.com/woman/talibanwomen.html

http://www.afghan.web.com/woman/waronwomen.html
Site covering various aspects of Afghan life including women's issues.

http://www.ige.apc.org/amnesty/women/womre/s.html
Amnesty International webpage – women's issues

http://www.best.com/-mlacabe/saran/afg.html
Human rights violations and various links.

http://www.europa.eu.int/en/comm/echo/womensday/press/press.htm
European Community Humanitarian Office (ECHO) website.

http://www.feminist.org/news/newsbyte/october96/1009.html
Feminist news group.

http://www.feminist.com/outrage/htm
Feminist news group.

http://www.humanitis.ucsb.edu/gallaghe/amnews.html
Association for Middle East Women's News

http://www.melink.it/n/dwpress/dww62/dw62~e.htm
Women's Press Agency

http://www.misc.activism.progressive

http://www.taliban.com/islam.forum.org/opedajah.html
Taliban, includes a section on women.

http://www.geocities.com/wellesley/33401
RAWA ! (Revolutionary Association of the Women of Afghanistan)

http://www.soc.culture.Afghanistan
http://www.soc.rights.human
http://www.derechos.org/saran/afg.html
US State Department Human Rights Report

http://www.chuma.cas.usr.edu/~rjayiz
United Afghanistan.

http://www.org/womenwatch/new.htm
United Nations women's watch.

http://www.washington post.com/wp-srv/wparch/1997-11/23/084r
Washington Post (will change)

http://www.ichr.org/zanweb
ZANWEB – an Afghan Women's Website edited by the International Centre for Humanitarian Reporting (ICHR)

Disaster Relief Websites:

http://www.cdc.gov
Centre for Disease Control and Prevention.

http://www.DisasterRelief.org
Joint website of American Red Cross, CNN and IBM.
Contributions welcome on:
TEL: +1 (703) 206 7199 FAX: +1 (703) 206 7139
E-mail: DisRelEdit@usa.redcross.org

http://hoshi.cic.sfu.ca/idndr/index.html
International Decade for Natural Disaster Reduction.

http://www.disaster.org
Internet Disaster Information Centre.

http://wwwnotes.reliefweb.int
UN Office for the Coordination of Humanitarian Affairs' ReliefWeb.

http://www.unhcr.ch/refworld/refworld.htm
UN High Commissioner for Refugees Database.

Telecommunications websites:

http://www.itu.ch
International Telecommunications Union (ITU).

http://www.remotesatellite.com/index.html
Provides a short course on satphones.

http://www.unog.ch/freq/icet.html
Latest draft on Convention on Emergency Communications.

http://www.wp.com/mcintosh_page_o_stuff/tcomm.html
Reviews on commercial communications systems.

Academic Websites:

http://www.columbia.edu/cu/libraries/idndiv/area/Middle East/ Afghanistan.html
Columbia University: links to relevant web sites.

http://www.phs.princeton.k12.oh.us/Public/Lessons/country/ afg.html
Princeton University: links to Afghan information.

http://www.rockbridge.net/personal/bichel/welcome.htp
Interactive Central Asia Resource Project links to Central Asian topics, very comprehensive.

E-mail lists for Afghanistan:

listserv@gwuvm.gwu.edu
AAAS Human Rights Action Network.

CCBAY-L@CMSA.BERKELEY.EDU
Campus Coalition for Human Rights and Social Justice.

CIPSHRIT@LISTSERV.UNB.CA
Discussions on Human Rights and Information Technology.

hrwatchnyc@igc.apc.org
Human Rights Watch news about Central Asia.

listserv@vm1.mcgill.ca
Information on Central Asia

HRS-L@BINGVMB.CC.BINGHAMTON.EDU
Systemic Studies of Human Rights.

Internet Publications:

The Essential Internet: Basics for International NGOs, Carlos Parada (InterAction)

Available from: InterAction,
1717 Massachusetts Avenue NW,
Suite 801, Washington, DC 20036, USA.
TEL: +1 (202) 667 8227 FAX: +1 (202) 667 8236
E-mail: ia@interaction.org
Website: http://www.interaction.org

Libraries

ACBAR Resource and Information Centre (ARIC), Peshawar

2 Rehman Baba Road, University Town, UPO Box 1084,
Peshawar, Pakistan.
TEL: +92 (91) 44392, 40839, 45347 FAX: +92 (91) 840471
E-mail: acbaar@radio.psh.brain.net.pk
Hours:
Mondays to Thursdays: 0800-1630;
Fridays: 0800-1230;
Saturdays and Sundays: closed.
ARIC is probably the best reference library on Afghanistan in the region. It contains nearly 4,000 books, agency reports, maps, journals and videos on every sector of interest in Afghanistan. The ARIC Bulletin, produced monthly, details all new acquisitions in English, Dari and Pashto languages. Photocopying for documents and maps is available for a small fee. A number of Nancy Hatch Dupree's books are for sale at ARIC. The *Essential Field Guide to Afghanistan* is also for sale.

Afghan Media Resource Centre (AMRC), Peshawar

2 Canal Bank Road,
University Town, Peshawar, Pakistan.
TEL: +92 (91) 41691, 45256
AMRC has an enormous collection of photographs, video and film footage, newspapers and magazines. Started by Boston University School of Communications in the 1980s and funded by the US State Department to train Afghan photographers and cameramen, the majority of its work has focused on documenting the Soviet-Afghan war.

British Council

The British Council is a developmental, educational and cultural organization with offices and libraries in over 100 countries. It promotes the exchange of ideas, expertise and knowledge between UK organizations and partners throughout the world.
ADDRESSES:
London: 10 Spring Gardens,
London, SW1A 2BN, UK.
TEL: +44 (171) 930 8466 FAX: +44 (171) 839 6347
E-mail: noned.enquiries@britcoun.org Website: www.britcoun.org
Pakistan: Block 14, Civic Centre,
G-6, Islamabad.
TEL: +92 (51) 829041-4 FAX: +92 (51) 276683
E-mail: (name)@bc-isb.sdnpk.undp.org

School of Oriental and African Studies (SOAS), London

Thornhaugh Street, Russell Square, London WC1H 0XG, UK.
TEL: +44 (171) 323 6009 FAX: +44 (171) 636 2834
Website: http://www.soas.ac.uk
Membership enquiries: jp6@soas.ac.uk
Other enquiries: libenquiry@soas.ac.uk
Library Hours:
Mondays to Fridays: 0900–1700 (2045 during academic term-time)
Saturdays: 0930–1700
One of the principal academic and research institutions in London covering the Middle East, Central Asia and Afghanistan. Publications relating to Afghanistan can be found on the ground floor under shelf-mark 'ON'; reference works (covering encyclopaedias, dictionaries and bibliographies) are found under 'ON' in the Islamic Reading Room, also on the ground floor. A charge is made for day tickets; six month or yearly membership is available. Information about the library is on the SOAS Web Page and on the following:
TELNET: 193.63.73.246 or Lib.soas.ac.uk
JANET: LON.SOAS.LIB (username is LIBRARY)

Stifthung Bibliotheca Afghanica: The Swiss/Afghanistan Archive, Liestal

Benzburweg 5, CH-4410 Liestal, Switzerland.
TEL/FAX: +41 (61) 921 9838
E-mail: afghannet@spectraweb.ch
Hours: by appointment with the director.
A scientific institution for documentation and research of Afghanistan's nature, culture and history (including contemporary history). For humanitarian and scientific matters use of the library is free of charge. All materials must be inspected on the library premises (there is no loaning of books). The library contains:
14,000 titles on Afghanistan/Central Asia in European languages;
A further 6,000 titles in Oriental languages;
Extensive collection of Afghan maps in different scales;
Phototheca Afghanica, a collection of over 7,000 black & white prints.

APPEAL FOR CORRECTIONS AND UPDATES

The editors would greatly appreciate if aid representatives, journalists and other readers could provide us with any changes and comments on information, statistical data and contact lists provided in this Essential Field Guide. Regular updates will be made available on the website of the International Centre for Humanitarian Reporting (http://www.ichr.org). New editions will include the corrected or updated material.

Bibliography

General books (alphabetical order by author)

Dictionary of Afghan Wars, Revolutions and Insurgencies, (Historical Dictionaries of Wars, Revolution and Civil Unrest, No. 1), Ludwig W. Adamec, The Scarecrow Press Inc.

Historical Dictionary of Afghanistan, Ludwig W. Adamec, The Scarecrow Press Inc. (Metuchen, NJ and London, 1997)

A Biographical Dictionary of Contemporary Afghanistan, Ludwig W. Adamec, Akademische Druck-u. Verlagsanstalt (Graz, 1987)

Afghanistan Crises, Tahir Amin, Holy Koran Publishing House

Afghanistan: Fighting for Freedom (Discovering Our Heritage), Mir T. Ansary, Dillon Press

The Tragedy of Afghanistan: A First-Hand Account, Raja Anwar, Fred Halliday, Khalid Hasan (Translator), Verso Books (London, 1988)

Afghanistan, The Definitive Account of a Country at Crossroads, George Arney, Mandarin (London, 1990)

The Politics of Social Transformation in Afghanistan, Iran, and Pakistan (Contemporary Issues in the Middle East), Ali Banuazizi and Myron Weiner (Editors), Syracuse University Press

Afghanistan, A Country Study, Sally Ann Baynard, Laurie Krieger, Robert S. Ford, Donald M. Seekins, Samuel Hayfield, United States Government

NGO Coordination at field level, Jon Bennett, ICVA (Geneva, 1994)

The World Factbook, United States Central Intelligence Agency (Washington, annually)

Danziger's Adventures; from Miami to Kabul, Nick Danziger, HarperCollins

Bridgehead Afghanistan, Wilhelm Dietl, South Asia Books

Afghanistan: Coordination in a Fragmented State, Antonio Donini, Eric Dudley, Ron Ockwell, United Nations Department for Humanitarian Affairs (New York, 1996)

Afghanistan, Louis Dupree, Princeton University Press (2nd Edition, 1980; reprinted by Oxford University Press, 1997)

State, Revolution, and Superpowers in Afghanistan, Hafizullah Emadi, Praeger publications (New York, 1990)

Shadow Over Afghanistan, Fazel Rahman Fazel, Western Book/Journal Press

Afghanistan: Highway of Conquest, Arnold Fletcher, Cornell University Press

---

***Editors' Note**: For further reading in French and German languages, contact AFRANE-CEREDAF in Paris or Stifthung Bibliotheca Afghanica in Liestal. Octagon Press in London specializes in publishing books written by Afghans but aimed at Western audiences. Their address is: Octagon Press Ltd., PO Box 227, London N6 4EW, UK. TEL: +44 (181) 348 9392 FAX: +44 (181) 341 5971 E-mail: octagon@schredds.demon.co.uk*

Islamic Fundamentalism in Afghanistan: Its Character and Prospects, Graham E. Fuller, Rand Corp.
Afghanistan: Agony of a Nation, Sandy Gall, Bodley Head
The Road to Kabul: An Anthology, Gerald De Gaury, Book Sales
Afghanistan: Key to a Continent, John C. Griffiths, Westview Press
Conflict in Afghanistan (Flashpoint), J. Griffiths, Rourke Publishing Group
Under a Sickle Moon: A Journey Through Afghanistan, Peregrine Hodson, Ulverscroft Large Print Books
Afghanistan, Michael Howarth, Chelsea House
Asia and Pacific Review: 58 Countries, from New Zealand to China to Afghanistan, Hunter Publishing
Afghanistan: Land in Shadow, Chris Johnson, OXFAM (Oxford, 1998)
Afghanistan Venture, Paul S. Jones, The Naylor Company
Afghanistan (World Bibliographical Series, Vol. 135), Schuyler Jones, Abc-Clio
Afghanistan in Pictures (Visual Geography), Lerner Publications Company
The light garden of the angel king: journeys in Afghanistan, Peter Levi, Collins
Caravan, Darryl Ligasan (Illustrator), Lawrence Jr. McKay, Lee & Low Books
The Land and People of Afghanistan, Lippincott-Raven Publishers
Afghanistan: A Profile, Ralph H. Magnus, Westview Press
Afghan Alternatives: Issues, Options and Policies, Editor: Ralph H. Magnus, Transaction Books (New Brunswick, NJ, 1985)
Fundamentalism Reborn? Afghanistan and the Taliban, William Maley (Editor), Hurst & Co. (London, 1998)
Caravans to Tartary, Sabrina Michaud, Roland Michaud, Thames & Hudson
Afghanistan, Sabrina Michaud, Roland Michaud, Thames & Hudson
Caravans: A Novel, James Albert Michener, Random House
The 3rd World: Afghanistan and Pakistan, E. Willard Miller, Vance Bibliographies
Afghanistan in Crisis, K. P. Misra, Stosius Inc./Advent Books Division
The Politics of Afghanistan, Richard Newell, Cornell University Press (1972)
Health Care in Muslim Asia: Development and Disorder in Wartime Afghanistan, Ronald W. O'Connor, University Press of America
Islam and Politics in Afghanistan, Asta Olesen, Curzon Press
Afghanistan (Country Guide Series Report from the Aacrao-Aid Project), Holly A. O'Neill, American Association of College Registrars
Adventures in Afghanistan, Louis Palmer, Octagon Press
La Nouvelle Asia Centrale (ou La Fabrication des nations), Olivier Roy, Editions du Seuil (Paris, 1997)
The Fragmentation of Afghanistan: State Formation and Collapse in the International System, Barnett R. Rubin, Yale University Press (New Haven and London, 1995)
The Search for Peace in Afghanistan: From Buffer State to Failed State, Barnett R. Rubin, Yale University Press
Regime Change in Afghanistan: Foreign Intervention and the Politics of Legitimacy, Amin Saikal, William Maley, Westview Press
Political Order in Post-Communist Afghanistan, Fazel Haq Saikal, William Maley, Lynne Rienner Publications
A Violation of Trust, Joseph S. Salzburg, Sovereign Books
Afghanistan of the Afghans, The Sirdar Ikbal Ali Shah, Octagon Press
Tales of Afghanistan, Amina Shah, Ishk Book Service
Kara Kush, Idries Shah, Octagon Press
Afghan Caravan, Safia Shah (Editor), Octagon Press
Superpower Detente and the Future of Afghanistan, Jasjit Singh, Eduard Shevardnadze, B.K. Shrivastava, B. Gupta, South Asia Books
Afghanistan, Alex Ullmann, Ticknor & Fields
Afghanistan: is there hope for peace? Hearings before the Subcommittee on Near Eastern and South Asian Affairs of the Committee on Foreign Relations, United States Senate, One Hundred Fourth Congress, second session, June 6, 25, 26, and 27, 1996.

War in Afghanistan, Mark Urban, St Martins Press
An Afghanistan Picture Show: Or, How I Saved the World, William T. Vollmann, Farrar Straus & Giroux
Afghanistan, Non-Alignment and the Super Powers, Mohammed Amin Wakman, Humanities Press
Pakistan & Afghanistan: Resistance and Reconstruction, Marvin Weinbaum, Westview Press
Pakistan and Afghanistan, Westview Press
Widener Library Shelflists, 19. Southern Asia: Afghanistan, Bhutan, Burma, Cambodia, Ceylon, Harvard University Press
The Bear Trap: Afghanistan's Untold Story, Mohammed Yousaf, Mark Adkin, Leo Cooper (London, 1992)
Devil's Playground, Said Yassin Zia, Morris Publications

Afghanistan and the Soviet war

Inside the Soviet Army in Afghanistan, Alex Alexiev, Rand Corp
Afghanistan: The Soviet Invasion in Perspective, Anthony Arnold, Hoover Institution Press (Stanford, CA, 1981 & 1985)
The Fateful Pebble: Afghanistan's Role in the Fall of the Soviet Empire, Anthony Arnold, Presidio Press
Afghanistan's Two-Party Communism: Parcham and Khalq, Anthony Arnold, Hoover Institution Press (Stanford, CA, 1983)
Russian Roulette: Afghanistan Through Russian Eyes, Gennady Bocharov. (Translated by Alyona Kojevnikov), A Cornelia and Michael Bessie Book/ HarperCollins
The Hidden War: A Russian Journalist's Account of the Soviet War in Afghanistan, Artyom Borovik, Atlantic Monthly Press
Afghanistan and the Soviet Union, Henry S. Bradsher, Duke University Press (Durham, 1983)
Guerrilla Strategies: An Historical Anthology from the Long March to Afghanistan, Gerard Chaliand, University of California Press
Out of Afghanistan: The Inside Story of the Soviet Withdrawal, Diego Cordovez and Selig S. Harrison, Oxford University Press (1997)
The Red Army on Pakistan's Border: Policy Implications for the United States, (Foreign Policy Report), Theodore L. Eliot (Editor), Brasseys Inc.
Gorbachev's Afghan Gambit (National Security Paper, 9), Theodore L. Eliot Institute of Foreign Policy Analysis
Afghan Resistance: The Politics of Survival, Grant M. Farr and John G. Merriam (Editors), Westview Press
Afghanistan, the Soviet Union's Last War, Mark Galeotti, Frank Cass & Co.
The Fall of Afghanistan: An Insider's Account, Abdul Samad Ghaus, Brasseys Inc.
Afghanistan: The Soviet War, Edward Girardet, Croom Helm, London and St Martins' Press (New York, 1985)
British and American Responses to the Soviet Invasion of Afghanistan, Gabriella Grasselli, Dartmouth Publishing Co.
Afghanistan: Politics, Economics and Society: Revolution, Resistance, Intervention (Marxist Regimes Series), Bhavani Sen Gupta, Francis Pinter Publishing Ltd. (London, 1986)
Red Flag Over Afghanistan: The Communist Coup, the Soviet Invasion, and the Consequences, Thomas T. Hammond, Westview Press (Colorado, 1984)
The Soviet War in Afghanistan: Patterns of Russian Imperialism, Milan Hauner, University Press of America
Afghanistan and the Soviet Union: Collision and Transformation, Milan Hauner, Robert L. Canfield, Westview Press
The Soldiers' Story, Anna Heinamaa, Maija Leppanen, Yuri Yurchenko, University of California International
The Afghan Rebels: The War in Afghanistan, D.J. Herda, Franklin Watts,
Afghanistan Under Soviet Domination, 1964-83, Anthony Hyman, St Martins Press, and Macmillan (2nd Edition, London, 1984)

War in a Distant Country, Afghanistan: Invasion and Resistance, David G. Isby, Arm and Armour Press (London, 1989)
Afghanistan: The Soviet Invasion and the Afghan Response, 1979-1982, M. Hasan Kakar, University of California Press (San Diego, 1992)
Soldiers of God: With the Mujahideen in Afghanistan, Robert D. Kaplan, Houghton Mifflin Company
Untying the Afghan Knot: Negotiating Soviet Withdrawal, Riaz M. Khan, Duke University Press (Durham, 1991)
Holy War, Unholy Victory: Eyewitness to the CIA's Secret War in Afghanistan, Kurt Lohbeck, Regnery Publishing, Inc.
Soviet-American Relations with Pakistan, Iran, and Afghanistan, Hafeez Malik, St. Martin's Press
Afghanistan: Soviet Vietnam, Naomi Marcus, Marianne Clarke Trangen (Translator), Vladislav Tamarov, Mercury House
Stumbling Bear: Soviet Military Performance in Afghanistan, Scott R. McMichael, Brasseys Inc.
Holy Blood: An Inside View of the Afghan War, Paul Overby, Praeger Publications
Afghanistan, Mongolia and USSR, Ram Rahul, Vikas Publications
War Without Winners: Afghanistan's Uncertain Transition After the Cold War, Rasul Bakhsh Rais, Oxford University Press
The Soviet Withdrawal from Afghanistan: Analysis and Chronology, Tom Rogers, Greenwood Publishing Group
Soviet Intervention in Afghanistan: Causes, Consequences and India's Response, Arundhati Roy, Stosius Inc./Advent Books Division
Afghanistan: From Holy War to Civil War, Olivier Roy, Darwin Press
Islam and Resistance in Afghanistan, Olivier Roy, Cambridge University Press (2nd Edition, Cambridge, 1990)
Soviet Policy Toward Turkey, Iran, and Afghanistan: The Dynamics of Influence, Alvin Z. Rubinstein, Praeger Publications (New York, 1982)
The Pulicharki Prison: A Communist Inferno in Afghanistan, Professor Mohammed Osman Rustar, Ehsanullah Azeri (Editor), Writers Union of Free Afghanistan
The Soviet Withdrawal from Afghanistan, Amin Saikal, William Maley (Editor), Cambridge University Press
The Afghan Syndrome: The Soviet Union Vietnam, Maj. Gen Oleg Sarin and Col. Lv Dvoretsky, Presidio Press (CA, 1993)
Soviet Expansion in the Third World: Afghanistan a Case Study, Nasir Shansab, Bartleby Press

Historical and cultural

Histoire de la Guerre d'Afghanistan, Assem Akram, Editions Balland (Paris, 1996)
Afghanistan (Cultures of the World), Sharifah Enayat Ali, Marshall Cavendish Corp.
Afghanistan of the Afghans, Shah Sirdar Ikbal Ali
Archaeology of Afghanistan: From Earliest Times to the Timurid Period, F. R. Allchin, N. Hammond (Editor), Academic Press
Buzkashi: Game and Power in Afghanistan, G. Whitney Azoy, University of Pennsylvania Press (1982)
The Central Asian Arabs of Afghanistan: Pastoral Nomadism in Transition, Thomas J. Barfield, University of Texas Press (1981)
A History of Afghanistan, Vitaly Baskakov (Translator), Firebird Publications
Among the Afghans (Central Asia Book Series), Arthur Bonner, Duke University Press
The History of the Saffarids of Sistan and the Maliks of Nimruz, Clifford Edmund Bosworth, Mazda Publications
The Later Ghaznavids: Splendour and Decay: The Dynasty in Afghanistan and Northern India, 1040-1186, Clifford Edmund Bosworth, Mazda Publications
Gemstones of Afghanistan, Gary W. Bowersox, Geoscience Press (1997)

Cabool in 1836-37 and 8, Being the Personal Narrative of a Journey to, and Residence in, that City, Sir Alexander Burnes, (London 1842. Reprinted by Ferozsons, Lahore, 1964 and by Akademische Druk-u. Verlagsanstalt, Graz, 1973)

The Road to Oxiana, Robert Byron, Macmillan (London, 1937; reprinted by Picador, London, 1981)

The Pathans: 500 BC-AD 1957, Olaf Caroe, Oxford University Press (Oxford, 1958; reprinted, Karachi, 1973)

Chroniques Afghanes, 1965-1993, Pierre Centlivres, University of Neuchatel, Switzerland (Paris, 1997)

Imageries Populaires en Islam, Pierre Centlivres & Micheline Centlivres-Demont, Georg Editeur SA (Chene-Bourg, 1997)

An Historical Guide to Kabul, Nancy Hatch Dupree (2nd Edition, Kabul, 1972)

The National Museum of Afghanistan, a pictorial guide, Nancy Hatch Dupree (Kabul, 1974)

An Historical Guide to Afghanistan, Nancy Hatch Dupree (2nd Edition, Kabul, 1977)

Heroes of the Age: Moral Fault Lines on the Afghan Frontier (Comparative Studies on Muslim Societies, No 21), David B. Edwards, University of California Press

An Account of the Kingdom of Caubul, Mountstuart Elphinstone, John Murray (London, 1815; reprinted by Akademische Druk-u. Verlagsanstalt, Graz, 1969 and by Oxford University Press, Karachi, 1972)

Afghanistan Dar Panj Qarn Akheer (lit. "English Afghanistan in the Past Five Centuries"), Mir M. Sediq Farhang, Sanai Publishing

Afghanistan (Enchantment of the World), Leila Merrell Foster, Childrens Press

Caravans and Trade in Afghanistan, Birthe Frederiken

Award Winning Low-Fat Afghani Cooking, Asad Gharwal

The Emergence of Modern Afghanistan: Politics of Reform and Modernization, 1880-1946, Vartan Gregorian, Stanford University Press (Stanford, 1969)

External Influences and the Development of the Afghan State in the Nineteenth Century, Zalmay A. Gulzad, Peter Lang Publishing

Afghanistan: The Synagogue and the Jewish Home, Zohar Hanegbi, Center for Jewish Art

Traditional Textiles of Central Asia, Janet Harvey, Thames and Hudson (London, 1996)

Government and Society in Afghanistan: The Reign of Amir' Abd al-Rahman Khan, Hasan Kawun Kakar, University of Texas (Austin, 1981)

Afghanistan: The Great Game Revisited, Rosanne Klass (Editor), Freedom House (New York, 1987)

The Constitutional Decade, Sabah Kushkaki, Cultural Council of Afghanistan Resistance (Language: Dari)

Life of the Amir Dost Mohammed Khan of Kabul, Mohan Lal, Oxford University Press

The 'Ancient Supremacy': Bukhara, Afghanistan and the Battle for Balkh, 1731-1901 (Islamic History and Civilization, No 15), Jonathan L. Lee, E J Brill

Permian Stratigraphy and Fusulinida of Afghanistan With Their Paleogeographic and Paleotectonic Implications, E. la Leven, Calvin H. Stevens, Donald L. Baars, Geological Society of America

Signal Catastrophe; The Retreat from Kabul, 1842, Patrick Macrory, Hodder and Stoughton (London, 1966)

Waqf in Central Asia: Four Hundred Years in the History of a Muslim Shrine, 1480-1889, R. D. McChesney, Princeton University Press

Afghanistan: Paradise Lost, Roland Michaud, Rizzoli International

Horsemen of Afghanistan, Roland & Sabrina Michaud, Thames and Hudson (London, 1988)

Oral Narrative in Afghanistan: The Individual in Tradition, Margaret Ann Mills, Garland Publications

Rhetorics and Politics in Afghan Traditional Storytelling, Margaret Ann Mills, University of Pennsylvania Press

Afghan Craftsmen: The Cultures of Three Itinerant Communities, (Carlsberg Foundation's Nomad Research Project), Ida Nicolaisen, Thames & Hudson

Afghan Nomads in Transition: A Century of Change Among the Zala, Khan Khel (The Carlsberg Foundation's Nomad Research Project), Ida Nicolaisen, Gorm Pedersen, Thames & Hudson

Amidst Ice and Nomads in High Asia, Edward F. Noack, National Literary Guild

Afghan Wars, 1839-1992: What Britain Gave Up and the Soviet Union Lost, Edgar O'Ballance, Brasseys Inc. (London, 1993)

Oriental Rugs: The Carpets of Afghanistan, R. D. Parsons

Reform and Rebellion in Afghanistan, 1919-1929: King Amanullah's Failure to Modernize a Tribal Society, Leon B. Poullada, Cornell University Press (Ithaca, 1973)

The Kingdom of Afghanistan and the United States: 1828-1973, Leon B. Poullada & Leila J. Poullada, Dageforde Publishing and the Center for Afghanistan Studies at the University of Nebraska at Omaha

Cultural Policy in Afghanistan, Shafie Rahel, UNESCO

Between Two Giants: Political History of Afghanistan in the Nineteen Century, Sayed Qassem Reshtia, Afghan Jehad Works Translation Centre (Peshawar, 1990)

Ancient Art from Afghanistan: Treasures of the Kabul Museum, Benjamin, Jr. Rowland, Ayer Co. Publishers

Revolutions & Rebellions in Afghanistan: Anthropological Perspectives, M. Nazif Shahrani, Robert L. Canfield (Editors), University of California Institute for International Studies (Berkeley, 1984)

Dust of the Saints: A Journey to Herat in Time of War, Radek Sikorski, Paragon House

The Minaret of Djam: An Excursion in Afghanistan, Freya Stark, Transatlantic Arts

Fire in Afghanistan: 1914-1929, Rhea Stewart, Doubleday & Co. (New York, 1973)

A History of Afghanistan, Percy Sykes, Macmillan (London, 1940, reprinted by Oriental Books Reprint Corp., New Delhi, 1981)

Afghanistan: An Atlas of Indigenous Domestic Architecture, Albert Szabo, Thomas J. Barfield, University of Texas Press

Beyond the Khyber Pass: The Road to British Disaster in the first Afghan War, John H. Waller, Random House

Charles Masson of Afghanistan: Explorer, Archaeologist, Numismatist, and Intelligence Agent, Gordon Whitteridge, Aris & Phillips

Ethnic & tribal

Islam, Ethnicity and the State in Pakistan: An Overview, R.Binder, in *The State, Religion and Ethnic Politics: Afghanistan, Iran, Pakistan,* A. Banuazizi and M. Weiner (Editors), Syracuse University Press (New York, 1996)

The Most Difficult Choice, R. Breen, in *Refugees*, UNHCR (Geneva, Issue 11, October 1997)

Ethnic, Regional and Sectarian Alignments in Afghanistan, R. Canfield, in *The State, Religion and Ethnic Politics: Afghanistan, Iran, Pakistan*, A. Banuazizi and M. Weiner (Editors), Syracuse University Press, (New York, 1996)

The Biggest Caseload in The World, R. Colville, in *Refugees*, UNHCR (Geneva, Issue 11, October 1997)

Dark Side of Moon, A. Jamal, in *Refugees*, UNHCR (Geneva, Issue 11, October 1997)

Government and Society in Afghanistan, H. Kakar, University of Texas Press (Austin, 1979)

The Pacification of the Hazaras of Afghanistan, H. Kakar, ACAS Occasional papers (New York, 1973)

Saire Dar Hazarajat, A. Laly, Ihsani (Qom, Iran, 1994)

The Hazaras of Afghanistan – An Historical, Cultural, Economic and Political Study, Dr Sayed Askar Mousavi, Curzon Press Ltd. (London, 1997)

The Struggle for Afghanistan, N. Newell and R. Newell, Cornell University Press (London, 1981)

The Kafir of the Hindu-Kush, George Robertson, Oxford University Press (1st Edition, 1896; reprinted, 1975)

State Building and Social Fragmentation in Afghanistan, N. Shahrani, in *The State, Religion and Ethnic Politics: Afghanistan, Iran, Pakistan*, A. Banuazizi and M. Weiner (Editors), Syracuse University Press (New York, 1996)

The Baluchis and The Pathans, V. Wrisling, Minority Rights Group Report (London, 1987)

Human rights

Report on the situation of human rights in Afghanistan by UN Special Rapporteur Choong-Hyun Paik (E/CN.4//1998/71)

Women in Afghanistan: The violations continue, Amnesty International (London, 1997)

Women in Afghanistan: A human rights catastrophe, Amnesty International (London, 1995)

Afghanistan: Torture of Political Prisoners, Amnesty International USA

Afghanistan: new forms of cruel, inhuman or degrading punishment, Amnesty International (London, 1992)

By All Parties to the Conflict: Violations of the Laws of War in Afghanistan, Published by Human Rights Watch

Afghanistan the Forgotten War: Human Rights Abuses and Violations of the Laws of War Since the Soviet Withdrawal, By Asia Watch Staff, Human Rights Watch

Afghanistan: A Nation of Minorities, Nassim Jawad, Minority Rights Group International (London, 1992)

A Nation is Dying, Jeri Laber and Barnett R. Rubin, Northwestern University Press (1988)

International Human Rights in Context, Henry Steiner and Philip Alston, Oxford University Press (Oxford, 1998)

The Universal Declaration of Human Rights

The Geneva Conventions (1949) and the **Geneva Protocols** (1977)

The International Covenant on Civil and Political Rights

The International Covenant on Economic, Social and Cultural Rights

The Convention Against Torture and Other Cruel, Inhuman or Degrading Treatment or Punishment

Report of the Independent Counsel on International Human Rights

Afghanistan, *in* **Country Report on Human Rights Practices,** United States Department of State (Washington, 1993)

Bibliographies

Additional bibliographies can be found in the following:

Historical Dictionary of Afghanistan, Ludwig W. Adamec, The Scarecrow Press Inc. (Metuchen, N.J. and London, 1991). Entries (47 pp) under: General; Cultural; Economic; Historical and Political; Juridical; Scientific; Social.

A Bibliography of Afghanistan, Keith McLachlan and William Whittaker, Middle East & North African Studies Press Ltd, Gallipoli House, The Cottons, Outwell, Wisbech, Cambridge, PE14 8TN (England, 1983). Entries (671pp) under: Bibliographies; General; Geology; Flora and Fauna; Water Resources; Geographical Studies; Travel; Historical Studies; History and Politics; Social Studies; Afghan Economy and Infrastructure; Agriculture and Forestry; Language and Literature; Supplement of Publications post 1979; Maps; Index.

The Fragmentation of Afghanistan, Barnett R. Rubin, Yale University Press (New Haven and London, 1995). Entries (17 pp) under: Books and Articles; Official Publications; Government Reports; Documents and Document Collections; News Sources.

Annotated Bibliography of Afghanistan, 3rd Edition, Donald N. Wilber, Human Relations Area Files Press, New Haven, Connecticut (USA, 1968), 252pp. Entries under: General Sources of Information and Reference Works; Geography; History; Social Organizations; Social Evolution and Institutions; Political Structure; Economic Structure; Languages and Literature; Art and Archaeology; Index.

Databases and directories

The Agency Coordinating Body for Afghan Relief (ACBAR) publishes:
Directory of Humanitarian Agencies. Annual publication (May) listing 170 NGOs working in Afghanistan (including agencies with offices in Pakistan). Contains alphabetical list of NGOs with details of sectors and areas of operations, budgets and principal donors.
Database of NGO Activities, *plus a* **Summary.** Updated each May, this breaks down agency operations by sector, province and district.
Telephone Directory of International NGOs, Afghan NGOs, UN Agencies, Press and Government Offices in Kabul. Updated each May.
All Available from:
ACBAR, 2 Rehman Baba Road, University Town, Peshawar, Pakistan.
TEL: +92 (91) 40839, 44392 FAX: +92 (91) 840471
E-mail: acbaar@radio.psh.brain.net.pk

Dictionaries

English-Pashtun Dictionary, Afghan National Islamic Council of Immigrants in America (1986)
Concise English-Afghan Dari Dictionary, S. Sakaria (Kabul, 1967)

Magazines

Afghanistan Forum. US-based magazine covering recent events and publications, NGO activities, chronology, and various articles. Discontinued in late 1997. *Available from:* The Afghanistan Forum Inc., 19 Fannine Avenue, East Hampton, NY 11937, USA
Afghanistan Info. Magazine of the Comite Suisse de soutien au peuple Afghan. *Available from:* Micheline Centlivres-Demont, Redacteur de Afghanistan Info. TEL/FAX: +41 (32) 724 7682
Aina (the "Mirror"). United Nations Afghanistan magazine. Produced quarterly to reflect the work of UN agencies and NGOs working in Afghanistan.
Paigham. Monthly UN magazine in Dari and Pashto.
Aina and Paigham are both available from: UNOCHA, House 292, Street 55, F-10/4, Islamabad, Pakistan.TEL: +92 (51) 211451-5
FAX: +92 (51) 211450 E-mail: sarah@undpafg.org.pk
Bulletin du CEREDAF. Published by the French Documentation and Study Centre on Afghanistan (CEREDAF), this is the most detailed monthly report available in French on current events and developments. *Available from:* AFRANE-CEREDAF, 16, Passage de la Main-d'Or, F-75011, Paris, France.
FAX: +33 (3) 80 55 21 45
Critique and Vision. An Afghan journal of culture, politics and history, dedicated to the publication of articles, research projects, and book reviews in the area of Afghanistan studies. Published twice-yearly. *Available from:* S. Wali Ahmadi, Editor, *Critique and Vision,* PO Box 478, Mount Eden, California 94557, USA.
Friends of Afghanistan (FOA). US-based quarterly publication. FOA was begun within the National Peace Corps Association and membership is open to all. Contents include articles and FOA membership information. *Available from:* Susan G. Aronson, Newsletter Editor, 9025 Chantal Way, Sacramento, CA 95829-1717, USA.
TEL: +1 (916) 682 0525 E-mail: aronson2@cwnet.com
Website: www.royalpages.com/~foa/
Khaharan Women's Journal. Pakistan-based magazine focusing on women's and children's issues. Published in Dari and Pashto. *Available from:* Editor, Khaharan, GPO Box 356, Peshawar Cantt., Pakistan
Les Nouvelles d'Afghanistan. French language quarterly published by the French humanitarian association AFRANE. Contents include: news; humanitarian aid issues; culture; quarterly chronology; bibliography & articles.
Available (FFr30) from:
Les Nouvelles d'Afghanistan, BP 254, 75524 Paris, Cedex 11, France.
Website: http://ourworld.compuserve.com/homepages/afghanistan_France/

FOR THE ROAD

J. Hartley/UNICEF

English-Dari phrasebook

The following information is taken from the Concise English-Afghan Dari Dictionary edited by S. Sakaria (Kabul, 1967), which can still be found in some Kabul bookshops. We are grateful to Gordon Adam for his help in editing this section.

PRONUNCIATION

Vowels

a as in father
e as in every
i as in ill
o as in orbit
u as in boot
aa as in market
ai as in ice
au as in our
dj as in pleasure

Consonants

Most consonants are pronounced as they are in Western tongues. A few, however, should be noted:

g is always hard, as in good.

q is not followed by ***u***, as in English; it is a somewhat more explosive, breathy sound, much as the **kh** in khaki, a Persian word long ago assimilated by English.

kh is quite a throaty, coughing sound, much as the **ch** in the Scottish loch, or the German **ch**.

GRAMMAR

Sentence Structure

In Dari, the sentence order is: SUBJECT-OBJECT-VERB, e.g.

Aan tefel khub ast	That child good is
Baks raa mekhaahad	He (she) the box wants
Khana-e-maa az erfaarat dur ast	House of us (our house) from the embassy far is

Articles

A, An and *the* are all expressed by *yak* (one) whenever it is deemed necessary. Generally, however, the article is used only when particular emphasis is placed on the subject.

Nouns

1. Plurals are formed by adding *haa*:

dars	lesson
dorshaa	lessons
tefel	child
tefelhaa	children

2. A word is attached to its modifier by adding *-e:*

dars-e-mushkel	difficult lesson
tefel-e khub	good child

3. Objective (accusative) case is indicated by *raa:*

Tefel khub ast	The child is good
Tefel raa mebinam	I see the child
Tefelhaa raa mebinam	I see the children

Prepositions

ba	to, at, into, on
baa	with, by means of
dar	in
az	from

Pronouns

1. Personal Pronouns

man	I
tu	you – intimate form
o	he, she
iin	it, this
aan	it, that
maa	we
shomaa	you – polite form for both singular and plural use
aanhaa	they

2. Possessive Pronouns. Possession is shown by adding *-e* to the thing possessed. Two forms are generally used: the formal and the shortened.

Formal		Shortened
baks-e man	my box	baks-am
ketaab-e man	my book	ketaab-am

3. Relative and Interrogative Pronouns

ki	who	-e ki, azki	whose
ki raa	whom		
che	what	kodaam	which

4. Demonstrative Pronouns

iin	this	innhaa	these
aan	that	aanhaa	those

Interrogative Adverbs

kai	when
kojaa	where
cheraa	why
chand	how many
cheqadar	how much
chetaur	how

Imperatives are usually indicated by the prefix ***be-***

raftan	to go	berau! (boro)	go away!
aamadan	to come	be'aa!	Come!
pak kardan	to clean	paak kon!	Clean (it)!

Questions

Shomaa ketaab daari?	Do you have a book?
Ketaab-e khub daari?	Do you have a good book?
Habib iin ketaab raa mekhaahad?	Does Habib want his book?
Che mekhaahed?	What do you want?
Chand daana ketaab daarand?	How many book(s) do they have?

Note: daana (piece) usually follows chand (how many).

Yes and No/Negation

bale (yes) often introduces a positive answer; ne, na-, and n' denote negation

Bale, man ketaab daaram	Yes, I have a book
Ne, ketaab na-daaram	No, I don't have any books
Bale, Habib iin ketaab raa mekhaahad	Yes, Habib wants this book
Ne Habib iin ketaab raa na–mekhaahad	No, Habib doesn't want this book

VERBS

Infinitive	to see	didan
Present	I see	man mebinam
Imperative	See!	bebin, loftan bebined
Past	I saw	man didam
Perfect	I have seen	man dida'am
Past perfect	I had seen	man dida budam
Past continuous	I was seeing	man medidam
Conjunctive	I want to see	man mekhaaham bebinam
	Perhaps I can see	shayad bebinam
	I ought to see	bayad bebinam
	I must see	man majbur hastam bebinam

THE VERB "TO BE": *BUDAN / HASTAM*

Present		**Optative**	
hastam	I am	baasham	I may be
hasti	you are	baashi	you may be
ast	he is	baashad	he may be
hastem	we are	baashem	we may be
hasted	you are	baashed	you may be
hastand	they are	baashand	they may be

USEFUL EXPRESSIONS

Greeting and Farewell

Salaam! Salaam a-laykum!	Peace! Peace to you!
Khub hasti?	Are you well? (Intimate form)
Shomaa chetaur hasted?	How are you? (Polite form)
Aaz amadan-e shomaa, khosh hastam	I am happy that you have come (lit. From your coming, I am happy)

Aaz didan-e shomaa, khosh shodam	I become happy to see you
Bubakhshed	Excuse me (*Note:* bakhshish, a present or gift)
Nam-e shomaa chist (che ast)?	What is your name?
Nam-e man Shikria ast	My name is Shikria
Famil-e shomaa khub ast?	Is your family well?
Bale, tashakor aanhaa khub hastand	Yes, thank you, they are well
Bisyaar tashakor!	Thank you very much!
Tefel-e man bisyaar mariz ast	My child is very ill
Bisyaar afsos!	(I am) very sorry!
Afsos!	Sorry!
Ba'aman-e Khoda	Goodbye (lit. Go in the safety of God)
Khodaa Haafez	Goodbye (lit. God be your protector)
Lotfan aasta gap beegee	Please speak more slowly
Man na-mefahmam	I do not understand
Lotfan tekraar ko	Repeat it, please

Driving and Directions

Lotfan aasta boro!	Please go slowly!
Lotfan zud boro!	Please go fast! Please hurry!
Rubaru	Straight ahead (lit. Face to face)
Dast-e raast	Right (lit. Right hand)
Dast-e chap	Left (lit. Left hand)
Baash! iinja baash!	Stop! Stop here!
Lotfan iinja baash	Please stop here
Sarak-e Bamiyan khub ast?	Is the road to Bamiyan good?
Baa shomaa chand nafar ast?	How many people are with you?
Che taklif/mushkil ast?	What's the trouble?

Shopping and Eating

Chand qimat?	How much (is the) price?
Qimat ast!	It is expensive!
Ne, qimat nist, arzaan ast	No, it is not expensive, it is cheap
Iin che ast? Aan che ast?	What is this? What is that?
Chist? (Che ast)?	What is it?
Kist? (Ki ast)?	Who is it?
Man yak otaq-e yak nafara mekhaaham	I want a single room
Otaq-e naan kojaast?	Where is the dining room?
Lotfan bishi	Please sit down
Loftan naan beegee	Please take food
Lotfan darwaaza raa waaz ko	Please open the door
Lotfan kelkin raa basta ko	Please close the window
Naan mehaahed?	Would you like some food?
Du, tokhme-e josh wa chai mekhaaham	I want two boiled eggs and some tea
Digar che mekhaahed?	What else do you want?
Man chai sabz mekhaaham	I want a cup of green tea
Ju'aab-e chai koja ast?	Where is the lavatory? (lit. Where is the answer to tea?)
Tashnaab kojast?	Where is the washroom?

TIMES, SEASONS, NUMERALS

waqt	time, early	hesaab kardan	to count
naawaqt	late	adad	numeral, number
baja	o'clock	pesh	before
saa'at	hour	baad	after
daqiqa	minute	ziyaad	too much
juma	Friday	kam-e	a little
shanbe	Saturday	bisyaar	many, much, very
yak shanbe	Sunday	sefer	zero
du shanbe	Monday	yak, awal	one, 1st
se shanbe	Tuesday	du, dowom	two, 2nd
chaar shanbe	Wednesday	se, sowom	three, 3rd
panj shanbe	Thursday	chaar, chaarom	four, 4th
saniya	second	panj, panjom	five, 5th
roz	day	shash, shashom	six, 6th
shab	night	haft, haftom	seven, 7th
diroz	yesterday	hasht, hashtom	eight, 8th
dishab	last night	noh, nohom	nine, 9th
emroz	today	dah, dahom	ten, 10th
emshab	tonight	yaazdah	eleven, 11
fardaa	tomorrow	duaazdah	twelve, 12
fardaa shab	tomorrow night	sezdah	thirteen, 13
pas fardaa	day after tomorrow	chaardah	fourteen, 14
har roz	every day	paanzdah	fifteen, 15
har shab	every night	shaanzdah	sixteen, 16
sobh	morning	hafdah	seventeen,17
chasht	noon	hajdah	eighteen, 18
baad az chasht	afternoon	nozdah	nineteen, 19
hafta	week	bisttwenty, 20	
	(*Note:* haft, seven)	bist-o yak	twenty one, 21
maah	month	bist-o du	twenty two, 22
saal	year	si	thirty, 30
mausem	season	chel	forty, 40
bahaar	spring	pinja	fifty, 50
taabestaan	summer	shast	sixty, 60
khazaan	autumn	haftaad	seventy, 70
zemestaan	winter	hashtaad	eighty, 80
dafa, yak dafa	one time, once	nawad	ninety, 90
yak dafa digar	once again	sadone hundred, 100	
hesaab	calculation	hazaar	one thousand, 1,000

Telling the time

Chand baja ast?	What o'clock is it?
Che waqt ast?	What time is it?

VOCABULARY

VERBS

Infinitive	Infinitive	Present
awake	bedar shodan	meshawam
bear	bordan	mebaram
beat	zadan	mezanam
become	shodan	meshawam
break	shekastan	meshkenam
bring	awordan	me'aaram
build	saakhtan	mesaazam
burst	tarqidan	metarqam
buy	kharidan	mekharam
can	tawaanestan	metawaanam
catch	greftan	megiram
come	aamadan	me'aayam
cost	arzidan	mearzam
creep	khazidan	mekhazam
cut	buridan	meboram
dig	kandan	mekanam
do	kardan	mekonam
drink	nushidan	menosham
drive	raandan	meraanam
eat	khordan	mekhoram
fall	oftaadan	me'oftam
flee	gorekhtan	megorezam
fight	jangidan	mejangam
find	yaaftan	meyaafam
fly	paridan	meparam
forget	faraamosh kardan	faraamosh mekonam
give	daadan	medeham
go	raftan	merawam
grind	maida kardan	maida mekonam
grow	ruidan	meroyam
have	daashtan	daaram
hear	shonidan	meshnawam
knit	baaftan	mebaafam
know	daanestan	medaanam
lay	maandan	memaanam
learn	amokhtan	me'aamozam
let	gozaashtan	megozaaram
light	bal kardan	bal mekonam
lose	gom kardan	gom mekonam
make	saakhtan	mesaazam
owe	qarzdaar budan	qarzdaar hastam
pay	pardaakhtan	mepardaazam
put	maandan	memaanam
read	khaandan	mekhaanam
recognize	shenaakhtan	meshnaasam
run	dawidan	medawam
say	goftan	megoyam
see	didan	mebinam

seek	paalidan	mepaalam
sell	frokhtan	mefrosham
send	frestaadan	mefrestam
set	neshastan	meshinam
shine	drokh'shidan	medrokh'sham
shut	bastan	mebandam
sing	saraa'idan	mesaraayam
slay	koshtan	mekhosham
sleep	khaabidan	mekhaabam
slide	lakh'shidan	melakh'sham
spin	residan	meresam
stand	estaadan	me'estam
steal	dozdidan	medozdam
stick	chaspidan	mechaspam
take	greftan	megiram
teach	dars daadan	dars medeham
think	feker kardan	feker mekonam
throw	andaakhtan	meandaazam
weave	baaftan	mebaafam
write	naweshtan	menawisam

EATING AND COOKING

apple	seb
apricot	zard aalu
asparagus	maarchoba
beans	lubiya
beef	gosht-e gau
beet	lablabu
boiling-water	aab-e josh
breakfast	naashtaa
bucket	satel
cabbage	karam
cardamom	hel
carrot	zardak
cauliflower	gole karam
cherry	gelaas
corn	jawaari
cucumber	baadrang
egg	tokhom
eggplant	baanjaane siyaah
flour	aard
fruit	mewa
grape	angur
icebox	yakh-chaal
kerosene	tel-e khaak
leek	gandana
lentil	daal
lettuce	kaahu
melon	kharbuza
mint	naanaa
mutton	gosht-e gosfand
okra	baamiyaa
onion	piyaaz
parsley	gashniz
peach	shaftaalu
pear	naak
peas	moshong
pepper	morch
pot	deg
potato	kachaalu
prune	aalubokhaaraa
radish	moli
raisin	keshmesh
rhubarb	rawaash
rice	brenj
sour-cherry	aalubaalu
spinach	paalak
squash	kadu
sugar cane	naishakar
tomato	baanjaane rumi
turnip	shalgham
veal	gosht-e gosaala
vegetables	tarkaari
water melon	tarbuz
wheat	gandom
yeast	kalpura

English-Pashto field vocabulary

n. noun, a. adjective, v.t. verb transitive, v.i. verb intransitive

accident	n. hadisa'h, afat	dark	a. tor
afraid	v.i. tarhedal	daughter	n. lur
angry	a. khafah	day	n. wradz
arable	a. shud-yar	dead	a. mar
army	n. lashkar	dirty	a. khiran
asleep	a. u-dah	donkey	n. khar
bad	a. kharab	dog	n. spaey
barley	n. aor-bushey	door	n. war
barren (land)	a. dag	dry (land)	a. wuch
bath	n. hammam	early	a. sahar
beggar	n. gada	earth	n. z'maka'h, zamin, mulk (land)
big	a. lo-e, ghat	empty	a. khali
bird	n. murgha'h	enemy	n. dushman
black	a. tor	evil	a. badi, ba'a
blanket	n. shara'i	excellent	a. shaeh
blood	n. winey	eye	n. starga'h
boil	v.i. aeshedal	face	n. makh
bone	n. had	far	a. bi-yartah
book	n. kitab	farmer	n. zamin-dar
bread	n. doda'i, nan	field	n. wand, kisht
canal	n. wala'h	fire	n. aor, balarn
chair	n. kursi, chauki	food	n. khwarah, shuma'h, n'mara'i
child	n. wor-kaey, halak	girl	n. jina'i
cold	a. sor	goat	n. wuz, psah (markhor: wild goat)
cook	n. bawarchi	God	n. Allah
corn	n. hala'h, danah	gold	n. zar
cotton	n. ma-luch	good	a. shaeh
cow	n. ghwa	government	n. daulat
cup	n. kandol	governor	n. hakim, sardar
danger	n. wera'h	grass	n. alaf, washah

green	a. shin
gun	n. topak
hand	n. las
happy	a. khwash
harvest	n. fasl
headman	n. malik
heavy	a. drund
herd (cows)	n. park
home	n. astogna'h
horse	n. as (asp)
hour	n. sa'at
hot	a. garm
husband	n. merah
ice	n. kangal
ill	a. najor
infant	n. tandaey
infidel	n. kafir
irrigate	v.t. lundawul
journalist	n. khabar'nigar
journey	n. safar
kill	v.t. wajlal
lady	n. bibi, merman
land	n. z'maka'h, zamin
law	n. shara, shari'at
leader	n. sardar, komand'r (mujahed)
light	a. roshna'i, rarna
mad	a. lewanaey
male	a. nar, merah
market	n. bazaar
meat	n. ghwasha'h
mountain	n. ghar, koh
mother	n. mor
much	a. der, frewan
news	n. khabar
night	n. shpa'h
noon	n. gharma'h, takkarna'h
numerous	a. der, garn, wadan
open	a. arat
ox	n. ghwayaey
pain	n. dard
pass	n. tangaey, dara'h (defile), ghashaey (mountain)
path	n. lar, wat
peace	n. sulha'h, ashti

plunder	v.t. tala'h, talanka
poor	a. khwar, tarah
quick	a. zaer
quiet	a. aram, karar
rain	n. baran
red	a. sur, surkh
rest	n. aram
rice	n. w'rijey
right (not left)	a. rast
river	n. sin, daryah
road	n. lar, rah
room	n. khuna'h, hujra'h
sad	a. zahir
safe	a. aman, salamat
salt	n. malga'h
salutation	n. salaam
sheep	n. majz (male), mejz (ewe)
shoe	n. parna'h, na'l (horse shoe)
sister	n. khor
sleep	v.i. khub ka
small	a. wor, lajz
snow	n. wawra'h
son	n. dzo-e, zo-e
state	n. daulat
storm	n. sila'i, tufan
straight	a. sam, sat
stream	n. lashtaey, wala'h
thief	n. ghal
time	n. waght
understand	v.i. pohedal
urgent	a. zarur
valley	n. dara'h
village	n. kalaey, dih
war	n. jang, jihad (religious war)
water	n. aobah, sakao
wood	n. largaey, jar (copse, small wood)
wound	n. parhar, zakhm
young	a. dzwan, halak

Sources: The Pushtu Manual (H.G. Raverty), personal notes (E.R. Girardet)

Glossary

adat: custom, habit.

AIG: Afghan Interim Government.

Afghani: Afghanistan's currency which varies in value between the north and the rest of the country: US$1.00 = c.20,000 *Afghanis* (Kabul/Taliban); US$1.00 = c.60,000 *Afghanis* (Mazar/"Northern Alliance" – the "Dostum Dollar")

Afghan Mellat: Afghan Social Democratic Party.

alim (plural: **ulama**)**:** graduate in higher Islamic studies from a *madrassa.*

amir: leader, lord, sometimes king.

basmachi: Islamic and traditionalist fighters who resisted Soviet rule in Central Asia; literally 'bandits.' The Soviets often referred to the mujahideen as *basmachi.*

buzkashi: violent sport played in northern Afghanistan by two teams of horsemen fighting to drop a decapitated goat inside a chalk circle.

chador: garment worn by women in accordance with Islamic law or local custom to cover required parts of the body.

Durand Line: boundary imposed by the British in 1893 on Amir Abdur Rahman which separated Afghanistan from British India. The line still splits Pashto-speaking tribes between Afghanistan and Pakistan's NWFP.

Durrani: Pashtun tribe living in southwestern Afghanistan, from which the Royal family came. Rivals of the Ghilzai.

Fundamentalist: "for fundamentalism it is of paramount importance to get back to the scriptures, clearing away the obfuscation of tradition. It always seeks to return to some former state; it is characterised by the practice of re-reading texts, and a search for origins. The enemy is not modernity but tradition…fundamentalism sits uneasily within the political spectrum, for the "return to first things" may take many different forms…in Afghanistan fundamentalism, defined as a desire to get back to *shari'at* as the sole authority, is the natural attitude of the educated clergy, the *ulama,* whereas the *mullah* of the villages, who have not mastered the whole corpus of the law, are traditionalists and not fundamentalists." (Olivier Roy) The Taliban movement is considered to be traditionalist not fundamentalist.

gelim: woven rug from Turkic tribes of northern Afghanistan. General Dostum's men were nicknamed the *gelim jam* (literally "carpet-baggers") because of their reputation for looting and pillaging.

hajj: Islamic pilgrimage to Mecca.

Ghilzai: Pashtun tribe in southeastern Afghanistan. Rivals of the Durrani.

hadith: Prophet Mohammed's sayings and doctrines, handed down through a line of authorities.

Harakat-e-Inqilab-e-Islami: Islamic Revolutionary Movement of Mohammed Nabi Mohammedi. The largest mujahideen movement in the early 1980s. A traditionalist party based on *madrassa* and tribal Pashtun support, many of its members have now defected to the Taliban. (SEE KEY PLAYERS)

Harakat-e-Islami: moderate *Shi'a* mujahideen party, led by Mohammed Asef Muhseni. Not currently a member of the 'united' *Shi'a* Hezb-e-Wahdat. (SEE KEY PLAYERS)

Hezb-e-Islami (Hekmatyar): Party of Islam (*Sunni*) led by Gulbuddin Hekmatyar; mainly radical Pashtun Islamists. (SEE KEY PLAYERS)

Hezb-e-Islami (Khalis): Party of Islam (*Sunni*) led by Mawlawi Younis Khalis; a splinter group from Hekmatyar's party; mainly moderate Pashtun Islamists. (SEE KEY PLAYERS)

Hezb-e-Wahdat-e-Islami: Party of Islamic Unity (*Shi'a*/Hazara) led by Karim Khalili. (SEE KEY PLAYERS)

hojra: guest room or house.

imam: leader of any Islamic community.

ISI: Inter Services Intelligence (Pakistani military intelligence).

Islam: literally, 'submission' to the commands of Allah, the omniscient and omnipotent God. A monotheistic religion which completes the prophetic Judaeo-Christian tradition and recognises Mohammed as the last of the prophets. The Five Pillars of Islam are: 1) *Shahadat*, the profession of faith in Allah and Mohammed; 2) *Salat,* prayer five times a day facing Mecca; 3) *Zakat*, almsgiving; 4) *Sawm* (*Ruza* in Dari), fasting during *ramadan* or *ramzan* (literally, "the month during which the Koran was sent down") 5) *Hajj,* pilgrimage to Mecca, a legal obligation of every adult Muslim of both sexes to conduct at least once in a lifetime.

Islamist movement: originated in the late 1950s in reaction to the process of Westernization and liberal secularization in Afghanistan. Professor Burhannudin Rabbani was pronounced Chairman in 1971 and it developed into the Jamiat-e-Islami. Puritanical reformists more than fundamentalists.

Isma'ilis: *Shi'a* Islamic sect led by the Aga Khan, numbering some 300,000 people living in northeastern Afghanistan, Pakistan, India, Tajikistan, Iran, Syria and Africa. They are 'Sevener' *Shi'as* as opposed to the 'Twelver' Hazaras. (SEE ETHNIC & TRIBAL)

Ittihad-e-Islami: Islamic Alliance (*Sunni*/Pashtun); an Islamist group led by Abdul Rasul Sayyaf. (SEE KEY PLAYERS)

izzat: honour (collective and individual)

Jamaat-e-Islami: Society of Islam (Pakistani *Sunni* party)

Jamiat-e-Islami: Society of Islam (Afghan *Sunni* party) led by ex-President Burhannudin Rabbani. Mainly moderate Tajik Islamists, its military commander is Ahmed Shah Massoud, a Panjshairi Tajik. Now one of the major parties in the anti-Taliban "Northern Alliance." (SEE KEY PLAYERS)

jihad: Islamic Holy War; struggle in defence of or to propagate Islam.

jirga: Pashtun tribal assembly for resolution of disputes and decision-making; literally, 'circle', denoting the equality of participants.

Jumbesh-e-Melli Islami: National Islamic Movement (*Sunni*/Uzbek) led by General Abdul Rashid Dostum. (SEE KEY PLAYERS)

kafir: non-Muslim, unbeliever; literally, 'denier.' The inhabitants of Kafiristan remained pagans until they were converted to Islam by the sword in 1896, after which their land became known as Nuristan, "Land of Light."

karez: underground gravity-fed irrigation canal.

KHAD: *Khademat-e-Ittela'at Dowlati*, State Information Services. The former Afghan communist government's East German-trained secret police. Once headed by Dr Najibullah.

khalifa: successor, caliph.

Khalq: one of the two main factions of the People's Democratic Party of Afghanistan (PDPA). Literally, "People" or "Masses," it was mainly Pashtun and military in its membership. Formed in 1967, it was led by Nur Mohammed Taraki (April 1978 to September 1979) and Hafizullah Amin (September to December 1979). (SEE KEY PLAYERS)

khan: leader of a clan, ethnic group, professional caste; socially/locally appointed (unlike a *malik*).

kuchi: nomads.

Loya Jirga: Great Council; highest representative institution in the Afghan state.

madrassa: school for secondary or advanced Islamic studies, usually attached to a large mosque.

malik: chief of a tribe or clan, usually one appointed by the state, as opposed to a *khan*; literally 'ruler.'

masjid: mosque; **Masjid-e-Jami:** Friday Mosque.

mawlawi: graduate from a *madrassa* (college of higher Islamic studies); similar to an *alim.*

mazar: monument built over the tomb of an important figure; literally, "place of pilgrimage."

melmastia: Pashtun hospitality, especially the feeding of guests.

mir: lord or ruler, especially of Hazaras.

mirab: someone elected and paid to ensure local water rights are respected.

mujahideen: soldiers of Islam or holy warriors. A **mujahed** is one engaged in *jihad; mujahed* is also an adjective.

mullah: a village-level religious leader and preacher.

namus: Pashtun honour, law, principle; those things a man must defend to preserve his honour.

Nasr: Victory, a radical Islamist *Shi'a* Afghan group once supported by Iranian Hazaras.

Northern Alliance: anti-Taliban military alliance between the mainly Tajik Jamiat-e-Islami party of Rabbani and Massoud, and the mainly Uzbek forces of General Dostum, centred on Mazar-e-Sharif. Replaced the earlier Shura-e-Hamahangi (Supreme Coordination Council, an alliance of the northern-based forces of General Dostum and Hezb-e-Islami-Hekmatyar) and Shura-e-Nezar Shomal (Supervisory Council of the North, an alliance led by Massoud).

NWFP: North West Frontier Province of Pakistan, largely Pashtun-inhabited. Part of Afghanistan since 1747 but assimilated under British control and divided up from Afghanistan by the Durand Line of 1893. Consisting of a number of tribal agencies it is today a semi-autonomous region not fully answerable to Islamabad.

PDPA: People's Democratic Party of Afghanistan. The Afghan Marxist party, founded in 1965 with the aim of turning the feudal society of Afghanistan into a socialist state. Rivalry led to a split in 1967, with Nur Mohammed Taraki creating the Khalq ('Masses') faction and Babrak Karmal forming the Parcham ('Flag') faction. Pressure from the Soviets caused the two factions to re-unite in 1977. The PDPA came to power after staging the April 1978 Saur Revolution which deposed (and killed) President Daoud. Taraki became President of the new Democratic Republic of Afghanistan, but was (murdered and) replaced first by Hafizullah Amin and then Karmal, on the eve of the Soviet invasion. Dr Najibullah replaced Karmal in 1986 and renamed the party Hezb-e-Watan ("Fatherland Party"), but it was ousted from power and dissolved when Najib's government fell to the mujahideen in 1992. The PDPA government is still referred to as the 'regime.' (SEE A BRIEF HISTORY)

Parcham: one of the two main factions of the People's Democratic Party of Afghanistan (PDPA). Literally, 'Flag' or 'Banner', its membership was mainly non-Pashtun intelligentsia and government officials. The party was formed in 1968 and led by Babrak Karmal, becoming dominant over the Khalq faction when Karmal was installed as the country's President by the Soviets in December 1979.

purdah: seclusion or separation of women from men; literally, 'curtain.'

Pashto: the language spoken by Pashtuns.

Pashtun: also called *Pakhtun, Pukhtun* and *Pathan*. The dominant political group in Afghanistan. *Sunni* Muslim. (SEE ETHNIC & TRIBAL)

Pashtunwali: Pashtun tribal code.

pir: religious leader of the Sufi order; literally "the old one."

qabila: large and established tribe.

qazi: Islamic judge.

qizilbash: literally "red head"; Dari-speaking *Shi'a* Afghans descended from the 18th Century Turkic contingent left behind by Iran.

sardar: chief or military commander.

sayyad: someone descended from the Prophet (through his daughter Fatima).

shah: king (Persian).

shari'a: Islamic law; literally, "the way."

Shi'a: Muslim sect which holds that leadership of the Islamic community should be by dynastic succession from Imam Ali (cousin and son-in-law of the Prophet Mohammed) and his descendants. Their view conflicts with the *Sunni* principle that Mohammed's successor or caliph should be elected. *Shi'as* divide into three main sects according to which of their *imams* is believed to be the "Expected One", who will return on judgement day: the 5th, 7th or 12th. In Afghanistan the Hazaras and Qizilbash are mostly 'twelvers', as in Iran; but the Isma'ilis are 'seveners.' The non-Pashtun *Shi'a* mujahideen refused to participate in the Afghan Interim Government. They represent around 15% of Afghanistan's population.

shura: council, assembly.

Sufism: Islamic mysticism; emerged in the 8th Century; seeks personal experience of union with God, rather than rational knowledge of God; long in conflict with more scholastic *Sunni* Islam. (Afghan contemporary *Sufi* orders include Qadiri and Naqshbandi).

Sunni: Muslim sect which holds that Mohammed's successor or caliph should be elected. Their view conflicts with the *Shi'a* principle that leadership of the Islamic community should be by dynastic succession from Imam Ali (cousin and son-in-law of the Prophet Mohammed) and his descendants. *Sunnis* constitute up to 85% of the population of Afghanistan, including most Pashtuns.

Taliban (singular: **talib):** religious students (literally, 'seekers') from a *madrassa*; the Taliban are a Pashtun-based traditionalist armed political group which emerged as a powerful force in November 1994 and took Kabul in September 1996. (SEE TALIBAN and *Traditionalist* below)

Traditionalist: "the desire to freeze society so that it conforms to the memory of what it once was: it is society as described by [our] grandfathers. In this vision history and tradition are merged; the historical development of society is effaced in favour of an imaginary timeless realm under attack from pernicious modernity. Traditionalism can never provide the basis for any coherent political programme; it is riddled with nostalgia and its politics naturally incline towards all that is conservative." (Olivier Roy) The Taliban movement is considered to be traditionalist not fundamentalist.

ulama (singular: **alim**): academics specializing in Islamic learning and traditions.

umma: pan-Islamic community, or Islamic nation.

Wahabism: puritan Saudi Arabian Islamic sect.

wali: governor of a province.

Watan: Fatherland Party (see PDPA).

zakat: Islamic tax on capital, payable to the poor, clergy etc.

Index

This index includes principal listings only. It does not include references that appear on a regular basis or are clearly cited in the contents and essential data listings.

About the ICHR and *CROSSLINES*

The International Centre for Humanitarian Reporting (ICHR) is a not-for-profit Foundation headquartered in Switzerland with a representative office in the United States, which is registered as a not-for-profit 501 (c)(3) organization. Founded in 1994 by a group of journalists, humanitarians and human rights advocates, the ICHR seeks to increase public awareness of humanitarian issues through the media. It also seeks to advocate greater and more effective use of the media to support humanitarian initiatives, and to facilitate increased cooperation and understanding between the media and other professionals involved in humanitarian work.

The ICHR's principal programmes and projects include the Weapons of War, Tools of Peace series of symposia, a Journalism Fellowship Programme to help improve humanitarian coverage, specialized seminars and workshops on media and communications, Humanitarian Reporting Awards, and ZanWeb (a website to help highlight women's issues in Afghanistan).

The ICHR is directly linked with the Radio Partnership, a long-term programme which initiates and facilitates field projects using radio and other broadcast media creatively to promote social and behavioural change and development. It highlights best practice in the use of radio for international public health, development and conflict resolution. In addition, it produces handbooks on the effective use of radio for HIV-AIDS awareness, public health issues, peace-building and distance education for children in war zones. The Radio Partnership is headquartered at the ICHR in Geneva, Switzerland.

The ICHR also aims to promote humanitarian awareness in partnership with other media or through publications and audio-visual projects, such as the Essential Field Guide Series and the Human Rights Handbook for Journalists.

CROSSLINES* Global Report**, the ICHR's independent flagship publication which co-founded the ICHR, seeks to promote greater public awareness of humanitarian issues through critical reporting, analysis, and special Focus series. Published six times a year, ***CROSSLINES is a unique newsjournal drawing on a growing network of experienced journalists, photographers and analysts to provide key coverage of issues often neglected by the mainstream media. While aiming to respond to the information requirements of the international humanitarian and media community, it also seeks to reach a broader audience of groups and individuals who would like to receive better and more consistent coverage of humanitarian issues. These include emergency relief, human rights, media and communications, environment, conflict resolution and security, health, education, and long-term development. ***CROSSLINES*** works in partnership with other news organizations as a means of making its coverage more widely available to the general public.

For further information on the ICHR, Radio Partnership or ***CROSSLINES***, please contact:

The International Centre for Humanitarian Reporting (ICHR)
Villa de Grand-Montfleury
1290 Versoix, Geneva
Switzerland
TEL: +41(22) 950 0750 FAX: +41(22) 950 0752
E-mail: info.ichr@itu.ch Website: www.ichr.org